Hokkeji and the Reemergence of Female Monastic Orders in Premodern Japan

STUDIES IN EAST ASIAN BUDDHISM 23

Hokkeji and the Reemergence of Female Monastic Orders in Premodern Japan

Lori Meeks

A Kuroda Institute Book
University of Hawai'i Press
Honolulu

Paperback edition 2022
Printed in the United States of America

Library of Congress Cataloging-in-Publication Data
Meeks, Lori Rachelle.
Hokkeji and the reemergence of female monastic orders in premodern Japan /
Lori Meeks.
p. cm.—(Studies in East Asian Buddhism ; 23)
"A Kuroda Institute Book."
Includes bibliographical references and index.
ISBN 978-0-8248-3394-7 (hardcover : alk. paper)
1. Buddhist nuns—Japan—Hokkeji (Nara-shi) 2. Buddhist monasticism and religious orders for women—Japan—Hokkeji (Nara-shi) 3. Monastic and religious life (Buddhism)—Japan—Hokkeji (Nara-shi) 4. Hokkeji (Nara-shi, Japan)—Religion. I. Title.
BQ6160.J32H656 2010
294.3'6570952184—dc22
2009032538

ISBN: 978-0-8248-9243-2 (paperback)

The Kuroda Institute for the Study of Buddhism and Human Values is a nonprofit, educational corporation founded in 1976. One of its primary objectives is to promote scholarship on the historical, philosophical, and cultural ramifications of Buddhism. In association with the University of Hawai'i Press, the Institute also publishes Classics in East Asian Buddhism, a series devoted to the translation of significant texts in the East Asian Buddhist tradition.

Cover art: Adapted from a scene from *A Poetry Competition among Skilled Workers in Seventy-One Rounds (Shichiju ichiban shokunin uta-awase),* 17th c. The nun on the right is identified as a Zen bikuni, and the nun on the left is identified as a Ritsu nun from Hokkeji. (Courtesy Tokyo National Museum)

University of Hawai'i Press books are printed on acid-free paper and meet the guidelines for permanence and durability of the Council on Library Resources.

Designed by University of Hawai'i Press production staff

Contents

Acknowledgments

My research on the nuns of Hokkeji grew out of a broader, cross-cultural interest in the nature of women's roles in the social lives of religious institutions. Exposed from an early age to doctrines preaching the inferiority of women, I struggled as a young adult to reconcile the moral insights of the tradition in which I had been raised with its oppressive views on social issues. In this sense, my academic research has allowed me to pursue a very personal interest in understanding how female actors in other times and cultures adapted, resisted, or made peace with religious traditions whose texts and institutions disparaged women. Although many of the arguments forwarded in this book address issues particular to the study of Japanese history and religion, I hope that it will also be of some value to nonspecialist readers interested in the dynamics that shape women's engagement with androcentric religious rhetoric.

In these pages, I would like to acknowledge the many individuals, foundations, and institutions that enabled me to write this book. To begin, this research would never have been possible without the pioneering work of Barbara Ruch, Nishiguchi Junko, and Katsuura Noriko, all of whom have provided generous mentorship over the years. I am also grateful to the abbesses of Hokkeji, Chūgūji, Reikanji, and Dōmyōji for sharing the stories and treasures of their convents with Westerners whose interest in the history of Buddhist convents must have come unexpectedly. Crucial financial and research support came from the Japan Society for the Promotion of Science, the USC College of Arts and Sciences, and the USC Provost's Office. The USC School of Religion provided a subvention that lowered the retail price of this volume. The Japan Fund postdoctoral program at the Stanford Institute for International Studies enabled me to spend a very enjoyable year at Stanford University. In Japan, the Center for the Study of Women, Buddhism, and Cultural History in Kyoto; the Historiographical Institute of the University of Tokyo; Shikoku University; and Ritsumeikan University provided institutional and administrative support.

Over the years, I have benefited from the kind and patient guidance of many teachers and mentors. Jacqueline Stone, my dissertation adviser, provided critical advice and incisive feedback. I am also indebted to Buzzy

Teiser and Martin Collcutt for their mentorship during my graduate school years, and to Ryūichi Abé, my undergraduate adviser. At Stanford and in Northern California, Carl Bielefeldt, Bernard Faure, Michael Zimmermann, and Bob Sharf created much-appreciated opportunities for provocative scholarly exchange. Colleagues and friends at USC and in Southern California have made Los Angeles an equally stimulating place to live, think, and write. Special thanks are due to Joan Piggott, whose efforts as the director of the Project for Premodern Japan have made USC a world-class center for the study of pre-1600 Japan.

In Japan, I learned under the tutelage of Taira Masayuki, Oka Yoshiko, and Manabe Shunshō. Harada Masatoshi, Minowa Kenryō, Patricia Fister, Hosokawa Ryōichi, Uejima Susumu, and Saeki Shungen answered numerous questions and arranged many introductions and site visits. Sasakibara Fumiko, Yoshida Kazuhiko, and Kawashima Masao also offered guidance and support. At the Historiographical Institute of the University of Tokyo, I received counsel from Kikuchi Hiroki, Yoshida Sanae, Katō Tomoyasu, Ishigami Eichi, Kondō Shigekazu, Kurushima Noriko, Kuriyama Keiko, and Uchida Mioko. I would also like to acknowledge the encouragement and kind advice of good friends Matsumoto Ikuyo, Kimura Saeko, and Naitō Mariko.

During the writing process, I was fortunate to receive feedback from many colleagues. William Bodiford and Paul Groner responded to this research at various stages and in various forms, always offering both encouragement and insightful critique. Robert Campany and Janet Goodwin read the manuscript in its entirety, and the final product owes much to their wise suggestions. Robert Borgen, Aileen Gatten, Charles Witke, Lisa Bitel, Michaela Mross, David Albertson, James Heft, James Ford, and Andrew Goble also read lengthy sections of the manuscript and shared their expertise in the form of generous comments. Christina Laffin, Asuka Sangō, Stephen Nelson, and David Quinter similarly contributed specialized knowledge at important junctures. I would also like to acknowledge the helpful advice of David Bialock, Tomoko Bialock, Maribeth Graybill, Niels Guelberg, James Robson, Shayne Clarke, Michael Jamentz, and Ryan Bonseok Joo.

Had it not been for the prompting of Richard Jaffe, I would not have had the courage to send my first book to the Kuroda Institute. I would also like to thank series editor Peter Gregory for guiding me through the submission process, executive editor Patricia Crosby, managing editor Cheri Dunn, and copy editor Ruth Homrighaus for their attentiveness throughout the editing process; and Celeste Newbrough for her work on the index. The anonymous readers who evaluated this manuscript also provided invaluable suggestions for improvement. One in particular provided an extensive list of detailed recommendations that saved me from many errors and oversights. Tomiko Jamentz and Katsura Michiyo obtained on my behalf the reproduction rights required to reprint all of the images found in this book, and Paul Swanson and the *Japanese Journal for Religious Studies* kindly allowed me to reprint in chapter 7 several paragraphs from my 2007 article on Chūgūji.

Finally, I would like to express my gratitude to those closest to me. My mother and father, Patricia and Chris Meeks, and my brother, Ryan Meeks, have patiently supported me through many years of education and exploration, all of which took me far from home. Thanks are due as well to Yukari Mitsuji (now Kawamura), who first introduced me to Japan, and to Julien Lee Kern and Natalie Carlson, whose friendships fortified me throughout my undergraduate, graduate, and postgraduate years. I am especially grateful to J.P. It was his humor and counsel that kept me grounded through years of late-night studying and frequent travel.

Abbreviations and Conventions

Chōmonshū	*Kōshō Bosatsu gokyōkai chōmonshū*
DDB	*Digital Dictionary of Buddhism*
DNBZ 1922	*Dai Nihon Bukkyō zensho*, ed. Bussho Kankōkai
DNBZ 1973	*Dai Nihon Bukkyō zensho*, ed. Suzuki Gakujutsu Zaidan
Gyōjitsu nenpu	*Saidai chokushi Kōshō Bosatsu gyōjitsu nenpu*
HMJE	*Hokke metsuzaiji engi*
KJGSK 1977	*Kongō Busshi Eison kanjin gakushōki*, ed. Kanshū Nara Kokuritsu Bunkazai Kenkyūjo
KJGSK 1999	*Kongō Busshi Eison kanjin gakushōki*, ed. Hosokawa Ryōichi
Nenjū gyōji	*Hokkeji metsuzaiji nenjū gyōji*
NKBT	*Nihon koten bungaku taikei*
NKBZ	*Nihon koten bungaku zenshū*
SEDS	*Saidaiji Eison denki shūsei*
SNKBT	*Shin Nihon koten bungaku taikei*
SNKBZ	*Shinpen Nihon koten bungaku zenshū*
T.	*Taishō shinshū daizōkyō*
TG	*Towazugatari*
X.	*Xu zangjing*
YKT	*Yamato koji taikan*

The best way to render classical linguistic forms of East Asia into roman letters remains controversial, especially among historical linguists. For the sake of convenience and immediate intelligibility I have chosen to employ modern conventions of romanization. For Japanese, I use a modified Hepburn style; for Chinese, pinyin; and for Korean, Revised Romanization of Korean (RR). Dates are given in the following format: Reign name and year (Gregorian equivalent) and lunar month/day. Japanese names appear with the surname first, except in cases in which the author has elected to follow Western convention.

women during the mid- and late thirteenth century (Ōishi 2001, 42–45; Ushiyama 1989, 264–269).[5] Driven by the conviction that their contemporaries had failed to take the *vinaya* precepts seriously and were thus practicing an inauthentic form of Buddhism, Eison and his followers called for a return to what they understood to be the original Buddhism of India and China. Above all else, they emphasized close adherence to the disciplinary codes of the *vinaya*. Adopting the motto *kōbō rijō,* "fostering the Dharma and benefiting sentient beings," Eison and his followers engaged in a variety of restorationist activities from the late 1230s. It was around this time that Eison also began to restore the Nara temple Saidaiji, where he eventually established a new ordination platform and launched a widely successful *vinaya* revival movement.[6]

In order to restore the precepts fully, Eison and his disciples believed it necessary to reestablish all seven divisions within the sevenfold assembly: fully ordained monks, fully ordained nuns, postulate nuns, novice priests, novice nuns, laymen, and laywomen. Four of these seven divisions were to be filled by women. By this time, however, Japan's Buddhist community had long accepted the absence of official, state-sponsored women's ordination lineages.[7] Although small, private hermitages for women did sometimes maintain their own forms of initiation or ordination, such rituals fell outside the domain of state-sponsored precepts ordination platforms and were, at least in the view of the major monastic centers like Nara and Mount Hiei, considered incomplete or unofficial (Katsuura 1989, 23).[8] Rejecting such unorthodox forms of ordination for women, Eison and his disciples believed that the *vinaya* could not be fully restored in Japan without the reestablishment of a nuns' precepts ordination platform sanctioned by the Buddhist order and the reopening of "official" convents (see Groner 2005, esp. 221–229).

In telling the story of their interactions with women at Hokkeji, Eison and his disciples portrayed their willingness to ordain women as exceptional and praised themselves for their generosity and compassion toward women. Given the greater rhetorical arc of Saidaiji writing, which emphasizes the extraordinary nature of Eison's commitment to the realization of a more rigorously "authentic" *sangha* in Japan, it is hardly surprising that Eison and his disciples portrayed their interactions with women as yet another indication of how they differed from the Japanese monastic mainstream. The self-aggrandizing function of Saidaiji literature thus skews its presentation of Hokkeji's restoration. That said, it is clear that Eison and his disciples did distinguish themselves from the monastic norm insofar as they offered full *bikuni* precepts to large groups of women. What Saidaiji literature is not clear about, however, is the degree to which nuns and laywomen were active in Japanese temple life long before the revival of Hokkeji. In particular, Saidaiji texts ignore the unofficial, less institutionalized, and more lay-oriented models of nunhood already in practice at small hermitages and temples before Eison's involvement with convents like Hokkeji. Stressing his ordinations of women as events of great magnitude, Eison tended to downplay both the efforts of the nuns themselves and the degree of organization already in place at temples like Hokkeji before his arrival on the scene.[9] In presenting the revival of Hokkeji and other convents in this fashion, Saidaiji literature attributes the successful revival of female monasticism almost entirely to Eison and his group of male clerics.[10] Contemporary scholarly analyses of Hokkeji's revival have also tended to privilege Saidaiji documents, thereby perpetuating the Saidaiji view that Buddhist women were dependent upon the mediation of male priests.

My study of Hokkeji attempts to balance the ideological significance of the Hokkeji restoration with careful attention to those aspects of the revival that did not engage Buddhist doctrine in a sustained or focused manner. In reading texts composed by Hokkeji nuns against the doctrine-oriented writings of Saidaiji's male monastics, I was first struck by the type of disjuncture observed by Caroline Walker Bynum in her studies of medieval Christian ascetics. Much as Bynum's work points to differences in male and female readings and usages of religious imagery in medieval Christian Europe, texts written by women involved in the Hokkeji revival suggest discrepancies between the ways in which men and women in premodern Japan received, interpreted, and used Buddhist teachings about gender (see Bynum 1991, 151–179). Documents written by women involved in the restoration of Hokkeji relate the story of their movement in ways that diverge, often radically, from Saidaiji narratives. Unlike Saidaiji texts, which emphasize both women's weak position in the Buddhist cosmos and their reliance upon the mercy of male priests, the texts associated with the women's order do not treat gender as a problem. They also downplay men's roles in the restoration of Hokkeji and other convents, focusing instead on the contributions of nuns—women whom they portray as self-reliant and confident.

The task of analyzing these differences is a worthwhile project in and of itself, especially given the fact that previous scholarship has interpreted Hokkeji's revival from a Saidaiji-centric perspective, failing to examine materials associated with Hokkeji's archives in any detail. But my project aims to move beyond this single task and to place the revival of Hokkeji in a broader sociocultural context. In doing so, it demonstrates that ideological disjunctures, even those pertinent to the relationship between gender and soteriological discourse, are not clearly split along gendered lines: that is, one cannot necessarily distinguish "male" and "female" views of women's salvation and religiosity. Other markers of difference—ordination status, social class, and educational background—also serve as indicators of how particular individuals viewed women, their salvation, and their place in the Buddhist order. We see a greater correlation between views of women's salvation held by male and female members of the aristocratic classes, for example, than between those held by male monks and ordinary laymen. Gender alone is not a reliable determinant of how individual historical actors understood women's salvation. So while Hokkeji materials do suggest that male scholar-priests and nuns, though both part of the monastic order in a large sense, tended to approach issues surrounding women's relationship to Buddhism in vastly different ways, these materials also demonstrate that gender difference was only one part of a complex social equation.

In addition to providing an opportunity to reevaluate the ways in which women interpreted and practiced Buddhism in premodern Japan, then, texts of Hokkeji and related convents also draw us toward a fuller understanding of Buddhism on the ground, Buddhism as it was understood and practiced by those not occupying scholarly positions at elite monasteries. Especially relevant in this regard is the fact that Hokkeji documents show little interest in doctrine. "Popular" and other nondoctrinal texts are central to this study, which understands Buddhism as a set of institutions, practices, and cultural motifs that is only partially informed by doctrine. The task of understanding how women understood and participated in Buddhism requires an interdisciplinary, intertextual approach that challenges the tendency of Buddhist studies to privilege doctrinal texts over social and ritual practice.

In piecing together the story of Hokkeji's medieval revival and its significance in the religious history of premodern Japan, I draw on a wide variety of sources, including materials ranging from state histories and Buddhist scriptures to ritual texts, popular narratives, temple origin stories *(engi)*, pilgrimage records *(junreiki)*, sermon collections, scriptural commentaries, biographies, diaries, fund-raising documents, name registers, and written prayer requests. Read in toto, these texts do not merely offer a new understanding of women's roles in Japanese Buddhist communities, they also challenge contemporary scholarly images of Japanese Buddhism. In particular, they speak to the social nature of Buddhist temple-shrine complexes,

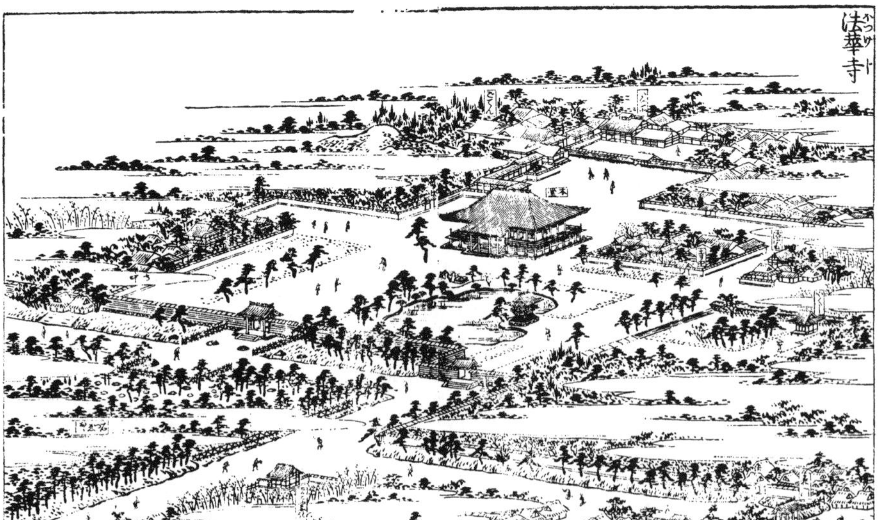

Map of the Hokkeji Temple (Hokkeji garanzu) from the *Yamato meishozue,* Edo period

thus providing a better sense of how monks and nuns actually lived and worked on a daily basis. These texts also reflect the everyday assumptions, hierarchies, and practices that structured the social and religious worlds of monastic life. They broaden our understanding of how Buddhist doctrine was transmitted on the ground, of how ordinary laypeople from different backgrounds came into contact with Buddhist teachers, doctrines, and practices. This book thus aims to contribute not only to growing literature on women and Buddhism but also to recent research on the social life of Buddhist temples and monastic communities.[11] Issues particularly relevant in the study include the function of the precepts in monastic life; the role of ritual and ceremony in temple life; the social and educational lives of monasteries; the relationship between Buddhism and other cultural values, such as courtliness and filiality; and the relationship between Buddhist doctrine and practice, both inside and outside the monastery.

The Question of Agency

Japanese scholarship on religious women in premodern Japan, especially that focusing on Buddhism, has flourished since the late 1980s. In 1984, Ōsumi Kazuo and Nishiguchi Junko founded a Japan-based research group devoted to the study of women and Buddhism in Japanese history. Just five years later, the group published *Shirīzu josei to Bukkyō* (Series on women and Buddhism), a four-volume collection of essays on women and Buddhism, broadly defined, in Japanese history and literature. These volumes, combined with Nishiguchi's groundbreaking 1987 work *Onna no chikara: Kodai no josei to Bukkyō* (The strength of women: Women and Buddhism in the ancient period), set the stage for the further development of the field over the course of the 1990s.

Interest in women and Buddhism in Japan—how women's bodies were represented in Buddhist texts, how women themselves understood and practiced Buddhism, how women interacted with Buddhist institutions—also grew in the West, where the field was established largely through the work of Barbara Ruch, a scholar of literature who also heads the Institute for Medieval Japanese Studies at Columbia University, as well as a recently established center in Kyoto devoted both to the study of women in Buddhist culture and to the preservation of imperial convents. In addition to authoring her own Japanese-language monograph on women and Buddhism in 1991 (*Mō hitotsu no chūseizō: Bikuni, otogizōshi, raise;* Another way of looking at the medieval period: Nuns, short story booklets, and the afterlife), Ruch also edited the 2002 volume *Engendering Faith: Women and Buddhism in Premodern Japan,* the first English-language volume to treat the history of women and Buddhism in Japan.

One of the major debates to emerge as this new field has developed has centered on the relationship between nunhood—and Buddhist practice more generally—and women's agency. Put simply, scholars have disagreed on this question: Did women's participation in Buddhist monastic life enable them to create meaning in a patriarchal society, or did it merely lend additional institutional and ideological support for their subjugation?

Approaches to the question of agency have varied, but most follow one of two trends: (1) that which describes convents as places of great oppression or (2) that which portrays convents as liberating, all-female spaces that allowed women to escape the constraints of marriage and family life. The first view, which understands Buddhist institutions as unilaterally oppressive of women, is the most dominant, especially in Japanese scholarship. This tendency can be attributed at least partially to the long-standing influence in the Japanese academy of Marxist analysis, which is inclined to view religious institutions as repressive. In Marxist-style Japanese scholarship, nuns and convents are described in the bleakest of terms. Convents, the argument goes, absorbed Japan's "used" and "unusable" women—the widowed, the sick, the aged, and the unmarriageable. Adding insult to injury, these institutions then forced already downtrodden women to pray both for rebirth into male bodies and for the salvation of the very fathers and husbands who had oppressed them throughout their lives (Hosokawa 1987, 1989a, 1989b; Matsuo 1989, 2001). Following this logic, several prominent historians in Japan have arrived at the conclusion that women living in medieval convents must have spent their years as nuns in misery. Some, citing disparaging views of the female body found in Buddhist literature, have commented that nuns must have suffered from a great sense of self-alienation. Others have gone so far as to argue that the severity of male domination in the monastic society of medieval Japan would have suppressed and even precluded women's personal investment in Buddhist training and study.[12]

On the other side are scholars who suggest that convents were places that afforded women a certain degree of freedom. Barbara Ruch, in particular, calls medieval nunhood a "radical" and "revolutionary path of freedom." This seemingly extreme stance is couched in caveats, however, as the freedom she speaks of here emerges only in contrast to what she describes as the harsh conditions of women's lives in premodern Japan. Through much of the premodern period, she tells us, there were few decisions that women could make for themselves, and for women unhappy in their domestic circumstances, the only viable options for escape were suicide, nunhood, and prostitution. For Ruch, then, nunhood represented a safe haven for women distraught or unhappy in their present circumstances. And for some women, such as the Zen nun Mugai Nyodai (1223–1298), she adds, convent life provided an opportunity for scholarly pursuits as well (1991, 22–25).

Katsuura Noriko, too, has spoken of nunhood as providing women with a certain degree of freedom, though she is more cautious than Ruch in making this claim. Katsuura does not use words like "revolutionary" or "radical" to describe nunhood in the premodern period, but she does conclude that in renouncing the world and taking on the epithet of "nun" (*ama* or *ni*), women were able to claim more freedom and social respect than ordinary laywomen. Using numerous examples from the Heian and Kamakura periods, she argues that women who became *shukke* (world renouncers) during these periods were no longer bound by wifely tasks and were free to leave their homes and husbands so as to focus their time and energy on religious endeavors. Although literary examples suggest that women were required to secure the permission of their husbands before renouncing the world, there are many stories of women who, eager to leave their homes and marriages, went to great extremes to secure the blessings of their husbands. There are also stories of women who ran away from husbands who refused to grant permission or who simply took the tonsure without spousal authorization. In addition to releasing women from the obligations of marriage, the status of nun, ambiguous as it may have been, also appears to have provided at least some women with a level of social authority not granted ordinary laywomen. To illustrate this point, Katsuura points to the fact that the women's names listed in medieval guild *(za)* registers were typically those bearing aristocratic titles or those bearing the epithet "nun." That "nun" was a socially powerful category is also demonstrated, she argues, by the fact that the prince Fushimi no Miya Sadafusa (1372–1456) began to use honorific language toward his own daughters once they attained *bikuni* status (1995, 150–153).[13]

Despite their willingness to entertain the notion that medieval convents provided women with a certain degree of freedom, refuge, and perhaps even social authority, Ruch and Katsuura are not naïve about the social and economic conditions that led many women to become nuns in the first place. Like those scholars who describe convents as institutions of oppression, Ruch and Katsuura also suggest that many women first took up nunhood because their husbands or fathers had died in violent conflicts, leaving them financially destitute. It is now common knowledge that a handful of convents, such as Zenmyōji, were established to house women whose husbands perished in the battles that marked the transition from the Heian period to the Kamakura (Ushiyama 1989, 231–238). Katsuura also cites examples of women who opted for nunhood when their husbands brought new women into the household. Ruch and Katsuura are thus sober in portraying the social constraints faced by women in premodern Japan. For many women, they suggest, the initial allure of the convent may have been less about pursuing a religious vocation than about escaping financial destitution or domestic humiliation.

Insofar as Ruch and Katsuura suggest that many women became nuns only because it was the best of several unattractive options, their perspective is not so different from that of the Marxist-influenced scholars described earlier. What distinguishes the approach of Ruch and Katsuura is that they view the convent itself in a different light. Whereas the other side understands the convent as an institutional arm of a dominant Buddhist ideology that offered women no respite, Ruch and Katsuura suggest that within the space of the convent, even those women who may have first become nuns for infelicitous reasons found ways to create meaning and dignity in their lives.

Moreover, their approaches, especially that of Ruch, allow for the possibility that at least some women may have become nuns not for wholly unhappy reasons, but rather because they were interested in studying Buddhist texts or in pursuing a life outside the confines of marriage and childbearing.

On this point, Tanaka Takako, in a personal account of experiences as a female scholar in Japan, has implied that many scholars working on women in premodern Japan are so inured to the social conditions of contemporary Japanese society that they cannot imagine how or why, barring coercion or desperation, a woman would choose life without marriage or children. Among male scholars of Buddhism in Japan, she points out, the tendency has been to assume that women who became nuns did so only because they had no other options and, furthermore, to describe the lives of women who did become nuns in the grimmest terms possible (2005, 166–171).

It is interesting to note, in contrast, that Western-language research on religious women in medieval Europe, especially that carried out by feminists, has tended to describe the motivations of female renunciants in a decidedly more positive way. An example: in her comprehensive study of Christian nuns, Jo Ann Kay McNamara argues that for many women in the early Christian movement, chastity represented a form of social protest; in embracing the status of virgin, she explains, women were able to declare themselves free from the obligations of marriage and family and to take on certain public roles typically reserved for men, such as teaching and social organizing. In other words, celibacy was thought to liberate women "from the disabilities of womanhood." As bishops and other male figures in the Christian movement wrote admiringly of women who, refusing to marry, rebelled against the wishes of their pagan families, virginity became the object of great celebration and was embraced by many young women, much to the chagrin of those representing the traditional Greco-Roman social order (1996, 23–26, 47–48, 59).

So while women who voluntarily gave up their sexual lives in order to pursue the Christian faith in the Late Antique West are described as rebels who boldly resisted established social norms, women who became Buddhist nuns in medieval Japan are described as the victims of a rigidly patriarchal society. Undoubtedly, Christian groups in the ancient Mediterranean world and Buddhist groups in premodern Japan imagined religious women in markedly different ways and ascribed different values to the renunciation of women. At the same time, however, the general tone of interpretation—and in this case, the choice to interpret renunciation as an indication of protest or as a sign of victimhood—surely reflects the historian's own biases.

In general, my study follows the approach of Ruch and Katsuura. Like Katsuura in particular, I have attempted to understand women's reception of Buddhist discourse and participation in Buddhist practice without characterizing their relationships with Buddhism as either oppressive or liberating. I view Buddhist convents as sites that both transmitted and reproduced (though often in piecemeal fashion) dominant ideologies while simultaneously offering the tools—knowledge in various forms, textual, ritual, economic—necessary for maneuvering through those ideologies. My study thus takes notice of ambiguities and incoherencies found in the histories of convents. Here I am indebted to Dorothy Ko, whose recent work (1994, 2005) provides a model of how women's contributions to dominant systems of power in historical societies might be understood in a way that recognizes women's agency without ascribing false consciousness.

Ko's work, which focuses on the histories of Chinese women, calls for a more nuanced understanding of the relationship between women and the dominant social ideology of Confucianism. Scholarship on women in China had long worked from the assumption that women struggled as "outsiders" against both the Chinese kinship system and the Confucian order that supported it. But Ko reasons that the very durability of Confucian social ideologies and institutions, which have been functioning and reproducing for so many centuries, implies that women had vested interests in their continuance. She demonstrates how women found contentment and meaning as they contributed to the success of the Confucian order, celebrating its moral ideals, embracing the roles it prescribed for them as women, and taking pride in gender-specific traditions like foot binding (1994, 8–9, 19; 2005). She also shows how, in exploiting the ambiguities of Confucianism, women crafted identities by cultivating their own artistic and literary talents and by creating societies of women that extended beyond the isolation of the "inner quarters," where elite women were expected to remain hidden (1994, 192). Similar dynamics are at work in this study, which shows how Japanese convents both served the needs of the androcentric social order—by housing widows and the secret daughters of forbidden unions, for example—and at the same time allowed women to create their own communities of practice, to transmit their own forms of knowledge and ritual authority, and to establish traditions in which they could take pride.

Saba Mahmood's work also encourages a reconsideration of the relationship between agency and resistance. In her study of women in Egyptian Muslim movements, Mahmood finds that the goals of liberal feminism often fail to recognize the "modalities of agency" found in non-Western and/or religiously fundamentalist cultures. She thus argues that scholars need to separate the analytical category of agency from the political project of feminism (2005, 153). Because liberal feminist understandings of agency are caught up in the telos of progressive politics, liberal feminists define agency through acts of resistance; that is, the liberal feminist scholar recognizes only those subjects who have defied, subverted, or manipulated the dominant patriarchal order (9). Mahmood urges scholars to reexamine liberal Western assumptions surrounding subject formation and to take up alternative approaches to the problem of agency. Her study forwards, in particular, the notion of "ethical agency," which recognizes that religious actors typically frame their identity not through reaction against, but instead through the adoption of, values specific to their tradition (34–39). In drawing attention to the ethical agency of Muslim women in Egypt, Mahmood helps readers understand how and why certain women may find practices based in androcentric or patriarchal teachings meaningful and even empowering.

Although this study does not apply the concept of ethical agency, it is inspired by the rationale behind Mahmood's approach, and particularly by her insistence that we learn to recognize the multivalent nature of agency. As this study will demonstrate, it is never clear that the women of Hokkeji consciously resisted or subverted androcentric Buddhist discourse. In some discursive arenas, such as those discussed in chapter 7, they did ignore, or "talk past," androcentric Buddhist teachings. And in others, such as those discussed in chapter 2, both male and female elites privileged practices downplaying the canonical notion that women faced great obstacles on the Buddhist path. But in many other instances, it was through the act of cultivating rather than resisting dominant ideologies that women in premodern Japan created meaningful social and religious lives. Women's contributions to Buddhist practice and discourse, both as laywomen and as nuns, were often made in collaboration with male priests or with male members of their own families or social groups.

Locating the Dominant Discourse

In this work, which considers the religious landscape of premodern Japan, it is also necessary to reexamine assumptions about who or what represented the "dominant discourse." Attention to the practical aspects of how Buddhist texts and ideas were disseminated, received, and put to use is also crucial. Although it may be tempting to assume that the writings of Buddhist scholar-priests represent the dominant discourse of the period, it is not clear that this was actually the case. When comparing the doctrinal texts of Japanese scholar-priests with contemporaneous literary materials, it is evident that doctrinal texts did not simply reflect mainstream cultural assumptions of the day. Instead, they represented the opinions of a special class of learned individuals who served as the mediators between difficult continental texts and broader Japanese society. While their interpretations of Buddhist texts were respected in certain circles, they did not always represent dominant or mainstream views of what Buddhism was in the everyday lives of ordinary laypeople. Laypeople, and especially commoners, did not necessarily share the worldview transmitted in—or even understand all of the terms and ideas central to—the doctrinal writings of elite scholar-priests.

Given the importance attributed to texts and doctrine in the Judeo-Christian traditions, it is not surprising that Western scholars of religion, biased toward doctrinal understandings of religion, have tended to overemphasize the role of sacred texts when studying other traditions. Western studies of Japanese Buddhism (and to some extent Japanese studies of Japanese Buddhism as well, given the strong influence of the Western academy in the development of Buddhist studies) have also suffered from this bias. In particular, scholars have tended to assume that ordinary laypeople internalized ideas found in the doctrinal texts of Buddhist scholar-priests and have sometimes been surprised by discrepancies between doctrine as conveyed in the writings of Japanese scholar-priests on the one hand and Buddhist ideas as reflected in contemporaneous popular literature on the other.

What one should keep in mind in noting such disparities, however, is that few lay Buddhists in Japan would have studied "Buddhism" as a holistic tradition: most had been exposed only to a smattering of disparate texts and rituals, and few had attempted to read and understand the contents of Buddhist texts on their own. Japan had no centralized Buddhist authority that dictated matters of doctrine. Knowledge of Buddhist texts was, on the whole, something transmitted via scholar-priests, who offered public lectures from time to time (some of which were later collected and transmitted in *setsuwa,* or short narrative, collections); explained Buddhist ideas through the explication of images *(etoki);* and sometimes, especially in the Kamakura period and later, exchanged letters with more educated lay followers. For most laypeople, Buddhism offered ritual practices thought capable of providing practical help in this life and the next. Buddhist priests were called upon to pray for the deceased and for the dying, to chant spells for the sick, to offer protective rites for women giving birth, and to carry out rituals aimed at granting the benefactor prosperity, long life, and rebirth in paradise. To seek comfort in this life and the next, laypeople carried out a variety of practices: simple chants and devotionals, pilgrimages to holy sites, and the commissioning of various Buddhist objects and rituals, including everything from temples and sutra sets to stupas, images, and multiday ceremonies. For most laypeople, Buddhist practice had little, if anything, to do with the study of texts and doctrines. Although wealthy laypeople sometimes produced extravagant copies of sutras, they did so primarily as a means of creating karmic merit. And while many did learn how to recite certain Buddhist sutras, emphasis was typically placed on the spiritual merit earned through the act of chanting and not on the explication of textual content.

Given the laity's uncertain grasp of doctrine, it remains unclear how widely known or influential the learning of Buddhist scholar-priests may have been. In evaluating the relationship between Buddhism and gender in premodern Japan, then, how much weight should be given to the writings of Buddhist scholar-priests? Were these texts of critical cultural influence, or should they be understood as the writings of an elite community of specialists whose ideas did not necessarily match those of the mainstream culture?

It is fair to assume that certain basic Buddhist concepts—the notion that all living beings experience rebirth through the six paths *(rokudō),* the impermanence of all things *(mujō),* the compassion of the bodhisattvas, the desirability of avoiding hell and gaining rebirth in heavens or pure lands, the notion that spiritual merit can be created and transferred, and even more complex ideas, such as original enlightenment *(hongaku)*—had, by the late Heian and early Kamakura periods, become part of the basic cultural knowledge of the educated classes (LaFleur 1983; Stone 1999, 40–46). Many of these ideas, spread through literary production, popular storytelling, and ritual practice, are reflected in literature from the Nara period onward, by which time they had already begun to figure importantly in the cultural activities of the literate. By the Heian period, ideas about rebirth, the Pure Land, and the creation of spiritual merit guided many of the everyday activities of courtiers and other educated elites. And as any student of the *Tale of Genji* knows, impermanence *(mujō)* was a concept Heian courtiers regularly invoked to describe personal experiences.

But even as these ideas began to take hold, their spread was neither seamless nor systematic, and few laypeople scrutinized the details of doctrinal texts. The reception of Pure Land teachings offers an instructive example. Even in the Kamakura period, by which time Pure Land teachings had flourished in Japan for several centuries, average laypeople did not typically concern themselves with the intricacies of Pure Land doctrine when formulating their own images of the afterlife. Although Pure Land scriptures clearly state that the Pure Land is devoid of all markers of gender and sexuality (and, indeed, devoid of women altogether), premodern writers regularly noted with joy the prospect of being reunited with a lover in the Pure Land. It was common, for example, to pray that one would be reborn on the same lotus pedestal as one's lover. In the *Tale of Genji,* Genji hopes that he and Murasaki will meet again in the Pure Land, where they will share a single lotus (*NKBT,* 4:174).[14] As Dobbins points out, "It is inconceivable to think that Genji expected Murasaki to appear in the Pure Land as a male. It was a female Murasaki whom Genji had known in this life, and certainly it was a female Murasaki whom he longed to join in the Pure Land" (2004, 104–105).

Dobbins (2004) suggests that those interpretations of the Pure Land that do not match doctrinal specifications convey a disjuncture between "idealized" religion and "popular" belief, or "practiced religion." In other words, while certain elite scholar-priests familiar with the intricacies of Pure Land texts—Chinkai (1091–1152), Hōnen (1133–1212), and Shinran (1173–1262), to name a few—did in fact emphasize, in their own treatises, that women did not exist in the Pure Land, most average laypeople were unaware of or uninterested in these doctrinal details. And although learned priests did sometimes seek to correct the doctrinal misunderstandings of laypeople, most appear to have been more or less tolerant of lay understandings of Buddhism. As long as laypeople exercised devotion by supporting local temples and clergy, few priests felt it necessary to ascertain the degree to which the views of ordinary laypeople corresponded to doctrinally orthodox positions.

In her innovative research on *kishinjō* (statements of a donors' intentions in making Buddhist offerings) and *ganmon* (prayer requests written by donors making offerings), Nomura Ikuyo argues to the same effect. Against earlier scholarship, such as that of Taira Masayuki and Hosokawa Ryōichi, which cites single mentions of androcentric Buddhist ideology, usually in elite scholarly texts, to suggest that *all* laypeople in premodern Japan necessarily understood the salvation of women to be a problem, Nomura undertakes a holistic study of offertory texts in order to survey the intentions with which laypeople made Buddhist offerings. In her study of 356 *kishinjō* and *ganmon* authored by women in the *Kamakura ibun* collection, Nomura discovers that only twenty, or a mere 6 percent, refer to androcentric Buddhist terms such as the five obstacles, the thrice following, and *henjō nanshi.*[15] This empirical data allows Nomura to confute the widely held assumption that laypeople in the Heian and Kamakura periods had fully internalized the androcentric rhetoric of elite scholar-priests. Nomura's research indicates that even educated laywomen in Kamakura Japan appear not to have been terribly concerned with the karmic burdens of womanhood; this rhetoric, which can be found in the texts of contemporaneous elite scholar-priests, is for the most part absent in the *kishinjō* and *ganmon* of women. On the whole, women asked for the same things that men asked for: long life, physical health, and rebirth in paradise (2004, 106–107).[16]

One of the most fascinating aspects of the Hokkeji-centered nuns' revival movement is that surviving records about the movement display no sustained interest in doctrines concerning soteriological challenges particular to women. Many of the scholar-priests associated with the *vinaya* revival movement, on the other hand, had, like their Tendai counterparts, studied doctrinal texts carefully and were determined to share their findings—that women were inferior to men and required special methods of salvation—with female followers. As Nomura has shown, and as the work of Abe Yasurō has also suggested, such ideas were alien to Japan, where women had to be taught that their bodies were problematic, that they should pray for rebirth in male bodies, and that they faced greater spiritual obstacles than men (Nomura 2004, 98, 101, 112; Abe 1998, 66–76). In studying the texts written by nuns affiliated with Hokkeji, then, we can interpret the fact that they do not mention the karmic obstacles of women in one of two ways: as evidence that, even as late as the mid-Kamakura period, androcentric ideology was not yet part of the mainstream Buddhist discourse in which educated laypeople engaged or as evidence that some women, though aware that the dominant discourse problematized women's bodies, chose to "talk past," or ignore, these ideas and to emphasize instead those aspects of Buddhist practice and doctrine that did not view womanhood as problematic.

Undoubtedly, the situation was mixed: while the observations of Dobbins and Nomura offer compelling evidence that ordinary laypeople had not fully internalized androcentric Buddhist doctrines, the nuns associated with the Hokkeji revival movement were not mere laywomen but were individuals who had sought an unusual level of textual and ritual training. Unlike ordinary laywomen, then, Hokkeji nuns—at least the more elite stratum of nuns at Hokkeji—had undertaken Buddhist study under the direction of scholar-priests. It is thus hard to imagine that they could have been unaware of the growing prominence among scholar-priests of Buddhist theories that problematized the female body. Why, then, did Hokkeji nuns not treat these theories in their own writings? Were they taking a stand against Saidaiji discourse, or did they feel that such discourse was peripheral to the more mainstream concerns of their followers—issues such as rebirth in the Pure Land, devotion to Buddhist deities, and the salvation of loved ones?

Revival activity at Hokkeji took place during an important historical moment, for up until this point, disparaging views of the female body were not yet part of those Buddhist teachings that had become truly mainstream in Japan. But during the very same years in which Hokkeji restored a precepts' platform for women and established itself as an important site in the southern capital, male scholar-priests intent on creating in Japan a more "authentic" *sangha* based more closely on foreign models became increasingly vociferous in their teachings against the female body. Eventually, the spread of Buddhist teachings that problematized the female body *did* enter the dominant discourse. By the late fourteenth century, the notion that women were fated to enter the blood bowl hell, a special hell that punished women for the bloody discharges of the female body, had begun to circulate within Japan.[17] By the early years of the Edo period (1603–1867), it had become standard protocol to bury women with copies of the *Blood Bowl Sutra* (*Ketsubonkyō* or *Ketsubongyō*).

This study thus focuses upon a period in which dominant social discourses, far from being fixed, were in flux. It further argues for greater attention to the dynamics of discourse formation: Buddhist scholar-priests, though influential in certain domains, did not have the last word when it came to determining mainstream beliefs and practices. This study challenges the assumption that scholarly Buddhist texts can be interpreted as representative of contemporaneously held beliefs and instead seeks to use more subtle means of determining the vectors of mainstream or dominant discourses in late-Heian and Kamakura Japan.

Terminology

Since the nineteenth century, Western scholars of Buddhism have relied upon the language of Christianity to explain the nature of Buddhist institutions and practices. This study, too, will employ the terms "monk," "priest," "nun," and "ordination," primarily for the sake of convenience. One should be aware, however, that these terms suggest only rough equivalents to the Christian case when used in the context of Japanese history. To warn the reader of important differences, this section will provide modified definitions of these terms.

Let us first consider the terms "monk" and "priest." Scholars have employed these terms almost interchangeably as translations of *seng* (Jpns. *sō*) and *biqiu* (Jpns. *biku*). Both *seng* and *biqiu* were Chinese neologisms that became part of the basic Buddhist vocabulary used in East Asia. Both terms were based on transliterations. *Seng* was an abbreviation for *sengqie* (Jpns. *sōka* or *sōgya*), meant to approximate the Sanskrit term *saṃgha,* or community. The term *biqiu,* on the other hand, was the most widely used

Chinese transliteration of the Sanskrit term *bhikṣu* and referred to individual members of the Buddhist community. The Sanskrit term *bhikṣu* was not associated with Buddhism in particular but was used more broadly to refer to world renouncers, or those who beg for food. *Bhikṣu* was often used, for example, to describe those who had entered the fourth and last stage of the brahmanic life cycle. In its Buddhist usage, however, the term came to refer specifically to men who had taken full vows of renunciation (that is, the 227 precepts of the Pali Vinaya or the 250 precepts of the *Four-Part Vinaya*), in contrast to novices. In Sanskrit, then, *saṃgha* referred to the Buddhist order as a whole, while *bhikṣu* referred to an individual member of the Buddhist order who took full vows and sustained himself through begging. In East Asia, however, *seng* and *biqiu* came to be used almost indistinguishably, with both terms referring to individuals who had renounced the world and joined a Buddhist order. Similarly, the Japanese equivalents of these terms—*sō* and *biku*—were both used to refer to male members of the Buddhist order. The primary difference between the terms was that *sō* came to be used in a broader sense and was eventually used to refer to anyone who had renounced the world (*chujiazhe,* Jpns. *shukkesha*). As the more generic term, *sō* was the word usually chosen for use in state documents and the like, while *biku* was chosen when an author wanted to emphasize the spiritual training or status of the *sō* in question.

As mentioned earlier, *sō* and *biku* have been rendered as both "priest" and "monk" in English. This method is imprecise, however, for while the English terms "priest" and "monk" suggest different occupations and ordination status, the terms *sō* and *biku,* if used to mark any differences at all, point only to different levels of commitment within the same occupation. In English, the term "priest" has long referred to members of the clergy who have received ordination from a bishop, granting them the authority to perform rites on behalf of a given community. "Monk," on the other hand, refers to religious, especially contemplatives, who separate themselves from the secular world to live under monastic rule. Unless ordained as priests, monks were not to perform those duties that required priestly authority, such as the Eucharist and confession. Unlike priests who served parishes, then, monks were ideally to distance themselves from the lay world, focusing instead on a life of prayer and study shared with other renunciants. Although abbots and other monks did often receive priestly ordination in order to perform rites on behalf of the monastic community, they tended to distinguish themselves from "secular" priests, who lived outside monastic rule and served lay communities.[18]

In the case of Japanese Buddhism, *sō* and *biku* sometimes behaved like priests, providing ritual services for the lay community, and sometimes behaved like monks, separating themselves from the secular world at large and concentrating on a life of secluded study. In his recent overview of Japanese religions, Richard Bowring addresses this issue by using the term "priest" to designate those *sō* who functioned primarily as state ritualists and the term "monk" to designate those *sō* who lived in religious communities and focused on scholarly pursuits. According to Bowring, early Japanese *sō* are best understood as priests, since their primary function was to perform rituals on behalf of the state. It was not until the eighth-century establishment of monastic centers in Nara, he suggests, that Japanese *sō* began to resemble monks in the Western sense of the term (2005, 98–99).

It should be noted, however, that even after Japanese *sō* began to take on monklike qualities, they tended to retain, at least as a group, the priestly functions that defined *sō* during Buddhism's earliest years in Japan. Unlike the Christian case, in which monks and priests pursued fundamentally different career paths, most Japanese *sō* spent time at monastic institutions and performed *both* priestly *and* monkish roles. In particular, those who had risen through the ranks of the *sangha* would usually split their time between serving members of the laity, usually in exchange for financial contributions or gifts; performing rituals at their home institutions, a number of which, especially from the early medieval period onward, were open to lay auditors; and teaching their own disciples. Their work, then, was aimed both at the lay public and at those training within the monastery. For this reason, I will refer to those *sō* who frequently undertook visibly priestly duties as "priests" and those who were less clearly engaged in public ministerial and ceremonial roles as "monks." It should be noted, however, that Buddhist institutions did not themselves distinguish between "priests" and "monks." Moreover, in the case of Nara- and early-Heian-period institutions, such as the state monastery-convent pairs discussed in chapter 1, monks and nuns at state temples performed rituals on behalf of the state—and thus had a priestly function—but appear to have had only limited involvement in the ritual lives of their local lay communities. For this reason, I tend to refer to these clerics as "monks" and "nuns" when treating them as a group, even though their positions required them to perform rituals for the state.

Ordination also carried a different set of meanings in the Buddhist case. Since the seventh century, Christianity has generally recognized a difference between taking vows, which monks and nuns do, and taking orders, or receiving priestly ordination, which bestows one with the authority to perform certain solemn rites (eventually designated "sacraments") like baptism, the Eucharist, and last rites. In the Buddhist case, there was no ritual category similar to that of the sacraments. In most Buddhist societies, there was a clear distinction made between taking vows as a layperson, which usually involved only a simple ceremony, and taking full vows and receiving initiation into the *sangha,* which was usually carried out in a more complex ceremony that required the participation of ten fully ordained *bhikṣu.* Among *bhikṣu* who had taken full vows, however, there was no further distinction between those allowed to perform public rites and those not; such opportunities were to be granted (and in many cases sought) in accordance with one's individual intellectual and spiritual progress and did not require additional ceremonies or ordinations.[19]

In Japan, as in many Buddhist societies, there were few general rules regarding teaching and the performance of rituals. What did develop in

Japanese monasteries, and at the Japanese court, was a system of official ceremonial positions that reflected the structure and logic of Confucian bureaucracy. Monk-priests who sought traditional advancement within state and monastic hierarchies strove to receive appointments as lecturers and cantors in large-scale ceremonies *(hōe)* held at monastic institutions and at court. Certain annual ceremonies, such as the Ceremony for the *Vimalakīrti Sūtra* (Yuima-e) performed at Kōfukuji, the Ceremony for the *Golden Light Sutra* (Saishō-e) performed at Yakushiji, and the Vegetarian Ceremony (Misai-e, also Gosai-e) performed at court, were especially prestigious (see Sangō 2007; Ruppert 2000, 360). Those granted visible roles in such ceremonies were marked as the most accomplished and celebrated figures in the monastic world and were more or less guaranteed secure positions for the remainder of their careers.

But while the lecturer and cantor positions of elite ceremonial performances were limited to a handful of privileged priests, there was nothing to prevent ordinary monks, or indeed anyone claiming the status of a world renouncer, from carrying out roles in less prestigious versions of major ceremonies, performing other types of rituals, or preaching. Thus, while advancement within the traditional monastic hierarchy did indeed reflect one's mastery of certain texts and ritual techniques, those occupying the lower echelons of the official monastic hierarchy, and even those who remained on its fringes, were not barred by state or religious law from engaging in priestly activities such as preaching and ritual performance. In this sense, the relationships between clerical status, ordination, and ritual authority were, on the whole, more fluid in Japanese Buddhist institutions than in Christian ones.[20]

Understanding this fluidity is especially important when considering the case of *ama,* usually rendered as "nuns," in Japan. In traditional Christian usage, nuns are viewed as the female counterparts of monks. And thus, like monks who have not received priestly ordination, nuns have not "taken orders" and are not recognized as having the authority to perform sacraments or to preach to members of the laity.[21] In the case of East Asia, however, Buddhism made no clear distinction between priests and monks; instead, *seng* and *biqiu* were used as practically interchangeable terms to refer to male members of the clergy who performed both priestly and monkish duties. The female counterparts of *seng* and *biqiu* were *niseng* (Jpns. *nisō*) and *biqiuni* (Jpns. *bikuni,* from the Sanskrit *bhikṣuṇī*). Just as male renouncers in Japan were often referred to simply as *sō,* female renouncers were often referred to as *ama,* the Japanese-style reading of the Chinese character *ni.*

Behavioral codes for the *sangha* made it clear that *bhikṣuṇī* were to answer to *bhikṣu.* In addition to the fact that *bhikṣuṇī* were required to take about one hundred more precepts than their male counterparts, they were also to uphold the *aṭṭha garu-dhammā,* or eight rules of respect (*bajingjie,* Jpns. *hakkyōkai*). Among these special rules was one that required *bhikṣuṇī* to bow down to all *bhikṣu,* even those who were their juniors; one that forbade *bhikṣuṇī* from rebuking *bhikṣu* (though *bhikṣu* could rebuke their female counterparts); and one that required *bhikṣuṇī* to take male, rather than female, members of the *sangha* as their preceptors. That the *sangha* was to be headed by its male members, then, was never in question. But what separates the Buddhist from the Christian case is that there were no Buddhist regulations that specifically forbade *bhikṣuṇī* from preaching to laypeople or from performing public rituals and ministerial services. In this sense, then, Buddhist nuns had the potential to act as what we might call "nun-priests."

In Christian Europe, by contrast, debates over the ordination of women, which have spanned nearly two millennia, have been bound up with concerns over the degree to which women should be granted teaching, ministerial, and sacerdotal roles in the church. As ordination came to be understood as a sacrament that bestowed one with public authority for teaching and ministry, church leaders did what they could to ensure that such authority would remain in the hands of men. Some of the first waves of censure came in the fourth and fifth centuries, when the Councils of Laodicea (mid-to-late fourth c.), Nimes (late fourth c.), and Orange (441) forbade women from acquiring clerical positions, including that of the deaconess, and from taking part in liturgical services (Rossi 1991, 83). In 494, Pope Gelasius I issued additional legislation, this time prohibiting the wives of bishops from performing services and ministries at the altar (McNamara 1996, 59). The issue gained broad attention again in the twelfth and thirteenth centuries, when a number of prominent church scholars began developing formal arguments against the ordination of women, this time providing various (and often contradictory) theological and philosophical views to support the position. Medieval canonists insisted that only priests had the right to preach and to perform sacraments: monks and nuns, no matter how learned they might be, were never to preach in public. Some forbade women, including nuns, from offering incense at the altar and handling ritual implements such as linens and vessels. Others prohibited women from even approaching the altar or entering the sanctuary. Faced with the task of interpreting canons from earlier centuries, which mention deaconesses in passing, a number of medieval commentators insisted that the deaconesses to which these canons refer did not "have orders," that is, that they had not gained authentic ordination and did not have the authority to do anything beyond singing or reciting prayers during certain services. Others denied that the position of deaconesses had ever been valid at all (Martin 1986, esp. 128–138; Macy 2008, 96–105).

In the thirteenth century, arguments against women's ordination moved from the mere citing of precedents and biblical passages (such as that in which Paul states that women are not to speak in church) to more abstract arguments about the inability to receive the sacrament of ordination in a female body. Eventually, the logic that gained most currency was that which holds that ordinands symbolize Christ when they receive ordination and that women, limited by the weaknesses associated with femininity, could not possibly represent Christ in his full masculine glory (Martin 1986, 148–154, 164–165; Macy 2008, 121–125).

A remarkable difference in the Japanese case is that while certain discourses disparaging the female body did indeed emerge, there was no central authority that systematically linked discourses on the female body to theological arguments about the ordination of women. Nor did Japanese Buddhist authorities use discourses on the female body to write laws that forbade women from preaching or performing rituals. That women's bodies rendered them unfit for the priesthood may have eventually come to form a kind of "commonsense" knowledge within certain monastic circles, but we do not know of any doctrinal records that articulate this idea in an explicit way. And thus we can observe that while Buddhist and Christian discourses gave rise to similar rhetoric about the inferiority of the female body, they defined the terms of women's inclusion and subordination in very different ways.

Buddhist nuns in premodern Japan faced obstacles on the path to ordination, as well as limited opportunities for monastic and scholarly training, but the question of whether or not nuns could teach or perform rituals emerges neither in the literature of Saidaiji nor in that of Hokkeji. Indeed, in the early Japanese state nuns were given roles very similar to those of male monks and priests and should thus be viewed as nun-priests: they performed official rites on behalf of the state, ministered to the sick, and carried out ceremonies for laypeople of both sexes. Nuns who executed priestly duties disappeared after the ninth century, when the state stopped offering women formal ordination, but lay and other types of privately professed nuns continued to preach and to conduct rituals, though in unofficial capacities. When monastic ordinations for women became common again from the time of Hokkeji's medieval restoration, nuns were once more able to serve in priestly roles. They did not have the visibility or numbers of male monastics, but there appears not to have been any widespread resistance to nuns who offered ritual services for lay patrons, performed ceremonies open to the public, or taught lay pilgrims. The warrior government even came to employ some medieval nuns—or nun-priests—in rites meant to protect the state from foreign invasion and to heal illnesses within the shogunal family. Chapter 6 will consider the ritual activities of Hokkeji and other medieval nuns in greater depth.

Another important issue worth clarifying here is that, as a rule, Buddhist nuns were not cloistered. Although there is ample evidence to suggest that, especially in the late medieval period, certain aristocratic and elite warrior families in Japan did send daughters to convents in order to maintain control over family wealth or because marriage partners of suitable standing were in short supply, women sent to convents were by no means forbidden from interacting with the outside world. Despite the fact that Buddhist monasticism, like Christian monasticism, requires celibacy of its monks and nuns (at least in theory), Buddhist groups in Japan did not idealize virginity or even chastity as a broad social value for women. It did become increasingly common, from the twelfth century or so, for widows to take vows as a way of displaying faithfulness to their husbands, but what was emphasized here was loyalty to the family group rather than sexual fidelity (Katsuura 1995, 102). There is also much Buddhist literature that advises monks to avoid interaction with women, but there is little evidence that Buddhist nuns, like Christian nuns, were cloistered in order to protect their own sexual purity or that of the male orders.[22]

This contrast did not go unnoticed by early groups of Westerners visiting East and Central Asia. The Portuguese Jesuit Luís Fróis (1532–1597), who arrived in Japan in 1563, observed that while Christian nuns ("our nuns") were expected to stay within their convents, Japanese *bikuni* were "going out at all times" of the day and night, sometimes even visiting battlefields.[23] Similarly, English diplomat Samuel Turner (1749?–1802), who visited Tibet in the late eighteenth century, seemed surprised by the fact that Buddhist nuns there were allowed male visitors: "Though nuns, the admission of male visitors among them during the day, is not prohibited."[24] In the case of Hokkeji, too, we will see that nuns interacted with men—monks from Saidaiji, men from court, and male patrons—on a regular basis.

Like nuns in the Christian West, *bikuni* at Hokkeji left home, took vows, and lived in a religious community. In this sense, "nun" is the English term that best approximates their the social position. But I use the term only with the qualifications mentioned above, namely, that Buddhist nuns at Hokkeji and other medieval convents were not cloistered and that these nuns were not theologically barred from performing priestly roles in their communities.

Overview

This book is divided into seven chapters. Following this introductory chapter, chapter 1 treats the history of Hokkeji from its initial decline in the Heian period through the various periods of neglect and semirevival it endured over the course of the Heian period and finally leading up to the years immediately preceding its large-scale revival in the mid-thirteenth century. Against previous studies (in Japanese) that have attributed Hokkeji's revival to the work of the priest Eison, this chapter traces Hokkeji's emergence in travel records from the early twelfth century and demonstrates how Hokkeji's restoration was rooted in the expansion of Nara pilgrimage routes during the late Heian period. Drawing on *engi* and other popular narratives associated with Hokkeji, I illustrate how nuns staying at Hokkeji during the early years of the Kamakura period used miraculous legends associated with Kōmyō to attract visitors and revitalize the convent. In approaching the story of Hokkeji's medieval revival from this angle, we are able to see that the reemergence of convents during this period was not simply the result of certain doctrinal innovations, such as those offered by Eison, which allowed for the ordination of women. Certain lay practices visible on the ground—such as pilgrimage to sites associated with legendary figures from Japan's past and the spread of *engi* and other popular religious literature—played key roles in the successful restoration of Hokkeji and other convents.

Chapter 2 focuses on individual women involved in the medieval restoration of Hokkeji. One of the most visible accomplishments of Hokkeji's medieval revival was the reinstitution of an ordination platform for nuns. Both this chapter and the one that follows seek to uncover how various communities surrounding Hokkeji understood the ordination of women, the problem of women's salvation, and the place of women in the Buddhist order during this period. Here, I am particularly concerned with understanding views of women and Buddhism popular in court society, for among the first rectors at the revived Hokkeji were a number of women who had served as ladies-in-waiting at court.

Chapter 3 contrasts courtly views of women and Buddhism with those widespread among male monastic groups. In this chapter, I examine how the monastic order viewed women and problems surrounding their ordination during the years preceding Eison's decision to create an ordination platform for women at Hokkeji in the 1240s. I begin with examples from monastic literature in which certain unorthodox priests—iconoclasts like Dōgen (1200–1253) and Myōe (1173–1232, also Kōben)—criticized the Tendai-Shingon orthodoxy for pandering to elite female patrons while failing to offer women official ordination. I then develop an examination of these critical comments into a larger argument about the ways in which women's ordination fit in to early-Kamakura-period debates about the authenticity of Japanese Buddhism vis-à-vis that practiced in China.

In chapter 4, I delve into Hokkeji's relationship with Eison and his widely popular movement to revive both the Ritsu school itself and the monastic practice of upholding the *vinaya* laws more broadly. The chapter begins with a summary of Eison's movement and a discussion of its significance in the religious landscape of Kamakura-period Japan. It goes on to explain how Eison and his disciples envisioned the role of Hokkeji and its nuns in the Ritsu order and to explore the details of how, exactly, Eison implemented Ritsu practices and teachings at Hokkeji. It further examines the question of whether or not Hokkeji nuns were under the management of Saidaiji monks during this period. Finally, the chapter argues that the relationship between Eison and his female followers, including both Hokkeji nuns and laywomen associated with Hokkeji or other temples, exemplified a new, distinctly Kamakura model of how monks were to interact with female followers.

Chapter 5 examines social and economic life at Hokkeji during the heyday of its medieval restoration. During the late thirteenth century, women came to Hokkeji from provinces near and far not only as world renouncers seeking ordination and monastic training but also as lay devotees, pilgrims, and patrons of ritual services. This chapter looks at the social composition of both those groups that took up residence at the convent and those brought to Hokkeji through networks of pilgrimage and patronage. Chapter 6 pursues similar issues but focuses in particular on the ritual programs in place at medieval Hokkeji. Close analysis of the *Hokke metsuzaiji nenjū gyōji* (Yearly events of the Lotus Temple for the Eradication of Transgressions), a lengthy ritual calendar from medieval Hokkeji, allows us to catch a glimpse of the daily liturgies and annual events that shaped everyday life at Hokkeji. Donor names included in the document also help us to better understand how ritual events held at the convent enabled Hokkeji nuns to gain the support of local laypeople.

Having examined the Hokkeji restoration from these numerous perspectives, I turn, in the final chapter, to consider how women and men involved in the convent's restoration articulated their views on the nature of women, their salvation, and their roles in the Buddhist community. Chapter 7 examines the degree to which literature composed by the Hokkeji nuns' community bypasses, or "talks past," the androcentric rhetoric espoused by Ritsu monks. Reading the literature of the male Ritsu community against that written by Hokkeji nuns, I suggest that Hokkeji nuns chose whenever possible to preserve a less doctrinal, more lay-oriented approach to salvation that downplayed soteriological obstacles related to the female body and focused instead on the saving power of their venerated patron goddess, Queen-Consort Kōmyō. I also examine representations of the nuns' order and its place in the Ritsu hierarchy, paying particular attention to the degree to which monks and nuns employed different language when describing the place of women in the order. While the members of the monks' order made it clear that they envisioned themselves as the stewards of the nuns' order, Hokkeji nuns barely mentioned Ritsu monks. Their texts hold Queen-Consort Kōmyō—and not any monk or group of monks—to be the leader of the nuns' order. Moreover, while monks tended to ground their views in scholarly and doctrinal texts, the nuns of Hokkeji focused instead on certain parallels between court life and life in the convent. Building on idealized views of the bygone Heian-era court, the nuns suggested that the venerated traditions of the old court survived in the daily activities of Hokkeji and in the memory of Kōmyō preserved there.

The book closes with a brief epilogue that reflects upon the place of Hokkeji and its medieval restoration in the wider history of women's religiosity in premodern Japan. It further considers the implications of this study for the field of Japanese Buddhism more broadly.

1

Pilgrimage, Popular Devotion, and the Reemergence of Hokkeji

LIKE MOST TEMPLES BUILT in the southern capital of Heijō-kyō (Nara) during the eighth century, Hokkeji's years of flourishing were limited. Although documentary and archaeological evidence indicates that construction continued on the grounds of the convent even into the early years of the ninth century, the convent lost its financial and political support base with the passing of its two major patrons, Queen-Consort Kōmyō and her daughter, the sovereign Kōken-Shōtoku, in 760 and 770, respectively. Moreover, Hokkeji, like many other great temple complexes that had been built in Nara, suffered when the court left the southern capital in 784, moving first to Nagaoka-kyō and then finally to Heian-kyō, in 794. This chapter examines the history of Hokkeji from the time of its initial decline in the early Heian period through the years preceding its large-scale restoration in the middle of the thirteenth century. How and why did Hokkeji lose visibility over the course of the Heian period, and what historical factors and processes allowed the convent to reinvent itself some five hundred years after its initial establishment?

As the work of Nishiguchi Junko has shown, Nara temples, especially those that had been built primarily by powerful local families, faced great uncertainty in the early years of the Heian period, when most politically important families relocated to the new capital of Heian-kyō (Kyoto). Even large-scale institutions like Saidaiji, Daianji, Hōryūji, Gangōji, Sōfukuji, Kenkōji, and Hokkeji—which had been designated "great temples" *(daiji)* by the state—fell into periods of desuetude from the late eighth century through the tenth (2004, 119–124).

Even for the so-called great temples of Nara, the early Heian period was a time of instability, for the state continued throughout this period to reassess its relationships with the temples of the Heijō capital. Official court documents, including the 927 *Engi-shiki* (distributed in 967), suggest that the court still depended on the great temples of Nara well into the Heian period. The twenty-first volume of the *Engi-shiki,* for example, frequently refers to the great Nara temples, including Hokkeji. But what exactly these textual references meant in terms of actual financial support is unclear. It is now known that many of the temples included among the fifteen great temples *(jūgo daiji)* in the *Engi-shiki* had in fact fallen into a state of dormancy, if not complete neglect, by the tenth century. Nishiguchi goes so far as to say that all the grand temples of Nara with the exception of Tōdaiji, Kōfukuji, and Yakushiji had "ceased to remain active" by the middle years of the Heian period (2004, 136).

When the history of Hokkeji is placed in this context, it becomes clear that Hokkeji did not lose stature *because* it was a convent, or at least not for that reason exclusively. Rather, the temple first lost visibility because it had been left behind in the Nara capital. Writers who referred to Hokkeji during the early years of the Heian did not convey any discomfort with the notion that Hokkeji was a temple for women; in fact, many recorded this detail rather matter-of-factly, as we will see in the discussion that follows.

As for early-Heian references to Hokkeji specifically, the convent is mentioned in the *Engi-shiki* and is also included in at least one royal command for ritual service. In the year 1017, supernumerary major counselor Minamoto no Toshikata (959–1027) issued an edict calling for the fifteen great temples (here defined as Tōdaiji, Kōfukuji, Yakushiji, Gangōji, Daianji, Saidaiji, Hōryūji, Hokkeji, Shin-Yakushiji, Moto-Gangōji, [Tō]Shōdaiji, Tōji, Saiji, Shitennōji, and Sōfukuji) plus Enryakuji to carry out quick readings *(tendoku)* of the *Humane Kings Perfection of Wisdom Sutra* (*Ninnō hannya kyō*, T. no. 245). These sixteen temples were to carry out this ceremony continuously for five days from the twenty-ninth day of the fifth month in order to quell an epidemic that was ravaging both capital and countryside. In addition to providing basic information about the epidemic, the document also indicates how many clerics each temple was to assign to the task of carrying out this particular ritual service. Hokkeji was among the eight small temples required to have fifteen clerics perform *tendoku* ceremonies; the largest temple was Enryakuji, which was to have sixty monks carry out the rite, followed by Tōdaiji, Kōfukuji, and Yakushiji, which were each called upon to offer the services of fifty monks (*Ruijū fusenshō*, 3:105–116).

Of the sixteen temples called upon to offer prayers in this 1017 command, Hokkeji was the only institution that might be identified as a convent. Given the fact that many convents had been converted into male monasteries by this period, can we be sure that Hokkeji was in fact operating as a convent in the year 1017 and that Toshikata, in issuing this commandment, expected Hokkeji to employ fifteen nuns in the performance of *tendoku* rites?

This question is a difficult one, and the few sources that might speak to the issue offer only ambiguous clues. As Ōishi Masaaki has pointed out, it is known that by the fifteenth century Hokkeji had two coexisting identities: there was the order of nuns that actually inhabited the convent, and then there was the male priest, usually someone from Kōfukuji, who occupied the post of Hokkeji *bettō*, or chief administrator priest. Since *bettō* posts were often held in absentia, it is likely that those men who occupied the Hokkeji *bettō* did not in fact live at Hokkeji but instead handled certain administrative matters related to the convent from afar, perhaps most often from living quarters at or near Kōfukuji. The *bettō,* Ōishi surmises, was the person who handled state requests for prayers and ceremonies. When the state called upon Hokkeji to perform rites, then, it was actually calling upon the Hokkeji *bettō* to perform rites, and these rites did not necessarily need to be carried out on the grounds of the convent itself; in fact, Ōishi speculates that the Hokkeji *bettō* carried out Hokkeji-related ceremonies somewhere at Kōfukuji (1997).

Knowing that this scenario existed in the fifteenth century, we might wonder if a similar arrangement—that is, a dual Hokkeji split between male administration and female occupation—was in place at Hokkeji four centuries earlier, at the time that Toshikata issued the 1017 command mentioned above. There is no conclusive evidence one way or the other, but careful attention to state documents from the early Heian period suggests that there may have been some kind of gender-based division of labor in place at Hokkeji during the ninth, tenth, and eleventh centuries. It appears to have been the case that male priests were charged with the performance of certain ritual and administrative functions at Hokkeji but that the convent retained its identity as a female monastic institution throughout, meaning that Hokkeji continued to be regarded as an institution that was to be inhabited by women.

First, on the matter of ritual activities at Hokkeji: the Daijōkan, or Council of State, issued a directive *(fu)* in the year 900 addressing Hokkeji specifically. According to this document, the provincial governor of Yamato had been allowing priests other than the Yamato provincial lecturer *(koku kōji)* to perform the *Lotus Sutra* recitations held at Hokkeji on the first and last days of the meditation retreat (the sixteenth day of the fourth month and the fifteenth day of the seventh month) (*Ruijū sandai kyaku,* 2:52). The position of provincial lecturer had been established in the late eighth century, when local administrators were finally, in accordance with Shōmu's 741 commands, erecting monastery-convent pairs *(kokubunniji)* in the provinces. Under the guidance of his provincial governor *(kokushi),* each provincial lecturer was to oversee the administration of the state monastery-convent pair in his province. This meant that while provincial convents were to house nuns, they fell under the jurisdiction of male priests and officials from their very inception.[1] That this command dated to the year 900 calls for the Yamato provincial lecturer to perform *Lotus Sutra* recitations at Hokkeji, then, should not be read as an indication that Hokkeji had been converted into a monastery. As temple administration became increasingly privatized over the course of the Heian period, the provincial lecturer position eventually gave way to the *bettō* title, which had more secular overtones and did not necessarily carry the same kind of ritual or pedagogical responsibilities that one might ascribe to an abbot or abbess.

Despite the changing nature of relations between the state and Buddhist temples, then, the Council of State continued to make efforts, even as late as the early tenth century, to control the activities of provincial monasteries and convents. What's more, these documents suggest that nuns may still have been in residence, both at Hokkeji and at some other provincial convents, as late as the late ninth and early tenth centuries. A separate Council of State directive dated to the year 839, for example, specifies that all provincial convents were to hold recitations of the *Lotus Sutra* during the summer retreat, when the provincial monasteries were to recite the *Golden Light Sutra*. Provincial monasteries, the document claims, were in fact still performing *Golden Light Sutra* ceremonies, but in recent years *Lotus Sutra* recitations were no longer being held at the convents. Calling for state convents to reinstate the performance of *Lotus Sutra* recitations, the directive notes that each monastery and convent had been staffed with clerics who were to carry out regular sutra recitations on behalf of the state (*Ruijū sandai kyaku*, 3:111–112).

In addition to this directive and the previously mentioned directive dated to the year 900, numerous other directives from the late ninth century mention both Hokkeji and provincial nunneries as a group. While it can be inferred from the content of the two directives examined above that activity was beginning to decline at Hokkeji and at provincial convents—rituals were not being carried out according to regulation, and lesser priests were being allowed to perform the *Lotus Sutra* recitations at Hokkeji—neither these two directives nor any others from this period suggest that nuns were no longer living in Hokkeji or in other provincial convents. The directives continue to speak of nuns *(ni)* in the abstract when discussing affairs at provincial convents, and they make no mention of priests having replaced nuns in the convents. One directive, dated to the year 818, states that the practice of monks and nuns cohabitating has become a problem at many provincial temples. It urges clerics to obey the rule that monks refrain from entering convents and that nuns refrain from entering male monasteries. Another directive, dated to the year 844, commands that the tonsure certificates of monks and nuns be returned to provincial government headquarters in the case of a cleric's death or laicization. Although Ushiyama Yoshiyuki's research has shown that the last public record of nuns receiving official state ordination dates to the year 828 (1990, 16), this directive implies that at least some nuns were still recognized as having received official state ordination and that they continued to possess verification of their ordinations as late as 844.[2] Taken together, these documents suggest that nuns were not forced out of convents immediately following their exclusion from the official ordination system. It seems safe to say that some convents remained home to nuns at least until the mid-ninth century, nearly a century after the court had last employed nuns in any of its official ritual services. And while, as Ushiyama's research has demonstrated, most of the convents that had been established during the Nara period were converted into monasteries during the early ninth century (63–65), it appears that a handful became hermitages or practice halls where privately professed nuns who had not received official ordination—female lay *shukke*—were permitted to live and to practice. Such, it would appear, was the case with Hokkeji.[3]

Hokkeji is mentioned again in an 898 entry in the *Fusō ryakki,* a history compiled by the Fujiwara-born Tendai priest Kōen in the late twelfth century. According to the entry, the retired sovereign Uda, having just abdicated the throne and taken precepts in the year 897, happened to pass by Hokkeji while visiting temples in the southern capital during the tenth month of Shōtai 1 (898). The entry says that Uda stopped at Hokkeji, paying obeisance to images of the Buddha there and making a donation of two hundred pounds of silk floss wadding. It also notes that the retired sovereign bemoaned the degree to which the various buildings on the grounds of Hokkeji had fallen into a state of disrepair (3:168). This brief reference to Hokkeji confirms the information conveyed in the directive dated to the year 900 mentioned above, namely, that Hokkeji was in operation around the turn of the tenth century but was not flourishing. Nevertheless, this entry suggests that the images installed in the temple halls were indeed being cared for and that there were clerics in residence who were able to accept Uda's offerings.

It was another century before Hokkeji appeared in surviving sources again. In the year 999, the celebrated calligrapher, supernumerary major counselor Fujiwara no Yukinari (also Kōzei, 972–1027), recorded in his diary, *Gonki,* a pilgrimage of his to the southern capital. On the fifteenth day of the tenth month, on his way back from visits to Daianji and Yakushiji, Yukinari surveyed the grounds at Hokkeji, noting that the buildings were in a heavily damaged state. These remarks are in contrast to those made with regard to Daianji, where he noted that numerous repairs had been made. The following year, on the twenty-first day of the eighth month, Yukinari sent an envoy back to Hokkeji to survey the extent of its physical decline (*Gonki,* Chōhō 1 [999] 10/15, Chōhō 2 [1000] 8/21, 140).

Neither the *Fusō ryakki* nor Yukinari's *Gonki* makes any direct mention of nuns at Hokkeji. But there is one contemporaneous collection that does mention nuns at Hokkeji around this time, and that is *The Three Jewels,* or the *Sanbōe kotoba,* compiled by Minamoto no Tamenori in the year 984. In *The Three Jewels,* written for Princess Sonshi (966–985; the second daughter of the Reizei Tennō) as an introduction to the fundamentals of Buddhism, Tamenori includes an entry devoted to the Ceremony for the *Flower Ornament Sutra* (Kegon-e) at Hokkeji (3.13). Within the space of this narrative, he notes, "Since the founding of this temple [Hokkeji] by the Empress [queen-consort], there has been no interruption in its habitation by nuns" (trans. Kamens 1988, 291; *Sanbōe kotoba,* 3.13). As mentioned earlier, the *Engi-shiki,* roughly contemporaneous with *The Three Jewels,* also mentions Hokkeji—and nuns—with regularity. But since it is known that many of the codes included in the *Engi-shiki* were taken from earlier codes, such as the 820 *Kōnin-kyakushiki* and the 869–871 *Jōgan-shiki,* we cannot assume that references to nuns in the *Engi-shiki* necessarily reflect tenth-century realities. The next major mention of Hokkeji appears in Minamoto no Toshikata's 1017 royal command for sutra recitations for protection from epidemics. His command, as we saw earlier, does not refer to nuns specifically. So while Tamenori's remark implies that nuns did indeed occupy Hokkeji throughout the tenth century, other textual references to Hokkeji during this period do not directly corroborate Tamenori's claim that the lineage of nuns at Hokkeji had remained unbroken even into the late tenth century.

Although they do not speak to the issue of whether or not nuns continued to inhabit Hokkeji, scattered references to the appointments of Hokkeji *bettō* in eleventh- and early-twelfth-century courtier diaries confirm that Hokkeji remained, if only barely, among those temples whose administration the court monitored during the mid-Heian period. An entry in the *Midō Kanpakuki,* for example, notes that the Hokkeji *bettō* was transferred from the priest Renshō to the priest Rinkai on the seventh day of the third month of 1004 (Kankō 1/3/7). Recent research has identified both Rinkai and Kyōri as Kōfukuji priests. This evidence supports the view that Hokkeji, like many temples in the Yamato area, had already come under Kōfukuji control by the eleventh century (Ushiyama 1990, 63).[4] A little over a decade later, in 1016, an entry in the *Shōyūki* records new *bettō* appointments. Here, the same Rinkai is named to the powerful post of Kōfukuji *bettō,* suggesting that the Hokkeji *bettō* may have been a stepping-stone to more prestigious posts within the ecclesiastical community of the southern capital. This same entry notes that a priest named Kyōri had been appointed to the Hokkeji *bettō* post (Chōwa 5 [1016] 5/16). Nearly a century later, in 1102, the *Chūyūki* mentions a Hokkeji *bettō* appointment. This reference, like those noted above, is brief. It simply notes that a priest named Jōkaku had been made *bettō* of Hokkeji (Kōwa 4 [1102] 1/14).

As these examples suggest, Hokkeji *bettō* appear to have been exclusively male. But one cannot use this detail to argue that nuns were no longer living at Hokkeji, since *bettō* titles were often bestowed upon priests as rewards. It was the prestige of the title and the right to annual income from the lands of the temple in question that made the *bettō* position attractive. Many *bettō* lived off-site. In particular, it was common for Kōfukuji priests who held *bettō* positions at other, smaller Yamato temples to remain living at or near Kōfukuji and to visit the temple whose *bettō* title they held only when their presence was necessary (Matsuo 2004b, 31; Ōishi 1997). In many senses, this arrangement mirrors the institutional arrangement in place at provincial convents during the Nara and early Heian periods, when male *koku kōji* (provincial lecturers) were the nominal heads of the convents, even though nuns occupied the convents and managed their daily affairs. We also know that a similar model was in place in the fourteenth and fifteenth centuries, when priests were assigned the Hokkeji *bettō* title despite the fact that nuns were living in the temple and appear to have been conducting their everyday activities independently of these *bettō.*[5]

In 1128, a couple of decades after the *Chūyūki*'s reference to the Hokkeji *bettō,* Hokkeji resurfaces in the written record, and this time the reference confirms the institution's identity as a monastic institution for women. The text in question is the *Bodai shinshū* (Collection on giving rise to the mind of enlightenment), a treatise on *nenbutsu* and other popular merit-making practices compiled by the Nara priest Chinkai (1091–1152). Here, Chinkai refers to Hokkeji in response to a question regarding the living quarters of nuns. The way he speaks of Hokkeji suggests that the convent was still being used to house nuns during his time:

> QUESTION: Must *ama* live in secluded areas?
> ANSWER: I have heard that it has been advised that temples for nuns be established inside the capital. Thus, in the Heijō capital [Nara], there is a temple for nuns [*ama no tera*] called Hokkeji. Nuns are to live there and carry out the reading of the *Lotus Sutra,* and so it is named the Lotus Temple [Hokkeji]. In each of the over sixty provinces, state monasteries [*kokubunji*] and convents [*kokubunniji*] have been built by the state. The convents were called Hokkeji, and the state also provided the nuns' food and clothing. Generally speaking, the residences of nuns must not be in secluded areas. The concern is that, should something happen, or if there were some kind of disturbance [such a situation would be dangerous]. (26a)

Admittedly, the description of Hokkeji that Chinkai provides here blurs the present and the past, failing to mention the changes that had taken place at Hokkeji since its establishment as the head of the provincial temple pair system that had been, by his time, long defunct. Given the fact that Chinkai spent much of his career at Tōdaiji, the monastery that had been paired with Hokkeji in the eighth century, it is unlikely that his understanding of this neighboring institution was based on textual sources alone; surely he had visited the convent and was kept abreast of its activities through colleagues in the southern capital. That said, his mention of Hokkeji leaves many details unexplained: are we to understand that Hokkeji nuns were still carrying out readings of the *Lotus Sutra,* or is this sentence simply repeating earlier descriptions of Hokkeji's founding? The text provides no clear answer. These ambiguities notwithstanding, Chinkai's words do imply rather clearly that Hokkeji's identity as a monastic institution for women had somehow persisted through the long centuries of the early Heian period, centuries that had seen the crumbling of the land administration system established through the *ritsuryō* (penal and administrative) legal codes, the gradual disintegration of the provincial temple network, the termination of official ordinations for nuns, and the transformation of women's renunciation practices.[6]

Hokkeji's Development as a Pilgrimage Destination

The turning point for Hokkeji was its reinvention as a site of elite pilgrimage. By the late twelfth century, Hokkeji had become one of the standard sites included in pilgrimage tours of the southern capital. Having gained a place within the Nara pilgrimage circuit, Hokkeji garnered greater attention from the elite, and especially from elite women. Moreover, legends of the convent's founding, its legacy of female leadership, and miracles associated with its founder, Queen-Consort Kōmyō, spread quickly, as pilgrims visiting Hokkeji studied and recorded these narratives to commemorate their journeys there.

Hokkeji's emergence as a sacred site can be understood as part of a larger reimagining of the southern capital and its ancient temples. As Tendai and Shingon establishments eventually came to absorb many of the official state functions that had once been the domain of the great Nara temples, ecclesiastical institutions in the southern capital had to find new ways both to remain relevant and to attract patronage. Those temples that survived the early centuries of the Heian period, which saw so many important patrons abandon Nara for the new capital of Heian-kyō, did so by shifting focus away from their original association with the state bureaucracy and toward identities based on sacred origins and spaces. In particular, they reinvented their institutions as efficacious pilgrimage destinations (Nishiguchi 2004, 119–128, 136–137).

Hokkeji was no exception. Its first widely recognized appearance as a pilgrimage site occurs in the 1191 *Kenkyū gojunreiki* (Record of a pilgrimage taken in the Kenkyū era [1190–1199], aka *Nanto shodaiji engi-shū,* Collection of founding tales for various temples in the southern capital [Nara]), a collection of temple *engi,* or founding tales, compiled by the Kōfukuji priest Jitsuei as he accompanied a *nyoin* on a pilgrimage of the great religious sites of the southern capital: thirteen Buddhist temples, including the Kōfukuji-Kasuga temple-shrine complex.[7] The identity of this *nyoin* has given rise to much debate, but scholars have recognized Hachijō-in (Princess Shōshi, 1137–1211) as a likely candidate. Hachijō-in had taken the tonsure in her early twenties and would have been in her mid-fifties at the time of the pilgrimage (Fujita 1972, 127–129; Koida 2004).

Records of pilgrimage to the southern capital gained popularity during the early twelfth century. The earliest well-known work belonging to this genre is the *Shichidaiji nikki* (Journal of [a pilgrimage to] the seven great temples), compiled by the scholar-aristocrat Ōe no Chikamichi (1081?–1151) in the year 1106. Chikamichi produced another Nara pilgrimage record, the *Shichidaiji junrei shiki* (Personal record of a pilgrimage to the seven great temples), several decades later in the year 1140. That these works were popular even during Chikamichi's lifetime is evident from the fact that they were widely circulated and cited. Later pilgrimage records and *engi* collections draw on Chikamichi's work with great frequency (Fujita 1972, 19–20, 29–30).

But Chikamichi's work was itself grounded in even earlier works of the same genre. To mention just one example, in a *Shichidaiji junrei shiki* entry on Yakushiji, he refers to an anecdote mentioned in "some person's pilgrimage record" *(aru hito no junreiki)* (58). It would seem, then, that pilgrimage records had been popular for some time even before Chikamichi created his own. The emergence of this genre reflects both the rise of pilgrimage from the central regions into outlying areas, a practice that becomes noticeable from the mid-eleventh century, and the related trend in which Nara temples came to reinvent themselves as sacred spaces associated with miracles *(reijōka)*. This process of designating specific temple sites as sacred depended on the creation of compelling *engi,* or foundational stories, narratives that attested to the miraculous origins and mysterious powers of a given temple. It was through the creation and distribution of *engi* narratives that temples in remote areas came to be recognized as places worthy of pilgrimage from the capital regions (Nishiguchi 2004, 88–90, 124–137). Although these narratives were not limited to their textual versions—it is believed that oral versions of *engi* were often performed by temple clerics as a way of entertaining lay guests—written accounts of temple origins allowed for greater spread, especially since would-be pilgrims often based their own itineraries on the written pilgrimage accounts of others.[8] For temples, then, the key to success lay in the production of an *engi* so impressive that visitors who heard it would record it in a pilgrimage record or *engi* collection, thereby putting the narrative into circulation and inviting additional pilgrimage and financial support.

The *Kenkyū gojunreiki* represents an elaboration of the Nara pilgrimage record genre popularized by Chikamichi. Whereas Chikamichi's works address only seven temples and no convents, the *Kenkyū gojunreiki* includes a greater number of religious sites, at least two of which can be identified with women specifically. Some have suggested that the attention given to stories associated with women's practice of Buddhism marks the *Kenkyū gojunreiki* as unusual within the genre of pilgrimage records (Koida 2004, 57). Close scrutiny of Chikamichi's texts reveals, however, that although he does not include any entries on convents, he does make frequent reference to women associated with the royal family and its court, many of whom he recognizes as having commissioned particular temple halls, stupas, and statues. Stories mentioning Queen-Consort Kōmyō, in particular, are scattered throughout the *engi* of various buildings and images at the seven great temples he documents. His section on Kōfukuji's Lecture Hall also includes the story of the Baekje (Paekche) nun Hōmyō, who is said to have healed Fujiwara no Kamatari (Kōmyō's grandfather and the founder of the Fujiwara clan) during a time of illness by offering teachings on the *Vimalakīrti sūtra.*[9] Despite the fact that he does not include convents among the temples on his pilgrimage route, then, Chikamichi's text does refer often to female patrons and even to a few nuns.

The *Kenkyū gojunreiki* differs, however, insofar as it tends to focus less on historical data and more on the miracles associated with particular buildings and images. Its stories are in many senses more exaggerated and more extraordinary than Chikamichi's. Unlike the stories of women related in Chikamichi's texts, which provide dates and biographical information, stories of women related in the *Kenkyū gojunreiki* tell of the ways in which women were miraculously rewarded for their faith. Much like Tamenori, who included a handful of stories about nuns and female devotees in his *Three Jewels,* compiled nearly two hundred years earlier, Jitsuei, the author of

Kenkyū gojunreiki, also appears to have believed that legends of extraordinary Buddhist women would be of special interest to his elite female travel companion. The two most obvious examples of such stories included in the *Kenkyū gojunreiki* are to be found in the text's entries for Hokkeji and Taimadera, which include lengthy narratives recounting miracles associated with Queen-Consort Kōmyō and Lady Chūjō (fl. mid-eighth c.; daughter of Fujiwara no Toyonari), respectively.

Hokkeji is the fourth stop on the pilgrimage route described in Jitsuei's *Kenkyū gojunreiki:* it is included directly after the Kasuga shrine, Kōfukuji, and Tōdaiji and precedes Saidaiji and Shōdaiji (Tōshōdaiji). Jitsuei's entry for Hokkeji strings together a series of narratives that are developed more fully in later *engi* and *setsuwa* collections. In general, pilgrimage records tended to organize information according to individual buildings: first the temple would be described in general terms, and then the compiler would go on to recount the miraculous origins of each structure on the temple grounds. Although the Hokkeji entry in the *Kenkyū gojunreiki* follows this structure, it describes only two buildings: the Golden Hall (*kondō,* also main hall) and the place where a bathhouse once stood:

> Hokkeji.
> Queen-Consort Kōmyō is the founding patron of this [temple]. She had [Hokkeji] built in response to her feelings of regret over the fact that those possessing women's bodies would not be allowed to enter the Great Buddha Hall of Tōdaiji. In that fifteen-*chō* space [approx. 1,635 meters] separating the two temples [Tōdaiji and Hokkeji], folding screens to fend off geese were set up along the north and the south [when she] made the journey [between the two temples]. It is said that in ancient times it was decided that this Golden Hall was too cramped for the performance of the Ceremony for the *Vimalakīrti Sūtra* [Yuima-e], and so it was commanded that the performance be moved to Kōfukuji. After [this command] was handed down, and after the ceremony was moved to that temple, the statue of the householder Vimalakīrti, which had been made to sit facing the western direction, turned to face the southeast direction, longing toward Yamashinadera [Kōfukuji]; now it is facing Kōfukuji like this. This is a moving thing. [But now] the ridges of the roof have become damaged and the tiles exposed; the altar has collapsed, and the doors [of the tabernacle housing the primary image] are hanging aslant; the [roof] does not keep out the rain of spring mornings, and there is no barrier against the early morning winds of autumn.[10] It is said that even the stone lanterns that were arranged here are now in a lamentable state. This temple is called a convent [*amadera*] because from the time of the founding patron, Queen-Consort Kōmyō, nuns have been appointed to its three main administrative positions [*sangō*]. That tradition continues through today, and in the more recent past they have been *sageama* [nuns who maintain shoulder-length hair]. In recent years, [these *sageama,*] even though they are women, have taken the names of abbot [*jōza*] and general administrator [*jishu*] and have governed the affairs of the temple's landholdings.

> Not too far southeast of this temple's *torii* [gateway], there is a place where a single pine tree is growing in a rice field. This is the place of the ancient temple Ashukuji. After Queen-Consort Kōmyō had built Tōdaiji, Hokkeji, and temples like this, when she thought she had fulfilled her merit-making [obligations], a voice came from above the clouds in the sky, saying, "You have not yet fulfilled your merit." The queen-consort said, "What merit have I not yet created?" To which it was replied, "The merit of [establishing] a [healing] bathhouse." And so she erected a bathhouse in that place. When the hot water had been prepared, she made a vow saying that she personally would scrub the dirt off the first person who came to bathe that day. Once she had made this vow, one person from Kiyomizuzaka [an outcast community] who was in a very unfortunate condition appeared. With residue falling off [his body], he entered the bath without hesitation. As the queen-consort, thinking that she must wash him in accordance with undifferentiating merit, gazed upon him, he immediately said, "Please scrub my back." Seeing that she was experiencing feelings of distress, he said, "If you do not scrub my dirt away yourself, then you will end up tarnishing your vow and will be blamed for this reason. This is surely not something a person should do." The queen-consort extended her hand and, without embarrassment, suppressed her [feelings of resistance] and touched him, and he directed her, saying, "Even though you have done this, you must not tell people that you yourself have scrubbed the dirt off me." After he made this request, this person said the following, "I, Ashuku Buddha [also Fudō Butsu, Skt. Akṣobhya Buddha, the Immoveable Buddha], will come again to this place and appear in this bath." When the queen-consort said that she would keep it confidential, he emitted a light and caused a pleasant fragrance to ascend into the heavens. At this time the queen-consort longed to preserve a remnant of this event. She made that bathhouse into a temple and named it Ashukuji. [This] is the ancient remains of that [temple].[11]

It is probably safe to assume that most of the narrative threads that emerge in Jitsuei's description of Hokkeji were already in circulation during his time. The *Three Jewels,* written nearly two hundred years earlier, contains similar passages attributing the founding of Hokkeji to Queen-Consort Kōmyō and noting that various Hokkeji offices had been entrusted to nuns (*Sanbōe* 3.13; trans. Kamens 1988, 291–294). It is also known that the *Konjaku monogatarishū* (Tales of times now past), likely compiled at least several decades before the *Kenkyū gojunreiki,* once contained a narrative describing Kōmyō's establishment of Hokkeji.[12] Stories emphasizing Kōmyō's role in the establishment of Hokkeji, then, were nothing new. That these narratives continued to underscore the notion that Hokkeji's lineage of female leadership had survived the centuries of the Heian period, however, is worth attention. That this thread is picked up again and again suggests that this particular motif—that is, that women had continuously served as the administrators of Hokkeji—appealed to lay audiences of pilgrims and potential donors.

Another significant aspect of Jitsuei's entry on Hokkeji is the way in which it chooses to explain why the Ceremony for the *Vimalakīrti Sūtra* (Yuima-e) was moved to Kōfukuji from Hokkeji, where it may have been held as late as the early years of the Heian period (Mizuno 1978, 62b). As Ushiyama and others have pointed out, official Buddhist ceremonies *(hōe)* held at court ceased to employ women sometime during the early eighth century (Ushiyama 1990, 54). Monastic institutions soon followed suit: it is clear that by the early years of the Heian period, men filled all of the elite lectureship roles of major ceremonies at large monastic institutions. That the Ceremony for the *Vimalakīrti Sūtra* was moved from Hokkeji to Kōfukuji can be understood as part of this larger shift toward increased male domination in late-Nara and early-Heian Buddhism.

While we know that this shift occurred, however, we still know very little about the doctrinal rationale that must have underlain or at least accompanied it. What is fascinating about Jitsuei's explanation of why the Ceremony for the *Vimalakīrti Sūtra* was moved out of a women's monastic institution and into a men's monastic institution is that he avoids invoking any kind of gender-based doctrinal explanation. Despite the fact that he has been identified as a Kōfukuji priest and despite the fact that he is a learned scholar, Jitsuei simply writes that the ceremony was moved because it had outgrown the rather small main hall of Hokkeji. According to Jitsuei, the ceremony was moved not because it was decided that women could no longer perform official ritual functions or because women's bodies had been deemed polluted (two explanations that one might expect a scholarly eleventh-century priest to suggest) but rather because Kōfukuji had a larger main hall.

Is it the case that Jitsuei was ignoring the elephant in the room by attributing the ceremony's move to issues of space rather than explaining obvious discrepancies between the roles granted to nuns in the ancient past versus those granted to nuns during his own time? A related issue, that of *nyonin kekkai* (later known as *nyonin kinsei* or *nyonin kinzei*), the barring of women from sacred sites, does in fact surface here: at the very beginning of the entry, Jitsuei relates the story that Kōmyō had Hokkeji built in reaction against the decision that those possessing female bodies would not be allowed to enter the Great Buddha Hall of Tōdaiji. Jitsuei appears simply to be recording the narrative of Hokkeji that he and his elite patron heard upon visiting the convent, and he does not offer any personal comment upon it. That this particular detail is not included in the *Three Jewels* suggests that it may have been added to the repertoire of Hokkeji narratives sometime after the start of the eleventh century, when *nyonin kekkai* practices were beginning to gain ground. The timing of this addition to the narrative suggests, then, that the stewards of Hokkeji's *engi*—most likely female *shukke* who were residing at Hokkeji—felt compelled to offer some comment on the relationship between Hokkeji and *nyonin kekkai* practices.

The practice of prohibiting women physical entrance to temple grounds is first documented in the ninth century but does not seem to have gained wider currency until the tenth and eleventh centuries (Ushiyama

1990, 51–55; Taira 2000–2002, 302a–b). *Nyonin kekkai* were not immediately established at all Buddhist temples. They were first instituted at male monastic centers situated atop mountains, and they typically prohibited women not from entire monastic complexes but from specific areas atop mountain centers.[13] The practice appears to have been rooted in particular interpretations of purification protocols used in Tendai and other *mikkyō* (esoteric) rituals. Katsuura Noriko (2009) has shown that many of these protocols drew on certain views of the female body found in a wide variety of Chinese texts, ranging from Daoist and Buddhist ritual manuals to legal, medical, and pharmaceutical texts. Within esoteric ritual contexts, *nyonin kekkai* practices would have been associated with the notion that female bodies stand to pollute ritual space. But this discourse appears to have remained localized within the context of mountaintop asceticism, at least during the initial stages of *nyonin kekkai* practice. Rhetoric disparaging women as inherently sinful and impure did not gain general currency outside this particular context and in lay communities until at least the twelfth century (Ushiyama 1990, 52).

We do not know exactly when women first came to be barred from certain areas within the Great Buddha Hall of Tōdaiji, but claims that the practice had existed from the time of the temple's founding are anachronistic.[14] There is no eighth-century evidence to support the explanation that Hokkeji was built in response to the exclusionary practices established at the Great Buddha Hall. But we can surmise that this particular claim may have appealed to a certain class of women making pilgrimages to Hokkeji in the late Heian and Kamakura periods. By the eleventh and twelfth centuries, many female poets had come to lament the fact that they were unable to ascend Mount Hiei. In addition to the well-known case of Izumi Shikibu (fl. eleventh c.), who used the *waka* form to poke fun at contradictions inherent in the *nyonin kekkai* system, Inpumon-in no taifu (1130?–1200?), another widely admired poet and lady-in-waiting, expressed regret, in a preface to a *waka* praising Mount Hiei, over the fact that *nyonin kekkai* was enforced there (Kubota 1993, 501; Kamens 1993). As her *waka* commemorating Enryakuji and its tutelary shrine Hie Taisha follow the same style as her other pilgrimage poems, which marked her visits to various religious sites, we can assume that she made some kind of pilgrimage to Mount Hiei, perhaps making offerings at sites near the base of the mountain, where women were allowed. That her works reflect numerous pilgrimage tours to Nara as well (she visited the same group of temples that Chikamichi recorded having visited in his pilgrimage records) suggests a close connection between women interested in visiting Mount Hiei but unable to do so because of *nyonin kekkai* and those who made pilgrimage rounds through the old temples of the Nara capital. Both destinations, in other words, were of interest to court women, and by the eleventh century women active as pilgrims and pilgrim-poets expressed regret over the fact that *nyonin kekkai* practices at Hiei prevented them from acquiring the positive karmic merit that pilgrimage there would have enabled them to create.

With this in mind, it is possible to surmise that elite female pilgrims would have appreciated this extra element integrated into the Hokkeji founding narrative, namely, the idea that Queen-Consort Kōmyō built Hokkeji in reaction against *nyonin kekkai* practices in place at the Great Buddha Hall of Tōdaiji. Emphasizing the notion that Hokkeji was the female Tōdaiji mirrors similar strategies adopted by institutions such as Murōji, which came to call itself "Mount Kōya for women" (Nyonin Kōya), and the Kumano shrine complex, which also billed itself as a pilgrimage destination open to women (Fowler 2005, 66–69; Moerman 2006, 180–199).

It is likely that both of the aforementioned narrative elements found in the *Kenkyū gojunreiki,* namely, that Kōmyō established Hokkeji in reaction to exclusionary practices at Tōdaiji and that the Ceremony for the *Vimalakīrti Sūtra* was moved to Kōfukuji only because Hokkeji was deemed too small, were based directly on narratives that Hokkeji nuns were themselves promoting to lay pilgrims who came to visit the convent. That Jitsuei simply recorded these narratives without drawing upon his own doctrinal knowledge to challenge them says a great deal about the nature of relationships between orthodox interpretations of Buddhist texts and the domain of accepted religious practice. Indeed, as these two examples suggest, Jitsuei's *Kenkyū gojunreiki* shows no interest in indoctrinating readers with orthodox views of the Buddhist teachings. If anything, Jitsuei seems to have shared many of the assumptions held among lay devotees: mainly, that Buddhist practice is above all else a matter of creating merit, or positive karmic connections, through efficacious acts such as pilgrimage and giving (*fuse,* Skt. *dāna*).

Over time, both the temples included on pilgrimage tours of old Nara temples and the narratives associated with particular temples came to be relatively fixed, as pilgrims continued to retrace the paths of earlier pilgrims and as certain narratives gained popularity and circulation. Evidence of the degree to which pilgrimage routes had become set can be seen in the case of Lady Nijō (b. 1258). When Nijō, who was active a century after Jitsuei and a century and a half after Chikamichi, visited the southern capital, she called at many of the same temples and shrines that Jitsuei and his patron had visited: Kasuga, Kōfukuji, Tōdaiji, Hōryūji, Hokkeji, and Taimadera (adding the convent Chūgūji, which, though not included in Jitsuei's record, had come to be included in later pilgrimage records).

Noting the many similarities between the stories of Hokkeji and Taimadera that Nijō relates in her memoir *Towazugatari* (Unrequested tale) and those that Jitsuei includes in the *Kenkyū gojunreiki,* Abe Yasurō has suggested that both of these works reflect a broader practice in which elite women—and especially women with court connections—visited Hokkeji and Taimadera in order to see artifacts and places associated with popular *engi.* By Nijō's time, Abe points out, seeing the *mandala* at Taimadera was recognized as one of the basic objectives of elite women's pilgrimages to Nara. Narratives about the *mandala* that foreground and praise the devotional practices of women had gained popularity by the early years of the Kamakura period. It was after having heard these stories many times over,

Abe suggests, that many court women decided to make pilgrimages to the southern capital to see Taimadera and its *mandala* for themselves. Similarly, the miraculous story of Ashuku Buddha revealing himself to Kōmyō once she agreed to wash him in his grotesque form appears to have spread far and wide by the early Kamakura period, attracting pilgrims, especially female ones, to Hokkeji, where they could see for themselves both the ruins of the old bathhouse and the newer bathhouse that Hokkeji had since established (1998, 7–11).

Entries on Taimadera and Hokkeji included in Lady Nijō's *Towazugatari* support Abe's thesis. Recalling her visit to Taimadera, Nijō relates the story of the *mandala* in abbreviated form:

> Later I went to Hōryū[ji] and then to Taima[dera], where the daughter of Lord Yokohagi had dedicated herself to the worship of the Buddha. Once a strange nun came to her and said, "Bring me ten bundles of lotus stems, and I will weave you a *mandala* depicting paradise." The nun took strands from the lotus stems and dyed them various colors, simply by dipping them in water from the Dyeing Well. When the fibers were ready for weaving a court lady appeared, requested some oil for her lamp, and wove from ten that night until four the next morning. As the two strangers were about to leave, Yokohagi's daughter asked, "Will we ever meet again?"
>
> She was told, "Long ago Kashō preached the Buddhist law; then, reincarnated as Hōki Bodhisattva, he came here to the Taima Temple and inaugurated Buddhist services. We have come here because you sincerely believed in the Western Paradise. If you trust in this *mandala,* you will not suffer." Then the two women disappeared into the western sky. I found inspiration in this tale, which has been transmitted in written form. (trans. Brazell 1971, 205–206, alterations indicated with brackets; *TG,* 193)

The last sentence of this passage indicates that the story of the *Taima Mandara* was indeed circulating in written form during Nijō's time. Nijō's reaction to the *mandala* is also significant: she speaks of the story, which does not problematize the soteriological prospects of women, as an "inspiration."

Although Nijō does not, in her remarks about Hokkeji, mention the bathhouse, she does mention, in many of her records of temples included on her long pilgrimage routes, miraculous founding tales associated with particular temples. Indeed, she leaves the impression that, as Abe has suggested, pilgrimages really were about deepening one's knowledge of—and in a sense *experiencing,* or having physical contact with—temples whose histories had been praised in *engi* spread by *hijiri,* by pilgrims, and by the compilers of pilgrimage records and *engi* collections.[15] In explaining her decision to visit the convent Chūgūji, for example, Nijō says that she went there because she "[wanted to hear] more about its connection with Prince Shōtoku and his consort" (trans. Brazell 1973, 205; *TG,* 192). Her remarks about the Wakamiya shrine at Kasuga also focus on a story she claims to have heard there, namely, that of the tenth-century Kōfukuji *bettō* Rinkai, who was reprimanded by the gods for having forbidden the music and dance of *kagura* at Kasuga.[16] From these examples, we can see that Nijō's visits to well-known religious sites were centered around miraculous narratives: she visited temples and great shrines not only to create merit but also to confirm stories she had already heard and to gather new ones.

We can safely assume, then, that Hokkeji's medieval revival was rooted in both the twelfth- and thirteenth-century rise of Nara pilgrimage tours and the development and spread of the related genres of *junreiki* and *engi*. As we have seen, both the *Three Jewels* and the *Kenkyū gojunreiki* claim that nuns had occupied Hokkeji since its establishment. The inclusion of Hokkeji in Nara pilgrimage routes and in *junreiki* and *engi* collections ensured that nuns who did occupy the temple could expect to receive guests and pilgrims who would provide some form of material support.

Hokkeji and Kōmyō Devotion in the Early Kamakura Period

Although Jitsuei's *Kenkyū gojunreiki* indicates that nuns were living at Hokkeji during the time of his visit there, he describes the convent as having fallen into a state of disrepair: "[But now] the ridges of the roof have become damaged and the tiles exposed; the altar has collapsed, and the doors [of the tabernacle housing the primary image] are hanging aslant; the [roof] does not keep out the rain of spring mornings, and there is no barrier against the early morning winds of autumn." Jitsuei leaves the impression that these damages simply reflect the ravages of time and the fact that those women currently living at Hokkeji did not have ample resources to fund repairs. Close attention to the diction of these lines, however, reveals the use of numerous stock phrases found in relatively contemporaneous Japanese works and in classical Chinese poetry. Both "the altar has collapsed" and "the doors are hanging aslant," for example, are phrases that were commonly employed by those describing the decline of ancient temples.[17] Jitsuei may have drawn on these phrases for their literary effect and not because they described the precise situation at Hokkeji. These phrases, which connote the sadness of a great institution having fallen into a state of desolation and neglect, both encourage others to value and patronize the convent and enable Jitsuei to display his learning.

But even while it may have been the case that Jitsuei described conditions at Hokkeji in a way that allowed him to make references to certain poetic motifs, it is unlikely that he was overstating the physical decline of Hokkeji altogether. Although left unmentioned in Jitsuei's pilgrimage record, it is known that Taira no Shigehira and his troops had ravaged the southern capital on the twenty-eighth day of the twelfth month of 1180, burning Tōdaiji and Kōfukuji to the ground and damaging numerous other temples and historic sites. This attack on Nara had taken place just over a decade before Jitsuei and his noble patron toured the old capital. We have reason to believe that Hokkeji also suffered devastation at the hands of Shigehira's troops, for the convent is listed among those institutions repaired by the priest Chōgen

(1121–1206) in the wake of Shigehira's attack. Chōgen reports in his 1203 *Namu Amidabutsu sazenshū* that he repaired the stupa and main hall at Hokkeji and, furthermore, that he restored the *honzon* (primary image) and its two attendant deities. This evidence suggests, then, that Hokkeji's main hall and its sacred images had indeed been damaged, either during Shigehira's attack or, as Jitsuei suggests, simply due to the passage of time.

Although early versions of the *Heike monogatari* do not mention Hokkeji in their descriptions of Shigehira's destruction of Nara, the *Genpei jōsuiki* (also *Genpei seisuiki*), a late and highly expanded version of the *Heike,* does mention Hokkeji in its description of Shigehira's attack. Here we are told that Shigehira and his men murdered everyone in their path, failing to distinguish between old and young, male and female, elite and commoner, lay and ordained. Some of the able-bodied managed to flee, the narrative continues, but few escaped alive: even nuns (here *nikō*) were beheaded en masse. Many of these nuns, the story implies, were associated with Hokkeji, for it was upon the gates *(torii)* of Hokkeji that Shigehira had over four hundred enemy heads hung (Jishō 4 [1180] 12).

Given the late compilation of the *Genpei jōsuiki* and the fact that these particular references to Hokkeji do not appear in earlier versions of the *Heike,* it is likely that these details represent embellishments added in the thirteenth and fourteenth centuries, embellishments that reflect Kamakura and Muromachi realities rather than actual events that took place during the Genpei Wars. Questions of historical accuracy aside, however, that the *Genpei jōsuiki* describes Hokkeji as a site of the battle reflects the fact that by the late Kamakura and early Muromachi periods, when the *Genpei jōsuiki* was taking shape, Hokkeji had gained visibility in the southern capital and was a well-known site suitable for use in dramatic narrative.

And thus, while Hokkeji appears to have suffered various levels of damage over the course of the late Heian period and as a result of Shigehira's attack on the southern capital, the convent recovered quickly, attracting elite pilgrims by 1191 and substantial aid from Chōgen in 1203. Although there is no indication that large numbers of women were living at Hokkeji during this time, the fact that the convent had earned the attention of pilgrims and Chōgen alike suggests that its medieval revival had already begun.

Linking Kōmyō to Hokkeji's Collection of Sacred Images

Following Chōgen's 1203 mention of repairs made at Hokkeji, the convent emerges in the historical record again in the year 1216, when it is included in the *engi* collection *Shoji konryū shidai* (Circumstances surrounding the establishment of various temples). This text contains a brief entry on Hokkeji that identifies Queen-Consort Kōmyō as the founder of the convent, lists her biographical data, and briefly explains the iconographical program in place at the convent's main hall. Here, we are told that the primary image in the main hall is Dainichi Nyorai (Skt. Mahāvairocana Buddha) and that a sandalwood image of the Eleven-Faced Kannon (Skt. Avalokiteśvara) stands behind him. The entry further states that the main hall contains foot-tall *(isshaku)* clay statues of the youth Sudhana (Sudhana-śreṣṭhi-dāraka; Jpns. Zenzai Dōji) and his *zenchishiki* (Skt. *kalyāṇa*), or virtuous friends in the Dharma. From the ceiling of the main hall, it continues, hangs a brocade with metal fittings and large lotus flowers at regular intervals. In the back of the hall, the entry adds, is an image of Nyoirin Kannon that is identified with the Yuge Dharma King (Yuge Hōō), otherwise known as Dōkyō (d. 772), the priest infamous for his close relationship with the female sovereign Kōken-Shōtoku, daughter of Queen-Consort Kōmyō and Shōmu Tennō.

The Hokkeji entry in the *Shoji konryū shidai* is important because it suggests that by the early years of the thirteenth century and at least thirty years before its affiliation with Eison and his Saidaiji-based movement, Hokkeji's caretakers had already managed to restore the convent's main hall so that pilgrims could come and pay homage to a number of deities there. Moreover, the particular images mentioned in this entry demonstrate that Hokkeji's administrators were emphasizing the convent's ties to popular narratives centered on Queen-Consort Kōmyō. The images of the youth Sudhana and his virtuous Dharma teachers, for example, recall the entry on Hokkeji from the *Three Jewels* in which Queen-Consort Kōmyō and her ladies-in-waiting, who had become nuns, are said to have created images of Sudhana and his fifty-something virtuous Dharma teachers. According to the *Three Jewels*, these images were used in the Ceremony for the *Flower Ornament Sutra* at Hokkeji: "On the day of the service [Queen-Consort Kōmyō and her nuns] dressed the images in garments made of silk and made offerings to them. Later this service introduced by the queen-consort came to be known as the 'Doll Service'" (trans. Kamens 1988, 291; see also *Sanbōe* 3.13).

The "sandalwood" (actually *kaya*, or Japanese nutmeg) statue of the Eleven-Faced Kannon mentioned here is also an image that had been popularized in earlier Kōmyō narratives. The provenance of this image, which continues to draw tourists to Hokkeji in the present day, is unknown, but art historians have dated its production to the early Heian period (Nishikawa 1978, 58b). The image was not always associated with Kōmyō, however. In the earliest known mention of the image, which appears in the entry on Kōfukuji's West Golden Hall (Nishi Kondō) in Chikamichi's *Shichidaiji junrei shiki* (1140), the narrative focuses not on the queen-consort but rather on the priest Gyōki (668–749), who is said to have created it, and on Jukō, a Kōfukuji priest said to have miraculously discovered it in the early Heian period. According to the story related here, Jukō was at a pond on the southern perimeter of Kōfukuji when he heard a voice call out his name and then witnessed the head of this Eleven-Faced Kannon spontaneously emerge from the earth. When Jukō exhumed the image and cleansed it of the dirt that had covered its body, a large divine child appeared and instructed him to install the image in the West Golden Hall (49).

Jitsuei's 1191 *Kenkyū gojunreiki* includes an abbreviated version of this same story but adds an identifying detail: Jukō, it says, was the disciple of the prelate *(sōzu)* Shuen (771–835). Although neither this text nor the

Statue of the Eleven-Faced Kannon Bodhisattva (Jūichimen Kannon Bosatsu ryūzō). Wood, early Heian period. (Photograph by Ueda Eisuke, courtesy Hokkeji, Nara, Japan)

Shichidaiji junrei shiki draws any direct link between Kōmyō and the Eleven-Faced Kannon, both texts do state that the West Golden Hall, where the Eleven-Faced Kannon was said to have been enshrined, was commissioned by Kōmyō in honor of her mother, Lady Tachibana. According to the *Shichidaiji junrei shiki* (50), Kōmyō used the hall to stage a large-scale rite, involving some four hundred priests, aimed at securing her mother's birth in the Pure Land. It is said that this ceremony was held on the eleventh day of the first month of Tempyō 6 (734).[18] The *Kenkyū gojunreiki* does not contain any discussion of this event, but it does add a narrative not included in the *Shichidaiji junrei shiki,* namely, the story of a Gandhāran king who had a divine vision in which it was revealed to him that Kōmyō was a living manifestation of the bodhisattva Kannon.

While the *Shichidaiji junrei shiki* includes a long list of images commissioned by Kōmyō on the occasion of her mother's services without providing any specific details about the individual images, the *Kenkyū gojunreiki* chooses to focus on one particular image: that of Śākyamuni. It claims that the image of Śākyamuni enshrined in the West Golden Hall was sculpted at Kōmyō's court by artisans from the Indian province of Gandhāra. Why were these Indian artisans at the Japanese court? It just so happened, the *Kenkyū gojunreiki* says, that these artisans had been sent to Japan by the king of Gandhāra, who, having voiced his desire to pay obeisance to a living manifestation of the bodhisattva Kannon, received a dream in which he was told, "Then you must worship the woman Kōmyō, consort of the king of the land of Japan, an island in the sea, to the east of here. She is a living manifestation of Kannon!" When he awoke from the dream, he is said to have dispatched artisans to Japan, telling them to go and capture her image in the form of a statue so he could worship her. It turned out, Jitsuei's *Kenkyū gojunreiki* informs us, that the Gandhāran artisans arrived just as Kōmyō was making plans to commission an image for her mother's memorial services. She sought their advice, and they told her that Śākyamuni would be a good choice for expressing filial piety. She thus asked them to create for her an image of Śākyamuni (136). Although the *Kenkyū gojunreiki* draws no clear connection between this story and the story of the Eleven-Faced Kannon, later, less abbreviated versions of the narrative say the Śākyamuni image was the product of an agreement Kōmyō made with the artisans: she told them that she would pose for them only under the condition that they first sculpt the Śākyamuni image she needed for her mother's service.

Later versions of the *engi* for Kōfukuji's West Golden Hall also go on to incorporate the miraculous tale of this Gandhāran king's vision into their remarks on the Eleven-Faced Kannon. In the *Kōfukuji ranshōki* (Record of the origins of Kōfukuji), for example, the Eleven-Faced Kannon is no longer identified as the work of Gyōki but is instead recognized as another creation of these Gandhāran artisans said to have visited the Japanese court.[19] Here, it is claimed that when Kōmyō looked at the sculpture that the artisans created in her image, it did not express her physical, female body but was instead a manifestation of the Eleven-Faced Kannon. This helps explain how the rather androgynous-looking statue could be widely regarded as having been sculpted in the image of Queen-Consort Kōmyō. This interpretation of the image's relationship to Kōmyō is a loaded one: although it does it identify Kōmyō as a manifestation of the bodhisattva Kannon, it denies femininity as an enduring part of her identity. In what seems like a preemptive rebuttal to those who might question whether a woman could be so venerated in the Buddhist cosmos, the author makes it clear that Kōmyō's true identity—Kannon—exceeds the boundaries and the limitations of femininity.

Finally, the *Kōfukuji ranshōki* explains that the Gandhāran artists made two additional copies of this image of Kōmyō. One they took back to India with them to give to the king who had sent them, another was given to the Japanese court, and the third was installed at a temple called Shiganji. The copy given to the court was installed at Hokkeji, and the copy originally enshrined at Shiganji is the one that Jukō discovered: it had been stolen by a thief and abandoned before it emerged from the earth before his eyes. He installed this copy of the Kōmyō / Eleven-Faced Kannon image at Kōfukuji in Tenchō 2 (825), sixty-six years after Kōmyō died, thereby miraculously fulfilling, we are told, a prediction that Kōmyō had made just before her death, when she said that her form would return to the West Golden Hall sixty-odd years after her passing (453–454).

The shifts that occur in this narrative over time—shifts that move toward increasing emphasis on Kōmyō as a divine figure—reflect the spread of Kōmyō devotion. In contrast with Chikamichi's 1140 pilgrimage record, which portrays Kōmyō as an esteemed but not divine historical figure, later records, starting with the 1191 *Kenkyū gojunreiki*, celebrate Kōmyō as a manifestation of Kannon. It is not known when exactly the Eleven-Faced Kannon was first installed at Hokkeji, but it is possible to speculate based on the dating of these various pilgrimage records and *engi* that the image was first added by Chōgen when he made repairs at Hokkeji in the early 1200s. The 1191 *Kenkyū gojunreiki* does not mention multiple copies of the Eleven-Faced Kannon, nor does it say anything about Hokkeji in connection with the image. The 1216 *Shoji konryū shidai* is the first text that clearly identifies the "sandalwood" Eleven-Faced Kannon as a statue enshrined at the main hall of Hokkeji. Chōgen's repairs date to the period separating these two distinct narrative threads used to explain the provenance of the Eleven-Faced Kannon.

Chōgen does not mention, in his brief record of repairs made at Hokkeji, the names of the images he restored there. He notes only that he repaired a sixteen-foot Buddha and its attendant deities. Given that his record predates the *Shoji konryū shidai* by just over a decade, it is likely that three main images he restored were those mentioned in the *Shoji konryū shidai:* Dainichi, the Eleven-Faced Kannon, and Nyoirin Kannon. Conventional iconography would not group these images together as a triad, however, and even the *Shoji konryū shidai,* which suggests a rather unorthodox grouping of images at Hokkeji, notes that the Eleven-Faced Kannon is at the back of the main hall and not situated up front next to the *honzon,* Dainichi. Later texts, such as the 1304 *Hokke metsuzaiji engi* (The karmic origins of the Lotus Temple for the Eradication of Transgressions) and the 1456–1466 *Shoji engishū,* offer a different configuration, saying that the Dainichi *honzon* was flanked by the bodhisattvas Kannon and Kokūzō (Skt. Ākāśagarbha, Wisdom-as-Vast-as-Space Bodhisattva).[20] It is thus possible to speculate that it was this latter triad that Chōgen repaired in the early 1200s. That the Kokūzō image is not mentioned in earlier documents suggests that it was likely added after Chōgen's time.

The *Shoji konryū shidai* indicates, then, that Hokkeji had on display in its main hall a number of images that had already been celebrated in pilgrimage records and *engi* collections as material links to the legacy of Queen-Consort Kōmyō. The images of Sudhana and his virtuous Dharma teachers, mentioned as early as the *Three Jewels* (late tenth century), and the Eleven-Faced Kannon image said to have been carved in the likeness of Kōmyō herself are the two most obvious examples. But the Dainichi image too was treated as a relic of Kōmyō: most texts listing the holdings at Hokkeji also identify this statue as the handiwork of Kōmyō herself. Even the Nyoirin Kannon image mentioned here leads back to Kōmyō, for it is identified with Dōkyō, the priest known for his close relationship with Kōmyō's daughter, the female sovereign Kōken-Shōtoku. It was not conventional iconography, then, but rather the shared goal of remembering and venerating Kōmyō that served as the common thread linking images at Hokkeji.

Records of images housed at Hokkeji affirm that Hokkeji had established itself by Chōgen's time as the center of Kōmyō devotion. Following his record of repairs at Hokkeji, Chōgen left a telling note in the margins of his *Namu Amidabutsu sazenshū:* "I heard that someone had a dream in which it was said, 'The Queen-Consort Kōmyō is delighted'" (48). This remark suggests that Chōgen and others regarded Kōmyō as a divine figure who yearned to see her temple restored and who, like other gods and bodhisattvas, revealed her will through dreams and visions. The *Hokke metsuzaiji engi* also includes a story in which Kōmyō uses divine possession—taking over the physical body of a nun—in order to make her will known. This story, which will be treated later, suggests, together with this brief remark in Chōgen's records, that Kōmyō devotees in medieval Japan regarded the queen-consort not as a mere historical figure but rather as an efficacious deity. Surely it was this connection to Kōmyō that enabled Hokkeji to gain visibility in the early Kamakura period, first as an important destination on Nara pilgrimage routes and eventually as the center of a large-scale revival of female monasticism.

On the Eve of Institutional Reinvention

Read in conjunction with popular *engi* and *junreiki* literature, records listing sacred images held at Hokkeji enable us to infer that the convent was in fact active, though only on a small scale, during the decades preceding its medieval restoration. The 1216 *Shoji konryū shidai,* in particular, makes it clear that that Hokkeji had not been abandoned but was in fact being well cared for: it had a number of images on display for pilgrims, and the main hall had been decked out with beautiful brocades and metal fittings. Increased attention to Hokkeji in *junreiki* and *engi* literature dating to this period also suggests that residents of Hokkeji shared—and most likely performed—oral versions of the miraculous narratives that linked the treasures of their institution to the venerated personage of Kōmyō.

Scholars know of only a single document related to Hokkeji that dates to the decades separating the early-thirteenth-century lists of Hokkeji images discussed above from the first records of Eison's involvement at the convent, which date to the mid-1240s. This document is a 1235 response to a call for soldiers. Kasuga shrine, which represented Kōfukuji, the most powerful landholder in Yamato during this period, had issued a call for militia. Signed by the residents *(jūninra)* of Hokkeji, the 1235 document states that Hokkeji was unable to contribute troops. Invoking earlier descriptions of Hokkeji, such as that found in the *Shoku Nihongi* and the *Three Jewels,* the document says that Hokkeji had been a convent *(amadera)* since antiquity. As such, it continues, all three *sangō* posts were filled by women. From the distant past, the authors claim, Hokkeji had never provided soldiers. The document also cites the decline of Hokkeji *(tōji no ryōchi),* claiming that the temple could not contribute any militia in any case, since the convent was not thriving and there were no residents who could be sent ("Hokkeji shin," *Kamakura ibun,* 4733).

What the document suggests, then, is that although Hokkeji had residents in the year 1235, it was inhabited by a relatively small group of women who had neither male servants they could send to battle nor financial resources to contribute to the military efforts of Kōfukuji. It is of course possible to speculate that the authors may have had a few male servants at their disposal but that they exaggerated the state of decline at Hokkeji so as to spare themselves from having to send their menservants. Even if this were the case, however, that this type of exaggeration would be overlooked does suggest that Hokkeji was small enough to escape the careful scrutiny of local officials.

The nun Enkyō's 1304 *Hokke metsuzaiji engi* reports additional repairs carried out at Hokkeji around 1243, just a couple of years before the convent's first interactions with Eison in 1245 (*HMJE,* 142a). It was Kōmyō herself, she explains, who convinced the Tendai priest Tankū (1176–1253), a disciple of Hōnen, to make a series of repairs at Hokkeji on this occasion.[21] We can gather from her narrative that Tankū had stopped by Hokkeji during a pilgrimage to the great temples of Nara. In particular, the fact that Enkyō connects this story to a lengthy discussion of the Eleven-Faced Kannon suggests that Tankū had stopped by Hokkeji to pay homage to this image, which, as we have seen, had been written up in many pilgrimage records and *engi* collections. The diction of the passage also suggests that Tankū sought lodging at Hokkeji during his visit. Jinen (d. 1298) and the other nuns tell him that although Hokkeji is a temple for women and does not usually accept overnight male guests, they would like for him to stay and help them rebuild Hokkeji's walls. His initial response, however, is negative:

> There was a person named Tankū the Exalted Person [Shōnin] from Saga, near the northern capital [Heian-kyō]. When he came to this temple [Hokkeji] on pilgrimage [*sankei*], the rector [*chōrō*] Jinen and the other nuns said to him, "This temple was originally a convent. Men are forbidden to share residency with us. But now each of the nuns in the order lacks even a [begging] bowl and [a complete set of] five robes. As a result, the four walls [of the temple] are poorly maintained, and even though we shut the gate, it is of no use [for keeping out intruders]. I beg you, Exalted Person, please help us [re]build our gate and walls." But the *shōnin* strongly refused and retreated.

Tankū displays a change of heart, however, when he experiences a miraculous vision of the Eleven-Faced Kannon weeping in disappointment:

> [Then] the *shōnin,* atop the raised seat [*raiban*], gave the precepts to people. When he honored Kannon during the *sanrai* [the first chant performed in the ordination liturgy], he saw that her face was filling with tears, which first looked like dew clinging to the bodhisattva's face. Other people did not see it; only the *shōnin* saw it. The *shōnin* choked on his tears and went further, sobbing loudly and intensely. Everyone thought it strange. [Then] the *shōnin* descended from the altar and agreed [to help rebuild] the gate and the walls. In tears, they told this story to people. Those who hear it cannot restrain themselves from being moved to tears. Finally, this karmic effect [*gō*] came to an end, and this place was restored as a convent. (142a)[22]

Read in conjunction with earlier narratives identifying the Eleven-Faced Kannon as Kōmyō and in light of Chōgen's report that Kōmyō appeared to someone in a vision to convey her delight with the repairs that Chōgen had carried out at Hokkeji, it is clear that Tankū's vision, too, was one of Queen-Consort Kōmyō. It was only after witnessing Kōmyō's tears of regret, Enkyō explains, that Tankū relented, finally agreeing to help Jinen and the other nuns make repairs at Hokkeji. Enkyō's portrayal of this episode clarifies that Kōmyō was the real hero of the Hokkeji revival, even from the start: Tankū is depicted only as a reluctant helper finally moved by Kōmyō's great will.

As for the precepts ordination ceremony that Tankū performs here, it is unclear who exactly received the precepts from him on this occasion. Most scholars have read this passage as evidence that Tankū bestowed the precepts on the nuns' group at Hokkeji (Hosokawa 1999a, 29). It is likely, however, that this ceremony also included members of the local community as well as other pilgrims undertaking tours of the great Nara temples. Public bestowals of the precepts upon laypeople had become popular during this period, especially in the southern capital (Meeks 2009). Given what

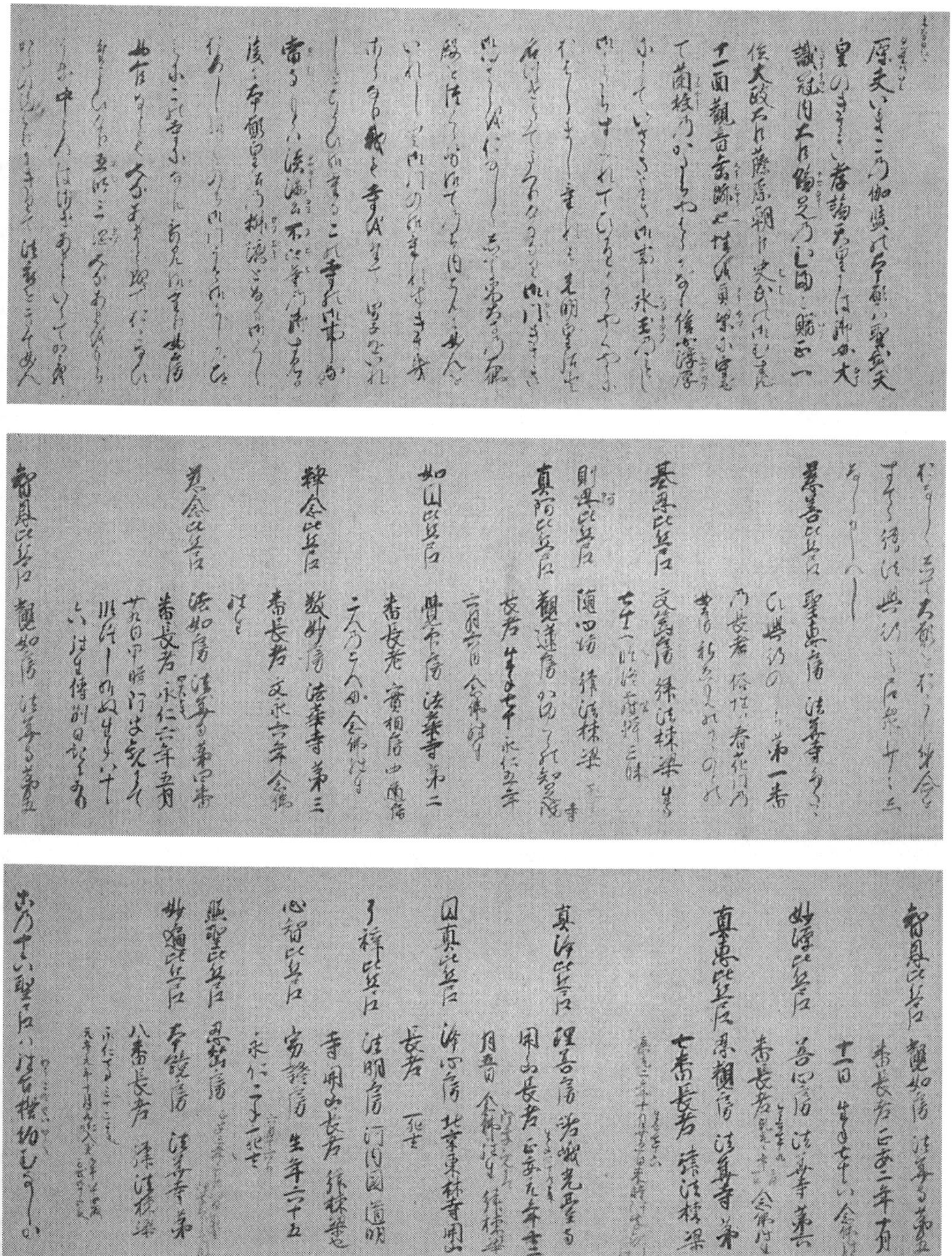

Excerpts from *The Karmic Origins of the Lotus Temple for the Eradication of Transgressions* (*Hokke metsuzaiji engi*), 1304. Ink on paper. (Photograph by Nara National Museum, courtesy Hokkeji, Nara, Japan)

we know about Tankū's training and ministry, we can be fairly sure that he would have used the perfect and sudden precepts *(endonkai),* the same set of precepts he had received from his master, Hōnen, when he ordained others. This passage thus implies that the small group of nuns residing at Hokkeji in the early 1240s (including at least Jizen, Jinen, Shakunen, Kinin, Shinmyō, and Zuikyō) had already received the perfect and sudden precepts from Tankū before they became involved with Eison a couple of years later (*HMJE,* 142a; Hosokawa 1999a, 29).

Building on the Kōmyō Cult: Miracles and Discoveries at Hokkeji

Like Chōgen before him, Tankū appears to have contributed to the restoration of Hokkeji only on a short-term basis. Enkyō does not leave the impression that the nuns established enduring ties with Tankū; she suggests that he simply offered Jinen and the other nuns assistance in the task of rebuilding Hokkeji's walls and gates—perhaps by donating funds or sending laborers—and then went on his way. He is not recognized as a teacher or leader in the movement.

Enkyō does suggest, however, that this assistance marked a turning point in the convent's restoration. Once help was acquired from Tankū, she writes, Kōmyō revealed, this time through spirit possession, her will that the Eleven-Faced Kannon image—her image—be taken off display and returned to its tabernacle *(zushi):*

> The circumstances surrounding Hokkeji's restoration in recent years
>
> The Eleven-Faced image of Kannon that has been placed in the lecture hall [*kōdō*] of this temple [Hokkeji] was the creation of the founder, the queen-consort [Kōmyō]. Originally, there was no manifestation buddha [*kebutsu*] on the crown of this statue's head.[23] When Monkyōbō [Kinin], a *bikuni* in residence here, noticed something strange about the statue on the twelfth day of the sixth month of Ninji 4 [1243], her fellow *bikuni* Shakunen and Jinen saw the following vision at the same time: rays of light shone from the tabernacle in which the Eleven-Faced Kannon was stored. At that time, they both faced the rector, Jizen Bikuni, and told her. As they were thinking something was awry, Monkyōbō performed the Kannon Kōshiki [Chanted Lecture on Kannon] in front of the image. When she looked up at the face of the statue, there was a vermillion-colored object about 2 *bu* [6 millimeters] in height on the crown of its head. She thought it miraculous, and it is said that when she looked and others looked at it more closely, they saw that it was a small image of Amida. Then it became white and grew to about 9 *bu* [2.7 centimeters]. It was fully endowed with the beautiful features of a buddha, and everyone looked it over carefully, touching and handling it. Then it disappeared into the shadows of the right and left faces of the Eleven-Faced Kannon. More and more [of the Amida image] kept disappearing.[24] After that, it is said that the novice nun Zuikyō delivered [the following] oracle [*takusen*] from the founder [Kōmyō]:

"That this statue was placed inside this tabernacle long ago was so that after the temple was destroyed, it could be opened up [that is, placed on display] until the present time for the purpose of benefiting sentient beings. But because the temple has already returned to its former [glory], now [the tabernacle] must be closed up and not opened." Therefore, the statue has been concealed in its tabernacle. (*HMJE,* 142a)

This passage, which relates an episode said to have occurred in the year 1243, tells us a great deal about how nuns at Hokkeji envisioned—and remembered—the story of their convent's thirteenth-century revival. Most telling here is the fact that Kōmyō is said to have deemed the restoration of Hokkeji already successful ("the temple has already returned to its former [glory]"), even though the group living there was still rather small and had not yet aligned itself with Eison's movement. Also noticeable, of course, is the degree to which the entire narrative focuses on Kōmyō: not only is the story about an image of Kannon that serves as a surrogate of Kōmyō herself, but it climaxes when Kōmyō delivers an oracle through the nun Zuikyō, thereby making her will known. Hokkeji's revival is remembered here not in terms of doctrinal or institutional accomplishments—not, for example, as the story of how a nuns' precepts platform was established. Instead, it is remembered in terms of how Kōmyō, a historical figure from the distant past who had taken on mythical status, remained a spiritual force in the history of the ancient Nara capital, weeping when her convent Hokkeji fell into a state of disrepair and using visions and possession to urge living beings to care for the convent in the way that she desired. Male priests may have told the story of Hokkeji's revival in terms of doctrinal and institutional change, but Hokkeji nuns themselves told the story as one of devotion to Queen-Consort Kōmyō.

And yet there is another layer of meaning discernible in this passage. While it is true that the passage focuses almost solely on Kōmyō, the oracle Kōmyō delivers through Zuikyō implies that this period in which Kōmyō devotion served as the primary function of Hokkeji has drawn to a close. Kōmyō's divine message states that the Eleven-Faced Kannon had been preserved in its tabernacle through the centuries precisely so that, following the convent's historical decline, the image could be placed on display to draw pilgrims. Now that the convent has been restored, she says, the Eleven-Faced Kannon's tabernacle doors should be shut, and the statue should no longer remain on display.

The message attributed to Kōmyō here most likely reflects the actual historical practice, also visible in pilgrimage records and the like, of temples placing their treasured icons on display so as to attract pilgrims and other visitors who were expected to make offerings when they came to pay homage to celebrated images. The implication here, which does match the details noted in the *Shoji konryū shidai* and similar texts, is that Hokkeji survived the difficult years of the late Heian and early Kamakura—though perhaps just barely—by putting this Eleven-Faced Kannon on display and using it to draw Kōmyō devotees. But when this oracle is placed within the larger context of the Tankū narrative to which it is attached, it becomes clear that the nuns did not view the practice of attracting pilgrims with the Eleven-Faced Kannon as a goal in and of itself; rather, the larger goal was to reestablish Hokkeji as a monastery for women. Using Kōmyō's icon was merely an expedient means. And thus when Tankū visits Hokkeji to pay homage to the icon, the nuns beg him to help them rebuild the convent, and Kōmyō, having lured him to Hokkeji to pay homage to her beautiful form as Kannon, does not allow him to leave until he has offered assistance.

Once this goal is accomplished, Kōmyō announces through Zuikyō that the doors of her tabernacle are to be shut. And thus we witness a shift: Kōmyō says that her image is to be used as an attraction no longer. This story centered on Kōmyō ultimately announces that devotion to Kōmyō is to take a backseat at Hokkeji; Hokkeji is now ready to expand into a movement that exceeds this interest. This passage, then, can also be understood as reflecting the changes that took place at Hokkeji from the 1240s onward, transforming the temple from a relatively small center of Kōmyō devotion into a large-scale training ground for Ritsu-school nuns.

But even when this shift began to take place, as Hokkeji aligned itself with Eison's *vinaya* revival movement from 1245 onward, Kōmyō devotion remained important at Hokkeji. Hokkeji's association with Queen-Consort Kōmyō was not only the most enduring aspect of its popular identity among laypeople, but this association also remained extremely important among nuns at Hokkeji and even among male priests. Eison too, as we will see later, regarded Kōmyō as a powerful spiritual force and participated in devotions carried out in her honor. It is worth noting here that even after Hokkeji nuns became involved with Eison and his Saidaiji group, they still tended to structure their memories of Hokkeji's revival around Kōmyō-centered narratives.

Case in point: the story of Zuikyō's possession by Kōmyō is followed by a report of materials discovered among the remains of Hokkeji's main hall on the twenty-fifth day of the tenth month of Kenchō 5 (1253), when the hall was in the process of being rebuilt. Although scholars believe that these repairs were completed with the help of priests and laborers from Eison's Saidaiji group, Enkyō's text makes no mention of them (Ōta 1978, 40a). Instead, she focuses solely on the task of listing for the reader (or perhaps for the listener, given that this *engi* was most likely read aloud to pilgrims during the medieval period) the many precious objects—the majority of them associated with Kōmyō in one way or another—exhumed when the main hall was rebuilt:

> During the time when the main hall was being rebuilt, on the twenty-fifth day of the tenth month of Kenchō 5 [1253], various treasures were exhumed from under the altars of the three sacred images. Among them was a golden tablet weighing 400 *ryō* [about 15 pounds]. It was a copy of the record [explaining the temple's founding] written by the founder [Kōmyō] that had been buried.

> [The nuns] copied this [the record visible on the tablet] by hand and then buried it just as it had been buried before. There were also two wish-fulfilling jewels [Jpns. *nyoishu;* Skt. *cintāmaṇi*]. They were inside a golden box. It is said that [the nuns] said [to each other], "The two jewels given by the dragon in the journal of the Tōdaiji treasury are said to be buried in the temple: are these those jewels?" They also buried these as they had been buried before. It is said that below the image in the center, there were twelve mirrors. The twelve gods of the Medicine Teacher Buddha [Yakushi Nyōrai] had been placed on the backs of these mirrors. There was one mirror under the Shō-Kannon of the left side. The inscription on the mirror is said to have read, "Precious Mirror that Reflects the Pure Mind." Next, it is said that there were many swords and also two strands of hair wrapped up in something purple. It is said that [the nuns] wondered if this was not the hair of the founder [Kōmyō]. As for treasures such as gold and silver, there were pearls from the pearl oyster, crystal, and *kaku* [small objects made of gold, silver, jade, and other precious materials used to adorn clothing, horse stirrups, and so on]—there were many of various kinds. [The nuns] used these to restore the main image. The principal image in the main hall is none other than a sixteen-foot, golden-colored Rushana [Skt. Vairocana]. Kanjizai [Kannon] and Kokūzō are sitting on his right and left. [Also,] there are Brahmā, Indra, and the Four Kings of Heaven. They were all carved by the founder Kōmyō herself. These were copies of [icons at] Tōdaiji. (*HMJE,* 142b)

This passage goes on to give a more complete inventory of the icons held at Hokkeji during the 1250s, an inventory that more or less matches that which we have seen in the 1216 *Shoji konryū shidai.* It also goes on to incorporate a reworked version of the miraculous episode, already seen in the 1191 *Kenkyū gojunreiki,* in which the image of the householder Vimalakīrti turns around on its own accord.

What is striking about this new material recounting various items discovered during repairs made at the main hall in the year 1253 is that it captures the degree to which Hokkeji nuns envisioned themselves as the stewards of an ancient tradition. Here, the nuns are portrayed as archaeologist-historians committed to the preservation of the past, and that past, while related to Buddhism, is more concerned with legends of Kōmyō and the ancient Nara capital she represents than with Buddhist doctrine or with Buddhism as a pan-Asian tradition. Many of the objects claimed as discoveries here seem to be the stuff of myth and fabrication, but they are mixed in with materials that likely were in fact recovered during medieval renovations at Hokkeji. Current scholarly consensus does hold, for example, that large-scale renovations of the type described in the *Hokke metsuzaiji engi* were carried out in the Kamakura period. Although the main hall was rebuilt at least twice after the Kamakura period (once in 1596 and more recently in the 1950s), these subsequent renovations tended to reuse earlier building materials. During renovations undertaken during the 1950s, it was discovered that many of the construction materials (various types of beams, rafters, and pillars) dated to the Kamakura period—so many, in fact, that those involved in the renovations concluded that the main hall had been rebuilt from scratch during the Kenchō period (1250s), as Enkyō's *engi* suggests (Ōta 1978, 40a; Okada 1978, 45–47). Another piece of evidence verifying the rebuilding of Hokkeji's main hall in the 1250s is a *waniguchi* (large circular bell hung near the entrance of temples and shrines), now held at Kōfukuji, that bears the inscription, "Humbly presented to the main hall of the capital's Hokkeji."[25] The inscription is dated to the tenth day of the seventh month of Kenchō 8 (1256) and carries the name of a female donor: "the nun Dō-Amidabutsu."[26] Since items of this nature were typically donated on the occasion of a new building's opening ceremony, it is believed that Hokkeji's main hall was likely completed around this time, in 1256 (Ōta 1978, 40a). In addition to evidence that corroborates the mid-Kamakura-period rebuilding of the main hall at Hokkeji, there is also much evidence to confirm the continued presence of Nara-period materials in and around Hokkeji: it has been shown, for example, that many of the tiles recovered from the Hokkeji site even in recent years date back to the late eighth century (Mori 1978, 52b). It is very likely the case, then, that Jizen, Jinen, and other nuns involved at Hokkeji during the time of this thirteenth-century reconstruction did in fact recover Nara-period artifacts from the site.

Archaeological evidence from other sites suggests that the various jewels, mirrors, swords, and other precious objects listed among the discoveries here were *chindangu* (Tanaka 1978a, 84b). According to Nara-period building practices, *chindangu*—small precious objects, including stones, jewels, coins, mirrors, small vessels, miniature swords, and the like—were intentionally buried at construction sites, especially beneath the stone platforms and altars of Buddhist temples, to appease the gods associated with the land and to secure their protection. *Chindangu* were discovered in great numbers both beneath the altar of the Great Buddha at Tōdaiji and beneath the stone platform of the Central Golden Hall at Kōfukuji.[27] (Indeed, at Kōfukuji well over a thousand *chindangu* items were found.) Enkyō says in the passage above that some of these items were used in the reconstruction of the *honzon* for the main hall, an image of Rushana. In light of the degree to which relic devotion *(shari shinkō)* became popular at Hokkeji, we might speculate that some of the relics the nuns claimed to have discovered at Hokkeji in the 1250s were comprised of *chindangu.*

There is also some evidence that the Tempyō Hōji 3 (759) tablet mentioned here was in fact unearthed during the Kamakura-period renovations. Although the whereabouts of the tablet are no longer known, a record from Hōryūji indicates that it was uncovered a second time in the year 1510. On this occasion, the inscription was copied again, and this 1510 copy survives in the Hōryūji document *Hōryūji kyūki ruijū*. Scholars recognize it as a Nara-period text (Ōta 1978, 35).

As DEMONSTRATED IN THIS CHAPTER, Hokkeji's medieval revival, though eventually aligned with Eison's campaign to revive the *vinaya,* first emerged as an effort to revive the memory of Kōmyō and to create a center for popular devotion centered on legends associated with her. This project in turn was bound up in the growing popularity of pilgrimage to ancient Nara temples and in one particular historical result of this mid-to-late-Heian boom in Nara pilgrimage: the spread of miraculous narratives about Kōmyō, narratives that first appear in *engi* collections describing icons and buildings at Kōfukuji, Tōdaiji, and the other great temples of Nara.

The medieval restoration of Hokkeji eventually expanded to include the goal of reviving a precepts platform for nuns, but this goal was not visible until the late 1240s and early 1250s, when Hokkeji nuns became active in Eison's movement. As suggested earlier, this shift toward the inclusion of larger doctrinal and institutional goals is reflected in Enkyō's record of the oracle delivered by Kōmyō through Zuikyō. But even as Hokkeji nuns did begin to turn toward the goal of reinventing Hokkeji as a large-scale monastery for women and training ground for nuns, they never lost sight of this initial vision of Hokkeji, which saw the convent as a sacred center of Kōmyō devotion. Records and memories of Kōmyō granting visions to and delivering oracles through nuns persisted, and the convent continued to use Kōmyō's legacy as a means of attracting patrons, devotees, and pilgrims. And thus we must not forget, as we examine in subsequent chapters the large-scale reinvention of Hokkeji as a Ritsu center for women, the significance of Kōmyō's legacy, both historical and mythical, at the convent.

Placing Hokkeji's medieval revival in the context of broader, on-the-ground religious practice also draws our attention to an alternative view of religious change in premodern Japan. Hokkeji's case provides a compelling example of the degree to which common lay practices—such as pilgrimage, spirit possession, and the veneration of images—drove transformation in the religious world. Growth and change in institutional Buddhism was not merely a question of doctrinal innovation or political struggle. For institutions eager to attract lay patrons, the key lay not so much in creating doctrines attractive to their target audience; more important, it would appear, was offering a set of practices that met the devotional needs and interests of that audience.

There is little reason to believe that Hokkeji's late-Heian- and early-Kamakura-period reinvention as a site of pilgrimage associated with a miraculous deity was exceptional. Even the fact that women inhabited and managed Hokkeji would not have made the temple all that unusual. Hokkeji was certainly the most visible convent of its time: given its prominent history as the head of the provincial convent system established during the Nara period and its long-standing connection to the Fujiwara family, Hokkeji attracted more attention than did other temples and small hermitages inhabited by women. Still, other temples controlled by nuns, such as Chūgūji, did come to gain visibility on Nara pilgrimage routes.

That Hokkeji's patron deity is female does set the convent apart from many male institutions (though some, including Saidaiji, also celebrated female founders). But the basic patterns of engagement with Buddhist devotional practice evident at Hokkeji in the late Heian and early Kamakura periods did not deviate from those evident at male institutions. And thus Hokkeji's revival does not merely reflect doctrinal innovations that allowed for the reintroduction of official ordinations of women. It also reflects the fact that Heian- and early-Kamakura-period laywomen, though barred from both official ordination and the ranks of elite monasteries, continued to perform, both as pilgrims and as the caretakers of temples, the same devotional practices that their male contemporaries also valued.

2
Envisioning Nuns
Views from the Court

Previous scholarship has viewed the revival of Hokkeji primarily through the lens of androcentric Buddhist rhetoric. Following the assumption that nuns and other female practitioners at Hokkeji internalized the androcentric Buddhist teachings propagated by Saidaiji monks and incorporated these doctrines into their daily lives and practices, earlier studies tend to view Hokkeji's nuns with pity (e.g., Hosokawa 1987, 1989b; Hosokawa and Tabata 2002; Matsuo 2001; Ishida 1978). But these studies overlook an important factor: Hokkeji's first medieval nuns approached Buddhism with a set of cultural assumptions that diverged from those held by scholastic priests. Many of the women involved in the restoration of Hokkeji had served as ladies-in-waiting under powerful royal women. As former ladies-in-waiting, they were well educated, well connected, and proud of the social status they possessed. The ties they had formed with each other as a community of cultural producers and patrons—ties supported by a shared sense of history that allowed them to feel connected both to each other and to ladies-in-waiting of times past—positioned them to formulate and support the restoration of Hokkeji both ideologically and economically.

This chapter will trace the role that the court women and the refined culture they represented played in the restoration of Hokkeji. It will further examine the ways in which members of court society viewed both nuns and the relationship between women and Buddhism more broadly. How did women like Jizen understand their roles as Buddhists vis-à-vis male monastics? What cultural assumptions did they bring with them to the convent, and how might these assumptions have affected their engagement with issues specific to their sex? The chapter will focus in particular on the ways in which male and female nobles viewed women's salvation, understood women's relationships with priests, and conceptualized the socioreligious roles of nuns.

Jizen and Her Lineage

Hokkeji's medieval lineage begins with Jizen, whom the convent's records recognize as its first postrestoration rector. The celebrated court poet Fujiwara no Teika (1162–1241) describes Jizen's renunciation in an entry in his

Meigetsuki dated Kenryaku 1 (1211) 12/23: "Saying that she was going out to bathe, Ukingo, a lady-in-waiting of the former *nyoin,* hired a carriage and set out for Kujō. She then sent a letter saying that she had made a mistake regarding the date and that she would return to court the day after next. It was [then] reported from Hachijō-dono [Kōmon] that when evening came, she [Ukingo] went to [the priest] Jiren-bō [of the southern capital] and entreated him to administer the precepts to her" (*Kundoku Meigetsuki,* 3:98b; *KJGSK* 1999, 213–215). Before her ordination, Jizen had been a lady-in-waiting (*nyōbō*) in the service of Her Highness Shunkamon-in (1195–1211). Teika refers to her as "Ukingo," a Chinese-style variation of the title "commander of the right gate guards" *(uemon no kami).* The *Hokke metsuzaiji engi* also uses this title in its description of Jizen: it says she was a lady-in-waiting in the service of Her Highness Shunkamon-in and that she was known as "new commander of the gate guards" *(shin'emon no kaunotono)* (142b). Since ladies-in-waiting often used sobriquets based on the posts held by their male relatives, one can assume that Jizen's father or one of her other male relatives had held this military position. That Jizen was the "'new' commander of the right gate guards" suggests that a woman using the same nickname had entered Shunkamon-in's service before Jizen.

It was likely through his sister, the poet and former lady-in-waiting Kengozen (b. 1157, aka Kenshunmon-in Chūnagon and Hachijō Chūnagon), that Teika first heard of Jizen's tonsure. Kengozen would have known Jizen because the two had served together at the Hachijō residence. Kengozen had been in the service of Her Highness Hachijō-in for over twenty years before retiring into nunhood at the age of fifty. Kengozen's mistress, Hachijō-in, had become the adoptive mother of Jizen's mistress, Her Highness Shunkamon-in, and Kengozen had been charged with the task of overseeing Shunkamon-in's upbringing. Kengozen was thus very familiar with Shunkamon-in's ladies-in-waiting and had most likely continued to act even after her retirement as one of their closest advisors.

Jizen's decision to renounce the world came in the wake of two tragic deaths. Hachijō-in had passed away just six months earlier, and Jizen's own mistress, Shunkamon-in, had passed away just over a month earlier, on the eighth day of the eleventh month, at the young age of seventeen. Although it had become common by this time to take the tonsure as an act of loyalty following the death of a mistress, master, lord, or husband, Jizen was only twenty-five years old when her mistress died (*KJGSK* 1999, 213–215). Since most members of court society considered it a great tragedy for a woman to renounce the world while still in the prime of her childbearing years,[1] Jizen likely believed that she would have faced opposition if she had made public her desire to take the tonsure. And so she left the Hachijō residence, Teika tells us, under the pretense that she was simply going out to bathe. Once she had left the company of those who might have challenged her decision, she traveled to Nara and took the precepts under the priest Jiren-bō. Following the custom of the day, she received one of the characters in her Buddhist name from the priest who gave her the precepts.[2]

In the sentences that follow the passage related above, Teika goes on to praise the young Ukingo for having displayed such profound loyalty to her mistress. By Teika's time, the tonsure had already come to signify personal loyalty, and as this passage suggests, the tonsure was taken not only to express conjugal fidelity but also, and perhaps more importantly, to express loyalty to one's household and its master. Unlike episodes from the *Genji* wherein the tonsures of young women are described with words of great regret, then, Teika, though saddened by the circumstances that led Jizen to take the tonsure at such a young age, clearly approves of her decision. The story of her tonsure is so moving, he writes, that he finds it "impossible to refrain from crying" (*Kundoku Meigetsuki,* 3:98b). And thus it is clear that social values surrounding the tonsure of young women were by this time rather mixed. While Teika's entry suggests that Jizen had to sneak away from the Hachijō residence in order to take vows without facing the objections of others, those who might have voiced opposition to her decision were in fact delighted to learn of it.

Between her flight from the Hachijō residence and her move to Hokkeji, Jizen began to study under the tutelage of the nun Kūnyo (b. 1176). Kūnyo, whose secular name was Takakura-dono (also Hachijō-in no Takakura), had also been called Daigo-dono, a moniker that reflected her long residence at Shōkutei-in, a nuns' subtemple *(shiin)* on the grounds of the great temple complex Daigoji in Kyoto. A former lady-in-waiting in Hachijō-in's service, Takakura-dono appears to have left the court and taken religious vows about six months before Jizen. Like Jizen, Takakura-dono, who had also served at the Hachijō residence, decided to take vows after learning of her mistress's death. Hachijō-in died in the sixth month of 1211, just a few months before the death of Jizen's young mistress, Shunkamon-in.

A number of Hokkeji-related documents suggest that Jizen and Kūnyo, who were eleven years apart in age, shared a teacher-student relationship.[3] According to an excerpt from Eison's *Hokkeji shari engi* (Karmic origins of the Lotus Temple relics), Kūnyo spent her final years at Hokkeji, where she practiced alongside Jizen and another disciple named Shakunen. The *Hokkeji shari engi* describes Kūnyo as follows:

> There was a *zenni* [privately professed nun] named Kūnyo (her original name was Takakura no tsubone). She had an intelligent character, and from a young age she entered the Buddhist path. She studied both the exoteric and esoteric doctrines and had the ability to read both Japanese and Chinese. She knew everything of the world and grieved for all people. After she became aged, she longed to see signs of the founder [Kōmyō] and retired to the meditation retreat [Skt. *varṣā*] hall [*angobō*] of Hokkeji. She earnestly developed the Buddhist cultivations of principle and phenomena. Once, when Kūnyo was together with Jizen Bikuni, the rector of this temple [Hokkeji] (who was first the disciple of this *zenni* [Kūnyo]), and Shakunen Bikuni, they cloistered themselves at Shōdaiji [Tōshōdaiji] in order to form positive karmic bonds [*kechien*] through the Shaka *nenbutsu.* (143b)[4]

Other textual evidence suggests that Jizen had studied under Kūnyo before either arrived at Hokkeji. During this time, the two appear to have resided at Shōkutei-in.[5] Piecing this evidence together, it is possible to speculate that Jizen followed Kūnyo to Shōkutei-in following Shunkamon-in's death. The two most likely practiced there along with other nuns until they decided to take up residence at Hokkeji.

Tanaka Takako demonstrated that Kūnyo was in fact the product of an illicit relationship between Her Highness Takamatsu-in (1140–1176) and the priest Chōken (1126–1203).[6] Indeed, as noted above, Eison's *Kongō Busshi Eison kanjin gakushōki* (Record of how the adamantine child of the Buddha [Eison] physically responded to the Buddha and studied the right doctrine; Eison's autobiography) refers to Kūnyo as the "royal daughter" Takamatsu-in.[7] A document from the Kanazawa Bunko archives also indicates that Kūnyo was a cousin of the Daigoji priest Jōken (1162–1231) (Tanaka T. 2006, 204). It was likely through these family connections that Kūnyo and Jizen gained entrée to Shōkutei-in.

Kūnyo's mother, Takamatsu-in, was the daughter of the Toba Tennō (1103–1156) and his queen-consort Bifukumon-in (Fujiwara no Tokushi, 1117–1160). She was also a full sister both to Go-Shirakawa Tennō (1127–1192) and to the powerful Hachijō-in. Takamatsu-in was herself granted the title *nyoin* in the year 1162. Since the relationship between Takamatsu-in, the lawful spouse of Nijō Tennō (1143–1165), and Chōken, a tonsured priest, was a forbidden one, Kūnyo's birth would have called for a full-scale cover-up (Tanaka T. 2006, 198-202).[8] But Takamatsu-in died soon after the birth of her illegitimate daughter, a distraction that would have aided in the concealment of her daughter's identity. Scholars believe that Hachijō-in also helped obscure her late sister's indiscretion by handing the infant Takakura-dono over to the great poet Fujiwara no Shunzei, who raised her until she was old enough to be returned to Hachijō-in as a lady-in-waiting (Tanaka T. 2006; *KJGSK* 1999, 210).[9]

Textual evaluations of Kūnyo's life and character reflect the influence of court culture. Eison's description of Kūnyo in his *Hokkeji shari engi,* for example, emphasizes her erudition. He mentions that she was able to read both Japanese and Chinese, an insight that suggests Shunzei may have directed her education. Kūnyo also authored a number of *waka* poems included in the *Shinchokusen wakashū* (New collection of waka compiled by imperial command). This accomplishment attests to her literary skill and suggests that she, like her disciple Jizen, was actively engaged in the *waka* writing circles of Shunzei and Teika (see *Hokkeji shari engi,* 143b).[10]

It should be clear, then, that a complex web of familial, social, and literary connections linked the most visible leaders of Hokkeji's thirteenth-century revival, Jizen and her master Kūnyo, to the royal court and its rich culture. In particular, the relationship between these women and the royal residences, or *gosho,* of *nyoin* is worth attention. As ladies-in-waiting in the *gosho* of *nyoin,* Jizen and Kūnyo would have been well educated and well connected, both in courtly circles and in the religious and literary circles linked to the court. The networks formed by women like Kūnyo and Jizen during their days at court were not forgotten once they had left the capital for the convent; they continued to draw upon these connections, to whatever degree possible, even after they had renounced the world.

Daigoji and the Nuns of Shōkutei-in

The nuns' lineage at Shōkutei-in, where Jizen and Kūnyo spent the early years of their monastic practice, can be traced back to the mid-thirteenth century. It was a cousin of Kūnyo, the Daigoji abbot *(zasu)* Jōken (1162–1231), who first bequeathed this subtemple to a woman. Before his death in the year 1231, Jōken wrote a land transfer document granting the rights to Shōkutei-in to his disciple and cousin Shin-Amidabutsu-ni (also referred to as the *bikuni* Shin-Amidabutsu and as Shin'a in related documents). As indicated by the epithet "*ni*," or "nun," Shin-Amidabutsu-ni was one of Jōken's female disciples.

The land transfer document indicates that the nun Shin-Amidabutsu was to receive the temple buildings and land, including both forests and rice fields, of Shōkutei-in. Following Jōken's death, she was to take up residence in the subtemple and to carry out certain Buddhist rites that had been Jōken's responsibility. In particular, she was to perform the *onki* for the ninth-century esoteric patriarch Ogurusu Jōgyō and for two twelfth-century Shingon priests: Shinkai, who had been Jōken's teacher, and Jitsuun. *Onki* are long-term *kuyō,* or commemorative rites, performed on regular dates extending over long intervals of time. They take place on death anniversaries, typically the thirteenth, seventeenth, twenty-fifth, fiftieth, centennial, bicentennial, and so on. In his document, Jōken bequeaths a special hall to Shin-Amidabutsu-ni—"the Continuous Nenbutsu Practice Hall" (Fudan Nenbutsu no Dōjō)—specifically for the performance of these rites. He also indicates his desire that Shin-Amidabutsu-ni use the hall to perform *onki* for him as well and that she pray for his posthumous salvation ("Jōken yuzurijō," *Kujō-ke monjo* 6, no. 1937: 278; "Shōkutei-in fuzoku shōmon funshitsu jōan," *Daigoji monjo,* no. 308, 56–57).

In addition to the land transfer document itself, Jōken left written instructions to the male members of his following warning that they must not dispute Shin-Amidabutsu's right to manage the affairs of Shōkutei-in and admonishing them to cooperate with her as she took over the administration of the subtemple.[11] Documentary evidence regarding the actual transfer of the temple property following Jōken's death suggests that the other disciples of Jōken did indeed respect his wishes, accepting Shin-Amidabutsu-ni as the rightful heir of Shōkutei-in (Tsuchiya 1989, 193–194).

Relevant texts indicate both that Jōken distinguished lay female patrons from nuns and that he considered Shin-Amidabutsu-ni to be a nun rather than a laywoman. As a priest with a considerable following, Jōken bequeathed Daigoji subtemples like Shōkutei-in to many of his disciples *(montei)*. But as he made clear in a 1209 land transfer document, he did not want these small worship halls to fall into the hands of "nonpriests" *(jisō ni arazaru no hito)*. In fact, he specifically noted that he did not want any such halls to be passed on to "lay [i.e., nonordained] ladies-in-waiting and the like" *(zoku nyōbō-ra)*. The fact that Jōken bequeathed Shōkutei-in to Shin-Amidabutsu-ni, then, suggests that he understood her not as a "nonpriest" laywoman but rather as a full-fledged member of his monastic following, that is, as a priest who had the right to inherit the administration rights to a subtemple and the authority to carry out ritual duties concomitant with the position ("Jōken shojō," *Daigoji monjo* 7, no. 1376; Tsuchiya 1989, 194).

That Jōken found it necessary to beseech his male followers to respect his decision to name Shin-Amidabutsu-ni the successor of Shōkutei-in suggests, on the one hand, that her status was contested. But the fact that Jōken's followers did indeed follow his wishes, allowing Shin-Amidabutsu to take over the management of Shōkutei-in without any clear signs of resistance, suggests, on the other hand, that Kamakura-period priests did not necessarily hold that women were barred from authentic discipleship. Insofar as the Daigoji community appears to have accepted Shin-Amidabutsu-ni's inheritance of Shōkutei-in, her case suggests that at least some late-Heian- and early-Kamakura-period monks did in fact recognize certain *ama* as members of monastic lineages prior to Eison's establishment of a nuns' ordination platform at Hokkeji.[12]

Having gained full bequeathal rights, Shin-Amidabutsu-ni legally transferred Shōkutei-in to Kūnyo.[13] The worship hall then remained in the hands of nuns—or female priests—well into the fourteenth century. Kūnyo and Shin-Amidabutsu had studied under Jōken together, and, as mentioned earlier, Jōken, Shin-Amidabutsu, and Kūnyo were all cousins. Kūnyo's disciple Jizen and her disciples, then, traced their learning not only through the lineages of Tankū and Eison but also through that of the Daigoji abbot Jōken and his cousins Shin-Amidabutsu and Kūnyo (Tsuchiya 1989, 194–197).

The case of Shin-Amidabutsu draws attention to the important role that familial connections played in temple affairs during this period. It is likely that Jōken chose Shin-Amidabutsu over other possible heirs because she was a cousin, a personal relative. In bequeathing properties or offices, people of the late Heian period tended to favor close female relatives over distant male relatives (Mass 1985, 67–77). It follows, then, that even as late as the mid-thirteenth century, Jōken may have preferred to hand Shōkutei-in down to an ordained female cousin rather than a male priest who had no connection to his family. And it is likely that Shin-Amidabutsu, in turn, decided to pass the hall on to Kūnyo because she too was a cousin.

As this section has demonstrated, Hokkeji's thirteenth-century female leaders were active in Buddhist religious circles for decades preceding their initial meetings with Eison. Long before meeting Eison, this first generation of nuns had already established a monastic lineage of their own, studied with a number of Buddhist teachers, and even maintained and managed the legal rights to the Daigoji subtemple Shōkutei-in.

Although it is not known how or why Kūnyo, Jizen, and their immediate disciples decided to move to Hokkeji around the year 1243, it is likely that, as former ladies-in-waiting who had served in the salon of Her Highness Hachijō-in, they had heard about Hokkeji at court or through court circles, since the convent had been incorporated into standardized pilgrimage routes through the southern capital. Indeed, some have even speculated that the *nyoin* whom Jitsuei, author of the *Kenkyū gojunreiki,* accompanied on a pilgrimage of the great temples of Nara in the year 1191 may have been Hachijō-in (Fujita 1972, 127–129; Koida 2004, 57). If Hachijō-in was in fact the woman who toured the great temples of Nara with Jitsuei, then Kūnyo, who was in Hachijō-in's service during the time of the pilgrimage, may have heard about Hokkeji directly from Hachijō-in. Regardless of whether these direct connections were in place, though, court and literary connections would have granted Jizen and Kūnyo access to Jitsuei's pilgrimage records, as well as to other, similar records and *engi* collections. They must have learned of Hokkeji both through word of mouth, as pilgrimages to Nara had become popular among courtiers during these years, and through literary collections that had begun to document the history of Hokkeji. There were also strong connections between Daigoji and the southern capital: it is well-known, for example, that Eison, who became a major figure in the Buddhist world of medieval Nara, was raised by monks at Daigoji and completed his initial training there. It is also likely, then, that in addition to having learned of Hokkeji and its association with Queen-Consort Kōmyō through their court connections, Jizen and Kūnyo again heard about various movements taking place in the southern capital of Nara during their time at Daigoji in Kyoto.

The Cultural Influence of the *Nyoin Gosho*

Insofar as texts related to Jizen and Kūnyo do not discuss doctrinal matters directly, it is impossible to access their views on female salvation or to obtain any direct insight into how they understood their roles as women vis-à-vis the male clergy. Attention to the cultural backdrop of the royal women's courts, however, can offer some insight into the attitudes and assumptions with which royal women and their ladies-in-waiting approached Buddhism.

Of special relevance here are the salons of *nyoin,* or royal women who had received an *ingō,* an "*in*" title that gave them rank and privilege similar to that of retired sovereigns *(in).* Women who received this title would take a new name that ended in the character "*in*" or the characters "*mon'in.*" The title was first granted in 991, to Ichijō Tennō's mother, the grand empress Fujiwara no Senshi (961–1001), following her decision to renounce the world *(shukke).* In this sense, the title was rooted in the notion that *in* was a title to be given to royalty upon their "retirement" into lives of religious devotion. But the title was soon dislodged from its association with world renunciation, and many subsequent *nyoin* received the title without having taken monastic vows. The title was granted to a range of royal women, from consorts, queen-consorts *(kōgō),* and princesses to grand empresses (*kōtaigō,* a title for the sovereign's mother) and senior grand empresses (*taikōtaigō,* a title for the sovereign's grandmother).

The political and cultural influence of the *nyoin* title reached its apex during the reign of Retired Sovereign Toba. Bifukumon-in, Toba's most beloved consort, received the title in 1149. As a favored royal consort and, in many senses, a co-sovereign, her cultural, political, and economic power was widely recognized (Nomura 1989, 144).[14] Since he favored Bifukumon-in so highly, Toba granted her an abundance of landholdings, and she in turn bequeathed these rich portfolios of landed estates to her daughter, Hachijō-in (Gomi 1984, 379–381).

The amassing of *nyoin* land portfolios did not begin with Bifukumon-in and her daughter Hachijō-in. Jōtōmon-in (Fujiwara no Shōshi, 988–1074) and Taikenmon-in (Fujiwara no Shōshi, 1101–1145) had also acquired many lands, and at least in the case of Taikenmon-in, it is clear that she entrusted the management of these lands to her ladies-in-waiting and then bequeathed these lands to them upon her death.[15] Hachijō-in, too, entrusted her ladies-in-waiting with the management of the lands she had inherited from her mother, Bifukumon-in. These lands increased greatly in number as local landholders *(zaichi ryōshu)* entrusted additional estates to Hachijō-in's protection. Having been placed in charge of the administration of these lands, Hachijō-in's ladies-in-waiting delegated actual on-site managerial work to male servant-guards *(saburai)* (379–390).

What is most significant about the immense land portfolios accumulated and managed by *nyoin* and their ladies-in-waiting is the degree of financial stability such assets provided. As the protectors *(honke)* of estates, *nyoin* provided lower-ranking land administrators with immunity from government officials and tax collectors; in return, they received a sizeable portion of the wealth from the estates under their shelter. Estates typically paid their protectors both with rice and foodstuffs, as well as with local products such as silks, handicrafts, and luxury goods. The accumulation of estates endowed late-Heian-period *nyoin* and their ladies-in-waiting with a firm economic base that allowed them to develop a broader sphere of cultural and political power. This pattern began with Taikenmon-in and was mirrored in the lives and activities of Bifukumon-in, Hachijō-in, Kenshunmon-in (Taira no Shigeko, 1142–1176), and Kenreimon-in (Taira no Tokuko, 1155–1213), among others (381–384). All those vying for power during this period—retired sovereigns, Fujiwara regents, heads of warrior families, and large Buddhist temple complexes—measured their success and their influence by the number and quality of estates under their control. As successful competitors in the struggle to acquire vast estate holdings, *nyoin* asserted their place among Japan's most powerful political figures and institutions. They had their own *mandokoro,* or administrative centers, and essentially functioned both politically and economically on the same level as retired sovereigns. *Nyoin* even had access to their own militias. In this sense, then, their political power rivaled that of their male contemporaries.[16]

The ladies-in-waiting of *nyoin* received many benefits. They were typically paid for their services with *shiki,* or rights to a portion of income from lands controlled by their mistresses. Sometimes, as was the case with several of Hachijō-in's ladies, ladies-in-waiting also inherited land rights from their mistresses.[17] Lady-in-waiting positions also offered much in the way of cultural stimulation and prestige. As reflected in Kengozen's *Diary of Chūnagon, Who Served the Nyoin Kenshunmon* (*Kenshunmon-in Chūnagon nikki,* also *Tamakiwaru*), the courts of *nyoin* tended to inspire a rich salon culture. Among the more than sixty women Kengozen mentions in her descriptions of Kenshunmon-in's ladies-in-waiting, one finds the sisters and daughters of those close to the royal family and the female relatives of those holding various court positions. Kengozen notes that some of these women were the daughters of women in the arts, such as *biwa* players and *asobi* (also *yūjo*), women who provided sexual entertainment. Also included among those listed are wet nurses and their daughters, as well as the daughters of priests, ladies-in-waiting, provincial lords, and even shrine administrators (*Kenshunmon-in Chūnagon nikki,* 85–90).[18]

Kengozen's diary demonstrates that the ladies-in-waiting at *nyoin gosho,* or the residences of *nyoin,* gained exposure to a thriving cultural scene and interacted within a diverse community, one that included court officials, poets, musicians, dancers, priests, nuns, wet nurses, and even pleasure women. Access to learning also seems to have been a primary advantage of this environment. That the inner court was a place where women had many opportunities to read and write is reflected in the fact that many of the great writers of the Heian period were the ladies-in-waiting of royal women. Having come of age in the cultural sphere of her highness Hachijō-in, Jizen and Kūnyo brought to Hokkeji deep knowledge of court tradition, literary and artistic skills, and awareness of recent trends in aristocratic society. One can also assume that these two women had formed, during their years at Hachijō-in's residence, substantive social networks that would continue to serve them beyond the secular world.

Buddhist Activity and Discourse in Female Court Salons

Nyoin gosho were also places in which women had the opportunity to participate in large-scale patronage practices. Royal women and their ladies-in-waiting regularly commissioned copies of the *Lotus* and other sutras, amassed and transmitted Buddhist relics, developed and performed relics assemblies, engaged in pilgrimages, and performed or commissioned *kuyō* services on behalf of their ancestors or other family members. Through these activities, they actively constructed a cultural sphere of influence that contributed both to contemporaneous Buddhist discourses in a broad sense and, in a narrower sense, to the ways in which such discourses depicted women.[19]

Brian Ruppert's study of Buddhist relics and their worship and transmission in premodern Japan, for example, illustrates the ways in which *nyoin* articulated and appropriated associations between women and Buddhist relics so as to divert attention from androcentric Buddhist doctrines, such as that of the five obstacles. Ruppert demonstrates that "court women were cognizant of both historical and literary" connections between women and relic worship. Many of the broader literary associations look back to Indian tales in which women are linked to Buddhist relics. The most powerful literary link was undoubtedly to the *Lotus Sutra*'s dragon girl, who will be discussed at greater length below. Ruppert explains that the dragon girl was "sometimes specifically described as protecting Buddha relics." By fashioning themselves as protectors of Buddha relics, *nyoin* were able to suggest that they, like the daughter of the dragon king, possessed both "secret access to the treasure house of Buddhism" and the "capacity to attain enlightenment." Narrating the history of the many relics assemblies that *nyoin* established, maintained, and even presided over, Ruppert shows how figures like Bifukumon-in, Kōkamon-in (Fujiwara no Seishi, 1121–1181), Hachijō-in, Senyōmon-in (Princess Kinshi, 1181–1252), and other Fujiwara women exploited literary associations between women and Buddhist relics as a means of fashioning their own ritual traditions and maintaining their own, often matrilineal, family lineages (2000, 203, 214–229, 278).

Past scholarship has also emphasized the degree to which Buddhist objects and services commissioned by female patrons reflected concerns and interests seemingly specific to women (e.g., Moerman 2006, 191). It has often been said, for example, that the lavishly ornamented *Heike nōkyō,* a copy of the *Lotus Sutra* produced by the Taira and donated to Itsukushima shrine in the year 1164, is illustrative of how elite court women read Buddhist doctrine in ways that allowed for female salvation.

As is well known, the twelfth chapter of the *Lotus Sutra* tells of a dragon *(nāga)* girl who achieves buddhahood in an instant, thereby astonishing all those in the assembly. Although this passage does suggest that women can realize buddhahood, its solace is only partial, as the text makes it clear that in her whirlwind ascent through the various perfections of bodhisattvahood, the dragon girl first attains a male body. The text does not argue that the five obstacles enumerated by Śāriputra just before the dragon girl's feat are merely empty designations; rather, it suggests that they can be overcome through the power of the Mahāyāna teachings. Even so, the dragon girl's instantaneous attainment of buddhahood remains just ambiguous enough to allow for innovative interpretation. First of all, while it is clear that the dragon girl attains a male body before achieving buddhahood, the text does not explicitly state that this step is necessary. Secondly, the passage does not indicate whether or not the attainment of a male body requires a separate birth. The dragon girl flashes through a series of accomplishments on the bodhisattva path that would typically require many lifetimes, offering the audience what might be understood as a fast-forwarded vision of the many births leading up to her buddhahood.

Does her attainment of a male body occur in a separate lifetime, or is it something that can be realized in this one? The text leaves this question open to the reader (trans. Hurvitz 1976, 200–202; T. 262, 35c6–21). Many have argued that court women, especially those poised to patronize large-scale artistic projects, tended to read the dragon girl's enlightenment as proof that they too could achieve buddhahood at the end of this lifetime and without having to pass through a separate lifetime in a male body. In the frontispiece to the twelfth (Devadatta) chapter of the *Lotus,* the *Heike nōkyō* cleverly avoids the question of whether or not the dragon girl's attainment of buddhahood required transformation into a male body. The image depicts her in the moments before her enlightenment not as a dragon but in the form of a female human being as she presents the Buddha with a jewel. Earlier Chinese and Chinese-style visual representations of the Devadatta chapter follow a standard iconographic sequence in which the dragon girl reappears following the Buddha's acceptance of her jewel as a male figure before finally being depicted as a buddha (Meech-Pekarik 1976, 251–253). In skipping over the scene in which the dragon girl is shown in male form, the *Heike nōkyō* implicitly dismisses the notion that the acquisition of a male body was a part of her enlightenment. Some have argued that this "deliberate misreading" of the text "entailed a constructive theological project and an assertion of [women's] religious agency" (Moerman 2006, 191).

Such readings of the *Heike nōkyō,* though compelling, lose sight of one important detail: there is little evidence indicating that women were the primary patrons of the *Heike nōkyō.*[20] To the contrary, the dedicatory text *(ganmon)* and the donor name register *(kechien kyōmyō)* associated with the *Heike nōkyō* suggest that the thirty-two individuals responsible for producing chapters for the collection were all male.[21] It is true that some of the donors may have had women in mind: a number of scholars have suggested that Taira no Kiyomori (1118–1181), in organizing and donating the work, envisioned it as a merit-making activity that would protect his daughter Tokuko (Kenreimon-in) and grant her success at court. Some of the men who contributed to the *Heike nōkyō* also conveyed in their *ganmon* that they wished the merit they accrued through this act of piety to benefit a female relative. Moreover, there is some evidence suggesting that women of the Taira family were involved at various levels in the production of certain chapters (Meech-Pekarik 1976, 143–147, 311–314). Evidence of women's participating in the project notwithstanding, it is difficult to make the argument that the *Heike nōkyō,* commissioned by men, represents the "assertion" of women's "religious agency."

Readings that understand works such as the *Heike nōkyō* as evidence of women's resistance or manipulation of the dominant discourse, then, may be missing the point. It is a stretch to argue that the *Heike nōkyō,* in offering positive readings of the dragon girl's enlightenment and optimistic views of women's salvation more generally, serves as evidence that certain court women actively forwarded their own interpretations of the *Lotus* and resisted "male" readings of the sutra. What the *Heike nōkyō* does tell us, however—and this is precisely because the work *did* involve so many male patrons—is that the broader culture of the late-Heian court tended to support interpretations of the *Lotus* holding that women could achieve salvation easily and without first having to attain birth as men. The modern reader, seeking to identify a battle of the sexes, might find it disconcerting that a work commissioned by men and in honor of both men and women would read against a canonical text in a way that seems to benefit women. But closer attention to the production of the *Heike nōkyō* suggests that elite men and women did not necessarily read the *Lotus* differently according to their sex. The *Heike nōkyō,* anyway, would suggest that court elites, both male and female, supported readings of the *Lotus* that granted women great potential on the Buddhist path.

The entire genre of the *Lotus ippongyō,* of which the *Heike nōkyō* is perhaps the most extravagant example, was developed largely within the salons of *nyoin* and other royal women. Although there is no element of this genre, in which thirty to thirty-two individuals each commission the copying and adornment of one scroll (the twenty-eight chapters of the *Lotus Sutra* plus two or four of the following: the *Sutra of Immeasurable Meanings,* the *Meditation Sutra on Samantabhadra* [*Guan puxian jing*], the *Smaller Sukhāvatī-vyūha Sutra,* and the *Heart Sutra*) that can be identified as essentially "feminine" or particular to women, many of the most famous examples of the practice of *ippongyō* were organized by women or involved important contributions from elite women.[22]

One of the earliest records of a *Lotus ippongyō* commemoration ceremony dates to Jian 1 (1021) 9/10, when thirty ladies-in-waiting in the service of Grand Empress Kenshi (994–1027, aka Kiyoko) dedicated an *ippongyō* they had produced both for the benefit of their mistress (to be used in a *gyakushu,* or predeath funeral service) and as a means of creating karmic merit for themselves. Fujiwara no Michinaga offered the ladies use of the Amida Hall on the grounds of his temple Hōjōji for the ceremony, and the ladies invited the priest Yōshō to serve as lecturer. The sixteenth chapter of *Eiga monogatari,* which describes the production of this *ippongyō* in great detail, indicates that the event, though planned by ladies-in-waiting and focused on the fruits of their own labors, was by no means limited to women: court men attended the dedication ceremony in great number and admired the lavish work produced by Kenshi's women (see McCullough and McCullough, 1980, 41–44). Minister of the right Fujiwara no Sanesuke even mentions the ceremony in his diary, *Shōyūki,* where he notes both that many nobles gathered to attend the event and that it was impossible to describe the beauty with which the sutra was adorned (*Shōyūki,* Jian 1 [1021] 9/10; Komatsu 2005a, 91–92).

Similar *ippongyō* projects, including those undertaken by elites of lower rank, can be found throughout courtier diaries (Komatsu 2005a, 92–93). Such projects were by no means limited to women—most, in fact, were produced through the joint efforts of elite men and women. It was especially common for royal women and their ladies-in-waiting to play significant roles in the organization and execution of these projects. In the case of the project undertaken by Kenshi's ladies, it is possible that women were involved not only in the commissioning of the scrolls but also in their actual artistic production.

Many ladies-in-waiting of the Insei-period (1086–1185) courts attained considerable expertise as painters. According to Akiyama Terukazu, "both the appreciation of painting and the ability to paint were considered requisite skills for the cultivated aristocratic lady or lady-in-waiting at court" (1990, 160). In fact, Minamoto no Moritoki mentions, in his *Chōshūki* (1130/9/17), that Toba Tennō and Her Highness Taikenmon-in (Fujiwara no Shōshi, 1101–1145) had established within their court a "painting atelier staffed by court ladies-in-waiting" *(nyōbō edokoro).* It was in this space, Akiyama surmises, that a lady-in-waiting and painter known as Lady Tosa produced the *meishoe,* or images of famous places, she had been commissioned to paint for Taikenmon-in's Hōkongō-in temple (1990, 162–163). Sources indicate that Lady Kii, another painter in Taikenmon-in's service, contributed to the production of a set of twenty illustrated *Genji* scrolls, a work that was likely regarded as a significant imperial commission. Akiyama further identifies Lady Kii as the "nun" involved in producing, along with the Emperor Goshirakawa (1127–1192), the *Menashikyō,* a set of sutra sketches resembling those that appear in *monogatari* illustrations (165–167). (The project was left unfinished because the emperor passed away before it could be completed.)

Lady Kii's participation in the *Menashikyō* project sheds light on the degree to which *monogatari*-style illustrations, such as those used in *Genji* scrolls, had become increasingly common in sutra projects, despite the fact that they were typically identified as examples of *onna-e,* or "women's[-style] painting" (Akiyama 1990).[23] The *Heike nōkyō,* too, includes a number of *monogatari-* and *onna-e*-style images in its frontispieces. While such designations do not mean that female artists were necessarily involved in the production of the images, they do suggest a certain admiration for styles associated both with court women and with *monogatari* (see Komatsu 1994, 116). It is also possible to speculate that, of the Taira men responsible for producing individual scrolls of the *Heike nōkyō* who chose to commission out some or all of the artistic labor required in the production of their contributions, some may have included female ladies-in-waiting among the artists they hired.

But even if a few women were in fact involved in the production of the *Heike nōkyō*—and we have no hard evidence to prove that this was the case—it would be a mistake to suggest that the *Heike nōkyō* is a "feminine" work or a women's theological project. Nor would it make sense to argue that the work is a male appropriation of a female art form. (Indeed, nearly half of the scrolls feature frontispieces painted in the so-called men's[-style] painting, or *otoko-e.*) The *Heike nōkyō* instead suggests that Heian men did not understand their own interests as opposed to those of court women; depicting on sutra frontispieces beautiful images of women in the *onna-e* style had, through the influence of female sovereigns and ladies-in-waiting, simply become a widely accepted practice popular among both men and women. The positive reading of the dragon girl's enlightenment found in the twelfth scroll of the *Heike nōkyō* should not be understood as an exceptional example of elite women "misreading" Mahāyāna doctrine in their favor, but instead as representative of a broader court discourse on women's salvation that was propagated and accepted among elites of both sexes during the late Heian period.[24]

Even more significant than the *Heike nōkyō*'s seemingly unorthodox interpretation of the dragon girl's attainment, however, is the related discourse on women's rebirth in the Tuṣita Heaven. This discourse, also based in the *Lotus Sutra,* emphasizes the vows of the bodhisattva Fugen (Samantabhadra) as conveyed in the twenty-eighth chapter of the *Lotus.* Here, Fugen promises that those who simply copy the *Lotus* will be granted rebirth into the Heaven of the Thirty-three Celestials (Skt. Devās Trayas-triṃśāḥ). Those who surpass this basic requirement by "accept[ing]," "uphold[ing]," "read[ing]," "recit[ing]," "memoriz[ing]," and "understand[ing]" the sutra are promised swift rebirth into the Tuṣita Heaven of Maitreya (trans. Watson 1997, 28). It is worth noting here that this chapter describes both the Heaven of the Thirty-three Celestials and the Tuṣita Heaven as home to thousands and millions, respectively, of female attendants, or ladies-in-waiting. This detail is of interest because there is much evidence that ladies-in-waiting of the late Heian and Kamakura periods had come to believe that they would be granted rebirth—as ladies-in-waiting—in these heavens, and especially in the Tuṣita Heaven.

Previous work on images utilizing the iconographical scheme known as *Fugen jūrasetsunyo,* which brings the bodhisattva Fugen together with the ten *rākṣasa* daughters, has suggested that many court ladies envisioned themselves as the attendants of the bodhisattva Fugen. That such was the case seems evident enough given the fact that a number of court ladies commissioned images in which the ten *rākṣasa* daughters were depicted in the clothing, hairstyles, and adornments of Heian noblewomen (see Fabricand-Person 2002, esp. 368–372).[25] But such studies have stopped short of clarifying the broader functions of *Fugen jūrasetsunyo* iconography: How were images bearing this iconography used, and to what end?

The recent work of Kimura Saeko offers new answers. Kimura suggests that these paintings were part of a larger discourse in which court women sought rebirth in Maitreya's Tuṣita Heaven. Juxtaposing a *Fugen jūrasetsunyo* painting held in the private collection of the Hinohara family with a text titled *Wagami ni tadoru himegimi* (A young noblewoman seeking [the karmic bonds within] herself, ca. 1271), Kimura offers compelling evidence that certain ladies-in-waiting sought rebirth as ladies-in-waiting in the Tuṣita Heaven. This goal is made explicit in *Wagami ni tadoru himegimi,* which portrays the ladies-in-waiting of a certain royal woman as continuing to serve their mistress, and even to hold poetry-reading parties, in the Tuṣita Heaven, where they have all been reborn together. Drawing both on imagery from the Hinohara painting and on a passage in *Wagami ni tadoru himegimi* that mentions a particular lady as appearing in the Tuṣita Heaven "still with beautifully tied hair," Kimura further argues that court women who sought rebirth in the Tuṣita Heaven believed that they could maintain in this heaven the long and beautiful hair that had marked their status during their earthly lives. Those familiar with the details of Pure Land doctrine would have known that rebirth in the Pure Land, by contrast, required women to sacrifice both their long hair and their entire female identity, for the Chinese Pure Land sutras state that female bodies do not exist in Amida's Pure Land. In fact, there is much evidence to suggest that Heian and Kamakura courtiers believed that women could, by taking full tonsure at the time of death, die as men, since the shaving of the head and the donning of monastic robes signified the loss of female identity (Mitsuhashi 2000, 628–631). That the Tuṣita Heaven is portrayed here as allowing the rebirth of court women, complete with their long hair, emphasizes that this heaven, unlike the Pure Land of Amida, did not require women to undergo rebirth as men.[26]

Although Kimura's work focuses on the Kamakura period, the view that women could attain rebirth in the Tuṣita Heaven without first having to attain male bodies can be found in Heian texts as well. In particular, Chinkai's 1128 *Bodai shinshū,* a text mentioned in the previous chapter, contains a passage in which he compares Amida's Pure Land with the Tuṣita Heaven:

> QUESTION: Which is superior, the Tuṣita Heaven or the Gokuraku [Amida's Pure Land]?
> ANSWER: The Gokuraku is a *completely pure* land. It contains neither the evil paths [*akudō*][27] nor women. But the Tuṣita Heaven is inside *sahā* [the samsaric world]. It contains spirits, gods, and women. For this reason, the Gokuraku is a bit superior.
>
> QUESTION: Which place is easier to get to?
> ANSWER: The Gokuraku is easier. (27)

Written in a question-and-answer format for a lay audience, Chinkai's *Bodai shinshū* offers a glimpse of how Heian laypeople encountered Buddhist teachings. Among the many questions he fields are the following: Is it necessary to visit Shitennōji when practicing the *nenbutsu?* Is there more merit earned in the building of a stupa or in the building of an image of the Buddha? How large, in terms of physical space, is the Gokuraku? and If one creates merit for deceased parents, will they know, even though they are dead? The nature of these questions suggests that the *Bodai shinshū* was aimed at educating laypeople by providing answers to commonly posed questions.

What is fascinating about the above sequence comparing the Pure Land with the Tuṣita Heaven is that it reflects lay confusion over the difference between these two postmortem destinations. Which paradise should a layperson seeking rebirth target? It is not surprising that Chinkai, who was aligned with the nascent Pure Land movement, deems the Pure Land superior to the Tuṣita Heaven. His reasoning, too, is worth attention: the Pure Land is superior because it contains neither women nor beings of the lower three realms, whereas the Tuṣita Heaven includes women, gods, and spirits. That said, he does not condemn the Tuṣita Heaven; he simply suggests that it is slightly inferior to the Pure Land and (yet) more difficult to attain. This particular stance thus leaves rebirth in the Tuṣita Heaven open as a desirable goal for women who are attached to their female bodies and who wish to be reborn as women, even if rebirth in the Tuṣita Heaven may be a bit more difficult to achieve than rebirth in the Pure Land of Amida.

Returning to the case of Kenshi's ladies, who hired the lecturer Yōshō to perform a commemoration ceremony following the completion of their *ippongyō* project, it is clear that these women did indeed have their sights set on rebirth in the Tuṣita Heaven. According to the *Eiga monogatari,* Yōshō's lecture began with the following remarks:

> Ten million people aspired to enlightenment while the Buddha lived on earth [Yōshō said], but never before, perhaps, have ladies entered into a compact, held consultations, and, like these, conceived a desire for enlightenment so fervent as to have written out, richly adorned, and presented a copy of the *Lotus Sutra,* "impossible to comprehend, impossible to penetrate." This is a rarity of rarities. Those who copy and dedicate the *Lotus Sutra* are assured of birth in the Heaven of the Thirty-three Divinities. What is more, it is unthinkable that any of these ladies-in-waiting should have failed to read the *Lotus,* and thus they will undoubtedly be born in the Tuṣita Heaven, there to lead a life of bliss. (trans. McCullough and McCullough 1980, 533; *Eiga monogatari,* 32:239–242)

Much attention has been paid to the fact that by the Heian period orthodox Tendai priests had long been teaching that Amida's Pure Land contained no women. In their explanations of why women were required to attain rebirth as men in order to achieve salvation, priests often cited the absence of women in the Pure Land. Both Chinkai's *Bodai shinshū* and Yōshō's lecture, however, suggest that orthodox priests recognized the Tuṣita Heaven as a heaven that contained women. Although there is no evidence that orthodox priests were actively promoting the Tuṣita Heaven as a place where women could attain rebirth as women, it is clear that many elites—male and female—did in fact understand the Tuṣita Heaven in these terms.

Indeed, diary entries from the Insei period indicate that lay patrons commissioned *Fugen jūrasetsunyo* images for use in women's memorial services. Taira no Nobunori mentions in his diary, *Hyōhanki,* two instances of elite men using *Fugen jūrasetsunyo* images in memorial services for their wives: an entry dated Kyūju 2 (1155) 10/9 reports that chancellor Fujiwara no Tadamichi used *Fugen jūrasetsunyo* images in a memorial service for his wife, Muneko, and a Kaō 2 (1170) 6/22 entry indicates that Nobunori used *Fugen jūrasetsunyo* images commissioned by his son for a memorial service in honor of his wife. Kujō Kanezane also reports in his diary, *Gyokuyō,* that the ladies-in-waiting of Her Highness Kōkamon-in painted—and here it appears that they did the actual painting themselves—an image of Fugen and the ten *rākṣasa* daughters for a memorial service they held in their mistress's honor (Fabricand-Person 2002, 370–371).

The fact that *Fugen jūrasetsunyo* images were being used in the memorial services of women suggests that many elites, male and female, understood the Tuṣita Heaven as a desirable postmortem destination for women. For women who hoped to maintain their female identities in the next life, beliefs surrounding rebirth in the Tuṣita Heaven offered an alternative to Pure Land discourse, which was by this time emphasizing with greater intensity the androcentric discourse of *henjō nanshi,* which taught that women should seek transformation into male bodies. In focusing on rebirth in the Tuṣita Heaven, however, aristocratic women and the men and women who arranged their funerary services managed to sidestep the notion, increasingly popular among Tendai priests, that women needed to seek male bodies before they could attain salvation.[28]

Attention to the Buddhist patronage practices and soteriological discourses that had become popular among elite women in the service of *nyoin* enables us to better understand the assumptions—social, cultural, and ideological—that Jizen and Kūnyo brought to Hokkeji. Here, it has been demonstrated not only that court ladies, and especially those in the service of *nyoin,* were well poised to make substantial contributions to elite society as poets, writers, artists, and patrons but also that they operated within an aristocratic subculture that tended to view the salvation of women as a given. The view that women were impure or that they did not belong in the heavens and pure lands may have become widely accepted among certain priests during this period, but late-Heian aristocrats, male and female, preferred to believe that the salvation of women was not a problem of any substance. They viewed the so-called obstacles of the female body as problems that could be overcome, either through a more thorough understanding of the dragon girl's story or by sending women to the Tuṣita Heaven rather than the Pure Land.

Perhaps this general lack of anxiety over issues particular to women's salvation among Insei-period aristocrats explains why Hokkeji nuns did not mention *henjō nanshi* or similar androcentric discourses in their writings.[29] Unlike Eison and his male followers, who expressed great concern over the salvation of women and who taught that rebirth in male bodies was indeed necessary, Hokkeji nuns appear to have been neither concerned with nor interested in such issues. This difference in perspective is undoubtedly rooted in the fact that Hokkeji's first medieval leaders, Jizen and Kūnyo, had grown up in a world in which the salvation of women was not viewed as a serious problem in the first place.

Hokkeji texts do not address the alternative soteriological strategies suggested in the *Heike nōkyō* or in *Fugen jūrasetsunyo* images, but a hall on the grounds of Hokkeji does contain an image of Fugen's descent dating from the late Heian or early Kamakura period (the *Raigōkabe Fugen Bosatsu yōgōzu*).

This hall, affectionately known as the Yokobue Hall, is named for a woman who had been in the service of Her Highness Kenreimon-in. According to *Heike* legends, Yokobue took the tonsure and fled for Hokkeji after discovering that her lover, Saitō Tokiyori, had become a monk. Unfortunately, the Fugen image has sustained such severe damage that its pictorial content is difficult to decipher. Scholars have managed to determine, however, that the painting follows the *Fugen raigō* iconography that had become more or less standard by this period, with the exception that women dressed in Tang-style clothing were added to the usual mix of Fugen, his attendant bodhisattvas, two heavenly kings, and the ten *rākṣasa* daughters (Miyamoto and Ariga 1978, 50–51). Extant sources do not allow us to judge the historicity of Yokobue's Hokkeji connection; if she did spend time at Hokkeji, however, she would have been there several decades before Jizen and Kūnyo arrived on the scene. Archeological evidence dates the Yokobue Hall to the Muromachi period, but the *Raigōkabe Fugen Bosatsu yōgōzu* painting has been dated to the late Heian or early Kamakura period. It is likely the case, then, that the painting has nothing to do with the figure of Yokobue. But its placement in this small private practice hall suggests that it may have been used for the performance of private deathbed devotions. It is known that similar *Amida raigō* were often used in death-preparation rituals performed in small practice halls by those who sought birth in the Pure Land. The existence of this painting and its placement in a private practice hall at Hokkeji suggests that beliefs surrounding rebirth in the Tuṣita Heaven persisted at the convent. It is possible to speculate, then, that at least some women at Hokkeji may have, like the women of the Insei court, sought rebirth in the Tuṣita Heaven, where they could retain their female identities.

Evidence from Eison's movement also supports the possibility that Hokkeji women may have been targeting rebirth in the Tuṣita Heaven, as opposed to Amida's Pure Land. Like many in the southern capital, Eison and his following tended to emphasize devotion to Śākyamuni Buddha (Jpns. Shaka) over and above devotion to Amida Buddha.[30] Shaka devotees practiced a version of the *nenbutsu*—the Shaka *nenbutsu*—aimed at rebirth in the Tuṣita Heaven. *Tosotsuten ōjō,* or birth in the Tuṣita Heaven, was in fact so highly regarded among adherents of Eison's movement that lay devotees of Eison's reported in the days following his death having had dreams confirming Eison's rebirth in the Tuṣita Heaven (Matsuo 2004b, 34–35).[31] That devotees who regarded Eison as a semidivine figure envisioned him as having attained birth in the Tuṣita Heaven suggests that Eison's group, in contrast to Pure Land thinkers like Chinkai, understood the Tuṣita Heaven to be equal, if not superior, to the Pure Land of Amida. The value placed on *Tosotsuten ōjō* within Eison's group might provide some insight into why Hokkeji nuns seem to have been more or less unconcerned with the notion that sexual transformation was prerequisite for salvation. For those seeking rebirth in the Tuṣita Heaven, the female body was not a major obstacle. Although there is no textual evidence that corroborates this connection directly, it is possible to speculate that the first generation of nuns at Hokkeji, most of whom had some court ties, found the devotional practices offered by Eison and other Nara priests more attractive than those offered by Pure Land priests precisely because they preferred the goal of *Tosotsuten ōjō,* which did not require separation from the female body, to that of *Gokuraku ōjō.*

The Patronage Model: Buddhist Priests as Employees of the Court

Given their exclusion from monastic hierarchies, powerful women of the Heian and early Kamakura periods sought to assert themselves in the Buddhist world not as priests or Buddhist officials but as great patrons of temples and rituals. In many senses, this approach was the same taken by men in their milieu; after all, in the Nara and early Heian periods, even the most powerful of priests was ultimately considered a servant of the sovereign and state. Women who grew up in the court were accustomed to calling on priests at whim to perform ceremonies and rites of all kinds. They could also expect generous reception from Buddhist institutions when they attended rituals or made official pilgrimages. *Nyoin,* in particular, were well positioned to commission large-scale Buddhist projects, such as the creation of lavish copies of sutras, the erection of statues and other images, and the construction of temples and subtemples.

That court women tended to view priests—even elite priests—as employees in their service can be seen throughout the literature of the Heian and early Kamakura periods. In the previously mentioned passage from *Eiga monogatari* in which the ladies-in-waiting of Grand Empress Kenshi produce an *ippongyō,* for example, the ladies express more interest in the details of how the artistic work itself will be carried out than in the question of which priest will perform the dedication ceremony once the work has been completed. *Eiga* suggests that the selection of a priest was almost an afterthought: only after Grand Empress Kenshi's ladies had made all of the more serious decisions regarding the ceremony and the sutra itself was nearly complete did they worry about choosing a priest to dedicate the sutra (2:233–236). The passage indicates that the project was not undertaken under the tutelage of any priest or religious institution but was instead initiated from the inside, by Kenshi's ladies-in-waiting. The passage also suggests that these ladies were not concerned over whether they would be able to find a priest to perform the dedication service on their behalf; they would simply hire the priest of their choice, paying him with fine silks. As mentioned previously, they elected to invite the priest Yōshō to perform the commemoration ceremony. Yōshō carried the prestigious Sōgō title *risshi,* or *vinaya* master (and was granted the even more prestigious title of *shōsōzu,* or junior priest general, shortly after this episode) (2:234n14).[32] Despite his high position, he was careful to keep his patrons in mind when he crafted his lecture: not only did he praise the ladies profusely, but he also assured them of their certain rebirth in the Tuṣita Heaven (2:239–242).

Much like Yōshō, the Tendai priest Ingen (954–1028), who was promoted to abbot *(zasu)* of Enryakuji in 1020 and then to supreme priest *(sōjō)* in 1023, also descended Mount Hiei regularly to provide services at court, primarily on behalf of Michinaga and his close relatives.[33] Within this broader context of serving the elite, Ingen frequently attended to the needs of aristocratic women, bestowing the precepts on and saying prayers for them, offering dedicatory ceremonies for Buddhist objects they had commissioned, and performing large-scale ceremonies, such as the Eight Chanted Lectures on the *Lotus Sutra* (Hokke Hakkō), at their request.[34]

Tendai priests had been serving court women, among their many elite patrons, throughout the Heian period. By the middle years of the Heian period, elite women were requesting ordinations with such frequency that Ryōnin (1072–1132) felt prompted to compile a set of standardized ritual procedures to be used in the ordination ceremonies of women (Shirato 1982, 61; Mitsuhashi 2000, 775; Meeks 2006, 62).[35] The notion that priests were the employees of the elite was not limited to the court: elites outside the court, including elite women, also employed priests regularly. The eighth scroll of the *Kasuga gongen genki,* for example, tells of an aristocratic nun *(nikō)* who, having moved to the Heian capital from Nara, called upon the chief administrator priest *(bettō)* at Seiryōji to make a proclamation to the gods *(keibyaku)* on her behalf (46b). Her status allowed her to take her concerns directly to the highest-ranking priest of this large institution.

Elites sometimes even hired priests to perform more mundane tasks for them. In the mid-eleventh-century *Sarashina nikki,* for example, the author's mother commissions a mirror that she wants to dedicate to Hasedera, but she does not have the time to make a trip to the temple and dedicate it in person. So she sends a priest in her stead, ordering him to cloister himself in the temple for three days and pray for a vision about her daughter, the author of the *nikki* (402–403). One similarly finds, throughout medieval records, numerous cases of low-level aristocrats hiring priests to perform a variety of personal services. It was particularly common for those who were unable to make pilgrimages on their own to send priests in their place so they could still acquire the merit of pilgrimage (see Hongō K. 2004, 224–228).

Power imbalances between elites and priests often enabled wellborn women both to act as the social superiors of priests and to criticize them openly.[36] That aristocratic women tended to identify themselves first as aristocrats and only secondarily as women and as laypeople is suggested in the *Sarashina nikki.* Here, the daughter of Sugawara Takasue, who served as a lady-in-waiting in the salon of Princess Yūshi (1038–1105, third daughter of Go-suzaku Tennō), tells her readers of a dream in which the details of her past life are revealed:

> I have heard that even for highly accomplished priests and the like, viewing one's own former life in a dream is extremely difficult; yet I, trivial and irreso-

lute as I am, saw my former life in the following dream: when I was sitting in the main worship hall [*raidō*] at Kiyomizu temple, someone who appeared to be the chief administrator priest [*bettō*] emerged and said, "In your last life, you were a priest at this temple. You were a carver of Buddhist images [*busshi*], and because of the great merit you created by carving so many images of the Buddha, you were born into a family whose rank greatly surpassed that of your former life." (*Sarashina nikki,* 26:327)

Against the conventional buddhalogical reading of the cosmos, which places male bodies above female bodies and priests above laypersons, Lady Sugawara offers the unexpected opinion that it requires more karmic merit—and thus that it is more desirable—to be born as an aristocratic woman than it is to acquire rebirth as a devout male Buddhist priest lacking in social rank.

Lady Sugawara's comments here reflect certain assumptions about the relationship between gender and class. In her last life, Lady Sugawara explains, she was a *busshi,* a priest who carved Buddhist images. Given the fact that most Buddhist priests were, by Lady Sugawara's time, preaching that women needed to be reborn in a male body in order to attain enlightenment, one might expect Lady Sugawara to have read this dream differently: Was she not better off in her previous life—as a man and as a Buddhist priest—than in this present one, in which she possessed a female body?

But Lady Sugawara does not even address the fact that her female body might be considered undesirable. Instead, she reveals rather matter-of-factly her assumption that birth as an aristocratic woman is preferable to birth in the body of a nonaristocratic male priest. The passage does not allow one to assess the dynamic between gender and class with any precision (Would it require more karmic merit, for example, to be born a middle-ranking aristocratic woman or a low-ranking aristocratic man?), but it does indicate that gender could not be understood outside the context of social class. Blanket statements about *all* women and *all* women's bodies would not have made sense within the rigidly stratified class system of Japanese court society. Surely Lady Sugawara's assumptions about her place in the world as an aristocrat would have affected not only the way that she interacted with priests but also the way that she received doctrines disparaging the female body.

That royal and aristocratic women felt confident in their superiority over those priests who needed their patronage is further suggested by the fact that many made light of and criticized priests rather openly. In *Makura no sōshi,* her collection of frank, if not arrogant, reflections, Sei Shōnagon (b. ca. 967), an accomplished poet who served as a lady-in-waiting in the service of Queen-Consort Sadako (976–1000), expresses words of pity for those men who have been sent into the priesthood: "That parents should bring up some beloved son of theirs to be a priest [here she uses the term *hōshi,* or teacher of the Dharma] is really distressing. No doubt it is an auspicious thing to do; but unfortunately most people are convinced that a priest is as unimportant as a [scrap] of wood, and they treat him accordingly. A priest lives poorly on meager food, and cannot even sleep without being criticized" (trans. Morris 1991, 25–26; *Makura no sōshi,* 8–9).[37]

But even while Sei Shōnagon criticizes others for their harsh judgment of priests, she is not above indulging in the practice herself. In one particularly famous passage, she comments, "A [priest who preaches on the sutras] ought to be good-looking. For, if we are properly to understand his worthy sentiments, we must keep our eyes on him while he speaks; should we look away, we may forget to listen. Accordingly an ugly preacher may well be the source of sin" (trans. Morris 1991, 53; *Makura no sōshi,* 39–42). These passages from the *Makura no sōshi* suggest that Sei Shōnagon, much like Lady Sugawara, tended to view priests with a sense of superiority.

Nearly three hundred years later, Lady Nijō, who served in the court of Retired Sovereign Go-Fukakusa (1243–1304), expressed similar attitudes toward priests in her memoir, *Towazugatari.* Of the priest who delivered remarks at the forty-ninth-day death commemoration service of her father, Minamoto no Masatada, she offers this candid assessment: "The priest from the Kawara temple read the usual phrases comparing the bereaved mourner with a mandarin duck whose mate had forsaken it, and alluding to the legendary one-winged birds; but today these customary metaphors struck me as trite" (trans. Brazell 1973, 31–32; *TG,* 32). For Lady Nijō, then, priests were not beyond criticism but were in fact considered fair targets of personal judgment.[38] Much like Sei Shōnagon, Lady Nijō took great pride in her refined sensibilities, and evaluating the skills of a Buddhist priest, much like judging the quality of a *waka,* offered her the opportunity to demonstrate just how cultivated her tastes were.

These passages from the writings of Lady Sugawara, Sei Shōnagon, and Lady Nijō demonstrate the degree to which the ladies-in-waiting of the court, first, understood themselves as the superiors of priests, whom they viewed as servants of the royal court and its aristocracy, and, second, felt comfortable evaluating, and often criticizing, priests in a public manner. Kūnyo and Jizen had been raised in a world in which priests were regarded less as the gatekeepers of salvation than as employees of the court. This power dynamic should not be forgotten when considering the relationships between Hokkeji nuns and Saidaiji priests. Documentary evidence does not suggest that Jizen or other aristocratic nuns at Hokkeji treated Eison with haughtiness or disrespect. But they did spend their young adulthood surrounded by women who tended to display confidence rather than intimidation in their interactions with priests. It was likely the case that Jizen and her master Kūnyo brought similar attitudes to their relationships with Eison and Saidaiji priests. Certainly Eison, a man of humble birth, recognized that Jizen's social standing greatly surpassed his own. As subsequent chapters will note, Eison used extremely polite language with Jizen, a sign that he was well aware of her superior place in the world.

Convents as Repositories of Court Culture

Having examined the attitudes and assumptions that characterized interactions between elite women and Buddhist monks, let us now turn to the ways in which court women of the late Heian and early Kamakura periods discussed convents and nuns. Of particular interest here are new views of the convent that begin to emerge in Kamakura-period literature. In earlier works, such as the *Genji,* the hermitages of nuns are portrayed as places of sadness and isolation. The image of the convent as a place of lonely despair is undoubtedly tied up in the fact that such places had long been viewed as the final holding place before death. They were the old folks' homes of the Heian period, and as such, Heian writers tended to regard them as depressing spaces hardly worth romanticizing. It was considered wasteful and tragic for a young woman in particular to spend her days among old nuns in some remote hermitage or practice hall.[39]

By the early Kamakura period, however, some female writers had begun to portray the convent in a different light. This alternative view does not comprise a radical reformulation of the convent, which retained its associations with solitude and old age, but rather a romanticization of the convent as a place where the memories of a more glorious age are preserved.[40] Having suffered great losses in the Genpei Wars of the 1180s and the Jōkyū Disturbance of 1221, the court of the Kamakura period lacked the wealth and power that had made the splendors of the Heian court possible. The financial power and cultural influence of *nyoin* and their ladies-in-waiting also waned during this period. By the mid-Kamakura period, the writings of ladies-in-waiting tend to ignore the harsh realities of the present and to focus instead on the bygone glories of the Heian court. It is in this context that the convent took on another layer of meaning as it came to be viewed as a repository of court culture.

At least a handful of the elite women who retired to convents in the early and mid-Kamakura periods had lived through the great changes that characterized the transition from the Heian to the Kamakura. As young women, they had served in the salons of *nyoin* during a time in which the court was still powerful. It was in the convent that these ladies, having retired from lay life after witnessing the diminishment of the court's influence, shared stories of the past with younger women longing to forge connections with the shining world of the Heian court. In this literature, which connects the world of the Buddhist nun with that of the erudite lady-in-waiting, convents are understood as extensions of the court, as places where the traditions of female salons are remembered and the grim facts of social and political change are ignored.

This new view of the convent can be seen in the early-Kamakura prose work *Mumyōzōshi* (Nameless tale), written by a woman known to us now only as the Daughter of Shunzei (1175?–1250?). The Daughter of Shunzei, who, historical sources suggest, was actually the granddaughter of Fujiwara no Shunzei, most likely knew both Jizen and Kūnyo personally.

Hachijō-in Sanjō, the mother of the *Mumyōzōshi*'s author, was the daughter of Shunzei, the sister of Teika, and a lady-in-waiting in the service of Her Highness Hachijō-in. Having been raised by her maternal grandparents, the Daughter of Shunzei seems to have been greatly influenced by Shunzei and Teika. In the year 1201, she appeared in a court poetry contest with her uncle Teika, and following his death in the year 1241 he bequeathed to her a mansion (Marra 1984, 116–117). Surely the Daughter of Shunzei was acquainted with Kūnyo, Shunzei's adopted daughter; Kengozen, Shunzei's birth daughter and sister of Teika; and Jizen, who had served with Kengozen at Hachijō-in's *gosho* and who was herself known as a poet who interacted with Teika on a regular basis.

The Daughter of Shunzei's *Mumyōzōshi* is not about nuns or Buddhism: it is a spirited commentary on Heian literature that focuses on the *Genji*. But it is of interest here because it is set in what appears to be a small hermitage where a group of highly educated ladies have gathered, apparently outside time and space, to remember the "dazzling world" of the Heian court that had "historically and socially disappeared, burned to ashes in the years of the civil [Genpei] war" (122–123). The text creates a fictional dialogue between these ladies and an elderly nun figure.

This elderly nun, like the first rectors at Hokkeji, had served at court during her youth: she had worked as a lady-in-waiting for Kōkamon-in's mother and for Her Highness Seishi. She had also worked in the *gosho* of two sovereigns, Rokujō and Takakura. The story begins when this elderly nun stumbles upon an "old, decrepit" residence that, though seemingly deserted, "retains an air of old-fashioned dignity." It is here that she finds a group of ladies eager to talk about the *Genji*. Michele Marra suggests that the nun's excursion to the crumbling but stately old mansion represents a return to the heyday of the Heian court, especially that period of prosperity represented by *Genji:* the mid-tenth to mid-eleventh centuries (119, 123).

This old villa could also be understood as a small hermitage for nuns. True, the ladies here are young and are not described as nuns. But, as Marra puts it, they are "ethereal" and exist "out of time and out of history" (123). They are perhaps the younger selves conjured up by old nuns. If placed in real time, they may in fact be old nuns, but in the context of this re-created past they take on the form of young ladies who remain forever in the glorious Heian past.

The hermitage this aged nun chances upon is located just behind the Saishōkō-in, a subtemple built through the patronage of Her Highness Kenshunmon-in on the grounds of Retired Sovereign Go-Shirakawa Tennō's Hōjūji residence. This type of temple, built by a *nyoin* on the grounds of a larger complex, was precisely the sort of place in which elite women who had renounced the world often took up residence. When *Mumyōzōshi*'s old woman notices the house, she begins to admire it immediately and soon becomes aware of a small chapel: "On the south of the residence there seemed to be a private oratory [*jibutsudō*] set between two pillars and it was closed off with white sliding doors. The smoke of constantly burning incense filled the place with a delicate fragrance that was truly wonderful. 'Here there is the Buddha,' I thought happily." As she approaches the Buddhist altar, a young woman calls out to her, praising her deep faith with references to passages from the *Lotus Sutra.* The nun responds with words that suggest the ladies of the house may be religious practitioners themselves: "Although you are young," she says, "your benevolence is indeed deep. Is it because you live so close to the Buddha?" References to the Buddha persist throughout the beginning of the narrative, as the young women themselves beg the old woman to tell them of her life's journeys: "Confess in front of this Buddha the things that have happened to you" (*Mumyōzōshi,* 177–178; trans. Marra 1984, 129–131). And thus the conversation begins, the old nun quite anxious to share the stories of her youth with this eager audience.

As the *Mumyōzōshi* narrative continues, it soon becomes clear that while the women have indeed studied the *Lotus* quite thoroughly, it is the *Genji* and the idealized past of the Heian court—not the Buddhist scriptures—that dominates their conversation. This conscious interest in the past (the nun herself admits, "I really wanted to speak of the past") can be found throughout elite women's writing of the Kamakura period. As Karen Brazell comments with regard to the *Towazugatari* of Lady Nijō: "One persistent attitude in Lady Nijō's world was nostalgia for a golden age in the past. . . . Lady Nijō and her friends revered the past. What they looked to as a model for their own lives, however, was not simply the historical past, but also the idealized past depicted in Heian period court literature" (1971, 223).

Like the old nun of *Mumyōzōshi,* Lady Nijō, who had spent her youth as a high-ranking lady-in-waiting in the service of Go-Fukakusa Tennō, also spent many years as a wandering nun. The type of religious pilgrimage in which she engaged—traveling around from temple to temple, writing *waka* in response to sad memories of the past, lodging in hermitages, convents, and small practice halls—was a practice common among Kamakura-period elites. Nijō visited several convents linked to the Hokkeji movement during her pilgrimages: Shōkutei-in at Daigoji, Hokkeji itself, and Chūgūji. Her *Towazugatari* illustrates the degree to which convents and small hermitages served as *yado,* or inns, for elite women seeking religious retreat or requiring a place to stay while on pilgrimage.[41] Her accounts of convents convey little interest in doctrinal matters and instead portray women's temples as miniature salons in the countryside, not unlike the villa described by *Mumyōzōshi*'s old nun. Consider, for example, Nijō's recollection of an evening spent at Daigoji's Shōkutei-in:

> One evening I was sitting with the nun Shinganbō. There were only three days left in the old year, and I was feeling unusually melancholy. "When will I ever have such peace and quiet again?" I wondered aloud. Thinking I was bored, she decided to cheer me up by calling in several of the older nuns and having them tell *stories about times past.* In the garden before us the water in the bamboo pipes leading to the cistern had frozen silent, and from the distant hill came the forlorn sound of someone chopping wood. *It was like a scene from a fairy*

> *tale.* I watched the lamps as they were lit one by one and listened to the early evening service. (trans. Brazell 1973, 41, emphasis mine; *TG,* 41)

For Nijō, then, there was something magical in this evening spent talking "about times past" with nuns at Shōkutei-in: her time at the small convent was "like a scene from a fairy tale."

Indeed, Lady Nijō speaks of her retreats at convents in the most appealing of terms. For her, convents were places full of aesthetic delight. Consider how she describes another scene at Shōkutei-in:

> The blossoms of a late-blooming cherry shone white against branches tipped by new leaves, and among the tree shadows cast by the brilliant moonlight, deer were wandering. If only I could have captured the scene on paper! Bells in nearby temples suddenly tolled the opening of evening services, and as we stood in a corridor beside the meditation hall we heard the chanting of the Buddha's name. I was touched by the pathos of the nuns in their rough hempen robes, leaving the hall after the service, and even Takaaki, normally unmoved by such things, was deeply affected. The glossy sleeves of his informal robe were damp with tears. (trans. Brazell 1973, 103; *TG,* 99)

Of another day at the same convent, she writes, "I spent the day viewing the summer scenery and learning of the true way from the head nun [*bōzu no amagozen*]" (trans. Brazell 1973, 105; *TG,* 101). Throughout *Towazugatari,* she conveys a yearning to take the tonsure, a feeling she expresses most acutely when her relationships with other courtiers become taxing. At these times she finds herself wanting to escape the court and take up a religious life "beyond the mountains" (trans. Brazell 1973, 121, 135; *TG,* 115, 128–129). Similar to the ways in which Lady Murasaki describes the quiet surroundings of the Kamo Virgin's (Saiin's) residence as a place conducive to the writing of impressive *waka* (Kamens 1990, 52–53),[42] Lady Nijō portrays Hokkeji as a tranquil place of study: "The next morning, on a visit to [Hokkeji], I went to the cloister, where I met the nun Jakuenbō, daughter of Lord Fuyutada. She talked to me about the relentless cycle of life and death, causing me to consider remaining in the cloister for a while. But realizing that it was not in my nature to quietly devote myself to scholarly pursuits, and aware of the unending confusion that still dwelled in my heart, I decided to leave" (trans. Brazell 1973, 204; *TG,* 192). Nijō may describe convents as places of serenity that offer respite from the stresses of court life, but she does not portray them as spaces entirely divorced from the ways of the world. The nuns Nijō describes do not shun the outside world and its ways; to the contrary, they remain enmeshed in the world and continue to embrace, in particular, those relationships and activities that lead back to the court. The nuns at Shōkutei-in grant Nijō lodging even when she is pregnant, and they do not protest when her lovers come to the convent in search of her. When her lover Saionji no Kanezane arrives, for example, the nuns do not merely permit his presence but actually welcome him in, delighting in his many gifts and allowing him to spend the day drinking with Lady Nijō and conversing with her nun-companions (*TG,* 40–43).

Another figure familiar to this network of writers, *nyōbō,* and pilgrims was the nun Abutsu-ni (1222–1283), who, like Lady Nijō, spent some time at Hokkeji. Although Abutsu-ni's writing does not directly contribute to the romanticization of the convent as described above, her life story is itself illustrative of the ways in which the social circles and activities of well-educated ladies-in-waiting were linked to and preserved within certain Kamakura-period convents. Abutsu-ni married the Daughter of Shunzei's cousin, Fujiwara no Tameie (1198–1275), who was the son of Teika. Like Jizen and Kūnyo, Abutsu-ni began her career as a lady-in-waiting and later took the tonsure and lived in a convent. But unlike Jizen and Kūnyo, who had also started their careers as ladies-in-waiting in the service of *nyoin,* Abutsu-ni's first tonsure was not permanent: she gave up the tonsured life in the early 1250s, when she became intimate with Tameie.

Abutsu-ni's years as a lady-in-waiting were spent at the court of Her Highness Ankamon-in, which was located near Kitayama. During these years, she is said to have had an affair with a nobleman that turned sour, and it was at this juncture that she decided to become a nun. In the years following her first tonsure, Abutsu-ni appears to have lived as a wandering nun. Like both Lady Nijō and the elderly nun of the Daughter of Shunzei's *Mumyōzōshi,* Abutsu-ni traveled around to various places, lodging at convents and hermitages. It is known that she stayed at Hokkeji for a while—during the time when Jizen was rector—and that "through the introduction of someone she had known at Hokkeji," she was hired by one of the ladies in Tameie's household to copy the *Genji monogatari.*[43] It appears to have been through connections made at Hokkeji that Abutsu-ni first met her husband Tameie (Wallace 1988, 391–392). It may have even been Jizen herself, who was known to have been close with Tameie's father, Teika, who introduced Abutsu-ni to members of Tameie's household (Hosokawa 1989a, 165–169).

The details of Abutsu-ni's everyday life during this period are unknown, and contemporaneous Hokkeji documents do not mention her name. Scholars do believe, however, that Abutsu-ni was living as a nun during her time at Hokkeji. They have also observed that she appears to have become pregnant during that period (Iwasa 1991a). It is likely, then, that Abutsu-ni was a novice or probationary nun at Hokkeji who did not attain any special rank. She probably lived not within the main halls of the convent but rather in a private hermitage near the grounds of Hokkeji. As a novice nun who joined activities at the convent only when she wanted to do so, Abutsu-ni would have remained free to engage with men as she pleased; the Hokkeji community did not monitor the sexual activity of its nuns closely, a fact that was especially true in the case of novice and semi-lay nuns, categories to be explained in greater detail in chapter 5.

Abutsu-ni's life story is suggestive of the cultural pull of the convent, for her involvement at Hokkeji does not appear to have been a function of economic destitution. Her tonsure did follow romantic loss, but the fact that she remarried after having been a nun underscores the fluidity of nunhood. Her time at Hokkeji, then, can be read as part of a larger pattern in which she pursued opportunities at various salons during different periods of her career: at Ankamon-in's *gosho* she learned to read and write, becoming both a poet and a *Genji* expert; as an itinerant nun who spent some time lodging at Hokkeji, she made new connections and was hired as a copyist of *Genji;* and finally, at the salon of Tameie, she gained recognition as the primary wife of Tameie himself. Abutsu-ni remained active in the world of poetry, dedicating herself to her husband's and sons' Mikohidari lineage of poetry. Once established as a literary figure in Tameie's salon, she wrote, among many other works, poems included in imperial anthologies and the *Menoto no fumi* (Nursemaid's letter), a guidebook for ladies-in-waiting.[44]

Abutsu-ni's case also illustrates how the networks of ladies-in-waiting operated in many directions: her literary skills and interests enabled her to interact not only with those ladies-in-waiting in the *gosho* of her mistress, the *nyoin* Ankamon, but also with a wide variety of women employed at other *gosho.* It was likely through people she knew at Ankamon-in's salon that she learned about Jizen and Hokkeji, and it was through Hokkeji connections that she landed the position at Tameie's residence, another *gosho*-like salon. Throughout all of these activities, Abutsu-ni remained in regular contact with other ladies-in-waiting through letters (Reischauer 1947, 293, 341–342, 382). Correspondence allowed her to stay in touch with ladies-in-waiting who had gone to other *gosho,* married, become pilgrims, or entered convents.

As the histories and writing practices of the Daughter of Shunzei, Lady Nijō, and Abutsu-ni demonstrate, the world of Kamakura-period ladies-in-waiting was bound up with that of nuns and convents, in some cases more intimately than in others, through texts and textual practices. By admiring natural beauty, writing *waka,* telling stories about times past, housing traveling women, and performing Buddhist rituals not unlike the ones that had been performed in the *nyoin gosho* where they served during their youth, nuns at certain elite convents and hermitages practiced a courtly form of Buddhism that, though perhaps quite different from the Buddhism described in the *vinaya* codes, had a historical and cultural legacy of its own. As the power and influence of both the court in general and *nyoin gosho* in particular waned in the Kamakura period, convents came to be viewed by many former ladies-in-waiting as repositories of *nyoin gosho* culture, as spaces in which the memories of a bygone age could be remembered. The *engi* of Hokkeji and Chūgūji reflect this identification of the convent as a place in which memories of all-female salons are to be preserved; chapter 7 will consider in greater depth these tropes and their role in the literature of Ritsu nuns.

Nuns as the Teachers of Women

Although Heian literature tends to portray nuns as desperate or forlorn characters—young women mourning lost love or older women retiring to lives of obscurity—more positive images of nuns emerge in early-Kamakura-period texts. In particular, a number of references to nuns both as the teachers of women and as the active leaders of religious communities suggest that many nuns were in fact held in high esteem, especially by elite women of the late Heian and early Kamakura periods.

In her *Towazugatari,* for example, Lady Nijō describes nuns—and female rectors, in particular—in favorable terms. Against the notion that priests managed convents during this period, she presents nuns as fully self-governed: neither priests nor monks appear in any of her descriptions of time spent at convents. Her references to nuns are often brief, but she describes Shingan-bō, the rector of Shōkutei-in, and Jakuen-bō, the rector at Hokkeji, as spiritual guides who offer both teaching in the sutras and personal counseling. In the first visit to Shōkutei-in she mentions in *Towazugatari,* Nijō says her pilgrimage to the convent was prompted by a desire to "[hear] some Buddhist teachings [*hōmon*]." Describing a later visit to Shōkutei-in, she states more explicitly that part of her time at the convent was spent in study with the rector: "I spent the day viewing the summer scenery and learning the true way from the head nun." At Hokkeji, too, she reports having received from the rector, Jakuen-bō, teachings on the "relentless cycle of life and death" (trans. Brazell 1973, 40–41, 105, 204; *TG,* 40–41, 101, 191–192).

Nijō's nuns, though well versed in the ways of the world, familiar with court life, and interested in news of the capital, are not merely elite ladies in retirement. She portrays nuns both at Hokkeji and at Shōkutei-in as fully engaged in the religious life: they fill their days saying prayers, chanting, copying sutras, presenting and listening to lectures, and performing various rituals. Nijō also makes it clear that the nuns living in the convents she visited performed regular services and lectures. Indeed, she writes that her decision to enter retreat at the Shōkutei-in convent was partially driven by her belief that participation in Buddhist services there would improve her postmortem fate (trans. Brazell 1973, 101; *TG,* 97). References to daily services at convents—predawn services, morning services, and evening services—can be found throughout her descriptions of Shōkutei-in. She says that the nuns at Shōkutei-in regularly awakened before dawn in order to carry out their liturgies and sutra readings; she also participated in these services when she was visiting the convent but only when, it should be added, she felt so inclined (trans. Brazell 1973, 40, 108–109; *TG,* 41–42, 104–105). In a passage dated to the year 1277, quoted above, Nijō evokes the sights and sounds of evening services at Shōkutei-in, in which nuns are the primary—and indeed only—religious actors mentioned (trans. Brazell 1973, 103; *TG,* 99). These references in Nijō's *Towazugatari* clearly suggest that nuns held their own services, without the guidance of priests, at convents like Shōkutei-in. The passages also imply that rectors like Shingan-bō and Jakuen-bō knew the sutras well and regularly shared their knowledge of doctrinal and liturgical matters with elite women like Nijō.

That nuns worked as teachers of women is also suggested in Abutsu-ni's *Menoto no fumi.* In advising her daughter on matters of propriety, Abutsu-ni suggests that it is unbecoming—and perhaps even dangerous—for a woman of status to devote herself to a Buddhist holy man *(hijiri)*. If a woman truly wants to learn the sutras and Buddhist liturgy, she should seek the instruction of a nun, Abutsu-ni writes:

> No matter how highly regarded and worthy of respect a *hijiri* may be, growing attached [to such men] by fraternizing with them and thinking that you would like to hear them teach the Dharma is an entirely unacceptable thing. It would be a mistake to tell [a *hijiri*] whatever half-formed, passing thoughts came through your head. Through these sorts of things arise bad things and bad reputations. As for such unacceptable matters [i.e., as for interacting with *hijiri*], no matter how cold you are and how much you distance yourself, it is a good thing. If you would like to clarify the words of the Dharma that must be received and upheld and the texts teaching the five virtues [*gōjō no hōmon*], place yourself before a beautiful image of the Buddha, gather many people around you, and take the tonsure. At this time, there are many wise and well-respected nuns. This being the case, after observing them carefully, make one of them your teacher of such [Buddhist] scholarly matters. Do not let others hear you say, even in jest, that such-and-such a priest is the most accomplished. (*Menoto no fumi,* sect. 19, 133–134)

Abutsu-ni's admonitions here are especially telling, for they introduce the notion that excessive interaction with priests of the opposite sex breaks with certain unspoken rules of propriety. This concern reflects the visibility gained by charismatic priests during the Kamakura period. More specifically, perhaps, her words build on memories of Hōnen's disciples Jūren-bō and Anraku-bō, both of whom had been put to death in the year 1207 on the order of Retired Sovereign Go-Toba. Go-Toba was angry that the men had spent the night in the quarters of his ladies-in-waiting under the pretense of offering them personal instruction in the *nenbutsu* teachings.[45] The case of Jūren-bō and Anraku-bō is an extreme example of the kind of social volatility recognized in close relationships between court ladies and priests. Private meetings between women and priests, even if centered on the performance of liturgy or on the act of teaching, are often misunderstood, Abutsu-ni warns her daughter. Better to seek training from a nun, she advises, than to risk one's reputation by socializing with male priests.[46]

Kamakura-period literature suggests many women were not as cautious as Abutsu-ni. As the next chapter demonstrates, it appears to have remained common, long after the beheadings of Jūren-bō and Anraku-bō, for women to favor and patronize individual priests. The Kegon priest Myōe, for example, is known for having attracted many female followers, and he often met with women individually, sometimes in response to invitations from *nyoin* and ladies-in-waiting.[47] Even Teika's wife and daughter were devotees of Myōe and would venture to faraway Toganoo and brave crowds of commoners in order to participate in his precepts ordinations for the laity (*Kundoku Meigetsuki,* Kangi 1/5/15, 28–29). Abutsu-ni's warning against female fraternization with male priests is directed, then, at a well-established model of female patronage. Against the long-entrenched model in which women hire male priests to practice Buddhism in their stead, a model still visible in much literature from the period, Abutsu-ni recommends that women study Buddhism on their own, under the tutelage of female teachers. She also suggests that it is unseemly for women to be showy in their patronage of male priests, for enthusiastic support for a particular priest may be taken as a sign of impropriety.

The degree to which nuns worked as the teachers and mentors of women is not well-known, nor is it well reflected in literature of the period. In saying that many women were allowed to take the precepts, to manage Buddhist institutions (with people in their service), and to practice the Dharma, Abutsu-ni may have been referring to those nuns who had taken vows under Ritsu or Zen priests in the mid-thirteenth century. If she was indeed referring to these nuns in particular, then it may have been the case that the Ritsu and Zen schools were responding to a growing feeling that female fraternization with monks was improper and even dangerous by ordaining nuns and training them to serve as the Buddhist teachers of other women.

There is some evidence, however, that nuns may have been active as the teachers of women even before the rise of women's ordination in the Ritsu and Zen schools. A Jishō 4 (1180) 8/18 entry in the *Azuma kagami* suggests that the practice was in place at least as early as the mid-twelfth century. Here, Hōjō Masako (1157–1225), still in her twenties, makes the decision to employ a nun named Hōon to perform the daily offerings and religious services that her husband, Yoritomo, now busy on the battlefield, was no longer able to perform on a regular basis. Hōon, the entry relates, was a privately professed nun *(zenni)* from Masako's home region of Izu and had been Masako's teacher in the sutras *(kyōshi)*. Although the term *zenni* was often used to refer to novice or lay nuns, this excerpt from the *Azuma kagami* presents the *zenni* Hōon as a nun who is professional in the sense that she is available for hire both as a ritualist and as a teacher. She is also described as a figure who could be counted upon to remain loyal to Masako over a lifetime; the inclusion of this description suggests that Hōon may have worked as a retainer of Masako's family. Much like the earliest Buddhist nuns to have practiced in Japan—women from the continent who served in the households of eighth-century aristocratic families—Hōon likely worked as a household employee placed in charge of family-related religious services and the education of children.[48]

Available sources do not allow us to reconstruct the theological views of Hokkeji's medieval nuns. Even the biographical details surrounding the lives of Jizen, her teacher Kūnyo, and her disciples are fragmentary. What we are able to determine, however, is that the women who restored Hokkeji in the thirteenth century had extensive connections to the court and its culture. It can be surmised, then, that certain attitudes and assumptions common within court culture shaped their perceptions of Buddhism and of their roles as female Buddhists. Art and literature from the Heian and early Kamakura periods indicate that many courtiers downplayed disparaging views of the female body found in Buddhist doctrine. Sex was in many cases less important than one's social class; or, as Lady Sugawara saw it, birth as an aristocratic woman required more karmic merit than birth as a non-aristocratic male priest. Some Heian- and early-Kamakura-period women did express dismay over the fact that that they were not granted access to official ordination platforms, a matter that will be explored in the next chapter. But as illustrated in this chapter, many elite women appear to have contented themselves with the role of the lofty female patron, especially those who considered the work of priests to be beneath them.

Views of nuns and convents began to change in the early years of the Kamakura period. It was during this period that women, including those of aristocratic birth, appear to have grown increasingly interested in the reestablishment of an official ordination platform for nuns. First, as the power of the court waned after the establishment of the warrior government in Kamakura, convents came to be romanticized as the repositories of court culture, as spaces in which the practices of a more refined age were preserved. Secondly, certain wellborn women began to show interest in studying under and patronizing female priests, especially as women's patronage of male priests came to be viewed with suspicion. These two trends are especially important in the story of Hokkeji's restoration. Hokkeji nuns continued to emphasize over the course of the convent's renovation their associations both with Queen-Consort Kōmyō and with court personages and culture more broadly. Hokkeji records also indicate that the nuns had attracted, in addition to numerous patrons of both sexes, a large following of local laywomen and female pilgrims. As we turn in later chapters to analyze the ways in which Hokkeji and Saidaiji texts treat gender-specific issues such as women's salvation, it will be clear that Hokkeji literature focuses on nuns' roles as the stewards of court culture and as the teachers of women while more or less ignoring doctrinal descriptions of women as disadvantaged on the Buddhist path. Male priests, however, would approach these issues in a very different manner. The next chapter will focus on their views.

3
Envisioning Nuns
Views from the Male Monastic Order

> In our country [Japan], there are women who, as daughters of emperors or of great ministers, are basically equal in rank to queen-consorts. Some have received titles as retired sovereigns *(in)* [making them *nyoin*]. Some have shaved their heads [become nuns], and some have not. Nevertheless, when priests appearing to be *biku* [properly ordained monks] who desire fame and love fortune hasten to the gates of nobles, they do not fail to prostrate themselves entirely at the feet of these women. It is even worse than the relationship between a master and his or her attendant. It goes without saying that there are many who pass the years having become the menservants of these women. Oh, isn't it a pity—having been born in this small and peripheral country, they do not know that this is a corrupt practice, and one that even now does not exist in India or China, but only in our country. We must lament this.
>
> —Dōgen, *Shōbōgenzō*

THE MOST POWERFUL POSITION in the Buddhist world that women of the Heian and early Kamakura periods could hope to attain was that of a great lay patron. As demonstrated in the last chapter, *nyoin,* as political players whose wealth and influence rivaled that of *tennō* and retired sovereigns, came to play significant roles in the Buddhist world from the late Heian period forward. But their model of female religiosity—that of the patron who conveys her faith through political and financial support—came under scrutiny during Kamakura period. This chapter examines the question of women's religiosity from the other side, that of the male monastic order. How did priests occupying positions of power within major monastic institutions envision women's roles in the Buddhist community?

In his *Shōbōgenzō* (Treasury of the eye of the true Dharma), Dōgen critiques the model of female religiosity described in the last chapter, namely, that of the great patron. In the passage above, taken from the "Getting the Marrow by Doing Obeisance" (Raihai tokuzui) chapter, Dōgen speaks against the obsequiousness of Buddhist priests who serve *nyoin* (36a4–15).[1] At the heart of his tirade is concern about the authenticity of Japanese Buddhism. That many Japanese priests are ignorant of true Buddhism, Dōgen writes, is evident from the fact that they are overzealous in their service of high-ranking female patrons, a situation that "true" followers of the Buddha should recognize as humiliating. The passage further reveals two anxieties also found in contemporaneous monastic texts: concerns about the propriety of close relationships between the *sangha* and rulers of state and uncertainties regarding the authenticity of Japanese nuns.

This first anxiety became noticeable in Japanese monastic literature during the Kamakura period. The idea that monks should steer clear of worldliness was hardly new: the issue is raised both in the *Lotus Sutra,* translated into Chinese in the early years of the fifth century, and in the *Brahma Net Sutra (Fanwang jing),* an apocryphal sutra composed in China, where it had gained wide circulation by the late fifth century. In the *Lotus,* the Buddha declares in the fourteenth chapter, "The bodhisattva-mahāsattva does not approach with familiarity kings or princes of realms, nor ministers or senior officials" (trans. Hurvitz 1976, 208; T. no. 262, 37a22). Closely related to the question of whether those on the bodhisattva path should associate with the politically powerful was the question of whether Buddhist priests should bow down to princes and kings when asked to do so. In China, this question had given rise to fierce debates that began in the early years of the fifth century and remained heated through the middle years of the Tang dynasty. The authors of the *Brahma Net Sutra* take an unambiguous stand on the matter, declaring in the fortieth of the text's forty-eight minor bodhisattva precepts that those who enter the Buddhist order should bow down neither to royalty nor to their own parents (1008c5).[2]

During the Nara and Heian periods, this issue attracted little attention in Japan, where the state had long established itself as the most powerful patron of Buddhism. The state and *sangha* were so intertwined in Japan that by the mid-Heian period, male relatives of royal and aristocratic families had come to dominate the ranks of the monastic elite (Okano K. 1998, 80–117). This state of affairs undoubtedly had much to do with the fact that warnings against monastic entanglements with secular sources of power were not widely invoked during the Heian period.

Things had begun to change by the thirteenth century, however. By this time, major monastic centers like Enryakuji and Kōfukuji had grown increasingly self-reliant both economically and politically and no longer required state or aristocratic patronage as a means of establishing power or influence (Adolphson 2000, 21, 193–195). Not only had temples become major landholders and tax collectors, they had also learned to raise funds through means independent of court and aristocratic patronage, such as offering services for local laypeople. This financial independence allowed for sustained reflection on the authenticity of Japanese Buddhism vis-à-vis that of China and India, an issue that came to the fore during this period. One sign of this trend is evident in the fact that both popular and monastic literature from this period often speaks of Japan as a small and peripheral country where Buddhism is not carried out properly. Such concerns were likely fueled by increased exchange with China and Chinese monks: sources indicate that hundreds of Japanese monks traveled to China for study from the twelfth century forward. At least twenty Chinese monks established themselves in Japan during this time as well (Verschuer 2006, 83, 100–101).

Dōgen, recognized as the founder of the Japanese Sōtō Zen lineage, is said to have spent several years (1223–1227) in Song China. Many of his critiques of Japanese Buddhism were based on the premise that his knowledge of continental Buddhism in particular made him an arbiter of authentic Buddhist practice. Like a number of his contemporaries, Dōgen chose to emphasize the fortieth minor bodhisattva precept, found in the *Brahma Net Sutra,* against bowing down to royalty.[3] Eison, who, like Dōgen, often boasted of his political aloofness, shared this concern. In a speech included in his collected admonitions or sermons, *Kōshō Bosatsu gokyōkai chōmonshū,* Eison says that the noble priest is one who rejects the patronage of the powerful: "It says [in the *Nirvana Sutra*] that those who have renounced the world should not bow down to laypeople [see T. no. 375, 12:640a29].... even though I receive invitations from all directions, I will not go [to those who have politely requested my services]. During his reign, the [retired sovereign] Go-Saga-in made several polite invitations through the mediation of Hamuro Nyūdō, but I did not accept any of them" (215).[4]

Although Eison did finally accept invitations from the most powerful figures of his day, including, among others, the retired sovereign Go-Saga and the warrior government regent Hōjō Tokiyori (1227–1263), he usually made a show of his resistance, turning down invitations numerous times before finally relenting.[5] He also made a point of explaining that when he did finally accept such invitations, he did not compromise his superiority as a Buddhist monk. He notes later in the same sermon mentioned above, for example, that when he at last accepted an invitation from Go-Saga, Go-Saga showed him the respect he deserved, preparing a high seat for him and treating him as an honored and respected guest (215). Eison believed that independence from worldly power was a fundamental prerequisite for authentic Buddhist practice. Like Dōgen, he was quick to assert his distance from the court and warrior governments.

The Kegon priest Myōe revealed similar concerns about accepting elite patronage, despite the fact that he, like Eison, did in fact accept a great deal of support from aristocrats. According to one of Myōe's biographies, *Toganoo Myōe Shōnin denki,* Myōe also invoked the principle that priests are not to bow down to laypeople. Consider the following passage, in which he refuses to be humiliated by Her Highness Shikikenmon-in (1197–1251), one of his many powerful female patrons:

> When Shikikenmon-in was to take the precepts, she requested the master [Myōe]. She herself sat within the bamboo blinds in her private room [*moya*]

> and put her hands forth, extending her fingers and allowing the master to fold them together in *gasshō*. The master was to be in a place one step [*nageshi*] lower [than she]: her taking of the precepts was a matter that she had expected to be carried out in such a way.
>
> At this time, the master said, "[I, Myōe] am a son of Yuasa Gon no Kami [the supernumerary lord of Kii, Yuasa Muneshige, Myōe's maternal grandfather], and although I am merely a worthless novice, I became a child of the Buddha and have practiced for a long time. Priests who enter the Buddhist path and uphold the precepts may bow down neither to the gods of heaven and earth, nor to kings, nor to great ministers, nor to [their own] mothers and fathers; in the same way, they do not ascend high thrones to bestow the precepts or to teach the Dharma. Because such actions lead to bad karma, both for masters and for disciples, they are severely forbidden in the scriptures. The reason [I will not perform the bestowal of the precepts in the way you have requested] is because I have always vigorously upheld this Dharma. I am without high position; if [you] can honor a *hinin* [outcast] Dharma master such as myself, there is surely great merit in it. If you look down [on me], the greatness of this crime is deep; regardless of what you say, such betrays the original master Śākyamuni Buddha's teachings..."
>
> Her highness, who had [up until then] thought that anyone would do and who had been inviting those [priests] whom she did not truly respect, saying that she needed to receive the precepts but then sending them away afterward, was aghast. She came out from behind the blind and apologized profusely, expressing her regrets. She [then] went over to the ritual platform [*raiban*] in the Gojibutsu Hall, climbed atop it, and received the precepts with ever truer faith. After that, she said she especially respected this master [Myōe], and until her death, she remained a deeply devoted patron. (*Toganoo Myōe Shōnin denki,* 354–355)[6]

This narrative, which praises Myōe's unwillingness to compromise his understanding of the Dharma when faced with an elite female patron, invokes this same debate over whether or not Buddhist clerics should pay obeisance to secular rulers. Indeed, Myōe's words at the end of this passage follow a line from the *Brahma Net Sutra:* "The Dharma of world renouncers is that they do not make obeisance to kings. They do not make obeisance to [their own] fathers and mothers" (1008c5).

This story portrays the *nyoin* Shikikenmon-in as a demanding patron who has a change of heart following Myōe's apparently unprecedented refusal to accept the terms of her request. The narrative contrasts Shikikenmon-in's court-centered emphasis on social standing with Myōe's conviction that the parameters of class should not operate within the Buddhist framework. Shikikenmon-in, who had grown accustomed to calling various priests into the court to perform rituals on her behalf, had been rather indiscriminate in her choice of priests, the narrator suggests. Her primary concern lay not with obeying the teachings and practices of the monastic order but rather with acquiring the merit (and accompanying worldly benefits) gained through the performance of various Buddhist rituals, such as that of the *jukai,* or the taking of precepts. What is more, she had expected to obtain such merit in the comfort of her own private, elevated quarters, as royal and aristocratic women typically did. Quite aware of her social eminence, she was at first unwilling to place herself in a position equal to or below that of Myōe, who was to bestow the precepts upon her. She had grown accustomed to protecting her position of power by keeping the priests who served her at a distance; her bamboo blinds and high platform served as the physical barriers marking this sense of superiority and detachment.

In a monastic setting, of course, Shikikenmon-in's request would have been implausible. A disciple receiving the precepts from his Dharma master would not have imagined placing himself above his master; to do such would have been regarded as wholly disrespectful. Yet according to the narrator, Shikikenmon-in clearly expected to take the precepts from behind a screen, as she sat on a platform situated above Myōe. Like the female patrons against whom Dōgen warns, Shikikenmon-in identifies herself not as a humble or subservient disciple of any given priest but rather as an autonomous consumer of priestly services.

It should be clear, then, that the first anxiety visible in the excerpt from Dōgen's *Shōbōgenzō*—namely, the fear that many Japanese priests had betrayed the basic principles of the Dharma in order to seek fame and fortune—was one shared by Eison and Myōe. But in addition to this fear that the Japanese *sangha* had lost integrity to priests willing to betray principle for fame and fortune, the *Shōbōgenzō* passage suggests that the problem was intensified by the fact that priests were behaving obsequiously to *female* patrons. Another concern that surfaces here, if only indirectly, is that the Japanese *sangha* had embraced a model of priestly interaction with women that Buddhists outside Japan would reject as inauthentic.

Although he does not treat the topic in any depth, Dōgen's commentary expresses considerable discomfort regarding the relationship between women and male priests in Japanese Buddhism. He mentions at the beginning of the passage that some of the royal women served by sycophantic priests had become nuns and some had not. In either case, though, the monastic establishment would have viewed these women as lay devotees, since they had not taken full *bikuni* precepts upon an officially recognized platform. The Tendai establishment had not demonstrated any sustained interest in the status of nuns. At least several Nara priests, however, appear to have felt uneasy about the fact that the Japanese *sangha* lacked an official ordination platform for women. An early example of this concern can be found in the 1128 *Bodai shinshū,* compiled by the Nara priest Chinkai (525b):

> QUESTION: How many precepts do those renouncing the world take?
> ANSWER: Novice monks and novice nuns take 10 precepts. Probationary nuns learn the 6 precepts. *Biku* receive 250 precepts and *bikuni* 500 precepts. However, in this realm [Japan], nuns [*ama*] are novice nuns [*shamini*]. They

> are not *bikuni*. Those who have ascended the precepts platform can be called *bikuni* afterward. But [nuns here] are novice nuns who have only received 10 precepts.[7]

Read as a whole, Chinkai's *Bodai shinshū,* which displays keen interest in comparing Japanese, Chinese, and Indian Buddhisms, reveals certain doubts about the authenticity of Japanese practice. Is it not the case, Chinkai seems to suggest here, that the Japanese *sangha* has failed to understand the rules governing the incorporation of women in the Buddhist order?

Certainly Eison, born several generations after Chinkai's death, understood the Japanese handling of the nuns' order as a sign of failure. Convinced that an authentic *sangha* had not yet been created in Japan, Eison devoted his career to establishing in Japan a sevenfold order that included four orders of women: laywomen, novice nuns, probationary nuns, and *bikuni.* According to his autobiography, Eison realized this goal on the sixth day of the second month of Kenchō 1 (1249), when he gave the *bikuni* precepts to twelve women on a platform established at Hokkeji. Eison says that this act marked the very first time in which the ordination of a sevenfold assembly had been completed "in accordance with the Dharma" in Japan *(Nihon koku nyohō shugyō no shichishū enman no hajimari nari)* (*KJGSK* 1999, 351). Nuns ordained in Japan before this time, Eison claims, were not ordained in accordance with the Dharma and thus could not be counted as members of an authentic sevenfold assembly. He makes this point clear in one of his sermons, where, echoing Chinkai, he notes that those women who had come to be known as "nuns" in Japan had not actually received full ordination: "Long ago, during the time of Bidatsu Tennō [538–585], the three nuns [*ama*] Zenshin, Zenzō, and Ezen, lacking teachers in Japan, crossed over to the Tang [China], took the precepts, returned, and took up residence at Toyuradera convent. . . . Even though [they were said to have been ordained] in accordance with the Dharma, it is hard to think that such was actually the case" (*Chōmonshū,* 218). Eison makes it clear throughout his writing that the establishment of a properly ordained nuns' order was essential to the authenticity of the Japanese *sangha.*[8] For both Chinkai and Eison, then, the fact that Japanese society had long referred to women who had received only novice precepts as "nuns" was a discredit to the Japanese *sangha.*

Earlier Attempts to Establish a Precepts Platform for Nuns

Members of the Heian court had attempted to establish precepts platforms for women on at least two occasions. The first case dates to the earliest years of the Heian period, when the Grand Empress Junna (Junna Taikō, born Princess Masako, 810–879) petitioned Ennin (794–864, aka Jikaku Daishi) to establish a bodhisattva ordination platform for nuns, and the second dates to the mid-Heian period, when Fujiwara no Michinaga made extensive plans to establish an official nuns' platform at his private temple

Hōjōji. Few details are known about either case—the debates surrounding each attempt, for example, or why exactly each ultimately failed—but both cases demonstrate that the issue of women's ordination was not forgotten over the long years of the Heian.

The first of these attempts, that spearheaded by the Grand Empress Junna, suggests considerable continuity with Buddhist institutional norms established during the Nara period. In particular, the story of Grand Empress Junna's life and practice mirrors that of Queen-Consort Kōmyō on many levels. Like Kōmyō, the Grand Empress Junna first focused on practices carried out in her private residential quarters before later expanding her Buddhist work to include public and charitable activities.

The Grand Empress Junna was a daughter of Saga Tennō (786–842). Betrothed to her uncle Junna Tennō (786–840) during her early teens, she took nun's vows at the age of thirty-four following the death of her father (Ōe 1989, 148–149). A fervent devotee, she used her influence to build Buddhist institutions and to further various causes, especially those related to nuns, within the monastic community. Her death record reports that her female servants and ladies-in-waiting followed her into the monastic life, becoming nuns themselves when the grand empress took her vows. She thus had an administrative staff of nuns who assisted her over the course of her religious career, which spanned more than three and a half decades (Shirai 1989, esp. 113–115; Ōe 1989, 149–153; *Sandai jitsuroku*, Jōkan 18 [879] 2/25).

The details surrounding Grand Empress Junna's plans to establish a bodhisattva ordination platform for women are not well-known. The plans appear, however, to have been born of her longstanding relationship with Ennin, whom she had supported as a patron. According to his biography, the instructions Ennin conveyed to his disciples just before his death contained the following statement: "Recently there has been talk that the Grand Empress Junna wishes to erect a bodhisattva precepts platform for nuns [female priests]. This would lead to a great flourishing of the Way [of proper Buddhist practice]. [But] my life will come to an end without having seen it established. I wrote the *Treatise in Praise of the Great* [*Mahāyāna*] *Precepts* [*Kenyō daikairon*] solely for the purpose of protecting the grand empress's vow [to establish the platform for nuns]. You all must inform her on these matters and enable her to fulfill her vow" (*Jikaku Daishi den,* 6/1, 64b; 69).

Ennin's lengthy *Treatise in Praise of the Great* [*Mahāyāna*] *Precepts,* which spans eight volumes, does indeed contain detailed explanations of nuns' precepts and ordination procedures. It also contains a number of anecdotes about women who became *shukke* during the Buddha's lifetime (e.g., T. no. 2380, 701a21). Although women and nuns do not constitute the primary focus of the text, the *Treatise in Praise of the Great* [*Mahāyāna*] *Precepts* does indeed demonstrate both that Ennin was deeply familiar with the textual precedents and ritual procedures surrounding the ordination of nuns and that he was in favor of the practice. That Ennin appears to have held nuns in high regard and to have supported the establishment of a bodhisattva ordination platform for nuns in Japan was likely a result of the fact that he had spent some time in China, where bodhisattva ordinations were conferred upon women during this period. Indeed, records of his travels in Tang-period China indicate that he visited a nuns' ordination platform at a temple called Shanguangsi in the year 840. Ennin also mentions in his diary having met and talked to at least a handful of nuns during his stay in China (*Nittō gubō junrei kōki,* 1:282–283).[9]

Grand Empress Junna's decision to take her concerns regarding the establishment of a bodhisattva precepts platform for nuns directly to Ennin was an astute one, for Ennin played a crucial role in shaping Tendai views of the precepts after Saichō passed away. He also served as the abbot of Enryakuji for more than a decade (Groner 2002a, 274). As a number of scholars have suggested, there appears to have been a causal relationship between the emergence and dominance of the Tendai and Shingon schools in the early Heian period and the obliteration of official nuns' orders (Shirai 1989, 106–112). Although it is unlikely that Grand Empress Junna was able to predict the enduring consequences of the Tendai school's failure to establish an ordination platform for nuns, she undoubtedly sensed that the growing influence of Tendai meant that nuns' orders would lose viability without its support.

Indeed, Grand Empress Junna appears to have forwarded her plans to establish a nuns' ordination platform just decades after the last recorded ordination of nuns. The last known public ordination of women took place in the year 828, just about fifteen years before Grand Empress Junna took her vows (Ushiyama 1990, 16). The grand empress may not have known what we do: namely, that it would be several centuries before public ordinations of *bikuni* would again take place in Japan. But we can imagine that she was keenly aware of the degree to which nuns' orders were losing ground in Heian society.

As far as the sources indicate, Ennin's disciples did not help the grand empress establish a bodhisattva ordination platform for nuns, despite the fact that Ennin had included this request among his dying wishes. It is not clear why Ennin's disciples did not feel obligated to follow this particular request. The sources leave one with the sense that there was simply a loss of momentum following Ennin's death in 864. But it would be another fifteen years before the grand empress passed away; one wonders, then, why she was unable to push the project through during these years. Perhaps Ennin's disciples simply did not share his personal commitment to supporting nuns. Unlike Ennin, most monks studying at Mount Hiei had not spent time in China and had no direct experience with professional nuns or with women's ordination platforms. Moreover, the monastic culture of Mount Hiei had already become markedly androcentric by the late ninth century. Unlike temples in the cities of Nara and Heian-kyō, which allowed women on their premises, Enryakuji had long barred women from the peak of Mount Hiei, where its main monastic complexes were located.

The Tendai and Shingon institutions, both of which were established in Japan during the early ninth century, emphasized mountain-based austerities and utilized ritual protocols, derived largely from continental texts, that viewed women's bodies as polluting forces. The presence of women, it was believed, would interfere with the purity of the ritual stage, thus rendering the ceremony or austerity in question ineffective. The implementation at Mount Hiei of *nyonin kekkai,* or the prohibition of women from sacred spaces, can be traced to the adoption of these protocols and of strict ascetic practices that forbade monks to interact with women during periods of austerity. Once *nyonin kekkai* was in place atop Mount Hiei, the training of nuns in the Tendai school became more or less impossible logistically. Even extensive interaction between Tendai monks and female practitioners was rendered difficult (Katsuura 2007; Groner 2002a, 245–265).

As this view gained ground, women—even elite women—came to be barred from most sites of monastic training, especially from mountains affiliated with esoteric practices. This barring of women from monastic training led aristocratic and royal women to assert themselves as patrons of Buddhism. Even as early as the ninth century, elite women appear to have been aware that patronage was the only means by which they could hope to contribute to the Buddhist community and advance toward salvation. This view is evident in documents as early as the mid-ninth century. In an 859 entry from the *Ruijū kokushi,* it is explained that although the Grand Empress Gojō (Fujiwara no Junshi, 809–871) "has the will of a 'manly person' [*jōbu*]," her female body prevented her from being able to practice austerities on her own. The text then goes on to state that she made arrangements for three men to be ordained every year so that they could "practice the path of Buddhism *in her stead*" and ensure her salvation (Shirai 1989, 114–117; *Ruijū kokushi,* 179, Jōan 1 [859] 4/18, emphasis mine).

Women's patronage of Buddhism, then, which remained important throughout the Heian period, first became noticeable in the ninth century, around the time that the growth of esoteric practices and lineages had given rise to *nyonin kekkai.* That Ennin's disciples failed to establish a bodhisattva precepts platform for nuns ensured that this trend toward redefining women as patrons of Buddhism who had men practice in their place would gain more ground. Over the course of the ninth century, many royal consorts built temples within their residences, donated estates *(shōen)* to temples, and had their own private family temples converted into public temples (Shirai 1989, 117–119). Grand Empress Gojō's wish to have monks practice in her place suggests that while ninth-century women were aware that their female bodies prevented them from training as full-fledged religious professionals themselves, they believed that they could earn the merit required for salvation by having men train and practice in their place.

By the mid-Heian period, patterns of female patronage were well established. But women never gave up interest in ordination; indeed, ordination became, over the course of the Heian period, a common life event, though the ordinations made available to women were only lay and novice ordinations targeted primarily at merit making and did not result in the making of female priests. Many women appear to have been largely content with these lesser forms of ordination, especially in elite society, where men tended to opt for lay and novice-style ordinations over full monkhood, since the former enabled them to remain involved in worldly life (Shirai 1989, 117–119).

That said, at least some elites remained eager to establish an official ordination platform for nuns. Michinaga began building an ordination platform for nuns at his private temple Hōjōji in the year 1025, over a century and a half after Ennin's death had put to rest Grand Empress Junna's nuns' ordination platform project. The details are recorded in the courtier diary *Shōyūki:*

> On the Nuns' Precepts Platform within Hōjōji.
> Eighth Day [of the Twelfth Month, Manju 2 (1025)],
> Senior Day of the Dragon
> Fujiwara no Yoshimichi Ason delivered the news that a nuns' precept platform was to be built within Hōjōji and that the building materials [for the project] were being prepared today.

According to the *Shōyūki,* the platform was completed within a little over one year. An entry dated to the twenty-seventh day of the third month of 1027 states that a nuns' precepts platform was successfully completed at Hōjōji and that plans were underway for the construction of a monks' platform there as well. The passage goes on to state that the project angered the monks of Enryakuji to such a degree that they banded together and demanded that the abbot Ingen do everything within his power to prevent Michinaga from realizing his plan.

Enryakuji monks viewed these attempts to build new ordination platforms at Hōjōji as an affront to their authority over the Tendai school. By this time, rivalries had intensified between the two branches of the Tendai school: the *sanmon* branch based at Enryakuji atop Mount Hiei and the *jimon* represented by the monks of Onjōji. Frustrated by the fact that their own monks had been barred from the Tendai abbotship, Onjōji monks eventually made formal appeals starting in the year 1040 to establish their own precepts platform, a move that would allow them to break away from the dominance of Mount Hiei. Placed in the context of these factional hostilities, it is clear that Michinaga's plan to establish new ordination platforms at Hōjōji was a bold move. Since the administrative positions at Hōjōji had long been granted to Onjōji monks, Michinaga's plans were essentially understood as measures that would allow Onjōji monks to acquire ordination on platforms other than those controlled by Enryakuji (Adolphson 2000, 65, 119).[10]

Pressured by this outcry from Mount Hiei, Michinaga conceded his plans to build a new monks' platform at Hōjōji. He ensured, however, that the nuns' platform was allowed to stand, at least briefly. The issue continued to be a source of great conflict between the two branches of the Tendai school, not only because Enryakuji did not want to grant the Onjōji school the authority to ordain official members of the *sangha* but also because the two schools could not agree on the many issues particular to the ordination of nuns: whether or not a platform for women should be established in the first place and, if such a platform were established, how the ordinations should proceed (*Shōyūki*, Manju 4 [1027] 3/27 and 4/26; Mitsuhashi 2000, 468).

According to the *Eiga monogatari*, the platform was built with the ordination of Michinaga's eldest daughter, Senior Grand Empress Jōtōmon-in (Princess Shōshi), in mind. She was to take vows on the platform as soon as its construction was completed in the year 1027. In an entry from the preceding year, *Eiga monogatari* reports that work on the nuns' platform was "being pushed forward day and night" in anticipation of Shōshi's ordination and that "nuns everywhere" were full of "great happiness" as they awaited the completion of the project (*Eiga monogatari*, 27.34, vol. 33, 65; trans. McCullough and McCullough 1980, 716).

Despite the fact that the *Shōyūki* reports the nuns' platform as having been completed in the year 1027, it is unclear whether or not women other than the Senior Grand Empress Shōshi managed to receive ordination there. Nor is it clear how long the platform was in operation. But it is known that the structure was destroyed by fire in the year 1058 and that the platform was never rebuilt (Matsuo 1995, 381–382). The Tendai establishment never again broached the topic of an official ordination platform for nuns (Nishiguchi 1987, 156–157). Tendai refusal to respond to calls for a nuns' precepts platform reflects both continued friction between the *sanmon* and *jimon* sects and a general lack of interest in extending official clerical status to women (Groner 2002a, 281–282).

Although these two cases vary considerably, they both point toward the reluctance of the Tendai school to ordain women on official precepts platforms. The Tendai position on women's ordination was mixed and, in many senses, incoherent: the school's resistance to *bikuni* ordinations, for example, was tempered by its support for lower levels of women's ordination. Tendai priests had actively ordained elite women as novices in private, lay-oriented ceremonies for centuries. Moreover, the two attempts to establish Tendai platforms for women mentioned above—those of Grand Empress Junna and Michinaga—both received the support of high-level Tendai priests. It does not appear to have been the case that Tendai priests had articulated opposition to the establishment of a nuns' precepts platform on doctrinal grounds. After all, even Ennin, one of the great shapers of Tendai doctrine, had supported the idea. But neither of the aforementioned attempts was successful in gaining the support of a wide base of Tendai monks. These attempts are thus best understood as the pet projects of certain Tendai monks whose elite patrons were eager to see nuns ordained officially. As such, neither represented the interests of the Tendai establishment as a whole. Despite the fact that Tendai priests never formulated a carefully articulated doctrinal argument against female ordination, they did maintain throughout the Heian period strong resistance to the notion of welcoming women into the priesthood. In other words, Tendai priests were happy to bestow novice-level precepts on elite laywomen but continued to resist any measures that threatened to bring professional religious women into the monastic fold.

The Influence of Zen Masters and Their Female Disciples

Over two hundred years passed between Michinaga's unsuccessful attempt to establish a nuns' precept platform at Hōjōji and Eison's bestowal of *bikuni* ordinations at Hokkeji in the middle years of the thirteenth century. Why, at this particular point in history, did Eison and his Saidaiji group become interested in ordaining women? Eison's writing indicates that he understood the ordination of women as part of a larger project aimed at establishing in Japan a sevenfold assembly. There is also much evidence to suggest that Saidaiji monks believed their work with women created karmic merit that benefited their own mothers, a subject that chapter 7 will consider in greater depth. In addition to these explanations, which Saidaiji monks explicitly invoked in their internal discussions of nuns, it is also necessary to examine the broader ethos of the Kamakura-period Nara monastic community. Attention to the activities of other Nara priests active during Eison's time suggests that the ordination of women was part of a larger set of concerns shared by the broader Nara community and that Eison was by no means the only priest in the southern capital who was reconsidering the role of women in the *sangha* during this time.

The timing of the resurgence of interest in women's ordinations—the reason why Eison and others were reconsidering the integration of nuns into the Buddhist community at this particular time—may be largely attributable to the increased influence of Zen (Chns. Chan) thought and practice. Although few associate the old capital of Nara with Zen, which flourished both in Kamakura and in Kyoto, Nara priests were in many senses among those at the forefront of the Kamakura-period Zen movement. A number of Nara priests had become interested in Chan texts and practices as early as the late twelfth century. Minowa Kenryō has even suggested that the influx of Chan teachings during this period was one of the forces driving calls for revival within the old schools of Nara Buddhism. Exposure to Chan compelled many Nara priests to reinvigorate their own schools and lineages, often by adopting certain aspects of Chan doctrine and practice (2005).

A number of Hossō monks demonstrated interest in Zen as early as the thirteenth century. The well-known Kōfukuji priest Jōkei, for example, wrote that meditation was an integral part of the Hossō tradition and suggested, if somewhat obliquely, a relationship between Zen theory and Hossō practice (Minowa 2005). Connections between Zen and Hossō are made clearer in the work of Ryōhen (1194–1252), one of Jōkei's disciples who was actively involved in revival activities at Saidaiji.[11] In his *Shinjin yōketsu* (Essentials of the true mind), which he presented to the Tendai-Rinzai priest Enni

Ben'en (1202–1280) in 1246, Ryōhen explicitly compared Hossō teachings and practices with those of Zen. Both the phrasing he used and the conclusions he reached—namely, that Zen and Hossō, though they take different approaches doctrinally, are "not different in the end"—demonstrate not only that Zen had caught the attention of priests in the southern capital but also that some felt it was a teaching to which the old schools in Nara had to respond (98c24–26). Ryōhen's response to Zen was mixed: he lamented the present condition of the Hossō school, which he said had long fallen out of practice and was no longer able to attract practitioners, but he did not reject the teachings of Hossō. Instead, he suggested that, if understood correctly, the doctrines of his school were as robust as those of Zen. In the end, then, his treatise is not merely a work written in praise of Zen but more importantly one that seeks to affirm the validity of the Hossō school through a positive comparison with Zen (108b17–18).

Shunjō (1166–1227) is another figure who bridged the interests and activities of Zen with those of the Nara schools. Shunjō is said to have spent twelve years studying Tian-tai, Vinaya, and Chan doctrine and practice in Song China. He returned to Japan in 1211, interested both in reviving the *vinaya* and in furthering Zen teachings in his own land.[12] Through the generous patronage of the retired sovereign Go-Toba, who became his devotee, Shunjō succeeded in launching, just seven years later, a full-scale revival of the Kyoto temple Sennyūji. At Sennyūji, Shunjō established an order that blended Tendai, Shingon, Zen, and Ritsu practices. Shunjō's commitment to Zen is apparent in the fact that he established periods of seated meditation *(zazen)* as part of the daily practice schedule for his disciples at Sennyūji (Minowa 2006, 55–56).

Like Eison, Shunjō believed that Japanese monks needed to keep the precepts with greater vigilance. In two of his sermons, Eison praises Shunjō as a forerunner of the *vinaya* revival movement.[13] In fact, early in his career Eison interacted with members of Shunjō's lineage who were practicing at Kairyūōji, an ancient Nara temple located next to Hokkeji.[14] Although Eison does not mention *zazen* with any frequency in his autobiography, he does suggest in a 1251 *hyōbyaku* (also *hyōhyaku*), or statement of intention presented at the beginning of a religious ceremony, that he, like Shunjō's disciples, set aside time in his daily schedule for the practice of seated meditation (Minowa 1999, 56–57). An entry in the *Kantō ōkanki* also mentions that Eison practiced seated meditation after performing a series of *dhāraṇī* (magical incantations) in the days leading up to his departure for Kamakura during the second month of 1262 (Minowa 1999, 57; *Kantō ōkanki,* Kōchō 2 [1262] 2/4, p. 70). And thus while ideas explicitly connected to Zen doctrines and lineages were not an overtly visible aspect of Eison's ministry or teaching, close attention to relevant sources indicates both that he was aware of Zen methods and that he incorporated them into his own ritual repertoire.

Connections between Zen and the Nara monastic community, and to Eison's group in particular, are even more apparent in the life of the Tōdaiji priest and Ritsu scholar Enshō (1221–1277). According to the *Tōdaiji Enshō Shōnin gyōjō* (Biography of the Exalted Enshō written by his disciple Gyōnen [1240–1321]), Enshō grew up in the monastic world of Nara: he was one of seven children born to the Tōdaiji scholar-priest Gonkan and took the tonsure at the young age of eleven. Among the many priests with whom Enshō studied during the early years of his career were Ryōhen, Kakujō, Eison, and Enni. Enshō had also stayed at the Zen temple Tōfukuji in Kyoto, where Enni hosted a number of Nara priests, especially those associated with Kōfukuji and Tōdaiji. Scholarly dialogue between Zen and Nara groups appears to have been both vibrant and commonplace during Enshō's time (Minowa 2005). Set against the backdrop of a Nara monastic community alive with debates over Dharma restoration, Enshō's biography makes it clear that Zen influence helped shape the contours of Nara revivalist activity in the Kamakura period (2a–b).

This interest in Zen among Nara priests of the Kamakura period is significant in studies of women's ordination because discussions of women's ordination began to emerge in the Nara monastic community around the same time that Zen masters were gaining attention and influence. In the eyes of those comparing the old Nara schools to the new Zen teachings, one of the more glaring differences between the two had to do with the ways in which these groups incorporated women. The Nara schools had long come to accept the absence of nuns in the Japanese Buddhist order, but Chan texts imported from China made frequent references to nuns of all ranks. Discomfort over the degree to which the Japanese Buddhism had failed to include women in the *sangha* can be seen throughout the Nara monastic community during this time, and much of that discomfort must have stemmed from comparisons made with what was perceived to be a more authentic Chinese standard.

The connection between the rise of Zen on the one hand and the establishment of women's ordination platforms on the other might not seem obvious, but when the lives and practices of those Nara priests who studied Zen during the Kamakura period are scrutinized, it is clear that those priests who were beginning both to take female students and to reconsider women's ordination were the very same men who were active in Zen circles. Zen's entry on the scene changed the terms of certain debates already brewing in the Nara monastic community. And one debate reformulated during this period was that which focused on the integration of women into the *sangha*.

Dahui Zonggao (1089–1163) is one of the earlier figures whose work is known to have been influential in Japanese Zen communities. In his *Dahui pujue chanshi yulu* (Teaching record of Chan Master Dahui Pujue), Dahui makes mention of the many women, including both laywomen and nuns, who studied Chan under his direction. He also speaks of all being equal in Zen—male and female, those of elite birth and those from humble backgrounds (833c25). Of even greater interest is the fact that Dahui draws on the story of the dragon girl's enlightenment not to illustrate the possibility of female salvation specifically but instead to illustrate the possibility of instantaneous enlightenment generally. In citing the narrative of her attainment, he makes reference neither to the five obstacles nor to *henjō nanshi* (Matsushita 2007, 35a; T. no. 1998a, 838a25). Still, while Dahui grants women a place within the *sangha,* his assessments of women remain unambiguously androcentric: "Among our female companions there are *daijōbu* [great manly persons]. They manifest those [female] bodies and enlighten those of the same sort [others with female bodies]" (872c9). For Dahui, then, women can be integrated into the *sangha,* but only insofar as they are understood as having "manly" characteristics. Ritsu monks associated with the Saidaiji order shared this view of femininity. Their views will be treated at greater length in chapter 7.

Dahui was not among those Chan priests who spent time in or relocated to Japan; it was nearly a century after his death that Chinese Chan masters began to immigrate to Japan. But his teachings were of great influence within Zen circles, and his work is noted in particular for having shaped that of Dōgen. Dahui's views of women are also visible in the work of later Zen and Ritsu writers. This notion that women can be "great manly persons," or *daijōbu,* which appears in the *Sutra on the Final Nirvana of Śākyamuni* (Chns. *Da banniepan jing,* Skt. *Mahāparinirvāṇa-sūtra*), surfaces regularly in Kamakura-period treatments of women and Buddhism. In one of his sermons, Eison uses a famous passage from the *Sutra on the Final Nirvana of Śākyamuni* to argue that the categories of "male" and "female" lack essence:

> According to the ninth chapter of the *Nirvana Sutra,* "If there is a person who does not know the Buddha-nature [*busshō*], then he or she hasn't the male aspect [*nanshō*]. . . . If there is a person who is incapable of knowing the Buddha-nature, I [Śākyamuni] would name this person a woman [*nyonin*]. If there is one who, on his or her own, realizes that the Buddha-nature exists, I would call this person a manly person [*daijōbu to nasu*]. If there is a woman who realizes, on her own, that she certainly possesses the Buddha-nature, one must thus call her a man [*nanshi*]." Since it is rare to receive a man's body, it is especially humiliating [for one who has received a man's body] to be called a woman. Also, even women, if they renounce the world now, pursue Buddhist learning and practice, take the tonsure, and reach enlightenment, are all manly persons. Truly this is a reason to rejoice! (*Chōmonshū,* 220)[15]

That this passage from the *Sutra on the Final Nirvana of Śākyamuni* was central to Chan views of gender is apparent from the degree to which priests use the terms *daijōbu* and *jōbu* (manly person) in their evaluations of women. Chan master Wuzhun Shifan (1177–1249), who trained the Japanese priest Enni during his 1235–1241 stay in Song China, for example, uses this terminology in a spirit similar to that employed by Dahui. In describing a certain woman in the order, he says, "Even though she is a female priest [*nisō*], she can be regarded as a manly person [*jōbu*]" (*Wuzhun Shifan chanshi yulu,* 258b17). Also like Dahui, Wuzhun suggests that narrative of the dragon girl's enlightenment is irrelevant in considerations of women's salvation. The bodhisattva Mañjuśrī may have used the story of the dragon girl to teach a method of women's salvation, Wuzhun argues, but the theory of emptiness renders such methods meaningless: "What method of transforming a woman into a buddha was it that Mañjuśrī taught? What buddha is it that one becomes? There is no method that can be taught, for there is no *buddha* that one can become" (269c7–9).

Similar rhetoric can be found in the work of Wuzhun's disciple Lanxi Daolong (Jpns. Rankei Dōryū, 1213–1278), who arrived in Japan in 1246. Among Lanxi's collected sayings are passages noting that within the women's group *(joryū)* there are those who manifest the actions of "manly persons" (*Dajue chanshi yulu,* 88b25). Another disciple of Wuzhun, Wuxue Zuyuan (Jpns. Mugaku Sogen, 1226–1286, posthumously known as Bukkō Kokushi), who settled in Japan in 1279, also employed similar language. When referring to Gunin, one of his female disciples, for example, Wuxue adds the epithet "female manly person" *(jojōbu)* (*Bukkō kokushi goroku,* 210b15). Japanese Zen masters continued to use this rhetoric, noticeable at least as early as Dahui's work, well into the fourteenth century. Muromachi-period Rinzai priests like Gidō Shūshin (1325–1388), Shun'oku Myōha (1311–1388), and Zekkai Chūshin (1334–1405) all invoked the term *daijōbu* regularly when delivering eulogies at the memorial services of nuns. These masters all indicated that those nuns most admired by their male peers were honored with the label "great manly person" or "strong woman" *(retsujobu)* (T. nos. 2556, 2560, and 2561; Matsushita 2007, 38–39; Bodiford 1993, 204–208).

This rhetoric, which suggests that nuns were expected to overcome their "female" qualities and manifest "manly" qualities to win the recognition of their male peers, remained a consistent theme in Zen discussions of women and nuns for at least several centuries. What is of special interest here is that Eison's own understanding of nuns and of women's place within the *sangha* was strikingly similar to that which appears in contemporaneous Chan and Zen texts. So while Eison never identified as a Zen scholar, it is clear that the Chan-influenced intellectual trends that swept through Nara during the Kamakura period influenced his thinking about the status of women within the order.

In addition to this discourse that identifies women as "great men," Zen texts of this period also use epithets such as "exalted one" *(shōnin)* and "great teacher" *(daishi)* to describe female members of the *sangha.* This trend is significant, since Japanese texts had not previously used these terms to describe women. Also noteworthy within these texts are references to nuns as *nisō* (nun-priests), which refers to fully ordained *bhikṣuṇī.* This semantic choice reflects a move away from terms such as *ama* and *nikō,* which were typically used to refer to privately professed nuns or laywomen who took partial vows and styled themselves as nuns. Early examples of this trend can be found in the work of Wuzhun, who uses the epithet "great teacher" to describe the "female priest" Ruyin, whom he identifies as a "manly person" in the passage noted earlier (T. no. 1382, 258b17).

Wuzhun's disciple Lanxi (posthumously known as Daikaku Zenshi) also uses this rhetoric. He refers to a number of women as great teachers and female priests in *Daikaku zenshi goroku* (Teaching record of Zen Master Daikaku, T. no. 2547). This collection of teachings includes several lessons directed at female disciples, demonstrating both that Lanxi allowed women to train under his direction—something that Tendai priests certainly did not allow—and that he recognized at least a handful of his female disciples as having achieved a level of spiritual attainment that qualified them to teach others. Wuxue's work suggests that he trained an even larger following of female disciples. His *Bukkō kokushi goroku* (Teaching record of National Master Bukkō) makes reference to at least a dozen female disciples whom Wuxue identifies as great teachers, junior monks *(koji)*, saints, rectors *(chōrō)*, and female priests (see T. no. 2549, 201b, 202a–210b, 220b, 223a–c; Harada 2004, 128b). One of Wuxue's most celebrated female disciples was Mugai Nyodai, who became the rector of Keiaiji. Not surprisingly, she is among the female disciples Wuxue refers to as a great teacher (T. no. 2549, 220b).

Chinese Chan masters like Wuxue and Lanxi influenced Japanese views of women's place in the Buddhist order both by directly training female disciples in Japan and by encouraging more inclusive attitudes among the male members of their lineages. Enni is one figure whose career established important links between Chan teachings—including Chan views on the incorporation of nuns into the order—and the monastic world of the southern capital. Enni, who had studied at Onjōji (the major Tendai temple in Ōtsu), in Kamakura, and in Nara before traveling to China in 1235, studied with Wuzhun during his time in China. While there is little direct evidence to indicate that Enni had his own female following, it is clear, as stated earlier, that Wuxue and Lanxi, two of Wuzhun's other disciples, both had significant female followings in Japan and that a number of other priests in Enni's immediate network also worked closely with women. Especially notable in this respect are the Tōdaiji priest Enshō, mentioned above, and the Rinzai priest Hakuun Egyō (1223–1297). Both Enshō and Hakuun spent time at Tōfukuji studying under Enni, and both recognized and interacted with female priests during their careers. Among the handful of nuns Hakuun is known to have interacted with is Mugai Nyodai, whom he refers to as a Zen master *(zenshi)* in his collected sayings (T. no. 2546, 36b21).

Enshō, whose case is of greater interest here, given his lifelong involvement with Ritsu priests in the southern capital, showed even more extensive engagement with nuns. His biography, *Tōdaiji Enshō Shōnin gyōjō,* counts 13 fully ordained nuns among his disciples. Since the text lists 239 individuals as disciples of Enshō, however, this number indicates that only about 5 percent of Enshō's disciples were *bikuni* (Horiike 1977, 17–20). But even while Enshō was not involved with a large number of nuns, his biography reports that he recognized three women with the Dharma anointment (*kanjō,* Skt. *abhiṣeka*) initiation, the highest form of esoteric ordination (14b). Given that many regard the bestowal of the *abhiṣeka* as recognition of a disciple's ability to attain enlightenment, the fact that Enshō performed the rite on three female disciples demonstrates that he held at least a handful of his female disciples in the highest esteem (Matsuo 2001, 377–379). Moreover, officially ordained nuns are not the only women mentioned in Enshō's biography: over a dozen laywomen, many of aristocratic or royal birth, are also listed as *zenni* or *ama* who took some form of the precepts from Enshō.[16] And thus while it cannot be said that nuns were at the center of Enshō's ministry, it is clear that he did count a significant number of women among his disciples and patrons (see *Tōdaiji Enshō Shōnin gyōjō,* esp. 14–15).

Enshō's biography also shows extensive involvement with nuns involved in Eison's movement and at Hokkeji. His mother, sister, and niece, in fact, all became leaders at Hokkeji and Hokkeji-branch convents. That Enshō was committed to the establishment of a nuns' order is suggested in the way his biography describes his relationships with those nuns to whom he was related. The story of his relationship with his mother is perhaps the most telling: here, Enshō's biographer Gyōnen writes that Enshō arranged for his mother, who had taken the Buddhist name Nyoen, to enter Hokkeji around 1247 or 1248, soon after Eison had begun to administer precepts to nuns at the convent. Following his mother's entry into Hokkeji, Enshō, who had been studying with Ryōhen at the Ritsu temple Chikurinji, moved to Kairyūōji (popularly known as Kakuji), which was adjacent to Hokkeji on the convent's northeast corner (1a).[17] It is said that Enshō moved to Kairyūōji because its physical proximity to Hokkeji allowed him to visit his mother on a daily basis, closely supervising her study of the Dharma. He performed dramatic readings of the teachings for her every day and even copied out in his own hand Daoxuan's lengthy *Biqiuni chao* (Compendium on bhikṣuṇī) and donated it to Hokkeji.[18] Sources also indicate that he performed lectures on this text for his mother, again on a daily basis. Enshō taught his mother, and she listened, absorbing these lessons for over three years, until she was finally able to recite the *bikuni* precepts on her own (1b).

Enshō's biographer does not reflect on the significance of Enshō's tutoring of his mother. But his biography does indicate that he encouraged all of the women in his family to study the sutras and to seek ordination as nuns. He even seems to have had a hand in grooming female members of his family to assume positions as rectors of Ritsu convents. After Jizen, it was Enshō's mother, Nyoen, who became the rector of the revived Hokkeji. And of his three sisters, at least two are said to have entered Hokkeji as nuns. One sister, who took the Buddhist name Nyoshin, entered Hokkeji with her daughter, who took the name Sonnyo. Sonnyo, who was Enshō's niece, eventually became the rector of Tōrinji in Kyoto's Higashiyama district. According to his biography, Enshō and his disciples were involved in the intellectual life of Tōrinji, too: in the early 1270s they lectured on several texts, including the *Bodaishinron* (Discourses on the mind of enlightenment, T. no. 1664) and the *Pini taoyao* (Requirements of the vinaya, X. 44, no. 743), for Sonnyo and her nun-disciples (1b, 8a; Hosokawa 1989a, 129–131; 1997, 97).

Chinese Chan priests who took up residence in Japan during the thirteenth century regularly accepted female disciples. Harada Masatoshi argues that Japanese Zen priests returning from study in China, as well as those who had studied with Chinese priests in Japan, eventually came to believe that "authentic" Zen practice included the practice of teaching female disciples. Added to this observation-based knowledge that Chan masters accepted female disciples was the fact that certain Chan texts that became popular in Japan make frequent reference to the nuns' order and to the female disciples of great masters. Japanese Zen priests, eager to establish in Japan a practice that simulated that of China, thus came to view the inclusion of female disciples as central to the task of creating an authentic form of Buddhism in Japan (1997).

One textual example of Zen concern over the absence of a women's ordination platform in Japan can be found in the work of Dōgen. Returning to his *Shōbōgenzō,* we find in the "Merit of Home Leaving" (Shukke kudoku) section a subtly put suggestion that nuns' orders should exist in an authentic *sangha.* Here, Dōgen attributes the following vow to Śākyamuni: "Vow 138: In the future, after I have attained perfect awakening, if there should there be a woman who wishes to leave home in accordance with my teaching, study the Way, and receive the great precepts [*daikai,* or Mahāyāna precepts], I vow to make her achieve [these things]. If it does not happen like this, I will not achieve perfect awakening" (77).

This passage represents Dōgen's interpretation of the vow as it appears in the *Karuṇā-puṇḍarīka-sūtra* (Compassionate flower sutra, Chns. *Beihua jing,* 208b18–21). The original text goes on to mention *bikuni* specifically, making it clear that this passage is not about ordaining women with the lay precepts. Dōgen treats only a handful of Śākyamuni's 500 vows, but he gives priority to this one, number 138, in which Śākyamuni vows to give women the opportunity to practice home leaving. That Dōgen selected this particular vow for close treatment in the "Merit of Home Leaving" section suggests that he wanted to underscore both the legitimacy and the necessity of the nuns' order. For Dōgen, authentic Buddhism was that which best approximated the practice of Śākyamuni himself. If Śākyamuni had vowed to offer ordination and home leaving to women, then surely an authentic Buddhist order needed to do the same (Matsuo 2002, 104). Dōgen also emphasizes, in the "Getting the Marrow by Doing Obeisance" section, that nuns' and laywomen's groups existed in the *sangha* during the time of Śākyamuni (*Shōbōgenzō,* 37b10-15).

Dōgen's treatment of women's ordination in the *Shōbōgenzō* reflects the broader religious concerns of his age. Like Dōgen and other Zen masters, Ritsu priests of the thirteenth century displayed great interest in creating an order of nuns. In attempting to reconstruct the links between these two groups and their discussions of women's ordination, it is useful to observe the degree to which members of the Nara monastic community were engaged in the Zen movement on some level, some as disciples of Zen teachers like Enni and Shunjō. Beyond tracing interpersonal connections between individual masters and disciples, though, one can also identify certain ideological trends in Nara and Ritsu movements as continuous with the interests of the Zen movement. Like Zen teachers, Ritsu revivalists were eager to establish in Japan a version of the Buddhist order that better duplicated what they understood to be the more authentic version of Buddhism practiced on the continent. This longing for a "return" to a more genuine form of Buddhism was also bound up in the conviction that the exoteric-esoteric *(kenmitsu)* establishment—and especially the Tendai and Shingon schools—had lost sight of certain foundational Buddhist practices and was, as a result, nothing more than a corrupted form of Buddhism.

Among Zen teachers and monks of the southern capital, then, we notice great interest in redefining patronage relationships, in instituting or reinstituting more rigorous codes of monastic discipline, and in importing Chinese texts not yet studied in Japan. Although Zen and Ritsu groups were interested in some of the same sutras—including the *Sutra on the Final Nirvana of Śākyamuni,* for example—their scriptural interests did diverge significantly, with Zen groups focusing more heavily on texts written in the "teaching records" *(yulu)* genre and Ritsu groups focusing on major *vinaya* commentaries written by Chinese and Korean monks. But both groups were importing texts from the continent that spoke of female disciples and nuns' orders. Close attention to the ideological trends of the Zen and Ritsu schools suggests that the reason Kamakura-period monks revisited the project of creating women's ordination platforms in Japan—a project that had lain dormant for over two hundred years—was precisely because they believed that by making room for women in the monastic order, they could establish a more authentic form of Buddhism in Japan.

The central role played by the Zen and Ritsu orders in establishing professional orders of nuns in Japan is well reflected in the *Shichijūichiban shokunin uta-awase* (A poetry competition among skilled workers in seventy-one rounds), an illustrated poetry collection depicting fictional poetry exchanges between skilled workers of various trades (Goto 2006, 193).[19] The sixty-seventh exchange pairs two nuns: a *bikuni* identified with the Rinzai Zen order and a Ritsu nun identified as a member of the "nuns' order" *(ama-shū).* What is so fascinating about this exchange is that it classifies these two groups of nuns as *shokunin,* or skilled workers. That is, the women are not depicted as laywomen but as professional members of the clergy with a specialized skill set. The illustrations depict both of the women as fully tonsured, the Zen nun wearing a hood and the Ritsu nun with an uncovered, shaved head. The content of the poems associated with each nun also emphasizes the fact that these women were professional rather than lay nuns. Both speak of the precepts they uphold and mention the meditative practices in which they engage. The frame poem used to introduce the exchange also includes a reference to the busyness of convent life: the six daily services (*otsutome,* or *gongyō*) keep the nuns at Hokkeji so busy,

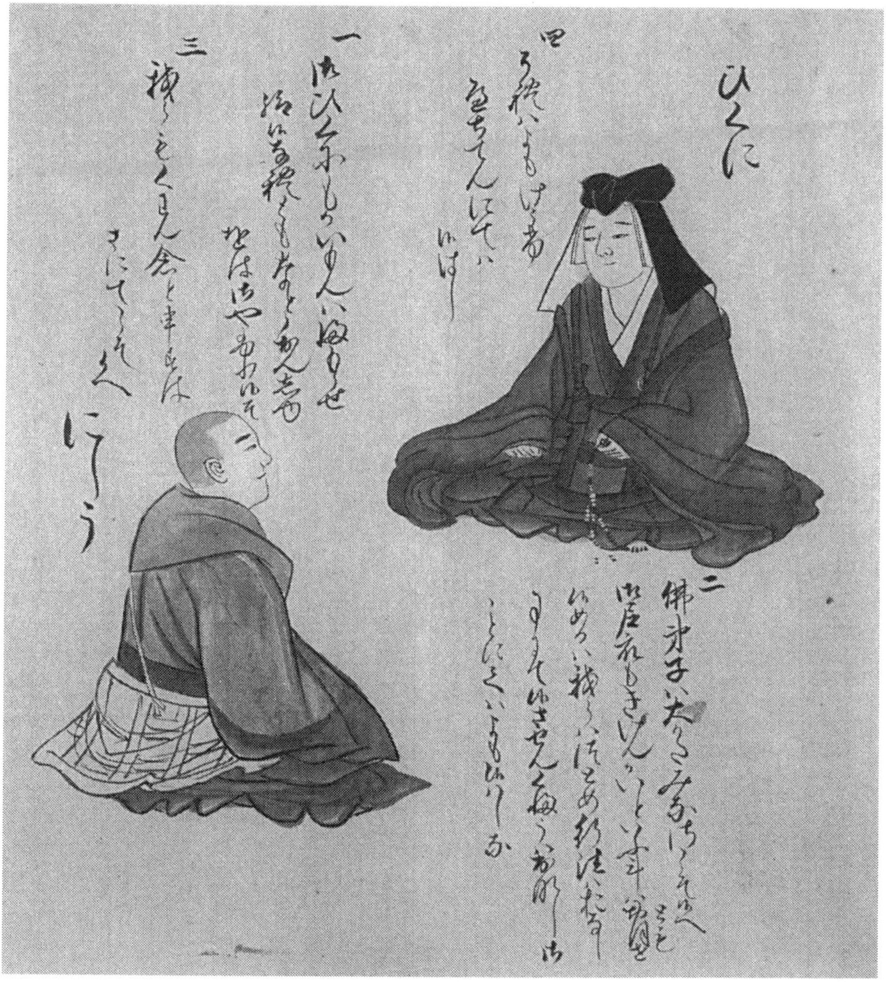

Scene from *A Poetry Competition among Skilled Workers in Seventy-One Rounds (Shichijū ichiban shokunin uta-awase),* seventeenth century. The nun on the right is identified as a Zen *bikuni,* and the nun on the left is identified as a Ritsu nun from Hokkeji. (Courtesy Tokyo National Museum)

the narrator suggests, that they have no break to gaze at the moon in the evenings (*SNKBT,* 61:136–137).[20]

Also worth noting here is the fact that the *Shichijūichiban shokunin uta-awase* associates its nuns with the Zen and Ritsu schools only. Although there are several other female religious professionals included in the scroll (among them an itinerant nun, a shrine worker, and two kinds of female shamans), the only nuns associated with particular schools of Buddhism are the two included in this pair, the Ritsu nun and the Zen nun. In depicting male religious professionals, by contrast, the scroll includes monks and priests representing a variety of other schools and sects. Admittedly, the scroll includes more male *shokunin* across the board; in the case of religious professionals, we find fifteen men but only six women. In this sense, then, the sectarian diversity of male religious professionals included in the scroll is at least partially attributable to the fact that the scroll simply includes more men and cannot be taken as evidence that professional nuns representing other sects were not in fact common during this period. Still, the choice to include nuns of these particular sects undoubtedly reflects the fact that these schools were the most actively involved in the re-creation of nuns' orders in the medieval period. A number of other schools did eventually create nuns' orders or allow for women's ordination, but it was nuns of the Ritsu and Zen orders that remained most visibly associated with nuns in the popular imagination, perhaps because these groups, in addition to having ordained women before other groups, had also established greater institutional infrastructure for professional religious women.

From Patronage to Discipleship: A New Model of Female Inclusion

It goes without saying that Zen and Ritsu efforts to incorporate women into the previously all-male monastic order led to a number of important changes in relationships between men and women in the *sangha*. But one of the most noteworthy changes on this front was the emergence of a new model of women's inclusion in Buddhist circles. Against the model of the great female patron who hired Tendai priests to perform various rituals on her behalf, Zen and Ritsu priests, wanting to emphasize their independence from worldly forms of power and prestige, sought to define female followers as disciples rather than lay patrons. In following the master-disciple model, priests like Myōe, Dōgen, and Eison entreated female followers, no matter what their rank, to regard their male teachers just as an ordinary novice would regard his master. Although the religious movements associated with these priests did not offer women opportunities within the *sangha* equal to those offered to men, they did offer women greater inclusion in the Buddhist order than Tendai and Shingon institutions had. There was, however, another side to this increased level of inclusion: elite women were expected to forget their social superiority and to venerate their Dharma masters, regardless of the fact that they often considered these men their social inferiors. These movements thus offered an ironic pairing: they granted women greater inclusion as disciples while simultaneously challenging the historically powerful roles of elite female patrons.

Reflecting this ideological shift, which was bound up in concerns over the authenticity of Japan's Buddhist order vis-à-vis those of India and China, Buddhist literature of the early Kamakura period moves away from portraying women as great patrons of Buddhism and toward portraying them as the disciples of illustrious male masters. In critiquing the "old" model of Japanese nuns—that of the elite lay devotee-patron—Dōgen, Myōe, and Eison convey their disapproval of the Tendai establishment, which had long accepted this model of interaction with women while forbidding the official ordination of *bikuni*. Increased emphasis on the discipleship model of female inclusion helps explain the dynamic growth over the course of the Kamakura period in the establishment of convents. Many of the new movements that emerged during this period offered women the opportunity to join their orders not as mere patrons but as nuns or nun-patrons.[21] Once the Ritsu school established a precepts platform for nuns at Hokkeji, hundreds of women trained at the convent, many taking full *bikuni* precepts and then proceeding to work at other temples or convents. During the very same years that all of this revival activity was taking place at Hokkeji and related Ritsu convents in Nara and Kyoto, Zen teachers were also attracting female students, many of whom also trained as nuns under the tutelage of male priests.

In emphasizing the model of woman-as-disciple as primary to that of woman-as-patron, both groups managed to incorporate women into their communities while at the same time ensuring that women within the orders were never allowed to challenge the authority of male priests in any substantial way. This master-disciple model of female integration was rooted in the assumption that women were always to be defined as the disciples, and therefore the social inferiors, of male masters. The relationship stressed was that shared between disciple and charismatic master, and the charismatic master was, without fail, male. Although there is evidence in both groups of female-to-female master-disciple relationships, the model of discipleship most frequently offered to women was that of the male master who offered instruction to both male and female disciples. The inclusion of the female discipleship model provided was tempered, then, by a view of patronage that sought to rein in noblewomen who might have used their privileges as patrons to exercise power over individual priests. And thus in characterizing the broader contours of female integration in the Zen and Ritsu movements, it is clear that even as they reached out to female disciples, both groups asserted the inferiority of women. They furthermore sought to place all women in a single category defined by sex alone, a move that worked against the cultural tendency of noblewomen to identify first as aristocrats and only secondarily as women.

Close attention to the nature of Eison's interactions with female followers—both nuns and laywomen—indicates that this new model of female discipleship played an important role in defining how the Saidaiji order would incorporate women. First, in the case of nuns, Eison offered them comprehensive doctrinal training comparable to that which he offered his male disciples. Eison's diaries indicate that he held a number of lengthy seminars at Hokkeji. During these seminars, which the next chapter will examine in greater detail, Eison taught Hokkeji nuns and female novices using highly specialized *vinaya* commentaries. The narratives examined above, in which Dōgen and Myōe critique the Tendai practice of serving noblewomen closely, suggest that it had become commonplace for Tendai priests to serve noblewomen. But in serving noblewomen, Tendai priests had tended to focus on the performance of various rituals, such as *jukai,* or bestowals of the precepts, and *kuyō,* or offertory ceremonies held to dedicate a newly commissioned item or to venerate the dead. One would be surprised to find an example of a Tendai priest taking several weeks to teach a noblewoman or a group of noblewomen the content of difficult commentaries.

This new model is also at work in Eison's unwillingness to place himself at the beck and call of nuns, regardless of their status. In a letter to be examined in the next chapter, Eison asserted distance between himself and Hokkeji's rector, Jizen. In the letter, Eison referred to complaints Jizen had been making within the Ritsu community. Apparently she was disappointed by the infrequency of Eison's visits to Hokkeji and had passed along a message asking that Eison meet with her at his earliest convenience. Although Eison responded to Jizen in an extremely polite way—that is, in a tone cognizant of her superior social standing—he did not yield to her wishes. For various reasons, he said, the timing was inconvenient, and he would not be able to meet with her. Some of the reasons he provided in the letter invoked the kind of rhetoric examined at the beginning of this chapter, namely, that Buddhist priests are not to affiliate too closely with members of the royal family *(Eison shojō santsū).* Hokkeji was, after all, known for its connection to the court. As we will see, Eison's interactions with Hokkeji nuns can be categorized according to a new model of female inclusion that offered women greater inclusion as disciples and more rigorous training while denying elite women many of the special favors and services that Tendai and other *kenmitsu* priests had long made available.

Eison's relationships with female lay patrons also followed this new model of discipleship. Consider, for example, the many women from warrior government families who came to support Eison's movement. As is visible in the case of Grand Empress Kenshi and her ladies calling the Tendai priest Yōshō to court to perform a *kuyō* ceremony on their behalf, court noblewomen who employed priests are portrayed as having expected the priests to come to them, and they are typically depicted as paying the priests with luxury goods, such as bolts of silk. But elite warrior women who entreated Eison to perform ritual services on their behalf did not call him to their personal quarters; instead, they are portrayed, at least in Saidaiji documents, as traveling out of their private quarters in order to seek audience with him at the temple where he was staying.[22] And their payment for his services was not limited to goods with clear exchange value; instead, their devotion suggests a relationship that was less transactional. In particular, some of Eison's female lay followers showed their support by contributing to his ideological campaigns, rather than merely providing basic forms of payment.

Some key examples can be found in the *Kantō ōkanki,* a record of Eison's sixth-month journey to Kamakura in the year 1262. This text mentions a large number of women associated with the warrior government who sought to receive the precepts from Eison. It is well-known that Eison made his journey to Kamakura in response to invitations extended by two male government officials: the scholar and Board of Councilors (Hōjō-shū) member Hōjō Sanetoki (1224–1276) and the regent *(shikken)* Hōjō Tokiyori. But close attention to the *Kantō ōkanki* indicates that many, if not the majority, of Eison's most prominent devotees in Kamakura were female: numerous women of the extended Hōjō network—wives, mothers, and daughters of government officials—visited Eison both with their male relatives and independently of them.

Among those women who acted as patrons of Eison were the principal wives of Sanetoki and Tokiyori (the daughters of Hōjō Tokimura and Shigetoki, respectively); the principal and secondary wives of Hōjō Tokimura, plus his mother and his principal wife's younger sister; Shigetoki's widow and her daughters; all of the ladies-in-waiting in the shogun's service; the shogun's wet nurse, Ichijō no tsubone (born the daughter of Dainagon Tsuchinomikado Michikata, 1189–1239); Mino no tsubone, identified as the mother of Tsuchinomikado Chūnagon Akikata;[23] a daughter of Ashikaga Yoshiuji; the principal wife of Fujiwara no Kin'atsu (1235–1287); a wife of Mutō Morosato; a wife of Hōjō Nagatoki; Uemon no kami no tsubone; and a wife of Hōjō Tokihiro. During his stay in Kamakura, these and other women sought a variety of services from Eison. Most attended various lectures that he gave and took some form of the precepts: the five lay precepts, the eight pure precepts, the ten major bodhisattva precepts, or the ten novice precepts. Some took multiple sets of precepts from Eison, sometimes with their daughters, mothers, sisters, or husbands. These precepts ceremonies were sometimes conducted on an individual basis or as part of a small group; at other times, however, these women received the precepts as part of a large group numbering in the hundreds. That their names were listed while others, male and female, were simply counted indicates that Eison's group valued the participation of these elite women.

Although a number of the women mentioned in the *Kantō ōkanki* visited Eison along with their husbands or fathers, many others appear to have first approached Eison on their own or to have visited him, perhaps after an initial introduction that included men, alone or with other women. The *Kantō ōkanki* indicates that Mino no tsubone, Ichijō no tsubone, and Uemon no kami no tsubone, in particular, visited Eison rather frequently. In an entry that lists the *jukai* (using the bodhisattva precepts) of hundreds of individuals, including regional military lords *(daimyō)*, members of the Board of Councilors *(hyōjō-shū)*, lower-level military government administrators *(bugyōnin)*, plus their wives and retainers, the record singles out Ichijō no tsubone for having given rise to especially firm faith and notes that Eison bestowed upon her and Mino no tsubone the ten novice precepts of the *Four-Part Vinaya* (Kenchō 2/5/19). In a record dated three days later, Mino no tsubone and Ichijō no tsubone appear again, this time to receive personal teaching, and are praised for having peerless faith (Kenchō 2/5/22). Just over two weeks later, Ichijō no tsubone performs a well-attended service in honor of the Sixteen Arhats (Rakan Ku) under Eison's guidance (Kenchō 2/6/8). This case is fascinating, insofar as it suggests that Eison was transmitting ritual knowledge to female lay disciples. About two weeks later, Ichijō no tsubone presented Eison with a set of documents declaring six lands in her possession *sesshō kindan,* meaning that all forms of killing sentient life, including fishing and hunting, were to be outlawed in these territories (Kenchō 2/6/23). *Sesshō kindan* declarations were an important part of Eison's movement, and Ichijō no tsubone's decision to declare six lands *sesshō kindan* demonstrates her commitment to the broader ideological goals of Eison's Ritsu community. The record also indicates that the wife of Mutō Morosato donated all of the Yamato lands in her possession to Saidaiji. While this donation was indeed a financially significant one, the fact that the wife of Mutō Morosato donated Yamato lands to Saidaiji, itself located in Yamato, points to her support of the Saidaiji movement as a whole. She was not merely paying Eison for his services but was demonstrating her commitment to helping him further his goal to revive the precepts. In donating all of her Yamato lands to Saidaiji, she enabled Eison to expand both the visibility and the economic and political foundations of his movement.

In short, Eison's relationships with nuns and laywomen alike were informed by a new model of female inclusion that emphasized discipleship while refusing to grant elite women any special treatment. On the one hand, this approach was good news for women seeking ordination as nuns: it meant that they would find in Eison's movement greater opportunities to take official ordination, to study Buddhist texts, and to gain ritual training. On the other hand, however, Eison's approach to elite patronage meant that noblewomen in his order could not expect from him the same special treatment they may have received from other priests.

Eison's approach to the nuns' order, which emphasized both the doctrinal necessity of establishing an order of officially ordained Ritsu nuns and an ideological commitment to distancing himself from institutions of political and worldly power, was quite different from the approach taken by many Hokkeji nuns themselves. As we saw in the last chapter, many of the women in Hokkeji's ranks were elite women who celebrated both their connections with the court and the culture that it represented. They expected a certain degree of service from priests like Eison, who was of relatively low social rank, and were not, we can presume, swayed by Eison's desire to remain aloof from courtly institutions.

4

Hokkeji's Place in Eison's Vinaya Revival Movement

THE LAST TWO CHAPTERS examined the historical development of two discrete discourses on nunhood and women's religiosity. The first, explored in chapter 2, was that adopted by men and women connected to the elite world of the court. Within these circles, women tended to downplay disadvantages ascribed to female practice in doctrinal texts and focused instead on the prestige afforded to powerful female patrons and on alternative methods of salvation, such as rebirth into Maitreya's Tuṣita realm. Chapter 3 treated issues of women's religiosity from the other side by looking at the ways in which members of the male monastic order handled issues surrounding the ordination of nuns and female patronage. There is much evidence to suggest priests outside the Tendai establishment had begun to view powerful female patrons with growing resentment by the middle years of the Kamakura period. Priests active in the Zen and Ritsu movements in particular believed that women had to be put in their place, as it were—something achieved, ironically, by granting women greater institutional inclusion through the establishment of nuns' orders.

The present chapter turns to consider how it was that the interests of these two groups—women with court connections on the one hand and revisionist priests on the other—converged in the large-scale restoration of Hokkeji in the mid-thirteenth century. Why did the women who had gathered at Hokkeji, many of whom had spent their young adulthood at court, become interested in Eison's movement? How did Eison interact with members of the Hokkeji community, and what place—ideological, political, and social—did Hokkeji come to occupy within his *vinaya* revival movement?

Eison, Saidaiji, and the Nara *Vinaya* Revival Movement

It was during the early years of his monastic career that Eison became interested in the restoration of the monastic precepts and joined a *vinaya* study group at Kōfukuji. Although initially one of the least-known members of this group, it was he who would eventually launch the most visible and successful movement to emerge from the medieval Nara monastic community. Over the course of his long career, Eison greatly expanded the scope of his ministry, which began with a strong focus on doctrinal matters related to the *vinaya* but eventually came to embrace a wide range of charity and fund-raising work. His disciples built on his work with commoners in the countryside, developing over the course of the late thirteenth and fourteenth centuries a vast network of Saidaiji-branch temples throughout Japan.

Unlike some new movements founded during the Kamakura period, such as the Pure Land, Zen, and Nichiren schools, Eison's lineage is no longer influential today. But at the height of his career, he was perhaps even more celebrated than any of the founders of the so-called new Buddhist schools of the Kamakura period. He ended his life as a well-loved public figure who had ordained nearly one hundred thousand people and who counted among his devotees the most powerful political figures of the day, including warrior government regents, *tennō,* and retired sovereigns. And unlike most of the founders of new schools, he was also esteemed by the old-guard monastic communities of Nara and Kyoto. This fact is well illustrated in records claiming that over seven hundred priests from these communities attended his memorial service when he passed away in the year 1290 (Nishiyama 2001, 43).

As mentioned in chapter 3, Eison began his monastic career at a young age. After years of apprenticeship under monks at Daigoji, he pursued ordination and initiation as a Shingon priest. By the age of twenty-five, his enlightenment had been confirmed by a Shingon teacher, and at the age of twenty-eight he received the *abhiṣeka,* or Dharma anointment (*KJGSK* 1999, 37, 44–45). Eison's career took a turn during his thirty-forth year, when, as he puts it in his autobiography, his faith faltered and he began to examine the doubts that had taken hold of him. Reflecting on this period, Eison says that he became disillusioned as he watched many members of his lineage fall into Māra's realm (46–47). These remarks reflect his longstanding critique that the Shingon establishment had fallen into corruption (see Hosokawa 1999b, 50).

Eison writes that it was during this period of intense reflection that he came to realize the importance of the precepts. Here, he cites Kūkai's admonition that those who fail to uphold the precepts cannot be counted among his disciples or among the children of the Buddha and are as useless as "clumps of dirt" or "tree stumps" (*KJGSK* 1999, 48). He thus resolved in 1234, at the age of thirty-four, to uphold the precepts completely and to dedicate himself to the salvation of sentient beings. That winter, he learned that the precepts revivalist Son'en, a Kōfukuji priest who had taken up residence at the Kaizen-in (also known as the Chisoku-in) of Tōdaiji, had undertaken an effort to place priests upholding the pure precepts in Saidaiji's Hōtō-in. Wishing to support this initiative, Eison went to Kaizen-in and met with Son'en, who, he reports, was delighted to learn of his interest (49–50).[1] Eison began staying with the others at Saidaiji's Hōtō-in during the first month of the following year, 1235. There, he studied the *vinaya* under Son'en, Kainyo (who had been a disciple of Jōkei), Kakuchō, and Ensen, attending regular lectures on the *Four-Part Vinaya* and its commentaries and arriving at the conclusion that his earlier training in the Dharma had been lacking (Nishiyama 2001, 7–8).

Statue of Kōshō Bodhisattva [*Eison*] *in a Seated Position (Kōshō Bosatsu zazō).* This image is said to have been created in the likeness of Eison during his eightieth year. (Photograph by the Nara National Museum, courtesy Saidaiji, Nara, Japan)

As Eison's interest in the *vinaya* deepened, he continued to pursue involvement with like-minded members of the Nara monastic community. The following year, he became an active participant in conversations about the *vinaya* taking place at the Kōfukuji cloister Jōki-in, an institution that Kakujō had built in 1212 in order to carry out Jōkei's wish to see the precepts revived in Japan. Twenty monks dedicated to the study of the precepts were in residence at Jōki-in, and as Nishiyama has pointed out, most were quite young. From this crowd emerged a group of four—Eison, Kakujō, Ensen, and Ugon—who decided to stage a self-ordination ceremony after spending a week in ritual seclusion at Tōdaiji's Kensaku-in. They took their ordinations in front of an image of Kannon in the Tōdaiji cloister Hokke-in on the first day of the ninth month of Katei 2 (1236) (*KJGSK* 1999, 63–64, 75–77; Nishiyama 2001, 8; Matsuo 2004b, 16–17).

As has been discussed elsewhere, this event marked a decisive break from the monastic norms of the day.[2] It was in accordance with texts such as the *Chanzha shane yebao jing* (Sutra on the divination of the effects of good and evil actions, Jpns. *Sensatsu zen'aku gyōhōkyō*), which stipulates that the precepts can be taken directly from the buddhas and bodhisattvas if and when ten priests cannot be assembled for an ordination ceremony, that Eison and his colleagues carried out this unusual ordination ceremony. Precepts priests were in fact widely available in Japan, and these four men had already received the precepts in formal ceremonies recognized as orthodox in the monastic circles of their day. In staging this self-ordination ceremony, then, these men were declaring their former ordinations—and the standard ordinations practiced within Japanese monastic society—inauthentic. Insofar as Japanese priests failed to uphold the precepts, Kakujō reasoned, they were not genuine precepts masters and could not bestow the precepts in an authentic manner. Self-ordination was necessary, the argument went, because those ordinations that had long been recognized as orthodox in Japan were in fact being performed by priests who lacked the spiritual power necessary to ordain others (Matsuo 2004b, 16–17).

Although this group of four had initially intended to continue their new, *vinaya*-centered practices at Kōfukuji, political turmoil rendered this plan impossible. Kōfukuji, which had long been the greatest landowner—and most powerful political presence—in the Yamato region, had recently mounted a *gōso*, or "forceful protest," against the warrior government in an effort to settle a land dispute (Hosokawa 1999b, 84; Matsuo 2004b, 17–18).[3] Rather than yielding to Kōfukuji's request, however, the government made the unprecedented decision to override Kōfukuji authority altogether and to place its own officials, land stewards *(jitō)* and military governors *(shugo)*, in the Yamato region. According to the records of Eison and other locals, these officials had begun to wreak havoc in the area, committing acts of violence on temple grounds and plundering whatever valuables they could find. When Eison and the other three men returned to Kōfukuji after their self-ordination ceremony at Tōdaiji, they found that the gates to the temple complex had been shut. They were thus forced to return to Tōdaiji, where they found lodging near an oil shed (*KJGSK* 1999, 75–76; Matsuo 2004b, 17–18; Nishiyama 2001, 10–12).

Through the mediation of Son'en, Eison began his new career as a *vinaya* monk at Kairyūōji, the Nara-period temple located just next to Hokkeji. Although Eison did manage to attract a few disciples at Kairyūōji, his debut there was more or less a failure, as many of the monks at Kairyūōji, though trained in the *vinaya* tradition established by Shunjō of Kyoto's Sennyūji, had little tolerance for the zeal with which Eison attempted to implement the *vinaya*. After suffering several acts of intimidation—he found graffiti denouncing him on the temple gates, as well as an arrow on the outer wall of his living quarters—Eison finally left. Son'en arranged for him to return to Saidaiji, where he took up residence in the seventh month of Ryaku'nin 2 (1238) (*KJGSK* 1999, 82–102).

Eison had his work cut out for him at Saidaiji. Like Kairyūōji, Saidaiji was an ancient temple that had been established during the Nara period. The establishment of Kairyūōji, in fact, is attributed to Queen-Consort Kōmyō, while her daughter, the female sovereign Kōken-Shōtoku, is recognized as the founder of Saidaiji. Like many of the great temples of Nara, Saidaiji had been devastated by the move of the capital to Kyoto in the early ninth century. By Eison's time, Saidaiji had been in a state of decline for some four hundred years. And as was the case with the majority of temples in the Yamato area, Saidaiji was kept afloat, if just barely, by Kōfukuji, which had long controlled its lands and administration.

In his autobiography, written decades later when he was in his mid-eighties, Eison remembered his early years at Saidaiji as a period of great difficulty. He was in his late thirties at the time, and Saidaiji, having been more or less neglected since the late Heian period, was in a state of ruin. "Words cannot describe," he remarks, the state in which he found Saidaiji. In this same entry, he tells of how he vowed, upon moving into Saidaiji this second time, to commit himself wholeheartedly to its restoration. He further vowed to spend his career in this temple, from which he would work for the flourishing of the true Dharma *(shōbō)* and the benefit of sentient beings (94).

During his first few months at Saidaiji, Eison studied Saidaiji temple records in an effort to better understand the temple's history. He then carried out various rituals meant to restore what he understood to be the ancient traditions of the temple. Just three days after having taken up residence there, for example, he performed a *tendoku,* or ritualized speed-reading, of the *Great Kings Sutra* (*Saishōōkyō,* also *Konkōmyō saishōōkyō,* Chns. *Jinguangming zuishengwang jing*) on the front altar of the Four Kings Hall (Shiōdō), one of the few buildings still standing at Saidaiji. Having learned, he explains, that this hall had been used in ancient times as the space in which the *Great Kings Sutra* was performed, he vowed that if the gods enabled him to establish an order of monks, he would offer regular performances of this sutra along with the monks in his order. Believing that Buddha relics had served as the primary object of worship at this hall, he also erected a stone stupa during his first month at Saidaiji, placing relics inside it and laying the groundwork for a relics cult meant to draw the interest of local laypeople (94–95; Hosokawa 1999b, 99).

Within two months of Eison's having taken up residence at Saidaiji, however, Son'en sent a messenger to Saidaiji with the news that the Nii estate (Nii no shō), one of the few estates in Saidaiji's possession, was in a state of rebellion. Since this estate served as Saidaiji's main source of financial support, this news meant that Eison had to begin thinking about fund-raising almost immediately upon his arrival at Saidaiji. He first returned to his hometown, raising funds among members of his family and adopted families. Although the Nii estate eventually came to yield financial support again, Eison's movement continued to draw heavily on the generosity of ordinary laypeople. He notes in this very early entry in his autobiography that it was through the combined efforts of many local supporters that his movement succeeded (*KJGSK* 1999, 95).

By the end of the tenth month of 1238—after less than three months in residence at Saidaiji—Eison began carrying out various *vinaya* rituals there. His first order of business was to establish the *kekkai,* or sacred boundaries, of Saidaiji; this ritual, which Eison performed with four other *biku* (including Kakujō and Ugon), marked as sacred the space that would be used for the two rituals Eison understood to be most central to the *vinaya* tradition: ceremonies in which the precepts were bestowed *(jukai-e)* and confession ceremonies, or *fusatsu.* Having established Saidaiji's *kekkai* on the twenty-eighth day of the tenth month, Eison and his colleagues went on to perform their first Shibun Fusatsu (Confession Ceremony Using the Precepts of the *Four-Part Vinaya*) at Saidaiji on the twenty-ninth. In the margins of his autobiography, Eison notes that this performance of the *fusatsu* represented a revival of the authentic practice of the ritual in Japan. Kakujō, who read the explanations of the precepts during the ceremony, is said to have cried tears of shame and joy throughout the entire ceremony; although Kakujō was elated to be a part of this momentous occasion, he lamented the fact that, despite having been a monk for decades, this was the first time he was able to perform the ceremony in an authentic way. He had chanted these same lines many times before, he explained to Eison and the others, but he had always done so as a monk who had broken the precepts (95–96).[4]

On the next day, the thirtieth, the group held another *fusatsu,* this time using the precepts of the *Brahma Net Sutra* (Bonmō Fusatsu). Eison's group, which drew upon both sets of precepts, would continue to follow this same pattern, holding *fusatsu* ceremonies four times per month, twice for each set of precepts. Once integrated into the Saidaiji movement, Hokkeji, too, incorporated these ceremonies into its ritual cycle (95–96; Hosokawa 1999b, 101–102).

Although Eison's movement started out small, it grew rapidly within the first several years of his tenure at Saidaiji. In the early years of the Saidaiji movement, he and his colleagues and disciples—mostly Hossō and Ritsu monks who gathered from Nara monastic circles—focused their work on ordinary laypeople, on the needy, and on small temples in the countryside. As Hosokawa Ryōichi has pointed out, during these early years Eison appears to have focused especially on those estates owned by Saidaiji. In addition to converting small countryside temples into *matsuji,* or branch temples of Saidaiji, Eison's group also began to work with groups of social outcasts known as *hinin* (literally "nonpersons") as early as 1240. During the early months of this year, for example, they are said to have given the eight pure precepts *(hassaikai)* to some four hundred *hinin* living near the temple Gakuanji. Entries dated to the year 1242 show Eison performing large public ordination ceremonies at other countryside temples as well: during the fourth month of 1242, for example, he is said to have bestowed the bodhisattva precepts upon some 104 people at Hasedera and 76 people at Minami Hokkeji. According to his autobiography, Eison also visited prisons in the eastern and western wards of Heijō-kyō (Nara), offering prisoners bathing money, food, and the pure precepts (*KJGSK* 1999, 110–111, 129–130; Hosokawa 1999b, 137–138).

Throughout the early 1240s, Eison continued to stage large-scale bodhisattva ordination ceremonies aimed at locals and offertory services aimed at *hinin.* In the year 1244, for example, he is said to have held two bodhisattva ordination ceremonies in which over three hundred people received the precepts at once. During this same year, he also held services in which he provided aid to over a thousand *hinin* (*KJGSK* 1999, 157–158). The early 1240s were also years during which Eison established his campaign to prohibit the killing of animals and fish *(sesshō kindan)* on as many lands as possible. As a part of this campaign, Eison's supporters would declare certain lands in their possession *sesshō kindan,* meaning that all forms of killing life—including fishing and hunting—would be forbidden on the lands in question (e.g., *KJGSK* 1999, 142, 158).

But even as his charity and outreach work continued to expand, Eison pursued his doctrinal interests in the *vinaya* as well. Much of his early work was aimed at transmitting what he understood to be the authentic *vinaya* practices established at Saidaiji to other Buddhist institutions; the goal was to spread these *vinaya* practices throughout Japan. To this end, Eison absorbed countryside temples into the growing Saidaiji network while ordaining new monks according to the rules of the *vinaya.* At those temples declared Saidaiji branch temples, Eison would establish *fusatsu* practices and perform lectures on important Ritsu texts, thereby providing the ritual and textual frameworks necessary for *vinaya* practice. Eison and Kakujō also continued to work together. After Kakujō decided to leave Kōfukuji and take up residence at Tōshōdaiji, which he vowed to restore, for example, Eison and other *biku* in his group participated in a *fusatsu* ceremony that Kakujō hosted at Tōshōdaiji (141–143, 157–158).

Eison's Use of Continental Commentaries on the *Vinaya*

Eison's commitment to creating an authentic practice of the *vinaya* in Japan is also reflected in the fact that he and Kakujō sent some of their closest disciples to Song China to retrieve additional *vinaya* texts. In 1244, they decided that Kakunyo, Ugon, and Jōjun would make a journey to China on behalf of the Ritsu group. The 1245 entry in Eison's autobiography mentions that he and Kakujō made a pilgrimage to the Sumiyoshi shrine during the ninth month of that year to offer prayers for the safe travel of these monks (158, 168).[5] These disciples are reported to have returned safely about four years later, in the year 1248, bringing with them a set of three major *vinaya* commentaries written by Daoxuan: the *Sifenlü shanfanbuque xingshichao* (Summary of services [achieved by] "shaving the thicket and supplementing the gaps" in the *Four-Part Vinaya,* Jpns. *Shibun ritsu sanpanhoketsu gyōjishō*) in twelve scrolls, the *Sifenlü biqiu hanzhu jieben* (Annotated *Four-Part Vinaya* prātimokṣa for bhikṣu, Jpns. *Shibun ritsu biku ganchū kaihon*) in three scrolls, and the *Sifenlü shanbusuiji jiemo* (*Four-Part Vinaya* priestly ritual proceedings with deletions and additions in accordance with capacities, Jpns. *Shibun ritsu sanpo zuiki konma,* T. no. 1808) in two scrolls (*KJGSK* 1999, 181; Hosokawa 1999b, 181–183).

As this particular selection of texts suggests, the Chinese priest and scholar Daoxuan (Jpns. Dōsen, 596–667) was among the masters Eison and his colleagues viewed as the great patriarchs of the *vinaya* tradition. In reviewing the texts Eison mentions in his sermons and autobiography, a certain number of titles emerge again and again. One of the texts commonly used by Eison, as mentioned in the last chapter, was the *Sutra on the Final Nirvana of Śākyamuni (Da banniepan jing).* But most of the lecture sessions he held at Kairyūōji, Saidaiji, Gakuanji, and eventually Hokkeji and other Saidaiji branch temples focused on *vinaya* commentaries written by Korean and Chinese masters. In addition to commentaries written by Daoxuan, Eison also drew heavily upon the commentaries of the Silla priest Taehyeon (also Taehyŏn, Jpns. Taigen, fl. mid-eighth c., affiliated with Faxiang or Hossō studies) and the Song priest Yuanzhao (Jpns. Ganjō, 1048–1116, affiliated with both Vinaya and Pure Land studies). Mentioned repeatedly in Eison's autobiography, for example, are two commentaries written by Taehyeon on the *Brahma Net Sutra:* the *Beommanggyeong gojeokgi* (Recorded ancient traces of the *Brahma Net Sutra,* Jpns. *Bonmōkyō koshakki*) and the *Beommanggyeong bosalgyebon jongyo* (Doctrinal essentials of the *Brahma Net Sutra* bodhisattva precepts prātimokṣa, Jpns. *Bonmōkyō bosatsu kaihon shūyō*). Other texts that appear to have shaped Eison's teaching and ministry are Daoxuan's *Jiaojie xinxue biqiu xinghu lüyi* (Instructing new bhikṣus in the rules and ceremonies they are to perform and uphold, Jpns. *Kyōkai shingakubiku gyōgoritsugi*), a manual for new monks, and the *Biaowubiao zhang* (Chapter on exposed and unexposed activity, Jpns. *Hyōmuhyōshō*), a *vinaya* commentary found in the eleventh section of the third scroll of Cien Ji's (Jpns. Jion Ki, 632–682) *Dasheng fayuan yilin zhang* (Chapters on the forest of meaning in the Mahāyāna Dharma garden, Jpns. *Daijō hōongirinshō,* T. no. 1861).[6] Eison also mentions with regularity the commentaries of Yuanzhao, including his *Sifenlü xingshichao zichiji* (The Zichi record of *Summary of services in the "Four-Part Vinaya,"* Jpns. *Shibun ritsu gyōjishōshijiki*), a commentary on Daoxuan's previously mentioned *Four-Part Vinaya* commentary *Sifenlü shanfanbuque xingshichao,*[7] and his *Fozhi biqiu liuwutu* (Jpns. *Bussei bikurokumotsuzu*), an illustrated explanation of Daoxuan's rules regarding the six personal possessions of monks and nuns (*liuwu,* Jpns. *rokumotsu,* which include three garments, a begging bowl, a sitting pillow, and a water strainer).

As their titles suggest, most of these commentaries are concerned with the monastic regulations, including both the precepts of the *Four-Part Vinaya* and the bodhisattva vows expounded in the *Brahma Net Sutra.* Eison does not merely mention these commentaries in passing: these are texts upon which he gave lengthy lecture sessions, sometimes spending weeks or even a month lecturing on a single commentary. It can be assumed, then, that Eison, his colleagues, and his disciples put a great deal of effort into the task of understanding and implementing the ideas contained in these texts. Of particular interest here is the fact that nearly all of these texts speak of the nuns' order *(nizhong)* and offer special teachings and rules aimed at nuns.

In other words, Eison and his followers had dedicated themselves wholeheartedly to the study of continental texts that took for granted the presence of a nuns' order. The dynamics at work in Eison's order, then, must have mirrored those described by Harada Masatoshi in his work on women in the Zen movement: as Harada explains, the texts used by Zen teachers and disciples in Kamakura Japan were, on the whole, texts written by Chinese masters who both accepted female students among their disciples and took for granted the existence of a nuns' order. Harada suggests that many Japanese priests studying Zen found it difficult to reconcile the inclusion of nuns in Chan texts coming in from the continent with the realities of Japanese Buddhist communities that did not recognize an official nuns' order (1997, 180). Dōgen's critique of Tendai practices that exclude female practitioners, such as *nyonin kekkai,* is one example of the ways exposure to Chinese Chan practice caused certain Zen monks to reevaluate stances toward women long accepted in orthodox Japanese monastic circles. It should come as no surprise, then, that Eison and his disciples also felt a certain contradiction between the texts they were reading, which spoke often and at length about nuns, and the social and institutional conditions of the Japanese order, which lacked fully ordained nuns, or *bikuni.*

The first widely acknowledged *bikuni* ordination performed in conjunction with the Nara *vinaya* revival movement was that of the celebrated nun Shinnyo (b. 1211). She appears to have taken *bikuni* precepts under Kakujō during or shortly after the year 1244 (Hosokawa 1999b, 149–153). Initially reluctant to bestow the *bikuni* precepts on Shinnyo, since there was no precedent within the Japanese monastic community of his time for doing so, Kakujō agreed to ordain Shinnyo on the premise that he had received a divine vision urging him that the time was ripe in Japan for the establishment of a nuns' order (Meeks 2007). Inspired perhaps by Shinnyo's ordination, Eison began making plans to establish a formal nuns' order the very next year, in 1245. Unlike Kakujō, Eison did not hint, as he set about these plans, at any anxiety regarding public reaction to this bold reenvisioning of the *sangha.* Perhaps it was because Shinnyo's case had tested the waters that Eison was able to move forward and establish a nuns' order without hesitation.

Instituting *Vinaya* Norms for Nuns at Hokkeji

Eison first mentions nuns at Hokkeji in the entry for the year 1245 in his autobiography. Here, he records having bestowed *shamini,* or novice nun, precepts on a total of eight women at Hokkeji: five took these precepts in the fourth month of 1245, and three took them in the eleventh month of that same year. This initial visit to Hokkeji appears to have been rather brief, for Eison mentions only that he gave the precepts at Hokkeji and nothing more. In the sixth month of the following year, 1246, he returned to Hokkeji to initiate *fusatsu* practice there. Since at this point he had only bestowed novice precepts on Hokkeji nuns, he carried out a *shamini fusatsu*, or a confession ceremony using the novice nuns' precepts. Following the summer retreat of 1247, Eison visited Hokkeji again, this time to lecture on the *Bikunishō* ([*Sifenlü*] *Biqiuni chao*, X. 724), Daoxuan's three-volume compendium on the nuns' precepts.

During the last month of that same year, Eison's records show that he gave the next set of precepts—the *shikishamana* precepts for probationary nuns—to eleven women at Hokkeji. He returned to Hokkeji again the next year (1248), this time spending a full month (from the nineteenth day of the eighth month through the nineteenth day of the ninth month) lecturing on the two Taehyeon commentaries central to his understanding of the *vinaya:* the *Beommanggyeong gojeokgi* and the *Beommanggyeong bosalgyebon jongyo*. Eison added here that there were twenty-five people in attendance at these lectures, plus another twenty-four who participated as members of the *kechien-shū*, which was likely made up of laypeople who hoped to create merit for themselves by forging karmic ties with his lectures (*KJGSK* 1999, 168–181).

In keeping with *vinaya* stipulations that required two years to pass between a woman's ordination as a *shikishamana*, or probationary nun, and her ordination as a full-fledged *bikuni*, Eison waited two years before offering *bikuni* ordinations to Hokkeji nuns who had taken *shikishamana* ordinations from him.[8] It was during the second month of 1249 that he conferred *bikuni* ordinations on twelve probationary nuns at Hokkeji. In the margins next to his record of this event, he proclaims, "In the country of Japan, this is the start of a complete sevenfold order practicing in accordance with the *vinaya*" (184; Hosokawa 1999b, 185–190).

In the years following these ordinations, Eison returned to Hokkeji with regularity. Particularly striking is the fact that he recorded having held a number of lengthy (three-to-four-week) lecture sessions at Hokkeji. In 1250, he spent three weeks at Hokkeji (from the second week of the third month through the early days of the fourth month) lecturing on two difficult *vinaya* commentaries: Daoxuan's *Jiaojie xinxue biqiu xinghu lüyi* and Cien Ji's *Biaowubiao zhang*. After having completed these lectures, Eison spent another day lecturing on Taehyeon's *Beommanggyeong bosalgyebon jongyo*. These texts are the very same ones that Eison used in his teachings to male monks. One can imagine, however, that Eison may have tailored his teachings on some of these texts to fit his female audience. The *Jiaojie xinxue biqiu xinghu lüyi*, a manual in which Daoxuan explains to new monks how they are to behave in the monastery on a daily basis, for example, contains gender-specific passages in which monks are specifically told not to talk with women or nuns on the street, not to visit brothels, and so on (T. no. 1897, esp. 873c–874a; *KJGSK* 1999, 199–200; Hosokawa 1999b, 200–203).

According to his autobiography, Eison returned to Hokkeji for another three-week lecture session in 1251, this time during the eleventh and twelfth months. He notes on this occasion, as in subsequent records of trips to Hokkeji, that he stayed at Kairyūōji, the *vinaya* monastery associated with Shunjō's lineage and located just next to Hokkeji, during the period when he was offering daily lectures at the convent. During this 1251 visit, Eison lectured on Yuanzhao's *Sifenlü xingshichao zichiji,* another difficult and lengthy *vinaya* commentary. It was during one of these lecture sessions, he notes, that Buddha relics first began to manifest at Hokkeji (*KJGSK* 1999, 205). In the *Hokkeji shari engi,* a separate document, Eison tells of the miraculous events surrounding the appearance and distribution of relics at Hokkeji. Although analysis of the relics-related narratives will be saved for a later chapter, it should be noted here that within the narrative framework of Eison's autobiography, the appearance of Buddha relics during a lecture at Hokkeji serves to demonstrate to readers that the buddhas and gods were pleased with Eison's decision to train Hokkeji nuns in the *vinaya.*

His next lectures at Hokkeji took place in 1254 (a seven-day lecture on Yuanzhao's *Sifenlü xingshichao zichiji*), 1256 (a nineteen-day lecture on Taehyeon's *Beommanggyeong gojeokgi*), and 1257 (a fifteen-day session, also on Yuanzhao's *Sifenlü xingshichao zichiji*). Reflecting the degree to which the Hokkeji order had grown, Eison's autobiography notes that sixty-four nuns and four monks were in attendance at this 1257 lecture (*KJGSK* 1999, 226–236). Also noticeable here is the fact that by the mid-1250s Eison was no longer introducing new texts at Hokkeji but was instead reviewing texts already taught there. The fact that a handful of monks also attended his lectures at Hokkeji further suggests that Eison offered Hokkeji nuns more or less the same training in *vinaya* texts that he offered his male followers. Although some might expect Eison to have used a simplified version of the teachings when addressing women, who, it has long been presumed, would have had fewer opportunities to gain the education necessary for work with such difficult texts, Eison's records show him devoting a great deal of time to teaching at Hokkeji the same rigorous texts he taught at male monasteries. The nonchalance with which Eison mentions the fact that monks, too, audited these lectures at Hokkeji suggests that his lecture sessions at Hokkeji were not perceived as intellectually inferior to those offered at male institutions; there is no obvious implication here that monks perceived participation in a lecture series targeted at women as beneath them in any way.

Conceptualizing the Nuns' Order

Those studying Eison's movement as a whole have often interpreted his efforts to train Hokkeji nuns in the *vinaya* tradition as a set of activities akin to his charity work with *hinin* and prisoners (e.g., Matsuo 1989, 2001; Tanaka 1978b; Hosokawa 1989b). It is true that Eison's work with nuns did overlap, temporally, with his outreach to socially marginal groups. And it is also true that Eison offered members of such groups ordinations in addition to more pragmatic things like food. But close attention to the sources does not support the logical leap necessary to arrive at the conclusion that Eison viewed all women, and thus all nuns, as impure beings comparable to *hinin* or prisoners. First of all, while Eison did offer outcast groups certain sets of precepts, he did not offer them precepts leading to full recognition as *biku*. Instead, he usually offered them only the eight pure precepts and, on some occasions, the bodhisattva precepts. By contrast, he offered a great number of nuns at Hokkeji complete ordination, which marked them as full members of the *sangha*. Secondly, as explained above, Eison spent a great deal of time training nuns in difficult *vinaya* texts. This activity suggests that he viewed nuns not as charity cases but as disciples, for the texts he taught Hokkeji nuns were the very same texts he used to train his male disciples. Although Eison did offer a number of special services for outcast groups, intensive doctrinal training was not one of them. Rather, as Hosokawa has suggested, it appears that Ritsu groups eventually came to train members of *hinin* communities to carry out certain unpleasant tasks, such as the handling of corpses during funerary services, that full priests trained in doctrinal matters did not ordinarily perform (1987, esp. 1–40).

In thinking through the question of how Eison conceptualized nuns as a group, a more helpful model is that of the elite patron. As demonstrated in the last chapter, elite women of the court (and, increasingly, from warrior government circles as well) had, like their male counterparts, long acted as the patrons of Buddhist priests. Especially during the Kamakura period, when members of the court and government were vying to discover and patronize charismatic priests and when numerous new, often unorthodox religious groups were emerging, women of means often took great interest in patronizing celebrated priests. Like Hōnen, Myōe, Eisai, and many others, Eison eventually became one of the most recognized priests of his day. By the middle years of the thirteenth century, he was in great demand, with invitations streaming in from both court and warrior government elites.

Studies of Eison's movement recognize the Lay Novice Hamuro (Hamuro Nyūdō) as Eison's first major aristocratic patron. The middle counselor Hamuro Sadatsugu (1208–1272), a Fujiwara who received the Buddhist name Jōnen, was a minister to Retired Sovereign Go-Saga (1220–1272). He had been born into a family of ministers and would hold over the course of his own career a number of high-level appointments within the retired sovereign's court.[9] Although the details of how exactly he came to learn of Eison's movement are unclear, Hamuro is known to have taken full precepts as a *biku* from Eison in the year 1260. In the years that followed, it became common for court elites to take lay and novice precepts from Eison, but Hamuro's case remained unusual, since most elites who took precepts from Eison remained laypersons.

What is interesting about Hamuro's case is that he made an effort to establish his own *vinaya*-centered ritual program soon after receiving full *biku* precepts from Eison. Early in his career as a *biku,* for example, he tore down a monk's hut *(bō)* that had been located at Tōdaiji and moved it to the grounds of Saidaiji. After residing there for less than a year, he hosted a summer retreat (*geango;* Skt. *varṣōṣita*) in the year 1261. During the same year, he went on to establish a temple on the grounds of his mountain villa in Kyoto. He asked Eison to perform *kekkai* and *fusatsu* services there, and these ritual performances rendered the temple, subsequently known as Jōjūji, a Saidaiji branch institution. Soon thereafter, Jōjūji came to serve as the center of Saidaiji-branch Ritsu activities in the Kyoto area (Hosokawa 1999b, 254–255).

In many ways, Hamuro's engagement with Eison's movement mirrored that of Hokkeji's first nuns. Although Hamuro, like Hokkeji's first group of nuns—Jizen and Kūnyo, especially—was of aristocratic birth, his involvement with Eison's group recalled older patronage models of lay-priestly interaction in certain respects but diverged from them in others. On the one hand, his status allowed him to ask special favors of Eison that ordinary laypeople would not have been able to ask: like courtiers who called priests to appear at court and perform rituals on their behalf, Hamuro called Eison to his mountain retreat and entreated him to carry out large-scale rituals on his behalf. On the other hand, Hamuro did not identify himself as a mere patron; instead, he sought acceptance as one of Eison's disciples, even taking up residence at Saidaiji for a period of time and placing his own temple under the jurisdiction of the Saidaiji group. He did not call upon Eison as a patron would call upon a client but instead treated Eison as a venerable master, committing himself and his private temple to the greater goals of Eison's Ritsu movement. In this respect, Hamuro's relationship with Eison departed from the types of patron-client relationships often seen among courtiers and Tendai priests, in which, if one can generalize from the aforementioned case of Shikikenmon-in's encounter with Myōe and from episodes related in the *Eiga monogatari,* high-ranking elites viewed Tendai priests as interchangeable providers of ritual services. Unlike Tendai priests, many of whom made themselves readily available to court elites, Eison appears to have expected more of his patrons. Like many of the Zen priests beginning to emerge around this time, he required his patrons to behave as disciples, and he managed to attract a number of elite patron-disciples, such as Hamuro, who were interested in more than having simple merit-making services performed on their behalf.

The case of Hamuro does not merely suggest parallels in terms of patronage relationships between Eison's group and newly emerging Zen groups. It also provides an important perspective for understanding Eison's work with Hokkeji nuns. Eison's work with Hamuro indicates that this pattern of performing Ritsu rituals at an outside temple need not be understood as an act of charity or dominance—as Eison's work at Hokkeji has often been read—but can also be interpreted as an act of obligation or favor to one's patron-disciples. It is clear that Eison's performances of Ritsu *kekkai* and *fusatsu* rituals at Hamuro's Jōjūji were not instances of either charity or dominance; Hamuro was a politically and economically powerful figure. It makes more sense to read Eison's performances at Jōjūji as attempts to bestow favor upon a patron-disciple who was extraordinary in terms of both his social prominence and the level of his religious devotion. Hamuro sought this kind of close affiliation with Eison's group, and Eison indulged him, likely because he had shown great commitment to the cause, both by taking full *biku* precepts and by spending time in residence at Saidaiji despite his pedigree. Eison also stood to gain much from the act of establishing Jōjūji as a branch temple of his movement. Not only did this move guarantee a close relationship with the well-connected Hamuro (who eventually introduced the retired sovereign Go-Saga to Eison), but Jōjūji also helped Eison's movement expand within the Kyoto area.

Hamuro's example is instructive when considering the Hokkeji movement as well. Like Hamuro, Jizen and Kūnyo were court figures of some status who personally sought affiliation with Eison's movement, inviting him to visit their temple and to perform rituals on their behalf. To assume that Eison viewed Jizen, Kūnyo, and the other nuns at Hokkeji as a group of women to whom he extended charity or over whom he sought to exercise dominance would require one to overlook the ways in which Hokkeji nuns identified, much like Hamuro, as patron-disciples of Eison. And it goes without saying that Eison gained even more from the reestablishment of Hokkeji than from the incorporation of Hamuro's Jōjūji, for Hokkeji came to serve, as we will see in the next chapter, as a training center for women and nuns within the Saidaiji network. Hokkeji and its ordination platform for nuns helped Eison's movement attract numerous female patrons and devotees who might otherwise have had little interest in his group.

Eison as a Charismatic Leader

If we view Hokkeji's thirteenth-century nuns as patron-disciples of Eison, then one question that must be addressed is the nature of Eison's appeal. What would have made Eison attractive to women with court connections? One obvious answer is that he offered women full, *vinaya*-style precepts. As demonstrated in the last chapter, certain groups of court women had been seeking full ordination for centuries. Certainly, Eison's willingness to offer these ordinations, a service that the *kenmitsu* orthodoxy had failed to provide, would have drawn many women to his movement. But literature surrounding Eison and his movement suggests that he also appealed to those who had little vested interest in taking formal monastic precepts. In other words, he also attracted men and women who simply wanted to create personal stores of good merit. His movement, aimed at the masses, was large in scale, and Eison himself, if one can trust his biographies and collected sayings, was a charismatic figure who had the power to draw large crowds.

Eison's most visible public performances were mass precepts ordinations. According to the 1290 Saidaiji document *Shien Shōnin donin gyōhō kechigeki* (Record of the ordinations, Dharma practices, and summer retreats carried out by Shien Shōnin [Eison]), Eison gave some version of the precepts to a total of 97,710 people. Of these, 1,694 were members of the five clerical groups: 784 were *biku,* or fully ordained priests; 442 were *bikuni,* or fully ordained nuns; 100 were *shikishamana,* or probationary nuns; 250 were *shami,* or novice priests; and 118 were *shamini,* or novice nuns. The remaining 96,016 were householders, lay believers *(zaike)* who took Eison's bodhisattva precepts (*SEDS,* 212–215). Although these numbers may have been inflated by Eison's disciples, the proportions suggest that his movement, despite its emphasis on the restoration of the sevenfold *sangha,* was primarily focused upon the laity: according to Saidaiji's own documents, a striking 98 percent of those who received the precepts from Eison were laypeople. A number of these ordinations took place at Saidaiji, but most took place during Eison's travels through the countryside. Eison traveled frequently, especially through the Kinai and Kingoku regions, and during his travels he made regular stops, during which he would perform rituals, especially bodhisattva ordination ceremonies, for large groups of ordinary laypeople.[10]

In his collected teachings, Eison sometimes reflects upon the nature of his encounters with lay folk in the countryside. In one passage, he speaks in a seemingly candid manner of his celebrity in the countryside as a source of personal and spiritual struggle:

> In pursuing my vow to advance the Dharma and benefit sentient beings, I have endured many hardships and visited many places. In the midst [of these travels], sometimes one hundred people, or fifty people, will run down from the peak of a mountain, or up from a valley, in hopes of seeing me. Among those people, there are some elderly people who bow deeply from the waist and devotedly venerate me, and there are others who, though they may be mature, have fewer expectations [of me] and look at me as an ordinary person. Some are young children who put their hands together in prayer [*gasshō*] and pay respects with a deeply faithful heart. When young and old first ran to gather around me, I thought it was only burdensome, and I worried about how I should handle it. But I came to realize that "people who see my body give rise to *bodhicitta;* people who hear my name stop committing the evil and begin to practice good; those who listen to my teachings gain great wisdom; those who know my heart can gain buddhahood in this very body" [Here, Eison is quoting the *Shengjun Budong Mingwang sishibashizhe mimi chengjiu yigui,* Commentary on successfully performing the secret [rites] of the Immoveable Luminous King who Conquers Armies and his forty-eight messengers, T. no. 1205, 33c4–7]. Sometimes, in response to requests for ordination and other things, I open the windows of my palanquin, raise my bamboo blinds, put my hands together in prayer, and pass by [the crowds] chanting, "All sentient beings have the Buddha Nature and will receive supreme, perfect enlightenment [Skt. *anuttarā-samyak-saṃbodhi*]." How many people have I encountered like this? (*Chōmonshū,* 211–212; Kōshō Bosatsu Onkyōkai Chōmonshū Kenkyūkai 2003, 134)

This passage suggests that Eison sometimes found the level of his own public celebrity bewildering. He suggests later in the same teaching that it required great patience to interact with large crowds eager to receive his blessings. While personal inclination would have led him to seek privacy, he says, he believed that his larger commitment to the salvation of sentient beings required him to sacrifice his desire for solitude.

Such passages might appear self-aggrandizing at first glance, but contemporaneous sources confirm that Eison had indeed become a highly visible and sought-after figure by the early 1260s. In 1261, a messenger from Kamakura arrived at Saidaiji with large gifts from Hōjō Sanetoki: a full set of Buddhist sutras *(issaikyō)* and a deed to Sanetoki's temple Shōmyōji. The gifts were accompanied by an order from Sanetoki that Eison visit Kamakura to perform ordinations on Sanetoki and his relatives and retainers. Although Eison refused Sanetoki's gifts, he found himself unable to refuse Sanetoki's order that he appear in Kamakura, and so he made a six-month sojourn to the eastern capital in the year 1262. In 1263, his popularity began to expand in court circles, and it was during this year that he finally agreed after much protest to visit and ordain Hamuro's lord, the retired sovereign Go-Saga (*Chōmonshū,* 215; *Saidai chokushi Kōshō Bosatsu gyōjitsu nenpu,* 146–147). Throughout the 1270s and 1280s, he made regular appearances in court, ordaining retired sovereigns Kameyama (1249–1305) and Go-Fukakusa (1243–1304), along with their female companions, ladies-in-waiting, and servants, on numerous occasions.

Eison's prominence as a religious figure is perhaps most evident in the fact that court and warrior government authorities bestowed upon him the prestigious position of chief administrator priest *(bettō)* at the popular and highly visible temple Shitennōji in the year 1284. This position had long been reserved for elite Tendai and Shingon priests; that government officials decided to grant it to the Ritsu priest Eison demonstrates that the power and prestige of his movement had come to rival that of the old orthodoxy (Matsuo 2004b, esp. 31–32; *KJGSK* 1977, 58–59).

Near the end of his collected sermons, Eison mentions that during a teaching lecture on the four poisons, one of which is pride, an aristocrat protested that Eison must himself possess pride. When pressed to clarify why he or she believed that Eison would have reason to be prideful, the individual explained that since Eison was "the foremost *hijiri* [holy man] in Japan" *(Nihon ichi no hijiri),* it could only be expected that he would harbor pride (*Chōmonshū,* 221). An isolated remark such as this, embedded as it is in Eison's teachings, might be interpreted as an attempt at self-promotion, but given the degree to which Eison's stature is corroborated in other sources, there is reason to believe that Japanese aristocrats did in fact consider Eison to be the most celebrated holy man of the late thirteenth century. Although Eison's prominence is especially visible in the fact that he was repeatedly invited to serve the most powerful warrior government and court officials of his day and granted the prestigious post of chief administrator at Shitennōji, his popularity was also felt on the ground. An account of Eison's funerary procession found among the Kanazawa Bunko archives, for example, claims that several tens of thousands of people, lay and clerical, male and female, participated in his funeral ceremonies ("Eison sōsōki," *Kanazawa Bunko komonjo,* no. 5975).

Nuns and laywomen were among Eison's most fervent supporters. The record of Eison's funeral mentioned above also notes that over five hundred women from the nuns' order were counted among the tens of thousands who attended Eison's funeral. Details of Eison's broad celebrity allow us to speculate that his popularity among women was not simply a result of the fact that he extended full ordination to women and supported the growth of a nuns' order. Although certain groups of women were clearly interested in this aspect of his ministry, we can assume that many women were attracted to Eison's movement for the same reasons that men were: he was a charismatic figure whose public profile grew increasingly impressive with time, and he offered a number of appealing services in the countryside, including ordinations of numerous kinds, Kōmyō Shingon (Mantra of Light) performances, and other large-scale lecture and chanting services.[11] While it is true that Hokkeji nuns like Jizen and Kūnyo first became involved with Eison perhaps a decade before he had achieved great fame, their involvement with his movement can in some senses be understood as an attempt to nourish young talent. That is, just as Hamuro recognized Eison's charisma and, predicting that he was on his way to becoming a major figure in the religious order of his day, chose to support him even before his movement had achieved recognition from high-level political authorities, Jizen and Kūnyo also recognized Eison as a person of great consequence even before he had become famous. They likely came to support his movement not only because he offered nuns full ordination but also because they were attracted to the broader messages and services offered by Eison and his innovative movement.

Were Hokkeji Nuns Under the Management of Saidaiji Monks?

Central to debates within Japanese scholarship on Hokkeji's thirteenth-century restoration is the question of Saidaiji's jurisdiction over and management of the convent and its order of nuns. What was the nature of the institutional relationship between Saidaiji and Hokkeji? And what did this relationship mean for individual monks and nuns in Eison's Ritsu group? Much previous scholarship, especially that influenced by Marxist historiography, has suggested that Hokkeji nuns were under the close control of Saidaiji leadership (e.g., Hosokawa 1989b; Matsuo 2001; Taira 1990; Ishida M. 1978). After examining such claims, this section will offer alternative readings of Hokkeji's relationship with Saidaiji.

To begin, a closer look at Jizen's relationship with Eison is in order. According to Hosokawa's calculations, Jizen was sixty-three years old when she took her first set of precepts from Eison. Having first taken precepts from the priest Jiren-bō in 1211, she had been living the life of a world renouncer for thirty-eight years before she received a conferral from Eison. In the interim, she had probably received precepts from Tankū as well, and perhaps from other priests in the Nara capital. Since she had also spent a number of years—indeed, perhaps as many as thirty-five or more years—living and studying at Shōkutei-in, where she was a student of Kūnyo and Jōken, it is likely that she had received precepts from these and other Daigoji teachers as well (see Hosokawa 1997, 93–95; 1999a, 31–37).

In other words, Jizen was not a single-minded follower of Eison, but rather a religious practitioner who had, like many male clerics of her day, sought education from masters representing a variety of different schools and lineages. Her multiple precepts ordinations also suggest continuity with the practices of royals and court nobles. Like the *nyoin* whom she served as a young woman—and like aristocrats of this period more generally—Jizen presumably considered it efficacious to take various types and levels of precepts numerous times. She acted more as a patron-disciple seeking the services of male priests than as a supplicant dependent on the mercy of the male clergy. This second characterization has been the one that modern scholars have tended, perhaps unwittingly, to project. Jizen and her group at Hokkeji seem rather to have envisioned themselves as an autonomous group that sought association with Eison's movement voluntarily.

Against the notion that Hokkeji nuns were the objects of Saidaiji proselytizing, Eison's records themselves actually suggest the opposite. Jizen and her followers, it seems, were actively seeking association with Eison and his group. Like the female retired sovereigns discussed in earlier chapters, and like Hamuro and other aristocratic patrons, Jizen and her growing group at Hokkeji most likely took the initiative with Eison, inviting him to Hokkeji and asking him to perform various services on their behalf: to bestow the precepts upon them and later to perform sutra readings, confession services, and lectures.

Although scholars suggesting that Saidaiji had the upper hand in interactions with Hokkeji tend to portray Saidaiji monks as having played a strong role in the day-to-day affairs of Hokkeji and other Ritsu-school nunneries, there is no documentary evidence to support this view (see Hosokawa 1989b, 141–158; 1997, 154; Matsuo 2001, 379–380; Taira 1990, 96–106). Close attention to Eison's autobiography suggests, in fact, that Eison's presence at Hokkeji was rather limited.[12] Moreover, aside from rare visits to Dōmyōji (which appear to have taken place before Dōmyōji was designated a convent), it seems that Eison rarely visited other convents.

As explained earlier, Eison did visit Hokkeji with some frequency, sometimes staying long enough to offer monthlong seminars on difficult doctrinal commentaries during the early years of the Hokkeji revival in the late 1240s and 1250s. But by the 1260s, his visits to Hokkeji had tapered off. His decision to spend less time at Hokkeji likely represents his faith in the convent's own leadership: having spent nearly a decade training Hokkeji nuns in both doctrine and practice, Eison appears to have been confident by this time in the ability of Hokkeji nuns to run their own affairs. It is also likely that Eison's successes in other sectors during this time simply left him with less time to devote to Hokkeji and its nuns. From the 1260s especially, Eison began traveling with increasing frequency. His periods of extensive travel are especially noticeable from 1262, when he made the long journey to Kamakura and back, making many stops en route to teach and to bestow bodhisattva precepts upon lay believers.

Indeed, by the middle years of his ministry, Eison had come to envision itinerancy as a primary component of the bodhisattva lifestyle to which he aspired. In one of his collected teachings, he expounds on the virtues of living without attachment to the place in which one resides and encourages followers to practice in the countryside, where, according to his logic, food shortages prevent monks from becoming complacent, thereby allowing the true Dharma to flourish (*Chōmonshū,* 192).

A quick glance at Eison's autobiography entry for this particular year indicates that he spent the first four months of 1281 performing services at a variety of different temples, shrines, and residences. The list does not, incidentally, include Hokkeji. Among the many activities that kept him busy during this period were a pilgrimage to the Hachiman shrines made at the request of the retired sovereign; lectures on Taehyeon's commentary *Beommanggyeong gojeokgi* delivered at a royal residence; a large-scale ceremony at Sangaku-in, a temple in the Nara countryside; and *kekkai* ceremonies at Saifukuji, another temple in the Nara countryside. During this same period, he is also said to have held bodhisattva ordinations at the Daijō-in of Iwashimizu Hachiman shrine (515 people); at Kyōkōji, a Saidaiji branch temple in Shimo Kawachi (248 people); at Ganpōji in present-day Hyōgō-ken (1,805 people); at Onsenji in present-day Kōbe-shi (221 people); and at Tadano-in, also in present-day Hyōgō-ken (432 people) (*KJGSK* 1977, 48–49).

The basic patterns visible in this three-and-a-half month outtake from Eison's autobiography are representative of the latter part of his career as a whole. Eison's records show that he spent these years primarily in transit, moving, as he notes in the teaching mentioned above, from place to place in accordance with the invitations and requests he received from followers and admirers. In his view, it was in enduring the hardships of this difficult schedule of travel, in giving so greatly of his time and energy by providing ritual services to those who made requests of him, that he was fulfilling the vows of a bodhisattva.[13] When this aspect of Eison's ministry is understood, it becomes clear that he was not himself interested in overseeing the day-to-day activities of specific institutions; the magnitude of his vision would not have allowed him to spend too much time focused on such small-scale matters. In establishing branch temples, Eison did offer ritual services on-site and would often inaugurate, as he did at places like Jōjūji and Hokkeji, certain rituals, such as the *kekkai* and the *fusatsu.* But once he recognized a given temple as having established a strong tie with the Ritsu order, he moved on to respond to the needs of other institutions and patrons.

In addition to the knowledge that, on the level of logistics alone, Eison's travel schedule allowed him to spend little time at Hokkeji, it is also clear that he had other, more ideological reasons for monitoring the amount of time he spent at Hokkeji. Eison hints at these reasons in one of the letters he wrote to Jizen while she was rector at Hokkeji. In this 1249 letter, written in a mix of Chinese characters and *kana,* Eison politely refuses to grant Jizen's request to meet with him and explains as justification for his refusal that it would be improper for him to be seen at Hokkeji too frequently. Notable here is his use of honorific language; he writes to Jizen in a deferential tone, begging her forgiveness as he refuses to fulfill her request:

> How have you been feeling after your illness? I have been worried about you.
>
> I have privately heard that you would like me to visit [Hokkeji] when it is convenient for me. You have been saying, "Since we are nearby [that is, since Hokkeji and Saidaiji are located near each other], it is important that we see each other," but as of late I do not casually go to visit people. The temple in Saga is a nunnery that everyone knows well [and feels comfortable with], and thus there are no objections [to my going there]; but it's just that Hokkeji is an old *gosho;* I sometimes find it difficult [as a priest upholding the *vinaya*] to go there. I especially do not [feel comfortable enough to] go to the *gosho* at [the temple] Ninnaji [the place of the *hōshinnō,* or retired prince].
>
> I've heard that you will come here tomorrow, but for various reasons it is inconvenient for me; I must say it seems impossible that I will be able to meet with you tomorrow. I deeply regret your inevitable disappointment, but since incurring people's slander would diminish [our ability to] benefit [sentient beings], it is not in my power [to do anything about it]. It is not that I think highly of myself [i.e., it is fine by me if people slander me], but we must preserve people's [confidence].
>
> By the way, the [statue of the] Buddha is being made, isn't it? I heard that it is almost done. But just what is the situation?
>
> I truly regret that I cannot meet with you this time.
>
> *(Eison shojō santsū)*

Both the tone and the content of this letter suggest that Eison understood his interactions with Jizen to be governed by the logic of the patron-client relationship. Far from showing interest in managing the daily affairs of Hokkeji, his letter suggests that both his schedule and his sense of propriety prevented him from visiting Hokkeji as frequently as Jizen desired. Tension between Eison's concerns over decorum and Jizen's expectations as a patron-disciple are apparent in his paraphrasing the complaint that, despite the proximity between Saidaiji and Hokkeji *(chikaki hodo nite mo),* she has not been able to meet with Eison all that often.

Eison explains his reluctance in several ways. He first suggests that he feels uncomfortable visiting Hokkeji since it is an old *gosho*—an old royal residence. The implication here might be that he feels unworthy, as a person of relatively low status, visiting a former royal residence. It is easy, he suggests, for him to visit the nunnery in Saga (Kōdaiji), as it is familiar and comfortable. (Here, the phrase "*mina shitaru amadera*" connotes a feeling of familiarity and ease.) He could be making an appeal of humility here, suggesting that he finds it intimidating to visit *gosho* like Hokkeji and Ninnaji. If Eison's suggestion is in fact that he finds it intimidating to visit a place associated with high social status, then it might be possible to read this letter as an attempt to flatter Jizen—basically by telling her that he feels lowly in her presence—even as he refuses to meet her request.

At the same time, however, Eison's explanation of his hesitation to visit Hokkeji should also be placed within the context of his teachings on the relationship between world renouncers and figures of worldly power. As mentioned in the previous chapter, Eison's collected teachings include a sermon in which he invokes the passage from the *Sutra on the Final Nirvana of Śākyamuni* in which it is stated that those who have renounced the world *(shukke)* are not to bow down before laypeople (T. no. 375, 640a29). Like Dōgen and Myōe, Eison was eager to demonstrate that his purity as a Buddhist monk would not be easily corrupted by the temptations created by association with worldly fame and fortune.

Although Eison did in the end accept patronage from the highest-ranking members of his society, he made a point of resisting such patronage, even though this protest may be read as a rhetorical conceit. As David Quinter has put it, Eison framed his response to attention from high within what might be termed a "rhetoric of reluctance," meaning that he accepted high-level patronage only after making a show of his reluctance to do so (2006, 4). A similar pattern is suggested in this letter to Hokkeji: if Hokkeji nuns (and Jizen in particular) are indeed understood as elite patron-disciples of Eison, then his hesitation to show too much interest in the convent, given its close association with the court and with elite society more broadly, resembles his reluctance to accept invitations from figures like the retired sovereign Go-Saga and warrior government regent Tokiyori. Were he to align himself too closely with Hokkeji, he suggests, he might place at risk his reputation as a holy man who placed principle above worldly reputation. In other words, since Hokkeji's status as an old *gosho* placed it in a category similar to that of the warrior government or the royal palace, Eison felt that he needed to maintain a certain distance from the convent.

Eison's letter states that his reluctance to visit Hokkeji has much to do with protecting the reputation of his movement: "It is not that I think highly of myself," he argues, but that "we must preserve people's [confidence]" *(Mi o oshimu nite sōrawazu, hito no kokoro o mamoran to omoite sōrō ni sōrō) (Eison shojō santsū)*. It is unclear in Eison's remarks about preventing slander here what issues exactly he believes will prompt gossip. Certainly one issue, as suggested above, was that of his association with figures representing political power: if he associates too closely with members of the highest elite, people may doubt his purity as a world renouncer. Another related issue, and one that was perhaps given greater importance in his relationships with ordinary laypeople, was how outsiders would perceive his interactions with female followers. As the leader of a movement to revive the *vinaya* precepts, Eison was likely concerned that people would misinterpret meetings with female followers as a deviation from his commitment to the precepts. The letter suggests that Eison believed that people may have been gossiping about his meetings with women and that he perceived such gossip to endanger the success of his movement.

Regardless of the precise dynamics at work between Eison's numerous motivations for maintaining a certain degree of space between himself and the nuns at Hokkeji, this letter makes clear that he expected Jizen to run affairs at Hokkeji independently of his guidance. Despite Jizen's resolution to see him, he refused both to visit Hokkeji and to allow her to visit Saidaiji as she had proposed. Thus, the letter suggests not—as Hosokawa and Matsuo, among others, have suggested—that Eison and his Saidaiji movement were actively seeking to take over the management of nunneries like Hokkeji but rather that Jizen, who was a patron-disciple of Eison's burgeoning movement in much the same way that Hamuro, Tokiyori, and Go-Saga were, pursued affiliation with him.

Read in conjunction with his autobiography, which records fewer than twenty specific trips to Hokkeji over a period of four and a half decades, Eison's letter suggests that the women at Hokkeji enjoyed relative independence from the Saidaiji institutional framework, at least during this early stage of Hokkeji-Saidaiji relations. After all, these sources, written by Eison himself, suggest that the nuns at Hokkeji received instruction only when they persistently requested it. Clearly, Eison was not managing daily affairs at Hokkeji.

But what about Eison's male disciples? Might it have been the case that a certain male priest or group of priests had been placed in charge of everyday administrative affairs at Hokkeji? Hosokawa has implied such a structure may have been in place at Hokkeji, but there is little evidence to support this view.[14] First of all, Hokkeji documents do not suggest that there were any male administrators active at Hokkeji. Although the *Hokke metsuzaiji engi* does mention Eison, it does so late in the text and does not suggest that he or any other Ritsu monks were personally responsible for overseeing the convent's daily affairs. Secondly, Saidaiji documents provide no evidence that Eison had placed any of his head disciples in charge of the nuns' order. Of all Eison's male disciples at Saidaiji, it was Sōji (1233–1312), a nephew of Eison who became one of his foremost disciples, who was most actively involved in what Hosokawa has termed the "education" *(kyōka)* of nuns. Hosokawa suggests, though not directly, that Sōji may have been one of the major male heads of the nuns' order, but close attention to the details of Sōji's life reveals that he was a mere teenager at the time of Hokkeji's initial revival. Although Sōji did, from the early 1250s onward, dedicate himself to the compilation and printing of doctrinal commentaries deemed relevant to women and nuns, a topic that will be treated in the final chapters, one can hardly imagine that Jizen, a woman of high birth who was at least forty years his senior, would have placed Hokkeji, the institution she had managed on her own before joining Eison's group, under Sōji's oversight.[15] At the time he first became engaged with the task of "educating" nuns, he was still an inexperienced young monk, perhaps even younger than twenty years old. Moreover, he was a man of humble birth. Jizen may have indulged his enthusiasm, but it is unlikely that she viewed him as a superior. By 1254, Sōji had been named rector of Sairinji in Kawachi (present-day Osaka). Although he continued to be active with nuns in Kawachi, most notably with those involved in the conversion of the temple Dōmyōji into a Ritsu convent, his dedication to Sairinji from this time forward would have precluded frequent engagements at distant Hokkeji, much less active management of the convent.[16]

There is some piecemeal evidence that the monks at Kairyūōji, the monastery located on the edge of the Hokkeji temple grounds, were engaged with the nuns' order at Hokkeji. As mentioned earlier in this chapter, Eison is known to have stayed at Kairyūōji when he gave lengthy lectures at Hokkeji. And as noted in the previous chapter, the Tōdaiji priest Enshō stayed at Kairyūōji during the period in which he performed daily chants of the *bikuni* precepts for his mother when she was in residence at Hokkeji. These examples hint at the possibility that certain monks at Kairyūōji were involved in the education of the Hokkeji nuns' order. That said, there is no direct evidence from the records of Saidaiji, Hokkeji, or Kairyūōji indicating that Kairyūōji monks were given any kind of jurisdiction over Hokkeji or its order of nuns.[17]

Indeed, all available evidence suggests that the dynamics governing Hokkeji's integration into the Saidaiji network as a branch temple were more or less the same as those operative in the case of other, male temples: the person holding the rights to the institution became a devotee of Eison (or, later, of one of Eison's disciples) and sought affiliation with the Saidaiji movement. Many of the most visible branch temples in the Saidaiji network had in fact been private clan or family mortuary temples *(bodaiji)*. When their lords became admirers of Ritsu monks, they sought to have their family temples converted into Ritsu institutions. In the Kantō area, enthusiastic support of Ritsu monks even led local lords to change the affiliation of their family temples from Pure Land to Ritsu. Two of the foremost Saidaiji-branch temples in the Kantō, Mimuradera and Gokurakuji, were both family temples converted into Ritsu temples by their owners, warrior government lords eager to display their devotion to Eison and his most celebrated disciple, Ninshō (1217–1303) (Matsuo 2004a, 53–86). And this same basic pattern follows in the case of Eison's aristocratic patron Hamuro, who asked that the temple that he had built, Jōjūji, be consecrated as a Ritsu institution. Just as Mimuradera and Gokurakuji became strongholds in the Kantō, Jōjūji became the major Ritsu center in the Kyoto area. When Jizen's devotion to Eison is placed within this context, it becomes clear that it was as a patron and devotee of Eison that she sought to identify her temple, Hokkeji, with the Saidaiji movement. Eison welcomed this affiliation, which supported his goal to create a sevenfold *sangha,* including nuns' orders, but there is no evidence that he or his male disciples sought to assume administrative roles at Hokkeji or to seek control over the everyday activities of the nuns' order there.

This view of Saidaiji's relationship with nuns diverges greatly from that presented by Hosokawa Ryōichi and Matsuo Kenji, who have both tended to assume that the institutional framework of Eison's movement consistently and uniformly subjugated women and nuns. Although it is true—as chapter 7 will demonstrate—that Eison's group promoted doctrines plainly favoring androcentric teachings such as *henjō nanshi,* it is not clear that the attitudes taken by Saidaiji monks in their everyday interactions with actual women were necessarily informed by the disparaging tone of these doctrines, many of which these men were themselves still struggling to understand as they continued to import texts from China. One of the oversights in Hosokawa's portrayal of the Saidaiji group's relationship with nuns is that he characterizes this complex relationship in overly simplistic terms, without taking into account the ways in which the institutional treatment of nuns within the Saidaiji movement differed according to region and changed over time.

An example of this kind of oversimplification is found in Hosokawa's claim that nuns active in the Saidaiji movement were expected to wash the robes of Ritsu monks. He bases this claim on an anonymous and undated document from the Kanazawa Bunko archives, a letter written by a nun affiliated with the Mimura convent (Mimura amadera). In the document, the nun mentions that she and her companions had a lot of laundry to which they had to attend. Hosokawa points to this letter as evidence that nuns at Saidaiji-affiliate convents were responsible for washing the robes of monks. Although he goes on to suggest, referring to recent scholarship by Katsuura Noriko and Nishiguchi Junko, that this duty may have been conceptualized as a sacred one, he ultimately uses this single undated document to support his larger argument that Saidaiji monks systematically subjugated nuns affiliated with the movement. Having women do their laundry was emblematic, Hosokawa writes, of the broader gender-based power dynamic within the movement that marked nuns as the subordinates of monks (1989a, 144–145).

It is of course possible that certain nuns within the Saidaiji network were in fact burdened with the task of washing monks' robes on a regular basis. But this undated letter, written by a nun affiliated with the Mimura convent in Hitachi (now known as northeastern Ibaraki-ken), which flourished later than Hokkeji, says nothing about the relationships between Saidaiji monks and Hokkeji nuns in Nara during the 1250s. Given their difference in social status, it is difficult to imagine that Eison would have dared to ask Hokkeji's first generation of nuns to wash his robes or those of his disciples. Out in Hitachi, where most of the nuns attracted to Ninshō's activities at the Mimura temple complex and its affiliate convent would have come from very different backgrounds—from warrior-class families, local landowning families, and agrarian households—it is easier to imagine that nuns may have in fact been expected to serve the movement in this way.[18] But it is also possible that the nuns at Mimura were talking about their own laundry; the document does not specify that the nuns were attending to the laundry of monks.[19]

Eison does mention Hokkeji once in a discussion of clerical robes, but the context and tone of his comments are different from what one might expect. In a lecture meant to emphasize the importance of maintaining detachment from the material things of everyday life, he laments the fact that so many of his disciples have been ordering increasingly luxurious robes for themselves. Once per year, he used to have his monks-in-training, who had yet to obtain their robes, draw lots *(kuji),* and he would order from Hokkeji a great robe *(daie)* for the winner. But in recent years, Eison says, his disciples had become so greedy that those who won this lottery only complained that the robe he provided was not thick enough. As a result, he discontinued this practice of having a great robe sewn at Hokkeji each year (*Chōmonshū,* 224).

This passage raises more questions than it answers. But Eison's words do allow for some educated guesses. First, it is clear from this passage that Eison did not expect Hokkeji nuns to supply great numbers of monks with robes. Rather, the fact that Eison ordered only one great robe from Hokkeji for his disciples per year suggests that these robes were precious commodities and that Eison did not obtain them free of charge. This line of reasoning allows for a second conjecture, namely, that certain nuns at Hokkeji or women in their employ may have sewn robes for profit. Given the many connections between Hokkeji nuns and ladies-in-waiting, many of whom were highly skilled weavers, it is not difficult to imagine that there were a number of expert garment makers among Hokkeji's ranks. This passage thus hints at one of the commercial skills that Hokkeji nuns may have offered members of the local lay and monastic communities. It is also suggestive of one of the means by which Hokkeji nuns may have maintained institutional and economic self-reliance.

Hokkeji as a Treasure House of Buddha Relics

Both the nuns of Hokkeji and the monks of Saidaiji had much to gain from Hokkeji's incorporation into the growing Ritsu movement. For the nuns, affiliation with the charismatic Eison and his increasingly popular movement promised to bring greater visibility to Hokkeji, its tradition of Kōmyō veneration, and its nuns' order. Eison also met the needs of Hokkeji nuns in more tangible ways, not only by aiding in the physical restoration of various buildings on the grounds of the convent but also by offering the nuns levels of ordination and training similar to that which he offered his male disciples.

For Eison and his disciples at Saidaiji, the project of restoring Hokkeji and cultivating its order of nuns was attractive for several reasons. First, as previously mentioned, Eison and his followers believed that the Japanese *sangha* would be neither complete nor authentic without the creation of an order of fully ordained *bikuni.* Their involvement in Hokkeji's restoration thus enabled them to work toward the creation of a *sangha* that better approximated their vision of continental Buddhism. Secondly, it is also possible to speculate that Eison's involvement with the creation of a *vinaya*-style nuns' order at Hokkeji had significant impact on his reception in elite social circles surrounding both the court and the warrior government. The nature of this influence is difficult to discern, but in examining Eison's interactions with members of the court and warrior government elite, it is clear that he had more female than male followers in these circles. It is true that invitations from powerful places like the court or the warrior government were always issued by men. But female devotees appear to have had a strong hand in these invitations, for when Eison made appearances in such sites of political power, he soon found himself surrounded by large numbers of elite women who wanted to receive ordination from him. This pattern may be observed both in records of his visits to the courts of the retired sovereigns Kameyama and Go-Fukakusa, in which he ordained large retinues of female consorts and ladies-in-waiting, and in the record of his trip to the Kantō, described earlier, in which he interacted closely with a large number of prominent warrior government wives and daughters. Many of these female patrons became involved in the social lives of Ritsu-affiliate convents as well, suggesting that some female patrons may have been drawn to Eison and his order specifically because his order offered them the opportunity to try their hand at monastic life, or at least to support the activities of convents. The degree to which convents in the Saidaiji network emphasized their connections to royal female personages, a topic to be treated at greater length in chapters 6 and 7, is also worth attention here. Eison must have been aware that Japan's most elite women would notice his work with convents, and especially his veneration of legendary court figures like Queen-Consort Kōmyō.

But looking past Eison's doctrinally driven motivations for establishing a nuns' order and beyond whatever social and political benefits may have resulted from his support of nuns and convents, it is clear that Hokkeji held yet another great attraction for Eison and his order. The nuns who had gathered at Hokkeji were well connected in the world of *shari shinkō*, or devotional practices centered on Buddha relics, and they had succeeded in producing a great number of relics.

Among the many eclectic practices that Eison integrated into his movement, relic veneration appears to have been especially close to his heart. Numerous reliquaries associated with Eison's movement, most of them quite ornate, are still held in the treasure houses of Saidaiji. Most celebrated is an iron reliquary Eison commissioned in the year 1284. As Naitō Sakae has explained, Eison is said to have enshrined in this beautifully crafted work over fifty-four hundred relics. The reliquary is recognized as the final product of Eison's long-standing interest in *shari shinkō*, for he had amassed these relics over the course of a long career (2004, 101).

What motivated Eison to collect so many relics? Insofar as Buddha relics had become, by the late twelfth century, prominent commodities in both court and monastic society, neither Eison's interest in acquiring these sacred objects nor his efforts to publicize his possession of them was extraordinary (Ruppert 2000, esp. 188–191). To possess Buddha relics was to bear the mark of authenticity: individuals and institutions that controlled great numbers of relics or particularly significant relics were regarded as having been ordained by the Buddha himself. This idea is readily visible in the many stories dating to the Kamakura period in which devoted practitioners are described as having received relics through *kantoku,* a specific kind of realization in which deities reward individuals of deep faith by manifesting treasures like Buddha relics before their eyes.

The idea that Buddha relics function as markers of legitimacy is also evident in medieval discourses on kingship. As Brian Ruppert's work has shown, royal ceremonies dating to the Heian and Kamakura periods drew on esoteric understandings of Buddha relics, and many sovereigns came to believe that the success of their rule—and especially their ability to maintain peace in the realm—was dependent upon their possession of and care for certain collections of Buddha relics. Some retired sovereigns even felt that the Buddha relics were synonymous with or perhaps even superior to the three royal regalia said to be held by the reigning *tennō* (Ruppert 2000, 90–91, 98, 168, 190–191, 209, 274–275; Tanaka T. 2006, 163–166).

But for Eison, amassing Buddha relics was not merely a matter of collecting tangible evidence that some greater force had sanctioned his religious movement. For while certain elites—the state, the *sangha,* and educated lay aristocrats—may have been concerned with these larger issues of legitimacy, there was another level on which Eison's possession of Buddha relics was of interest to an even broader audience: Eison's collection of relics heightened his appeal as a charismatic religious leader and especially as a figure capable of offering practical or worldly benefits *(genze riyaku)* to lay followers. Over the course of the Heian period, Shingon priests had developed elaborate theories identifying Buddha relics as wish-fulfilling jewels (*nyoishu* or *nyoi hōju;* Skt. *cintāmaṇi*), magical gems said to fulfill their possessors' every wish. Buddha relics thus came to be regarded as powerful objects capable of accomplishing a variety of feats ranging from the pacification of political territories and the protection of sovereign rule to rainmaking, the production of jewels and other riches, the lengthening of life spans, and the healing of illnesses (Ruppert 2000, 172–173, 363).[20] By the twelfth century, educated laypeople were well aware of the abundant supernatural powers ascribed to Buddha relics. Seeking out venues that would allow one to view and venerate Buddha relics thus became a common element of medieval religious practice.

This-worldly-oriented uses of Buddha relics are evident throughout Eison's ritual practices. Eison regularly performed a number of elaborate rituals that utilized relics and reliquaries, primarily as *honzon,* or primary images. Among the most significant of these rituals are the Godai Kokūzō hō (Rite for the Five Great Manifestations of Ākāśagarbha Bodhisattva), the Kinrinbucchō hō (Rite for the Golden Wheel Buddha Crown Bodhisattva [who is a manifestation of the syllable *bhrūṃ*]), and the Nyoihōringe hō (Rite for the Brilliant, Sparkling Wish-Fulfilling Jewel), all three of which drew on Shingon theories and doctrines specific to the Ono lineage.[21] In a careful study of Eison's ritual engagement with relics and reliquaries, Naitō Sakae demonstrates that Eison viewed Buddha relics as wish-fulfilling jewels capable of fulfilling the needs and desires of their possessors. His use of relics thus focused on the performance of elaborate, often lengthy rituals in which he would ask the relics to perform miraculous tasks (2004, 110).

This particular approach to relics and relic worship accords with one of the broader claims Eison frequently made in his interactions with lay followers: namely, that the many rituals he performed were directed not at his own salvation but at improving the world around him. According to his *Chōmonshū,* for example, Eison delivered one of his sermons to a crowd of 270 laypeople who had gathered at Saidaiji to pray for rain. He bestowed the eight pure precepts *(hassaikai)* on the group and led it in the incantation of Kannon *dhāraṇī* aimed at producing rainfall. Following his explanation of the rainmaking ritual, Eison told the crowd that the fundamental work of Buddhist priests was to employ expedient means aimed at benefiting laypeople. He also noted that his performance of the seven-day Nyoihōringe hō,[22] one of the annual relic ceremonies he carried out at Saidaiji, was similarly aimed at creating worldly benefits for sentient beings. He performed the ritual not to achieve birth in the Western Pure Land of Amida or in the Tuṣita Heaven, he said, but rather to create peace throughout the land and to benefit and comfort sentient beings (197).

This broader context allows for a better understanding of the role that Buddha relics played in Eison's appeal to lay followers. Access to and control over Buddha relics enabled Eison not only to make certain claims to authenticity as a religious figure but also to perform rituals aimed at protecting the state and comforting laypeople. His use of relics increased his visibility at all levels of society, from the heights of court and warrior government society to the margins of the Kinai countryside.

Given the important role that relic veneration played in the Saidaiji movement, it is hardly surprising that Saidaiji records reflect a sustained commitment on Eison's part to the development and promotion of Hokkeji relics. Both of the primary biographical narratives of Eison—the *Saidai chokushi Kōshō Bosatsu gyōjitsu nenpu* (Chronological record of the activities of the posthumously named Bodhisattva Kōshō [Eison] of Saidaiji, hereafter *Gyōjitsu nenpu*) and the *Kongō Busshi Eison kanjin gakushōki*—make numerous and extended references to the relics at Hokkeji and the nuns who care for them.[23] Moreover, the *Gyōjitsu nenpu* includes the text of a handful of separate documents, most of them authored by Eison, that focus on matters related to Hokkeji's production and maintenance of Buddha relics.

The *Gyōjitsu nenpu* reports, for example, that Eison made a pilgrimage to Hokkeji in order to worship relics held at the convent on the twenty-fifth day of the first month of Bun'ei 7 (1270). On this occasion, the text continues, the nuns at Hokkeji begged him to record the story of the karmic origins of Hokkeji's Buddha relics. In response to this request, Eison is said to have written out in his own hand the text of the *Hokkeji shari engi* (159).[24]

According to the *Hokkeji shari engi*, Hokkeji's relic collection had its origin in the religious practices of Jizen's teacher Kūnyo, or Takakura-dono. After introducing Kūnyo and establishing her worthiness as a recipient of Buddha relics, the text goes on to explain how she transformed a single relic into a handful:

> Once, Kūnyo; the [current] rector of Hokkeji, *bikuni* Jizen (originally she was the disciple of the *zenni* Kūnyo); the *bikuni* Shakunen; and others together made a pilgrimage to Shōdaiji [Tōshōdaiji], where they cloistered themselves in prayer to form good karmic bonds through the practice of Shaka *nenbutsu*. During that time, Kūnyo said, "I have one relic from Tōji that I received through *kantoku*. I will test it to determine whether it is authentic or forged; I wish to use it to purify my faith." She then placed the relic atop a rock, and grasping an iron hammer, she violently struck it three times. But it was firm and was not damaged. When she struck the relic a fifth time, however, it was crushed and became like tiny specks of dust. Each of those shattered pieces emitted a ray of light. At that time, Kūnyo grieved to the point of tears and felt remorseful. She collected the fine, shattered pieces, believing in and revering them single-mindedly. (143b–144a)[25]

The story begins on an inauspicious note: failing to accept the authenticity of her relic after three strikes of the hammer, Kūnyo continues to strike it until it finally gives way on the fifth blow. But from this tragedy, miraculous events soon emerge. Having collected the shattered bits of her precious relic, Kūnyo continues to venerate the dustlike particles as Buddha relics. Then, recognizing the virtue of Shakunen's mother, Kūnyo bestows upon her one of the tiny fragments left from her original Tōji relic: "After that, Shakunen's mother, Shū-Amidabutsu (she was a member of the *saikaishū*[26] and lived at Hokkeji), had the aspiration to request [a relic]. Kūnyo felt the steadfastness of the woman's sincere heart and gave her one piece of the fine, shattered relic. At first, because the piece was so fine that it was difficult to worship, the woman took black-colored paper and placed the relic inside it. Afterward, the fragments naturally and gradually increased in number" (143–144).

Over time, the *engi* continues, the relic first splintered by Kūnyo's hammer bore hundreds, and eventually thousands, of new relics (143b–144a). The *engi* goes on to describe a number of miraculous events that ensued in the meantime, the most noteworthy being the spontaneous appearance and multiplying of relics during a series of *vinaya* lectures Eison delivered at Hokkeji in the spring of Kenchō 3 (1251):

> And then, when Eison opened his book and wished to [continue the] lecture, one tiny relic appeared atop the book. On top of that, relics manifested

> themselves everywhere in the center of the enclosure and atop the desk. They put the relics in a jar and stored them there at Hokkeji. This was at the very beginning. After that, it is said that the relics naturally divided and that their number doubled by the day. It is quite impossible to describe these miraculous transformations and auspicious signs using brush and ink. When people prayed with firm faith, the relics arose on their own, like a mist, from within the jar, reached the place where people were sincerely and joyfully praying, and then appeared before their eyes like grains of sand. As a result of this, clerics and laypeople alike bowed their heads in devotion. Many relics were given away and distributed throughout the capital and provincial areas. (143b–144a)

Of particular interest here is the degree to which the relics at Hokkeji are described as having attracted widespread attention. As we saw in chapter 1, Hokkeji residents used *junreiki* and *engi* literature to popularize the convent as a pilgrimage destination. Eison's biography states that the nuns begged him to write the *Hokkeji shari engi* out for them, a detail that suggests rather clearly that they were interested in publicizing as widely as possible the particulars of their miraculous relic collection.[27] This interest in popularizing the convent's Buddha relics fits well within the context of pilgrimage practices, since stories about the miraculous relics at Hokkeji would have even further augmented the convent's appeal as a pilgrimage site. The last detail mentioned in the excerpt above, namely, that many of the relics at Hokkeji were distributed to devotees far and near, suggests that pilgrims visiting Hokkeji may have visited the convent with the expressed hope of receiving their own relic.

Eison's biographical narratives indicate that he monitored the Hokkeji relics with great interest. According to the *Gyōjitsu nenpu,* Eison made another trip to Hokkeji to venerate the convent's relics on the fourth day of the tenth month of Kenji 1 (1275), five years after he had recorded the *Hokkeji shari engi.* On this occasion, he also performed the important task of determining the number of relics held at the convent, apparently in response to the nuns' concern that there was something amiss about the count carried out during the previous year.[28] To determine the exact number, Eison counted the relics numerous times. He made a record of his calculations, which resulted in a count of 2,063 relics, 500 of which were "large grains" and 1,563 of which were "small grains" (167).

Six years later, Eison visited Hokkeji for yet another counting of the relics there. On this occasion, a new shrine had been built for the relics, and Eison helped move the relics from their previous holding place into this new shrine. In the process of installing the relics in their new home, Eison counted them several times. As he had previously, Eison composed a separate document in which he recorded the details of his accounting. Having counted the relics several times over, he determined that there were, in Kōan 4 (1281), only 2,040 relics. In the document, he went on to say that while there had been some confusion over why the counts were resulting in different numbers at different times, it was not the case that there had been some kind of mistake in the counting process. Instead, he said, it was clear that the relics simply appeared and disappeared according to the time and that their number did not remain constant (178).

Attention to other entries about Hokkeji relics found in Eison's biographical narratives suggests that Hokkeji's abundant relics were sometimes used at other Ritsu temples. The clearest example is one mentioned in the *Gyōjitsu nenpu.* Here, an entry for the first day of Shōō 3 (1290) reports that Eison visited Kairyūōji on this date in order to install 37 relics donated from Hokkeji's collection within Kairyūōji's new golden pagoda. According to the entry, these relics were enshrined there in order to offer the temple protection. As one might expect, Eison recorded the details of this event in a separate document, the text of which is included in the *Gyōjitsu nenpu.* In this record, Eison explained that the relics at Hokkeji were counted again at this time. After 37 relics were counted out and distributed to Kairyūōji, 2,020 remained in Hokkeji's possession, meaning that the convent had held 2,057 relics before donating 37 to Kairyūōji. Because only 2,040 had been counted in Kōan 4 (1281), this new count revealed, Eison pointed out, an increase of 17 (196).

Another, more ambiguous reference to the practice of using Hokkeji's relics at other Ritsu temples can be found in Eison's autobiography, the *Kanjin gakushōki.* According to this account, on the sixth day of the seventh month of Bun'ei 8 (1271), Eison prepared for a seven-day relics offering by placing on a single altar all of the Buddha relics held within the Saidaiji complex, together with the two-thousand-odd relics that had miraculously appeared at Hokkeji. On the day of the service known as the *kechien* day (most likely referring to a day on which laypeople were invited to observe the ceremony as a means of creating good merit), the entry continues, the nuns from the Hokkeji order attended the ceremony, and yet another count of the Hokkeji relics was performed. Although the details of the episode are imprecise, it appears that Eison returned Hokkeji's relics soon after completing the ceremony (*KJGSK* 1977, 37). In other words, this installation of Hokkeji relics at Saidaiji was only temporary.

These entries both suggest that Eison and other Ritsu priests viewed the Hokkeji relics as important sources of ritual and protective power. The entries also indicate that unlike other branch temples, Hokkeji supplied relics to other institutions within the Saidaiji network, sometimes temporarily and sometimes on a long-term basis. Given the central role that Buddha relics played in the performance of popular Ritsu ceremonies, the significance of Hokkeji's role as a fecund source of Buddha relics cannot be overemphasized. Hokkeji's relics tradition enabled the convent to occupy important political and symbolic roles within the Ritsu network.

What is the significance of the fact that the Ritsu temple most closely associated with Buddha relics was Hokkeji, the movement's primary temple for women? What, if any, role did gendered understandings of relics and relic worship play in the success of Hokkeji's relics tradition? Contemporaneous sources suggest that within the broader culture of Heian and

Kamakura Japan, at least some women were perceived as having special roles as the bearers and guardians of Buddha relics. But what exactly were these special roles, and how were they constructed?

The question of how women and female sexuality were understood in traditions surrounding the Buddha relics can be approached from at least two perspectives: First, one might examine the ways in which relics were discussed on an abstract or symbolic level, in literature of various kinds. Secondly, one might consider the ways in which specific social practices surrounding the veneration of relics incorporated nuns and female devotees.

Much work has already been done on the first level. Ruppert has explored how Buddha relics and wish-fulfilling jewels operated as signifiers of female sexuality, both in Buddhist narratives across Asia and in Japanese literature dating to the Heian and Kamakura periods. Textual representations of women's relationship to Buddha relics can be divided into three categories: (1) Stories that depict women as having the ability to manifest Buddha relics spontaneously. These narratives tend to build on continental Buddha tale collections and suggest, however obliquely, connections between the fertility of the female body and the production of Buddha relics. (2) Narratives that portray women as the bearers and protectors of Buddha relics. The most celebrated version of this narrative is that found in the Devadatta chapter of the *Lotus Sutra,* in which the daughter of the dragon king achieves enlightenment following her presentation of a rare jewel to the Buddha. Given long-standing associations between the wish-fulfilling jewel and Buddha relics, the rare jewel here, typically identified as a wish-fulfilling jewel, could also be identified as a Buddha relic. As Ruppert explains, the dragon girl was understood not merely as a bearer of jewels or relics but also as their guardian. This association stems from the widespread notion, seen throughout East Asian Buddhist literature, that dragons serve as the protectors of Buddhist treasures. (3) Narratives that invoke the motif of the "Jade Maiden" (Gyokujo or Gyokunyo) in discussions of women's relationship to Buddha relics. The Jade Maiden is usually identified with Nyoirin Kannon, a manifestation of Kannon long associated with the wish-fulfilling jewel. In esoteric Buddhist sources from both China and Japan, the Jade Maiden is often described as a beautiful woman who uses her sexual appeal to guide men toward salvation (2000, esp. 197–214).[29] Although few stories linking women to Buddha relics focus on associations between women's bodies and sexual desire, this second aspect of the Jade Maiden motif, namely, that which identifies women associated with relics as imbued with spiritual authority that allows them to offer guidance to men and even Buddhist priests, is certainly present in a number of narratives linking women and Buddha relics.

How and to what degree did these associations manifest themselves in social practice? Ruppert has also done extensive work in this area. In particular, he emphasizes the role of court women, especially those of royal and Fujiwara lineage, in the creation and promotion of relic veneration practices at court.[30] In a close study of court diaries, he demonstrates that royal and Fujiwara women constructed relic veneration traditions that gave them visible roles as the guardians and managers of these Buddhist treasures. For Fujiwara women, he argues, this role was intimately linked to notions of lineage maintenance: in assuming the role of protecting and venerating the relic collections of their lineages, Ruppert argues, these women asserted themselves as the guardians of prized family treasures and were subsequently held in high regard by the male members of their lineages. Although male monks performed the relic ceremonies held at major monastic centers like Enryakuji, royal and Fujiwara women (especially *nyoin*) came to play increasingly dominant roles in the sponsorship and performance of these rites within the sphere of the court. Ruppert judges their roles to have been at least "as great" as those played by their male peers, and he suggests that in some areas women were regarded as having an even more dominant role than their male counterparts. After a Fujiwara chapel housing a large collection of Buddha relics burned down in 1174, it was the women of the lineage, Ruppert explains, who were trusted with the task of locating the relics in the ruins of the burned building. This "gendered division of ritual labor" confirms that the Kujō lineage of the Fujiwara held that women were to fulfill the "prominent role of protecting the stock of relics" (219–220).

Ruppert ultimately makes the case that royal and Fujiwara women were successful in creating for themselves roles of authority within the sphere of relic veneration not by emphasizing the ways in which relics had been gendered female but rather by "degendering" relic veneration. In particular, he demonstrates that royal and Fujiwara women emphasized relic veneration as a means of maintaining lineages, a concern that linked the interests of men and women bound through familial connections. Along these lines, he notes that Japanese narratives connecting women and relics tended to downplay associations that linked "female reproductive capacities with the fecundity symbolically associated with relics" (227–229).

But there is another sphere of social practice linking women and Buddha relics that Ruppert does not address: that of nonelite religious women who traveled the countryside bearing Buddha relics. There is some evidence that these women, many of whom presented themselves as Buddhist nuns, may have exploited symbolic connections between women and Buddha relics in noticeably different ways.

Consider, for example, the following anecdote from *Heikoki,* the diary of popular affairs minister Taira no Tsunetaka (1180–1255). According to an entry dated to 1240/12/14, Tsunetaka commissioned a priest called the Exalted Shibutsu (Shibutsu Shōnin) to perform on his behalf a seven-day *gyakushu,* or a predeath funeral rite aimed at saving him before his death. The ceremony, held in Kitayama on the northern outskirts of Kyoto, was open to the public and attracted a number of auditors. Among these funeral crashers was a young woman of humble background who appeared bearing relics in a small bag she wore around her neck. Delighted by her offer to grant him one of her relics, Tsunetaka listened as the woman told of a dream she had experienced that morning. In the dream, she said, she saw Tsunetaka in a lotus pond standing behind a dancing bodhisattva. She asked him for a lotus flower, but he replied that she needed to wash her head before taking a flower. Upon awakening, she interpreted this dream as meaning that she needed to take the tonsure before she could pursue enlightenment. Since awakening from the dream, she had been seeking out a priest who could give her the precepts, but she had yet to find anyone appropriate (Hongō K. 2004, 246–255).

The young woman and her faith captivated Tsunetaka, who showered her with hospitality and invited her to his home for an evening. The next day, she declared that she wanted to take vows as a world renouncer *(shukke).* Tsunetaka's retainers were unable to dissuade her, and Tsunetaka, saying that it would be a sin to prevent someone of such deep faith from taking the tonsure, ordered them to take her to Shibutsu Shōnin. She made her intentions clear to Shibutsu, confessed her transgressions, and took vows from him straightaway. Tsunetaka's diary says that the priest Shibutsu was himself so moved by the depth of this young woman's faith that he took off his own *kesa* and bestowed it upon her (246–255).

The anecdote is pertinent here, insofar as it confirms the suggestion in Japanese scholarship that associations between women and Buddha relics were also linked to the social practices and religious roles of *miko,* or spirit mediums (see Tanaka T. 2006, esp. 171–192; Abe 1987).[31] What is particularly interesting about this story is that the young woman, though not identified as a *miko,* serves the same social function that *miko* serve in so many contemporaneous stories of male practitioners seeking divine guidance. Much like the *miko* who deliver divine revelations to priests (Eison and Myōe, for example, are among the many priests who claimed that they received revelations through *miko* at critical points in their monastic careers), this young woman enters Tsunetaka's life at just the right point, offering him the divine guidance he has been seeking. She is not possessed by a deity, but she does tell him of a dream in which he appears in an efficacious light.[32] In this sense, her role as a conveyor of divine guidance—a role typically associated with *miko*—merges with images of the Jade Maiden, who is also deemed capable of offering divine guidance. Her role as a bearer and distributor of relics can also be viewed both as an extension of the mediating function of *miko,* who open channels between the human and divine realms, and as an extension of other, disparate discourses that identify certain women, such as the dragon daughter of the *Lotus,* as the bearers and protectors of Buddha relics.

Narratives describing the relics tradition at Hokkeji combine these various symbolic connotations and social models. Hokkeji nuns, too, appear to have exploited different aspects of their association with Buddhist relics in their relationships with different members of the Buddhist community. There is much evidence to suggest, for example, that historical practices linking *nyoin* with the stewardship of Buddha relics benefited both Hokkeji and Saidaiji. The most compelling evidence in this regard is found in the case of Muromachi-in (1228–1300). Numerous narratives dating to the thirteenth and fourteenth centuries state that Muromachi-in possessed a precious Buddha relic known as the Buddha Tooth Relic, said to have once been possessed by the Chinese master Daoxuan, a figure whom Ritsu priests held in the highest regard. They viewed Daoxuan as a patriarch of their tradition: not only did Eison and his disciples rely heavily on his *vinaya* commentaries, but they also venerated him as an individual, holding regular memorial services in his honor. Hokkeji nuns also held regular ceremonies in honor of Daoxuan. According to legendary accounts, it was through *kantoku* that Daoxuan first received the Buddha Tooth Relic that eventually came to be held by Muromachi-in (*Gyōjitsu nenpu,* 192).

Medieval records report that Muromachi-in received the prized Buddha Tooth Relic through a series of esoteric transmissions. Nearly all of the nine individuals said to have held the relic before Muromachi-in also held significant roles within their lineage, which combined royal and Fujiwara lines: (1) Shirakawa Tennō (1053–1129); (2) his lady-in-waiting Gion no Nyōgo (d.u.); (3) Toba Tennō (1103–1156); (4) his queen-consort Bifukumon-in (1117–1160, a Fujiwara who was named *nyoin* in 1149); (5) their daughter Hachijō-in (1137–1211, a princess named *nyoin* in 1161); (6) Fujiwara Shunzei no Kami (most likely a daughter of the poet Shunzei); (7) Retired Sovereign Go-Takakura (1179–1223, a prince named retired sovereign following his son's ascension as sovereign); (8) his consort Kita Shirakawa-in (1209–1283, a Fujiwara granted *nyoin* status in 1222); and (9) their daughter Ankamon-in (1209–1283, also a Fujiwara, named *nyoin* in 1224) (Hosokawa 1989a, 89–96).

Muromachi-in, who received the relic from Ankamon-in, was herself born a princess but received the title of *nyoin* at the young age of sixteen. Ankamon-in was one of the royal consorts of Muromachi-in's father, Go-Horikawa Tennō (1212–1234). She was also Muromachi-in's aunt, since Go-Horikawa and Ankamon-in were siblings. Muromachi-in was also related to the retired sovereign Go-Takakura and his consort Kita Shirakawa-in: they were her grandparents and the parents of Go-Horikawa and Ankamon-in. Above Go-Takakura in the lineage is Fujiwara Shunzei no Kami, whose identity is ambiguous, though the title is thought to refer to a daughter of the poet Shunzei. In the cases of Shunzei no Kami and Hachijō-in, one can infer connections with the Hokkeji nuns Kūnyo and Jizen, both of whom are said to have served in the court of the *nyoin* Hachijō-in and to have been close with Fujiwara no Shunzei and his son Teika. In this sense, then, the Buddha Tooth Relic embodied intimate links between Muromachi-in's own biological lineage and the court ties of Hokkeji's first nuns, Kūnyo and Jizen.

Muromachi-in's interest in protecting her biological lineage and her conviction that Hokkeji nuns were well positioned to offer the kind of protection she sought are visible in the *Hokke metsuzaiji nenjū gyōji,* a liturgical calendar used by Hokkeji nuns following the medieval revival of the convent. The document mentions that Hokkeji nuns had been commissioned to perform Kōmyō Shingon services on the death anniversaries of four royal figures in Muromachi-in's line: for her grandfather, the retired sovereign Takakura, on the fourteenth day of the fifth month; for her father, Go-Horikawa Tennō, on the sixth day of the eighth month; for her grandmother, the *nyoin* Kita Shirakawa-in, on the seventh day of the tenth month; and for her aunt, the *nyoin* Shikikenmon-in, on the second day of the first month. In the case of Shikikenmon-in's service, the *Hokke metsuzaiji nenjū gyōji* notes that the service was ordered by Muromachi-in. The donor's name is not specified in the other cases, but careful analysis of the document indicates that Muromachi-in had a hand in commissioning all four of these services. When the document is examined in its entirety, it is clear that the *only* major royal personages whose names are included in the annual liturgical calendar are the four mentioned above, all of whom are tied to Muromachi-in through familial relationships.[33] That Muromachi-in entrusted the performance of these memorial rites to Hokkeji nuns demonstrates not only that she was deeply committed to the protection of her lineage but also that she held Hokkeji nuns and their ritual services in high esteem.

Muromachi-in's high regard for the Hokkeji nuns' group is also evident in her decision to transmit the Buddha Tooth Relic outside the royal sphere. In Kōan 10 (1287), Muromachi-in bequeathed the prized relic to Eison. The decision was a major boon for the Ritsu group, which installed the Buddha Tooth Relic at Jōjūji (*Gyōjitsu nenpu,* 192). Eison's disciples are said to have treasured the relic to such a degree that they boldly refused a royal call for the Tooth Relic to be returned to court. Saidaiji documents report that Fushimi Tennō (1265–1317) issued a royal order following the death of Eison in 1290 asking for Muromachi-in's Tooth Relic to be removed from Jōjūji and installed at court. But Eison's foremost disciple, Ninshō, then acting as the primary leader of the Saidaiji group, strongly advised that the group refuse to return the relic. Ninshō argued that the relic should not leave the Ritsu temple Jōjūji, since it was the will of both Eison and Muromachi-in that the relic remain there (Hosokawa 1989a, 94–95).

Why, given her strong connections to Hokkeji, would Muromachi-in have transmitted the Buddha Tooth Relic to Eison rather than the nuns of Hokkeji? Since surviving documents do not address the issue, we can do little more than speculate. One of the more obvious answers might be that within the Saidaiji group, Hokkeji was understood as the source of—and not a recipient of—Buddha relics. Having such an extensive collection of its own, Hokkeji was hardly in need of an extra relic. Jōjūji, on the other hand, needed relics, as this institution is not known to have produced Buddha relics on its own. Perhaps it was in keeping with Hokkeji's perceived role as provider of Buddha relics that Muromachi-in, having aligned herself with Hokkeji, bestowed her family treasure on Eison. One could perhaps even make the case that she made this gift to Eison and Jōjūji *on behalf* of the Hokkeji group and that her gift can be understood within the broader context of Hokkeji's role of supplying Buddha relics to Saidaiji and its branch temples.

But regardless of how one interprets Muromachi-in's gift, two matters are clear. First, Muromachi-in understood her role as guardian of the Buddha Tooth Relic to be inseparable from the broader goal of protecting and serving her lineage. Both of these goals intersected at Hokkeji, where she commissioned numerous services for members of her lineage and found a home for the prized relic that represented her family line. Secondly, this case demonstrates one of the more tangible ways in which Eison and his Saidaiji group benefited from their ties with Hokkeji and its relics tradition. Given Muromachi-in's patronage of Hokkeji, it seems extremely likely that Hokkeji nuns facilitated her relationship with Eison. Without the intercession of Hokkeji nuns, it is unlikely that Eison would have received the Buddha Tooth Relic that he and his disciples cherished so deeply.

The case of Muromachi-in also demonstrates that both Hokkeji and Saidaiji benefited from associations between Buddha relics and the maintenance of elite lineages. But this face of relic veneration at Hokkeji was only one of many. There is much reason to believe that in their interactions with other members of the Buddhist community, Hokkeji nuns emphasized other aspects of their relics tradition, aspects that drew on gendered associations quite directly. (And thus here we see that while court women may have "degendered" the veneration of the relics, Hokkeji nuns drew on both gendered and degendered understandings of them.) At least two other sides to Hokkeji's relics tradition can be identified: first, at least some nuns at Hokkeji promoted themselves within monastic circles as *miko*-like figures capable of delivering divine messages. Secondly, to both monastic and lay audiences, Hokkeji nuns presented their relics tradition as one that was indeed about fecundity. Although surviving records do not indicate that the nuns used language that made overt associations between the relics and the fertility of the female body, narratives such as the *Hokkeji shari engi* do indeed emphasize the great generative power of the Hokkeji relics.

That Hokkeji nuns presented themselves as *miko*-like figures capable of transmitting divine messages is evident in a number of sources. The nun Shinnyo, for example, is famed for having conveyed to Eison in the year 1243 the details of a dream that confirmed the gods' approval of his project to restore the *vinaya*. Eison was delighted to hear of the dream and of Shinnyo's interpretation of it. He held her in high esteem from that point forward and appears to have viewed this revelation as an important affirmation of his movement (*KJGSK* 1977, 18–19; *KJGSK* 1999, 141–142). There are many other episodes mentioned within Hokkeji literature of Hokkeji nuns who deliver oracles and visions from Queen-Consort Kōmyō. Eison appears to have taken these revelations and visions quite seriously (*Hokkeji shari engi*, 144a; *HMJE*, 142a).

Evidence that Hokkeji nuns may have presented their relics tradition as an extension of their ability to transmit divine messages is suggested in the story of the priest Chōzen (1227–1307), who was affiliated with the temple Kōryūji. Chōzen was actively involved in relic veneration and is known to have written several documents in which he promotes his involvement in the veneration of Buddha relics. In one 1297 document, he tells the story of a relic of his that disappeared from his care and mysteriously appeared with rays of light shining forth from it in the relic collection of the Hokkeji nun Monshō (Hosokawa 1989a, 75–85).[34] The story parallels another narrative thread present in the *Hokke shari engi,* namely, a story in which Gyōgu, the brother of the nun Shakunen, demands that his mother, Shū-Amidabutsu, give him one of the relics she had received from Kūnyo. Because Gyōgu's spiritual capacity is not worthy of relic possession, the relic disappears from his reliquary and returns of its own accord to his mother's reliquary. When he notices that his relic has gone missing, he visits his mother and learns that it has manifested itself in her collection. She interprets this supernatural event as a sign of his inferior capacity and offers him guidance (144a). Chōzen's story, too, is one in which a relic spontaneously disappears from one location and manifests itself in the reliquary of a nun with profound spiritual capacity. In searching for the lost relic, the priest or practitioner in question arrives at the door of a nun who can offer both the kind of divine message that a *miko* might offer and the spiritual guidance that the Jade Maiden was believed to provide to struggling priests. Especially noteworthy in the case of Chōzen is the fact that he used these documents about relics in fund-raising appeals. This detail suggests that he believed his claims of affiliation with the Hokkeji relics tradition would attract patronage even as late as 1297 (Hosokawa 1989a, 75–85). The case of Chōzen thus suggests not only that Hokkeji nuns promoted their relics tradition to priests as an extension of their *miko*-like ability to offer spiritual guidance but also that the relics tradition at Hokkeji was of such broad appeal to laypeople that Chōzen believed his own association with Hokkeji relics would win him new patrons.

Outside Chōzen's writings, there is not a lot of documented evidence bearing witness to the broader appeal of Hokkeji's relics tradition. But the very fact that Hokkeji nuns entreated Eison to record the *Hokkeji shari engi* serves as a powerful indicator that the nuns were in fact promoting their relic collection as an attraction for ordinary laypeople and pilgrims. Some, as suggested earlier, may have hoped to obtain their own relics by visiting Hokkeji. But one can imagine that for most, the goal was simply to create good merit by viewing and venerating the relics. Close attention to the content of the *Hokkeji shari engi* suggests that for pilgrims and other lay folk, much of the appeal of the relics tradition at Hokkeji was based in the sheer number of relics held there and in the mysterious quality of their rapid multiplication. In a passage introduced earlier, the *engi* suggests that the relics grew in response to the faith of pilgrims and devotees: "When people prayed with firm faith, the relics arose on their own, like a mist, from within the jar, reached the place where people were sincerely and joyfully praying, and then appeared before their eyes like grains of sand. As a result of this, clerics and laypeople alike bowed their heads in devotion. Many relics were given away and distributed throughout the capital and provincial areas" (144a). The fact that numbers mattered is evident in the many documents offering official tallies of the number of relics at Hokkeji. Eison's involvement in those counts underscores his interest in monitoring Hokkeji relics, for their number ultimately reflected the success of the wider Ritsu group.

Hokkeji nuns did draw on aspects of relic veneration and protection that had been gendered female both in texts and in popular practices on the ground, especially in their interactions with ordinary lay devotees and members of the monastic community. They promoted themselves both as spiritual guides and as the guardians of a fecund source of Buddha relics. And, as we have seen, the Ritsu community gained much from the Hokkeji relics tradition. Not only did Ritsu monks use Hokkeji as a source of relics, they also stood to gain from the guidance and authenticity that Hokkeji nuns offered in connection with their relics, as well as from the popular appeal of stories and practices centered on the relic collection at Hokkeji.[35]

As demonstrated in this chapter, Hokkeji's place in Eison's order was not merely that of a token women's order created to meet certain doctrinal ideals. Yes, Eison believed that an authentic revival of the *vinaya* could not take place until an officially ordained order of nuns had been created. It is also true that he regarded the ordinations and training he carried out at Hokkeji as part of a larger project culminating in the establishment of the first genuine *vinaya*-style monastic order in Japan. But Hokkeji's role within the Saidaiji order clearly exceeded these modest doctrinal goals. As an institution headed by women with powerful court and warrior government ties, Hokkeji attracted elite patrons to the Saidaiji movement. And as an order that produced and cared for a vast store of Buddha relics, Hokkeji also contributed precious ritual and symbolic capital to the Saidaiji movement, capital that increased the Ritsu movement's claims to spiritual authority as well as its institutional visibility on all levels of society.

Hokkeji nuns also had a great deal to gain from interaction with Eison's group: not only did Eison offer Hokkeji nuns ordinations that were widely recognized as "official" in the eyes of the Dharma, but he also offered them serious doctrinal and ritual training. Official training and ordination gave Hokkeji nuns even more standing in the eyes of their donors and patrons. Moreover, association with Eison's movement—and especially with his charismatic person—gave the Hokkeji order increased visibility as a site of pilgrimage. Although Hokkeji nuns did show great interest in seeking advice and counsel from Eison, there is little evidence that Ritsu monks managed their day-to-day affairs. Hokkeji nuns appear to have enjoyed relative autonomy vis-à-vis Eison's group and to have gained nearly as much from their association with him as he and his disciples gained from their association with the women of Hokkeji.

5
Social and Economic Life at Hokkeji and Its Branch Convents

> Some [nuns] pushed through the mists of the eastern barbarians [*tōi*] to come [here]. Some endured the waves of the western seas to gather here [at Hokkeji]. Some abandoned the light indigo [robes worn] in the sovereign's quarters of the royal palace. Some forgot about the radiance of the moon of the royal family. Even the ladies and ladies-in-waiting of the high aristocracy carry hand water on their shoulders, and even beloved children of many fortunes and pleasures take single begging bowls and offer them up to the home of enlightenment. Even though the court ladies of high-ranking officials who are able to gain audience with the sovereign are refined, we do not consider them superior; even though unconnected folks of humble birth are coarse, we cannot disregard them as inferior. It is the same for all four *varṇāḥs* [Jpns. *shishō;* the four castes]: when they become home leavers [*shukke*], they all become sons of the Buddha [*shakushi*]. They are like the waters of many rivers, which come to share a single flavor [that of salt] when they enter the ocean.
>
> —Enkyō, *Hokke metsuzaiji engi*

WERE IT NOT FOR SUBTLE CLUES found in passages such as the one above, the *Hokke metsuzaiji engi* might leave readers with the impression that Hokkeji's medieval restoration was a rarefied event, a small-scale revival undertaken by a handful of elite women committed to the veneration of Queen-Consort Kōmyō.[1] Insofar as her primary goal was that of a hagiographer, *Hokke metsuzaiji engi* author Enkyō did not treat the institutional or social history of Hokkeji in any depth. Her concerns were twofold: first, she enumerated the noble and miraculous qualities of Kōmyō, and secondly, she explained how the nun-architects of Hokkeji's Kamakura-period revival succeeded in reviving and embodying Kōmyō's "original vow" *(hongan).* Because she focused on only a handful of individuals, her narrative of Hokkeji says almost nothing about the scale of the convent's Kamakura-period restoration. If anything, she tended to recount miraculous events in ways that suggest the privacy and intimacy of convent life. When she tells of the time when Zuikyō delivered an oracle from Kōmyō, for example, only three other nuns—Jizen, Shakunen, and Monkyōbō (aka Kinin)—are said to have been present. And when she describes the lives of Hokkeji nuns near the end of the *engi,* she compares her nun-contemporaries at Hokkeji to Queen-Consort Kōmyō's ladies-in-waiting: "Long ago, [Kōmyō's ladies-in-waiting-turned-nuns] decorated green banners here, offered poetry, and performed music in the queen-consort's deeply-recessed room [*hi no mado no uchi*]; now, in the residential rooms of the *vinaya* temple, they use the Mahāyāna and Hīnayāna sutras of the expedient and true teachings to enjoy themselves. Some, on rainy days and stormy evenings, go in front of the Buddha and pray that the Dharma will flourish and that sentient beings will receive merit [*kōbō rijō*]. Others, on frosty evenings, prostrate their bodies on the ground and repent for the obstructions caused by the sins of their infinite pasts" (143a).

In contrast to Enkyō's narrative, which portrays Hokkeji as an intimate, courtlike salon of elite women, outside sources dating to this same period indicate that by the height of its revival in the 1280s, Hokkeji had grown into a large-scale institution that housed hundreds of women. These same sources further suggest that the majority of Hokkeji's population was comprised of women with little or no exposure to the court and its culture. In the passage quoted at the beginning of the chapter, Enkyō makes an oblique reference to the diversity of Hokkeji's medieval population. Although this passage does not mention the size of the nuns' order, it does suggest that Hokkeji was home to women of varied social backgrounds. Enkyō draws the reader's attention to those women of high birth—to those with access to royalty and wealth—while describing other women with rather broad strokes, either as women from the eastern provinces (who, readers might assume, had connections to the warrior government in Kamakura) or simply as "unconnected folks of humble birth."

This second category likely included the majority of Hokkeji's medieval population, which was made up primarily of women who grew up outside the refined worlds of Kyoto and Kamakura. Enkyō did not discuss these women in great depth, perhaps because the details of their lives seemed irrelevant to her larger project of praising Hokkeji's founding nuns, or perhaps because she preferred a romantic view of Hokkeji that emphasized its ties to the elite world of the court. But her remarks here suggest, however subtly, that there was in fact a discourse of social integration in place at Hokkeji. Eison, too, hinted at the existence of such a discourse: in a 1262 letter to Hokkeji's rector, he commended the nuns' order for its social harmony: "I am happy," he wrote, "to hear that the nuns' assembly is working together in harmony, young and old, pursuing both scholarship and practice. This is especially outstanding" (*SEDS,* 410–411). Read in conjunction with Enkyō's words—and in light of knowledge about the social diversity of the nuns' order at Hokkeji in the mid-1200s—Eison's reference to the nuns' success in working together suggests that achieving and maintaining harmony among women of various classes and backgrounds was not an easy task.

Kūnyo, Jizen, and their immediate disciples may have spent the early years of their renunciant lives living in refined circumstances akin to those to which they had grown accustomed at court, but the demographics of the Hokkeji community changed dramatically as the convent's revival continued to gain momentum in conjunction with Eison's missionary activities. While the exact details of Saidaiji's involvement in the physical aspects of Hokkeji's restoration are not entirely clear, it is believed that the Saidaiji group helped Hokkeji nuns restore the buildings and grounds of the convent. These improvements, combined with the visibility that came through affiliation with Eison's charismatic movement, helped the convent grow by leaps and bounds. In 1245, when Hokkeji nuns first took ordinations from Eison, they were a small group of thirteen. But by the year 1280, hundreds of women—including *bikuni,* novices of various levels, and laywomen—were active at Hokkeji. Moreover, a number of new Ritsu convents emerged as Eison's movement continued to expand and to absorb new temples into its network. These new convents were configured as the branch convents of Hokkeji, which came to serve as a training ground for nuns active throughout Saidaiji's network of temples. In particular, it appears that women chosen to serve as rectors at Ritsu convents in other parts of Japan trained at Hokkeji before assuming their posts. By the end of the thirteenth century, Hokkeji was no longer a small pilgrimage site dedicated to the veneration of Queen-Consort Kōmyō: it had become a large-scale institution and was widely recognized as the center of the Ritsu nuns' order.

These changes meant that the rector (*chōrō;* sometimes translated as "abbot," "abbess," or "superintendent") position at the convent became one of considerable responsibility. By the year 1280, the rector of Hokkeji was in charge of a monastic community exceeding 250 women. Like her male counterparts at Ritsu monasteries, a rector at Hokkeji would have been in charge of all aspects of monastic life related to Buddhist training and teaching. She would have been responsible not only for the training and guidance of the scores of women under her tutelage but also for overseeing the temple's arduous ritual program, the details of which will be explored in the next chapter. Added to these responsibilities were more practical concerns, such as promoting social integration among the diverse groups of women who had gathered at Hokkeji, managing the temple's finances, and directing fund-raising efforts. As the stories of Hokkeji nuns and their rectors are pieced together, an alternative image of nunhood emerges. Against the common image of nuns invoked throughout Heian and Kamakura literature, in which nunhood is portrayed as a mode of retirement, historical materials related to Hokkeji's revival provide evidence of nuns who acted as religious professionals: as administrators, teachers, fund-raisers, and performers of ritual. Representing diverse backgrounds and age groups and interacting on a regular basis with large, often public groups of priests, patrons, and laypeople, the nuns at Hokkeji pursued not retirement but active engagement as practitioners of Buddhism.

This chapter has two aims: First, it will clarify, to the degree that sources permit, the social and economic conditions at Hokkeji during the height of its revival, from the 1260s through the 1280s. How was the Hokkeji community organized? What kind of women entered the convent and in what capacity? How did various members of the community interact with one another, and how did they support themselves financially? Second, it will examine the smaller convents affiliated with Hokkeji and analyze the nature of their relationships with Hokkeji. This in-depth look at Hokkeji and its branch convents will demonstrate the degree to which Hokkeji nuns succeeded creating a wide-reaching monastic institution that enabled women to pursue careers as religious professionals.

This model of the nun as a religious professional stands in stark contrast to the well-known images of nuns that emerge so frequently in the literature of premodern Japan. In Heian and Kamakura literature, the most visible model of nunhood is that of the woman who takes vows as a method of retiring from the household life. In Heian literature, women typically take vows after a certain age to devote themselves to spiritual preparation for death, while in Kamakura literature it is the *goke ama,* or "widow nun," who becomes most prominent. The ideal "widow nun" was the woman who took the tonsure following her husband's death as a way of displaying loyalty to his lineage.[2] In the case of Hokkeji's medieval revival, however, nuns were not focused simply on private rituals aimed at their own salvation or at the benefit of family members. Hokkeji nuns engaged in serious training and study and undertook a range of activities targeted at patrons, pilgrims, and other lay devotees. Living communally in a large-scale religious institution, these women undertook a lifestyle that had not been visible among women since the mid-ninth century.

Classes of Ordination within Eison's Order

Name registers provide considerable insight into the internal social organization of Hokkeji during the height of its revival. There are five surviving name registers of particular importance here. Four contain the names of women counted among the nuns' order at Hokkeji *(ama-shū meichō).* These registers, attached to *kekkaiki,* or records describing the temporary establishment of sacred space for the purpose of bestowing the precepts, date to the years 1249, 1259, 1265, and 1272. A fifth name register, the *Jubosatsukai deshi kyōmyō,* lists the disciples upon whom Eison had bestowed the bodhisattva precepts. The list, compiled in the year 1280, was stored in an image of Eison produced in honor of his eightieth birthday (Matsuo 1996, 78; Nara Rokudaiji taikan kankō kai 2001).

Most telling about these name registers is the fact that they categorize women according to the type of ordination they had received from Eison.[3] The registers indicate that the Hokkeji nuns' order contained the following suborders: the *bikuni-shū,* comprised of full-fledged nuns who had taken a complete set of precepts; the *shikishamana-shū* (sometimes *shikishamani-shū*),

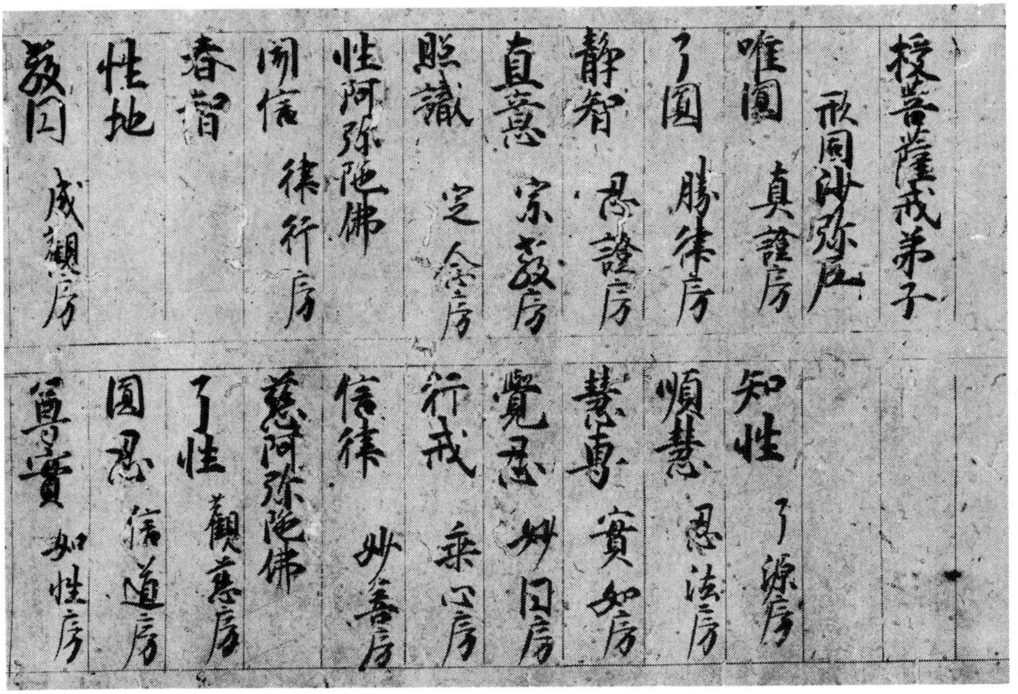

Selections from *Name Register of Disciples upon whom* [*Eison*] *Conferred the Bodhisattva Precepts (Jubosatsukai deshi kyōmyō),* 1280. Ink on paper. (Photograph by Nara National Museum, courtesy Saidaiji, Nara, Japan)

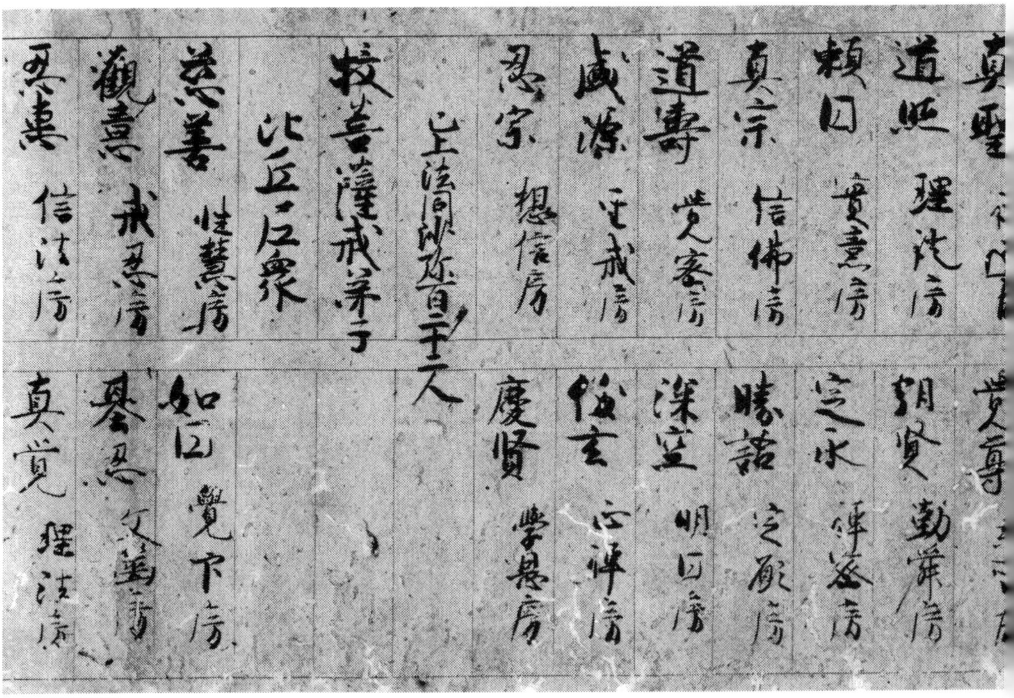

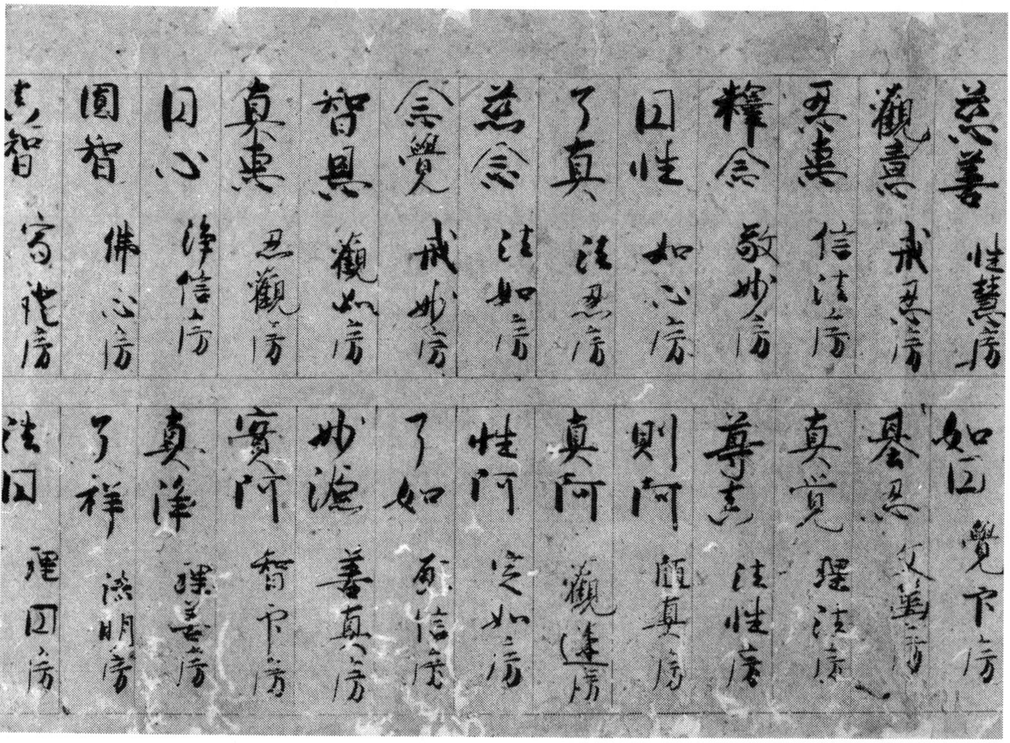

慈善 性慧房
観意 戒忍房
忍恵 信法房
禅念 敬妙房
円性 如心房
了真 法忍房
慈念 法如房
念覚 戒妙房
智具 観如房
真恵 忍観房
円心 浄信房
円智 仏心房
恵智 寂忍房

如円 覚了房
曇忍 [illegible]房
真覚 理法房
尊恵 法性房
則阿 願真房
真阿 観達房
性阿 定如房
了如 所信房
妙證 善真房
寂阿 智了房
真浄 理善房
了禅 浄明房
法円 理円房

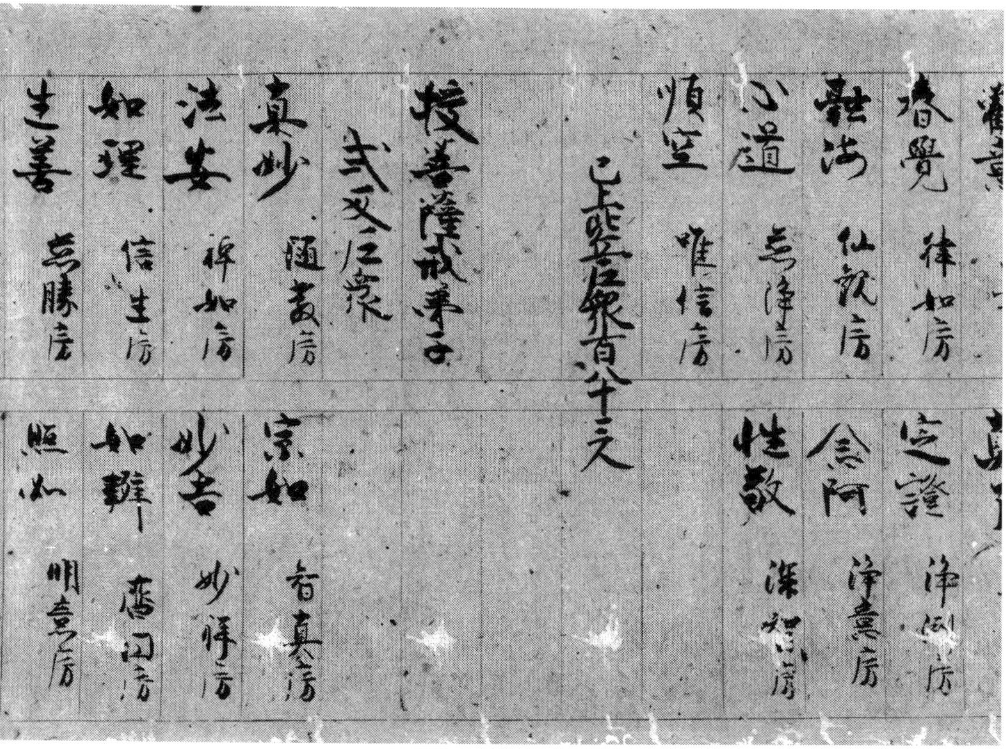

観意
春覚 律如房
融法 仙観房
心道 慈浄房
順空 唯信房
已上比丘衆百八十人

授菩薩戒弟子
式叉尼衆
真妙 随喜房
法妙 禅如房
如理 信生房
生善 恵勝房

真
定證 浄観房
念阿 浄意房
性敬 深智房
宗如 音真房
妙音 妙蓮房
如蓮 忍円房
照如 明意房

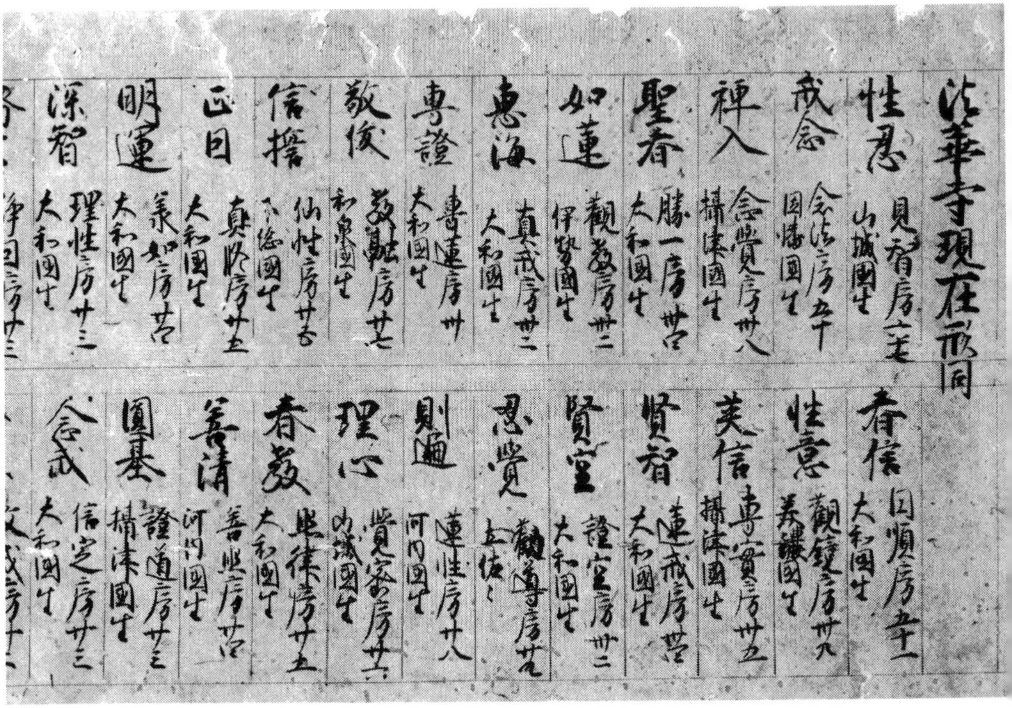

法華寺現在衆

性恩 見有房 六十七 山城国生
春信 因順房 五十一 大和国生
戒念 念法房 五十 因幡国生
性意 観鏡房 卅九 美濃国生
禅入 念覚房 卅八 摂津国生
英信 専実房 卅五 摂津国生
聖春 勝一房 卅四 大和国生
賢智 蓮戒房 卅四 大和国生
如蓮 観教房 卅二 伊勢国生
賢宣 證宣房 卅二 大和国生
恵海 真戒房 卅二 大和国生
恩覚 観尊房 廿九 土佐
専證 善蓮房 卅 大和国生
則遍 蓮性房 廿八 河内国生
教俊 教観房 廿七 和泉国生
理心 覚寂房 廿六 山城国生
信擇 仙性房 廿六 丹後国生
春教 明律房 廿五 大和国生
正円 真照房 廿五 大和国生
善清 善照房 廿四 河内国生
明蓮 義如房 廿四 大和国生
円基 證道房 廿三 摂津国生
深智 理性房 廿三 大和国生
念戒 信定房 廿三 大和国生
浄円房 廿三
文戒房 廿

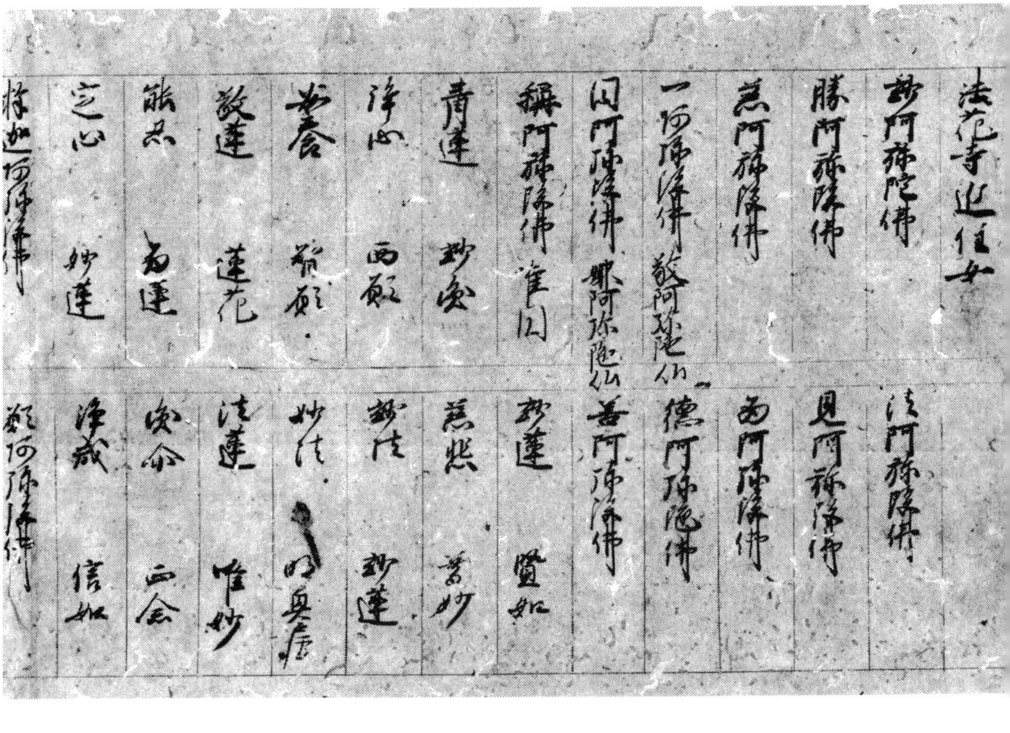

法花寺近住女

妙阿弥陀仏
法阿弥陀仏
勝阿弥陀仏
見阿弥陀仏
慈阿弥陀仏
西阿弥陀仏
一阿弥陀仏 教阿弥陀仏
徳阿弥陀仏
円阿弥陀仏 那阿弥陀仏
善阿弥陀仏
禅阿弥陀仏 唯心
妙蓮 賢如
善蓮 妙慶
慈照 善妙
浄心 西観
妙法 妙蓮
妙養 観願
妙法 明真
教蓮 蓮花
法蓮 唯妙
能忍 如蓮
慶命 西念
定心 妙蓮
浄戒 信如
修如阿弥陀仏
観阿弥陀仏

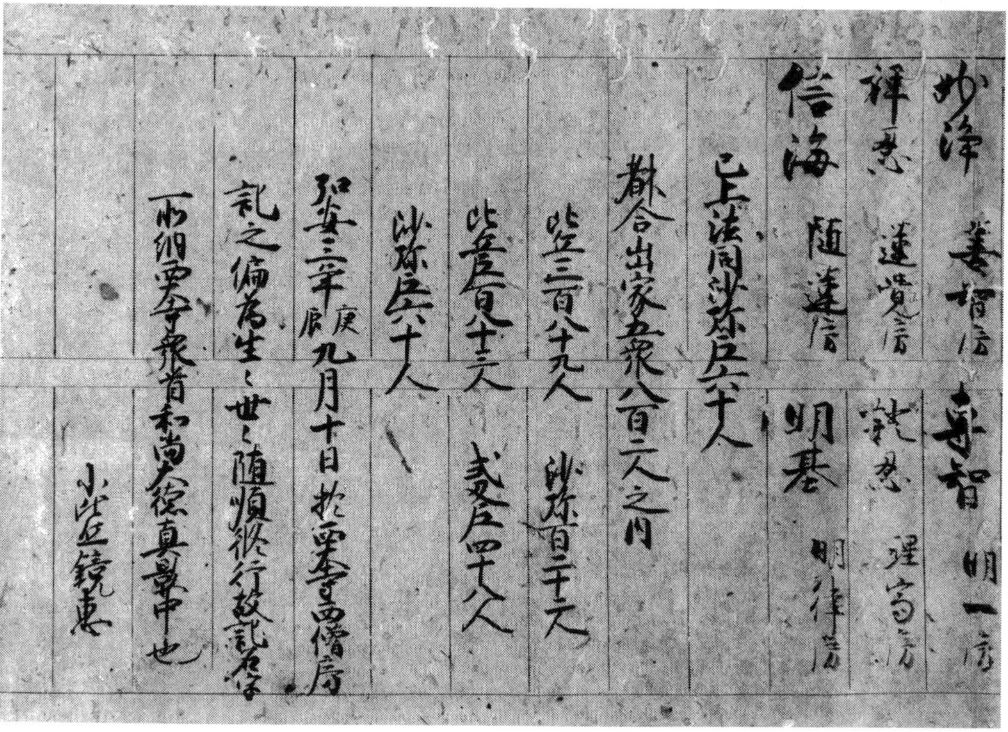

已上法同沙弥尼六十人
惣合出家衆八百二人之内
比丘三百八十九人　沙弥百二十人
比丘尼百八十人　式叉尼四十人
沙弥尼六十人
弘安三年庚辰
記之偏為生々世々随順修行故記名字
小比丘鏡恵

or probationary nuns; two groups of *shamini,* or novices, namely, *hōdō shamini,* full novices, or "novices in accordance with the Dharma," and *gyōdō shamini,* "female novices in outward form"; and, finally, an order of committed female lay devotees known as *gonjūnyo* (local laywomen, or "devout lay believers").

Suborders within the Ritsu monks' and nuns' orders followed the same logic, with one exception: the rank of *shikishamana,* a stage meant to screen novices for pregnancy before allowing them to take full precepts, existed only within the nuns' order. Standard *vinaya* literature speaks of a sevenfold *sangha* that includes *biku, bikuni,* probationary nuns, novice monks and nuns, and male and female laypeople. Although Eison also spoke of a sevenfold *sangha,* he created additional suborders, primarily by dividing both his male and female novice orders into "full novices" *(hōdō shami/ni)* and "novices in outward form" *(gyōdō shami/ni).* He also subdivided the lay order, distinguishing highly committed local lay followers who lived on the grounds of a Ritsu temple *(gonjū)* from more ordinary lay followers (*gonshi* or *gonji*) (Minowa 1996a, 78–81).[4]

Although the systems of ordination used by Eison and his disciples are not entirely clear, it is known that the rules governing the various suborders of the Ritsu *sangha* embody Eison's efforts to combine the traditional precepts of the *Four-Part Vinaya* with the bodhisattva precepts of the *Brahma Net Sutra.* All of Eison's disciples took the ten major bodhisattva precepts of the *Brahma Net Sutra,* as well as the three sets of pure precepts *(sanjujōkai),* in which ordinands promise to avert evil, to advance good, and to benefit sentient beings (see Groner 2005, 218). They also took, often in the same ceremonies, sets of traditional precepts from the *Four-Part Vinaya.* Because the bodhisattva precepts were widely available within Eison's group, and because the bodhisattva precepts made fewer distinctions among ordinands, it was the traditional precepts that tended to set one suborder apart from another (Minowa 1999, xiv–xv, 316–330, 372–381; 1996b).

This principle is noticeable even at the level of lay followers. The difference between *gonshi* and *gonjū,* for example, is that the *gonshi* took the five traditional lay precepts in addition to the bodhisattva ordination. They did not shave their heads or live on the grounds of Ritsu temples, but in taking the five lay precepts they distinguished themselves from the lay masses that took only the bodhisattva precepts from Eison. Above the level of the *gonshi* was that of the *gonjū.* These followers received the eight pure precepts, or *hassaikai,* of the traditional *vinayas.* Although most *vinayas* required that lay followers were to observe the eight pure precepts only six days per month, Eison required members of Ritsu *gonjū* orders, also known as the *saikai-shū,* to commit themselves to these precepts for life (Minowa 1999, 316–330).[5] Members of this group combined the attributes of laypeople and home leavers *(shukkesha):* they did not shave their heads, but they did take up residence on the grounds of Ritsu temples. As I will discuss below, this group was instrumental in providing Ritsu communities with both financial support and manual labor.

The next rank within the order was that of the *gyōdō shamini.* These "female novices in outward form" took the appearance of those who had taken the ten novice precepts of the traditional *vinayas*—that is, they shaved their heads and donned the robes of novices—but unlike full novices, they did not take the ten novice precepts of the traditional *vinayas.* Novices at the *gyōdō shamini* level took only the ten bodhisattva precepts. *Hōdō shamini,* by contrast, took the ten novice precepts of the traditional *vinayas* as well as the ten bodhisattva precepts. Once this step was complete, the women were given Buddhist names and were regarded as world renouncers rather than lay believers. The fact that they had taken the ten novice precepts of the traditional *vinayas* qualified *hōdō shamini* for ordination as *shikishamana* or *shikishamani.* At this stage of ordination, they would take the six laws (*liufashi,* Jpns. *roppōji*).[6] To advance to the rank of full *bikuni,* a nun would have to practice as a *shikishamana* for two years and then take the 348 vows of the *bikuni gusokukai* (Minowa 1999, xiv–xv, 316–330). The conditions that distinguished these various levels of ordination are outlined in table 1.

The *Bikuni* Order

Close attention to the particulars of these suborders sheds light on the nature of the social order at medieval Hokkeji. To begin, it is clear that the *bikuni-shū,* the female parallel of the *biku-shū,* made up the most elite

TABLE 1 Precepts and levels of commitment in the Hokkeji community

	Ten major bodhisattva precepts	Five lay precepts	Eight pure precepts	Tonsure	Temple residency	Novice precepts	Six laws	*Bikuni gusokukai*
gonshi	X	X						
gonjū (saikai-shū)	X		X		X			
gyōdō shamini	X			X	X			
hōdō shamini	X			X	X	X		
shikishamana	X			X	X	X	X	
bikuni	X			X	X	X	X	X

Sources: Ōishi 2004, 184–189; Matsuo 1996; Tanaka Minoru 1978c, 89.

stratum of nuns at Hokkeji. It was this group of women that headed the administration of the convent. In following with the guidelines of the *vinaya,* the convent's rector position, as well as all of the ritualist positions necessary for the performance of official *vinaya* ceremonies, were filled by members of the *bikuni* order.

Very little is known about the personal backgrounds of women who joined the Ritsu order. The *Jubosatsukai deshi kyōmyō,* which lists the names of 183 Ritsu *bikuni,* is an invaluable resource, but it provides no biographical data. And because it includes only the Buddhist names of those ordained, the list allows for no speculation based on surnames. For detailed knowledge on the *bikuni* order, we are thus left to cobble together information gleaned from a variety of other sources, including both documents internal to the Ritsu movement and literary works external to it. Perhaps the most logical place to start is with the *Hokke metsuzaiji engi,* written by Enkyō, who identifies herself as a sixty-four-year-old *bikuni* who has been a *shukke,* or "home leaver," for thirty-three years. Near the end of her compilation, Enkyō provides basic biographical data for the sixteen *bikuni* she regards as the founders of the Hokkeji nuns' order:

> Jizen Bikuni [also known as] Shōe-bō. After Hokkeji was restored for the second time, she was the first rector [*chōrō*]. As for her secular name, she was the lady-in-waiting [*nyōbō*] of Shunkamon. She was known as Shin'emon no kaunotono [New Commander of the Gate Guards].[7]
>
> Kinin Bikuni [also known as] Monkyō-bō. A pillar of the *vinaya* [*rippō tōryō*]. Died in *zazen samādhi* [meditation] at age seventy-two.
>
> Sokunin [Sokua, according to a correction made in the margins] Bikuni [also known as] Zuishin-bō. A pillar of the *vinaya* [*rippō tōryō*]. (Died [*shikyo*]).
>
> Shin'a Bikuni [also known as] Kanren-bō. Rector of the Kamakura temple Chisoku'in [Chisokuji, according to a correction made in the margins]. At age seventy, she attained *nenbutsu ōjō* on the sixth day of the sixth month of Einin 5 [1297].

Nyoen Bikuni [also known as] Kakuin-bō. Second rector of Hokkeji. Mother of the two *shōnin* [exalted ones, or celebrated priests] Jissō-bō and Chūdō-bō. Attained *nenbutsu ōjō.*

Shakunen Bikuni [also known as] Kyōmyō-bō. Third rector of Hokkeji. Attained *nenbutsu ōjō* in Bunei 6 [1269].

Jinen Bikuni [also known as] Hōnyo-bō. Fourth rector of Hokkeji. Died during the hour of the monkey on the twenty-ninth day of the fifth month of Einin 6 [1298] (after forty-eight summer retreats [i.e., having been a member of the *sangha* for forty-eight years]) while visualizing the Sanskrit letter "A" [*ajikan*]. She was eighty-six years old. The account of her *nenbutsu ōjō* is in another diary.[8]

Chion Bikuni [also known as] Kannyo-bō. Fifth rector of Hokkeji. On the eleventh day of the tenth month of Shōan 2 [1300], (she attained *nenbutsu ōjō*) at the age of seventy-six.

Myōgen Bikuni [also known as] Zenshin-bō. Sixth rector of Hokkeji. (On the thirtieth day of the third month of Kengen 1 [1302], she attained *nenbutsu ōjō* at the age of seventy-nine.)

Shin'e Bikuni [also known as] Ninkan-bō. Seventh rector of Hokkeji. A pillar of the *vinaya* [*rippō tōryō*]. (During the hour of the ram on the twenty-fifth day of the tenth month of Kagen 2 [1304], she attained *ōjō* while visualizing the Sanskrit letter "A" [*ajikan*] at the age of seventy-six.)

Shinjō Bikuni [also known as] Rizen-bō. Founder [*kaisan*] and rector of the Saga temple Kōdaiji. On the fifth day of the twelfth month of Shōan 1 [1299] (after forty-nine summer retreats), she attained *nenbutsu ōjō.* [A note in the margins offers the correction that she attained *ōjō* while visualizing the Sanskrit letter "A."] A pillar of the *vinaya* [*rippō tōryō*].

Enshin Bikuni [also known as] Jōshin-bō. Founder and rector of the temple Tōrinji in the northern capital [Heian-kyō or Kyoto]. Died [*shikyo*].

Ryōshō Bikuni [also known as] Hōmyō-bō. Founder and rector of the temple Dōmyōji in Kawachi Province. A pillar of the *vinaya* [*rippō tōryō*].

Shinchi Bikuni [also known as] Jakushō-bō. Died [*shikyo*] at age sixty-five (on the sixteenth day of the sixth month of Einin 2 [1294]).

Shōshō Bikuni [also known as] Ninkyō-bō. (Died [*shikyo*] on the eighth day of the second month of Shōan 3 [1301].) [A note in the margins offers a correction saying that she died while visualizing the Sanskrit letter "A" [*ajikan*].][9]

Myōpen Bikuni [also known as] Honkyō-bō. The eighth rector of Hokkeji. A pillar of the *vinaya* [*rippō tōryō*]. (In Einin 7 [1299], she had [completed] thirty-two summer retreats. At the age of eighty-four, she entered final nirvana during the hour of the snake on the nineteenth day of the tenth month of the first year of Genkō [1321].[10] This adds up to fifty-six years in the *sangha.*) (142b–143a)[11]

One trend visible in this list of women is that many were from families or groups that would have been able to provide them with a high level of education. Although there is no clear indication that high birth was required for ordination as a *bikuni,* many members of the *bikuni* order did come from elite or semi-elite families. Several had connections to the court or to priests affiliated with one of the great temples of the Nara capital. This tendency is clearest in the case of Jizen. As discussed in chapter 2, Jizen spent her young adulthood as a lady-in-waiting in the court of Her Highness Hachijō-in. A woman of considerable learning, she continued her postcourt education at Daigoji, where she studied under the direction of the nun Kūnyo. Jizen's education was important at Hokkeji: she corresponded with Eison regularly and hosted as guests a number of female court poets, including Abutsu-ni and Lady Nijō.

Sokua, the third woman on the list, was from a local elite family that managed the estates of Kōfukuji. She took her first set of precepts from Eison in the year 1244, in her father's residential quarters. On this occasion, recorded in Eison's autobiography, Sokua received the *saikai,* or eight pure precepts, from Eison. Sokua's father is given the Buddhist name Renshin-bō here, suggesting that he was also a home leaver. The level of his commitment to the monk's life is unknown, but the fact that Eison made a personal visit to his residence suggests both that he was a man of some standing and that he was an early patron of Eison's movement (*KJGSK* 1999, 158; Hosokawa 1999a, 29–30; 1999b, 167). The style of Sokua's first ordination stands in contrast to the many countryside ordinations in which Eison bestowed the precepts in large temples or outdoor spaces. She took the precepts in the comfort of her own home, an arrangement that evokes court models of patronage in which the elite called priests into their private quarters.

Nyoen, the fifth *bikuni* listed here, had been married to Tōdaiji scholar-priest Genkan. As noted in chapter 3, Nyoen had three sons—Enshō, Shōshu, and Kenshun—and a daughter, also named Enshō but spelled using a different character for "shō." Her first two sons went on to successful careers as Tōdaiji scholar-priests. Her daughter, Enshō, also pursued a monastic career, becoming a nun at Hokkeji after having lived an ordinary household life and giving birth to a daughter of her own. The male Enshō's biography, *Tōdaiji Enshō Shōnin gyōjō,* indicates that his sister's daughter Sonnyo also entered Hokkeji. After Jizen, Nyoen became the second rector of the revived Hokkeji. Her granddaughter Sonnyo was eventually selected as the rector of the Ritsu branch convent Tōrinji in Kyoto's Higashiyama district (Hosokawa 1989a, 129–131; 1997, 97). Although neither Nyoen nor Sokua was of aristocratic birth, they both hailed from privileged backgrounds. Nyoen was associated with the Minamoto, and scholars speculate that she was from a local warrior family in Yamato Province. Some have even identified her as having come from a family of military generals (Ōishi 1997, 193–195; Hosokawa 1999a, 37). Her proximity to the world of Tōdaiji scholar-priests—she was married to one and gave birth to two—also points to a certain set of advantages. The men in her life were extremely well educated and had far-reaching connections in the monastic world of the southern capital. And as is evident in her son's biography, the men in Nyoen's life shared their doctrinal knowledge with her, expending great effort on her education. One can imagine that she did the same for her daughter and granddaughter, thereby preparing them for successful careers as *bikuni.*

Another notable case among the women listed in the *Hokke metsuzaiji engi* is the *bikuni* Ryōshō, also known as Hōmyō-bō. Enkyō notes that Ryōshō was the first rector of Dōmyōji, an ancient temple in Kawachi Province that the Ritsu group restored and converted into a convent. Few details about Ryōshō's background can be found in surviving records, but careful study of Ryōshō's activities at Dōmyōji has allowed Robert Borgen to speculate that Ryōshō had an elite background similar to that of Jizen. His analysis is based in two observations: first, a postscript listing the names of patrons who contributed funds to one of Eison's woodblock printing projects indicates that Ryōshō had considerable wealth, as she is listed as having donated a sizeable sum to the project. Secondly, a cache of texts dating to the year 1286 found in a Dōmyōji statue of Prince Shōtoku attests to Ryōshō's great learning. Five of the texts included in the image and four of the five colophons added to the texts are written in Ryōshō's own hand, and, as Borgen observes, Ryōshō's practiced script, as well as her skill in Chinese, confirm her erudition (2007, 39–42).

Little is known about the backgrounds of the other *bikuni* included in Enkyō's list. But evidence about nuns who became active at Hokkeji in the late 1200s and early 1300s suggests that wellborn women continued to enter the *bikuni* order. Among the 183 *bikuni* whose names are listed in the *Jubosatsukai deshi kyōmyō,* there are at least 2 cases in which outside evidence identifies specific *bikuni* as elite women who had taken up residence at Hokkeji.

One example is found in the case of Jakuen-bō Son'e. Lady Nijō mentions Jakuen-bō in her memoir *Towazugatari.*[12] During a visit to Hokkeji in the year 1290, Nijō writes, it was Jakuen-bō who "talked to [her] about the relentless cycle of life and death, causing [her] to consider remaining in the cloister for a while" (trans. Brazell 1971, 204; *TG,* 191–192). In her brief summary of the encounter, Nijō also mentions that Jakuen-bō was the daughter of court minister Fujiwara no Fuyutada (Oonoimikado Fuyutada), a detail corroborated in the *Hokke metsuzaiji nenjū gyōji,* where an entry for the sixth day of the fourth month says that the Kōmyō Shingon is to be performed on this day annually for the benefit of Jakuen-bō's grandfather, the late inner palace minister *(naidaijin)* Fujiwara no Ietsugu (87a). Following a number of scholars, Hosokawa Ryōichi posits that Jakuen-bō was also the half-sister of Lady Nijō. According to this theory, the two women were born of different fathers to the same mother, Dainagon no Tenjichikako (d. 1259), a female court official who served in the court of Go-Fukakusa Tennō (1987, 137–140).

Hosokawa goes on to note that Jakuen-bō was orphaned in 1268 at the age of sixteen when her father passed away. He uses this information to suggest that Jakuen-bō entered Hokkeji when, having become an orphan, she found herself without a stable means of support. It may indeed have been the case that Jakuen-bō took up life as a nun at Hokkeji because she found herself struggling to survive in court circles without strong familial backing (140–141). But it is also plausible to imagine that she, like many of her peers, was an enthusiastic supporter of Eison's movement. Indeed,

Nijō's brief reference to Jakuen-bō in the *Towazugatari* presents her as a teacher of Buddhist doctrine whose words were so compelling that Nijō found herself tempted to join the order. Against Hosokawa's reading, then, it seems possible that Jakuen-bō, like other *bikuni* at Hokkeji, styled herself as a professional member of the Buddhist order. It is likely that her social status would have granted her access to a number of leadership positions at the convent. As a woman who had grown up in courtly circles, Jakuen-bō likely entered Hokkeji with a high level of education. Compared to women of lesser backgrounds, she would have been especially well poised to study Buddhist texts and to teach others.

Shingen Ryōshō-bō was another elite member of the *bikuni* order whose name appears in the *Jubosatsukai deshi kyōmyō* but not in the *Hokke metsuzaiji engi*. Additional information about Ryōshō-bō can be found in Hokkeji's liturgical calendar, the *Hokke metsuzaiji nenjū gyōji*. This text indicates that Hokkeji nuns were to perform the Kōmyō Shingon on the twenty-second day of the eighth month in honor of Ryōshō-bō's father, the Dewa Nyūdō, who was given the Buddhist name Dōga. In secular life, he had been known as the warrior government bureaucrat Nikaidō Yukifuji (1246–1302). Ryōshō-bō's father, Yukifuji, held a number of prominent positions over the course of his career, including head of the administrative headquarters *(mandokoro no shitsuji)*, commissioner of appeals *(osso bugyō)*, and head of the high court *(hikitsuke tōnin)*.[13] The details surrounding Ryōshō-bō's decision to become a *bikuni* are unknown, but her father's standing in Kamakura would have placed her into a class similar to that of Jakuen-bō. Both women serve as examples of noblewomen who trained as *bikuni* at Hokkeji during the latter decades of the thirteenth century.

Two details about Enkyō, the compiler of the *Hokke metsuzaiji engi*, are also worth consideration here. First, she writes in her colophon to the *Hokke metsuzaiji engi* that she, like many of the *bikuni* she describes in the list above, served as the founding rector of a new temple, which she refers to as Enkōji of the northern capital (Kyoto). It was at this new temple, she writes, that she finished her work on the *Hokke metsuzaiji engi*, which she compiled for the purpose of "fostering the Dharma and benefiting sentient beings" *(kōbō rijō)*. Little is known about this temple Enkōji, but a temple of the same name does appear in biographical accounts of the Shin-shū priest Zonkaku (1290–1373), who was the eldest son of Kakunyo. Zonkaku had eight children, and the first, a daughter named Mitsume (b. 1319), is said to have renounced the world at the age of seventeen. According to one account, Mitsume became the disciple of a *bikuni* named Yūgan and was given the Buddhist name Eizen. Another account says that she became the rector of Enkōji. Given the fact that her father, Zonkaku, was both a Kyoto native and a priest with considerable ties in the southern capital (he had studied at both Kōfukuji and Tōdaiji), it seems possible to suggest that the temple Eizen came to preside over may have in fact been the same Enkōji that Enkyō had founded in Kyoto. And in light of Zonkaku's ties to the Ritsu community, it also seems possible to speculate both that his daughter

Eizen may have taken her *bikuni* precepts with the Ritsu order and that this temple was still affiliated with the Ritsu sect during Eizen's tenure there.[14] There is no evidence that Enkyō and Eizen knew each other personally; indeed, Enkyō would have been ninety-seven years old at the time of Eizen's tonsure. But perhaps the *bikuni* Yūgan, who is listed as Eizen's teacher, was among Enkyō's disciples at Enkōji. Her teachings may have linked Eizen with the nuns' order at Hokkeji.

As for the situation at Hokkeji in the early fourteenth century, it is not known who was made rector following the 1321 death of Myōpen, the last rector *bikuni* included in Enkyō's list. A Genkō 2 (1332) 5/4 entry from the diary of Hanazono Tennō, *Hanazono Tennō shinki,* offers a clue, however.[15] According to this entry, Hanazono went to the Nakazono residence on this day, where he met in secret with the eldest daughter of his grandfather Go-Fukakusa. He identifies this aunt with the nuns' order at Hokkeji (Genkō 2 [1332] 5/4). A second document, the *Sanbōin teikeizu,* refers to this same royal woman as the "Rector of Hokkeji in the Southern Capital" (qtd. in Ōtsuka 1967a, 63).

Although it is not known why exactly Hanazono Tennō met with Go-Fukakusa's first daughter at the Nakazono residence, the two may have met to discuss doctrinal matters. Hanazono dedicated much of his life to the study of Buddhist doctrine, and he regularly sought counsel with Buddhist teachers and adepts representing a variety of schools and lineages.[16] Moreover, there is reason to believe that he may even have counted nuns among his teachers. In a passage in his diary dated Genkō 3 (1323) 9/2, Hanazono writes that he received a visit from the rector of the Nonomiya convent. One of Hanazono's aunts, another of Go-Fukakusa's daughters, is said to have founded this Rinzai Zen convent in Yamashiro (Ushiyama 1989). Known as Her Highness Eiyōmon-in (1272–1346), she received her title in 1294 and took Buddhist vows in 1304. Hanazono praises his visitor, who may have been the founding rector Eiyōmon-in, for her doctrinal knowledge: "This evening the rector of Nonomiya convent came and delivered teachings on the *nenbutsu.* Her explanations were not those of a woman, and I must say that she was an extremely learned and clever person! Surely the *nenbutsu* teaching is something that must be understood correctly. If there is a misunderstanding, one invites blame for having slandered the Dharma. [But] she expounds the true principles and never disparages the Dharma. One who is learning must give [her teaching] great consideration."[17] Hanazono's bias is visible here: he expects to find a woman's understanding of Buddhist doctrines inferior and is surprised by this rector's erudition. But he also acknowledges this nun's wisdom and recognizes her as a teacher from whom he can learn. Moreover, his characterization of her underscores the degree to which *bikuni* of the late thirteenth and early fourteenth centuries, especially those affiliated with the Ritsu and Zen schools, often dedicated themselves to serious doctrinal study.

Of the nearly two hundred women who had taken *bikuni* precepts from Eison, surviving documentary evidence provides biographical details for only a handful. Some of these women had clear ties to the court and warrior government—especially figures like Kūnyo, Jizen, Jakuen-bō, Ryōshō-bō, and the eldest daughter of Go-Fukakusa Tennō. Others were the daughters or wives of priests, or they hailed from powerful local warrior or land-management families. Insofar as the records that provide details of these women—temple documents and courtier diaries—tend to focus on those individuals with particular social or political influence, it is probably safe to assume that the most elite group at Hokkeji was made up of the women most visible in the documentary record. If this reasoning holds true, one might also speculate that the majority of the women in the nuns' order at Hokkeji—even the majority of the convent's *bikuni*—did not have close connections to the court, the warrior government, or particularly famous priests. Most were probably women from powerful local warrior and land-management families. Women whose parents were involved in local government, especially as land stewards or governors, would have had some ties to the cultural centers of Kyoto and Kamakura and would have been able to provide their daughters with a basic education. Women born to scholar-priests, though often impoverished, also had an advantage when it came to obtaining an education. The picture that begins to emerge, then, is that the *bikuni* order at Hokkeji, at least as it was structured from the mid-thirteenth through early fourteenth centuries, was by no means limited to women of aristocratic birth. If the *bikuni* order as a whole shared anything besides religious devotion, it was likely an interest in learning, something to which many of the *bikuni* would have had access long before training at Hokkeji.

Attention to the internal diversity of the *bikuni* order allows for a better understanding of Enkyō's subtle reference, in the *Hokke metsuzaiji engi*, to the ideal of social harmony. To the degree that it brought women from vastly different social backgrounds together in the name of "fostering the Dharma and benefiting sentient beings," Hokkeji was an unusual social experiment for its time. Women with experience at court may have interacted with priests or even nuns on a regular basis, and they were certainly used to having women of humbler backgrounds serve them as attendants and servants. But at medieval Hokkeji, hierarchies appear to have been more fluid, as evidenced by the fact that nonaristocratic women often held the rector position. Surely the social dynamics at work, even within the *bikuni* order, must have been complex, given the cultural differences among women from various class and regional backgrounds. Enkyō's invocation of the Buddhist ideal that members of the *sangha* leave social class behind and become equals as children of the Buddha speaks, ever so gently, to the challenges of social integration—challenges that must have been very real at Hokkeji.

The *Gyōdō Shamini* Order

The name registers mentioned earlier—the four included in the *Hokkeji kekkaiki* (Record of the sacred boundaries of the Lotus Temple), plus the

Jubosatsukai deshi kōmyō—indicate that in the early years of the revival, the Hokkeji community consisted primarily of women training for ordination as *bikuni*. In other words, during the early years of Hokkeji's revival, the majority of the convent's nuns were on the "*bikuni* track": they first took traditional novice precepts (as *hōdō shamini*) and then proceeded to advancement as *shikishamana* and *bikuni* by taking additional precepts. As illustrated in table 2, this began to change in the year 1259, after which the

TABLE 2 Nuns and laywomen at Hokkeji

Year	*Gonjūnyo* (*saikai-shū*)	*Gyōdō shamini*	Novice nuns (*hōdō shamini*)	Probationary nuns (*shikishamini*)	Fully ordained nuns (*bikuni*)	Total
1245			13			13
1247				11		11
1249		2	5	7	12	26
1259		21	14	2	27	64
1265		41	6	7	25	79
1272						119
1280	118 (all at Hokkeji)[a]	89 (56 at Hokkeji)[b]	30[c]	29[d]	31+? (183)[e]	>264[f]

Sources: Ōishi 2004, 184–189; Matsuo 1996; Tanaka Minoru 1978c, 89.
Note: Blank spaces indicate that numbers are unknown.

[a]The name register lists 204 *gonjūnyo* living near Hokkeji, but 86 are listed as deceased members, leaving a living group of 118 (Matsuo 1996, 104–105).

[b]A total of 140 *gyōdō shamini* are listed, but 51 are listed as deceased. Of the remaining 89 living at this time, 56 are listed as Hokkeji novices, 10 as Keishō-in novices, 7 as Dōmyōji novices, and 16 as Kōdaiji novices (Matsuo 1996, 100–101).

[c]The register lists a total of 60 *hōdō shamini* but indicates that 30 were deceased (Matsuo 1996, 96–97).

[d]The register lists a total of 48 *shikishamani* but indicates that 19 were deceased (Matsuo 1996, 96).

[e]The number 183 refers to the total number of women who had taken *bikuni* precepts from Eison before 1280. Some of the *bikuni* listed here may have been deceased at the time that the document was composed. Shakunen, for example, is listed as a member of the *bikuni* order in this 1280 document but is also described in the *Hokke metsuzaiji engi* as having passed away in the year 1269. (In the other categories, lists are split between deceased members and living members, but the *bikuni* order list is not divided into these categories.)

[f]This number is difficult to estimate, since we have no way of determining how many of the 183 *bikuni* included in the 1280 name register were living at this time and how many of the *bikuni* ordained by Eison living at this time were in residence at Hokkeji. But according to the name register *Saidaiji nishi sōbō zōei dōshin gōriki hōga chō*, 194 women at Hokkeji contributed money toward the building of a new residence for Eison in 1280. Of these 194 women, 146 are listed as members of the nuns' order, 30 as *saikai-shū*, and 18 as laywomen. Even if every member of the nuns' order contributed to this effort, that would mean the nuns' order was at least 145 in number. And if we were to assume that every probationary nun (29), full novice nun (30), and *gyōdō shamini* (56) was included in this number (146), that would still leave 31 *bikuni*. See Ōishi 2004, 332–333.

TABLE 3 Male and female disciples of Eison in 1280 (including the deceased)

	Men	Women
Fully ordained *biku/ni*	389	183
Novices[a]	122	108
Gyōdō shami/ni	280	140
Gonjūnan/nyo	121/159[b]	204

Sources: Ōishi 2004, 184–189; Matsuo 1996; Tanaka Minoru 1978c, 89.

[a] In the nuns' case, I include both novices *(shamini)* and probationary nuns *(hōdō shamini)* in this figure.

[b] There are two sets of numbers here because the 1280 *kyōmyō* (name register) found inside a statue of Eison lists 121 local laymen *(gonjūnan),* plus 38 *gyōja* and *jōnin* "outside the priests' order." If these groups are included, the total number comes to 159. Since these *gyōja* and *jōnin* are mentioned as people who live at Saidaiji, it is most likely the case that they were all men. (Women listed in the *kyōmyō* are typically listed as nuns or laywomen associated with or living at Hokkeji or other convents.)

number of *gyōdō shamini* in the order rose steadily. By the year 1265, over half of the Hokkeji nuns' order was composed of *gyōdō shamini,* or "female novices in outward form." This growth in the *gyōdō shamini* order mirrors a similar growth in the male order: as indicated in table 3, Eison had ordained some 280 *gyōdō shami* (novices in outward form) by the year 1280. *Gyōdō shamini* also came to populate several of the provincial convents headed by former Hokkeji *bikuni.* The *Jubosatsukai deshi kyōmyō* indicates that groups of *gyōdō shamini* were living at Keishō-in, Dōmyōji, and Kōdaiji in the year 1280. Although little is known about the first convent, the second two are both mentioned in Enkyō's *Hokke metsuzaiji engi:* she says that the *bikuni* Ryōshō-bō established a lineage at Dōmyōji in Kawachi and that it was the *bikuni* Shinjō who converted the temple Kōdaiji in Saga into a Ritsu convent. As the rectors of these institutions, Ryōshō and Shinjō would have taught and managed the *gyōdō shamini* orders in residence there.

Details about the *gyōdō shamini* in Eison's order come primarily from the previously introduced *Jubosatsukai deshi kyōmyō,* which dates to the year 1280. This document lists 140 *gyōdō shamini* in all. The first grouping contains only the names of 51 members of the *gyōdō shamini* order and no further information; these 51 *gyōdō shamini* may have been deceased.[18] The remaining 89 names, which presumably refer to members of the *gyōdō shamini* who were still active in the year 1280, are grouped into subcategories organized by convent. Four convents are included: Hokkeji, which is described as the home of 56 *gyōdō shamini;* Keishō-in, home to 10; Dōmyōji, home to 7; and Kōdaiji, home to 16. The register also provides information regarding the birthplaces and ages of these *gyōdō shamini.*

Because they identify the women's home provinces, these sublists allow us to observe that many members of the *gyōdō shamini* order came from distant places. In the case of Hokkeji, the majority of the women, as one might expect, are listed as having come from Hokkeji's own province of Yamato: 36 of Hokkeji's 56 *gyōdō shamini* were born in Yamato. But the other 20 women came from a diverse range of provinces, some quite remote. Three are from Yamashiro; 5 from nearby Settsu; 1 from neighboring Izumi; 1 each from the distant provinces of Inaba, Shimōsa, Tosa, Aki, and Bitchū; 2 from Kii; and 4 from Kawachi, the latter two places being rather close to Yamato. At Keishō-in, 5 women came from Settsu, the province in which Keishō-in was located. Two were from Kawachi, and the remaining 3 were from Izumo, Kii, and Suruga. Of these provinces, Suruga is the only one of significant distance. For the convent Dōmyōji in Kawachi Province, a total of 7 *gyōdō shamini* are listed, with 5 of them hailing from Kawachi, 1 from Tanba in the north, and another from Izumi in the south. Sixteen *gyōdō shamini* are listed as residents of Kōdaiji, a convent in Saga, an area in Yamashiro Province. Six of the women are listed as natives of Yamashiro, while the other 10 came from other provinces: 1 from Mino, 1 from Kawachi, 1 from Izumi, 1 from Ise, and 2 from Yamato. The final 3 all came from more distant provinces: one from Hōki to the south on the Japan Sea, 1 from Sanuki in northern Shikoku, and 1 from Iyo in southern Shikoku.

These *gyōdō shamini* sublists also include ages for each of the women listed. The range of the numbers is eleven to sixty-seven, the average being twenty-four.[19] A typical entry reads like this: "Shōnin Kenchi-bō, sixty-seven, born in Yamashiro Province." This woman, who is listed as a resident of Hokkeji, seems to be the oldest in the group. The women's names are for the most part given in order of age, starting with the eldest and ending with the youngest, suggesting that age may have been an important indicator of rank at the convent. But what is surprising is that there are few older *gyōdō shamini* at these convents: of the 89 *gyōdō shamini* living in the year 1280, only 2 were over the age of forty, and these were 2 women at Hokkeji aged fifty and sixty-seven. All of the other women were in their teens, twenties, and thirties, with the majority in their twenties. While most of the *gyōdō shamini* groups were comprised mostly of women in their twenties and thirties, Hokkeji's list includes a number of especially young women: an eleven-year-old, several fourteen- and fifteen-year-olds, and many other teenagers, for a total of over 20 women under the age of twenty (*Jubosatsukai deshi kyōmyō,* 100–101).

Based on what is known about their male counterparts' order, it is thought that *gyōdō shamini* assumed the appearance of full novice nuns, that is, that they shaved their heads and wore Buddhist robes *(kesa),* even though they had taken only the ten major bodhisattva precepts. Eison classified *gyōdō shamini* and their male counterparts as laypeople rather than home leavers. But we can imagine that ordinary people unfamiliar with the unusual ordination classifications of Eison's group would have viewed the women as home leavers, since they took on the appearance of female novices (Matsuo 1996, 88; Minowa 1999, 316–338).[20]

Placing Nonlocal Regional Elites in the Provinces

What do the regional affiliations of *gyōdō shamini* tell us about the nature and function of this suborder? Ōishi Masaaki and Matsuo Kenji, among others, have suggested that this rise in the number of *gyōdō shamini* at Hokkeji reflects the degree to which the convent's sudden growth from the 1250s onward was made possible through the incorporation of women from provincial management, warrior, and even farming families. But women brought into the Hokkeji network from provincial families did not necessarily enter convents in their home provinces. As noted above, at least 36 percent of the *gyōdō shamini* at Hokkeji had come to the convent from provinces outside Yamato, where the convent was located. In other words, at least a third of the *gyōdō shamini* at Hokkeji did not represent the incorporation of the local community but rather the incorporation of women from families that held regional power in areas outside Yamato. In the other three convents listed, the percentage of women from outside provinces fluctuates greatly: at Dōmyōji, only 28.5 percent of the *gyōdō shamini* were from outside provinces, but in the case of Keishō-in, this number jumps to 50 percent, and in the case of Kōdaiji, 75 percent of the *gyōdō shamini* were from outside provinces. In these cases, it seems clear that *gyōdō shamini* positions were not made widely available to locals as a way of integrating them into the community. To the contrary, these numbers suggest that the *gyōdō shamini* position was actually one of some privilege. These women had to have the freedom and means to leave their homes behind and to take up residence in religious communities that were often far from home.

But why would Ritsu institutions seek to install women from powerful regional families in convents outside their home provinces? Attention to the political situation on the ground at Saidaiji during this time provides some tentative answers. In his detailed analyses of the social dynamics in place at Saidaiji in the mid-Kamakura period, Ōishi has suggested that Eison worked to create a presence of "nonlocal" provincial elites at Saidaiji as a means of asserting control over the Saidaiji complex. This was necessary because prior to Eison's arrival at Saidaiji the temple was a small institution whose land had been occupied and managed by farmers and estate lords. Although their actual daily work was that of farming, land management, and tax collecting, these local men comprised what was known as the *jisō* order at Saidaiji. They had been assigned titles, as well as management duties, by the Kōfukuji priests who held the position of Saidaiji *bettō*. Eison was eventually granted the *bettō* position in the year 1278, but until that time he would have faced some struggle on the ground there, for while he was recognized as the rector of Saidaiji (Saidaiji *chōrō*) soon after his arrival there, this position was primarily religious and academic in nature. It was the *bettō* who had the power to manage the financial and political affairs of an institution.

Eison established at Saidaiji the Rikke, a priestly occupational group based on the study of the precepts. The group included Eison as rector, plus the suborders of *biku,* full novice monks, *gyōdō shami* (novices in outward form), and members of the *saikai-shū.* By 1278, the members of the Rikke had succeeded in asserting enough power over local *jisō* monks to win the *bettō* title for Eison. Eison's strategy, Ōishi (2004) suggests, was to incorporate into the Rikke numerous individuals from powerful nonlocal families. The inclusion of such men asserted that the Saidaiji complex did not belong to local families but was instead the center of a vast network of temples that stretched through many provinces. Viewed from this perspective, the *gyōdō shami* order served as a constant reminder of the regional breadth of Eison's movement and worked against local claims to the temple and its land.

Was there a local *jisō* order on the ground at Hokkeji against whom the nuns had to assert themselves? The documentary record provides no clues on this issue, but it is clear that in the case of Hokkeji and its branch convents, the interregional nature of the Ritsu network was always emphasized. This interregionality is evident on a number of fronts: not only did women from provinces outside Yamato go to Hokkeji for extensive training, some taking up long-term residence there, but nuns installed at small branch convents in the provinces maintained close communications with the order at Hokkeji, sometimes traveling long distances to participate in collaborative undertakings, such as precepts ordinations or fund-raising endeavors. The nature of Hokkeji's relationship with its branch convents will be explored in greater depth in the sections that follow. Important here is the observation that the Ritsu nuns' order, like its male counterpart, worked to integrate provincial families into its ranks while at the same time emphasizing the degree to which its institutional scope exceeded the local.

At Saidaiji, this infusion of "outsiderness" was accomplished at all levels of the Rikke, including the *biku* and novice suborders. Close attention to the provincial ties of men in the Saidaiji order reveals that the greatest influx of non-Yamato Rikke members came from areas in which Eison did the most traveling and teaching, and in particular from areas within the Kinai region and along the Tōkaidō, Tōsandō, Nankaidō, and Sanindō highways (Ōishi 2001, 2004). One can thus imagine that Eison attracted attention from provincial elites—members of warrior, local government, land-management, and powerful farming families—as he traveled through the countryside and that he encouraged those with interest in the monastic life to follow him back to Saidaiji, where they could begin monastic training. Similar patterns are visible at Hokkeji. Indeed, 86 percent of the convent's *gyōdō shamini* came to Hokkeji from the five provinces in the Kinai region. This number suggests that the Hokkeji order, like its male counterpart, was comprised of folks from elite and semi-elite provincial families who had decided to try monastic life after encountering Eison in the Kinai area, where he did most of his proselytizing work.

Another relevant observation that can be made from the *Jubosatsukai deshi kyōmyō* is that at regional temples, it appears to have been the case that the Rikke was comprised *only* of a rector, who was a *biku* or *bikuni,* and a small group of *gyōdō shami* or *gyōdō shamini.* This impression may reflect certain idiosyncrasies in the name register, but it would appear that, at least in the year 1280, *biku* and full novices focused their training at Saidaiji, while *bikuni,* probationary nuns, and full female novices took up residence at or near Hokkeji. Most likely this is because ordinations beyond the bodhisattva precepts had to take place on special platforms and would typically be bestowed only upon those undertaking a formal training program. Since one needed only the bodhisattva precepts to attain *gyōdō shami* or *gyōdō shamini* status, this status required much less commitment and could be attained with much greater ease.

In the male order, only 55 of 280 *gyōdō shami* were in residence at Saidaiji in the year 1280; the other 225, or 80 percent, were distributed among fifteen other temples in the countryside, including places like Daianji, Sairinji, Jōjūji, Kairyūōji, and Hannyaji. These numbers suggest that the *gyōdō shami* and *gyōdō shamini* orders were especially important at regional temples, where their presence provided a visible presence of "outsider" monks who linked the temple to Saidaiji. This order could be created quickly: it required only that its members receive bodhisattva precepts, which could be taken rather easily and without great preparation, as well as shave their heads and don Buddhist robes. In using *gyōdō shami* and *gyōdō shamini* to populate regional temples, rectors did not need to wait for monks or nuns to train at Saidaiji or Hokkeji and then return; they could instead create an order almost instantly.

The *Saikai-shū*

The *saikai-shū,* made up of *gonjūnan* and *gonjūnyo,* or men and women who "lived nearby," served as a powerful counterbalance to the *gyōdō shami* and *gyōdō shamini* orders. While the latter represented nonlocal groups at Hokkeji and Saidaiji, the former served to incorporate members of the local population into the Rikke. As explained earlier, members of Eison's *saikai-shū* maintained the appearance of laypeople but were to make a lifetime commitment to the eight pure precepts. They were also to live on temple precincts, a practice that distinguished them from the non-Rikke *jisō* groups, who typically maintained private households outside temple grounds (Ōishi 2004).

The social composition and function of the *saikai-shū* is somewhat elusive. According to Hosokawa, the *saikai-shū* was a group of menials who undertook various forms of undesirable work on behalf of Ritsu priests. *Saikai-shū* were created not only at Tōshōdaiji but at all of the major Ritsu centers in the Nara capital, including Saidaiji, Tōdaiji, and Kairyūōji. At Tōshōdaiji, the group was made up of local villagers *(muranin),* and Hosokawa speculates that the same was true of *saikai-shū* at other Ritsu institutions. He argues that the *saikai-shū* formed an underclass at Ritsu temples. While these men were granted a place in the temple community, they were not given the opportunity to advance through the priestly hierarchy

(1987, 11–24). Instead, they were entrusted to perform the work that full *biku* found defiling, namely, matters associated with money and with dead bodies. The late medieval flourishing of the Ritsu school, built on fund-raising campaigns and on the offering of funerary services to ordinary laypeople, was made possible through the work of the *saikai-shū*. Ritsu school *biku* performed the rituals associated with death rites and offered other ceremonies and services meant to attract donations, but the dirty work of handling corpses and collecting money, Hosokawa suggests, was carried out by the *saikai-shū*. He further speculates that much of the labor required for Ritsu projects—building and rebuilding temple structures, bridges, and the like—was also carried out by the *saikai-shū* (13–25).

Hosokawa argues that a *mibun*, or class, system in place at Ritsu temples enforced this division of labor. As evidence for the existence of such a system, he cites the 1347 document "Itemized Rules for the Kairyūōji Hassaikai-shū." Hosokawa points to one regulation in particular: the fifth item says that when the Rikke was bathing in the Hokkeji bath, members of the *saikai-shū* were forbidden to bathe with full priests *(sō)*. They were to wait until the priests had finished bathing before entering the bathhouse. This same set of regulations also mentions that members of the *saikai-shū* were not to entertain or to spend leisure time with members of the *jisō* or village communities associated with the temple. The list further contains an article that forbids members of the *saikai-shū* to leave temple grounds before sunrise or after sunset (qtd. in Hosokawa 1987, 11–12). These rules suggest that the Ritsu community wanted to ensure that members of the *saikai-shū* would remain allies of the Rikke and would not, through close relations with local families or with members of the *jisō* community, form local, anti-Rikke alliances.

These rules certainly do suggest that a rigid, and perhaps even oppressive, form of class regulation was in place at Kairyūōji during the mid-fourteenth century. Although Hosokawa argues that the function and structure of the *saikai-shū* was consistent among all Ritsu groups in the Kamakura period, details from the female *saikai-shū* at Hokkeji suggest that the class composition and social positionality of the group may have been more fluid at Hokkeji, or perhaps at all Ritsu temples, during the mid- and late thirteenth century.

Ōishi speculates that many who joined the *saikai-shū* at Hokkeji were local warrior-class and peasant women (2004, 332–333).[21] The inclusion of these groups would have made Hokkeji's *saikai-shū* demographically diverse: while women from peasant families would have had little education, those from warrior families often had considerable access to learning. And at least some, Ōishi points out, had expendable wealth: female members of the Hokkeji *saikai-shū* made numerous financial contributions to Saidaiji during the late 1200s. Donor records dating from 1261 to 1282 indicate that twenty-two women contributed parcels of land to the Saidaiji movement during these years. Thirteen—more than half—of these women are listed as members of the *saikai-shū* in the 1280 *Jubosatsukai deshi kyōmyō* (334).

Other records of donations made by Hokkeji nuns to various Ritsu fund-raising campaigns also indicate that members of the *saikai-shū* made regular and significant financial contributions to the Ritsu order. A particularly notable case is that of the *saikai-shū* member Hōmyō, who donated 10,100 *mon,* or copper coins (the equivalent of 10.1 *kan,* or 101 strings of cash), to a campaign aimed at printing one of Eison's commentaries on the *Brahma Net Sutra.*[22] Compared with those made by other monks and nuns for the same project, this donation was extremely large (Hosokawa 1989a, 133). Ōishi estimates that many of the women who came to live at Hokkeji as *saikai-shū* donated private funds to the Ritsu order upon taking up residence at the convent. He even posits that contributions made by the *saikai* and *gyōdō shamini* orders comprised the single most important financial base at Hokkeji: without the help of these women, Ōishi argues, the convent would not have had the financial means to stage a revival so large in scale (2004, 332–334).

Evidence of the *saikai-shū*'s financial power at Hokkeji seems to work against the notion that these women represented an underclass at the convent. But there might be another way to interpret the fact that the names of *saikai-shū* women appear so frequently in fund-raising records. Nagamura Makoto's work on Tōdaiji has shown that members of the *saikai-shū* order there were routinely placed in charge of fund-raising. He argues, in fact, that fund-raising was the primary duty of the *saikai-shū* at medieval Tōdaiji (1976, 54–77). Given the frequency with which their names appear in fund-raising records, it seems possible to suggest that the *saikai-shū* at Hokkeji may have been charged with similar duties. Work with money serves as one possible bridge between Hosokawa's view of the *saikai-shū* as an oppressed underclass and Ōishi's observation that members of the Hokkeji *saikai-shū* appear to have been women who enjoyed some degree of financial latitude. Perhaps the donations of at least some of these women represent funds that they had raised rather than personal resources. Still, even if the *saikai-shū* at Hokkeji was given the task of collecting money—a task that may have been viewed as inferior to the ritual work carried out by other members of the order—there is no direct evidence to suggest that its members prepared corpses or guarded burial sites, as did members of the *saikai-shū* at Tōshōdaiji.

There is also little evidence to suggest that rigid social boundaries separated the Hokkeji *saikai-shū* from members of the nuns' order. We know that at least several members of the *bikuni* order had in fact been members of the *saikai-shū* at one time or another: as mentioned earlier, Sokua, the third *bikuni* included in Enkyō's list of sixteen, is said to have first joined the Ritsu order by taking the *saikai* (pure precepts) from Eison in the year 1244. Her case thus provides at least one clear example of a woman who advanced from the *saikai-shū* to the *bikuni* track. Another detail suggesting that the social boundaries separating *bikuni* and *saikai-shū* were not strictly drawn is found in the *Hokkeji shari engi,* discussed at length in the last chapter. Among the narratives in this text is the story of Shakunen's mother, Shū-Amidabutsu, who is identified in the margins as a member of the *saikai-shū*. Like many members of the *saikai-shū*, Shū-Amidabutsu's Buddhist name has a "lay" sound to it: unlike conventional monastic names, which are composed of two Chinese characters, hers is simply a single Chinese character followed by the popular epithet "Amidabutsu" (Amitābha Buddha). But the *Hokkeji shari engi* suggests that Shū-Amidabutsu had close personal relationships with members of the *bikuni* order. Not only was her daughter a *bikuni* in the order, but the text also states that Shū-Amidabutsu received her first relics from the nun Kūnyo, who, as the teacher of Jizen, was arguably the most revered nun in the order. These two examples suggest that, at least at the beginning of the Hokkeji revival movement, members of the *saikai-shū* were not necessarily regarded as the social inferiors of the *bikuni* order. When speaking of general trends, it is probably safe to assume that members of the *bikuni* and novice orders did tend to come from more elite families than did members of the *saikai-shū*. But the boundaries between these groups appear to have remained rather fluid, at least at late-thirteenth-century Hokkeji. Hokkeji materials do not suggest the kind of rigid social segregation seen in the "Itemized Rules for the Kairyūōji Hassaikai-shū."

Social Class and Mobility in the Nuns' Order

One question that emerges when the various suborders at Hokkeji are compared is the degree to which women were free to choose their ordination levels or to move across or through different suborders. It is clear that nuns on the "*bikuni* track" were marked by the stages of full noviceship, probationary noviceship, and finally *bikuni*-hood. But were the other ranks in the order—specifically those of *gonjūnyo* and *gyōdō shamini*—commonly perceived as part of the progression to *bikuni* ordination, or were they viewed as terminal ranks that did not allow for greater advancement? And were women of certain classes or regional affiliations bound to specific orders?[23]

None of these questions can be answered with full certitude, but several observations are possible. To begin, it does appear to have been the case that, on the whole, the level of ordination attainable by a given woman reflected her class and regional background. Women from elite backgrounds tended to achieve *bikuni* status more readily than did those from more humble backgrounds. Similarly, Hosokawa and Ōishi both suggest that the *gyōdō shamini* came from more prestigious backgrounds than did members of the *gonjūnyo* order or *saikai-shū*. If *gyōdō shamini* did indeed come from more elite families, then it may be possible to speculate that as a general rule *gyōdō shamini* were from the land-managerial and warrior classes, while members of the *saikai-shū* tended to be from the homes of villagers and farmers. Hosokawa's analysis of the men's *saikai-shū* would support this possibility, as would the fact that many of the *gyōdō shamini* listed in the 1280 name register are shown as having come from remote provinces rather than from local areas. This view also follows the general principle that the *gyōdō shamini* order brought a sense of outsiderness to the nuns' order, whereas the *saikai-shū* served as a link between Hokkeji and its local community (Ōishi 1997, 187).

That said, it does not appear to have been the case that women who had the social background required to seek ordination as *bikuni* necessarily pursued that status. As mentioned earlier, there are several known cases of women who attained the status of *bikuni* who began their religious careers as members of the *saikai-shū*. Similar examples can be found in the case of the *gyōdō shamini* order as well. In its record of Eison's 1249 ordinations at Hokkeji, the *Hokkeji kekkaiki* indicates that Sonnyo, the woman who eventually became the rector of the convent Tōrinji in Kyoto, was ordained as a *gyōdō shamini* in the same ceremony that rendered both her grandmother, Nyoen, and her mother, Enshō, *bikuni*.[24] Recent scholarship has also made it possible to suggest that the great poet Abutsu-ni, who had served in the courts of royal women and who eventually married Fujiwara no Tameie, received conferral either as a *gyōdō shamini* or as a member of the *saikai-shū* during her time at Hokkeji, likely around the year 1252. Matsumoto Yasushi has identified Abutsu-ni's ordination name as Ji-Amidabutsu, and this name appears in both the *gyōdō shamini-shū* and *saikai-shū* registers in the 1280 *Jubosatsukai deshi kyōmyō* (Hosokawa 1989a, 168; *Jubosatsukai deshi kyōmyō*, 100, 104–105). Names comprised of a single Chinese character followed by "Amidabutsu" are more common in the *saikai-shū* than among members of the *gyōdō shamini* order, but this particular name does appear near the top of the list of *gyōdō shamini* included in the *Jubosatsukai deshi kyōmyō*, suggesting that this particular "Ji-Amidabutsu" was ordained as a *gyōdō shamini* before the order became more regularized and gave all of its ordinands more formal Buddhist names.

Both of these cases make it clear that women who had the social and educational background required for access to the stages of ordination leading to *bikuni* sometimes chose ordination as *gyōdō shamini* or *gonjūnyo* instead. In Sonnyo's case, it may have been her relatively young age that prompted her to seek ordination as a *gyōdō shamini* rather than a *hōdō shamini* in 1249. She would have been about twenty-eight years old in 1249. Although this age is well beyond that required for ordination as a full novice, it is possible that Sonnyo was still unsure of whether she wanted to pursue married life before making a full commitment to the life of a nun. Both her mother and grandmother had married and raised children before entering Hokkeji. It is possible that Sonnyo first sought ordination as a *gyōdō shamini* to test the waters of monastic life before making a more binding commitment. This same theory holds in the case of Abutsu-ni, for it is known that she left Hokkeji for employment in Tameie's household, an opportunity that did, despite her advanced age, lead to marriage. This view of the *gyōdō shamini* order might also explain why the average age of women in the order was so low: as related earlier, over twenty of the women in the *gyōdō shamini* order at Hokkeji were under the age of twenty years.

For women of a certain birth and education, then, ordination as *gyōdō shamini* and *gonjūnyo* offered the opportunity to give monastic life a trial run before making a less alterable commitment. Women of this category who discovered following these ordinations that they did want to become home leavers could go on to seek ordination as full novices, probationary novices, and finally *bikuni,* as did Sokua and Sonnyo. But it is likely that women who did not meet certain requirements of birth or education would not have been permitted to advance through the ranks in the same manner. Although such social barriers are never made explicit in Ritsu texts, which tend to speak instead of the great egalitarianism of the Buddhist order, Hosokawa finds evidence of a glass ceiling in passages describing the early years of the Hokkeji movement. Pointing to the fact that thirteen nuns took the novice precepts in 1245, while only twelve were granted the full *bikuni* precepts in 1249, he speculates that the woman who did not receive the full precepts in 1249 was Zuikyō (whose full name, according to the *Jubosatsukai deshi kyōmyō,* was Zuikyō-bō Shinmyō). Indeed, the *Jubosatsukai deshi kyōmyō* indicates that Zuikyō-bō passed away without having advanced to *bikuni* status; the register lists her as the first of nineteen women who died as probationary nuns. What is noteworthy about Zuikyō-bō's case is the fact that, despite describing her in the *Hokke metsuzaiji engi* as one of the nuns who had been living at Hokkeji with Kūnyo, Jizen, Shakunen, and others even before the group became involved with Eison, Enkyō did not include her in the list of Hokkeji's sixteen matriarchs. This detail suggests that Enkyō viewed Zuikyō-bō as a nun who, despite her presence at Hokkeji from the earliest years of its revival, did not deserve recognition as one of the founders of the revival.

One possible explanation would be that Zuikyō-bō passed away sometime between 1247, when she was ordained as a *shikishamana,* and 1249, when the *bikuni* ordinations were first held. Hosokawa offers another interpretation, however. He speculates that Zuikyō-bō did not receive the full precepts in 1249 because she was a servant woman who followed her mistress to Hokkeji. To support this argument, he points out that it was Zuikyō-bō who delivered an oracle from Queen-Consort Kōmyō in the *Hokke metsuzaiji engi.* Spirit possession, Hosokawa argues, was something typically performed only by women of lower status; when *bikuni* received spiritual direction, they tended to receive visions or dreams rather than oracles requiring spirit possession. Indeed, Hosokawa does appear to be right on this issue when it comes to *bikuni* affiliated with the movement: when Eison mentions in his autobiography a divine message revealed to him by the *bikuni* Shinnyo, he refers to it as a *musō* (dream) (*KJGSK* 1977, 18). The message Jitsua receives from Kōmyō in the *Hokkeji shari engi* also comes in the form of a dream (*Hokkeji shari engi,* 144a). Zuikyō-bō's failure to attain *bikuni* ordination, as well as her function as an oracle, Hosokawa suggests, marks her as a woman of lesser birth, while her proximity to the elite *bikuni* at Hokkeji suggests that she may have worked as a servant. A servant woman responsible for serving the more privileged women at the convent, Hosokawa suggests, would not have been able to receive the highest ordination, since this privilege would have threatened the hierarchy in place at the convent. Hosokawa's argument is highly speculative, but he does bring attention to an important issue. "Servant nuns" had been a part of the culture of convents since the Heian period, and there are many literary examples of high-ranking women who brought servants along when they took the tonsure and entered a religious community (1997, 98–99).

Hosokawa's analysis might also help explain why so many women at Hokkeji appear to have passed away as members of lower orders. Given the fact that the training period of *shikishamana* was only meant to last two years, it is difficult to explain why some 19 women are listed, in the *Jubosatsukai deshi kyōmyō,* as having passed away as *shikishamana.* The text also indicates that 30 women died as full novices. It is of course possible to speculate that some of these women were destined for full *bikuni* status but simply died from natural causes before advancing through the *bikuni* track. But it also seems likely in light of Hosokawa's interpretation that some women were barred for reasons related to their class or level of education from advancing through the ranks. Among the *gyōdō shami* and *shamini,* in particular, it is clear that many died in this status without advancing toward novicehood. In the nuns' order, 51 women are listed as having passed away or left the order as *gyōdō shamini;* in the monks' order, 139 men are said to have passed away as *gyōdō shami* (*Jubosatsukai deshi kyōmyō,* 97–98). That so many men died without receiving higher levels of ordination suggests that a large percentage were not granted access to full novice and *biku* ordinations. Similar limitations were likely placed on certain members of the *gyōdō shamini* and *gonjūnyo* suborders at Hokkeji: while some of these women moved on to higher levels of ordination, many were likely bound—by class, regional background, or educational level—to the lower suborders of the Hokkeji community. But even if these women did occupy the lower ranks of the Hokkeji hierarchy, their numbers made them a majority in the community: nearly half of the total population of Hokkeji in the year 1280 was made up of *saikai-shū* women, and nearly half of the nuns' order was comprised of *gyōdō shamini.* This means that *saikai-shū* and *gyōdō shamini* made up about 75 percent of the entire order in the year 1280.[25]

The Branch Convents

During the heyday of the *vinaya* revival movement, Hokkeji operated as the head convent of the Saidaiji network. Most of the convents involved in the movement appear to have been configured as *matsuji,* or branch temples, of Hokkeji, which was the only convent that had an ordination platform of its own.[26] Among the convents listed in the 1280 name register, it is clear that Hokkeji was at the center of the group: of the 89 *gyōdō shamini* shown to be residing at a Ritsu convent in the year 1280, 56 were at Hokkeji. Moreover, Hokkeji's group contained the greatest range in ages (eleven through sixty-seven), suggesting the convent served as a training center for nuns.

Enkyō's list of nuns in the *Hokke metsuzaiji engi* confirms this understanding of Hokkeji. She depicts eight of the nuns listed as having gone on to become rectors of Hokkeji and four as having gone on to become the rectors of other convents. The *bikuni* Shin'a, for example, became the rector of Chisokuji in Kamakura. The *bikuni* Shinjō ventured out to Saga, in Yamashiro Province, to become the founding rector of the convent Kōdaiji; the nun Enshin became the founding rector of Tōrinji in the northern capital (Heian-kyō, or Kyoto); and the nun Ryōshō went to Kawachi to convert the ancient temple Dōmyōji into a convent and to become its founding rector (143a).

Although information about those convents connected to Hokkeji is limited, available data does allow for several observations.[27] First, we are able to see that, on the whole, the kind of demographic diversity found at Hokkeji in the mid-to-late thirteenth century is also found in the groups of women who took up residence at Ritsu branch convents. Even more significant, however, is the degree of communication and cooperation that linked various convents within the network. Not only were nuns sent from Hokkeji out to branch convents following their training, but those nuns sent to outlying convents remained active both in Hokkeji rituals and in broad-based Ritsu fund-raising campaigns. These branch convents thus provide a wider view of the Hokkeji movement and demonstrate the degree to which the Hokkeji nuns' order succeeded in creating a broad-based, interregional community for Ritsu nuns.

Ritsu Convents in the Capital Regions: Yamato and Yamashiro

In the western capital regions of Heijō-kyō and Heian-kyō, or Nara and Kyoto, there were at least four other convents of Ritsu affiliation: Kōdaiji, Tōrinji, Chūgūji, and Shōbōji. The first two, located in or near the northern capital of Heijō-kyō, appear to have been configured as branch temples of Hokkeji. The other two, located in the southern capital, did not identify as Hokkeji branch convents but were instead affiliated with Tōshōdaiji. But it is clear that these two convents, both of which were affiliated with the nun Shinnyo, had long-standing ties both with Eison and with Hokkeji.

Kōdaiji was the more visible of Hokkeji's two branch temples in Kyoto. According to Enkyō's *Hokke metsuzaiji engi,* the nun Shinjō established the convent Kōdaiji after training at Hokkeji. In Hosokawa's estimation, this convent, which was in the Saga area of Yamashiro Province (northwestern Kyoto), maintained especially close ties with the court and the aristocratic class. Although it is unclear whether or not Shinjō herself had any direct connection to the court, her talent for attracting large contributions suggests that she may indeed have been a member of elite circles.

In 1278, Eison's disciple Kyōe organized an effort to collect funds for the printing of Eison's *Brahma Net Sutra* commentary *Bonmōkyō koshakki hokō monjū* (Collection of secondary works on the ancient records of the Brahma Net Sutra). In conjunction with this campaign, Kōdaiji raised as much money (in rice) as Hokkeji, and both of the convents significantly outperformed the monasteries.[28] Both Hokkeji's Shin'e and Kōdaiji's rector, Shinjō, raised and contributed 11.6 *mon* each, a hefty sum when compared to the amounts raised by Saidaiji-branch priests, who raised sums in the range of 0.8 to 3.3 *mon* each (*Saidai chokushi Kōshō Bosatsu gyōjitsu nenpu,* 169–170; Hosokawa 1989a, 133).

An undated document from the Kanazawa Bunko archives also indicates that at least one princess or woman otherwise close to the royal house had entered Kōdaiji as a *bikuni.*[29] This document tells of a noble's daughter *(himemiya)* named Chōken who entered a "convent near the Shakadō in Saga." The document mentions that she had no progeny and furthermore emphasizes that her rights regarding the inheritance and bestowal of property had been rendered invalid as a result of her renunciation of the world. The document portrays Chōken as a career nun who had forsaken family life and taken all 348 *bikuni* precepts (Hosokawa 1989a, 135).

Few details of Chōken's life are known. Hosokawa speculates that she may have been the product of an illicit relationship between Princess Rinshi, the elder sister of Her Highness Eikamon-in, and Minamoto (Rokujō) no Arifusa (1251–1319). Arifusa, a poet of the legendary Rokujō line of the Fujiwara family, was the grandchild of former prime minister *(daijō daijin)* Koga no Michimitsu and a cousin to Lady Nijō. According to the 1338 collection *Masukagami,* Rinshi, who had become the royal consort of Retired Sovereign Kameyama, was unable to win his affections, despite her great beauty. In frustration, she left the palace and took up residence near Zenrinji, a temple in the Sakyōku district of the capital. It was there that she is said to have caught the eye of Arifusa. Chapters 11 and 12 of the *Masukagami* tell of how the two began to meet secretly from the year 1290 and of how they ended up having a child together. Rinshi later returned to the palace, serving Kameyama's son, Go-Uda Tennō, and ultimately giving birth to a prince fathered by Go-Uda. Her return to court, of course, would have required her to hide the child born of her affair with Arifusa. Hosokawa suggests that Chōken, who emerged as a major figure at Kōdaiji, was in fact this secret child of Rinshi (Hosokawa 1989a, 135–138; Gomi 1988, 369).

Another woman with courtly connections who entered Kōdaiji, likely before Chōken's time, was a nun named Kyōmyō. Kyōmyō is mentioned in a series of letters found in the *Tōji hyakugō monjo* as having possessed and transferred, in 1305, the Kami no Katsura estate in Yamashiro. According to the documents, Kyōmyō served as a lady-in-waiting in the household of regent *(kanpaku)* Konoe Kanetsune (1210–1254) before entering the convent (*Dai Nihon shiryō,* sect. 6, vol. 9, 43–47). This evidence suggests that Kōdaiji, like Hokkeji, housed both the daughters of *nyoin* and the ladies-in-waiting of royal and aristocratic families.

But court ties were by no means a prerequisite for women wishing to enter Kōdaiji. The *Jubosatsukai deshi kyōmyō* lists sixteen *gyōdō shamini* in residence at Kōdaiji in the year 1280, and only 25 percent of these women were from Yamashiro. Two were from Yamato, but all the others had been born in remote areas, suggesting that they were at best the daughters of provincial elites. It is probably safe to assume that Kōdaiji, like Hokkeji, housed a diverse group of women.

Tōrinji, located in the Higashiyama district of the capital, is another convent that seems to have been regarded as a branch convent of Hokkeji. Enkyō mentions the temple briefly in her *Hokke metsuzaiji engi:* according to this account, Enshin Jōshin-bō, who had first trained at Hokkeji, founded the convent (143a). But according to the literature of the temple Kaikōji, Tōrinji had originally been a monastery, a branch temple of Kaikōji (*Ritsuen sōbōden,* chap. 11). This claim would suggest that the nun-rector Enshin converted the temple into a convent. Unfortunately, little is known about Enshin and her role in the conversion of Tōrinji, if it had indeed been a monastery before her arrival there. Much more is known about the rector Sonnyo (1221–1277), who was the daughter of the Hokkeji *bikuni* Enshō, the niece of the priest Enshō, and the granddaughter of the Hokkeji *bikuni* Nyoen. Sonnyo took her first vows as a *gyōdō shamini* at Hokkeji in 1249. According to the *Tōdaiji Enshō Shōnin gyōjō,* which recounts the life of Sonnyo's uncle Enshō, Sonnyo prospered at Tōrinji, where she administered the affairs of the convent and trained a number of her own disciples. She and Enshō appear to have been quite close, as Sonnyo frequently invited her uncle and his disciples to perform lectures on difficult commentaries for her disciples at Tōrinji (1b, 8a; Hosokawa 1989a, 129–131; Hosokawa 1997, 97; Ushiyama 1986). This detail suggests that Tōrinji nuns, like their counterparts at Hokkeji, were interested in serious doctrinal study.

In addition to Hokkeji, there were at least two other Ritsu convents located in the southern capital active during the thirteenth century: Shōbōji and Chūgūji. The nun Shinnyo, mentioned briefly in chapter 4, was active at both of these convents. Shinnyo appears in the earliest of Ritsu documents and is known in particular for having revealed to Eison in 1243 the contents of a dream that affirmed the righteousness of the larger Ritsu campaign to revive the *vinaya* in Japan (*KJGSK* 1977, 18–19). She supported the efforts of Eison and Kakujō alike and is believed to have taken the *bikuni* precepts from Kakujō during or shortly after the year 1244, just before Eison began ordaining women at Hokkeji (Hosokawa 1999b, 149–153). After taking the precepts from Kakujō, who was by that time in residence at Tōshōdaiji, Shinnyo identified her own temples and groups of disciples as belonging to the Tōshōdaiji lineage of the Ritsu school, but her activities clearly overlapped with those of the nuns at Hokkeji.

Shinnyo's first major undertaking as a *bikuni* was to establish the convent Shōbōji, also known as Tatsuichi Shōhōji and as Seihōji.[30] According to the *Shōdai senzai denki* (Transmitted record of Toshōdaiji's thousand years), Shinnyo opened the temple with a *kekkai* service on the first day of the third month of Kenchō 1 (1249). Just over a month later, she is said to have hosted at the new convent a large Shaka *nenbutsu* service "to save people and spread the *vinaya.*" The size of Shinnyo's order at Shōbōji is not known, but according to this same text, there were always dozens of people scattered throughout the temple's buildings. The text also reports in a different section that twelve nuns from the Shōbōji nuns' order took *bikuni* ordinations at Hokkeji on the twenty-first day of the third month of Kōan 8 (1275). They then continued to Shōdaiji (Tōshōdaiji) and received ordination there (424b). This record reveals not only that Hokkeji's ordination platform served women from other Ritsu lineages but also that the nuns' order had begun to practice *betsuju* ordinations in accordance with the rules of the *Four-Part Vinaya,* which states that *bikuni* vows are to be taken first in the presence of ten *bikuni* and then in the presence of ten male masters (Matsuo 1995, 384).

Although the record of these 1275 ordinations is brief, it provides great detail about the nature of the Ritsu ritual community. In the margins, the compiler lists the names of the eleven monks and eleven nuns who performed the ceremonies. Here it is stated that Eison performed the *konma,* Shōgen of Tōshōdaiji the questioning, Sōji of Sairinji the explanation of the precepts, Kōson of Kairyūōji the leading of the chants, and so on. These details indicate that the ritual was deemed important enough to attract priests from a number of different Ritsu temples. Indeed, some, like Sōji, must have traveled considerable distances to be present at the ceremony. On the nuns' side, all of the women participating in the ceremony with the exception of one are identified with Hokkeji. The exception is Ryōshō, the rector of Dōmyōji, who performed the *konma* on behalf of the nuns' order. Like Sōji, Ryōshō would have traveled a considerable distance to attend these ceremonies at Hokkeji and Tōshōdaiji. The precepts master *(wajō)* on the Hokkeji side was Shin'e, the tenth nun to appear in Enkyō's list of sixteen in the *Hokke metsuzaiji engi.* The high position assigned to Shin'e suggests that she was the rector at Hokkeji during the time of these ordinations. The marginal notes also indicate that the nuns' ceremony followed the basic protocol of the monks' ceremony but with nuns performing the various ritual duties, such as the performance of the *konma* and the questioning of ordinands. A handful of the nuns listed in these notes are women mentioned in Enkyō's *Hokke metsuzaiji engi.* In addition to Shin'e and Ryōshō, the notes indicate that Shōshō and Myōpen, the fourteenth and fifteenth nuns on Enkyō's list, also participated in the ceremony. The other nuns mentioned here are not included in Enkyō's list, but their names can be found in the *bikuni-shū* portion of the *Jubosatsukai deshi kyōmyō* name register, which means that they had all taken full *bikuni* precepts by the year 1280 (95–96). Many of these women had clearly risen to senior positions in the nuns' order by the year 1285: Chigen served as the *kyōju,* or teacher of the precepts, and Chihen as the *dōtatsu,* or transmitter of liturgical documents (*Shōdai senzai denki,* 424b).[31]

The document ends by stating that when the group members took their second set of precepts at Tōshōdaiji, it marked the first time in ages that nuns' precepts had been granted at the temple. The ceremony, it continues, marked the efforts of the Kakujō's disciple and successor, Shōgen, to revive the precepts for monks and nuns at Tōshōdaiji (11:424b). The planning and execution of this ceremony, like so many of the activities in the broader Ritsu movement, reflected an interest in spreading *vinaya* practices and protocols as widely as possible. The nuns' group centered at Hokkeji, like its male counterpart at Saidaiji, was anything but parochial: this ceremony, like most of the Ritsu ceremonies and activities we know about, was aimed at the creation of a far-reaching, large-scale nuns' order with well-established institutional and ritual practices.

Narratives of Shinnyo's work to revive Chūgūji also attest to Ritsu nuns' interest in gaining external support for their newly created order. Of particular interest here is the fact that Shinnyo actively campaigned in court and Kamakura circles alike to raise funds for the restoration of the convent. Like Hokkeji, Chūgūji, built on the edges of the Hōryūji complex, had a long history of association with the royal house. Chūgūji's origins predate those of Hokkeji: the temple is said to have been originally been built by Prince Umayado (popularly known as Prince Shōtoku, 574–622) on behalf of his mother, Anahobe no Hashihito no Himemiko (d. 621). Analysis of the temple's tiles indicates, however, that Chūgūji was constructed only after the prince's death, most likely around the middle of the seventh century.

According to Shinnyo's *Ama Shinnyo ganmon,* which gives an account of her vow to restore the convent, Chūgūji, though once a grand institution, had fallen into a state of severe neglect by the thirteenth century (82b–83a). Shinnyo frames her lament for Chūgūji's lost glory in terms very similar to those employed by Enkyō in the *Hokke metsuzaiji engi.* Both women emphasize the ancient splendor and current neglect of the convents they were involved in restoring (*HMJE,* 142a–b, 143a). This narrative strategy was common in appeals used for fund-raising purposes, especially when those appeals were aimed at court and warrior government elites who saw themselves as the stewards of tradition.

Shinnyo appears to have taken up residence at Chūgūji around the year 1262. It was over a decade later, however, that her fund-raising campaign there gained great momentum. Shinnyo's efforts began to yield results when in the year 1274 she claimed to have recovered from the storehouse of Hōryūji the *Tenjukoku mandara,* a silk *mandala* said to have been produced by the ladies-in-waiting of Tachibana no Ōiratsume, a consort of Prince Umayado, in his memory. According to popular accounts of its "discovery," Shinnyo's initial encounter with the *mandala* came about in connection with her efforts to learn the death anniversary of Prince Umayado's mother, who was to be celebrated as the patron saint of the temple. Seeking this information so she could carry out a proper commemorative service *(kuyō)* in Hashihito's honor, Shinnyo is said to have cloistered herself in prayer during the second month of Bun'ei 10 (1273). Her answer finally came in the form of a revelatory dream: the date of Hashihito's death was not revealed to her immediately, but she is said to have learned in the dream that she could find the date inscribed on a *mandala* in the treasury of Hōryūji. Unfortunately, the treasury of Hōryūji was sealed by royal order and could not be accessed without royal permission. According to the story,

Shinnyo managed to overcome this obstacle when, about one year later, a thief broke into the treasury and a group was allowed to enter the treasury to assess damages. Shinnyo is said to have joined this group and to have recovered, on this occasion, the *Tenjukoku mandara.*[32]

Shinnyo's fund-raising efforts centered from the year 1274 on the *Tenjukoku mandara.* She is known to have taken the *mandala* to Kyoto during 1274 and 1275, visiting a number of priests, aristocrats, and members of the court. To decipher the text inscribed on the *mandala,* she sought the help of the Dharma Seal priest Jōen of Ryōzenji, a temple in the Higashiyama district of Kyoto, and the scholar Middle Counselor Kazan-in Morotsugu. She also took the *mandala* to the court of the retired sovereign Kameyama.[33] Eison also frequented Kameyama's court during this period, bestowing precepts on Kameyama-in and his consorts and servants. Although no such details are provided in any of the narratives linking Shinnyo with Kameyama-in's court, it is possible to speculate that Eison may have introduced Shinnyo and her project to Kameyama-in and perhaps to Kameyama-in's brother, Go-Fukakusa. Emphasizing Chūgūji's connection to court women, Shinnyo appealed for funds both to make a replica of the *mandala* and to hold a *kuyō* service for Hashihito. She had accomplished these goals by the year 1282, when she wrote the *Ama Shinnyo ganmon* (Hosokawa 1987, 115–116; Abe 1987, 79–80). Shinnyo's primary audience appears to have been made up of women with court ties: indeed, the *Shōtoku Taishi denki* says that it was through the patronage of high-ranking ladies-in-waiting *(jōrō nyōbō tachi)* that Shinnyo was able to produce a replica of the *mandala* (88b1). Many sources suggest, however, that her fame extended beyond court society. The author of the *Shōyoshō,* for example, writes that "everyone in the capital and in Kamakura, from the noble to the base" knew of Shinnyo (23a; Hosokawa 1987, 144; 1999b, 149–152). It seems possible to speculate, then, that she may have taken the *mandala* to Kamakura as well.

Lady Nijō knew Shinnyo, most likely from her days in the courts of Go-Fukakusa and Kameyama-in. In *Towazugatari,* Nijō records her thoughts after visiting Chūgūji in the year 1290 and interacting with Shinnyo, who was by this time eighty years old: "Later I went to visit the Chūgū Temple [Chūgūji], curious to learn more about its connection with Prince Shōtoku and his consort. The head of the cloister [*chōrō,* rector] there was a nun called Shinnyobō [i.e., Shinnyo], whom I had seen once at the palace. She was older than I, and my acquaintance with her scarcely went beyond knowing her name, so I was not sure how she would react to my visit. But she greeted me kindly, and I remained there for a time" (trans. Brazell 1973, 205; *TG,* 193). In mentioning the fact that she had known the nun Shinnyo from her days in service at court, Lady Nijō confirms that Shinnyo had indeed made herself known within court circles. This evidence thereby lends credit to the thesis that Shinnyo's 1274–1275 campaign in Kyoto had been targeted at women of the court.

The narrative of Shinnyo's life—her early interest in the teachings of Kakujō and in the revival of the *vinaya,* her involvement in the revival of a nuns' order, her restoration of Chūgūji, and her fund-raising campaign at court—is suggestive of the ways in which the leaders of Ritsu nuns' communities successfully mixed doctrinal and scholarly interests with broader interests in the culture of the court. Shinnyo appears to have moved fluidly between elite court circles and Buddhist scholarly circles. This ability to mediate between various social spheres undoubtedly made her an effective leader at Shōbōji and Chūgūji.[34]

Convents in Other Kinai Provinces

In addition to affiliate convents in the capital regions, Hokkeji's network also extended to include a number of convents in the greater Kinai area, the region where Eison focused most of his early outreach activity. These other Kinai-area convents include Dōmyōji, in Kawachi, and two temples in Settsu: Keishō-in (also known as Sanka-in) and Shana-in.

Little is known about the two convents in Settsu, although both appear in Eison's autobiography. He visited both convents on the same day in 1281: he went to Keishō-in in the morning and to Shana-in in the evening, suggesting that the two were close in proximity. At Shana-in, he performed a *mandara kuyō* and gave the bodhisattva precepts to forty-seven people (*KJGSK* 1977, 61). It is also known that both convents, like many contemporaneous temples claiming affiliation with Saidaiji, were commissioned by the warrior government in 1298 to say prayers aimed at protecting Japan from the threat of a Mongol invasion (Ushiyama 1986, 22–23). Although little information regarding either of these convents has survived, the *Jubosatsukai deshi kyōmyō* suggests that Keishō-in, at least, was one of the more important convents connected to Hokkeji, as it is one of only four convents listed in the register. The register indicates that ten *gyōdō shamini* were in residence at Keishō-in in the year 1280. Another 1280 document, this one listing donors who contributed to an effort to build a new residence for Eison at Saidaiji, also suggests that Keishō-in was an important convent in the Ritsu network. According to this document, the nuns' order at Keishō-in donated 10 *kan* (100 strings of cash, or 10,000 copper coins) to the effort, a respectable donation for a small temple.[35]

Much more is known about Dōmyōji, primarily because this temple has such a long history and appears in such a wide variety of sources. The site of the temple, which continues to operate as a convent today, was first established as early as the seventh century. As Robert Borgen (2007) has pointed out, the temple is located near the ancient provincial capital of Kawachi. The temple is also near the Yamato River, which provided easy access both to Ikaruga, the site of Hōryūji and Chūgūji, and to Heijō-kyō, or Nara, where Saidaiji, Hokkeji, and Tōshōdaiji are located.[36]

During the Heian years, Dōmyōji appears to have operated as a family temple of the Sugawara, whose great ancestor Michizane (845–903) was recognized as the god Tenjin. Like many ancient temples, Dōmyōji appears to have endured cycles of flourishing and neglect during the long centuries of the Heian period. Although the Sugawara restored the temple during the eleventh century and introduced at that time cultic practices associated with Tenjin, Dōmyōji appears to have again fallen into a state of disuse by the middle years of the Kamakura, when Eison and his disciples converted the temple into a Ritsu convent (32).

This process likely began around the year 1246, when, according to his autobiography, Eison is said to have performed offering services *(kuyō)* for the bodhisattva Mañjuśrī at Dōmyōji. Over thirty years later, around 1278, the Hokkeji-trained *bikuni* Ryōshō was sent out to Dōmyōji to serve as the temple's rector. She would have been about forty-six years old at this time. What transpired between 1246 and 1278 is unknown, but Ryōshō's dispatch to the temple in 1278 appears to have marked its official debut as a Ritsu institution, for she is regarded as the founding rector of the temple.

Subsequent records suggest that Ryōshō's tenure at Dōmyōji saw the successful conversion of Dōmyōji into a Saidaiji-branch convent. The 1280 name register reveals that seven *gyōdō shamini* had taken up residence at the convent just a few years after her arrival. Evidence dating from a few years later—1286—suggests that the nuns' order at Dōmyōji continued to expand; indeed, Borgen estimates that as many as twenty-seven nuns were living at the convent by this time (43). In this year, Ryōshō and the nuns in her following copied out several sutras, wrote dedications for them, and placed them inside an image of the Sixteen-Year-Old Filial Prince Shōtoku.[37] In one of the sutra dedications, Ryōshō lists the names of more than ninety female donors (sixty-four living and twenty-eight who had passed away) from Dōmyōji, Keishō-in, and Hokkeji. Presumably, these women wished to create karmic bonds with Shōtoku by supporting this effort.[38] This document thus suggests not only that Dōmyōji itself had grown as a women's community but also that the nuns at Dōmyōji, most of whom had been trained at Hokkeji, continued to maintain close ties with Keishō-in, a small affiliated convent in Settsu, and with Hokkeji (Kobayashi and Sugiyama 1960; Sawa 1990; Hosokawa 1999a, 40–41).

Lady Nijō, who mentions many Ritsu convents in her *Towazugatari,* also makes a brief reference to Dōmyōji. She claims to have learned in 1276 that the fan-maker's daughter, a woman whom Go-Fukakusa had dallied with and humiliated a year earlier, had joined an order of nuns "who take the 500 precepts" (an exaggeration of the 348 *bikuni* precepts). The temple she entered was Sarara in Kawachi Province (84). Scholars have identified "Sarara" as a copyist's error for "Hajiji," another name for Dōmyōji (Tomikura 1967, 413; Borgen 2007, 44; Hosokawa 1987, 139–141).

The narrative of the fan-maker's daughter raises the question of class once again. To which precepts would such a woman have had access? On the one hand, it is clear that she was not a member of the aristocracy. But on the other, her proximity to the palace and to court life itself—her education, her artistic skill, her knowledge of how the court operated—suggests that she was more urbane and more comfortable among elites than a local woman from the provinces would have been. Although Lady Nijō comments upon the poor quality of this woman's robes, as well as her lack of subtle refinement (she makes too much noise when getting out of her carriage, Nijō comments), it is clear that the fan-maker's daughter was prepared for visits to court: she did have access to the requisite robes and carriage, and she knew how to write the morning-after poem court women were expected to present to their lovers. In other words, she had clearly been educated in the ways of the court (see Tokimura 1967, 413). The demographic she represents—that of a woman who has knowledge of elite culture but is not herself a member of the aristocracy—resembles that of many women in the *bikuni* order. Having been brought up in the capital, the fan-maker's daughter had a certain level of education and sophistication that would have separated her from most provincial women. But the fact that she was not a member of the aristocracy rendered her more or less unnoticeable. Like so many members of the *bikuni* order, her life passed with little attention from the elites whose diaries and documents constitute the bulk of surviving historical sources for this period.

Convents in the Eastern Provinces

As Eison's movement began its eastward spread from the early 1250s, a nuns' movement modeled on that of Hokkeji began to take root in the eastern provinces. It was Ninshō, the most celebrated of Eison's disciples, who built a Ritsu stronghold in the provinces directly surrounding the warrior capital in Kamakura. Though a native of Saidaiji's own Yamato Province, Ninshō was chosen by Eison, apparently through a divinatory practice involving the drawing of *kuji,* or strips of bamboo, to go to the eastern provinces and spread the teachings of the *vinaya* there.[39] Ninshō arrived in Kamakura in 1252 at the age of thirty-six. He spent the first ten years at Mimuradera in distant Hitachi Province (present-day Tsukuba, in Ibaragi Prefecture) and from there became active at a number of other temples, the most visible of which included Gokurakuji in the Kamakura area of Sagami Province and Shōmyōji in the Kanazawa area of Musashi Province. Ninshō also established refuges for the sick and needy in Kamakura. One such place was the Daibutsu refuge (Daibutsu *hiden*) located in the Hase area of Kamakura, where the Great Buddha of Kamakura was erected.[40]

Convents emerged in all four of these areas. On the whole, these convents were configured as the sister institutions of Ritsu monasteries and were built on or near the grounds of male institutions. Most of these convents were established at least several decades after Ninshō's arrival in Kamakura and after the monastery with which they would be paired had already been established. It is possible to speculate that Eison's visit to the Kantō in 1262 helped create a need for Ritsu convents in the east, for his record of the trip indicates that many women took the precepts from him during his six-month stay in the region.

The convent least visible in surviving sources is the Mimura convent (Mimura amadera or Mimura niji), which appears to have been established on the grounds of the Hitachi temple Mimuradera, where Ninshō spent his first ten years in the Kantō. Early records of his activities there do not mention a convent, but archaeologists have found among the remains of the Mimuradera site an epigraph that reads "convent entrance" *(amadera irui)* (Matsuo 1995, 109–130; 2004a, 65; Hosokawa 1989a, 178). Additional evidence of a convent at Mimuradera is found in the form of an undated letter held in the Kanazawa Bunko collection. The letter, addressed to Ken'a (1261–1338), the second rector of Shōmyōji, is signed by a *bikuni* who identifies herself as Ryōshō of the Mimura convent (*Kanagawa kenshi shiryōhen,* vol. 3, no. 3417).[41] Since Ryōshō's name appears among the members of the *bikuni* order in the 1280 *Jubosatsukai deshi kyōmyō,* one can surmise that Ryōshō, like several of the *bikuni* listed in the *Hokke metsuzaiji engi,* was dispatched to the Kantō to help establish a *bikuni* order there.[42]

A nuns' order also emerged at Gokurakuji, the Kamakura temple built by military commander Hōjō Shigetoki (1198–1261). Ninshō entered the temple as its founding rector in the year 1267. Although the details remain unclear, it appears that a convent named Hokkeji and modeled on the Hokkeji convent in Nara was built on the grounds of Gokurakuji. This Hokkeji appears on a late Kamakura-period map of the Gokurakuji complex *(Gokurakuji garan kozu).* There is also much evidence to suggest that the second and third rectors of Gokurakuji, Eishin and Junnin (1266–1326), respectively, were committed to the project of establishing of a nuns' order in Kamakura. Eishin, a disciple of Eison's who arrived in the Kantō sometime in the 1260s, followed Sōji's lead by printing texts aimed at distribution to nuns. He is known to have printed in Bun'ei 7 (1300), for example, Yuanzhao's *Abbreviated Notes on the Four-Part [Vinaya] Bikuni Precepts* (*Sifen shanding biqiuni jieben,* X. 722) (Nōdomi 1982, 91–97). Junnin, on the other hand, was actively engaged in the ordination of *bikuni.* Like Eishin, Junnin was a priest who had studied under both Eison and Ninshō. He became the third rector of Gokurakuji in the year 1315. On the epigraph of a bronze urn at the Yamato temple Gakuanji, it is written that Junnin ordained some 117 *bikuni* (64 of whom had never received *bikuni* ordinations from other masters), 61 *shikishamana,* and 74 novice nuns (*Kanagawa kenshi shiryōhen,* vol. 2., no. 2585). Hosokawa surmises that most of these ordinations took place at the Kamakura Hokkeji convent that was paired with Gokurakuji (1989a, 143, 178).

Additional evidence from the Kanazawa Bunko archives suggests both that the nuns' movement at Gokurakuji's Hokkeji was large in scale and that it offered women opportunities for advanced study and ordination. Of particular note here are several documents that list nuns who received the *denbō kanjō* (Dharma transmission initiation), the highest form of *mikkyō* (esoteric) initiation. Recipients of this ordination earn the title *ajari* (eminent master, Skt. *ācārya*). One undated document (no. 5868), for example, lists fourteen nuns who received the Dharma transmission initiation. Although the document does not indicate the institutional affiliations of the women it lists, one, a nun named Zennin, has been identified with both Junnin and Gokurakuji. In fact, recent archaeological work at Gokurakuji has brought to light an epigraph on a funerary stupa at the temple that bears both her name and the name of the Gokurakuji priest Junnin. This five-wheeled stupa contains five separate receptacles containing the remains of individuals. One bears an inscription stating that it contains the remains of Junnin, who died in 1326, and another bears an inscription saying that it holds the remains of the *bikuni* Zennin, who passed away in Enkyō 4 (1311) (*Nihon rekishi chimei taikei,* s. v. "Ninshōtō, Ninkōtō"). The fact that her remains were put to rest within such a large monument, and that the high-ranking Junnin would be placed within the same structure some fifteen years later, suggests that Zennin was an important figure at Gokurakuji. It is probably safe to assume that she had served as the rector of Hokkeji in Kamakura. It is even possible to speculate that she was the founding rector of this convent, for her name appears in the *Jubosatsukai deshi kyōmyō* as one of the novice nuns *(hōdō shamini)* who received her precepts from Eison (97a). Perhaps she, like so many other nuns active in the southern capital, was sent eastward to aid in the establishment of a nuns' order in Kamakura.

Another convent close to Gokurakuji, though not in its immediate environs, was Chisokuji. Records indicate that this temple was located in the Daibutsu-dani area of Kamakura, also known as Hase. This area was home to the Great Buddha project and to the Daibutsu refuge, one of the places where Ninshō aided the needy, such as those suffering from debilitating illnesses like Hansen's disease (leprosy). Kanren-bō Shin'a (1228–1297),[43] a disciple of Eison who had trained at Hokkeji, is recognized as the founding rector of Chisokuji. She is listed fourth on Enkyō's record of early Hokkeji leaders and would have been senior both to Ryōshō of the Mimura convent and Zennin of the Kamakura Hokkeji. In the years following Shin'a's tenure at Chisokuji, the convent came to be increasingly associated with the warrior class. The second rector of the convent was Gyōen-bō Enchi, whose father was the prominent Amano Kagemura, father-in-law to Hōjō Sanetoki and elder brother to Hōjō Saneyasu. As his daughter, Enchi would have had close connections to powerful figures in the warrior government. Shin'a's ascension to the Chisokuji abbacy was followed by the continued presence at Chisokuji of women with links to the warrior government (Hosokawa 1989a, 141–142).

As was the case with other convents in the eastern provinces, Chisokuji's rectors appear to have maintained close contact with other nearby Ritsu orders, male and female. Records indicate not only that Shin'a and Junnin were in regular contact but also that the Chisokuji nuns participated in rituals that involved monks and nuns from other Kamakura Ritsu orders.[44] There is also evidence to suggest that the members of the nuns' order at Chisokuji, like the nuns at other Ritsu convents, were actively involved in patronage projects. An image of Bishamonten (King Vaiśravaṇa) now held at Shōmyōji contains a record identifying its patron as the *bikuni* Ryōshin-bō Shunnin of Chisokuji. Hosokawa has argued that Chisokuji's proximity to the Daibutsu refuge suggests that the nuns of Chisokuji were involved in various forms of social charity, perhaps under the direction of Ninshō

(1989a, 139–141). Although this possibility seems likely, no conclusive documentary evidence is available.

Finally, there is evidence that a fourth convent was established near Shōmyōji in the Kanazawa area of Musashi Province. Hōjō Sanetoki founded Shōmyōji in 1259 in honor of his mother. He first designated it a hall for *nenbutsu* recitation *(nenbutsudō)* but decided to configure it as a Ritsu temple once he became a devotee of Eison. He initially offered Shōmyōji to Eison, but Eison would not accept the gift. Sanetoki then asked Ninshō to recommend a founding rector of the temple, and Ninshō suggested Shinkai, who refused three times before finally accepting the position in 1267.[45] Shōmyōji's sister convent, Kaiganji, must have been established sometime thereafter. Although few details about the institutional history of the convent can be gleaned from surviving records, documents from the Kanazawa Bunko archives confirm that Shinkai bestowed the Dharma transmission initiation upon a number of nuns. The first such ordination took place in the year 1300, when he ordained a nun named Shōkaku. He bestowed the same rite on four other nuns in 1302 (*Kanazawa Bunko komonjo,* nos. 6480, 6488; Nōdomi 1982, 431–432).[46] Documents from the Kanazawa Bunko further illustrate that nuns' groups from the Kamakura region regularly interacted both with each other and with priests from area Ritsu temples. A document titled "Record of Those upon Whom the Initiation Was Bestowed at Shōmyōji," which includes entries ranging from 1316 to 1345, contains sections dedicated to the "nuns' order" *(ama-shū).* In some instances, the institutional affiliations of particular individuals are indicated in the margins. Nuns from Chisokuji, as well as monks from a number of other temples, are included in the list (*Kanazawa Bunko komonjo,* no. 5888).

Other Affiliate Convents

Convents affiliated with Hokkeji were by no means limited to the ones described here. Iwashimizu Gubodai'in is another convent about which very little is known. A Gubodai'in nun named Shinkaku is listed in Saidaiji records as having donated the enormous sum of thirty *mon* to the 1278 project to print Eison's *Bonmōkyō koshakki hokō monjū.* The size of her contribution is especially noticeable when contrasted with the average contribution of Saidaiji priests, which was less than three *mon* (*Saidai chokushi Kōshō Bosatsu gyōjitsu nenpu,* 169–170; Hosokawa 1989a, 133). In addition to Gubodai'in, there were a number of other small hermitages and practice halls where nuns connected to the Hokkeji-centered movement took up residency. The temple Toyuradera, attributed to the female sovereign Suiko Tennō (554–628), for example, seems to have housed nuns during the late thirteenth century; a *bikuni* identified with Toyuradera donated land to Saidaiji in the year 1277.[47]

This period also witnessed the opening of many Zen, Jōdo-shū, and other convents that were not directly affiliated with Hokkeji or the Ritsu school but that may have had some loose connections with the Hokkeji movement. During the Kamakura and Muromachi periods especially, royal princesses, women of eminent aristocratic families (such as the Kujō branch of the Fujiwara), and women hailing from families connected to the warrior government (especially the daughters of the Ashikaga), opened many new convents, many of them small-scale chapels or hermitages tailored to the lifestyles of elite women.[48]

As seen in the many examples above, the convents affiliated with Hokkeji—including Chūgūji, Kōdaiji, Dōmyōji, Chisokuji, Shōbōji, Keishō-in, and Tōrinji, among others—tended to count among their residents women from elite backgrounds who had connections either in the world of the court or in warrior government circles. At the same time, however, the social makeup of these convents remained rather fluid during the Kamakura period: although women from elite backgrounds emerged in the stories of the convents, there is no sense that these communities of nuns were restricted to women of high birth.

Fund-Raising and Economic Activities

As the number of *gyōdō shamini, gonjūnyo,* and laywomen listed in Hokkeji name registers for the year 1280 indicates, Hokkeji had, by the last decades of the thirteenth century, become the center of a popular movement whose members came from all social classes. Although evidence of a few sizeable donations from elite patrons can be found among Ritsu records, it appears that small donations made by low-ranking nuns, lay devotees, and pilgrims comprised the bulk of the convent's income during this period. In this sense, Hokkeji appears to have followed the basic mode of operation that characterized Saidaiji at this time: lacking major landholdings from which they could draw tax earnings, nuns relied heavily on the accumulation of large numbers of small donations. Some of these donations were made by women who joined the order as nuns, while others were made by lay patrons and devotees.

Like monks in the Saidaiji order, Ritsu nuns were actively involved in fund-raising campaigns. As seen above, both Ryōshō, a rector at Dōmyōji, and Shunnin, a rector at Chisokuji, raised funds for the production of Buddhist images. We also know that in addition to raising funds for internal projects, nuns in the Ritsu order participated in broader campaigns in which the rectors of various Ritsu temples would offer support toward the funding of a single project. As has already been mentioned in the sections above, Ritsu nuns contributed to a number of large-scale campaigns headed by Saidaiji monks. In the previously mentioned example from 1278, in which Eison's disciple Kyōe appealed for support to print Eison's *Brahma Net Sutra* commentary *Bonmōkyō koshakki hokō monjū,* the largest contributions came from the female members of the Saidaiji-affiliated institutions. The Hokkeji rector Shin'e contributed 11,805 *mon* she had raised, a considerable sum, especially when set against the 3,000 *mon* contributed by Saidaiji. Added to these sums were large contributions from the rectors of convents affiliated with Hokkeji: Dōmyōji's Ryōshō (7,300 *mon*), Kōdaiji's Shinjō (11,600 *mon*), and Gubodai'in's Shinkaku (30,000 *mon*). What is more, two nuns from the *saikai-shū* and lay orders also made large contributions: a *saikai-shū* member known as Myohō contributed 10,100 *mon*, and Shin-bō, identified as a *gonjinyo*, donated 10,000 *mon* (*Saidai chokushi Kōshō Bosatsu gyōjitsu nenpu*, 169–170; Hosokawa 1989a, 133).

Similar patterns can be found in a 1280 record of contributions to the project aimed at erecting a new residence for Eison on the grounds of Saidaiji. For this project, which was much larger in scale than the printing project mentioned above, the total amount raised exceeded 715 *kan*. In this particular case, the nuns' orders raised only a small portion of the total sum: Hokkeji contributed 75 *kan*, 360 *mon*, and some change; Keishō-in, 10 *kan*; and Kōdaiji, 30 *kan*. A contribution from a *gonjūnyo* order (17 *kan*, 620 *mon*) is also listed.[49] The money contributed by the women's groups comprised just under 20 percent of the total amount raised. That said, the amount that Hokkeji raised far surpassed that raised by many other branch temples: the aristocratic temple Jōjūji, for example, contributed only 35 *kan*; Gokurakuji in Kamakura, 70 *kan*; Gakuanji, 8 *kan*; Futaiji, 18 *kan*; Kairyūōji, 15 *kan*, and so on. In this sense, it is clear that Hokkeji's contribution was much more significant than that of most male branch temples; the total contribution of the nuns' order is diminished by the fact that only three female orders contributed to the campaign, while a much larger number of male orders participated (*Saidaiji hishi sōbō zōei dōshin gōriki hōga chō*, 383–389).

Most remarkable about the Hokkeji donations recorded in this document is the degree to which they differ from donations made by male donors and institutions. First, the sections recording Hokkeji donations include large subsections in which offerings from lay donors are listed. Male temples, by contrast, list only donations submitted by male priests. While it may have been the case that some of these male priests were submitting funds they had raised among the laity, the names of individual lay donors are not indicated. The Hokkeji donor lists include 18 *bikuni*, 4 *shikishamana* and *hōdō* novices, 10 *gyōdō shamini*, 138 female members of the *saikai-shū*, and 45 laywomen.[50] As donors, then, *saikai-shū* members and laywomen clearly outnumbered full-fledged nuns. Secondly, additional details about the types of donations contributed by members of the Hokkeji community are included in the document. The document indicates, for example, that many of the 18 *bikuni* who contributed to the effort donated materials other than cash. There are a few instances in the Kairyūōji list in which male donors also offered gifts other than cash, but this is a phenomenon that appears to have been more prevalent among women. Of particular interest is the fact that many of the *bikuni* are recorded as having donated robes, fabrics, and other goods commonly used by monastics: an ink stone, several begging bowls, a mallet, and so on. But fabrics and robes are by far the most common items listed. Several *bikuni*, novice nuns, and *gyōdō* novice nuns are said to have contributed bolts of silk and cotton, as well as *kesa*, great robes *(taie)*, upper body robes *(hensan)*, and small sacks *(kobukuro)* (386b–387a).

These observations raise larger questions about the nature of fund-raising and economic life at Hokkeji. How was it that Hokkeji nuns managed to mobilize so many laywomen and female *saikai-shū* to contribute resources to Ritsu projects? In short, what can be known about the processes by which Hokkeji attracted and maintained lay support? Secondly, what do the kinds of gifts offered by the nuns at Hokkeji say about the kind of work that they may have been engaged in on the grounds of the temple?

Written records hint at the various means by which Hokkeji nuns attracted patronage and support from the laity. First, as emphasized in chapter 1, during the early years of Hokkeji's medieval revival, nuns likely depended on the support of pilgrims who visited the convent to view—and seek karmic connection with—the images held there, particularly the wooden Eleven-Faced Kannon popularly regarded as having been made in the likeness of Queen-Consort Kōmyō herself. Enkyō's *Hokke metsuzaiji engi* suggests that the image was left on permanent display only during the early years of the revival. In 1243, Zuikyō delivered an oracle from Kōmyō, who instructed that her image was to be taken off public display and returned to its tabernacle. During periods of crisis, the oracle suggested, the image could be left on regular display so as to attract support, but now that the convent had returned it its glory, the image should be allowed to rest. Since this time, Enkyō stated, the Eleven-Faced Kannon has been kept in its tabernacle (142).

But there is evidence to suggest that the image was taken out on special occasions, most likely for *kaichō,* or "openings." *Kaichō* are short-term public displays of images typically hidden from view. As anyone who has spent time in Kyoto knows well, *kaichō* are still held at many temples today. They are major events attracting devout members of the laity who wish to form a connection with an image deemed both rare and efficacious. Although there are no records that directly mention *kaichō* of Hokkeji's Eleven-Faced Kannon during the Kamakura period, the diary of the Kōfukuji Daijōin Monzeki Jinson (1430–1508) makes several references to such events in the fifteenth century. He notes in one such entry, dated Meiō 3 (1494) 6/18, that huge crowds gathered at the convent to view the image: "It was said that there was a public viewing [*kaichō*] of the Hokkeji Kannon today; apparently the image was open to the public from the early morning, and crowds of all kinds of people gathered [at Hokkeji to view the image of Kannon]" (*Daijōin jisha zōjiki,* 396). According to Jinson, the Eleven-Faced Kannon, which had drawn so many pilgrims to Hokkeji in the late Heian and early Kamakura periods, still managed to attract crowds in the late fifteenth century. Surely nuns active at Hokkeji during the Kamakura period also relied upon the image—and miraculous narratives about it—as a means of drawing the devout to the convent.

The Eleven-Faced Kannon was not the only attraction that Hokkeji offered pilgrims, however. The bathhouse at Hokkeji was another source of popular appeal. As related in the first chapter, the *Hokke metsuzaiji engi* identifies this bath with Queen-Consort Kōmyō herself. According to the *engi*, Kōmyō built the bath in response to a miraculous voice from the sky that instructed her to build it as a way of creating karmic merit. Having taken a vow that she would personally scrub the dirt off the first person who came to bathe on the bathhouse's opening day, Kōmyō was dismayed, the *engi* continues, when the first person who appeared at the bathhouse was a man suffering from the advanced stages of leprosy. Once she pulled herself together and washed him, he revealed that he was Ashuku Buddha. She had passed his testing of her vow. According to the *engi*, Kōmyō converted the original bathhouse into a temple for Ashuku Buddha. The temple has since fallen into ruin, the *engi* continues, but the kettle used for boiling bathwater at Kōmyō's bathhouse survives. And that same kettle, we are told, has been installed at a newer bath at Hokkeji. Since the kettle contains the gods of the Medicine Teacher Buddha, water boiled in it, Enkyō explains, has the power to heal Hokkeji's bathers: "The hot water kettle [used at that bath] is now at Hokkeji. It is expected that the twelve gods of the Yakushi [the Medicine Teacher Buddha; Skt. *Bhaiṣajya-guru tathāgata*] can be encountered within it. People who touch this hot water to their body even once are healed of sicknesses such as the three poisons [*sandoku:* covetousness, anger, and delusion]. There should be no doubt that many sick people will be fully healed and that their bodies and minds will gain comfort" (141b).

Variations of the narrative in which Kōmyō washes a leper with her own hands abound in medieval literature, a fact that has prompted Abe Yasurō to suggest that the bath at medieval Hokkeji was a major attraction for pilgrims who wished to form bonds with Kōmyō (1998, 21). What exactly the bathhouse was like during this period, both in terms of its physical size and the conditions placed on its use, are not well-known, but it is clear that Hokkeji did have a bath during this period and that the bath served both male and female members of the local community. The earliest mention of Hokkeji's medieval bath appears in the *Hokkeji kekkaiki.* Near the end of the document, it states that one day after the sacred boundaries of the convent were declared in the second month of Hōji 3 (1249), the Hokkeji bathhouse was similarly declared a place of sacred waters (138).[51] Nearly a century later, Hokkeji's bathhouse is mentioned in the 1347 document "Itemized Rules for the Kairyūōji Hassaikai-shū." As mentioned earlier, there is listed among the rules here a guideline forbidding members of Kairyūōji's *saikai-shū* order to enter the bath at Hokkeji along with fully ordained priests. Here, the water of the Hokkeji bath is described as the "meritorious bathwater" *(kudoku no yu),* phrasing that clearly suggests that people viewed the Hokkeji bath as an attraction that offered pilgrims the chance to gain positive karmic merit ("Kairyūōji hassaikai-shū kishiki jōjō," qtd. in Hosokawa 1987, 11–12).

The salvific qualities of the Hokkeji bath are again invoked in the diary of the previously mentioned priest Jinson. In a 1464 diary entry recounting one of his visits to Hokkeji, Jinson writes that he entered the bath there because he had been told about its miraculous saving powers: "After that, I entered the great bathhouse [*daiyuya*]. The significance of this bathwater is explained in a written divine oath [*onkimon*], which says that to avoid the three evil realms [of rebirth], one really should enter [this bath]" (*Daijōin jisha zōjiki,* 316, Kanshō 5/6/7). Over the course of the late fifteenth century, Jinson made numerous trips to Hokkeji. Most of his visits centered on the Bonmō-e, or Ceremony for the *Brahma Net Sutra,* an annual ritual event held in Kōmyō's honor. The nature of this ceremony and its role in ritual life at Hokkeji will be discussed in the following chapter. What is worth attention in the context of this chapter is the fact that Jinson appears to have viewed bathing in the Hokkeji bathwaters as an essential element of any visit to the temple. Nearly every entry in his diary that mentions a trip to Hokkeji also mentions, usually quite briefly, that he entered the bath during his visit to the convent. An abbreviated entry from the year 1484, for example, suggests that attending the Bonmō-e at Hokkeji and entering the bath there were, in Jinson's mind anyway things to be done together: "Today there was [i.e., I participated in] the Bonmō-e Ceremony at Hokkeji and the bath [at Hokkeji]" (Bunmei 6/6/7).

These various anecdotes suggest that Hokkeji nuns relied on both the Eleven-Faced Kannon and the bathhouse throughout the medieval period as means of attracting pilgrims. In addition to these two long-standing attractions at Hokkeji, there is also ample documentary evidence that the nuns of Hokkeji succeeded in winning patronage through the performance of ritual. The ritual life of Hokkeji appears to have been quite rich during the medieval period, and many of the services Hokkeji nuns performed were likely public events aimed at the entertainment of lay devotees. Narratives extolling the virtues of Kōmyō and promoting the Eleven-Faced Kannon and bathhouse connected with her may have brought many pilgrims to Hokkeji, but one can imagine that it was the ritual life at the convent, which offered devotees the opportunity to observe and participate in a variety of events, that ultimately led certain members of the laity to make large financial contributions. The particulars of rituals performed at Hokkeji, as well as the nature of such performances, will serve as the focus of the next chapter. What is notable here is the degree to which donors' names appear in documents describing the ritual calendar of medieval Hokkeji, for these details allow for several observations about the role that ritual played in the economic life of the convent during this period.

The document central to this discussion is the *Hokke metsuzaiji nenjū gyōji* (hereafter *Nenjū gyōji*), a lengthy ritual calendar that lists the various ceremonies and rites nuns at Hokkeji were to perform on an annual basis. According to its colophon, the only surviving copy of the text was copied out in the year 1322 by the *bikuni* Yūshi, who held the title of *kōi,* or elder (87b).[52] Close analysis of this document, which contains long lists of complex rites and ceremonies, will be offered in the next chapter. Only the final section, "Annual Rites, Offering Services for the Dead, and the Like," will be treated here. Many of the rites listed in this final section, which is in fact the longest section in the document, are offering services for the dead *(mōja kuyō).* When such rites are listed, the document often provides marginal notes indicating the name of the deceased, as well as his or her relationship to the convent.

Services for the dead have always been among the most important rites carried out at temples in Japan; such is true not only today but also of the earliest Buddhist institutions established in Japan, most of which were first erected to pacify the spirits of the deceased. Indeed, the Ritsu revival groups of the Kamakura period, much like the Zen movements that emerged around this time, offered funerary and memorial services as a means of broadening their appeal to ordinary lay folk in the countryside. Although there is no documentary evidence indicating that Hokkeji nuns performed funerary services involving the handling or preparation of corpses, it is clear that they performed offering services for the dead on a regular basis.

Many of the offering services for the dead included in this final section of the *Nenjū gyōji* were to be performed for patriarchs in Ritsu lineages, for the relatives of Hokkeji nuns, and for Hokkeji nuns who had passed away. The document lists, for example, services for Daoxuan (tenth month, third day), recognized as one of the founding patriarchs of the Ritsu tradition, as well as for the Tripiṭaka Master Xuanzang (Jpns. Genjō Sanzō) (second month, fifth day), who was associated with the Hossō school (Chns. Huayan), also important in Nara.[53] The nuns also performed services for at least nine different Saidaiji rectors, as well as for at least two Kairyūōji rectors. Added to these were regular services for the former rectors of Hokkeji, as well as for other members of the nuns' order who had passed away (86b–87b).

The *Nenjū gyōji* also mentions memorial offerings for patrons *(seshu)* and their relatives, suggesting that Hokkeji nuns performed a number of annual rites on behalf of donors who paid for ritual services. At least a handful of these donors were elites. As mentioned near the end of the last chapter, Muromachi-in, for example, commissioned Hokkeji nuns to perform Kōmyō Shingon services on the death anniversaries of four royals in her lineage: her grandfather, the retired sovereign Takakura (5/14); her father, Go-Horikawa Tennō (8/6); her grandmother, Kita Shirakawa-in (10/7); and her aunt, Shikikenmon-in (1/2). Inner palace minister Fujiwara no Ietsugu, the grandfather of Hokkeji *bikuni* Jakuen-bō, was also included in Hokkeji's ritual calendar (4/5). Since this inclusion is exceptional (the ritual calendar does not include the death anniversaries of relatives of all former Hokkeji *bikuni*), it suggests that either Jakuen-bō or a member of her family made a significant financial contribution to the convent so the services would continue even after her death.

The last section of the *Nenjū gyōji* also includes a number of Kamakura figures, suggesting that Hokkeji had acquired a significant number of donors from among the warrior government elite. As explained earlier in this chapter, the parents of Hokkeji *bikuni* Shingen Ryōshō-bō are both included in the *Nenjū gyōji*. Shingen's father, Nikaidō Yukifuji, was a member of the ruling elite and held a number of prominent posts. Another warrior government figure who emerges in the *Nenjū gyōji* is Sakyo Gon no

Daibu Hōjō Tokimura (1242–1305). Like Nikaidō Yukifuji, Tokimura held a number of important posts within the warrior government. Hokkeji nuns made offerings in honor of Tokimura's death on the twenty-third day of the fourth month, the day Hōjō Munekata had killed him in 1305. The nature of Tokimura's connection to Hokkeji is unknown, though we can speculate that a member of his family, perhaps a wife or daughter, commissioned Hokkeji nuns to perform annual services on his behalf. It is also possible, of course, that a female member of his family had entered Hokkeji as a nun.

Some beneficiaries of death memorial offerings are actually labeled as donors or are identified by their relationships to donors. On the eleventh day of the fifth month, for example, the *Nenjū gyōji* instructs that a death offering service was to be performed on behalf of "the Kantō patron who donated 200 *kan*." And on the twenty-first day of the same month, a service was to be held for "Dōsei, the father of the Kamakura patron-novice Dōin."[54] Other figures who are more difficult to identify but whose names suggest that they were warrior government elites include the "great patron Kiyohara Hyōgo no Suke," for whom services were to be performed on the twenty-ninth day of the ninth month, and the "spirit of Masahiro," who was to be remembered on the first day of the fourth month.

A significant number of donors included in the *Nenjū gyōji* appear to have taken vows of some kind, a detail suggested by the fact that they are referred to by Buddhist-style names. From the fourteenth day of the fifth month through the twentieth day of that same month, for example, a *tendoku* of the thousand sections of the *Lotus Sutra* was to be carried out on behalf of "the patron Zen'en-bō." And on the sixth day of the twelfth month, a Kōmyō Shingon was to be performed on behalf of "the nun Son'nin-bō, the donor who repaired the jeweled stupa at Saidaiji." Added to these cases are more than a dozen death offering services for individuals bearing "Amidabutsu" names such as Hō-Amidabutsu, Nishi-Amidabutsu, Zen-Amidabutsu, Ji-Amidabutsu, Kai-Amidabutsu, Hon-Amidabutsu, Yaku-Amidabutsu, and so on. Since some of these same names also appear among the *saikai-shū* and lay order *(zaike-shū)* name registers included in the 1280 *Gonjū nannyo kyōmyō* (104–105), it seems likely that many of these names refer to donors who had joined the Hokkeji community as members of the *saikai* or *zaike* orders.

Also worth attention here is the fact that the *Nenjū gyōji* mentions a couple of larger rituals to be held in honor of all Hokkeji donors as a group. One such occasion is the Urabon-e, or Ghost Festival, which was scheduled to begin on the thirteenth day of the seventh month and to last for fifteen days. In the marginal notes describing this event, it is stated that the nuns are to make offerings of the Kōmyō Shingon continuously for three days and three nights on behalf of the "hungry ghosts" of all "great patrons" *(daise no gaki)*. In other words, the nuns were to say prayers for the deceased family members of the temple's great donors. Another event for patrons and pilgrims was a Butsumyō (Recitation of the Buddha's Name) ceremony in the main hall to take place for three days starting on the eighth day of the twelfth month. According to the *Nenjū gyōji,* the ceremony was to be held for those "outside the order" who wanted to create karmic ties with the convent.

Well over 165 names are included in this last section of the *Nenjū gyōji;* the examples shared above are representative of the broader trends found in the ritual calendar, but the treatment here is far from exhaustive. What should be visible from this abbreviated treatment, however, is the degree to which Hokkeji nuns succeeded in attracting donors from various backgrounds. That individuals of means who could afford to have death offering services performed at prestigious male temples chose to commission rites from Hokkeji nuns says a lot about medieval views of nuns. The *Nenjū gyōji* attests to the fact that many entrusted Hokkeji nuns with the task of extending postmortem salvation to themselves and their loved ones. Clearly these individuals believed Hokkeji nuns capable of performing efficacious death offerings. The text also demonstrates the degree to which Hokkeji nuns relied upon the performance of ritual work for income.

Careful attention to the *Nenjū gyōji* also reflects on another theme of this chapter, namely, the diversity of the Hokkeji community. In addition to a handful of royals and court aristocrats, there are numerous warrior government figures and even more individuals who appear to be ordinary laypeople. Worth mentioning here is the fact that several heads of *asobi* (also *yūjo*) guilds are also included in the *Nenjū gyōji. Asobi* comprised a female occupational group that provided sexual entertainment and services for male patrons (Goodwin 2007, 1, 6). One of the *asobi* included in the document was the head of the *asobi* guild at the Kagami post-station (Kagami no shuku no kami chōja). A complete *tendoku,* or quick reading, of the *Lotus Sutra* was to be performed for her posthumous merit on the twenty-fifth day of the second month. On the twenty-eighth day of that same month, the Kōmyō Shingon was to be recited twenty-one times on behalf of her father. The guild head at Kagami had provided for her mother as well: according to the ritual guide, a lecture on the *Brahma Net Sutra* was to be performed in honor of the death of the "compassionate mother of the Kagami no shuku no kami no chōja" on the second day of the eleventh month. Another *chōja* mentioned in the Hokkeji ritual calendar is the head of the guild at Hashimoto (Owari no kuni no Hashimoto chōja).[55] A complete *Lotus Sutra tendoku* was to be performed in honor of her death on the third day of the third month. And on the twenty-eighth day of the sixth month, "a single-day copying of the [*Lotus*] *Sutra* with questions and answers" was to be performed in honor of her daughter, the head of the *yūkun* (another term for *yūjo*) guild at the Hashimoto post-station.

Insofar as *asobi* cultivated certain arts, such as song, dance, and poetry, to entertain elite men, they might be regarded as the forerunners of geisha. *Asobi* established and operated inns along major highways and waterways, offering elite travelers entertainment, conversation, lodging, and sex (Gotō 2002; Goodwin 2007). Female guild heads, or *chōja,* headed these inns. As Gotō (2002) has explained, *asobi* mimicked court women in appearance:

they maintained long, flowing hair and wore clothing commonly worn by *nyōkan* or other elite women. They also kept their eyebrows in the *tsukurimayu* style popular with court women, meaning that they shaved their eyebrows and then penciled them in with black ink *(sumi)*. Based on their appearance, Gotō writes, *asobi* could have easily been mistaken for court women. (The difference was that while elite women hid their faces for reasons of propriety when venturing outdoors, *asobi* did not.) *Asobi* did not simply try to look like court women: they also worked to achieve a level of training in the arts that would allow them to interact with the elite. This meant that in addition to entertaining guests with song, poetry, and dance, many *asobi* hosted drinking parties, for example, in which they wrote *renga*, or linked-verse poetry, with their guests.

As innkeepers, *asobi* played an important role in pilgrimage networks and in the larger economic landscape of religious pilgrimage. It is well-known, for example, that *asobi* regularly lodged and entertained elites who traveled by water on their way to pilgrimages at Sumiyoshi shrine, Shitennōji, Kōya-san, and Kumano. The *asobi* mentioned in the *Nenjū gyōji* were from two *shuku,* or post-stations, along Tōkaidō highway: Kagami post-station in Ōmi Province and Hashimoto post-station in Tootōmi Province. Both of these post-station towns flourished during the Kamakura period, when traffic between the cities of Kyoto and Kamakura increased.[56] Both post-stations were places where pilgrims traveling from Kamakura to Nara on religious pilgrimage commonly lodged en route. These post-stations were also places where Ritsu priests traveling between Ritsu centers in the Kantō and Kansai would have stayed. It is likely, then, that the *asobi* guild heads at Kagami and Hashimoto heard about the Ritsu movement—and about its hand in restoring the Hokkeji convent—from pilgrims and preachers traveling between the two capitals. Guild heads may have heard about Hokkeji from female travelers as well, for court women, like court men, often stayed at these same inns when they were on pilgrimage (Gotō 2002). Lady Nijō, for example, wrote of staying at several inns during her pilgrimages, and she identified one of them as Kagami post-station (*TG*, 169). The inn may have been managed by the same Kagami guild head who appears in the *Nenjū gyōji*.

How did *asobi* fit into the broader social context of Hokkeji? Tanaka Minoru, like many historians of the Ritsu movement, has suggested that the *asobi* mentioned in the *Nenjū gyōji* likely became affiliated with Hokkeji through Eison's influence. The assumption here is that *asobi* occupied low social positions during the time and would have fallen into a social category similar to that of *hinin* and other marginalized groups Eison and Ninshō targeted in much of their outreach work (1978, 86).

But Tanaka's view, which works from the presumption that *asobi* occupied a social position similar to that of *hinin* during the late thirteenth and early fourteenth centuries, overlooks the cultural affinities that may have linked *asobi* with nuns at Hokkeji, a good number of whom were active in circles of former *nyōbō,* or ladies-in-waiting. First of all, as the work of

Amino Yoshihiko (1989) confirms, one can view *asobi* and *nyōbō* as having existed on a continuum of sorts, with *nyōbō* occupying a glorified *asobi* position. Some *asobi* even managed to reinvent themselves or their daughters as *nyōbō.* The diary of Kengozen, for example, notes that one of the *nyōbō* in Kenshunmon-in's service was the daughter of an *asobi,* and Amino (1989) writes that it was quite common for the daughters of *asobi* and *shirabyōshi* to become *nyōbō* (*Tamakiwaru zenchūshaku,* 87). Since *asobi* mixed with elite society frequently, often hosting royal and aristocratic guests and receiving amorous attention from elite men, they traversed many of the same social circles as ladies-in-waiting. Indeed, it was common for aristocratic men to father children through *asobi,* and historical records suggest that children born of *asobi* did not suffer any hindrance when they wished to pursue careers at court; that is, there was no particular stigma, at least in the late Heian and early Kamakura periods, to having been born the child of an *asobi* (Gotō 2002).[57]

That many *asobi* enjoyed relatively high social positions is perhaps most evident when one considers cases of *asobi* who amassed great material wealth. Like many priests, *asobi* supported themselves through court patronage. Payments to *asobi* were typically given to guild heads in the form of rice and silk. Guild heads, in turn, would divide that wealth among the members of their community. Those women who had performed especially well or who had special talents were rewarded with valuable silks and clothing. Because they reserved the right to decide how such rewards were parceled out among members, guild heads obviously stood to gain the most from large payments, as they could retain significant portions for themselves (Matsuhara 1998, 13–15).

This wealth allowed some *asobi* guild heads to act as patrons of Buddhism. Of particular interest here is a *ganmon* found inside an image of the guardian deity Bishamonten at Ōgaji, a temple located near the Hashimoto post-station in Ōmi (present-day Shizuoka-ken). According to this document, dated to the twenty-fifth day of the ninth (intercalculary) month of Bun'ei 7 (1270), the *asobi* guild head of the Hashimoto post-station, a woman by the name of Myōsō, commissioned an image of Bishamonten.[58] The *ganmon* states that Myōsō copied out, in her own hand, a number of sutras, which she enshrined along with the *ganmon* and two relics in the statue of Bishamonten. Given the expense associated with the act of commissioning and enshrining a Buddhist image, this example suggests that the *asobi* guild head of the Hashimoto post-station had a great deal of spending power. The *ganmon* also illustrates her interest in Buddhist patronage.

The information about the Hashimoto and Kagami post-station guild heads contained in the *Nenjū gyōji* is not extensive enough to allow for an in-depth analysis of the relationship between these women and the nuns at Hokkeji. Some have suggested that *asobi* guild heads may have entered Hokkeji as nuns, perhaps after retiring from their posts (Hosokawa 1997, 97–98). It is also possible that they simply acted as high-profile donors who commissioned memorial services from Hokkeji nuns. In either case, it is clear that a number of *asobi* guild heads contributed funds to the Ritsu movement, and most likely to Hokkeji directly, for regular services were typically offered only for former rectors of Hokkeji and Saidaiji, for great Ritsu patriarchs, and for donors.

There is also much evidence to suggest that ordinary *asobi*—that is, those who were not guild heads—were also active in the Hokkeji community, both as vow takers and as patrons. Close attention to the types of names that emerge in Ritsu name registers and donation records make this observation possible. As *Gashō roku* and other texts have pointed out, *asobi* often took the names of Buddhist deities or names that otherwise drew upon Buddhist language *(shakke no kotoba)*. Thus, as seen in Ōe no Masafusa's (1041–1111) *Yūjoki* (Record of *yūjo*), the name "Kannon" (as in the bodhisattva Avalokitēśvara) was commonly used among *asobi* (157–159). *Asobi* names also appropriated words like *yashame* ("[Buddhist] demon-god girl," from the Sanskrit *yakṣa* with the Japanese "*me*," or "girl," added) and *nyoi* ("wish-fulfilling jewel"; Skt. *cintāmaṇi*) with some frequency. *Asobi* often added the character "*me*," or "girl," to the ends of their names, creating monikers like "White Girl" (Shirome). Another common tendency was to draw on animal names. Examples of this practice include names like "Small Horse" (Koma) and "Peacock" (Kujaku) (Gotō 2002; *Yūjoki*, 157–159).[59]

Many names bearing these same tendencies emerge in Hokkeji-related documents, suggesting that the convent's ties with *asobi* was by no means limited to the several *chōja* listed in the calendary ritual guide *Hokke metsuzaiji nenjū gyōji*. At other places in the *Nenjū gyōji*, for example, appear names like the "Dog Star Girl" (Doyōme), the "King of Bulls Girl" (Goōme), the "Pearl Girl" (Shinjume), and "Kichijōme" (from the Sanskrit Śrī-mahādevī or Mahāśrī, referring to the Indian goddess). According to the *Nenjū gyōji*, all of these women were to receive the same service: the nuns at Hokkeji were to perform the Kōmyō Shingon on their respective death dates for their postmortem benefit (see entries for 2/8, 5/16, 6/7, and 8/1, 86a–87b). Although the only information given about these women is their names and death dates, their names alone suggest that they may have been *asobi*.

Names following similar patterns also appear in many of the name registers *(kyōmyō)* associated with Eison's movement. In a *kechien kyōmyō* (name register of those wishing to form karmic ties) placed inside a statue of Śākyamuni at Saidaiji, for example, are many names that sound like those belonging to *asobi*. "Bull King Girl" appears again, as do other female names such as "Me Seishi" after the Bodhisattva Mahāsthāmaprāpta and "Vermillion Sparrow Girl" (Me Shujaku) after one of the deities of the four directions. Hundreds of examples such as these appear throughout the name register.

The *kechien kyōmyō*, dated to the seventh day of the fifth month of Kenchō 1 (1249), is nearly three hundred pages long in the edited version found in the *Dai Nihon shiryō* collection, and the majority of the names it lists belong to women. What is more, while many of the names include the expected epithets "*ama,*" "*bikuni,*" or "Amidabutsu," others resemble those of *asobi:* they use animal names like "horse," "dog," or "tortoise," or Buddhist language like "*yakushi*" (a reference to the Medicine Teacher Buddha). These women are listed alongside well-known nuns like Shinnyo, Jizen, and others (*Dai Nihon shiryō,* sect. 5, vol. 30, 10–285).

All of this evidence suggests that *asobi* were active at Hokkeji both as patrons and as nuns at various levels. There is no evidence from within Hokkeji documents to suggest that the nuns' order looked down upon *asobi.* To the contrary, the *Nenjū gyōji* treats the guild heads of Hashimoto and Kagami as elites, since it lists only those who have achieved a certain status as donors or devotees. Rather than viewing *asobi* as having entered the Hokkeji community through Ritsu outreach targeted at outcast groups, it might make more sense to understand them as having learned about Hokkeji and the Ritsu movement more broadly through regular contact with pilgrims traversing the increasingly traveled path between Kyoto and Kamakura. As women who envisioned themselves as stewards of arts connected to the culture of the court—and as women who had the financial power to act as patrons of Buddhism—*asobi,* and especially their guild heads, were well poised to support the Hokkeji movement. Many did so by commissioning ritual work from the nuns' order.[60]

Finally, in addition to the religious labor of performing rituals, at least some Hokkeji nuns may have been engaged in more quotidian forms of labor as well. To return to the 1280 record of contributions made to the campaign to erect a new residence for Eison, this record indicates that many of the *bikuni* at Hokkeji donated to the campaign textiles of various kinds, including robes of different sizes, small bags, and bolts of cotton and silk. As Wakita Haruko has observed, many convents in premodern Japan developed businesses of their own, especially during the late medieval period. By the late fifteenth century, for example, nuns at Dōmyōji had come to be known for their *hikimeshi,* a gruel made from the scraps of rice used for offerings. Nuns at the convent Mieidō (also known as Shin Zenkōji), she adds, were talented fan makers who exported their works to China, Korea, and the Ryūkyū Islands, in addition to selling them throughout Japan. By the Edo period, a number of convents are said to have specialized in the production of particular local specialties *(meibutsu),* such as the *kazukiwata,* a type of woman's hat; the ropelike straps used to make traditional sandals; and a variety of local delicacies (1995, 169–170). Given this broader history, it seems possible to suggest that at least some nuns at Hokkeji may have been involved in the production of textiles and robes. As we have seen, Eison does mention in one of his sermons that he used to have robes made at Hokkeji (*Chōmonshū,* 224). The Kōfukuji Daijōin Monzeki Jinson also mentions, in a 1475 inventory of expenses incurred during the planning of the Ceremony for the *Vimalakīrti sūtra* (Yuima-e), that three hundred *mon* were spent having *kesa* made by the nuns' order at Hokkeji (*Daijōin jisha zōjiki,* Bunmei 7/12/5, 219a).[61] Out of context, these brief references are difficult to interpret, but placed alongside evidence of multiple donations of robes and similar products from Hokkeji nuns and in view of the fact that many convents did develop small businesses over the course of the medieval period, it seems likely that the nuns' order at Hokkeji did in fact create and maintain a long-standing tradition of weaving textiles and sewing robes for profit.[62]

THE PICTURE OF MEDIEVAL HOKKEJI that emerges as evidence from surviving sources is pieced together and placed within the larger context of the Ritsu movement overturns many assumptions about the nature of nuns' lives in premodern Japan. In sources like the *Genji* or *Heike monogatari,* nunhood is often depicted as a state of retirement or withdrawal from the world, as a means of retreating into a distinctly *private* mode of living. In the case of Hokkeji, however, surviving records suggest that the women who entered the convent as nuns, novices, and members of the lay and semi-lay orders joined what was in fact a complex religious society that interacted with the laity and with other segments of the Ritsu order in very public ways.

What also becomes evident is that the *bikuni* at Hokkeji and at its branch convents were regarded not as "lay nuns" who had taken only private vows of some kind but as full-fledged members of the clergy. Unlike the nuns we see in well-known *monogatari*—nuns who focus on private devotions—the nuns of Hokkeji dedicated themselves to projects much larger in scope. Not only were they active as institution builders, aiding in the establishment of branch convents and contributing to fund-raising projects that benefited the entire Ritsu group, but they also performed significant ritual duties, fulfilling key roles in ordination ceremonies for other nuns and carrying out death offering rites, as well as a number of other rituals, on behalf of the lay community. The *bikuni* ordained at Hokkeji, unlike women who took private vows, envisioned themselves not as private devotees of the Buddhist tradition but rather as professional members of the clergy. Their ordinations as *bikuni* were ordinations in the true sense of the word: they were rites that "publicly designat[ed] and se[t] [them] apart" as "persons for religious service and leadership, granting them religious authority and power to be exercised for the welfare of the community."[63]

Although there is some evidence, as suggested at the end of chapter 2, that some women who had taken private vows did in fact work as teachers and as the performers of semipublic rituals, the Hokkeji community is the first known example since the Nara period of a large-scale religious institution directed and operated by women. While it is true that the Ritsu order as a whole was under male leadership, the everyday affairs of the Hokkeji community appear to have been entrusted to the convent's rector and the orders under her management. During the last half of the Kamakura period, the community under the rector's charge was significant, actively involving hundreds of women. The large population at Hokkeji made the convent's rector position a highly visible and political one. But added to the sheer size of the job was the ritual, pedagogic, and financial responsibility it entailed: the Hokkeji rector was required to stage official *vinaya* rituals of numerous kinds; to train *bikuni,* at least some of whom would be sent to other convents; and to attract donors and raise funds. Nuns who entered Hokkeji, especially those who advanced to the rank of *bikuni,* were not leaving the world behind. To the contrary, they were embarking upon a professional path that would give many of them the opportunity to seek advanced levels of education and ritual training, to become skilled administrators, and to exercise political and financial power.

In short, medieval Hokkeji flourished as a center of wealth and culture run by women. Its social constitution, as emphasized at the beginning of this chapter, was remarkably diverse. It is this diversity, perhaps, that best speaks to the public nature of life at medieval Hokkeji. The *bikuni* order was not simply a group of elite women who retired as nuns into lives of obscurity. It was composed of women from a variety of regional areas, social classes, and life experiences who had to learn how to interact with and manage large groups of women from backgrounds often radically different from their own. The nuns of Hokkeji succeeded not only at the task of creating an order for women that followed the rules of the *vinaya* but also at establishing a harmonious community of women who under other circumstances would have never shared a life together. Above and beyond these accomplishments, they also cultivated Hokkeji as a site of religious pilgrimage attractive to both men and women seeking karmic merit, and they won the trust of donors, many of whom commissioned them to perform death offering services. Added to this, there is evidence to suggest that they drew upon the talents of Hokkeji nuns and laywomen to produce textiles and robes for sale.

In other words, there is much reason to believe that Hokkeji offered women attractive professional, academic, and religious opportunities not readily available in other sectors of premodern Japanese society. Against the common assumption that women of this era pursued nunhood only as a last resort, the evidence provided in this chapter is sufficient to suggest that Hokkeji offered many women, especially those who met the requisites necessary for promotion to *bikuni,* the chance to pursue religious and political ambitions on a level not typically accessible to women of the period.

6
Ritual Life at Medieval Hokkeji

> To the east of Mount Awata, north of the village of Yamashina, there is a Buddhist temple called Fujiodera. To the south of this temple is another practice hall [*dōjō*], and there is one nun [*ama*] in this practice hall. Last year, this nun had an image of the Iwashimizu Hachiman Great Bodhisattva built, and she installed it [in this practice hall]. From the beginning, the miracles this image manifested were numerous and frequent. And so from near and far, monks and nuns, elites and ordinary folk, men and women [came and] clung like a grove of trees in devotion to this image. The spokes of their carriages gathered to form a marketplace [i.e., many people gathered at the practice hall where the image had been installed]. As for the Iwashimizu main shrine, on the fifteenth day of the eighth month of every year, it prepared a ceremony called the Releasing of Life [Hōjō]. Of the many people of high and low rank, there were none who did not attend this ceremony. And then the aforementioned nun also established this [same] ceremony to be held on the same day [at her practice hall]. During the afternoon, she sent for musicians, and they committed themselves fully to the production of exquisite music. In the evening, she invited famous priests to transmit the great bodhisattva precepts. The provisions of food and drink were of utmost goodness and beauty. The offerings made were [so numerous that they were] like mountains and hills. Because of this, the priests and musicians found it difficult to go to the main shrine, and [so] the [Releasing of Life] Ceremony at the main shrine was left very neglected.
>
> —Fujiwara no Michinori, *Honchō seiki*

THE ABOVE NARRATIVE, recounted in a 938 entry from Fujiwara no Michinori's (1106–1160) state history, *Honchō seiki,* goes on to tell how the main shrine of Iwashimizu Hachiman punished a charismatic nun for ritual performance. By the year 938, it had been at least a century since Japanese nuns had been given the opportunity to receive official state ordinations as *bikuni*. But according to this story, the disappearance of an official ecclesiastical path for nuns did not prevent women from styling themselves as unofficial members of the clergy or from organizing popular religious activities—and rituals—on the ground. The nun in the narrative above is described as someone who possessed a popular appeal that drew people of all backgrounds, including priests and members of the elite, to her practice hall. Though neither an officially ordained member of the clergy nor a member of a large monastic institution, she attracted large crowds when she staged opulent ceremonies in honor of the Great Bodhisattva Iwashimizu Hachiman.

What is most telling about the story of this nun is that her downfall, though the result of ritual performance, did not hinge on questions of ordination status or ritual authority. The problems began when she decided to hold her own version of the Releasing of Life Ceremony on the same day that the Iwashimizu Hachiman main shrine held its ceremony. Had her ceremony remained a modest and quiet affair, it most likely would have gone unnoticed. But this nun invited prominent priests and musicians to her ceremony, and the payments she offered them were so great that everyone—including the priests and performers—came to favor her ceremony over that held at the main shrine. In short, her ceremony became so popular that people stopped attending that held at the main shrine. Dismayed, the main shrine requested that she move her ceremony to another day. But she refused. As a result, the main shrine sent "several thousand" strongmen to her practice hall. They tied her up, confiscated her image of the Iwashimizu Hachiman bodhisattva, and took both her and the image into custody at the main shrine.

In describing this nun, the text's twelfth-century compiler Michinori does not imply that she overstepped her boundaries by performing or staging Buddhist rituals as a woman or as a privately professed nun. Her confrontation with the main shrine was simply about competition: the main shrine felt threatened by the visibility and popularity of the rituals she had been staging and wanted to protect the viability of its own ritual program. Especially telling here is the fact that the representatives of the main shrine began with diplomacy. They did not immediately forbid the nun to hold a ceremony in honor of their deity but simply asked her to hold the ceremony on a different day. It was only when she declined to reschedule her ceremony that the main shrine punished her. This case reveals a great deal about the role that underlying interests, such as prestige and material wealth, play in the formation of orthodoxy. Doctrinal issues, at least in this narrative, play no apparent role. Even as the main shrine struck to define and ban unorthodox ritual practice, it did so only with self-preservation in mind. In describing the shrine's actions against this nun, Michinori frames the issue simply as one of noncompliance; he invokes neither her gender nor her ordination status.

What does this tenth-century example tell us about the state of women and ritual authority in the thirteenth century? Although some caution is necessary, I argue that this indifference toward the gender identity of those leading rituals represents a larger trend that continued to linger in the medieval period. Indeed, it is telling that Michinori presents the story of this nun in the way that he does, without introducing issues of gender or ritual authority.[1] The passage also points to a certain orientation toward ritual performance—namely, one that valued entertainment and spectacle—that remained extremely important throughout the history of religious practice in premodern Japan. On the level of popular religious practice, few consumers of religious ceremony expressed sustained interest in issues of ritual authority. Few questioned the notion that women, or specifically unofficially ordained nuns, could organize and perform large-scale ceremonies. The issue for ordinary lay folk was more pragmatic: they tended to value miracles and pageantry.

A similar case from the Kamakura period is found in a 1233 description of the Ceremony for the Large *Prajñāpāramitā sūtra* (Daihannya-e) performed at the Hachiman shrine near Tōdaiji. The *Tōdaiji zoku yōroku* (Essential records of Tōdaiji, continued) states that the tradition of offering this ceremony at the Hachiman shrine was first established by a nun named Jōadan. It further explains that on the twenty-third day of the third month of Kangi 4 (1233), the day that the nun Jōadan began to perform the ceremony, she gave voice to an oracle of the god *(shintaku)* and, possessed by the power of the Dharma and encouraged by Dharma friends *(chishiki)* of the ten directions and four groups of Buddhist disciples, she wrote sixteen volumes of "true texts" *(shinmon)*. These texts, the entry continues, were installed in the three altars to the deities at the shrine. On the day of the ceremony, this nun also hired two priests, one to lead the chanting and another to lead the reading of the sutras. Sixty other priests were also invited (258–259). The nun Jōadan is portrayed as the primary organizer and patron of this Buddhist ceremony held at the Hachiman shrine near Tōdaiji, but she engaged Buddhist activity in a manner different from that of a typical male priest: she was possessed by the Hachiman deity and in a state of possession copied out sixteen volumes of *shinmon*, a term used to describe Buddhist texts written in a Sanskrit script.

In comparing the case of Jōadan with that of the first nun introduced in this chapter, several observations are relevant. First, both of these women, though they called themselves nuns, organized their activities outside strictly monastic structures. Although they interacted with and employed Buddhist priests, their Buddhist ceremonies were in fact staged at shrines to the Hachiman deity. A second, related observation is that both women drew on a kind of charismatic appeal: the first nun had an image that performed miracles, and the second was possessed by a deity that allowed her to produce spirit texts in a state of trance. In other words, both women claimed access to the miraculous, and these claims appear to have compensated for the women's lack of traditional monastic training. That they were able to stage Buddhist rituals outside the strictures of ordinary protocol was likely related to their exceptional qualities. Both appear to have been wealthy women who were able to act as generous patrons and hosts, and both exhibited a kind of personal charisma that enabled them to gain recognition as the performers of miracles.

Especially noticeable in the case of Jōadan is that her role in the Ceremony for the Large *Prajñāpāramitā sūtra* was similar to that of a *miko*. While she was clearly given a part to perform in the ceremony, it was a role distinct from that performed by male priests. The passage thus suggests a division of ritual labor that reflected Jōadan's status as a woman who had not taken full vows. Again, as in the first example, there is no suggestion that as a woman she should not have been allowed to perform or preside over a Buddhist ritual. But the role that she performed here—that of a spirit medium—was typically associated with women.[2]

Assessing the relationship between gender and ritual authority in medieval Japan is a difficult task. As seen in the narratives above, there is little evidence to suggest that ordinary laypeople were aware of or concerned with discourses about the relationship between gender and ritual performance. Laypeople do not appear to have viewed rituals performed or staged by women with any greater suspicion than those performed or staged by men; emphasis was instead placed on identifying which rituals were most efficacious. That said, women's opportunities for Buddhist ritual training had greatly diminished over the course of the Heian period. With the fall of the state convent system in the early Heian period and the subsequent disappearance of a state ordination system for women, women lost access to systematic forms of Buddhist training and education. Some who were blessed with wealth or social status were able to hire Buddhist priests as private tutors and to learn from these priests how to perform *kuyō* offering rites and how to chant sutras and *dhāraṇī*. But because the most powerful monastic institutions of late-Heian- and early-Kamakura-period Japanese society—those affiliated with Tendai and Shingon lineages—were closed to women and did not accept female disciples, the institutional structures of the day did not allow women to pursue the kind of serious, extended training in Buddhist ritual available to men.

What is so remarkable about the ritual lives of women at medieval Hokkeji, then, is not that they were allowed to perform the same traditional Buddhist rites that men performed. Nor is it that they managed to attract, through the ceremonies and ritual performances they frequently staged, numerous lay donors and devotees. What is striking in the case of nuns at medieval Hokkeji is that they created an institutional structure that enabled women to pursue extensive ritual training as full-fledged members of the Buddhist clergy. At some places in Hokkeji materials, there is evidence of spirit possession and other charismatic activities akin to those seen in the cases of the two nuns mentioned above. But on the whole, Hokkeji nuns did not need to rest on such appeals to validate their authority as the performers of ritual. They were instead able to derive authority from the orthodox and systematic nature of the Buddhist training they received both from Saidaiji monks and from the senior nuns who headed their community.

This chapter will examine the ritual life of the medieval Hokkeji community. The study and performance of ritual served Hokkeji nuns on a number of levels. It was through ritual practice that Hokkeji nuns were able to claim a place in the broader Ritsu community, to work toward their own salvation and that of their loved ones, and, finally, to serve lay communities both near and far. Indeed, the centrality of ritual in the lives of Hokkeji nuns and in their relationships with lay patrons is so striking that it raises the question of whether or not the Hokkeji nuns' order is best described as a female priesthood. The final section will consider this question in depth.

Performing the Priestly Rituals of the Ritsu Sect

Hokkeji's Kamakura-period alliance with Saidaiji provided nuns with the opportunity to study and perform most of the same rituals that male Ritsu priests performed.[3] Hokkeji nuns were thus able to engage in ritual performance not simply as patrons or charismatic figures forced to work outside traditional monastic procedures but rather as fully ordained *bikuni* trained to perform roles that had long been dominated by male priests. One of the earliest examples of such ritual activity is found in the *Hokkeji kekkaiki*, a document mentioned in the last chapter. According to this record, the Hokkeji nuns' order held a ceremony marking the sacred boundaries of Hokkeji on the sixth day of the second month of Kenchō 2 (1249). This ceremony, which established the sacred space necessary for the performance of official Ritsu rituals, such as confession ceremonies *(fusatsu)* and ordination ceremonies *(jukai-e)*, is also mentioned in Eison's records. As seen in other examples in which Eison established Ritsu practice at temples that sought incorporation into the Saidaiji network, *kekkai* ceremonies were performed to mark as sacred the spaces where the fundamental rituals of a given Ritsu community were to be performed.

What is revealing about the *Hokkeji kekkaiki* is that it clearly indicates that the nuns themselves, with their rector Jizen leading the way, performed the ritual acts comprising the *kekkai* ceremony. Following the main body of the document, which describes in detail the stones and walls marking the physical boundaries of Hokkeji's sacred space, is this epigraph:

> Hōji 3 [1249], the year of Tsuchinoto Tori
> On the sixth day of the second month, during the hour of the monkey [3:00–5:00 p.m.], we established these boundaries. (Today, after twelve [nuns] first received the great precepts [as *bikuni*].)

Bikuni: Jizen (priestly ritual proceedings [*konma*])	Gyōdō Novice Nun: Sonnyo
Bikuni: Nyoen	Gyōdō Novice Nun: Zenmyō
Bikuni: Kan'i	Hōdō Novice Nun: Shōnyo
Bikuni: Kinin	Hōdō Novice Nun: Hōen
Bikuni: Shinhō	Hōdō Novice Nun: Jōshin

Bikuni: Shinkaku (chorals [*shōsō*])
Bikuni: Shakunen
Bikuni: Sonshin
Bikuni: Enshō
Bikuni: Gyōa
Bikuni: Nenshun
Bikuni: Kan'a
Hōdō Novice Nun: Chimyō
Hōdō Novice Nun: Shinjō
Probationary Novice Nun: Zen'e
Probationary Novice Nun: Zenshin
Probationary Novice Nun: Chion
Probationary Novice Nun: Ganshin
Probationary Novice Nun: Kaimyō
Probationary Novice Nun: Jōnyo
Probationary Novice Nun: Jinen

Hōji 3 [1249], the year of Tsuchinoto Tori
On the fourteenth day of the second month in the hour of the rooster [5:00–7:00 p.m.], we read the *kekkai* again. The members of the nuns order [who performed this ceremony] were all the same as listed above, except that the *konma* was performed by Shinkaku and the chorals by Gyōa. (Kenchō 2 [1249])

As the order of the names makes visible, the person who performed the *konma* held the leading role in the ceremony. The *konma* master was to recite the purpose of the ritual *(hyōbyaku)* and was also responsible for directing the ceremony as a whole. The second most important role was that of the choral leader. This person was to lead the group in the chanting of the verses that comprised the ceremony. As a point of comparison, it is worth noting that when the same *kekkai* ritual was performed by male monastics at Saidaiji in the year 1238, it was the senior priest Kakujō who served as the *konma* master and Eison who fulfilled the role of choral leader (*KJGSK* 1999, 95; Hosokawa 1999b, 101). That the *bikuni* Jizen, Shinkaku, and Gyōa are listed here as having fulfilled these roles in two different *kekkai* ceremonies at Hokkeji, then, indicates that these three women were regarded as leading figures of the Hokkeji community in the year 1249.

This document illustrates the degree to which Hokkeji nuns were committed to and actively engaged in the performance of the very same rituals that occupied Ritsu priests. It also suggests that nuns at Hokkeji acquired ritual training that enabled them to fulfill the various roles central to the performance of traditional Buddhist ceremonies, roles like *konma* master and choral leader. These observations, like those that follow in the sections below, challenge the idea, well entrenched in the study of women in Japanese Buddhism, that women did not perform "serious" Buddhist rituals (e.g., Ishida M. 1978).[4]

The Ritual Calendar

The *Hokke metsuzaiji nenjū gyōji* provides extensive insight into the ritual program in place at Hokkeji in the years following its medieval revival. As explained in the previous chapter, the only surviving copy of this text contains a colophon stating that it was copied out in the year 1322 by the *bikuni* Yūshi. The fact that this copy contains a reference written in the same hand as the main body of the text to the twenty-ninth day of the ninth month of Jōwa 3 (1347) indicates, however, that it must have been recopied on or after this later date. Still, other references within the text, especially those mentioning donors and former rectors, allow one to speculate that some version of this same ritual program was already in place at Hokkeji during the heyday of its thirteenth-century revival (Tanaka Minoru 1978b, 85–86a).

The *Nenjū gyōji* is divided into six sections: (1) Daily Rites, which is further divided into Morning, Midday, and Evening Rites; (2) All-Day Rites of Offering; (3) All-Day and All-Night Continuous Ceremonies; (4) Twice-a-Day Vinaya Discussions; (5) Ceremonies for the First Month of the New Year; and (6) Annual Ceremonies, Death Memorial Services, and the Like. The longest and most substantial sections, which will be treated in this chapter, are sections 1, 5, and 6. The full document is rather long, some sixteen single-spaced pages when translated into English, and it offers almost no detail about the actual content of the rites and ceremonies it mentions. Essentially, the *Nenjū gyōji* is a long list of rituals arranged in the form of a calendar. It is not a manual as such; that is, it does not explain *how* to perform the rites it lists. Rather, it is a document that was meant for the eyes of insiders, a reference work or schedule that provided Hokkeji nuns with guidelines and reminders. The *Nenjū gyōji* outlines when the nuns' order was to perform what rituals and for whom. The content of individual rites and ceremonies would have been learned elsewhere—primarily through instruction and practice, but likely with the help of manuals containing written versions of the chants to be performed in various rituals. Although no such manuals dating to this period survive at Hokkeji, detailed manuals dating to the fifteenth and sixteenth centuries, many of them containing the same rituals, can be found within the archives of Saidaiji.[5] Nearly all of the rituals listed in the *Nenjū gyōji* had been standardized by the twelfth and thirteenth centuries and can be found in contemporaneous documents associated with other temples and lineages.

Daily Rites

The first section of the *Nenjū gyōji* lists the rites that Hokkeji nuns were to perform on a daily basis. As will be made clear below, most of these rites consist of *shōmyō,* or Buddhist chants.[6] Most common are *shōmyō* pieces based on standardized liturgical texts, usually passages from well-known sutras, although a few can be categorized as *dhāraṇī,* or magical incantations. Together, these rites make up the *gongyō,* the daily ritual tasks to be performed by the priest or priests of any given temple. Typically, priests have performed these chants and sutra readings in front of the Buddhist images enshrined in their temple. Because the act of offering the Dharma to these images is understood as one of tasks most fundamental to the daily operations of temples, contemporary priests often refer to such activity as *otsutome,* a polite way of saying "work."

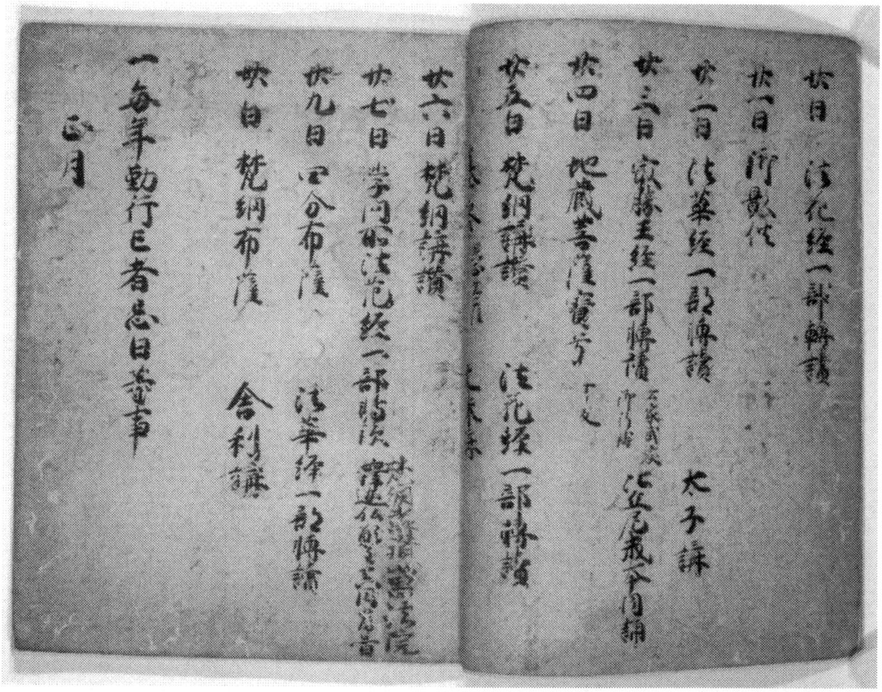

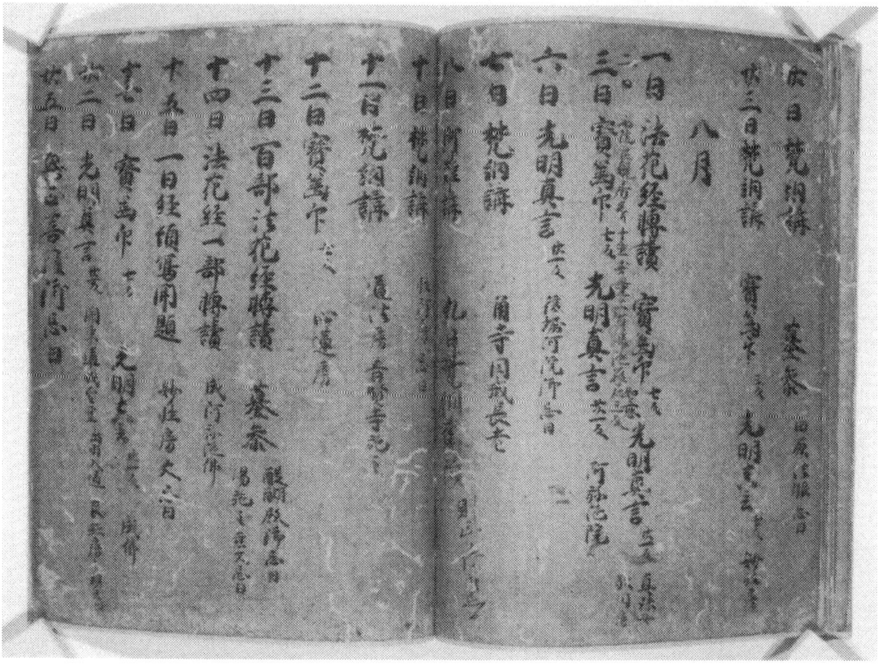

From *The Yearly Events of the Lotus Temple for the Eradication of Transgressions (Hokke metsuzaiji nenjū gyōji)*, fourteenth century. Ink on paper. (Photograph by Nara National Museum, courtesy Hokkeji, Nara, Japan)

According to the *Nenjū gyōji,* morning, midday, and evening *gongyō* were performed in the lecture hall, and an additional midday *gongyō* was also to be performed in the main hall:

Item: Daily Rituals

Morning

Raimon [Includes seven sections: Honoring All Buddhas, Praising the Nyorai, Confession of Karmic Obstacles, Rejoicing in Karmic Merit, Praying for the Turning of the Wheel of Dharma, Praying for a Sight of the Buddha, and Merit Transfer; in Chinese.]

Chant of the Monk's Staff in Nine Parts [Kujō Shakujō; in Chinese]

Lotus Confession and Lotus Hymn [Hokke Sen narabi ni San]

Wish-Fulfilling Dhāraṇī of the Bodhisattva Mahāpratisara [Zuigu Dhāraṇī], twelve times[7]

Merciful Savior Fudō [Fudō Jiku], twenty-one times

The above is to be carried out in the lecture hall.

Midday

Raimon [same as above]

Kannon Sutra [*Kannonkyō,* the title of twenty-fifth chapter of the *Lotus Sutra;* in Chinese]

Thousand-Armed [Kannon] Dhāraṇī [Senju Darani], five times [in Chinese]

Eleven-Faced [Kannon] Great Incantation [Jūichimen Daiju], thirty-three times [in Chinese]

Relics Respects [Shari Rai(mon)], three times [to be read in *kundoku* style]

Relics Hymn in Japanese [Shari Wasan]

Precious Name of Śākyamuni [Shaka Bōgō], one hundred times

The above is to be carried out in the lecture hall.

Raimon

Twelve Respects for Śākyamuni [Shaka Jūni Rai; in Chinese]

The Sutra of the Deathbed Injunction [*Yuigyō,* Chns. *Fochui boniepan lüeshuo jiaojie jing*][8] (Sometimes in the study room. The place where this service is to be performed is not fixed.) [in Chinese]

Thirty Verses on the *Vijñapati-mātra Treatise* [*(Yuishiki) Sanjū (ron)ju,* Chns. *Wishisanshilunsong,* T. no. 1586; in Chinese]

[Amida's] Precious Box Seal Dhāraṇī [Hōkyō Darani; in Sanskrit]

Incantation for All the Four Kings [Shiō Sōju; in Chinese]

Precious Name of Śākyamuni, one hundred times

Relics Respects, three times [same as above]

The above is to be carried out in the main hall.

Evening

Raimon [same as above]

Twelve Respects for Amida [Mida Jūni Rai]

Amida Sutra [*Amidakyō;* Skt. *Amitābha-sūtra,* aka *Smaller Sukhāvatī-vyūha Sutra;* in Chinese]
Great Incantation of Amida [Amida Daiju], seven times [in Chinese]
Great Incantation of King Aizen [Rāgarāja] [Aizen-ō Daiju], seven times [in Chinese]
Noble and Excellent Dhāraṇī [Jpns. Sonshō Darani], three times [in Sanskrit][9]
Five Syllable [Arapacana] Mañjuśrī Incantation [Goji Monju Ju], twenty-one times
Kōmyō Shingon, seven times [in Sanskrit]
Precious Name of [A]mida [Mida Bōgō], one hundred times
Seated meditation [*zazen*] after the evening service
The above is to be carried out in the lecture hall. (86–87)

Two important observations can be made from this list of daily liturgies. First, in comparing Hokkeji's chants with those in place at male monastic institutions, it is evident that Hokkeji nuns were performing the same chants and sutra incantations as their male counterparts. For the most part, the chant pieces listed here are all standard ones that can be found in the contemporaneous liturgies of most Japanese monastic institutions, regardless of sectarian affiliation. Because the liturgical texts of these chants had been standardized by the time the Hokkeji liturgical calendar was compiled, both the textual content and base language of each chant can be extrapolated from contemporaneous or nearly contemporaneous outside texts.

The Raimon offered at the beginning of each service refers to the Sanrai, a chant in which the activities of body, speech, and mind are offered up in praise of the buddhas. Based on passages from Śikṣānanda's Tang-period translation of the *Flower Ornament Sutra in Eighty Fascicles* (*Dafangguangfo huayan jing,* aka *Bashi huayan*), this *shōmyō* piece was already in wide usage within Japan by the early Heian period. Another *shōmyō* piece included in the Hokkeji liturgies, the Chant of the Monk's Staff in Nine Parts (Kujō Shakujō), also contains text taken from the *Flower Ornament Sutra in Eighty Fascicles.* By the time of Hokkeji's restoration, Japanese monks had been employing both of these chants for some time. The Chant of the Monk's Staff in Nine Parts, which was introduced to Japan in the tenth century, had gained circulation within China many centuries earlier. Some other chant pieces, especially native ones like the Relics Hymn in Japanese (Shari Wasan), were of later compilation but were also used widely by the thirteenth century. At least two versions of the Shari Wasan were in circulation. One is attributed to the Nara scholar-monk Yōkan (1033–1111) (Iwahara 1986, 221–251).[10]

With only a few minor exceptions, all of these chants and sutra readings appear in the earliest surviving lists of daily liturgy at Saidaiji, which date to the sixteenth century.[11] Although the order in which the chants are arranged in the *Nenjū gyōji* varies from that evident in these Saidaiji liturgies, the basic selections of chants are similar both in content and in number, despite the fact that the liturgical records from Saidaiji postdate the Hokkeji records by at least three hundred years. In other words, the records show that centuries after the Hokkeji revival Saidaiji monks were still performing the same liturgies contained in the early fourteenth-century *Nenjū gyōji*. This consistency over time suggests that the liturgies carried out by Hokkeji nuns in the medieval period were based on those practiced by Ritsu monks. It further indicates that women were both allowed and expected to draw on the same repertoire of *shōmyō* as their male counterparts.

On the one hand, this revelation may not seem terribly surprising. In contemporary Japan, where the sight of elderly widows reading sutras on behalf of deceased husbands is an everyday one, the fact that laywomen have long chanted sutras as an act of devotion or on behalf of the dead is accepted as common knowledge. Chanting a sutra in front of an altar requires neither a male body nor ordination; it is a task that anyone can perform, and it is known that educated Japanese laywomen have been performing chants and sutra readings for well over a thousand years. Consider, for example, the descriptions of his grandmother's daily devotions that Heian aristocrat Fujiwara no Munetada (1062–1141) includes in his diary, *Chūyūki*. Following the custom of elite Heian women, Munetada's grandmother, known as the (Lay) Nun of Ichijō, spent the last thirty years of her life in retirement as a privately professed nun. She spent these decades performing regular liturgies and offerings as a means of preparing for a favorable death. As Munetada explains:

> She carried out 7,100 recitations of *The Lotus Sutra,* and each day without fail she made offerings to Amida in the prescribed manner and recited *The Daizuigu Dharani Sutra* [*The Sutra on the Wish-Fulfilling Dhāraṇī of the Bodhisattva Mahāpratisara*]. In the course of thirty years, she carried out the one million recitations of the *nenbutsu* [the invocation of Amida's name] a total of twenty times. Every month on the fifteenth day [or twenty-fifth day; the text is unclear] she recited the *Amida Daiju* [*The Great Incantation of Amida*] ten thousand times, and on the eighteenth day she recited *The Thousand Arm*[*ed Kannon*] *Dharani* a thousand times. (trans. Watson, in Obara 2002, 443–444; *Chūyūki,* Kōwa 5 [1103] 3/23)[12]

The three *dhāraṇī* mentioned here—the Thousand-Armed Kannon Dhāraṇī, the Wish-Fulfilling Dhāraṇī of the Bodhisattva Mahāpratisara, and the Great Incantation of Amida—also appear in the *Nenjū gyōji* (*Chūyūki,* Kōwa 5 [1103] 3/23; qtd. in Obara 1989, 114). The Nun of Ichijō also recited a number of sutras. Insofar as there were no rules forbidding women and laypeople from chanting sutras and *dhāraṇī,* there is perhaps nothing extraordinary about the fact that Hokkeji nuns were performing the same chants as their male counterparts. As laypeople or as unofficially ordained nuns, women had been chanting the same sutras and *dhāraṇī* as men for centuries.

And yet there is something remarkable about the *Nenjū gyōji*'s liturgical program, and that is the fact that it does not contain any extra chants or other ritual activities meant to alleviate problems associated with the female body. Although certain sutras aimed at rendering the female body male were in fact available at this time, the liturgies of Hokkeji did not take up such discourse.[13] There is no evidence that passages from [*The Buddha Teaches the*] *Sutra on Transforming the Female Body* (*Bussetsu tennyoshingyō*, or *Tennyoshingyō*, T. no. 564), for example, were included in the liturgical programs at Hokkeji, despite the fact that the text had been circulated in thirteenth-century Ritsu circles. The lengthy esoteric *(mikkyō)* compendium *Mahāsaṃnipāta-sūtra* (Great collection sutra, Chns. *Dajijing*) also offers a number of discussions relevant to women's attainment of male bodies (Katsuura 2003, 52; T no. 397, esp. fasc. 13, 132–133, 146–149, 217–219), but readings from this sutra are not included in Hokkeji liturgies either. None of the *shōmyō* pieces included in the daily liturgies at Hokkeji draw on sutra passages that mention the soteriological obstacles of women. The longer Pure Land sutras mention that women do not exist in Amida's Pure Land and that women seeking rebirth in the Pure Land should despise their female bodies and pray for male bodies, but the Pure Land passages included in these Hokkeji liturgies are taken from the *Amitābha sūtra* (*Amidakyō*, T. no. 366), the shortest of the Pure Land sutras. Like the other sutras invoked in Hokkeji's liturgical program, the *Amitābha sūtra* offers no comment on women's bodies.

Given the absence of texts emphasizing the problematic nature of the female body in the *Nenjū gyōji*, one can speculate that such discourses were not of primary concern to the nuns' community at Hokkeji. The sutra passages that Hokkeji women internalized through the repeated physical practice of chant were no different than those consuming the days of their male counterparts. In many cases, these chants contain ambitious vows emphasizing the spiritual potential of the cantor. Consider, for example, the first few lines from the lengthy Chant of the Monk's Staff in Nine Parts (Chns. Jiutiao Xizhang):

> With my hand I grasp the monk's staff
> I vow [to help] sentient beings
> Prepare a great offering ceremony and
> Reveal the Path of Truth [Jitsudō]
> Let us make offerings to the Three Jewels,
> Prepare a great offering ceremony,
> And reveal the Path of Truth,
> Let us make offerings to the Three Jewels. . . .
> With a heart pure of karmic defilement,
> Let us make offerings to the Three Jewels. . . .
> I vow [to help] sentient beings
> Become the teachers of heavenly and human beings,
> Fulfill unceasing vows,

And rescue suffering sentient beings,
Bringing them into the Dharma Realm.
Let us make offerings to the Three Jewels,
Directly encounter all of the buddhas
And quickly achieve enlightenment! . . .[14]

The Chant of the Monk's Staff in Nine Parts invokes the power of an ordained member of the *sangha*—one with a monk's staff—both to teach and to save sentient beings. Against earlier descriptions of nuns as passive figures requiring the mediation of male priests, then, this *shōmyō* piece, included in the morning services at Hokkeji, suggests that at least some nuns may have in fact envisioned themselves as having the potential to teach, and yes, even to extend salvation to, sentient beings.

Attention to the textual content of *shōmyō* chanted at Hokkeji leads to another important observation: the chants included in the *Nenjū gyōji*'s daily liturgies were not easy ones. As seen in chapter 4, Eison did not simplify Ritsu teachings when faced with an audience of women: he offered Hokkeji nuns multiweek seminars on the same difficult texts that he taught his male disciples. Perhaps it comes as no surprise, then, that the textual content of the Hokkeji liturgy was also extremely rigorous. There is no indication that Hokkeji's liturgical program was simplified in any way so as to make it more accessible to female practitioners.

Among the more difficult sutras included in the Hokkeji liturgical program is the *Yuishiki sanjū* [*ron*]*ju* (Thirty verses on the Vijñapati-mātra Treatise, T. no. 1586), which appears in the midday service at the main hall. Attributed to Vasubandhu, one of the founders of the Indian Yogācāra school (known as Hossō in Japan), this text was translated by Xuanzang in the seventh century. A difficult philosophical text, the *Thirty Verses on the Vijñapati-mātra Treatise* expounds concepts such as the processes by which conditioned phenomena *(uihō)* arise, the three kinds of subjective transformations in consciousness *(sannōhen),* and the methods by which illusions are removed in enlightenment (*DDB,* s.v. "Sannōhen").[15] The inclusion of this text—a text that is also included in Saidaiji liturgies—in the Hokkeji liturgical calendar reflects the continued influence of the Hossō school in Nara Buddhism. It also suggests that at least some nuns at Hokkeji were very learned. That nuns in the Hokkeji network were familiar with Yogācāra texts is further supported by a rare artifact from the Chūgūji convent: a copy of the *Yuqie shidi lun* (*Discourses on the stages of concentration practice,* Jpns. *Yugashijiron,* Skt. *Yogacāra-bhūmi-śāstra,* T. no. 1579) believed to have been used by the nun Shinnyo. What is especially remarkable about this text is that its colophon attributes to Shinnyo the *katen,* or marks used to render Chinese texts into Japanese grammatical form, which had been added to the text in red ink (*YKT,* 1:80). That Shinnyo had added *katen* to the text implies that her understanding of this unpunctuated text was so sophisticated that she was able to parse it according to the conventions of Japanese grammatical form, which requires verbs to come after, instead of before, their objects.

The fact that the chants included in the Hokkeji liturgies are written in several different languages—Chinese, Sanskrit, hybrid Sino-Japanese, and Japanese—also suggests a high level of learning among Hokkeji nuns. As mentioned earlier, the *shōmyō* pieces included in the *Nenjū gyōji* all incorporate liturgical texts whose content had been standardized during the Heian and Kamakura periods. Comparison with outside texts thus allows us to determine both the textual content and the base languages of Hokkeji liturgies. In examining the languages of these various chants, we find all but two are based on Chinese or Sanskrit texts. One exception is the Sino-Japanese Relics Respects (in both midday services), which was to be read in *kundoku* style, meaning that its Chinese text was to be read aloud in a stylized form of Japanese as it was performed. The other is the Relics Hymn in Japanese (Shari Wasan), a Japanese-language hymn in praise of the relics (from the first midday service). The other texts were to be read aloud according to the original Chinese or Sanskrit word order. That these other texts were Chinese or Sanskrit-based does not, of course, mean that the Hokkeji nuns performing them were necessarily proficient in these languages. Japanese phonetic glosses would have been available for all of these chants, and it is likely that most who performed the chants—male and female—relied upon such glosses until they had memorized the chants. Still, that Hokkeji nuns were trained to perform such a great number of foreign-language-based chants is significant, especially given the deeply entrenched view, at least within the contemporary academic world, that women who attempted to read or write in foreign languages were regarded as unfeminine.[16]

The one ritual event listed among these daily services that does not represent a chant of some kind is the seated meditation *(zazen)* included at the end of the evening service. The *Nenjū gyōji* indicates that this meditation was to take place after all of the chants had been performed. The inclusion of seated meditation here is fascinating for two reasons in particular. First, it reflects the degree to which Zen studies and practices had been absorbed within Ritsu institutions. Although *zazen* was among the meditative techniques practiced within the Tendai school, the Ritsu group had closer ties with institutions and figures associated with the new Zen movements than with Tendai groups. Even Eison's Saidaiji group, as mentioned earlier, was known to have incorporated some Zen-style meditation practices into its ritual repertoire. The *zazen* listed here, then, most likely refers to the seated meditation practices reintroduced in the late Heian and early Kamakura periods by advocates of the Zen school.

The second point worth mentioning with regard to the inclusion of seated meditation in the *Nenjū gyōji* is that it suggests a certain rigor of practice not commonly associated—in contemporary scholarly assessments, anyway—with female practitioners in medieval Japan. That Hokkeji nuns were actively engaged in difficult practices such as meditation is further indicated in the *Hokke metsuzaiji engi,* where the text's author, Enkyō, includes in her list of sixteen founding *bikuni* at medieval Hokkeji information regarding how many of the women died. Here, she says that a number of Hokkeji nuns died while performing ascetic practices. The inclusion of this information demonstrates that many Hokkeji nuns, like great male masters, aspired to achieve certain idealized forms of death that required diligent training in the years leading up to one's death. Enkyō records *bikuni* Kinin, for example, as having died at the age of seventy-two while performing seated meditation *(zazen samadhi).* She also says that the *bikuni* Jinen, Shinjō, and Shōshō all died while carrying out *ajikan,* or meditation on the Sanskrit letter "A" (143a).[17]

Surviving sources do not reveal how exactly these daily liturgies were performed. It is unlikely that all women in residence were required to participate in each and every daily service, but we can speculate that the rector supervised these performances and that women in residence were encouraged to attend as many services as possible. Information from outside sources, such as Lady Nijō's *Towazugatari,* also suggests that these services were open to outside auditors and especially to female pilgrims lodging at the temple. When visiting the Daigoji convent Shōkutei-in, Nijō attended daily services, reading "sutras and such" alongside the nuns there.[18] The nuns at Shōkutei-in often rose before daybreak to perform these morning sutra-reading services, Nijō writes (*TG,* 104; trans. Brazell 1973, 108). This example from Shōkutei-in, as well as knowledge of similar practices in place at monastic institutions during this time, allows us to speculate that Hokkeji nuns, too, likely began their preparations for morning services as early as four or five in the morning, depending on the season (Sugimoto and Koga 1979, 97).

Nijō's descriptions of services at the Shōkutei-in convent also offer another insight relevant here: she mentions that when listening to the morning services one day, she was moved when she heard the nuns chant the line, "Even a cakravartin [wheel-turning king] who is of high rank is ultimately bound to the three evil paths [*sanzu*]."[19] Because she cites this line in Japanese, one can assume that it is taken from a *wasan,* or Japanese hymn. In citing a line from a chanted text like this, she suggests that she was familiar enough with the content of chants to recognize their textual meaning upon hearing them recited. Whether or not this was actually the case and whether or not laywomen who lacked Nijō's education would have been able to make sense of difficult Buddhist terms like "cakravartin" upon hearing them recited is another matter. But the assumption underlying Nijō's citation of this *wasan* is that chants were, at least in the case of hymns composed in Japanese, intelligible to auditors. Sanskrit texts may have been like *dhāraṇī,* or magical incantations, valued primarily for the sounds they created when chanted rather than for their linguistic meaning. Chinese texts, however, would have been at least partially intelligible to nuns who chanted them on a daily basis. If one accepts that Shinnyo had read and analyzed the difficult *Yuga shijiron,* it is easy to imagine that educated groups of nuns at Hokkeji would have been able to comprehend the simpler Chinese phrasing that appears in Chinese-language chants such as the Relics Respects, the Kujō Shakujō, and the *Amitābha sūtra.*

And thus, notwithstanding their brevity and lack of detail, these lists outlining daily liturgies at Hokkeji reveal a great deal about lives of medieval nuns there. First, the lists demonstrate the overall parity between the liturgical programming in place at Hokkeji and that found at male monasteries. Secondly, they suggest that the ritual program in place at Hokkeji was a rigorous one: four separate services were to be performed each and every day without break. The rigor of ritual life at Hokkeji will be made even clearer as additional sections of the *Nenjū gyōji* are analyzed. The fact that most of the chants comprising these services were based on Chinese and Sanskrit texts also suggests that extensive educational structures were in place at Hokkeji.

Large-Scale Ceremonies

The second major category of rituals included in the *Nenjū gyōji* consists of *hōe,* or large-scale Buddhist ceremonies. A sample of these many ceremonies includes the following:

Main Hall Service of the First Month (Kondō Shushō-e; first through seventh days of the New Year)
Yakushi Hall Service of the First Month (Yakushidō Shushō-e; first through third days of the New Year)
Lecture Hall Service of the First Month (Kōdō Shushō-e; first through seventh days of the New Year, and again on the ninth day for lay donors)
Great Benevolent Kings Ceremony (Dainin'nō-e; tenth day of the New Year; first day, fifth month, "for protection from foreign invaders" [*ikoku kitō*])
Four-Part [Vinaya] Confession Ceremony (Shibun Fusatsu; fourteenth and twenty-ninth days of the New Year)
Brahma Net Confession Ceremony (Bonmō Fusatsu; fifteenth and thirtieth days of the New Year)
Chanted Lecture on Kannon (Kannon-kō; eighteenth day of the New Year)
Ceremonial Offerings to Kōbō Daishi, or Kūkai (Mieku; twenty-first day of the New Year)
Chanted Lecture on Prince Shōtoku (Taishi-kō; twenty-second day of the New Year)
Chanted Lecture on Mañjuśrī (Monju-kō; twenty-fifth day of the New Year)
Chanted Lecture on the Relics (Shari-kō; thirtieth day of the New Year, third day of the third month, twenty-fourth day of the fourth month)
Chanted Lecture on Rāhula (Ragora-kō; eighth day, first and seventh months)

Service of the Second Month (Shuni-e;[20] first three days of the second month)
Praises Expounding the *Nirvana Sutra* (Nehankyō Kōsan; first through twelfth days of the second month)
Praises Expounding the *Brahma Net Sutra* (Bonmōkyō Kōsan; fourteenth day of the New Year, twenty-fifth through twenty-seventh days of the New Year, second day of the second month)
Chanted Lecture on Ānanda (Anan-kō; eighth day of the second and eighth months)
Eight Chanted Lectures on the *Lotus Sutra* (Hokke Hakkō; from the seventh day of the second month for four days)
Reciting the Name of Śākyamuni (Shaka *nenbutsu;* from the thirteenth day of the second month for three days and nights continuously)
Nirvana Ceremony (Nehan-e; fifteenth day, second month)
Goza Chanted Lectures (Goza-kō; fifteenth day, second month). These consisted of four major *kōshiki* written by Myōe: Chanted Lecture on the Buddha's Nirvana (Nehan-kō), Chanted Lecture on the Sixteen Arhats(Jūroku Rakan-kō), Chanted Lecture on Historic Sites (Associated with the Buddha) (Yuishaku-kō), Chanted Lecture on the Relics, and (most likely) Chanted Lecture on Upholding the Sutras (Jikyō Kōshiki). This elaborate liturgy uses the four standardized *shōmyō* pieces *bonbai, sange, bon'on,* and *shakujō.*
Ceremony for the Buddha's Birthday (Busshō-e; eighth day, fourth month)
Ceremonial Quick Reading of All Sutras (Issaikyō Tendoku; twenty-third day, fourth month, for three days)
Great Brahma Net Ceremony in Honor of the Death Anniversary of Our Founder [Queen-Consort Kōmyō] (Hongan Onkijitsu Bonmō Dai-e; first seven days of the sixth month). According to the entry, *gigaku* music was to be performed on the last day of the rite.
Chanted Lecture on the Favorable Birth of Our Founder [Queen-Consort Kōmyō] (Hongan Ontsuizen Ōjō-kō; seventh day, sixth month, for seven days). According to the entry, this was to be performed using the four standardized *shōmyō* pieces.
Ghost Festival Ceremony (Urabon-e, Ullambana; thirteenth through fifteenth days, seventh month). The entry notes, "As a part of the ceremony, a continuous three-day-and-night Kōmyō Shingon is to be performed."
Recitation of the Buddha's Name (Butsumyō; eighth and twenty-third days, twelfth month, for three days each)

Analysis of the numbers and types of *hōe* performed at Hokkeji sheds light both on the institutional stature of the convent during its medieval revival and on the nature of the nuns' relationships with local laypeople.

On the whole, the *hōe* included in sections 5 and 6 of the *Nenjū gyōji*—the majority of which are cited in the list above—refer to lengthy public ceremonies open, at least partially, to local lay followers. Many, as indicated above, were multiday ceremonies, some lasting as many as seven days and others requiring continuous practice all day and all night over several days. If knowledge from outside examples of these ceremonies holds true in the case of Hokkeji, multiple-day services would have also required extensive preparation. Consider, for example, the Shuni-e, which is listed among those ceremonies to be performed during the second month at Hokkeji. Ethnographic and historical studies have described Tōdaiji's well-known Shuni-e celebration, also known as the Omizutori (Water-Drawing Festival), as a great ritual undertaking that called for weeks of preparation (see Nara National Museum 2001b, 2006, and Irie 1996).[21]

The performance of *hōe* also required significant financial resources: dancers and musicians had to be hired, adornments had to be purchased, and, for large *hōe* especially, grand ritual spaces and dance platforms had to be erected. Although *hōe* could be scaled down in times of economic hardship, the frequency with which a given temple held *hōe* reflects the scope of its financial resources. Large temples that enjoyed court patronage held great numbers of *hōe*, while smaller temples of lesser political import may have sponsored only several, if any, such grand occasions per year. The large number and wide range of *hōe* included in Hokkeji's ritual calendar reflects the convent's status as one of the great temples of Nara. In fact, a quick comparison with the medieval ritual calendar at Tōdaiji suggests that Hokkeji's annual calendar was only slightly smaller in scale than that of Tōdaiji. What is more, Hokkeji's calendar appears to have been significantly larger in scale than that of the male monastic institution Daianji, long recognized as one of the seven great temples of the southern capital.[22]

It is probably fair to say that *hōe* were the most visible events undertaken by Buddhist temples. Nagamura Makoto has referred to them as the "pillar" of temple activity (2001a, 87–88). As such, they carried a great deal of prestige and were recognized as the primary vehicle for professional promotion within the monastic community. The successful performance of a *hōe* required a sizeable team of professionals, each of whom was given a specific role according to his (or, in the case of Hokkeji, her) position within the hierarchy of the Buddhist community. In *hōe* centered on the reading of sutras, the highest positions were those of *kōshi,* or lecturer, and *dokushi,* or reader. In sutra-centered ceremonies such as the Great Benevolent Kings Ceremony, the *kōshi* and *dokushi* would both take seats of honor atop high platforms. In repentance ceremonies, the highest position was that of *dōshi,* officiating priest (Yamagishi 2004, 194–195). Within the great monastic institutions of Nara, members of the *gaku-shū,* or order of scholarly priests, typically filled these three positions. This tendency likely resulted from the fact that the performance of such ceremonies required great erudition: those occupying such positions had undergone extensive training in the reading and chanting of Chinese and Sanskrit texts and possessed specialized knowledge of liturgical music. Being chosen to occupy a position of leadership in a given ceremony was thus regarded as a great honor. It was primarily through such invitations that male priests advanced professionally.[23]

This bureaucratic aspect of *hōe* reflects the historical origins of these ceremonies, which first emerged in Japan during the eighth century. As Uejima Susumu has shown, the Nara court, which held knowledge of sutras and commentaries in high esteem, created a system that rewarded those who had successfully performed an ordered series of *hōe* with titles as state lecturers and readers (*shokoku kōshi* and *shokoku dokushi*) (2004, 232). In the early years of Japanese Buddhism, *hōe* appear to have been performed primarily for the protection of the court and its realm. The spectacle of the *hōe*—which included grand performances of song, dance, and recitation—was meant both to generate great karmic merit and to please the gods and buddhas. *Hōe* also served a didactic purpose, insofar as they offered explications of sutras and commentaries.

Around the tenth century, the social meaning of *hōe* performance changed significantly. First of all, *hōe* grew in number. Many new *hōe*, such as the Shushō-e and the Shuni-e, emerged around this time. Secondly, the ceremonies gradually gained popularity among the laity. By the middle of the Heian period, most religious institutions, unable to rely on state patronage, had been forced to seek out private support to stay afloat. One of the primary means by which temple-shrine complexes came to attract the regular financial support of local laypeople was by offering the public numerous occasions to make merit. *Hōe* were opened to the public and made as amusing as possible, and various forms of music, dance, and teaching were also made available for public consumption. Members of the laity—first aristocrats, but eventually commoners as well—found *hōe* attractive not only because they offered the opportunity to create good merit but also because they promised a variety of sensual delights: ornate decorations, brightly colored costumes, song, dance, storytelling, and sutra recitation. Clergy, in turn, prized the opportunity to teach the masses about Buddhism and to earn their loyalty and financial support. Outside the capital, *hōe* played an important role in the acceptance of Buddhism among commoners in the countryside (234–236, 250).

Recent scholarship on the nature of *hōe* in the social history of medieval Japan has demonstrated that these events often took on the character of festivals. Beyond the chants, lectures, dances, and musical performances that constituted the basic structure of major *hōe*, other forms of popular entertainment were often added. In particular, it is known that *etoki*, or the explication of images, and popular dances, such as *dengaku* and *sarugaku*, were commonly performed for pilgrims during large-scale *hōe*. *Hōe* performances thus involved people of all classes: the top lecturer positions were filled by elite scholar-monks, while those who danced and provided musical accompaniment were often hired from organizations outside the temple.[24] *Dengaku* and *sarugaku*, in contrast, were often performed in less formal contexts, by artisans who presented themselves as monks but who had no formal institutional status or affiliation *(hōshi)*.

Over the course of the Kamakura period, many temple-shrine complexes expanded *hōe* performances into *kanjin kōgyō*, multiday festivals that offered visitors a smorgasbord of spiritually edifying amusement (*etoki*, lectures, rituals, song, and dance) in exchange for a small fee *(chōmonryō)*. By the fourteenth and fifteenth centuries, *kanjin kōgyō* had become one of the primary means of fund-raising carried out at religious institutions (Fukuhara 1987, 220a). These events were the precursors of the Tokugawa theater industry: even the staging, seating, ticketing, and admission practices of the Tokugawa *kabuki* houses had their roots in the practices developed in medieval *kanjin kōgyō* (Ogasawara 1987).

The religious logic underlying these festivals was that of merit making. Of particular importance in this context was the concept of *kechien*, or positive karmic connections, an idea rooted in the notion that it was possible to transfer religious merit from one being to another. It was widely held that laypeople unable to dedicate themselves to austerities or to the maintenance of the precepts could access religious merit—thereby improving their future rebirths—by forming *kechien* with the religious undertakings of others. In concrete terms, this teaching meant that one could accumulate merit toward birth in the Pure Land and other Buddhist paradises by listening to Buddhist priests chant sutras and preach the Dharma, by taking in an *etoki* performance, by contributing to the reproduction of a sutra, or by observing any number of rituals. The theory of *kechien* thus doubled the worth of such performances: that is, not only were the various types of entertainment offered at temple-shrine complexes amusing in their own right, but they were also seen as soteriologically beneficial. As Lady Nijō, reflecting upon a service she attended at the Wakamiya shrine at the Kōfukuji-Kasuga complex, explains, "The night was spent in song and dance, for the Buddha, who joins us in this corrupt world out of his deep compassion, uses songs and stories to guide us to paradise" (trans. Brazell 1973, 203; *TG*, 190–191).

Outside sources do not reveal how public or how festive ceremonies held at Hokkeji were. Nevertheless, historical research on *hōe* as a category of ritual does indicate, as explained above, that nearly all of these ceremonies had already become entertaining public events long before Hokkeji's restoration. Although the *Nenjū gyōji* does not offer detailed information about particular rites and ceremonies, it does include the phrase "patrons from the lay order" *(zaike-shū seshu)* in the margins next to the Lecture Hall Shushō-e (ninth day of the New Year) (*YKT*, 5:86b). Unlike some *hōe* that were targeted at lay audiences in particular, the Shushō-e, like the Shuni-e, had historical connections with the state and had been performed since at least the early Heian period to ensure peace in the realm. Certain portions of the ritual, then, were carried out within the temple and were not open to lay auditors; it was only at certain points in the ceremony that lay audiences would be granted the opportunity to participate. At Tōdaiji, where the Shuni-e spans two weeks, lay groups are included only at certain points. With this information in mind, one can speculate that the marginal note in Hokkeji's *Nenjū gyōji* means that unlike the Shushō-e ceremonies carried out in the main and Yakushi halls, which may not have been fully open to the public, the Shushō-e held in the lecture hall on the ninth day of the New Year was performed specifically on behalf of lay donors and welcomed their participation. Although it is not known whether Hokkeji charged *chōmonryō,* or admission fees, for lay auditors, studies of medieval *hōe* have shown that auditors were always expected to make contributions of some kind (Ogasawara 1987).

The *hōe* included in the *Nenjū gyōji* at Hokkeji represent a broad sampling of medieval religious ceremony as practiced within institutions representing the *kenmitsu* (exoteric-esoteric) orthodoxy. Many of the ceremonies—including the Shushō-e, the Great Benevolent Kings Ceremony, the Shuni-e, and the Nirvana Ceremony—date back to the Nara and early Heian periods, when they were performed on behalf of the state at the great temples of the southern capital. Others, such as the Eight Chanted Lectures on the *Lotus Sutra,* the Ghost Festival Ceremony, the Ceremony for the Buddha's Birthday, and the Recitation of the Buddha's Name, had more popular roots and were more explicitly geared toward lay audiences (Uejima 2004, 232–234).

Chanted Lectures

Hokkeji's list of annual ceremonies also includes a great number of *kōshiki,* or chanted lectures. This ritual genre, which first emerged in the historical record during the late tenth century, flourished during the medieval period.[25] They always involved the veneration of a *honzon,* or primary image, which typically consisted of a statue or hanging image of a deity. In the early stage of their development, *kōshiki* services tended to be smaller in scale and more intimate than many of the older forms of *hōe.* As such, they commonly allowed not only for lay auditing, but also for lay participation.[26] By the Kamakura period, *kōshiki* were frequently performed at temples as a means of educating and entertaining lay audiences.

Medieval sources suggest that temples often staged *kōshiki* as grand events that attracted large crowds. Guelberg mentions a scene from the forty-second scroll of the *Genpei jōsuiki* (Account of the rise and fall of the Genji and Heike) in which Minamoto no Yoshitsune (1159–1189) and his men interrupt a *kōshiki* service in honor of the bodhisattva Kannon just as it is about to begin.[27] Although the episode is set at a rural temple in Shikoku, the narrative describes the *kōshiki* service as both large and diverse, involving hundreds of participants, male and female, lay and ordained, young and old. Even children are present. The text further describes the occasion as a merry one that included generous quantities of food and alcohol. Guelberg posits that the readers of the *Genpei jōsuiki* likely participated in similarly festive chanted lecture services, even if they lived in areas remote from the capitals of Kyoto and Kamakura. Myōe, who performed *kōshiki* regularly, also describes them as events attracting hundreds of devotees, including men and women of all ages and walks of life (Guelberg 2006, 31–32; *Genpei jōsuiki,* fasc. 42; *Kōzanji Myōe Shōnin gyōjō*).

The texts chanted during *kōshiki* services were written in Chinese, but they were performed primarily in *kundoku* style, which required the performer to render the text into Japanese word order and pronunciation as he or she chanted it aloud.[28] This style of performance meant that even lay participants could easily understand the textual import of the liturgy (Ford 2006, 74–75). But while this reading style made the textual content of rituals more accessible to laypeople, it required both great erudition and well-honed technical skill on the part of the performer. Guelberg estimates that priests who performed *kōshiki* most likely learned the techniques of performance directly from their masters. Some extant copies of *kōshiki* liturgical texts dating from the premodern period contain pronunciation glosses, grammatical marks (*kaeriten* and other *katen*), and marginal notes that demonstrate the relative difficulty of *kundoku* readings (2006, 36).

In looking through the texts of *kōshiki,* it is immediately apparent that the content and narrative style of these texts were indeed more accessible than those of sutras. They not only offered Buddhist teachings in concise, digestible form, but they also tended to exclude complex philosophical discussions. Consider, for example, the Chanted Lecture on the Buddha's Nirvana, a *kōshiki* written by Myōe. This *kōshiki* opens with an expression of sorrow over the Buddha's death:

> Firstly, to express the sorrow of the Buddha's entrance into *nirvāṇa:*
> The Buddha lived for eighty years, was born in Kapilavastu, reached enlightenment at Buddha-gayā,
> Preached a sermon at Vulture Peak Mountain, and entered *nirvāṇa* at the Śala Grove.
> All of these things came from his great compassion,
> and represent his skillful means of bringing salvation.
> His teachings brought both joy and sorrow,
> but they were all for the benefit of sentient beings.
> His pledge to escape the sufferings of the three realms of existence in his first life
> alleviates the sufferings of the children of this burning house
> in which the unenlightened dwell.
> His statement that we were never to see him again after his entrance into *nirvāṇa*
> adds further tears of sorrow to the sea of sufferings
> in which those of this world are drowning. . . .[29]

The text goes on to relate the story of the Buddha's death, first explaining how the Buddha announced his impending death to Ānanda, how various beings reacted to this news, and how the Buddha comforted them in their sorrow. It then describes the scene of the Buddha's death, noting the response of the universe: living beings cried in anguish, and the earth expressed grief with great winds, earthquakes, and other natural disasters. Finally, the text adds commentary, saying that the sadness felt in being separated from the Buddha serves as a reminder of just how true his teachings are: it is, after all, because living beings are mired in the world of *saṃsāra* that they find separation so painful. The text ends with words of encouragement and appeal:

> So, let us wipe away our tears,
> put away our sadness,
> intone a verse,
> and make worship. (247)

Myōe's Chanted Lecture on the Buddha's Nirvana appears in the *Nenjū gyōji* as part of the Goza Chanted Lectures (fifteenth day of the second month). The Goza Chanted Lectures also included the Chanted Lecture on the Sixteen Arhats, on Historic Sites Associated with the Buddha, on the Relics, and on Upholding the Sutras. In addition to these five lectures, the *Nenjū gyōji* also includes a number of other chanted lectures: one on the bodhisattva Kannon (eighteenth day of the New Year), one on Prince Shōtoku (twenty-second day of the New Year), one on the bodhisattva Mañjuśrī (twenty-fifth day of the New Year), one on the Buddha's son, Rāhula (eighth day, first and seventh months), one on the Buddha's favored disciple Ānanda (eighth day, second and eighth months), and a series of Eight Chanted Lectures on the *Lotus Sutra* (seventh day, second month, for four days). The Chanted Lecture on the Relics, included in the Goza Chanted Lectures, was also to be performed at four other times during the year: the thirtieth day of the New Year, the third day of the third month, and the twenty-fourth day of the fourth month. This means that chanted lecture ceremonies were to be offered at least twelve days per year at Hokkeji. Most of the chanted lectures listed in the *Nenjū gyōji* were written by Nara priests active during the time of Hokkeji's revival. With the exception of the Chanted Lecture on Ānanda, all of these *kōshiki* were rites also performed regularly at male monastic institutions in the southern capital.[30]

The Chanted Lecture on Ānanda

This exception, the Chanted Lecture on Ānanda, represents perhaps the only ceremony in the *Nenjū gyōji* that was gender-specific. The Chanted Lecture on Ānanda belongs to a particular genre of chanted lectures that can be traced back to an Indian practice in which different orders within the *sangha* offered *pūjā* (Chns. *gongyang*, Jpns. *kuyō*) for disciples of the Buddha with whom they were believed to have had a special karmic connection. In the record of his trip to India (ca. 399–414 CE), Faxian (320?–420?) says that in Madhurā he witnessed a practice in which monks made elaborate offerings of flowers and incense to *stupas* of Śāriputra, Maudgalyāyana, and Mahākāśyapa one month after the end of the meditation retreat (Skt. *varṣa,* Chns. *anju*). In the same way, he wrote, "the various *bhikṣuṇī* [Jpns. *bikuni*] make great offerings to a *stupa* of Ānanda." Faxian continued: "This is because Ānanda entreated the World Honored One, asking him to let women leave home [*chujia*]. The various novices make great offerings to Rāhula.... Every year these *pūjā* are offered once, and each has its own day" *(Gaoseng Faxian zhuan).*[31]

When Xuanzang visited India over two centuries later, he noted a similar practice, also in the province of Madhurā. The practice as he describes it had changed in several ways, however. First, additional groups honoring other figures were specified:

> The Abhidharma group makes offerings to Śāriputra; those who study meditative concentration make offerings to Maudgalyāyana; those [who specialize in] intoning and upholding the sutras make offerings to Pūrṇa-maitrāyaṇī-putra; the order studying the *vinaya* makes offerings to Upāli; the various *bhikṣuṇī* make offerings to Ānanda; those who have not yet received the full precepts *(śīla-saṃpad)* [i.e., novices] make offerings to Rāhula; and those who are studying the Mahāyāna make offerings to the various bodhisattvas. (*Datang xiyuji,* Jpns. *Daitō saiikiki,* 890b13–b17)

Secondly, Xuanzang describes the offering services, or *pūjā,* as taking place more frequently. They are to be performed during the first fifteen days of the three months of abstinence (the first, fifth, and ninth months), as well as on the following days every month: the eighth, fourteenth, fifteenth, twenty-third, twenty-ninth, and thirtieth. Finally, Xuanzang also mentions that for the *pūjā* he witnessed, each group making an offering prepared an image of the disciple they were honoring and would use it, along with banners, jeweled canopies, incense, and flowers, to adorn the disciple's *stupa* (890b17–b19; Katsuura 2008, 104–107).

In the excerpt from Xuanzang's account, the logic underlying the association between specific groups and the disciples to whom they are said to have made offerings is made more explicit. Groups studying particular disciplines—such as meditation, *vinaya* studies, or sutra recitation—are shown to venerate those disciples of Śākyamuni regarded as having most excelled in those particular areas. In the accounts of both Faxian and Xuanzang, nuns are depicted as venerating Ānanda. Faxian reports that nuns venerated Ānanda because it was he who convinced the Buddha that women should be admitted into the order as home leavers.

The story of Mahāprajāpātī, celebrated in Buddhist literature as the first woman to gain entrance into the *sangha,* is well-known. The story appears in the *Cullavagga* (10.1) and *Aṅguttara Nikāya* (8.6.1) of the Pāli canon; in the *Middle-Length Āgama Sutras* (Skt. *Mādhyamāgama,* Chns. *Zhong ahan jing*); and in a long list of *vinaya* texts, most of which are included in the Taishō canon.[32] The basic story, consistent throughout these various versions, begins when Mahāprajāpātī, sister to the Buddha's mother and the woman who cared for the Buddha following his mother's early death, approaches the Buddha together with a large retinue of female disciples (in many versions the number is five hundred) and asks that he allow them to enter the *sangha.* The Buddha refuses, even after (according to many versions) she repeats her request three times. Then Ānanda, one of the Buddha's closest disciples, intervenes, asking the Buddha to reconsider his response. The Buddha finally relents, but only after he admits at Ānanda's prompting that women are capable of attaining the four fruits, and Ānanda reminds him of the debt he owes Mahāprajāpātī for having raised him.[33] In some versions, Ānanda offers yet another point that works to persuade the Buddha, namely, that all earlier Buddhas had allowed women into the order (Heirman 2001, 279–281).

The records of Faxian and Xuanzang suggest rather clearly that the nuns' order in fifth-through-seventh-century Madhurā had incorporated this narrative into its routine ritual practices and that in connection with this narrative the nuns made regular offerings to Ānanda, while other, male groups within the *sangha* made special offerings to different disciples of the Buddha. Whether or not the practice of nuns making special offerings to Ānanda ever became widespread within China is not well-known. Several later Chinese texts, including the *Fayuan zhulin* (Jade grove in the Dharma garden) and the *Shijia fangzhi* ([On the spread] of Śākyamuni's [teachings] in the provinces, T. no. 2088), do refer to the observations of Faxian and Xuanzang, but they do not comment on whether the same practice was carried out in China. Katsuura finds evidence in another text, the *Dafangbian baoen jing* (Sutra on compassionate recompense, T. no. 156), that the practice may have been initiated in China sometime around the fifth century. In a careful textual analysis of this text, Katsuura demonstrates that the *Dafangbian baoen jing,* which appears to have been largely reconstructed by its Chinese translator or translators in the fifth century, added at least three elements not included in early descriptions: that *all* women, and not only nuns, were to make special offerings to Ānanda; that Ānanda would bless with positive karmic merit those women who performed offering rites for him in conjunction with the upholding of the eight pure precepts *(ba zhaijie);* and that offering rites for Ānanda should be held on the eighth day of the second and eighth months of the year (2008, 107–109).[34]

In Japan, some version of the practice in which nuns made offerings to Ānanda appears to have been established at Junna-in (also known as Sai-in), the convent established by Grand Empress Junna during the early Heian period. Minamoto no Tamenori mentions the rite, which he refers to as the Confession Ceremony for Ānanda (Anan Keka), in *Sanbōe* (984). There, he describes the rite as one that seeks both to ask Ānanda for divine protection and to acknowledge women's debt to him. In the *Sanbōe,* Tamenori also specifies that the rite was carried out on the eighth days of the second and eighth months and in conjunction with the eight pure precepts (Katsuura 2008, 101–104). Katsuura shows that the rite as Tamenori describes it was inspired by the *Dafangbian baoen jing,* but Tamenori also includes clear references to the Mahāprajāpātī narrative as it appears in both the *Four-Part Vinaya* and the *Mādhyamāgama* (Middle-length sayings, 102–103, 113).

How exactly the rite Tamenori described in the year 984 is linked to the Chanted Lecture on Ānanda is unclear. Both rites share the same raison d'être: they are both meant to acknowledge the debt owed to Ānanda and to ask for his blessings. Moreover, the Chanted Lecture on Ānanda, much like the rites described by Faxian and Xuanzang, also served the function, at least within the Ritsu group, of providing the nuns' group with a distinct sense of identity vis-à-vis other subgroups within the order.

Numerous versions of the Chanted Lecture on Ānanda survive today, but as Katsuura has demonstrated, the textual content of each is similar enough to suggest that they were all based on a single original. Myōe, who authored many *kōshiki,* was long regarded as the author of the Chanted Lecture on Ānanda, but recent scholarship has called that attribution into question. Close textual and doctrinal analysis suggests instead that it was a Tendai priest who first created the Chanted Lecture on Ānanda. Katsuura is even more specific: she speculates that the author was likely a Tendai priest who was inspired by the earlier Anan Keka rite at Junna-in (118).[35]

Little is known about the fate of nuns' offering rites to Ānanda in the years separating the close of the nuns' tradition at Junna-in and the reemergence of convents in the thirteenth century. But there is much evidence to suggest that Myōe reintroduced the practice in the early years of the thirteenth century. Myōe founded the Zenmyōji convent in 1223 for elite women whom the battles of the Jōkyū uprising (1221) had left widowed and orphaned.[36] Entries related to Zenmyōji found in the *Kōzanji engi* mention that an image of Ānanda was installed at the convent in the year 1244. Additional evidence of devotion to Ānanda at Zenmyōji is found in the case of the nun Zen'e, who was widowed following the death of her husband, the supernumerary middle counselor *(gon no chūnagon)* Fujiwara (Hamuro) no Mitsuchika (1176–1221). Zen'e erected a *stupa* in honor of Ānanda in the year 1265. Although Zenmyōji has since fallen into ruin, this *stupa* still stands, bearing witness to the brief revival of Ānanda devotion among nuns at Zenmyōji (119).

According to the *Nenjū gyōji,* the Chanted Lecture on Ānanda was performed at Hokkeji on the eighth day of the second and eighth months. The liturgy used at Hokkeji most likely employed the same textual source that has been associated with Myōe, namely, that entitled the *Anan Sonja kōshiki* (Katsuura 2008, 113–115, 120). This *kōshiki* text is divided into three primary segments and one final segment *(dan),* each of which has a theme. The first offers an explanation of why women should feel indebted to Ānanda, the second praises the many virtues of Ānanda, the third praises Śākyamuni, and the fourth is comprised of a merit transfer. *Kada,* or Chinese verses, are included after each *dan.*

The first section of the Chanted Lecture on Ānanda is of particular interest, for it is here that the ceremony makes an appeal to Indian precedent.

In these lines, the liturgy draws a clear connection between nuns in ancient India and those in premodern Japan, suggesting that Japanese nuns were encouraged to think of themselves as part of a tradition that exceeded the boundaries of the Japanese islands:

> First, as for the reason why women must repay a debt to Ānanda. It is due to Ānanda's request that women [may] leave home and gain ordination in the first place. If Ānanda had not made the request three times, then it would not have been decided that women, having encountered the Buddhist teachings, would be allowed to gain ordination! Therefore, we must repay this debt to him, praise his virtues, and bow down before his image. In all of the provinces of India, women who have left their homes [and become nuns] make offerings to the stupa of Ānanda on the six pure days of every month.[37] The traffic [they create in honoring the *stupa*] is like that of a market. According to the *Baoen jing* [Sutra on Compassionate Recompense, Chns. *Dafangbian baoen jing,* T. no. 156)], the Buddha said to Gautamī, "In the future, should there be in the world *bhikṣu, bhikṣuṇī,* or any women, they must always and wholeheartedly remember the debt of Ānanda. They should intone his name, pay obeisance to him, hold him in awe and reverence, and make offerings to him. If unable to do so during the six times of the day and evening, then they should not allow their hearts to forget Ānanda. Also, if there are women who wish to receive good fortune, they should receive and uphold the eight pure precepts on the eighth day of the second month and on the fourth day of the eighth month and should establish great zeal during the six times of day and night on these days. Ānanda will then use his great divine power to respond at the appropriate time with help and protection; as it is needed, so it will be received." (*Anan Sonja kōshiki;* Katsuura 2008, 115)[38]

In identifying itself as an ancient tradition that can be traced back to the very first nuns in the order, the Chanted Lecture on Ānanda reminds its performers and auditors that they are part of a long-standing tradition founded outside Japan. Also worth attention here is the fact that the chanted lecture spends very little time on the details of the exchange between Ānanda and Śākyamuni. In canonical versions of the narrative, Śākyamuni explains at great length why it is that he opposes the entrance of women into the order. He cites numerous reasons, most of which are disparaging to women. The gist of his argument, as Heirman has pointed out, is that women would weaken the doctrine and the *sangha* (2001, 280–284). But in the Chanted Lecture on Ānanda, those aspects of the narrative critical of women are skipped over, and the liturgy focuses instead on Ānanda as a divine figure who has promised to aid and protect all women who honor him with offerings. On the one hand, one cannot overlook the fact that the Chanted Lecture on Ānanda serves as a constant reminder of the fact that nuns were not regarded as equal members of the *sangha:* they were admitted only on an exceptional basis and were required to express regular gratitude for having been granted access to the *sangha* despite their female state. On the other hand, however, the Chanted Lecture on Ānanda text downplays the soteriological obstacles faced by women. Compared with conventional scriptural teachings on women, the chanted lecture offers a markedly positive view of women's practice, as it skips over, or "talks past," canonical views of nuns that explicitly disparage women. The chanted lecture instead stresses the notion that women shared a special bond with Ānanda. The rite thus provided the nuns and laywomen at Hokkeji with a means of celebrating their identity as members of an ancient tradition protected by the venerable Ānanda.

The Chanted Lecture on Rāhula

In their records of observations made in India, Faxian and Xuanzang both mention that novice groups, namely, those who have yet to take the full precepts, venerate Rāhula as the disciple with whom they have a special connection, just as the nuns' group honors Ānanda. In the excerpts from their records included above, there is no indication that novice group or groups honoring Rāhula include both men and women. But the Ritsu group clearly interpreted the rite of making offerings to Rāhula as one that should be performed by both male and female novices, for the Chanted Lecture on Rāhula (Ragora-kō) appears in the *Nenjū gyōji* as a ceremony that was to be performed by Hokkeji nuns on the eighth days of the first and seventh months. Following each of these entries is the detail, "This is to be performed by the order of novice nuns."

Within Japan, the earliest surviving copy of the liturgy for this rite is a copy held in the archives of Tōshōdaiji. This copy of the text, titled *Raun kōshiki,* bears an epigraph dated 1312.[39] There is little evidence to suggest that special offerings to Rāhula were held in Nara- or Heian-period Japan; all surviving references to the practice point to Shingon and Ritsu groups active from the mid-Kamakura period onward. Eison and his disciples at Shōmyōji, Tōshōdaiji, Hokkeji, and other Ritsu institutions appear to have instituted the Chanted Lecture on Rāhula as a relatively new practice. It was likely meant both to encourage novice monks and nuns and to emphasize the Ritsu order's connection to ancient Indian practices.

According to an epigraph found on another, later copy of the Chanted Lecture on Rāhula, the original text used in the liturgy was written by the Exalted Yuishin, a Shingon master who served as a Buddhist priest at the Iwashimizu Hachiman shrine. The epigraph is attributed to the Nara priest Gyōnen, who writes in it that Yuishin composed the Chanted Lecture on Rāhula during a stay at the Tōdaiji Kaidan-in in 1257. Gyōnen, who was a young novice training at the Kaidan-in during the time of Yuishin's visit there, says that Yuishin wrote the Chanted Lecture on Rāhula in response to a request made by two members of the novice order (Sekiguchi 1998, 6–7).[40]

The textual content of the Chanted Lecture on Rāhula makes it clear that Rāhula's role as the protector of novices is based on the premise that he left home and acquired ordination at a very young age. According to

Portrait of the Bikuni Shinnyo [according to temple tradition] (*Shinnyo Bikuni zō* [*den*]), Kamakura period. Color on silk. (Photograph by Nara National Museum, courtesy Chūgūji, Nara, Japan)

the Chanted Lecture on Rāhula, Rāhula was only nine years old when he entered the novice order.[41] The child novice Rāhula is thus offered as a representative of all child and teenage novices awaiting full ordination (9). The basic structure of the Chanted Lecture on Rāhula resembles that of the Chanted Lecture on Ānanda: in the first section, the disciple's relevance for the group in question is explained, and in the subsequent sections, he is exalted as a guardian of the Buddhist teachings in general and as a protec-

Portrait of an Eminent Priest (*Kōsō zō*), also called *Portrait of the Venerable Rāhula* (*Raun Sonja zō*), Nambokuchō period. Color on silk. (Courtesy Shōmyōji and the Kanagawa-kenritsu Kanazawa Bunko, Yokohama, Japan)

tor of the group in question in particular. In the case of the Chanted Lecture on Rāhula, the first section focuses on the tender age at which Rāhula shaved his head and entered the *sangha* as a novice, while subsequent sections focus on praising him as a guardian of all novices (15–18).[42]

By the year 1262, Eison had incorporated the Chanted Lecture on Rāhula into his liturgical program. According to the *Kantō ōkanki,* members of Eison's novice order performed the Chanted Lecture on Rāhula in

Kamakura on both the fourteenth and fifteenth days of the seventh month of 1262. On both occasions, large groups auditing the ceremonies are said to have responded with great joy (87–88). That Eison had his novices perform the Chanted Lecture on Rāhula in Kamakura suggests that this chanted lecture had become part of the standard Saidaiji liturgical repertoire by this time. Indeed, the colophon on a 1266 copy of a text called the "Raun kuyō gi" states, "[This is a] book common among the novices of Saidaiji." Chanted lectures in honor of Rāhula also appear to have been known at Shōmyōji: Ken'a, the second rector of Shōmyōji, received between the years 1277 and 1279 initiation into a series of *gatha,* or Buddhist hymns, that included the text of the "Raun-kō" (Sekiguchi 1998, 8).

That the *Nenjū gyōji* included the Chanted Lecture on Rāhula, a relatively new liturgy popularized by Ritsu groups, emphasizes the extent to which Hokkeji nuns had come to identify themselves as members of the Ritsu order. Like residents of other temples in the Saidaiji network, the nuns of Hokkeji added the Chanted Lecture on Rāhula to their liturgical calendar. What is more, they viewed Rāhula's protection of novices as a guardianship that covered both male and female novices. One can imagine that the Chanted Lecture on Rāhula may have gained popularity among the many teenaged and young adult women who entered Hokkeji and its branch convents as *gyōdō shamini* during the height of the convent's revival. Sekiguchi even goes so far as to suggest that the image of the young novice included above, an image that has long been identified as a portrait of the *bikuni* Shinnyo, was in fact an image of Rāhula that was used in performances of the Chanted Lecture on Rāhula at Chūgūji. A painting held in the Shōmyōji archives, *Image of the Honorable Rāhula (Raun Sonja Zō),* depicts Rāhula as a beautiful young novice whom one could, at least in Sekiguchi's view, easily mistake for a young woman. Scholars believe that the Shōmyōji image of Rāhula was used in performances of the Chanted Lecture on Rāhula. Sekiguchi suggests that the Chūgūji painting, too, was once used as the main image in performances of the Chanted Lecture on Rāhula and that it was only much later, after the original purpose of the painting had been forgotten, that its main figure came to be identified as the *bikuni* Shinnyo (Sekiguchi 1998, 9; Nishikawa 1988, 52).

The Great Brahma Net Ceremony in Honor of Queen-Consort Kōmyō

Another ceremony of particular importance in the *Nenjū gyōji* is the Great Brahma Net Ceremony performed in honor of Queen-Consort Kōmyō during the first seven days of the sixth month. According to the *Nenjū gyōji,* this ceremony included, in addition to the Brahma Net (Fanwang) liturgy itself, an offering of *gigaku* music on the day of the death anniversary, as well as a full seven days during which quick readings *(tendoku)* and explanations *(keisan)* of the *Lotus Sutra* were to be performed one thousand times.[43] Moreover, the *Nenjū gyōji* states that this seven-day rite was to be followed by another seven days of performances in honor of Kōmyō: from the seventh day and for seven days, the nuns were to perform the Chanted Lecture on the Favorable Birth of Our Founder [Queen-Consort Kōmyō]. This ceremony offers an instructive example of the ways in which Hokkeji nuns blended Ritsu scholastic and liturgical practices with long-standing traditions that predated the convent's association with Saidaiji. As illustrated in chapter 1, Hokkeji had long been recognized as the holy grounds of Queen-Consort Kōmyō, and the nuns who worked to restore the convent in the late Heian and early Kamakura periods emphasized Kōmyō's role as the patron saint of the temple. The Great Brahma Net Ceremony in honor of Kōmyō appears to have been the most elaborate ceremony undertaken at Hokkeji on a regular basis, and records indicate that nuns at Hokkeji continued to perform this ceremony well into the fifteenth century. That the ceremony is defined as an offering of the *Brahma Net Sutra*—a *vinaya* text—is in keeping with Hokkeji's identity as a Ritsu institution. But the fact that the largest ceremony held at the convent was one that celebrated the founder, Kōmyō, makes it clear that Hokkeji nuns viewed the worship of the queen-consort as the primary task of the convent.

Evidence that Hokkeji nuns continued to perform this Great Brahma Net Ceremony well into the fifteenth and sixteenth centuries can be found in the *Daijōin jisha zōjiki* (1450–1508), which contains the diaries of the priests Jinson, Seikaku, and Kyōjin, all of whom held the title of Kōfukuji Daijōin Monzeki. The *Daijōin jisha zōjiki* mentions Hokkeji with great frequency and demonstrates the close relationship shared between the Daijōin Monzeki and the nuns at Hokkeji. In particular, the *Daijōin jisha zōjiki* makes it clear that the priest filling the Daijōin Monzeki post regularly attended the Great Brahma Net Ceremony held at Hokkeji on the seventh day of the sixth month (a date that corresponds, incidentally, with those given in the *Nenjū gyōji*).

We know from examples at Tōshōdaiji that the Great Brahma Net Ceremony typically involved hanging an image of the person being honored—at Tōshōdaiji, it was Kakujō; at Hokkeji, it would have been Kōmyō—in the lecture hall and then chanting certain *shōmyō* pieces (including the *bai* and *sange*) as well as portions of the *Bonmōkyō,* or *Brahma Net Sutra.* Also included was the offering of several types of dance, including the *bairo* and the *bosatsu.*

The *Daijōin jisha zōjiki* focuses only on the seventh day of the sixth month, suggesting that by the fifteenth century the *hōe* had either been reduced to a one-day affair or the most important part of the ceremony—and the part well attended by the public—was the part held on the seventh, or last, day. In the year 1464, Jinson described his visit to the festivities at Hokkeji:

> Today Queen-Consort Kōmyō's memorial service was carried out in the lecture hall [of Hokkeji]. I made a pilgrimage to Hokkeji's [performance] of the queen-consort's memorial service. I made the rounds, paying homage at every hall, and then settled down in the private room [provided for me]. After that, I entered the great bathhouse [*daiyuya*]. The significance of this bathwater is

> explained in a written divine oath [*onkimon*], which says that to avoid the three evil realms [of rebirth], one really should enter [this bath]. Next, I listened to the *hōe* in front of the Golden Hall, then I visited the rector's quarters, met with her, and presented an offering. Then I returned to the Zenjō-in [at Kōfukuji]. My guards prepared my small perfumed robe and my palanquin, and my procession came to an end. (Kanshō 5 [1464] 6/7)

According to this entry, the Great Brahma Net Ceremony at Hokkeji was known primarily for its connection to Queen-Consort Kōmyō, the patron goddess of the convent. As Nagamura's research has shown, the Great Brahma Net Ceremony was a *hōe* typically associated with the royal court. It also had strong associations with Kōmyō herself, as it was her spouse, Shōmu Tennō, who first established the Great Brahma Net Ceremony (at Tōdaiji, where he ordered that it be performed annually for the salvation of Kōmyō's mother) (2001a, 64).

This particular rite appears to have been the *hōe* most strongly associated with Hokkeji, at least during the fifteenth century. It is the only *hōe* at Hokkeji that Jinson mentions regularly and the only one that he made a point of attending each year. His attendance was a grand event: he was carried in by a handful of servants on an *itagoshi* (palanquin), he wore his finest perfumed robes, he was given a special room in one of the halls at Hokkeji, and he presented an offering. That he put such care into his attendance suggests that Hokkeji's Great Brahma Net Ceremony was a major event in the old capital of Nara.

The fact that the Great Brahma Net Ceremony was so closely associated with the royal court should not be overlooked here. Surely the nuns at Hokkeji wanted to emphasize this *hōe* above all other performances at the nunnery, for this ceremony not only marked the commemoration of their founder, Queen-Consort Kōmyō (whom popular narratives and Hokkeji texts alike had deified as the bodhisattva Kannon), it also drew attention to Hokkeji's close affiliations—historical and contemporaneous—with the elite world of the court. It was, in other words, a ceremony that allowed Hokkeji nuns to display the prestige of their institution. And given the care with which the rector and her underlings appear to have prepared for and executed the ceremony, the occasion also enabled the nuns to affirm, physically and mentally, the significance of their roles as stewards of a long tradition they traced back to Kōmyō.

Jinson's record of this particular trip to the Great Brahma Net Ceremony at Hokkeji provides a sense of how elite guests might have experienced the ceremony. His visit encompasses a standardized set of activities: first, he takes a tour of the entire complex, which involves prayers at each hall within the convent; next, he enjoys a bath at Hokkeji's famous bathhouse; then, he attends at the *hōe* itself, which he watches from a place in front of the main hall; and finally, he visits the rector's quarters, has a formal meeting with her, and presents an offering. (The rector at this time was Sonshun, a daughter of Ashikaga Yoshimitsu.)

Another entry, from the sixth day of the seventh month of 1476, reflects a similar protocol: "I made a pilgrimage to the memorial service [for Kōmyō] at Hokkeji. I visited the rector's quarters, entered the great bathhouse, and listened to the Brahma Net Ceremony. [Her] disciple served as the reader [*dokushi*] [in the ceremony], and musicians also performed. Everything was carried out properly" (*Daijōin jisha zōjiki*, Bunmei 8 [1476] 6/7). Jinson also mentions in this entry that musicians *(gakunin)* served in the ceremony. This detail suggests that the nuns at fifteenth-century Hokkeji were hiring musicians to perform at the ceremony, as the *Nenjū gyōji* instructs.[44] The festivities were thus attractive on many fronts: in attending the Brahma Net Ceremony, visitors to Hokkeji were able to forge karmic merit by auditing the liturgy itself, to enjoy a musical performance, and to enter the efficacious waters of the Hokkeji bathhouse.

Returning to the protocol mentioned earlier, it is worth reiterating that Jinson's visits included not only entering the bath and auditing the Brahma Net Ceremony but also meeting with the rector and making an offering. This part of his visit is mentioned in many of his entries on the Brahma Net Ceremony at Hokkeji. In an entry from 1483, for example, he says that he presented the rector with three hundred units of cash: "I visited the Brahma Net Ceremony at Hokkeji, traveling together with the administrator [*jimu*] and [priest of] Tōrinji. . . . I presented an offering of three hundred *hiki* [the equivalent of 3,000 *mon*, 3 *kan*, or 30 strings of cash] to the rector and entered the bath" (Bunmei 15 [1483] 6/7). (In 1483, Sonshū Kōei-bō, a daughter of chancellor [*kanpaku*] Ichijō Kaneyoshi, was rector.) Although it is likely that such formal offerings were made only by elite figures such as Jinson, the fact that monetary donations appear to have been a standardized part of attending the Brahma Net Ceremony confirms that one of the functions of such events was to garner financial support.

Finally, Jinson's records mention that it was typical for the rector of Hokkeji to carry out the leading roles in the performance of the ceremony. Entries from 1478 and 1480 refer to the Hokkeji rector as having performed in the ceremony as the *okashira* (head of ceremonies) on one occasion and as *dōshi* (officiating priest) in another:

Bunmei 10 [1478] 6/7
The memorial service for Queen-Consort Kōmyō was carried out in the lecture hall [of Hokkeji] according to custom. It was said that today the rector performed the leading role [*okashira*] in the ceremony.

Bunmei 12 [1480] 6/7
Today, the memorial service was behind schedule. During the time in which the manager of *hōe* offerings *(kumokudai)* had not yet been determined, there were no assignments of ritual duty, and so ultimately the service was delayed. It was said that the rector served as the officiating priest [*dōshi*] in the Hokkeji memorial service.

By the late fifteenth century, the nuns' order at Hokkeji was much smaller than it had been at the height of the convent's medieval revival some two centuries earlier. Records suggest that only a handful of nuns, most of them extremely elite, occupied the convent at this time. Moreover, Jinson's entries date to the years surrounding the eleven-year Ōnin War (1467–1477), which ravaged the city of Kyoto. The war was felt keenly in Nara too, and most of the temples in the old capital found themselves in dire straits during this period. Most lacked funds to keep the grounds of their institutions in good repair; money for extravagant ceremonies was even harder to come by. That Hokkeji nuns managed to continue staging the Brahma Net Ceremony despite a decreased population of nuns and difficult economic times serves as a testament to their long-standing dedication to Kōmyō. That Jinson identified the rector of the convent as the person who performed the leading roles in the ceremony is also important here. From this detail, we are able to ascertain that even as Hokkeji came to be dominated by increasingly elite women over the course of the late fourteenth and fifteenth centuries, these women were not simply sent to the convent to languish there: Jinson suggests that they were actively engaged in the transmission of ritual knowledge. They performed rituals of great importance, such as the Brahma Net Ceremony in honor of Kōmyō, which can be traced back to Hokkeji's more prosperous days in the thirteenth and fourteenth centuries, and they passed this ritual knowledge on to their own disciples.

The Female Priesthood

This chapter has examined only a handful of the numerous rituals and ceremonies included in the *Nenjū gyōji.* What this brief sampling aimed to convey is the sheer richness of ritual life at Hokkeji. The *Nenjū gyōji* indicates not only that Hokkeji nuns were trained to perform the same rituals and ceremonies as their male peers but also that they had created an extremely extensive ritual program that allowed for regular interaction both with other monastic orders and with lay groups. Additionally, the *Nenjū gyōji,* especially when read in conjunction with outside texts such as Jinson's diary, suggests that Hokkeji nuns established pedagogical structures that allowed them to transmit ritual knowledge to subsequent generations.

Close attention to the *Nenjū gyōji* raises important questions about the social roles of nuns in medieval society. Ritual activity at thirteenth- and fourteenth-century Hokkeji—in terms of both its public nature and its sheer scale—suggests that the nuns' order there could in fact be described as a female priesthood.

Even the most conservative definition of the term "priest," which uses the term only to describe religious figures who perform sacrifices at an altar on behalf of a community, is more or less applicable in the case of Hokkeji nuns. As is true in the Christian case as well, the Buddhist clergy was not involved in the offering of blood sacrifices, of course. But Hokkeji nuns, like male Buddhist priests, did make offerings (including not only offerings of the Dharma but also gifts of fruit and other food items that did not involve the taking of life) on behalf of the lay community, both to Buddhist deities and to the spirits of the dead. When a wider definition of "priest" is employed, the priestly qualities of their roles are even clearer: Hokkeji nuns took ordinations that set them apart from members of the lay community, underwent special training in the performance of liturgical chants and other skills used in ritual, performed public religious functions, served as intermediaries between the human and divine realms (especially through the performance of death offering rites), and offered laypeople instruction in Buddhist theories and doctrines (most notably in the form of chanted lectures).[45]

What the *Nenjū gyōji* reveals that is not apparent in earlier cases of women's religious practice in Heian- and Kamakura-period Japan is evidence of a *vocational* Buddhist priesthood for women. Numerous examples of nonordained or seminovice laywomen women undertaking private, devotional Buddhist practices can be found in Heian and Kamakura literature. There are also many examples, as noted at the beginning of this chapter, of nonordained women who drew on spirit mediumship and other forms of charismatic religious practice to perform public rituals. But at Hokkeji women performed public rituals as ordained members of the Buddhist clergy that drew on well-established Buddhist liturgical and ritual traditions. In other words, their ritual activities exceeded those typically associated with women of the Heian and Kamakura periods: they limited themselves neither to rituals involving mediumship nor to personal devotions. Hokkeji nuns, like the male members of in the Saidaiji order, acted as members of a vocational priesthood who made their living through the performance of ritual.

Even the warrior government recognized Hokkeji nuns as fulfilling a priestly role vis-à-vis the state. Evidence to this effect can be found in the *Nenjū gyōji,* which lists at several points that special prayers were to be offered on behalf of the state for protection from foreign invaders. The *Nenjū gyōji* states that the Great Benevolent Kings Ceremony, for example, was to be performed on the tenth day of the New Year, as well as on the first day of the fifth month, for the expressed purpose of protecting the state from foreign invaders *(ikoku kitō).* A colophon included at the very end of the *Nenjū gyōji* also suggests that the military government sometimes called upon Hokkeji nuns to perform rituals in times of crisis: "Outside of this, prayers for the shogunal household. Also prayers and *gongyō* as needed in times of emergency. Depending on the time, these things are decided following the event or in accordance with the [particular] difficulty" (87b).

Hokkeji's role in providing ritual services to the warrior government was bound up in its identification as a Ritsu temple. During the years of the Mongol threat (the two attempted attacks on Japan occurred in the years 1274 and 1281), the court and warrior government, searching for an effective means by which to protect Japan, began to look back to the *kokubunji* (state temples in the provinces) established during the Nara era, for these temples had long been conceptualized as institutions established for the specific purpose of offering prayers for the protection of the state. Most *kokubunji* had fallen into ruin by the early years of the Heian period, but Eison and Ninshō had, by the 1260s and 1270s, gained recognition for their work in restoring several of these *kokubunji,* including, of course, Hokkeji. From the mid-1270s and throughout the years of the Mongol threat, Eison and the revived *kokubunji* affiliated with Saidaiji were among the many priests and temples that offered rituals for the protection of the Japanese archipelago. Since the Mongol fleets that attempted to enter Japan did not succeed (being blown away, legend has it, by "divine winds," or *kamikaze*), these ritual performances were deemed successful, and the state recognized Eison and his Ritsu order for having played a role in the protection of Japan (Inoue M. 1985). In subsequent years, the warrior government acknowledged many Saidaiji-branch Ritsu institutions as "Kantō *kitōji,*" or temples that offered prayers on behalf of the Kamakura warrior government.

Ninshō in particular made a successful appeal to the military government in the year 1298. In a plea dated to the second month of 1298, Ninshō asked the military government to protect Saidaiji-branch temples from incursion by land stewards *(jitō)* and military governors *(shugo).* Clerics living in Saidaiji temples, Ninshō wrote, had been aiding the hungry during times of famine, saying prayers for peace in the land, and praying for the welfare of the shogunal household. And yet despite these many good deeds, he explained, the government's land stewards and military governors had been wreaking havoc on Saidaiji-branch temple lands: renegade warriors destroyed temple property and harassed monks and nuns in a variety of ways. Ninshō asked the warrior government to keep its retainers off the premises of thirty-four Ritsu temples, seven of which were convents. In exchange for granting them "non-entry" status, he wrote, these temples would all continue to say prayers on behalf of the military government. The government accepted Ninshō's proposal, sheltering all thirty-four temples from land stewards and military governors (*Kamakura ibun,* nos. 19616, 19668–19670, 19798–19803).[46] In performing the Great Benevolent Kings Ceremony twice a year to protect Japan from foreign invaders, then, Hokkeji was fulfilling its priestly obligation to the government; it was this ritual work that enabled the convent to maintain autonomy vis-à-vis the local warrior government. That the nuns' order made itself available for ritual services in times of state emergency also reflects the priestly relationship that Hokkeji maintained with the military government. It was only by offering the state a set of valued priestly services that Hokkeji was able to guard its interests from rogue warriors.

That the state recognized Ritsu convents as capable of offering prayers worthy of "Kantō *kitō*" status suggests, of course, that the warrior government accepted the notion that women could perform priestly services. This view appears to have gained great currency in subsequent years. As women continued to gain access to higher levels of ordination and monastic training, their roles as the providers of Buddhist priestly services continued to expand as well. This trend is also visible in the case of the Nakahara family in the early Muromachi period (1336–1573). The Nakahara was a scholarly family that specialized in the Confucian classics.[47] As Nishiguchi Junko has shown, the family had long maintained a mortuary temple called Ryōzenji in the Higashiyama district of Kyoto. Although the temple was originally affiliated with the Tendai sect, the family had become followers of the Ji sect by the early Muromachi period, when they invited the priest Kokua (1314–1405) to take up residence at Ryōzenji. His entry into the temple marked its conversion to the Ji sect (1999a, esp. 168).

Worth attention in the case of the Nakahara family and its conversion is the fact that several members of the family, including a number of women, entered the clerical order of the Ji sect. Using the *Shishuki* (1339–1374), the extensive personal diary of Nakahara no Moromori, Nishiguchi traces the activities of women in the Nakahara family who became nuns in the Ji order. Her close analysis of the text indicates that numerous women from the scholarly Nakahara family became Ji sect nuns, trained at numerous Ji sect practice halls and temples in Kyoto, and offered priestly services alongside male Ji sect priests. The Nakahara family was especially active at the Rokujō practice hall (Rokujō *dōjō*), also known as Kankikōji, a temple in Yamashina. Moromori's aunt, the nun Kyōbutsu-bō, joined the nuns' order at the Rokujō practice hall. Unlike Hokkeji, the Rokujō practice hall was not a convent as such but housed both men and women. Kyōbutsu-bō spent most of her time at the practice hall, returning home perhaps once a week, often in order to perform a ritual of some kind. At the practice hall, she attended regular lectures on the sutras and received liturgical training (166–172).

When the Nakahara family was in need of private priestly services—when they needed to have a death offering service performed, or when a family member was facing death—Moromori's aunt Kyōbutsu-bō would return to the household, usually with several other nuns from the Ji order in tow, to prepare for the service. In the case of death memorial offerings *(kijitsu kuyō),* the nuns would typically arrive the day before the actual death anniversary and would read sutras and perform the *nenbutsu* on behalf of the deceased. Then, on the next day, male priests from the order would arrive, and the male and female clerics would perform a more elaborate service together. Nishiguchi demonstrates that Ji nuns appear to have been given preparatory tasks not assigned to male priests; that said, they are also described as having performed the actual offering ceremonies alongside male priests, a detail indicating that Ji nuns were in fact performing priestly duties, even though their rank within the order remained lower than that of the male priests. In instances of deathbed services, however, Moromori suggests that female priests often acted alone, especially when the dying client was female. When one of Moromori's other aunts (the wife of Morosuke) was on her deathbed, for example, Kyōbutsu-bō and another Ji nun (who was not a member of the family) came to the house to act as her deathbed *zenchishiki,* or "good and virtuous friends [in the Dharma]." They tended to her bedside and aided her as she said her final prayers. As Nishiguchi points out, this detail is remarkable, for it had long been assumed that deathbed *zenchishiki* were always male priests. In the case of this same woman, Morosuke's wife, Kyōbutsu-bō performed even her gravesite ceremony: acting as the mourning priest *(kōsō),* she offered sutra readings and *nenbutsu* incantations at the grave (171–174; *Shishuki,* esp. Ryakuō 2 (1339) 7/5 and 10/15).

The stories of Kyōbutsu-bō and her fellow Ji nuns shed light on the degree to which women continued to succeed throughout the post-Kamakura era in defining themselves as members of the vocational clergy. The Buddhist activities performed by nuns in Moromori's diary, Nishiguchi emphasizes, are of a different quality than those performed by nuns in the Heian period: Kyōbutsu-bō and Ji nuns like her were not focused on private devotions but had become professional members of the clergy who were commissioned to perform rituals for others, including patrons outside their own families (1999a, esp. 172, 175).

Similar cases can be found in the Edo period as well. Although the priesthood remained overwhelmingly male—and despite the fact that men continued to hold all positions of power within visible monastic hierarchies—there are still numerous examples from the Edo period in which Buddhist nuns were commissioned to perform priestly functions. One such example is found in the case of the nuns' order at Mantokuji. Mantokuji, also identified as a Ji sect convent, was established in Kōzuke Province (present-day Gunma Prefecture). Similar to the way in which the Kamakura warrior government granted Hokkeji and other Ritsu convents "non-entry" status in exchange for their prayers on behalf of the state, nuns at Mantokuji offered prayers for the welfare of the Tokugawa family in exchange for various gifts and benefits. As Diana Wright (2002) has shown, Tokugawa Iemitsu (1604–1651), the third of the Tokugawa shoguns, was personally involved in the patronage of Mantokuji. He had skilled carpenters rebuild the convent and provided the nuns with an annual stipend of one hundred *koku* (about 512 bushels of rice, which was theoretically enough to feed 100 people for a year). In return, they were to carry out regular prayers for the protection of the realm and for the welfare of the Tokugawa family. Iemitsu also relied upon Mantokuji nuns in times of personal crisis: when his daughter Chiyohime (1637–1698) faced grave illness at the young age of two, Iemitsu personally appointed Mantokuji rector Shunchō (1615–1650) to perform rituals aimed at healing the toddler. Because Chiyohime survived, Iemitsu continued to patronize the nuns' order at Mantokuji, commissioning, in particular, monthly rites of gratitude for Chiyohime's recovery (253–254).[48] Shunchō and other Mantokuji nuns also gained great popularity among the women of the shogunal women's quarters *(ōoku).* Wright shows that the shogunal household came to rely on Mantokuji nuns as consultants who offered medical care, spiritual guidance, and ritual services of all kinds. Iemitsu's wet nurse even gave Shunchō a room in the women's quarters of the Edo castle, and Iemitsu further recognized Shunchō's service by donating to Mantokuji a house and lot in the city of Edo, as well as another gift of land (256–257). The Tokugawa family clearly regarded the nun Shunchō as a powerful and worthy provider of priestly services.

This later evidence suggests that Hokkeji nuns, in studying and carrying out ritual programs that paralleled those of male priests, and in serving as ritualists for both lay communities and the state, were in fact part of a broader historical trend that saw women enter the Buddhist priesthood as professionals. Subsequent generations of nuns in Japan never gained the political power or visibility that male priests did, but as indicated in the examples above, the priesthood did become an occupational choice for some women. Although these women never had the same spectrum of choice when it came to monastic training and were never allowed to attain any monastic rank above that of a convent rector, they were often recognized both by laypeople and by powerful members of the state as priests capable of offering Buddhist prayers that would protect the nation, heal the sick, and extend salvation to the dead.

7
Representations of Women and Gender in Ritsu Literature

PREVIOUS CHAPTERS have demonstrated the success with which Hokkeji nuns re-created an institutional framework for female monastic life. In restoring Hokkeji, they tended to adopt the structures and practices of male institutions. Before association with Eison, women at Hokkeji revived the convent as a pilgrimage site, following the broader patterns by which male temples in Nara also re-created themselves as pilgrimage destinations. In the mid-Kamakura period, when Hokkeji nuns joined Eison's movement, they integrated Ritsu texts, practices, and ordination categories. As chapters 5 and 6 illustrate, the economic and ritual operations in place at Hokkeji also followed patterns evident at male temples. In short, nuns appear to have been engaged in the same type of daily work as their male counterparts: they performed liturgies and ceremonies, carried out memorial rites for the dead, maintained sacred objects meant to attract pilgrims, and taught laypeople.

Despite these many similarities on the level of praxis, however, the fact remains that scholarly Buddhist discourse was unequivocally androcentric. How did Ritsu nuns reconcile their faith and vocation with the rhetoric of the *vinaya* tradition? And how did Ritsu priests familiar with the condemnations of women that appear in so many doctrinal texts interact with women in their order? This final chapter will examine and analyze Ritsu discourse on gender as it developed over the course of the mid-to-late Kamakura period. Here, I will argue that male and female members of the Ritsu order drew upon largely divergent paradigms as they struggled to understand the practical ramifications of Buddhist discourses on gender.

Leading scholars of Eison's movement have argued that Ritsu nuns were dependent upon the salvational work of Saidaiji priests. Matsuo Kenji argues that Eison and other *tonseisō* (reclusive priests) understood themselves as savior figures willing to reach out and save women and other "impure" beings (1988, 257–278; 1989, 99; 2001, 372–380). Hosokawa Ryōichi also depicts Ritsu nuns as having suffered under the patriarchal control of Saidaiji priests (1987, 154; 1989b, 146–151). Matsuo and Hosokawa presume that women in the Saidaiji group fully internalized androcentric Buddhist rhetoric that rejected female bodies as nonreceptacles of the Dharma.[1]

Attention to the texts associated with Ritsu nuns, supplemented with closer and more contextualized readings of the literature produced by

Saidaiji priests, reveals that the views of women and gender produced by Ritsu groups were far more diverse and far more complex than Matsuo and Hosokawa have suggested. First of all, an examination of the literature composed by Ritsu nuns reveals a set of themes and concerns that tend to ignore, or "talk past," the androcentric claims evident in Saidaiji literature. Secondly, close readings of the texts produced by Eison and his immediate disciples suggest that male Ritsu priests were struggling to reconcile various textual understandings of gender and the place of women within the Buddhist cosmos. So while one cannot deny that androcentric views of women, some more extreme than others, emerge regularly in the writings of Saidaiji priests, it is evident that Eison and his disciples did not articulate a systematic ideology of gender robust enough to silence dissenting voices. The flexibility inherent in thirteenth-century Saidaiji discourses on gender allowed the nuns associated with the group to formulate and disseminate their own views on women and women's salvation without directly contesting the claims of the Ritsu establishment.

Indeed, the narratives Ritsu women promoted offer no direct protest: the nuns do not address issues related to women's salvation in a straightforward manner, nor do they offer candid criticism of their male counterparts. But the evidence they provide does contradict the claim that Ritsu nuns had fully internalized the androcentric rhetoric of Eison and his disciples. Their texts offer an altogether different set of concerns and values, presenting the reader with a view of the cosmos and of women's bodies that chooses not to concentrate on—and in many cases not even to acknowledge—the concerns of Saidaiji priests.

As discussed in chapters 1 and 2, fascination with the court and its culture was an important theme in the literature associated with Hokkeji. This observation holds true in the discussions of women and gender offered by Ritsu nuns as well. Many of the Ritsu nuns' most compelling rejections of androcentric views are arguments that simultaneously glorify queen-consorts, ladies-in-waiting, or the Japanese court more generally. This persistent emphasis on the court suggests not only that Ritsu nuns envisioned themselves as women hailing from a tradition fully embedded in the culture of the court but also that they were aware of the wide appeal that stories about the court continued to hold in the Kamakura world and that they were able to exploit connections to the court to their benefit. Moreover, by placing themselves in a wider historical narrative of court women's encounters with Buddhism, these women were able to reinterpret androcentric Buddhist discourse in a spirit quite similar to that of women in the Heian *gosho,* women who, as illustrated in chapter 2, were able to actively contribute to various cultural expressions of Buddhism, including Buddhist representations of women, through patronage and writing.

This chapter explores textual discussions of women at three levels: (1) gender, women, and mothers in the abstract; (2) specific women of the remote past who had acquired an exalted and almost mythic stature; and (3) actual women who were contemporaries or near contemporaries of the writers in question, that is, nuns who were active in the revivals of Ritsu convents. While the texts of Saidaiji priests tend to focus on the first level—that of women, gender, and mothers in the abstract—the nuns' writings ignore doctrinal texts and focus on the second level, producing powerful images of queen-consorts who have been reconfigured as female bodhisattvas. Rather than directly arguing against the notion that female bodies are karmically burdened and incapable of progressing on the Buddhist path, these texts simply portray specific women as pure and illustrious bodhisattvas.

While both groups offer discussions of women at the third level, that of actual contemporary women, they construct these treatments in considerably divergent ways. Saidaiji priests tend to refer back to the first level, to textual discussions of women in the abstract, when addressing present-day women. Ritsu nuns, on the other hand, place their contemporaries or near contemporaries in a framework that understands them not in relation to the abstract women who emerge in doctrinal literature but instead in relation to specific legendary women of the past. It was by taking this step—by ignoring abstracted, doctrinal treatments of women and by concentrating on the connections between present-day women and celebrated women of the past—that Ritsu nuns were able to circumvent androcentric Saidaiji discourse.

Thus, any specific representation of women in Ritsu literature must be understood within the context of the particular level at which the author had chosen to engage in his or her discussion of women, gender, or motherhood. For even Eison, in the rare examples in which he discussed women at the second level mentioned above, admired legendary women like Queen-Consort Kōmyō. In thinking through images of women and gender in Ritsu texts, then, a full consideration of context is of utmost importance. From a doctrinal standpoint, Eison probably believed that men had a soteriological advantage over women, but this understanding of women in the abstract did not prevent him from praising Kōmyō when attempting to associate his own movement with Hokkeji's relics tradition, from using humble language in the presence of women who outranked him, like Jizen, or from honoring oracles delivered by female *miko*.[2] In other words, there were many situations in which Eison did not deploy abstract doctrinal positions on women. He and his disciples may have understood men to be superior to women in the abstract, but other, circumstantial factors would have come into play when they interacted with particular women.

This chapter is divided into three sections. The first section examines Ritsu representations of the relationship between gender and salvation, illustrating how Saidaiji priests and Ritsu nuns constructed this relationship in markedly different ways. The second section discusses images of motherhood and argues that while Saidaiji priests fashioned themselves as the saviors of their passive mothers—and of all women—Ritsu nuns tended to deemphasize this biological motherhood, reinterpreting maternal characteristics in ways that served to legitimate their own roles. By portraying the founding women of their own convents as savior figures, they also dismissed the notion that women (and mothers) needed to rely upon male-granted salvation. The second portion of this chapter also offers a brief discussion of the degree to which Eison supported a mythical understanding of Kōmyō's "motherliness" in the context of the Hokkeji-centered Buddha relics tradition. In contrast to the wider suggestion made in this chapter, which is that Ritsu priests and nuns represented women in markedly divergent ways, this section on relics literature serves as an example of one of the rare cases in which the views of each side overlap. The section thus serves as a reminder that the opposition between priests' and nuns' representations of women was not as monolithic or systematic as one might expect. The last section of this chapter addresses the ways in which the texts of these institutions envisioned the role of nuns in the Buddhist community. While Saidaiji priests clearly represented themselves as standing above the women's groups in an unyielding hierarchy, the literature of the convents emphasized the leadership of women and tended to ignore discussions of male priests altogether.

Finally, a few words on sources are in order before turning to specific passages from Ritsu literature. To my knowledge, there are no thirteenth- or fourteenth-century Ritsu sources that treat issues of women and gender systematically or in great detail. The representations of women and gender put forward by Ritsu priests and nuns are embedded within other texts, and only a limited number of passages address these issues directly. For Saidaiji examples, I have relied primarily on the collected sermons of Eison (*Kōshō Bosatsu gokyōkai chōmonshū,* Collection of admonitions heard from Kōshō Bodhisattva [Eison]); on the three surviving letters that chronicle Eison's correspondence with Jizen, Hokkeji's first rector; on documents preserved in the biography of Eison compiled by the Edo-period priest Jikō *(Saidai chokushi Kōshō Bosatsu gyōjitsu nenpu);* on Eison's autobiography *(Kongō Busshi Eison kanjin gakushōki);* and on several sutra inscriptions written by Eison's disciples Sōji and Eishin. I also draw on two of Eison's commentaries, the *Bonmōkyō koshakki kamon bugyō monjū ehon* and the *Bosatsu kaihon shūyō bugyō monjū,* as well as on several later Ritsu biography collections, including the *Shōdai senzai denki.* The excerpts I have culled from these sources and treat below represent a limited source base from which we may perhaps infer more general attitudes. As for the literature of Ritsu nuns, this chapter focuses primarily on the representations of women and gender found in Enkyō's 1304 *Hokke metsuzaiji engi* and in Shinnyo's 1282 *Ama Shinnyo ganmon,* the two main sources containing Ritsu nuns' portrayals of women. Two texts thought to have been written in the early-to-mid-1270s by the priest Jōen, who appears to have been a friend of Shinnyo's, are also treated briefly: the *Chūgūji engi* and the *Taishi kōshiki mandara.*[3]

Gender and Salvation

Women as Preying Snakes and Potential Men

As previously discussed, the *vinaya* texts so central to Eison's movement presume the existence of nuns' orders in the Buddhist community, a condition that encouraged Saidaiji's incorporation of female believers. At the same time, however, other continental texts valued by the Ritsu tradition, such as the *Jingxin jieguan fa* (Methods for purifying the mind and restraining [from evil] in order to see things as they really are) of Daoxuan, list and describe the "grave transgressions" associated with women and their bodies in great detail, thereby promoting, one might assume, disregard for Saidaiji's female followers. The "vices" Daoxuan attributes to women include not only character flaws such as jealousy, greed, and desire, among many others, but also biological offenses. He writes, for example, that "smelly, unclean [things] are constantly flowing from women's bodies" (824b25). Given the Ritsu school's indebtedness to Daoxuan, one might expect to see comparable condemnations of the female body in Saidaiji literature, especially since such denunciations of the female body were commonly recognized in monastic circles at the time.[4]

Views similar to those of Daoxuan can be found in at least one of Eison's texts. In his *Bonmōkyō koshakki kamon bugyō monjū ehon,* a well-known treatment of the Silla priest Taehyeon's *Fanwang jing* commentary *Beommanggyeong gojeokgi,* Eison warns male priests of the "weakness for women." Quoting the *Great Wisdom Treatise (Dazhidu lun),* Eison's commentary states, "Of the multitude of weaknesses, the weakness for women is the most grave." While lightning bolts and packs of feuding, poisonous snakes "can be approached briefly," one should never "draw close to" the many vices of women, which range from jealousy and greed to flattery, bickering, and anger. The reason, according to the *Great Wisdom Treatise,* is that women are of "shallow heart and meager wisdom." Moreover, women ensnare and bind people (presumably men, given the monastic context), and the resulting "stain" is ineradicable: "Once one sinks into this ignorance [of involvement with women], it is impossible to gain release. Of all the various diseases, the disease of [involvement with] women is the most grave.... Even poisonous vipers can be caught with the hand. [But] a person lost in affection for a woman cannot be restrained" (*Bonmōkyō koshakki kamon bugyō monjū ehon,* 314b–315a; *Dazhidu lun,* 165c27–a13).

Much of the imagery invoked in this quotation of the *Great Wisdom Treatise* corresponds to that used in Daoxuan's *Jingxin jieguan fa,* which also compares women to "poisonous snakes" and describes them as excessively jealous, deceitful, greedy, full of desire, and eager to "entrap" men (824a12–c24). But unlike Daoxuan, who writes that the bodies of women are physically foul, this quotation from the *Great Wisdom Treatise* does not emphasize the impurity of women's bodies. And while the misogynistic language of this warning against involvement with women cannot be dismissed, it should be clear that Eison quotes this passage only within a certain context. In the passage above, his audience is male monastics who are to remain celibate. Following in a long tradition of Buddhist doctrinal literature that demonizes women in the abstract for arousing the carnal desires of men, Eison cites metaphors that convey a loathing for the sexualized female body.[5] But his message does not address actual female members of the Buddhist community, nor does it consider the soteriological prospects of women.

The context of this passage suggests that its purpose is not to discourage women on the Buddhist path—though it may have had that effect in some cases—but instead to discourage priests from breaking the precept against sexual activity.

Such hyperbolic condemnations of women, even in the abstract, are rare in the literature of Eison and his immediate disciples. Many Saidaiji discussions of gender, while they admittedly assume that "female" is implicitly inferior to "male," separate the *categories* of gender from actual gendered bodies. Moreover, they often suggest that the "sins" of womanhood can be overcome through arduous Buddhist practice, arguing that women can transform themselves into "men" through faith and discipline and "rise above" the obstacles posed by their sexuality. In contrast to the singular warning mentioned above, in which Eison suggests that women's bodies are a dangerous threat to monastic practice, other Saidaiji views of women understand women not as enemies but as substandard human beings—latent men, as it were—who can, through great effort, join the ranks of the male. In these examples, women are represented as lesser beings, but they are treated neither as adversaries who jeopardize the Buddhist practice of men nor as physically impure beings who defile the priests with whom they come into contact.

During the central years of the nuns' revival movement, in the mid-to-late thirteenth century, priests affiliated with the Saidaiji movement were developing various views of women, of their role within the Buddhist community, and of their prospects for salvation. While Eison may have stressed the dangers of women's sexualized bodies to monastics when emphasizing the importance of celibacy, these views of women tend not to appear in writings and sermons destined for the eyes and ears of actual women in the order. When treating the category of women to audiences of *real* women, Eison and his disciples supported the view that women need to seek transformation into men, but their suggestions regarding this transformation were vague at best and even allowed for the possibility that women could achieve buddhahood in their own bodies, and in this lifetime. In this context, it is worth emphasizing that at least six nuns affiliated with Eison's movement were granted certificates of *denbō kanjō,* or *abhiṣeka* anointment, which acknowledges their achievement of buddhahood (*Shien Shōnin donin gyōhō kechigeki;* Matsuo 1998, 288–293).

To begin, a closer look at the ways in which Saidaiji priests discuss "male" and "female" as abstract categories suggests that they were not necessarily committed to a view that understood gender as an unchanging state inextricably linked to the physical body. Indeed, some Ritsu writings suggest that Eison's movement challenged accepted understandings of "male" and "female." The priest Jishin, a disciple of Eison who is said to have revived the Yamato temple Gakuanji in honor of his mother in the year 1260, wrote in an epigraph to the *Kōmyō Shingon'e ganmon* that the Kōmyō Shingon ritual espoused by the Saidaiji movement transcended the categories of gender and social status. From the time when this rite first began, he tells the reader, in its performance, "There is neither noble nor base; neither man [*otoko*] nor woman [*onna*]; [like] clouds, [they] gather together at the meeting place. The karmic bonds [*kechien*] [thus formed] are inexhaustible. What is more, from the ancient days of this *kaibyaku* [written blessing of the ritual] until now, [everyone] from the sovereign, his consorts, the high aristocrats, and those above the fifth rank on down to cultivators and artisan women, together with the virtuous eminent priests of various Buddhist schools, join their hearts together here" (qtd. in *Saidai chokushi Kōshō Bosatsu gyōjitsu nenpu,* 151).

This notion that the Buddhist community does not recognize worldly categories of social division such as those of rank can be seen in the literature of Hokkeji as well. As briefly mentioned in chapter 5, the nun Enkyō, who recorded the *Hokke metsuzaiji engi* (Karmic origins of the Lotus Temple for the Eradication of Transgressions) in 1304, also argued that class divisions were irrelevant in the Hokkeji community. Court ladies are not considered superior, she says, nor are those born without impressive social connections considered inferior. When people renounce the world *(shukke),* Enkyō writes, "they all become sons of the Buddha. They are like the waters of many rivers, which come to share a single flavor [that of salt] when they enter the ocean" (143a).

The rhetoric of equality under Buddhism may have gained great popularity by Enkyō's time, but we know that this notion of class equality, while it may have had some effect on the degree to which individual women were accepted into the community, did not eradicate all vestiges of the class system at Hokkeji. As explained in chapter 5, class consciousness seems to have played an important role in the social lives of Hokkeji women, and it is likely that a woman's class affected not only her reception at the convent but also her chances of advancement and her role within the community.

At Saidaiji too, this notion that there is "no male or female" in the Buddhist community is misleading. But the move toward "oneness" is revealing. In both cases, a dichotomy is presented: high status versus humble status and male versus female. And in both cases, a specific hierarchy is presumed: it is better to be of high status than to be of low and better to be male than female. Enkyō admits that "high-ranking maidens who are able to gain audience with the sovereign" are "refined" and that "unconnected folks of humble birth are coarse." The function of her rhetoric here is not to dismiss the perceived *real* differences of the highborn and the humble; rather, her objective is to argue that Buddhist rites and the Hokkeji community are so powerful that they are able to fuse these groups together, to make them "one." This act is accomplished not by diluting the grandeur of the highborn but rather by elevating the virtues of the lowborn, an act accomplished through *shukke.* Once a woman takes the tonsure, Enkyō suggests, she is no longer bound by the limits of her class, but becomes a member of the Buddhist family.

In the Saidaiji literature, this notion that there is "neither man nor woman" is perhaps best understood as "there is only man in Buddhism";

that is, there is neither man nor woman not because the tradition understands the male/female dichotomy as fundamentally flawed or as a false hierarchy but rather because it holds that the female state can be overcome through devout faith and arduous practice. The same can be said for this notion that there is "neither noble nor base": these dualistic categories are indeed considered operable ones, but it is understood that the category of "base" can be overcome through the extraordinary power of Buddhist practice.[6]

Eison's use of the *Sutra on the Final Nirvana of Śākyamuni (Da banniepan jing),* mentioned in chapter 3, is worth further consideration here:

> According to the ninth chapter of the *Nirvana Sutra,* "If there is one who, on his or her own, realizes that the Buddha-nature exists, I would call this person a great manly person [*daijōbu*]. If there is a woman who realizes, on her own, that she certainly possesses the Buddha-nature, one must thus call her a man [*nanshi*]." [And thus] even women, if they renounce the world now, pursue Buddhist learning and practice, take the tonsure, and reach enlightenment, are all great manly persons. (*Chōmonshū,* 220)[7]

Eison understands the male/female dichotomy as an absolute hierarchy but offers, at the same time, a view of gender that can be abstracted from the somatic body. That is, he suggests that women can become men without undergoing any kind of physical or sexual transformation: the real transformation is an internal one. Gender, he implies, is a state of mind and is not biologically determined. Men who lack spiritual awareness are "women," and women who take the tonsure and practice Buddhism are "great manly persons." What is more, this particular view of gender transformation suggests that the metamorphosis can happen in this lifetime. Taken further, this view suggests that women do not need to pray for rebirth into male bodies in a future lifetime in order to reach enlightenment, for they can achieve "manliness" in this lifetime if they are willing to follow the Buddhist path with complete devotion.

This seemingly malleable view of gender transformation diverges from some of the more dogmatic views on the issue found in later discourses on gaining rebirth in a male body. The excerpt above appears in the *Collected Sermons Received from the Bodhisattva Eison (Kōshō Bosatsu gokyōkai chōmonshū),* a collection of sermons Eison is said to have delivered during lectures to his followers and on certain ritual occasions, such as precepts ordinations. Although this particular passage reinforces the notion that male is superior to female, its view of gender transformation is notable in its flexibility. In understanding gender primarily as a metaphor for one's spiritual understanding, it does not commit to the notion that femaleness is a characteristic innate to those inhabiting female bodies and thus allows for the possibility that women can gain buddhahood as "men" in women's bodies.

Sōji, who is known to have distributed copies of the *Sutra on Transforming the Female Body (Tennyoshingyō)* to nuns active in Ritsu-affiliated convents, also offers a view of gender transformation that leaves some room for interpretation.[8] In the second year of Kōgen (1257), Sōji donated a copy of the *Tennyoshingyō* to the nuns' group at Hokkeji and the laywomen's groups associated with Hokkeji. Because the sutra was a gift to the women, he personally inscribed it with the following message:

> This *Sutra on Transforming the Female Body* conveys the complete truth of the Mahāyāna teachings. It is a guide for liberating women. How regrettable that until this time in our land, we have not yet developed but have repressed nuns! The karmic burdens of women are heavy—just use this [sutra]. Entrust [yourselves] to the great teacher Śākyamuni Buddha's compassion, and you will lose [this unfortunate] collection of aggregates. As for its wondrous intent that has been transmitted and translated, by relying on this, you can not only repay your indebtedness to the sages and worthies but also redeem the heavy karmic burdens of women. I urge that you respectfully print copies; earnestly ask that you will distribute it in perpetuity; and deeply hope that [you] nuns and women will earnestly receive and uphold [this sutra]! If, in accordance with this sutra, women perform the ten practices related to scriptures [*jūhōgyō,* Skt. *daśa-dharma-caritam*][9] and they have deep faith in this text, then [as it says in the *Konkōmyōkyō, Golden Light Sutra*]:
>
> > May all women [*nyonin*] be transformed into men [*otoko*],
> > Courageous, intelligent, and full of wisdom.
> > May they practice the bodhisattva path at all times,
> > Cultivating the Six Perfections until they reach the realm of
> > enlightenment.
>
> First year of Kōgen [1256], senior year of the dragon, twelfth month, fifth day. Recorded by your fellow practitioner the *biku* [monk] Sōji. (qtd. in Ōya 1987, 189–190)[10]

Although the title of the text Sōji donates, the *Sutra on Transforming the Female Body,* refers not to transforming "women" (*onna* or *nyonin*) but specifically to transforming "women's *bodies*" *(nyoshin)*—the character *shin* connoting the fleshy, physical aspects of the body itself—Sōji's preface does not draw an absolute equation between "femaleness" and female bodies. His use of the compound "women's karma" *(nyogō),* translated here as "the karmic burdens of women" (but which could also be understood as "the karma that has caused one to be born a woman") does imply that women have stores of bad karma simply by virtue of the fact that they inhabit female bodies, that is, that grave karmic debts are an inherent part of the female condition. At the same time, however, his text does not preclude the possibility that women can be reborn as "men" in this lifetime through a spiritual—rather than physical—transformation from female to male. Sōji's words allow for the possibility that women can escape their karmic fate by overcoming their (nonphysical) femaleness. While those born into women's bodies are by biological default faced with the "karmic burdens of women," those who overcome such burdens through ardent practice can, it would seem, do so while remaining in their female bodies.

The language of the stanza Sōji quotes from the *Golden Light Sutra* is worth attention here. The line "May all women be transformed into men" uses only the single character *nan* (also pronounced *otoko*) for "men"; it does not specify that women need male *bodies (nanshin)*. Furthermore, the set of dualities here defined across the male/female divide would describe disposition rather than sexualized bodies. If men are "courageous, intelligent, and full of wisdom," then women, the reader is to infer, are not. Only after one has attained transformation into a "man," the verse proposes, can she (he) display these positive traits, practice the bodhisattva path, and attain enlightenment. But while these lines are clearly androcentric in their open preference for the qualities they define as masculine, they do not preclude the possibility that women can attain "manly" characteristics. That is, Sōji's preface is open to the reading that women can enter the bodhisattva path simply by acquiring the character traits described as masculine, a process that would not necessarily entail any physical transformation.

Thus, while the logic developed in Saidaiji discourse is clearly androcentric, it also leaves itself open to several distinct readings. Jishin, Eison, and Sōji all suggest the female state is something that can be overcome, perhaps through a nonphysical change. By distinguishing the category "woman" from the specifics of the female body, these positions allow for the possibility of gender transformation through nonphysical means. Sōji's inscription, too, insofar as it describes maleness primarily through references to certain qualities of character or disposition, offers a reading of gender that does not firmly locate the female state in the physical bodies of women. Transformation into a man, then, may not have necessarily entailed a miraculous cessation of blood flow, but only a strong commitment to Buddhist practice.

This view of women as potential men contrasts with the first view of women discussed in this section, namely, that of women as preying snakes who threaten male monastic practice. Although Eison did draw upon the well-entrenched Buddhist view of women as the enemies of the monastic order, it is worth emphasizing that this view is not the one articulated in other Saidaiji representations of women. The vision of women that appears to have gained wider acceptance among Saidaiji priests is that which understands women not as the enemy but as lesser beings who, through great effort, can be brought into the monastic fold as quasi-men. While Eison does invoke the image of women as sexual temptresses in his *Bonmōkyō koshakki kamon bugyō monjū ehon,* he quotes the *Sutra on the Final Nirvana of Śākyamuni* passage that distinguishes gender from physical bodies both in his commentary *Bosatsu kaihon shūyō bugyō monjū* and in his collection of sermons, which appears to have had a wider and more public audience. Perhaps it was necessary for Saidaiji priests to stress this second view over the first, given the fact that their desire to create a sevenfold *sangha* required the incorporation of a women's order. As the Saidaiji order brought women into its community, its leaders tended to downplay teachings that presented women as the enemies of the Buddhist order. In addition to supporting the need of Ritsu priests to incorporate women into their movement, this treatment of women as potential "men" likely reflects the fact the demonization of female biological processes had not yet progressed as far or extended as universally in Eison's time as it would in subsequent centuries.

But even while this second view of women as latent men is more inclusive than the first view, which understands women as dangerous adversaries, the texts of Saidaiji priests do emphasize that the inclusion of women into the order rests upon an understood hierarchy in which men are superior to women. And while Eison and his disciples tended not to appeal to the notion that female bodies are physically defiled, they *did* suggest that there is something about the condition of being born as a woman that damns women to an inferior status that must be overcome. Although these men may not have described women's bodies in terms of impurity or uncleanliness, as later priests would, they associated character flaws and ethical shortcomings with women precisely because women inhabit female bodies. The connection between female bodies and the use of the category "woman" in Saidaiji texts, then, is always implicit. As Sōji's inscription makes clear, these priests were all working from the assumption that the physiological state of inhabiting a woman's body was indicative of past karmic defilement. For Jishin, Eison, and Sōji, then, the female state did not prevent one from entering the Buddhist order, but it did represent a particular position of spiritual disadvantage.

Divine Female Bodies

Since it is known that Ritsu nuns were familiar with the texts circulated by Eison and Sōji, these women's views provide particularly compelling evidence of dissent from Saidaiji discourses of male superiority. And yet Ritsu nun-authors did not internalize but instead pointedly ignored those aspects of Saidaiji discourse that problematize the female body. Rather than directly addressing Saidaiji claims, these nuns sidestepped them, creating and furthering their own understandings of women's bodies and salvation. The rhetorical strategies that make this sort of contestation possible deserve closer analysis.

First, to return to the preface Sōji included on the copy of the *Tennyoshingyō* he presented to the nuns' group at Hokkeji, it is clear that while his words do leave room for the reading that women could in effect become "men" without transforming the female body, he does not promote this interpretation directly. Instead, he emphasizes that men are superior to women, who have "heavy karmic burdens," and that women must be transformed into men in order to gain enlightenment. A remarkable contrast may be seen in the 1304 *Hokke metsuzaiji engi* compiled by the Hokkeji nun Enkyō.

Although undoubtedly aware of Sōji's position, Enkyō does not acknowledge his dismissal of women's bodies.[11] Essentially talking *past* Sōji's text altogether, Enkyō offers a radically divergent vision of women and their role in the Buddhist cosmos in her history of Hokkeji, one that undoubtedly reflects a long-standing narrative tradition at the convent. In telling the story of Hokkeji's initial founding and of its most recent revival, Enkyō makes many important textual moves, suggesting not only that women need not worry about the question of sex change but also that salvation does not require the mediation of male priests. Enkyō's women are capable both of securing their own salvation and of extending salvation to others, regardless of their sex.

Nowhere in her lengthy text, which summarizes narratives celebrating Hokkeji as they were collected and retold by nuns and pilgrims during the Heian and Kamakura periods, does Enkyō problematize women's bodies. She makes no mention of "female karmic burdens," nor does she speak of the five obstacles, the thrice following, or the notion that women need male bodies. Enkyō avoids the concepts of female bodily impurity and sinfulness, as well as the notion that women arouse lust in men. Indeed, she ignores unfavorable representations of women altogether. What is more, she describes the body of Hokkeji's ancient founder, Queen-Consort Kōmyō, in terms Sōji might have found incongruent with the female form: "She [Queen-Consort Kōmyō] had a chaste and pure character and a gentle, noble form. Her purity was like ice and jade. Her faith was pure and devout. Her form was unsurpassed, and it is said that because she was like rays of light shining forth, she was called Kōmyō Kōgō [the Rays of Light Queen-Consort]" (140a).

In addition to possessing a body described both as female *and* as pure, Enkyō's Kōmyō exhibits those qualities labeled "masculine" by Sōji—intelligence, wisdom, and the ability to advance along the bodhisattva path quickly: "During the time when Shōmu was the designated royal heir, at age sixteen, she was in charge of managing ladies-in-waiting. With sincerity, she held fast to the teaching of propriety and worshipped the Buddha-Dharma enthusiastically.... Benevolent and compassionate, Kōmyō's wish was to save living beings in a profound way" (140b). One particularly noteworthy characteristic of Enkyō's Kōmyō is her potency as a female political figure and as a foundational patron of Buddhism. Throughout the *Hokke metsuzaiji engi,* Enkyō treats Kōmyō not as a figure secondary to that of the sovereign but rather as one of the most central figures—if not the most central figure—in the royal house. Enkyō grounds her praise of Kōmyō's leadership in contemporary mythologies of kingship. Here, she explains Kōmyō's divine right to rule: "[Kōmyō's] body was bright and balanced, and she displayed miraculous qualities. Long ago [in a past life], she consumed a freshly discovered red jewel, and yellow clouds as vast as the sea enveloped her. Therefore, she moved into the queen-consort's place and exquisitely manifested the ability to rule the country. While she was sitting in her quarters, the dragon offered her his jewel" (140b).

Enkyō's claims about Kōmyō's right to rule most likely refer to a narrative from the *Great Wisdom Treatise (Dazhidu lun)* in which the bodhisattva

Śākyamuni, in a former life as an royal prince, seeks the wish-fulfilling jewel in order to help save his people from poverty. The dragon king, noticing the virtue of the prince, invites Śākyamuni to come and stay in his palace for a month. At the end of the month, he presents the bodhisattva with his wish-fulfilling jewel (316b). Enkyō's use of the story implicitly compares Kōmyō to Śākyamuni Buddha, suggesting not only that she too is a bodhisattva but also that she is a rightful and compassionate ruler. In Enkyō's telling, Kōmyō does not even have to travel to the dragon king's palace to acquire the jewel; instead, the dragon king notices her majestic qualities from afar and comes to her palace without any prompting from her side to grant her the jewel. This reading suggests that Kōmyō's virtue as a ruler exceeded even that of the Buddha himself.

Of particular significance in Enkyō's vision of Kōmyō is the fact that the queen-consort's validity as a ruler is inextricably linked to her role as a Buddhist patron. Directly following explanations of Kōmyō's majestic qualities, Enkyō makes Kōmyō's role as a bodhisattva-ruler even stronger: Kōmyō, she says, "had a longing for the bamboo grove [for the ascetic life of Buddhism]. Her mind was always journeying to the golden lands [to thoughts of Buddhist temples]. It is said that the queen-consort also sought to promote reputation and virtue, spreading the teachings of the six schools [Tendai, Sanron, Hossō, Kusha, Kegon, and Jōjitsu]." At other places in the text, Enkyō speaks of Kōmyō as "a scholar of the Kegon [Chns. Huayan] school." Since the queen-consort "was skilled at writing," Enkyō notes, "she copied out all of the sutras by herself with a single stroke of the brush" (141b).

According to the *Hokke metsuzaiji engi,* Kōmyō was concerned not only with the success of Hokkeji and its nuns' group but also with the spread of Buddhism more widely and with the protection of Japan. Having "advanced the scholarship of priests and nuns," Enkyō writes, Kōmyō advised people to study under a "strict master" and issued a decree in the year 739 ordering the heads of temples throughout the land to contribute capable clerics from their provinces to the central Bureau of Priests (Sōgō) every year. In this way, Enkyō portrays Kōmyō as a bodhisattva leader responsible for the spread and management of Buddhism in early Japan.

Through this image of queen-consort Kōmyō as female bodhisattva-ruler, Enkyō ultimately sidesteps the question of sexual transformation, begging the question of whether or not women can progress along the Buddhist path and achieve bodhisattvahood in female bodies. Following earlier *junreiki* (pilgrimage record) accounts, Enkyō presents Kōmyō, an unambiguously female character, as a bodhisattva. Her view of women's bodies does not rely upon a sophisticated critique of Saidaiji discourses, nor does it depend upon the argument of Eison and his disciples outlined above, namely, that women can spiritually become "men" in women's bodies. Instead, Enkyō simply bypasses the question of women's transformation into men by describing Kōmyō as a figure who is unmistakably female and simultaneously unmistakably divine. Consider, for example, the following episode from her *Hokke metsuzaiji engi:*

> There was a king of the Indian province of Gandhāra who apparently made a vow that he would worship the living body of [the bodhisattva] Kannon. He then had a dream in which it was said, "If that is so, then you must worship the woman Kōmyō, the consort of the king of Japan, the island country in the eastern sea; she is indeed the living body of [the bodhisattva] Kannon." He awoke from the dream and dispatched an artisan to go as an envoy, to copy the [bodhisattva's] form and bring it back [to India].... Saying that they wanted to copy Kōmyō's image, six artisans came from Gandhāra to Japan. Thereupon the queen-consort summoned each of them, and each of them sketched her. It is said that when they finished the images, lined them up, and looked at them, they saw before them nothing other than the Six Manifestations of Avalokiteśvara Bodhisattva [Rokkannon]! (141a)[12]

In adopting from earlier *junreiki* literature this image of Kōmyō as a bodhisattva recognized even outside the Japanese islands, the *Hokke metsuzaiji engi* contributed to broader discussions about the relationships among local deities, buddhas and bodhisattvas, and the inhabitants of Japan. As Japan moved into the twelfth and thirteenth centuries, local and other popular gods came to play an increasingly larger role within the Japanese Buddhist imagination, as the theory of *honji/suijaku* (original ground/subsidiary manifestation) identified ostensibly "non-Buddhist" deities with specific buddhas and bodhisattvas. The *honji/suijaku* theory, which held that all gods were the "subsidiary manifestations" of buddhas and bodhisattvas perceived as Indian or Chinese in origin, was one method through which Buddhism mapped itself onto the Japanese landscape and asserted ideological dominance over other visions of the cosmos.[13]

Honji/suijaku discourse was used in a variety of ways. Some deployed the theory to argue against the necessity of traveling to India or China in search of more "authentic" forms of Buddhism. A skillful application of *honji/suijaku* theory allowed for the assertion that local gods were indeed Buddhist deities from the outset: these deities simply took on local forms so as to better reach their Japanese audiences. Enkyō uses the term *suijaku* when she writes of Kōmyō: "She [Kōmyō] is the subsidiary manifestation [*suijaku*] of the Eleven-Faced Kannon" (141a). On the one hand, Enkyō invokes the theory of *honji/suijaku* in conventional ways both to illustrate how local gods are in fact Buddhist in origin and to assert that Japanese Buddhism was just as authentic as that practiced on the continent. On the other, however, she suggests, in identifying Kōmyō as a manifestation of Kannon, that the theory of *honji/suijaku* may in fact offer a means of evading Buddhism's male body requisite for liberation.

Insofar as Kōmyō is described as a "subsidiary manifestation" *(suijaku)* of Kannon, one might argue that her female form is merely an expedient means, that she is "actually" male. The *Vimalakīrti sūtra*'s goddess, for example, is a bodhisattva who uses the female form as a tool to teach others about emptiness. Similarly, in a series of texts on the *Taima mandara chū* written by Japanese Pure Land priests, female bodies are understood as manifestations of Amida Buddha. In the *Taima mandara chū* of Hōnen's disciple Shōku (1177–1247), for example, Amida, out of great compassion, manifests himself in female bodies so as to save sentient beings (Taira 1990, 96–97). Kōmyō's female body, too, could be understood as an expedient means appropriated by a bodhisattva who had already achieved birth in a nonfemale body.

But neither Enkyō nor the texts from which she drew as she compiled the *Hokke metsuzaiji engi* frame Kōmyō's identity in this manner. The miraculous stories about Kōmyō that had been circulating since the late Heian period viewed Kōmyō as a female bodhisattva and showed no concern over the queen-consort's "true" gender. In short, Kōmyō functioned as a female character in the narratives associated with Hokkeji: her femininity is neither problematized nor explained away as the expedient means of a bodhisattva.

In a similar way, Shinnyo's 1282 *Ama Shinnyo ganmon* identifies the queen-consort Anahobe no Hashihito, mother of Prince Umayado (later known as Shōtoku), as a manifestation of Amida Buddha.[14] Queen-Consort Hashihito had been mentioned briefly in a number of earlier works, including the tenth-century (917) *Shōtoku Taishi denryaku,* the early-Heian-period *Jōgū Shōtoku Taishi den hoketsuki,* the 984 *Sanbōe kotoba* (2.1), the tenth-century (985–987) *Nihon ōjō gakurakuki,* the 1040 *Hokkekyō genki* (1.1), and the twelfth-century *Konjaku monogatarishū* (11.1). But this earlier literature describes her only as the mother of Shōtoku Taishi. It presents Shōtoku as a divine figure—he is described as the bodhisattva Kannon—and his mother as a passive figure whose womb the prince "borrows." Moreover, in these versions of the narrative, she describes her own body as defiled and expresses concern that her womb is too "filthy" for the prince to inhabit (see Meeks 2007).[15]

Shinnyo's *Ama Shinnyo ganmon,* however, displaces Shōtoku and centers on Hashihito instead. Although Shōtoku worship had gained great popularity by the year 1282, when Shinnyo wrote her *ganmon,* she barely mentions Shōtoku, who is said to have built Chūgūji in honor of his mother. Instead, her *ganmon,* which is addressed to the royal court, concentrates on the spiritual power of Queen-Consort Hashihito, whose past deeds, Shinnyo writes, "unfailingly generate [benevolent] responses [*kannō*]" (82b).

As mentioned in chapter 5, Shinnyo's own narratives emphasize that one of her primary goals in reestablishing Chūgūji was to hold death-date memorial rites *(kijitsu kuyō)* on behalf of Hashihito. The obstacles Shinnyo is said to have faced as she pursued this goal serve to create dramatic tension in popular narratives about her work at Chūgūji. According to most accounts, Shinnyo was at first unable to hold a ceremony for Hashihito because she was unable to verify the queen-consort's death date. She finally accomplished her goal after cloistering herself in prayer for eight days, receiving a vision in which she was told that she could find the date inscribed on the *Tenjukoku mandara* held in the sealed treasure house of Hōryūji and finally acquiring the image when an unrelated theft at the temple enabled her to gain entrance into the otherwise forbidden treasure house there. After this long string of miraculous events, Shinnyo finally succeeded in staging a death offering service for Hashihito in the year 1282. Shinnyo's *ganmon,* which was likely read aloud during the full day of rituals for Hashihito, declares, "I, Shinnyo, have revived the holy legacy of Anahobe no Hashihito, planting Buddha seeds in the dew of Amida's Western Pure Land. Already we have known the efficaciousness of [Hashihito's] original vow" (83a; see also *Chūgūji engi* and *Taishi mandara kōshiki*).

Shinnyo's portrayal of Hashihito asserts that the queen-consort is a bodhisattva: she has an "original vow" *(sogan)* that has already proven to be "efficacious" *(yūkō),* meaning that she has been successful on the bodhisattva path. And her past deeds, like the past deeds of other gods and bodhisattvas, "generate [benevolent] responses" *(kannō)* in the karmic world. Shinnyo also suggests that Shōtoku's eminence was the result not of his own karmic merit but rather of his mother's guidance: "As for the queen-consort's acts of faithfulness," Shinnyo writes, "she herself made the temple [Chūgūji] her own residence and aroused in the prince feelings of mercy and humanity throughout his life" (82b). This reading represents a significant departure from earlier narratives, which portray Shōtoku as an enlightened being who merely "borrows" Hashihito's womb for a few months and then begins to perform miraculous deeds as an infant.

In summary, the texts of Enkyō and Shinnyo are suggestive of the ways in which Ritsu nuns sidestepped the question of whether women could attain salvation in women's bodies. While Enkyō and Shinnyo did not directly argue against the doctrine, so evident in Saidaiji texts, that women must overcome their female states in order to progress along the Buddhist path, they effectively refuted this view simply by portraying the women who founded their convents as bodhisattvas, as divine beings who are visibly female. This indirect approach allowed them to "talk past" the dominant discourses of Saidaiji priests without even acknowledging them.

Mothers and Saviors

This strategy of "talking past" certain Saidaiji representations of women in the abstract may be seen again in the examples below, which illustrate contrasting views of motherhood put forth by Ritsu priests and nuns. Ritsu revivalists were writing during a period in which patrilineal family structures were becoming increasingly normative, and as a result, perhaps, idealized images of motherhood were gaining popularity (Tabata 1985). Ritsu constructions of motherhood, then, reflect both views of motherhood outlined in Buddhist literature and valorizations of mothers and motherliness visible in wider discourse. While Saidaiji priests tended to draw on abstract views of mothers in monastic literature, Ritsu nuns discussed motherhood in relation to the legendary founders of their convents, women they portrayed as divine mothers whose maternal qualities did not depend on biological processes. In the end, male Saidaiji clerics tended to promote images of mothers as passive figures in need of male salvation, while Ritsu nuns portrayed mothers as active figures who, far from relying on others for salvation, were themselves capable of saving sentient beings.

Filial Piety and the Salvation of Women as Mothers

One thread that emerges frequently in Saidaiji discussions of women is the role that priests play in the salvation of their mothers. Many Ritsu priests specified the desire to earn merit for the salvation of their mothers as one of the primary goals motivating their participation in certain religious projects, such as the restoration of a temple, the printing of a text, or the performance of a ritual. The priest Jishin, for example, is said to have revived the temple Gakuanji in honor of his mother. Sōji printed sutras for Ritsu nuns in honor of his mother, and Ninshō is said to have taken the tonsure so as to win his mother's salvation. Eishin, the second rector of Gokurakuji, like Sōji, also wrote that he wished to save his mother by printing texts for nuns. Eison himself, who lost his mother at age seven, had a lifelong concern for her salvation. Indeed, he carried out many of his virtuous deeds with the expressed intent of accruing karmic merit on her behalf.[16]

Taken together, passages about motherhood extracted from the works of Saidaiji priests like Eison, Ninshō, and Sōji suggest a certain biological determinism that understands all women as inherently disadvantaged in matters of spiritual import. These Saidaiji clerics constructed a discourse that assumed (1) all mothers are destined for hell and in need of salvation, (2) children owe a great filial debt to their mothers, (3) all women are manifestations of a single mother figure, and (4) by working toward the salvation of all women, Buddhist priests can save their own mothers.[17]

While the particular set of arguments outlined above does not emphasize the notion of physiological impurity per se, the essentializing move insisting that all women are mothers and that all mothers are destined for hell suggests that women are indeed bound by their physiological circumstances and biological roles. It furthermore identifies mothers—and all women—as wholly other and as wholly dependent on male priests as the brokers of their salvation.

Such assumptions were already well established by Eison's time, as seen most prominently in the widespread adoption of the Chinese legend of Mulian (Skt. Maudgalyāyana, Jpns. Mokuren), a disciple of the Buddha who seeks to save his mother. The narrative of Mulian, which had become popular among Japanese priests as early as the eighth century (*Daizōkyō zenkaisetsu daijiten*, 208), is based on the *Yulanpen jing* (Jpns. *Urabongyō*, T. no. 685). This sutra, which praises the filial piety of Mulian, who goes to great lengths in order to save his sinful mother from the depths of hell, had gained widespread popularity among commoners in China by the Tang period (608–907). Stephen Teiser (1998) and others have explained the emergence, circulation, and eventual popularity of the *Yulanpen jing*, which seems to have been a Chinese creation without significant Indian precedent, as an example of Buddhism's "Sinicization." As a tradition that emphasized leaving one's family behind in favor of an ascetic life free from attachment, Buddhism when imported into China inevitably required its new adherents to construct interpretations of the tonsured life that could accommodate Confucian conceptions of family life and filial piety.

In his heroic salvation of his mother, Mulian resolves the inherent contradiction between Buddhism's stress on a life free from familial and other attachments and Confucianism's central tenet that a son's primary duty is to father a son and to care for his parents. The fundamental logic of the *Yulanpen jing* is that Mulian is able to save his mother precisely because he is a Buddhist priest. So while non-Buddhists might criticize Mulian for his failure as a Confucian son, the *Yulanpen jing* argues that Mulian's Buddhist brand of filial piety is actually much more effective than its purely Confucian counterpart. The salvation of Mulian's mother rests, after all, on the offerings to the Buddhist monastic community Mulian makes on her behalf.

Images of women as polluted, sinful beings can be found throughout Indian Buddhist texts, but the Mulian narrative does not simply argue that women's bodies are helplessly in need of salvation; rather, it complicates the issue by building on the notion that women, as mothers, are simultaneously praiseworthy and sinful. Given the degree to which the story of Mulian and his mother, as well as the Ghost Festival it inspired, gained widespread popularity in Tang China, it is not surprising that Heian- and Kamakura-period Japanese priests, many of whom traveled to China and brought back Chinese Buddhist texts and rituals, seem to have grown increasingly concerned with the problem of saving their mothers.[18] As early as the eighth and ninth centuries, there are many examples of Japanese Tendai priests who expressed concern about their mothers, some even deciding to return to lay life so as to care for aging mothers. Ryōgen (912–985) and Genshin (942–1017), for example, both indicated a desire to save their mothers through Buddhist practice.[19]

In an insightful article that traces the historical development of ideas about hell and women in Japan, Katsuura Noriko (1986) argues that images of Mulian saving his mother, as originally depicted in Chinese transformation tales (*bian-wen,* Jpns. *henbun*), were brought together with visual depictions of women in hell, such as those presented in the *Mandala for Contemplation of the Ten Realms (Guanxin shijie manchaluo)* and the Song-period (960–1279) *Diagram for the Perfect and Sudden Contemplation of the Ten Dharma Realms (Yuandun guanxin shifajie),* to form a group of images and concepts about mothers and hell particular to Japan. In the center of the *Mandala for Contemplation of the Ten Realms,* a hell attendant stabs a woman as she suffers in an iron pot full of boiling water. Nearby, a tearful priest laments her situation. Similarly, the *Diagram for the Perfect and Sudden Contemplation of the Ten Dharma Realms* shows a woman in an iron pot being tortured with a lance as a crying priest grieves over her fate. Katsuura recognizes this same theme in a *Konjaku monogatarishū* tale about the mother of a priest named Ren'en (19.28). In this story, Ren'en, like Mulian, sets out to find his mother in hell. Aiding him in his search, a guardian of hell sticks a pike into a boiling iron pot and, pulling out the head of Ren'en's mother with the sharp end of the pike, presents it to the horrified Ren'en. Katsuura argues that it was this particular visual image of mother and priest—a woman boiling in an iron pot in the depths of hell as her son looks on—that had captured the imaginations of Japanese priests by the early twelfth century.

Saidaiji literature suggests that these gruesome images of mothers in hell were a matter of significant personal concern for the priests involved in the restoration of convents. In several surviving sources, Saidaiji priests suggest that they were interested in establishing a nuns' order precisely because they believed that the merit accumulated from their work in encouraging women's practice could be applied to eradicating the karmic debts incurred by their own mothers. In working toward the salvation of nuns, they reasoned, they were working toward the salvation of their own mothers.

The tonsure scene of the priest Ninshō is illustrative of Saidaiji views of the relationship between priests and their mothers. Celebrated primarily for his work with *hinin,* his fund-raising and social works projects, and his popularizing of the Monju Kuyō services, Ninshō was also known for his deep devotion to his mother. In his autobiography, Eison tells the story of Ninshō's tonsure, describing the episode with great emotion. This scene reflects two widely held assumptions: that mothers face certain suffering in the next life and are in need of redemption and that sons are greatly indebted to their mothers:

> On the eighth day of the ninth month, I gave the ten major precepts (including that forbidding the consumption of alcohol) to Ninshō [Ryōkan-bō]. At the time when I encouraged him to leave the household, tears rolled down his face, and he replied, saying, "Because I was my parents' only son, my mother and father together did nothing but cherish me. My mother in particular experienced sorrows exceeding the ordinary. When Mother had been invaded by disease and the end of her life was approaching, she wished to see me in the form of a novice, and for that reason I hastily shaved my head and put on priestly robes. [*But she only*] *began to despair more and more about* [*my*] *future; summer and winter, she asked for nothing. She neither cultivated distaste for* [*this*] *defiled realm nor delighted in the Pure Land; she only despaired about Ninshō's* [*my*] *future, filling herself with anguish. And* [*it was in this state of mind that*] *her breath ended and her spirit departed.* At that time, I was only sixteen years old, and I hadn't the power to repay my debt of gratitude [to her]. I missed the opportunity to save her from suffering and to give her comfort. All I can do is to look to the divine power of the primary deity Mañjuśrī [Jpns. Monju]. On the thirteenth-year anniversary of her death, I will offer up seven images of Mañjuśrī and enshrine them in seven outcast communities [*shuku*] in this province [Yamato]. Then, on the twenty-fifth day of each month, I will intone Mañjuśrī's precious name continuously for one day and one night, and *I will send the karmic merit thereby produced to the place where my deceased mother has been reborn.* This will be the excellent karmic condition that will liberate her from the six realms of rebirth. Only after I have

fulfilled this long-cherished vow will I take the tonsure and study the Way." (*KJGSK* 1977, 14–15; emphasis mine)[20]

One sentiment that stands out in Ninshō's tearful monologue is the notion that his mother's suffering both before and after her death was a result of her attachment to him. Ninshō invokes here what Wakita Haruko has described as a popular literary motif known as *kokoro no yami,* or "darkness of the heart," the excessive love of a child that creates attachment in a parent's—and especially in a mother's—heart. According to Wakita, narratives about monks and mothers gradually came to incorporate, over the course of the late Heian and Kamakura periods, the notion that mothers were bound for hell precisely because they tended to love their sons too much. Numerous narratives from this period tell of how women, having become so personally invested in the welfare of their male offspring, became more deeply entrenched in the world and in some cases even wished harm on others (Wakita 1985, 178–186; Glassman 2001, 16, 96–130). Stories about monks and their mothers dating to this period also emphasize the notion that mothers urged their sons to become monks because they expected their sons to win their salvation. The story of Genshin's mother, which appears among other places in the *Konjaku monogatarishū,* is a case in point. In the tale, Genshin's mother sends Genshin a letter in which she admonishes him for having pursued a reputation among the elite. The reason she encouraged him to become a monk, she says, was because she had no other sons. She sent him to Mount Hiei so he could become an accomplished priest and win her salvation (15.39).

Ninshō suggests that his mother, much like Genshin's, was depending on her only son to become a monk so he could offer her salvation. The logic underlying this desire recalls the sentiment of Grand Empress Gojō, who made arrangements for three men to be ordained each year so they could carry out Buddhist austerities in her stead (*Ruijū kokushi,* 179, Jōan 1 [859] 4/18). As discussed in chapter 3, the disappearance of convents in the early Heian period led to a situation in which women eager to earn merit toward their salvation had to turn to others for help. Shirai Yūko (1989) argues that it was at this juncture that elite women began to focus on patronage, the idea being, as Grand Empress Gojō's actions suggest, that one could employ others to practice Buddhism on one's behalf. But Ritsu narratives about the relationships between monks and their mothers suggest that patronage was not the only method by which a woman could have a man practice Buddhism on her behalf: another option was to send one's son to do the job.

Eager to please his dying mother, Ninshō hurriedly shaved his head and styled himself as a monk. But this action alone did not allow his mother to relax; so worried was she about her son's future—and, presumably, his ability to save her—that she died in a state of despair and anxiety. It was her attachment to Ninshō and her preoccupation with his success on the Buddhist path that prevented her from dying in a soteriologically efficacious manner. Not only did Ninshō's mother fail to cultivate distaste for the impure realm and to delight in the prospect of birth in the Pure Land, but she also died in a state of attachment and anguish. Since contemporary beliefs about death held that one's state of mind at the moment of death determined one's rebirth, Ninshō feared the worst. He believed not only that his mother had fallen into a state of postmortem torment but also that it was his responsibility to rescue her from suffering.

Also relevant to Ninshō's presentation of his relationship with his mother are the broader discourses about motherhood circulating during his time. The growing consensus among Japanese social historians is that motherhood first gained strength as a social ideal during the early Kamakura period (1186–1336), the very age during which Ninshō was living. Tabata Yasuko (1985), for example, has argued that as the patriarchal *ie* (corporate household) model of family life gained importance and marriage systems became more and more solidly patrilineal, women came to be appreciated primarily for their ability to give birth to male heirs. As a result, motherhood, which had enjoyed less attention during earlier periods of Japanese history, became fully romanticized during the thirteenth century.

A number of Japanese scholars have pointed to the following passage from the 1219 *Gukanshō* of Jien as emblematic of the degree to which values associated with motherhood had gained discursive weight by the early years of the Kamakura period:

> The truth of the old saying that women "provide the finishing touches" in this country was revealed by the appearance of these reigning Empresses [female *tennō:* Kōgyoku, who reigned a second time as Saimei, and Kōken, who reigned a second time as Shōtoku]. In trying to understand the basis for this in Buddhist teachings, I conclude that the phrase "birth of the human world" clearly points to the meaning of the fact that people are all born from the wombs of women. The pain that a mother suffers in childbirth is indescribable. Since causal effects [*inga*] are both good and bad, persons born of women include those who are good as well as those who are bad.... All have received female, motherly blessings. (trans. Brown and Ishida 1979, 37; *NKBT,* 86:243)

As a Fujiwara, Tendai priest Jien had a vested political interest in promoting the significance of motherhood: the Fujiwara had gained political power by marrying its daughters into the royal family and exploiting the positions of those daughters as mothers of *tennō.* Still, his appeal to the physical aspects of motherhood suggests that by the thirteenth century, fixation on the suffering endured by mothers had entered popular discourse.

Jien's glorification of mothers also coincides with another claim made in Saidaiji literature, namely, that *all* women can be understood as mothers. That Jien collapses the categories of "woman" and "mother" is evident when he describes the sovereign Kōken, who had no biological children, as one of the women who has bestowed "female, motherly blessings" on the people of Japan. This move toward identifying all women as mothers regardless of whether they had actually given birth to children in this lifetime is based in a particular reading of the twentieth minor bodhisattva precept in the *Brahma Net Sutra*. Here, in an explanation of the twentieth precept, the text states, "All men have been our fathers, and all women have been our mothers. We are born into what we are according to birth and rebirth. Thus, all living beings on the six paths are our parents. Therefore, killing and eating [living beings] is the same as killing our fathers and mothers and also the same as killing our [own] bodies" (trans. Osuka 2005, 103, with slight revisions; *Fanwang jing*, 1006b9–12).[21]

In its original context, this notion that all women have been one's mothers in past lifetimes is used together with the parallel notion that all men have been one's fathers to illustrate the immorality of killing sentient beings. The passage is not about parent-child relationships per se, nor does it single out the role of the mother. But in Japan, priests came to cite this passage as evidence that they should regard all women as their own mothers. Jien does not cite the *Brahma Net Sutra* directly in the passage related above, but it is likely that he too had this passage in mind when he mentioned, in his praises of motherhood, the fact that all beings are born from the wombs of women.

The notion that all women can be regarded as mothers and, moreover, as manifestations of a single mother figure can be found throughout Saidaiji literature. Invoking the passage from the *Brahma Net Sutra* mentioned above, Eison himself vows that he will treat all living beings as if they were his own mother or father (Nōdomi 1977, 32–36).[22] Sōji, Eison's nephew and one of his foremost disciples, makes a similar proclamation, focusing solely on the mother figure: "When I was young, my mother died, and I continually mourned for her. [Because she died when I was so young,] I lost the opportunity to repay the gratitude I felt toward her, and I have long regretted this fact. But my heart of filiality [must be] so feeble: for as it has been taught, *every woman—all women—are themselves Mother;* it is merely the difference in time between the past and the present [that makes them seem otherwise], and that is all" (*Shibun ritsu chū bikuni kaihon,* 115; emphasis mine).

Sōji included these words as an inscription on his precepts manual for nuns, the *Four-Part Vinaya Notes on the Bikuni Precepts (Shibun ritsu chū bikuni kaihon).* He compiled and printed the text for the nuns who had taken the precepts under Eison and begun to establish monastic centers for women. In criticizing the weakness of his "heart of filiality," Sōji suggests that the regret he felt in the past, which was based upon his perceived inability to repay his mother's kindness, was in fact ill founded. After all, if he had followed the logic of Eison and of the *Brahma Net Sutra,* he reasons, he would have realized that his mother is very much still alive: she lives in all the women who surround him in daily life. By aiding these women, he can repay the filial debt he owes his mother. That he has realized this truth so late, he reflects, reveals his lack of true filial piety.

This excerpt from Sōji's inscription illustrates a third assumption found in Saidaiji discourse on motherhood, namely, that all women are manifestations of a single mother figure. It also hints at a fourth, that Buddhist priests can save their own mothers by working toward the salvation of all women. For many Saidaiji priests, working toward the salvation of all women appears to have meant encouraging nuns in their practice of Buddhism. Many of Sōji's printing projects, such as the one mentioned above, in which he printed copies of a four-part *vinaya* manual for nuns, and the one mentioned in the previous section, in which he raised funds to print and distribute the *Tennyoshingyō,* were said to have been carried out in an attempt to gain karmic merit for his own mother. Likewise, the priest Eishin, the second rector of Gokurakuji in Kamakura, also printed, in the year 1302, the *Four-Part Vinaya Notes on the Bikuni Precepts* edited by Sōji. Much like Sōji, Eishin indicates in his preface to the volume that by dedicating the text, he wishes to aid his mother in her passage to the next life *(jibo no meiro)* while simultaneously contributing to the cultivation of a nuns' order *(ama-shū no gyōke)* (qtd. in Hosokawa 1989b, 144).

It is clear, then, that Eison's male disciples contributed to the construction of a soteriological model in which Buddhist priests were understood both as responsible for and as capable of saving their mothers. But while Saidaiji priests did assume that their mothers, and women in general, faced severe karmic burdens, they did not tend to articulate the sinfulness of women in terms of physical impurity, nor did they connect the karmic burdens of their mothers to the blood of childbirth and menses.

This distinction is significant. While it has sometimes been assumed that all priests understood women's bodies as impure,[23] a close reading of the Saidaiji representations of gender suggests that while Saidaiji priests clearly understood women as inferior, as soteriologically challenged, and perhaps even as sinful *(zaigōteki),* they did not stress the notion that women's bodies were themselves defiling or polluting. Concerns about the uncleanliness of women's bodies, which are not really addressed in Ritsu texts, came to a head during the late fourteenth and early fifteenth centuries, when the *Blood Bowl Sutra (Ketsubonkyō)* began to circulate and the notions of the five obstacles and the thrice following came to be associated not only with the social practices or circumstances that marked one "female" but also with the biological condition of inhabiting a female body.[24] The notions that the blood of women's menstrual cycles, as well as the blood lost during childbirth, was polluting and that as a result of their intimate ties to these impure biological processes all women were unclean then gained widespread popularity.

Although Eison and Sōji were certainly aware of the Mulian narrative, later versions of which became conflated with the *Blood Bowl Sutra,* it is unlikely that they were familiar with the *Blood Bowl Sutra* itself.[25] The texts of Eison, Ninshō, Sōji, and Eishin all agree that mothers are a soteriologically problematic category, which is the primary theme of the Mulian story, but they do not emphasize the notion that women are physiologically impure in the way that later priests would. The idea that women's bodies were defiled was not foreign to Eison's place and time: as mentioned in earlier chapters, many Japanese temples had established *nyonin kekkai,* which prohibited women from entering temple grounds on the premise that their bodies were ritually polluting. Furthermore, Daoxuan, whom Ritsu priests regarded as one of the patriarchs of their tradition, had included in his list of women's grave vices the filth of women's blood. Mujū Ichien, a contemporary of Eison, cites the seventh of Daoxuan's accusations against women as follows: "[Women's] bodies are forever unclean, with frequent menstrual discharges. Seeing that both pregnancy and childbirth are both foul and the afterbirth unclean, the evil demons vie for possession while the good deities depart. The foolish find these things attractive, but the wise are repelled" (trans. Morrell 1980, 67).[26]

Given the degree to which Eison and his disciples venerated Daoxuan, holding regular death offering services on his behalf and mentioning him frequently in their own works, it is safe to assume that they were familiar with Daoxuan's view that women were physically impure. If the text cited above, Daoxuan's *Jingxin jieguan fa,* was circulating widely enough that Mujū Ichien, a Rinzai Zen priest, was reading and commenting upon it, then surely Eison and his disciples, who were contemporaries of Mujū and who considered themselves members of Daoxuan's lineage, must have studied this text as well.

But Eison, Ninshō, and Sōji do not address this notion of impurity originating from biological processes. Still, their writings allude to a type of biological determinism that connects women's postmortem fate to their anatomical condition: it is, after all, the physiological similarity of all women that defines them as manifestations of a common mother, separates them from male priests, and places them in the passive category of those requiring salvation.

It is impossible to determine the degree to which Eison and his disciples were genuinely concerned with the salvation of their own mothers, as available records do not allow scholars to separate personal sentiment for their own mothers from a collective desire to mimic the rhetorical structures of earlier Buddhist narratives. But one matter is clear: the views of motherhood forwarded in the literature of the Saidaiji movement project a dynamic in which male priests are responsible for the salvation not only of their mothers but of *all* women. This rhetorical move allowed Saidaiji priests both to claim authority over the women's order and to assert that women must rely upon the teachings of men. What is more, these claims to authority and power over women were made in the name of compassion and filial devotion.

Motherliness and the Creation of a Hokkeji-Centered Relics Tradition

In contrast to earlier sections, in which Saidaiji representations of women were shown to oppose those offered by Ritsu nuns, this section will focus on an example in which Ritsu monks and nuns both contributed to the valorization of the mythicized Kōmyō. In this instance, Eison stepped back from discussions of women and mothers in the abstract to help promote the

Kōmyō cult, most likely in conjunction with efforts to associate his movement with the relics tradition of Hokkeji. Ritsu discourse on the relics is of special interest here because it serves as an example of the degree to which Saidaiji conceptions of motherhood were multivalent. While the examples mentioned in the section above suggest that Saidaiji priests understood mothers as helpless, pitiable women in need of salvation, the literature that emerged in conjunction with the Buddha relics tradition of Hokkeji worked from an altogether different reading of "mother"—one that gave certain mothers salvific power.

As discussed in the last section of chapter 4, nuns involved in the thirteenth-century revival of Hokkeji envisioned the convent as a center of relic veneration. Eison, who was himself highly invested in devotional practices using Buddha relics, actively supported the relics tradition there. The success of the relics tradition at Hokkeji contributed in turn to the broader success of the Saidaiji movement, which regularly invoked the power of the relics in its appeals both to the state and to ordinary laypeople. Of particular interest here is the way in which the *Hokkeji shari engi,* which Eison is said to have recorded at the behest of Hokkeji nuns in the year 1270, handles images of motherhood. This text associates Kōmyō with *prajñā-pāramitā,* or the perfection of wisdom (144a).

Wisdom is one of the six *pāramitās,* or practices that bodhisattvas must perfect en route to buddhahood (the others are charity, morality, forbearance, effort, and meditation).[27] Wisdom is in fact regarded as the most important of the six, for without it, the scriptures explain, one cannot perfect the other five. To illustrate the degree to which the perfection of the *pāramitās* is driven by the perfection of wisdom, scriptures on the perfection of wisdom describe this one perfection as the "mother of all buddhas." The metaphor is used not only to describe the generative nature of wisdom, which "gives birth to all the buddhas," but also to describe the pain of bodhisattva practice. Just as the greatest pain of pregnancy is experienced in the final weeks preceding birth, when the mother experiences great discomfort and is rendered more or less immobile, so are the final stages of the bodhisattva path, when bodhisattvas are about to experience delivery into buddhahood, exceedingly painful and trying (Nagata 1985, esp. 278–283; T. no. 220, 888c24–27; T. no. 223, 315b20–23; T. no. 227, 554c1–7; T. no. 228, 622a5–8). One of the most well noted passages from this literature describes *prajñā-pāramitā,* or the perfection of wisdom, as a mother whose children adore her. Feeling great debt toward their mother, these children (like Ninshō) are eager to offer their mother comfort when she is stricken with illness:

> The Buddha said to Subhūti, "Consider, for example, a mother with children, whether five or ten or twenty or thirty or forty or fifty or one hundred or one thousand children. If the mother were to become ill, each and every one of her children would toil in search of a method to save her.... These many children would constantly strive to furnish with comfort and serve their mother. Why

> is this? Because she gave birth to them and raised them, showing them their world. In this same way, Subhūti, does the Buddha, always use his Buddha eye [of omniscience], to focus on the deep perfection of wisdom. Why is this? It is because the deep perfection of wisdom reveals the characteristics *(xiang)* of the world. The Buddhas in the Ten Directions also focus on the deep perfection of wisdom with their Buddha eyes [in this same way]. Why is this? It is because the deep perfection of wisdom is able to give birth to many buddhas. It is able to give the many buddhas omniscience. It is able to reveal to them the characteristics of this world. It is for this reason that the many Buddhas always use their Buddha eyes to focus on the deep perfection of wisdom." (T. no. 223, 323a23–b5)[28]

This metaphor describing the perfection of wisdom as the mother of the buddhas offers a rich set of interpretative options. In Buddhist treatments of motherhood in premodern Japan, two interpretations are particularly visible. One speaks to the biological nature of motherhood: mothers are praised both for their fecundity and for the pain they endure in childbirth (a point also made in Jien's *Gukanshō*). Another builds on the fact that this mother is the personification of wisdom and that she creates buddhas by enabling wisdom to pervade the practices of bodhisattvas. This point allows for another avenue of interpretation, namely, that which portrays mothers—and women—as spiritual guides. While the first approach is that most commonly seen in the work of priests, the second can be found in the *Hokkeji shari engi.*

The first approach to this metaphor can be found in *Gyokuyō,* the diary of Kujō Kanezane (1149–1207). In an entry for the twenty-eighth day of the eleventh month of Juei 1 (1182), Kanezane summarizes a sermon given by the priest Chōken (who, incidentally, was the father of the nun Kūnyo):[29]

> All women are the true mothers of all the buddhas of the triple world, but it is not the case that all men are the true fathers of all the buddhas of the triple world. Why is this? Because when a buddha emerges in the world, he absolutely must reside in a womb temporarily. For example, in the case of [a buddha manifesting himself in] a transformation body [*nirmāṇa-kāya*], it goes without saying that this happens through birth from a womb but is not a matter of a father having a part in the coming together of *yin* and *yang* essences [i.e., there is no sexual intercourse involved]; the skin and hair of the body is not received from the father.[30] And thus because there is no natural principle shared between father and child [in this case], can we not conclude that women are superior to men? (2:584)

Here, Chōken draws upon phrasing from the *Tennyo jōbutsukyō* (Sutra on transforming women into buddhas) to present a view of motherhood that reconciles those found in the *Brahma Net Sutra* with those found in *prajñāpāramitā* literature.[31] In describing *all* women as mothers, he is of course drawing on common interpretations of the previously mentioned passage from the *Brahma Net Sutra.* But instead of viewing all women as ordinary mothers, he uses the metaphors developed in *prajñā-pāramitā* literature to assert that *all* women are the mothers of the buddhas. He then moves into a rather pragmatic discussion of why it is that fathers are excluded in discussions about the birth of buddhas: this, he asserts, is because buddhas, when they are born in manifestation bodies, are born through supernatural means and not through sexual intercourse. So while the ability of buddhas to manifest themselves in the human realm does in fact depend on the use of women's bodies—wombs, after all, are necessary in this scenario—neither men nor their seed is required. Fathers, then, have no role in the birth of buddhas, and thus women, the contrarian Chōken asserts, are superior to men.

Kanezane notes in his summary of the lecture that Chōken's words were "strange and unexpected" (2:584). Surely, Chōken's conclusion that women are superior to men would have been viewed as unusual (Wakita 1985, 172). His approach to the passages from the *Brahma Net Sutra* and *prajñā-pāramitā* literature to which he indirectly refers is also unusual, especially insofar as he forces a great deal of pragmatic thinking on the metaphor of *prajñā-pāramitā* as the mother of all buddhas. For while the metaphor is used within canonical literature to illustrate the *spiritual* birth of buddhas, Chōken applies it instead to the process by which buddhas physically manifest themselves in the world by being born into manifestation bodies. His approach to the subject of motherhood thus shares the emphasis of Jien, who several decades later praised women for their biological function as mothers. Chōken, too, asserts that women are praiseworthy—and indeed even superior to men—precisely because of their biological bodies: namely, they possess the wombs upon which buddhas depend when they manifest themselves in the world.

In the *Hokkeji shari engi,* by contrast, we see a different approach to the metaphor of *prajñā-pāramitā* as mother. As discussed in chapter 5, the *Hokkeji shari engi* portrays Kōmyō, the founder—and, one could argue, "mother"—of Hokkeji, as personally causing the Buddha relics enshrined at the convent to reproduce. She also punishes the nuns when they fail to obey her will and distribute the relics freely. Of particular interest is a passage near the end of the text, in which Kōmyō is identified with the *prajñā-pāramitā* and her function as the spiritual guide of Hokkeji nuns is emphasized. Here, the biological aspects of motherhood are wholly ignored, and the text chooses instead to emphasize the role that *prajñā-pāramitā* plays in leading beings toward buddhahood. In other words, the spiritual rather than biological functions of the "mother" *prajñā-pāramitā* are emphasized:

> Meanwhile, in the spring of Kenchō 5 [1254], the *bikuni* Jitsua became sick and was bedridden for many days. She stopped sleeping and eating. As the days passed, she grew increasingly exhausted. Then finally, late at night when everyone was quiet, as she was anxious and unable to sleep, the founder Kōmyō, without manifesting her bodily form, expressed these words in a clear and friendly voice: "I take the relics, together with great wisdom [*daihannya,* Skt. *mahā-prajñā*], as my two eyes. As for great wisdom, the nun [Shū]-Amidabutsu

> has already carried out that work.[32] As for the relics, I use expedient means to cause them to be enshrined in this temple [Hokkeji]. Entrusting them [the relics] to you was my original intent, [but you] have distributed them in many directions, and this greatly violates my will." After Jitsua heard these sacred words, her illness immediately dissipated, and her body and mind were restored to their prior state. Truly, this is a matter of a miraculous age, for it does not distinguish between noble and base, those who are close and those who are not. When [Kōmyō] firmly gave them the clear warning that the distribution of the relics must be brought to an end, those who had first distributed the relics were frightened of the divine feelings [*meiryō*] of the founder [Kōmyō]. Gradually [the relics] were sent back [to Hokkeji].

Once the nuns collected the distributed relics and stored them properly, Kōmyō was satisfied and caused them to multiply again. The *engi* claims that they increased from 656 to 2,073 pieces between 1254 and 1268 (144a–b).

The *Hokkeji shari engi* suggests not only that Kōmyō, the "mother" of Hokkeji, uses *mahā-prajñā,* or great wisdom, to exercise control over the relics at Hokkeji but also that there is a broader connection between motherhood and relic possession. In another episode of the *engi,* discussed in chapter 4, Shū-Amidabutsu, the mother of the nun Shakunen, receives small shards of Buddha relics from Kūnyo. Meanwhile, her son (and Shakunen's brother) Gyōgu desires a relic but has been unable to receive one, despite his many prayers. Upon hearing that his mother had been given a relic that split into two, Gyōgu approaches her and asks for one relic. Shū-Amidabutsu bequeaths one of her relics to him, but he loses it, revealing that he does not yet have the spiritual capacity necessary for relic possession:

> After several months passed, at one time he wanted to look at the relics, but there was only an empty vessel [where the relics had once been], and he could not see any relics. Gyōgu was completely and visibly stupefied. He felt ashamed of the baseness of his past karma. As he was deeply harboring thoughts of lament, he saw a dream in which there was a five-colored light atop a high parapet of a residence hall on Mount Shigi. He thought it strange and asked someone who was standing to his side about it and was given the following response, "This is the mysterious light of the relics that your mother possesses." As he was listening to these words and feeling increasingly ashamed of himself, these rays of light all became relics and filled up the parapet. He took refuge in his joyous heart and awoke from the dream. He went to the place of his mother, and in tears, he told her the content of the story above. His mother then revealed to him that the relics had already returned to her place, and Gyōgu was both saddened and overjoyed. Over and over, Gyōgu begged to receive [a relic]. His mother informed him, saying, "I heard that your relic disappeared and thought it was strange. [This indicates] that your mental capacity [is unripe] and relationship [to the Buddha] [*kien*] is distant.[33] Carefully consider that which your dream told you. Whether it is logical or not, it is surely a matter of [karmic] rectification! Now, as in the beginning, you are again wishing to be given one relic." At

> that very moment, the relic that had been lost before unexpectedly appeared in the reliquary. At the same time, two relics were received through *kantoku* [merciful response from the gods and buddhas]. Gyōgu finally attained a mind of firm belief. During the time that he exclusively and arduously cultivated the path of Buddhism, there was more than a single miraculous transformation of these relics. They split into innumerable pieces, and gradually they doubled and exceeded several hundred pieces. (144a)

This episode suggests that while Gyōgu's mother was fully entitled to possess and care for the relics, he was not—at least not in the beginning. His relic vanished, the text implies, because he was undeserving of it; relics, after all, were regarded as objects that verified the spiritual accomplishments of those who bore them. They were received from the buddhas and deities through *kantoku,* or from an accomplished Buddhist master like Kūnyo who had the ability to discern the spiritual capabilities of others. And thus, when Gyōgu's mother, Shū-Amidabutsu, learns that the relic she had bestowed upon her son disappeared, she declares the situation a "matter of [karmic] rectification." Gyōgu, who is "distant" from the Buddha, does not earn the right to possess Buddha relics until he learns through his mother's guidance how to attain a "mind of firm belief" and how to improve his "mental capacity," matters that the text portrays his mother as having already mastered.

The second of the first two sentences uttered by Kōmyō in the divine message she delivers to Jitsua may refer to Shū-Amidabutsu's role as a spiritual mother: "I take the relics, together with great wisdom, as my two eyes. As for great wisdom, the nun [Shū]-Amidabutsu has already carried out that work." Shū-Amidabutsu, in leading her son toward a more correct form of practice, does indeed exercise the nurturing wisdom characteristic of *prajñā-pāramitā.* After accepting his mother's admonitions, Gyōgu finally succeeded in cultivating the faith required for relic possession. Shū-Amidabutsu's wisdom, then, led to Gyōgu's "birth" as a disciple of the Buddha. Shū-Amidabutsu may have been Gyōgu's biological mother, but the *Hokkeji shari engi* emphasizes her role as his spiritual mother. This portrayal of Shū-Amidabutsu as spiritual guide to her son echoes Shinnyo's description of Queen-Consort Hashihito in the *Ama Shinnyo ganmon.* There, as mentioned earlier, Shinnyo says that the queen-consort "aroused in the prince [Umayado, her son] feelings of mercy and humanity throughout his life" (82b). In both of these narratives, it is the mother who offers her son spiritual guidance. Read against more commonly known trope of a monk who saves his mother, these portrayals of mothers in the literature of Ritsu nuns offer a striking reversal of roles in the mother-son relationship.

The relics tradition at Hokkeji thus inspired a distinct reading of mothers and motherliness, one that likely appealed to nuns and noblewomen more than that of the passive priest's mother. The *Hokkeji shari engi,* which is said to have been written by Eison at the prompting of Hokkeji nuns, configures motherliness in a way that contradicts the passive, powerless motherliness of the Saidaiji priests' mothers examined earlier. Not only is Kōmyō depicted as a divine mother capable of saving others, but Gyōgu's mother is depicted as a devout believer whose success on the Buddhist path greatly exceeds that of her son. The *engi* alludes to some of the more creative readings of motherhood and motherliness that emerged in the Ritsu texts. The next section will consider how Enkyō built upon and reformulated those values associated with motherhood in the *Hokkeji shari engi.*

Re-imagining Ideal Motherhood

Enkyō's 1304 *Hokke metsuzaiji engi* further develops the idealization of Kōmyō evident in Eison's *Hokkeji shari engi.* Shinnyo, too, elaborates upon the mythical nature of Chūgūji's founding queen-consort, Hashihito, in her 1282 *Ama Shinnyo ganmon.* But while Eison's valorization of Kōmyō serves to associate his *vinaya* movement with the Hokkeji relics tradition, which would gain wide recognition given its ties to the relics of *nyoin,* the motherly virtues of Kōmyō and Hashihito play another legitimizing role in the texts of Enkyō and Shinnyo. Attention to the virtuous motherliness of legendary female founders allows these nun-writers to construct representations of motherhood that work against the image of mothers as passive beings in need of salvation and in support of an image of mothers as wise women who use certain maternal qualities to save sentient beings.[34] While Saidaiji priest-mother narratives tend to portray mothers as helpless figures who need to be rescued, Enkyō and Shinnyo portray Kōmyō and Hashihito as active, *saving* mothers—mothers who, far from needing their sons to save them, are actually enacting salvation both for their own children and for sentient beings more widely. Thus, while Ninshō makes it his life's mission to "win [his deceased mother's] liberation" through the production of karmic merit, Enkyō and Shinnyo understand the mothers Kōmyō and Hashihito as having attained divine status at death. Now that they are gods and bodhisattvas, Kōmyō and Hashihito are capable of interacting with and saving those who call upon them. Kōmyō and Hashihito may be mothers, but their posthumous fate is altogether different than that of a Saidaiji priest's mother.

Moreover, it is interesting to note the degree to which Enkyō and Shinnyo, building on the sorts of notions of motherly wisdom developed earlier in the *Hokkeji shari engi,* abstract the "motherliness" of Queen-Consorts Kōmyō and Hashihito from the biological context. The mothers of Saidaiji priests are given only flat characterizations: they are mothers in need of spiritual liberation, and their sons, whose very births are tied up in the karmic burdens of their mothers, look to them with feelings of pity and indebtedness. For Enkyō and Shinnyo, however, Kōmyō and Hashihito are mothers in a broader sense, and their motherliness has more to do with wisdom, guidance, and self-sacrifice—all venerable qualities from a Buddhist standpoint—than with karmic quandaries or feelings of guilt.

Although descriptions of Kōmyō in the *Hokke metsuzaiji engi* do not use the word "mother," they generally correspond with the *Hokkeji shari engi* in portraying Kōmyō as a divine mother figure. Following images of Kōmyō from *junreiki,* as well as from Hokkeji *engi* that had likely been in circulation for centuries, Enkyō's *Hokke metsuzaiji engi* describes Kōmyō as a queen-consort who ruled Japan with compassion and guidance during her earthly life and who continues to lead the nuns at Hokkeji and to protect Japan. Enkyō's Kōmyō, like the Kōmyō of the *Shoku Nihongi,* for example, washes a leper with her own hands and builds the dispensary halls Hiden and Seyaku to "nurse all of the malnourished and diseased crowds under heaven back to health." She is also a teaching "mother" who educates, guides, and motivates. The *engi* says that Kōmyō instructed those under her service with the "teaching of propriety" and that the queen-consort herself "went out into the market areas [*ichi*] and taught all of the many merchants [*akibito*] how to use standardized measurements." Kōmyō "helped the country and sympathized with the people," Enkyō writes. She adds that Kōmyō was so committed to the project of building temples for the protection of her people that she and her ladies-in-waiting would go to the Tōdaiji construction site at night, "put[ting] earth into the sleeves of their robes and then pil[ing] it atop a platform" (141a).

Enkyō's Kōmyō, like the Kōmyō described in the *Hokkeji shari engi,* also delivers oracles to—and through—the nuns at Hokkeji. In the *Hokke metsuzaiji engi,* Kōmyō's spirit again guides the nuns in a maternal fashion. In an episode that will be examined at greater length below, Kōmyō speaks to the nuns through the matronly Eleven-Faced Kannon, a statue that, according to legend, was built in the image of Kōmyō herself (142a). Enkyō writes that during her lifetime, Kōmyō personally led the nuns' assembly at Hokkeji, assigning the nuns to specific posts and positions within the convent and leading them through certain rites and rituals, such as the Doll Ceremony inspired by the *Kegon Sutra* (Flower ornament sutra, Chns. *Huayan jing*) (141b). Enkyō clearly suggests that Kōmyō's guidance of Hokkeji affairs did not end with her death: her divine spirit continued to lead, advise, and inspire the nuns in residence at the convent. And like the children of the mother described in the *Mahāprajñāparamitā sūtra,* the nuns at Hokkeji are portrayed as "constantly striv[ing] to furnish with comfort and serve" Kōmyō (cf. T. no. 223, 323a27–28). In praising the new nuns at Hokkeji who have revived the institution, Enkyō writes, "We are pursuing the same intention that was in place here in the beginning and awakening the great will [of the Queen-Consort Kōmyō]" (*HMJE,* 142b).

In examining the connection between Kōmyō and the Mother of Wisdom, it is worth noting Enkyō's emphasis on the ways in which the thirteenth-century nuns who reestablished Hokkeji endured suffering in order to follow Kōmyō's will. According to Enkyō, many royal women made great sacrifices in order to pursue Kōmyō's calling. Enkyō says that many of Hokkeji's women traveled to the convent from distant provinces, a notion substantiated by the name register discussed in chapter 5, which contains lists of women living at Hokkeji who had indeed come from distant provinces. She also says that many women came from elite backgrounds and gave up rare privileges—the opportunity to spend time with the sovereign and other extraordinary personages, the opportunity to participate in court rituals or to enjoy the beauty of the palace—in order to live at Hokkeji. Women from extraordinary backgrounds, Enkyō writes, were reduced to performing arduous tasks (such as carrying water) once they came to Hokkeji. They were required to endure a simple life free from the comforts of excessive wealth (143a).

The sacrifices made by Enkyō's contemporaries recall the great sacrifices made by Kōmyō in her own work for the Buddha-Dharma. If Kōmyō, as a queen-consort, physically carried dirt in the sleeves of her garments in order to help build Tōdaiji, if she washed a leper with her own precious hands, if she went out into the boisterous marketplaces to teach her subjects, how can women who want to carry out her will not make sacrifices as well? Enkyō suggests that like the children in the *Mahāprajñāparamitā sūtra* who care for their mother with the utmost devotion because they realize that she endured great suffering when she gave birth to them, the nuns at Hokkeji, realizing the great pains that the "mother" of their convent went to in founding their institution and in guiding Japan along the Buddhist path, are willing to serve her with the greatest of loyalty. Thus, while Enkyō's Kōmyō shows distinct signs of motherliness, her motherliness exceeds the one-dimensionality of mothers described by their priest-sons.

It should be noted that amid all of these implicit associations made between Kōmyō and motherhood, her birth child, Kōken, is never mentioned. In the Saidaiji accounts of priests saving their mothers, the biological connection between mother and son is always made clear. But in Kōmyō's case, her motherhood is abstracted from the physiological processes that define motherhood in its biological sense.

Several texts associated with Chūgūji also elaborate upon the deification of Queen-Consort Hashihito: the *Chūgūji engi* (Karmic origins of Chūgūji), thought to have been written around the year 1273 by the Tendai priest Hōin Gondai Sōzu Jōen; the *Shōtoku Taishi denki,* a 1274 text of unknown authorship that was likely produced in collaboration with Shinnyo's campaign to revive the convent; and Shinnyo's 1282 *Ama Shinnyo ganmon.* Jōen, the reputed author of the *Chūgūji engi,* appears to have been a friend and teacher of Shinnyo. It is known that she visited him at the temple Ryōzenji in 1274–1275 during her trip to the capital to raise funds to make a replica of the *Tenjukoku mandara.* She probably asked him to write out the *Chūgūji engi* in much the same way that Hokkeji nuns are said to have asked Eison to record the *Hokkeji shari engi* (Pradel 1997; Hosokawa 1987, 114–116; Mori 1976, 57).

The *Chūgūji engi* declares outright that Shōtoku's mother, Hashihito, was a manifestation *(keshin)* of the Thus Come One Amitābha (Amida Nyorai): "The great compassionate mother who bore and raised me," the text cites Shōtoku's epigraph as having read, "was the founder of the Western [Pure Land], the honored Amida." The *engi* goes on to describe a complex understanding of Shōtoku and his mother, Hashihito, in which both are manifestations of Buddhist deities. (She is Amida, and he is Kannon.) At one point in the narrative, Hashihito manifests a Pure Land in rays of light right before her son Shōtoku's eyes (87a).[35] When Hashihito passes away, she is described as having returned to her Pure Land and is praised for having been compassionate and self-sacrificing enough to have lived in this defiled world for as long as she did. Moreover, once the *Tenjukoku mandara* is installed at Chūgūji, Hashihito's earthly dwelling place, the convent, is understood as "the Lotus Palace of Amida [Buddha]," a "Pure Land amid the world of impurity," and a "paradise within the world of *saṃsāra*" (86, 87a).

In her 1282 *Ama Shinnyo ganmon,* Shinnyo emphasizes the importance of Hashihito even further. Unlike Jōen, whose *engi* also deifies Yōmei Tennō as Shōtoku's father, Shinnyo does not mention Yōmei in her *ganmon,* which devotes full attention both to Hashihito and to the author, Shinnyo.

The degree to which Shinnyo promotes herself in her *ganmon* predicts the way in which her own image would eventually overtake that of Hashihito in later Chūgūji literature. Even texts written during her lifetime—the 1273 *Chūgūji engi,* mentioned above, and the 1274 *Taishi mandara kōshiki,* both thought to have been written by Jōen—treat Shinnyo as a celebrated model of Buddhist practice, if not a full bodhisattva. In a popular sixteenth-century account of Chūgūji that appears in the Saidaiji document collection, Hashihito is all but ignored as the narrative draws attention to Shinnyo as the primary personage associated with Chūgūji.[36] The veneration of Shinnyo is especially noteworthy, as she is neither a woman of royal origins nor a birth mother. While narratives describing her do indeed suggest that she has those qualities that had come to be understood as "motherly" (wisdom, guidance, and self-sacrifice), she is said to have taken the tonsure and to have given up traditional family connections from a young age. Records suggest that she never married or gave birth to children. The popularity that Shinnyo narratives eventually gained, then, is particularly striking, for her story suggests that a woman who was not a biological mother could still achieve popular appeal in medieval Japan, at least in the realm of literature.

The writings associated with Ritsu convents not only divert attention away from the biological aspects of motherhood and toward positive, active character traits associated with motherliness, but they also offer a compelling refutation of the view, inherent in portrayals of Saidaiji priests' mothers, that women must rely on men (and specifically on priests) as the brokers of their salvation. Enkyō and Shinnyo both portray former queen-consorts as beings who, though markedly female, have salvific powers. The *Hokke metsuzaiji engi* further implies that nuns, too, are capable of securing salvation for themselves and for others. Enkyō is unequivocal in identifying Hokkeji's first rectors as savior figures: "Because of these sixteen holy nuns, the ancient vow [of Queen-Consort Kōmyō, the founder of Hokkeji] is not in vain. Now they [the nuns] are good friends cultivating the Buddhist path just as the Buddha taught.... they are purifying their minds with the single suchness that is the Dharma nature. *Therefore, they join their minds and combine their strengths in order to revitalize the Three Jewels and save sentient beings*" (142b; emphasis mine). For Enkyō, then, the Mulian model, which holds that women must rely upon the efforts of male clergy, was clearly not the only model of women's salvation available in the religious landscape of medieval Japan.

Shinnyo, too, suggests that nondivine women can act as savior figures; indeed, in her *ganmon,* she portrays herself as an fully engaged cleric, a bodhisattva of sorts. Selflessly committed to "encourag[ing] people on the Buddhist path," she restores Chūgūji to its former glory, receives divine insights, revives the "holy legacy" of Hashihito, and "plant[s] Buddha seeds in the dew of Amida's Western Pure Land." Shinnyo emphasizes the centrality of her own role, just as Enkyō emphasizes the centrality of Hokkeji's first group of devoted nuns. She notes that it was her determination and her prayer-induced vision that restored Chūgūji. She also mentions that the temple she has revived contributes to the salvation of living beings. At one point in the text, she explains, "In [the temple's] natural surroundings, the opportunities for encountering the Dharma are not at all shallow" (*Ama Shinnyo ganmon,* 83a). The tone of the text is not suggestive of a woman who understood herself to be dependent upon salvation offered by a male member of the clergy.

The *Chūgūji engi* makes this argument even more explicit, stating that Chūgūji itself—as a physical locale—is capable of extending salvation to any who step onto its premises. Chūgūji's main hall, for example, is described as an earthly manifestation of Mount Potalaka, a legendary site in the Buddhist cosmos thought to be an entrance to the Pure Land. Those who enter the hall and wish to be born in the Pure Land, it argues, will surely be granted birth there (86b). Acknowledging Shinnyo's role as the nun who revived Chūgūji, the text portrays her as actively working for the salvation of others.

In summary, the representations of motherliness offered in the texts of Enkyō and Shinnyo divert attention away from the Saidaiji model of mothers as pitiful figures requiring the salvation of male priests. By refusing to engage the topic of motherhood in the abstract and instead focusing on the maternal qualities of certain legendary women, Enkyō and Shinnyo produce a reading of motherhood that understands it only in terms of its merits. They de-emphasize biological motherhood and instead draw attention to the character traits associated with exemplary mothers: wisdom, guidance, compassion, and salvific power. The qualities underlined as motherly in the nuns' writings stand in stark contrast to Daoxuan's "vices of women"; what is more, they clearly overlap with those traits described as masculine in Ritsu doctrinal literature. This particular view of women and motherliness dismisses the notion that women must rely on salvation by their sons and suggests instead the ways in which women can themselves extend salvation to sentient beings.

The Place of Women in the Order

This last section will examine how the contrasting views of Ritsu priests and nuns unfold not in discussions of women or mothers in the abstract or of powerful female founding figures but in connection with actual living women who were involved in the Ritsu movement. In particular, it will consider how Ritsu priests and nuns envisioned the role of women in the Buddhist community. Sources suggest that Ritsu priests and nuns drew on largely different paradigms when interacting with *real* women in the monastic community. While Eison's treatments of Ritsu nuns tended to refer back to abstracted doctrinal concerns about proper ordination procedures or to assume the inferiority of women's Buddhist practice, for example, the writings of nuns connected the present-day inhabitants of Hokkeji and Chūgūji to romanticized images of court life or to the valorized personages of Kōmyō and Hashihito. By placing present-day women within different interpretive frameworks, Ritsu monks and nuns arrived at different conclusions about the governance of the nuns' order. Eison's answer, of course, was that he himself had final authority over the convents affiliated with Saidaiji, especially Hokkeji. But Enkyō and Shinnyo suggested that Ritsu nuns managed their own communities, which were ultimately governed by the divine will of their miraculous female founders.

Who Governs the Nuns' Order? Saidaiji Visions of the Priest-Nun Hierarchy

In perpetuating the idea, whether literally or metaphorically, that women need to seek birth as men in order to achieve salvation, Eison and his disciples asserted their own superiority as men. They constructed a dynamic granting them the authority to decide how—in what capacity and to what degree—women would be incorporated into the Ritsu school. In their writings, Eison and Sōji created a model in which they were compassionate mediators who brought women into the Buddhist fold. For example, in Sōji's preface to the *Tennyoshingyō,* the deliverance of women is achieved through the intercession of male priests. Like Mulian, who serves as a medium between his sinful mother and the Buddha himself, Sōji indicates that his gift to the nuns' group at Hokkeji has the power to "redeem" the "karmic burdens of women." Women in the Ritsu movement may be able to take all of the precepts and even become "men" in this very lifetime, but according to Sōji they cannot accomplish such feats without the help of the male clergy.

Indeed, one of the more noticeable aspects of Ritsu discourse on women's salvation is that it creates an essential role for the male clergy vis-à-vis the nuns. While Eison may have drawn women into the movement by offering them both salvation and social roles within the movement, he eventually makes it clear not only that the nuns' group is subordinate to the priests' group but also that the nuns' group cannot exist without the larger *vinaya* movement. As mentioned in chapter 3, Eison offers in one of his sermons commentary on popular narratives about Japan's first Buddhist nuns, Zenshin, Zenzō, and Ezen, who are said to have traveled to the Korean peninsula in the sixth century to take precepts. The most visible versions of these narratives are those included in the *Nihon shoki* (21:2) and the *Gangōji garan engi narabi ruki shizaichō* (The karmic origins of the Gangōji monastery and a list of its treasures).[37]

In his sermon that mentions these nuns, Eison reveals disregard for those not ordained according to the rules of the *vinaya.* Against narratives that praise these three women and use their example as evidence of the roles that women played in Japanese Buddhism, Eison emphasizes that these women were not *authentic* nuns: "Even though [they were said to have been ordained] in accordance with the Dharma [*nyohō*], it is hard to think that such was actually the case" (*Chōmonshū,* 218). According the *Nihon shoki* and the *Gangōji garan engi,* Zenshin and her disciples went to Baekje (Paekche) to study the *vinaya,* but Eison, arguing the women did not receive proper *vinaya* ordination, disregards the weight that others had given their accomplishment.

Eison's sermon thus dismisses the tradition of tonsured women that had existed in Japan prior to his own involvement in establishing a nuns' order. The comment above, juxtaposed with the following entry from Eison's autobiography, suggests that Eison considered only those nuns he had himself ordained to be "real" nuns: On the sixth day of the second month of Kenchō 1 [1249], Eison gave the *bikuni-kai* to twelve women at Hokkeji, claiming that this act marked "the first time in which the ordination of a sevenfold assembly had been completed in Japan in compliance with the Dharma" [*Nihon koku nyohō shugyō no shichishū enman no hajimari nari*] (*KJGSK* 1999, 351).

Eison's narrow definition of "nun" trivializes the long-standing practice in which women styled themselves as nuns following private profession ceremonies. Although it is clear that many of the women who became active at Hokkeji in the Kamakura period were drawn to the convent precisely because nuns there were being given the opportunity to take full *bikuni* precepts according to the proper method, it is also clear that Hokkeji nuns were not as narrowly focused on the *vinaya* as Eison. In praising Kōmyō as a great patron of Buddhism and incarnation of Kannon, for example, they did not even mention the queen-consort's ordination status. Whether she and her ladies-in-waiting had received the full precepts of a *bikuni* does not appear to have been a matter of concern in the eyes of Hokkeji's medieval nuns. Moreover, many of the women who first worked to revive Hokkeji in the 1240s and 1250s prided themselves on their roles as stewards of these traditions. They valued the opportunity to take full precepts, but unlike Eison they did not disparage the Buddhist practices of earlier court women.

As mentioned in chapter 2, Lady Nijō's *Towazugatari* portrays Shōkutei-in, a small convent at the temple Daigoji, as a place where nuns managed their own affairs with great competence and autonomy. She speaks of the nuns who resided there with much respect, admiring the devotion with which they carried out their daily prayers and rites. She mentions no priests but instead suggests that the nuns of the temple handled their own affairs independently of the male clergy (40–43). As discussed earlier, several of Hokkeji's first nuns had trained at Shōkutei-in. Lady Nijō's portrayal of Shōkutei-in suggests that women who had trained as nuns there would have felt confident in their practice of the Dharma. But another of Eison's sermons implies that he did not accord the nuns in his order the same level of respect that court ladies like Nijō did. The following passage, taken from his collection of sermons, suggests that he was worried about the degree to which the nuns in the movement were conforming to his vision of the nuns' order: "More than anything, it is the nuns' assembly that worries me. I greatly fear that something might happen while I am away. [When] Saimyōji-dono [Hōjō Tokiyori] said, 'As for putting the benefit [of sentient beings] first [i.e., preaching the Dharma], since it is the same everywhere [i.e., it does not matter where you preach], stay here [in Kamakura]; please do not return to the capital,' I said, 'As for the priests, nothing will happen [if I leave them to practice on their own], but the nuns are probably unable to manage without me; the women may all end up losing the Dharma. Since that would be pitiable, I will return to the capital'" (*Chōmonshū*, 214).

This passage refers to Eison's 1262 visit to Kamakura, when the Hōjō had summoned him for a visit. Although warrior government officials showered Eison with attention, offering him large gifts of land and lavish accommodations and begging him to stay in Kamakura, Eison declined such offers and hurried back to the capital region (see Inoue M. 1985; Nakao 1987). Urged by warrior government regent *(shikken)* Hōjō Tokiyori to extend his stay in the Kantō, Eison used his concern over the nuns' group as an excuse for his refusal.

As discussed earlier, Eison wrote a letter to the Hokkeji rector Jizen in the year 1249 refusing her request to meet with him. In that letter, Eison suggests that he cannot meet with Jizen or with the Hokkeji nuns as a group frequently. His tone in the letter implies that he would prefer the nuns to handle their affairs independently of him, a hypothesis that his entries from his autobiography support, for they record only infrequent trips to Hokkeji, suggesting that he was not actively involved in the day-to-day life of the nuns' assemblies. It is possible that Eison never actually made the aforementioned argument to Tokiyori or that if he did he was merely feigning concern over the nuns' group in order to excuse himself from an extended stay in Kamakura. But a letter written by Eison to the nuns at Hokkeji, most likely during this visit to the Kantō in 1262, suggests that his attitude toward the nuns' group had indeed shifted between the years 1249 and 1262. The following 1262 letter, written in a more paternalistic tone, suggests not only that Eison was concerned over the nuns' commitment to the Dharma but also that he saw himself as playing a central role in guiding the training programs of the nuns in residence at Hokkeji:

As per your letter dated the tenth day of the third month, I opened its seal at the hour of the cock [around 6:00 p.m.] on the third day of the fourth month. I received various detailed explanations from you, and I now humbly offer my reply. *I presume that when you receive my letter, you will read what I've written about the Buddhist path. It will not be otherwise. I am happy to hear that the nuns' assembly is working together in harmony, young and old, pursuing both scholarship and practice. This is especially outstanding.* As for my return to the capital, usually I return once the summer has ended, but what will I do this year? *I am just praying that you all will work to promote the Dharma and to benefit sentient beings. Your work is important both for yourselves and for others. The benefit you will reap at your death is truly great.* I was sorry to learn that the rector of Sennyūji entered nirvana [i.e., died]. *Please continue working hard in your studies and in your practice. If my work to benefit sentient beings [i.e., my missionary work here in the Kantō] is successful, I will hurry to return to the capital. But in the case that I return late, you must wait for me, continuing to practice without distraction.* Convey this message widely within the nuns' assembly. In this letter, I used both Chinese characters and *kana,* mixing them together, but since there are many people there now [I am confident that someone can read the letter]. Since benefiting [others] should come first, in the case that I am late [in returning to the capital], you must take delight [in the fact that I am spreading the Dharma]. I will write again later.

fourth month, tenth day [no year indicated]
Eison (*SEDS,* 410–411; emphasis mine)

In his 1249 letter to Jizen, discussed in chapter 2, Eison had written in an almost deferential tone, insisting that he felt uncomfortable at Hokkeji since it was an old *gosho* and he was of humble birth. Although he did nudge Jizen about the progress of the statue of the Buddha she had commissioned, he did not assume the position of a religious leader, urging her and her disciples to remain committed to the Dharma and to work together in harmony. Instead, he seemed intent upon letting Jizen manage Hokkeji with as little guidance from him as possible.

But this second letter suggests a change in Eison's attitude toward the nuns' assembly. In this letter, Eison elevates his own position, making it clear that he understands himself as the final leader of the nuns' assembly. He praises the nuns for "working together in harmony" and admonishes them to read what he has written about the "Buddhist path." Moreover, he expresses concern over his long absence, suggesting that the nuns may stray from the path if he remains in Kamakura too long. "You must wait for me," Eison insists, implying that the nuns cannot practice the Dharma correctly and with devotion unless he is there to guide them. At one point, Eison says that he is "just praying" that the nuns will remain focused without him. Read against Eison's earlier letter to Jizen, this letter suggests that his words to Tokiyori may have revealed a larger shift in his attitude toward the nuns' assembly.

Sentiments similar to those found in the 1262 letter emerge in a third letter, written by Eison nearly two decades later, in the year 1279:

> The other day I sent a letter to you—did it arrive?
>
> I reached Kamakura on the twenty-seventh day of the second month. From the twenty-ninth day, I stayed temporarily in a temple in which a copy of the Saga Nyorai had been placed. As I said before at your place [Hokkeji], it seems that I am [working to] benefit sentient beings in my own way [and that it is going well]. *Please, each of you must reside in the will to revive the Dharma and benefit sentient beings and practice with great effort.* Although I do not have anything specific to say, I am writing since you had inquired [after me]. At your convenience, in addition to notes on viewing the Chanted Lecture on [Queen-Consort] Kōmyō [Kōmyō-kō Kenchū],[38] if someone has a report, I would very much like to receive it, as I am sure that someone will be coming to Kamakura soon.
>
> Kōan 2 [1279]
> third month, nineteenth day
> Eison (*SEDS*, 331)

This letter resembles the earlier letter, in that it suggests that Eison saw himself as being in a position to exhort the nuns. Based on a reading of these three letters (which are unfortunately the only of Eison's letters to the Hokkeji community that have survived), it seems that Eison envisioned himself as having assumed a more prominent leadership role in the Hokkeji community sometime between 1249 and 1262 and that he continued to view himself as the spiritual leader of the Hokkeji group well into his later years. By the year 1262, of course, Eison was much more famous and well established than he had been in the year 1249. The nuns' order had also grown much larger: Hokkeji was no longer just a small temple that served pilgrims who wanted to pay their respects to Kōmyō. It had become the center of a large-scale nuns' order invested in the ordaining and training of nuns in accordance with the *vinaya.*

Another record suggestive of Ritsu priests' attitudes toward women involved in the *vinaya* movement dates from the ninth month of Bun'ei 10 (1273). According to this entry from Jikō's edition of the Eison biography, Ritsu priests met following a Kōmyō Shingon service held around that time and issued a statement declaring that nuns visiting Saidaiji on the occasion of all-night Kōmyō Shingon, New Year's *Dhāraṇī* (Shōgatsu Darani), or other major Buddhist rituals were to stay at the temple only temporarily. They were not to stay overnight, nor were they to interact closely with male priests. Such behavior, the statement warns, is the origin of slander *(kibō no minamoto nari).* Henceforth, the announcement reads, women participating in all-night rituals would be required to seek lodging outside the temple. Moreover, not only nuns but all women were ordered to exit the temple by the hour of the boar (10:00 p.m.); women were not to be roaming through the halls of Saidaiji during this hour (*Saidai chokushi Kōshō Bosatsu gyōjitsu nenpu,* 260).

Hosokawa has read this letter as evidence that Saidaiji priests understood themselves as the guardians of women's sexuality. Because the statement seeks to control the behavior of women—by forcing them out of the temple after 10:00 p.m.—rather than that of men, he argues that it places the blame for all sexual misconduct on the side of women, thereby justifying the priests' management of women affiliated with Saidaiji. He argues that this example is linked to the larger tendency of patriarchal societies to value chastity (1987, 154–155). But while the 1273 statement clearly suggests that Ritsu priests were in control of affairs at Saidaiji (it does not appear, for example, that nuns were a part of the meeting that issued this decision), the statement says nothing about the ways in which affairs at the convents themselves were to be conducted.[39] There is no indication, then, that Saidaiji priests attempted to "control" the "chastity" of nuns living at Hokkeji or other Ritsu convents. Moreover, the concern seems to be one based on the notion—clearly conveyed in the precepts—that priests and nuns should avoid excessive contact, since it might lead to sexual misconduct. The priests did not forbid nuns and laywomen to participate in Saidaiji rituals or to enter Saidaiji; they simply forbade women to stay overnight at the temple and to wander around the temple halls late at night. This ruling in and of itself does not seem unreasonable given the large size of the groups that would have been assembling at Saidaiji for major ritual events. Nevertheless, Hosokawa's basic point is well taken: the statement does suggest that the Ritsu priests envisioned themselves—the male priests—as the leaders of the community. The tone taken in the statement is a stern and commanding one, indicating that the Ritsu priests were indeed positioning themselves as the ultimate leaders of all Ritsu nuns and laywomen, even those of high clerical rank or social class.

Despite the rhetoric that finds "neither man nor woman" in the *vinaya* movement, then, one's physical identification as male or female was clearly an important marker of status from the perspective of Saidaiji priests. And although evidence suggests that Eison may have treated women of high social status with great respect, his sermons reveal that he did not regard as authentic the private precepts conferral ceremonies undertaken by women who sought to define themselves as nuns before the revival of an ordination platform at Hokkeji. Instead, he insisted on defining the category "nun" on his own, *vinaya*-centered terms and on molding the assemblies of women he had ordained into an order that matched his own vision of the sevenfold assembly. Moreover, he and other Ritsu priests began to portray themselves, in their writings at least, as the final spiritual leaders of the movement. Their texts further suggest that the male priests believed that it was their place both to exhort the nuns in their practice and to define the nature of their visits to Saidaiji.

But if the literature composed by the nuns themselves is any indication, many of the women who became active in monastic life at Ritsu convents did not share Eison's vision of the nuns' order completely. While Eison viewed the nuns' order as essential to his goal of realizing the *vinaya* in

Japan, Ritsu nuns tended to focus instead on the goal of realizing the vows of the women they regarded as their institutions' ancient female founders. Constructing their own understandings of women's roles and opportunities in the Buddhist cosmos, Enkyō and Shinnyo ignored the claims of priests who represented themselves as the ultimate leaders of the nuns' communities. The next section will explore how Ritsu nuns portrayed their convents as institutions led by women.

Under the Leadership of Women

As discussed above, Eison's autobiography, letters, and sermons suggest that he and his leading disciples spearheaded the thirteenth-century revival of Hokkeji and other convents. But the literature of Hokkeji and Chūgūji suggests not only that the nuns were themselves the main actors in this revival movement but also that they asserted their own autonomy vis-à-vis Eison's movement.

The *Hokke metsuzaiji engi*, for example, ignores Eison and his disciples almost entirely. It mentions Eison once, noting that he was "spreading the *vinaya* far and wide" and that people "revere him," but it does not suggest that Eison alone was responsible for the renovation of Hokkeji, nor does it mention any of his fellow priests or disciples at all (142b). What is more, the one other male figure it does mention is the priest Tankū, who, as noted in chapter 1, aided the nuns' group in repairing some of their temple buildings. A disciple of the Pure Land priest Hōnen, Tankū was not associated with Eison, nor was he a member of the Ritsu movement. The fact that the *Hokke metsuzaiji engi* actually devotes more space to Tankū than to Eison suggests that Hokkeji nuns did not conceptualize their convent as falling under the domain of Saidaiji's institutional authority. Rather, it seems that Enkyō envisioned the Hokkeji community as a group of relatively autonomous nuns who interacted with male priests voluntarily, and only when they perceived such interactions as beneficial to their own interests.

Indeed, Enkyō's *Hokke metsuzaiji engi* suggests that Hokkeji fostered a strong tradition of female leadership. As explained in chapter 5, Enkyō lists near the end of the *Hokke metsuzaiji engi* sixteen nuns who "cast aside their own lives in order to revive the *vinaya*" (142b). Most of the women whose names Enkyō records died in the late 1290s or early 1300s and represent the first generation of Hokkeji leaders. In describing their contributions to the movement that began at Hokkeji, Enkyō writes (as discussed at the beginning of chapter 5): "Some [nuns] pushed through the mists of the eastern barbarians to come [here]. Some endured the waves of the western seas to gather here [at Hokkeji]. Some abandoned the light indigo robes worn in the sovereign's quarters of the royal palace.... Even the ladies and ladies-in-waiting of the high aristocracy carry hand water on their shoulders, and even beloved children of many fortunes and pleasures take single begging bowls and offer them up to the home of enlightenment" (143a). Stressing that many of Hokkeji's first leaders were aristocratic women whose commitment to the Dharma inspired them to forfeit lives of leisure and to take up residence in the "dilapidated remains" that comprised Hokkeji, Enkyō makes it clear that the nuns who gathered at Hokkeji in the mid-twelfth century were anything but passive recipients of male-granted salvation. Assigning distinctively *active* roles to the nuns, Enkyō suggests not only that the nuns themselves contributed to the "revitalization of the Three Jewels [the Buddha, the Dharma, and the Sangha]" but also that the nuns themselves guided others along the Buddhist path: their altruistic actions inspired others to "give rise to the mind of enlightenment" and to "praise" the buddhas and bodhisattvas. Enkyō also portrays nuns as missionaries and as leaders who establish new institutions and seek new patrons. Of the sixteen nuns for whom Enkyō provides personal information, all are said to have served as leaders of Hokkeji, and four are described as having established and led other convents (142b–143a).

The degree to which Hokkeji narratives praise the leadership skills of nuns might be read as part of a larger narrative meant to argue for the autonomy of the convent. Asserting that Hokkeji nuns should enjoy the right to handle their affairs independently of priests, the *Hokke metsuzaiji engi* traces their right to self-rule back to the very beginning of Hokkeji's history: "After the *tennō* and his consort, with equal sincerity, built the Tōdaiji Daibutsuden [Great Buddha Hall of Tōdaiji], the *tennō* said, 'I do not want to put women in its inner altar area [*naijin*].' The queen-consort then made a vow, saying, 'If that is so, [then] I will surely build a temple, too, and will not allow men to be placed within it.' That is how this present temple [Hokkeji] was founded" (140b).[40] According to these narratives, then, Kōmyō intended from the very beginning for Hokkeji to be understood not only as the female counterpart of Tōdaiji but also as an institution built *exclusively* for women. Hokkeji narratives also take up the theme of autonomous women when they claim that Kōmyō assigned all of the posts within Hokkeji's hierarchical system to women. Consider, for example, the following passage from the *Hokke metsuzaiji engi:* "The positions of the five masters [*goshi*] and the three deans [*sangō*] were all entrusted to nuns. Sometime after that, they were called *sageama,* and they cut their hair about shoulder-length and wore Buddhist robes. While still women, they took the positions of head priests [*jōza*] and temple administrators [*jishu*]. It is said that they all divided up the domains and responsibilities of the temple and practiced the path of Buddhism" (140b).[41] These claims were not unique to Enkyō's version of the Hokkeji *engi:* they had been circulating in Hokkeji pilgrimage and miracle narratives since at least the late twelfth century. They point, then, to long-standing narratives promoted among women and laypeople associated with the convent. That Hokkeji nuns continued to tell and retell these particular narratives about the founding of their convent suggests that they sought to disregard any claims of authority over the nuns' order made by Ritsu priests.

Competing Versions of the Shinnyo Narrative

Narratives about the Chūgūji nun Shinnyo also bring to the fore issues of leadership and of the ways in which it was constructed and perceived.[42] As mentioned earlier, Shinnyo, in her own *Ama Shinnyo ganmon,* portrays herself as the sole person responsible for Chūgūji's revival. But versions of the Shinnyo narrative that appear in Eison's autobiography and in later Ritsu literature tend to insert Ritsu priests into her story, thereby deflecting from her centrality. In several Ritsu versions of the Shinnyo narrative, the priest Kyōen is credited for having encouraged Shinnyo in her initial decision to take the precepts. The juxtaposition of these contrasting accounts of Shinnyo's role in the revival of Chūgūji illustrate the degree to which Ritsu priests and nuns used writing as a way to legitimate different visions of the relationship between priests and nuns in the Ritsu movement.

Some of the more fantastical accounts of Shinnyo's ordination claim that the monk Kyōen, one of Kakujō's disciples, transformed himself into a female-bodied nun in order to encourage Shinnyo in her efforts. These versions of the Shinnyo narrative, which appear in the mid-sixteenth-century *Shōyoshō* as well as in a number of other texts, downplay Shinnyo's own determination to become a nun. They credit Kyōen both for encouraging Shinnyo to seek nunhood and for reviving the nuns' order in Japan. According to these accounts, Kyōen received a divine message instructing him to turn himself into a female-bodied *bikuni* and to realize the birth of a nuns' order in Japan. Following these instructions, he transformed himself into a woman and then returned to his home village, where he encouraged his elder sister Shinnyo to leave home and take the precepts. Once she did so, thereby initiating a movement resulting in the reestablishment of the sevenfold *sangha* in Japan, Kyōen's work was complete, and he returned to his male form. The narrative does not indicate that Shinnyo had wanted to become a nun prior to her brother's prompting, nor does it acknowledge her own contributions to the nuns' revival movement.[43]

In short, this narrative downplays Shinnyo's agency.[44] Crediting the male order of Ritsu monks—rather than the initiative of Shinnyo and other nuns—with the restoration of the *bikuni* precepts in Japan, this tale of Kyōen's transformation emphasizes that it was the male monastic community and not the activities of Shinnyo and her fellow nuns that finally enabled Japan to establish all seven of the official positions within the *sangha* as described in the *vinaya.* A reference to this miraculous feat even appears in Eison's autobiography, the *Kongō Busshi Eison kanjin gakushōki.* Under an entry dated to the fifth day of the first month of 1251, Eison remarks, "As for the case in which [the Sixteen Arhats (Jūroku Rakan)], saddened that none of the great and small nuns' orders had yet been revived, transformed a *biku* [fully ordained monk] into a *bikuni* [fully ordained nun], this miracle exceeded the ordinary" (*KJGSK* 1977, 23–24). Even Eison tends to credit others—here the Sixteen Arhats—and not the nuns themselves when commenting on the small steps that had been taken toward the revival of convents. The Sixteen Arhats and Kyōen are lauded for this exemplary transformation, and Shinnyo is rendered a passive, and less visible, historical actor.

The 1274 *Shōtoku Taishi denki* strikes an interesting balance between the view that the revival of Chūgūji can be attributed to the work of Ritsu priests and that which grants all credit to Shinnyo. In this text, it is Eison's disciple Sōji who first comes up with the idea of restoring the temple, but he is told in a vision that Chūgūji is a convent and that its restoration should be headed by *bikuni* from the nuns' order:

> Over 600 years after my entry into nirvana [death], the *mandala* will first be discovered in the world. This record will not be incorrect. [This came to pass] over 640 years after the prince's death, during the time of the ninety-first sovereign, Go-Uda, when the two brothers Go-Fukakusa-in and Kameyama-in were ruling the realm, in Bun'ei 11 [1274]. In the province of Yamato to the east of Hōryūji is Chūgūji, the holy place established by the prince's mother. Five hundred years after the prince's death . . . the temple had fallen into a state of decay; all that remained was a two-story main hall and a treasure stupa. At that time, there was Nichijō Shōnin [Eison's disciple and nephew Sōji], rector of the temple Sairinji in Kawachi Province. Although, having seen the way in which Chūgūji had fallen into a state of disuse, he had the will to restore it, he had not the means to effectively benefit the temple. So during the Bun'ei period [1264–1275], he cloistered himself in Chūgūji's main hall and prayed for the means to rebuild the temple. In a dream, Shōtoku Taishi appeared to him and said, "Teacher of the Dharma, your kind will is worthy of praise. But this temple, from days of old, is a place maintained by nuns. Now there is again a nuns' order that can revive it. Do not lament!" Sōji was moved to tears. He met with the Saidaiji rector, Eison, and reported this message to him, saying, "It is my wish that you choose the precepts-upholding nuns' order and have them maintain this temple." Eison was moved by this, and he selected the Ritsu nun Shinnyo and made her rector. (88a)

According to this account, Eison was so moved by Sōji's vision that he agreed to help with the revival of Chūgūji and decided to appoint the nun Shinnyo, who was already one of his disciples, as its rector (Hosokawa 1987, 114).

In Shinnyo's account of the Chūgūji revival narrative as it appears in her 1282 *ganmon,* Sōji plays no role whatsoever: she alone is the protagonist, the sole force behind the convent's restoration. Moreover, her move to Chūgūji occurs before she receives any kind of authorization from Eison or Sōji; the version of the Chūgūji revival recorded in the *Shōtoku Taishi denki,* by contrast, downplays Shinnyo's role so as to foreground the centrality of Sōji and Eison.

Shinnyo's own version of the Chūgūji restoration, much like Enkyō's account of the Hokkeji revival, does not focus on Eison and his movement but instead emphasizes the convent's ties to the royal court. Having acknowledged the sponsorship of the court and of the sovereign specifically, Shinnyo declares in her *ganmon:*

> Outwardly, I have studied the virtue of nurturing children [Confucianism]; internally, I have sought to form ties with the Buddhist path. Here I, the *bikuni* Shinnyo, as a way to encourage people on the Buddhist path, state:

In the capital of Nara near Hōryūji, there is an excellent place called Chūgūji [the Queen-Consort's Temple]. As I warmed myself [by sitting on] its outer steps, I learned that it is the holy ground established by the queen-consort of Yōmei Tennō, the late mother of Prince Shōtoku [Anahobe no Hashihito].[45] ... But [now] the fences are used to dry laundry; pine trees take root in roof tiles. The flowers and incense [used for offerings] have gone unused for many years. In the morning, there is no [ringing of the] bell, and in the evening, there is no *kei* [a metonym for Buddhist ritual music].[46] The altar is infested by lizards and frogs, and stags and flying squirrels fight in the rock garden. When I, Shinnyo, saw this current state of shabbiness, I cried and thought of the temple's prosperity in ancient times. I took over the administration of this temple and vowed to return it to its ancient state. Entreating the gods, I entered into a holy dream state while sleeping alone. Unexpectedly, I discovered a *mandala* made up of two panels. [...]

Here, Shinnyo has revived the holy legacy of Anahobe no Hashihito, planting Buddha seeds in the dew of Amida's Western Pure Land. Already, we have known the effectiveness of this basic vow; all this is entirely the result of the karmic ties of a servant girl! (*Ama Shinnyo ganmon,* 82b–83a)[47]

Shinnyo's *ganmon* does not mention any Ritsu priest even once. She portrays herself as the sole force behind Chūgūji's revival, and the priests who are mentioned in the text appear only when they are following her lead. She is bold in asserting her centrality, as well as that of Queen-Consort Anahobe: "Here, Shinnyo has revived the holy legacy of Anahobe no Hashihito," she writes. In the section where she enters a "holy dream state," she learns that the death date of Anahobe, for which she had been searching, could be found on the *Tenjukoku mandara.* When she finally discovers the location of the *mandala,* a group of monks gathers around and begins to worship it. And when Shinnyo, having found Hashihito's death date on the *mandala,* decides to hold a memorial service *(kuyō)* for her, she, just as a woman of the court would do, invites a high-ranking priest to participate in the service. She appoints the Junior Great Master of the Righteous Dharma Seal Genga to preside over the service.

Shinnyo emphasizes female leadership at Chūgūji. Although she does not list an entire group of women who helped restore Chūgūji, as Enkyō did for Hokkeji, she suggests rather clearly that any assistance received from priests was secondary to her own leadership of Chūgūji. According to Shinnyo, priests became interested in the legacy of Hashihito only *after* she had discovered the *mandala.* At this point, she writes:

A group of priests all gathered together within the temple. They searched after [the *mandala* that Shinnyo had discovered] and obtained it. They worshipped it fervently and cried profusely. With the tortoise pattern embroidering, it showed the detailed images of dragons [i.e., the *mandala* had been made and/or used by the royal family]. They not only showed concern over whether Chūgūji would prosper or decline, but they also began to make it known that the queen-

> consort's past [deeds] would unceasingly generate [benevolent] responses. Their joy in the Dharma was so limitless that they committed to the effort their own implements, their three cloaks and their single bowls [to engage in raising funds to repair the *mandala* and restore the temple]. And before long they had filled [the bowls] entirely and undertaken splendid construction work. Entreating donors in the ten directions, they strived to rebuild the temple in an exquisite manner. (82b–83a)

In this passage, Shinnyo acknowledges the help she receives from priests, but the way in which she crafts the narrative suggests that the priests became involved only after they realized there was something of value to them at Chūgūji. Had Shinnyo not cloistered herself in prayer and discovered the *Tenjukoku mandara,* these priests would never have learned of Hashihito's efficacious power, nor would they have become involved in the restoration of Chūgūji. It is through Shinnyo's leadership that the priests first discover Hashihito and Chūgūji for themselves and under her guidance that they decide to contribute to the restoration effort, worshiping Hashihito, collecting funds, and contributing labor to the project.

In concluding this section, a third account of Chūgūji's founding, that of Shinnyo's friend Jōen, is worth noting. This text offers further insight into the complexity of gender constructions and their contexts. Jōen's 1275 *Taishi mandara kōshiki* follows Shinnyo's own writing, in that it places her at the center of Chūgūji's revival. The text is the second of a three-part liturgy designed for use in conjunction with the *Tenjukoku mandara.* Jōen, who is also thought to have been the author of the *Chūgūji engi,* wrote the *Taishi mandara kōshiki* on Shinnyo's behalf, likely in response to a request. Here, at the beginning of the text, Jōen tells the story of Shinnyo's recovery of the *mandala:*

> First, to reveal the origin story of its manifestation, this *mandala* is a record that the prince of the upper court [Prince Shōtoku] was led by his mother to birth in the Pure Land. It is the illustration [of the Pure Land] that Suiko Tennō ordered her maidservants [*uneme*] to weave. Over fifty reigns later, the karmic opportunity was not yet ripe. Over six hundred calendar years passed, and the *mandala* was uselessly buried in Hōryūji. For a long time, it was decaying in a storehouse that could not be opened without the permission of the *sangō* priests. The world knew nothing of the *mandala;* people did not know of its existence. *At this time there was a single bikuni. She was wholly faithful to the prince of the upper court. She deeply lamented the old temple Chūgūji's state of decay. Crying, she made plans to repair the temple by restructuring its main hall. But her begging bowl was still empty, even of mist.* How could it possibly become the foundation of a high-eaved temple hall? Although the robes [of the nuns had become so thin that] they could feel the cold wind, they [sacrificed in order to] just barely keep the three-tiered bell stupa running [i.e., in order to keep the temple operating, if only just barely]. They swept the long-neglected moss-covered paths running between the nuns' quarters and the Buddha Hall. They also performed *tendoku*

> [ritualized quick sutra readings] and incantations, laying out incense and flowers. The prince had already built this lofty hall for his honorable mother. We also wanted to open the temple right on the day that a memorial service should be held in her honor, but we did not know the date of her death. We wanted to pray for the knowledge of the date that she achieved enlightenment [died]. Even though we asked wise people about this, none of them knew. We also looked for the date in old records, but there was no record of it. (88b; emphasis mine)

The account goes on to describe the story that Shinnyo herself tells in her *Ama Shinnyo ganmon,* namely, that she was so determined to find the *mandala* that she cloistered herself in prayer, received a vision in which the location of the *mandala* was revealed, and eventually acquired it.

Jōen styles Shinnyo as the single person responsible for Chūgūji's revival both in the *Taishi mandara kōshiki* and in the *Chūgūji engi,* which he is thought to have written around the same time. He describes Chūgūji as the manifestation of the Western Pure Land, the earthly dwelling place of Amida (Hashihito) and Kannon (Shōtoku), thereby suggesting that Shinnyo's revival of Chūgūji was an act of bodhisattvalike proportions. In the *engi,* as in the *kōshiki,* Jōen follows Shinnyo's lead and does not mention Sōji or any other Ritsu personage, such as Kyōen. The degree to which Jōen describes Shinnyo as working independently of priests is particularly striking. Employing rhetoric similar to that used in the *Hokke metsuzaiji engi,* Jōen suggests that Chūgūji, like Hokkeji, was first renovated by a group of women so wholly devoted to the cause of restoring the convent that they were willing to sacrifice material comfort and to perform physical labor to do so. And just as Enkyō describes her Hokkeji nuns as selflessly committed to the original vow of Kōmyō, so too does Jōen describe Shinnyo and her disciples as entirely dedicated to the will of Hashihito and her son Shōtoku. Not only are the women portrayed as having exercised great autonomy in the reopening of the convent, but they are also shown as ritual experts in their own right, performing *tendoku* (speed readings of sutras) and making offerings on their own without the guidance of male priests.

The following excerpt from the *Chūgūji engi* offers additional insight into Jōen's approach to establishing the legitimacy of the Chūgūji nuns' order:

> Our Dharma king and merciful bodhisattva [Prince Shōtoku] was also the one who, in the village of Wakaki [Village of Young Trees], first spread the teachings of the Tathāgata and ordained the three nuns Zenshin, Zenzō, and Ezen. [These three nuns] were the first to renounce the world [*shukke*] in our country. Women have the obstructions of the five obstacles [*itsutsu no sawari*] and the thrice following [*sanjū*]; the mountain of obstructions caused by their transgressions is high, and their sea of vanity that is the cycle of life and death [*saṃsāra*] is deep. Grieving over these matters, [he, Prince Shōtoku] first encouraged women [to renounce the world and practice Buddhism], and thus

> [he] ordained about five hundred nuns [*nisō*]. They all made this Ikaruga nunnery [Chūgūji] their main temple [*honji*]. (87b1–4)

This excerpt, when read in the context of Jōen's larger valorization of Shinnyo and Chūgūji, is striking. Although neither Jōen nor Shinnyo mention any of the karmic burdens linked to women in any of their other Chūgūji-related works, Jōen appeals to women's associations with the five obstacles and the thrice following in this passage, which is found at the very end of the *Chūgūji engi.*

Jōen's references to the five obstacles and the thrice following can be read in several ways. On the one hand, his handling of the terms confirms that the notion that women faced soteriological obstacles specific to their sex was, by the thirteenth century, a well-entrenched one. At the same time, however, the context in which he employs this rhetoric is especially worthy of notice. For here, Jōen offers a rereading of the historical narrative that recognizes Japan's first three female monastics, Zenshin, Zenzō, and Ezen. In the sermon mentioned above, Eison dismisses these three nuns as women who were not ordained properly. Jōen reappropriates the narrative by arguing that these first nuns—whom he further identifies as the first nuns of Chūgūji—received ordination from the legendary Shōtoku himself. The *Chūgūji engi* thereby rejects the view that Japan's, and Chūgūji's, first nuns were not legitimate members of the Buddhist *sangha.*[48] Jōen does not call these women *ama* (as Eison does), but *nisō,* the inclusion of the character "*sō,*" or priest, suggesting that the women were fully ordained clerics. Against Eison's description of Japan's first nuns' order as a pitiful sight (he says that the nuns "had barely shaved their heads" and "had not as much as five robes"), Jōen describes the order established at Chūgūji as a flourishing one that counted over five hundred women among its ranks. He furthermore argues that these first nuns, and indeed Chūgūji's current nuns, had a special relationship with the deified Shōtoku himself. How could anyone, including Eison, fail to recognize as legitimate those ordained by Shōtoku?

Conspicuous is the fact that this particular argument for the legitimacy of Chūgūji hinges on the connection between Chūgūji nuns and Shōtoku, which is described in terms of the five obstacles and the thrice following. While more conventional doctrinal treatments of these teachings had tended to cite the heavy karmic burdens as arguments for the exclusion of women from the monastic order,[49] Jōen invokes the five obstacles and the thrice following for the opposite purpose. He suggests that these karmic burdens actually serve to legitimate the nuns' order, for it was precisely because women were understood as having faced the five obstacles and the thrice following that Shōtoku forged a special relationship with them.

It is furthermore worth noting that Jōen's use of the five obstacles and the thrice following is not understood as incongruous with the larger purpose of the *Chūgūji engi,* which valorizes Shinnyo and Chūgūji. Given the degree to which the *Chūgūji engi* venerates Shinnyo for her commitment to

Buddhist practice, her miraculous recovery of the *Tenjukoku mandara,* and her leadership at Chūgūji, it is clear that Jōen does not understand the heavy karmic burdens of women as having hindered Shinnyo's practice. Since Jōen celebrates Shinnyo in her female state as a model Buddhist practitioner and leader, his handling of the five obstacles and the thrice following can be read as one that recognizes the assumption that women face heavy karmic burdens while simultaneously rejecting the idea that these karmic burdens are of any real consequence in women's practice of Buddhism.

It is worth note that while Jōen included references to the five obstacles and the thrice following in the *Chūgūji engi,* Ritsu nuns avoided the topic of women's heavy karmic burdens in their own narratives. Perhaps Jōen, as a Tendai priest familiar with doctrinal understandings of womanhood, was not in a position to deny the concept of women's karmic burdens altogether. In any case, the way in which Jōen invoked the five obstacles and the thrice following to argue in *support* of Shinnyo's leadership at Chūgūji accentuates the complexity and multivalence of rhetoric about women and gender in the Ritsu nuns' revival movement and illustrates the ways in which arguments in support of the nuns' own interests may have overlapped with, appropriated, or even been embedded within certain androcentric assumptions.

THE TEXTS EXAMINED ABOVE illustrate the degree to which Ritsu priests tended to address the themes of gender, motherhood, and women's roles in the Buddhist community in markedly different ways than did Ritsu nuns. Even as Eison and his disciples were eager to ordain a nuns' order so as to complete the full *vinaya*-style *sangha,* they appear to have struggled with doctrinal concerns about the sinfulness of women and the soteriological helplessness of mothers, as well as with pragmatic concerns regarding the mixing of the sexes. Although Eison did draw upon well-entrenched images of women as the enemies of the Buddhist order in one of his *Brahma Net Sutra* commentaries, this particular representation of women appears to have been rare in Saidaiji discourse. That this image of women rarely emerged in Saidaiji literature is hardly surprising. After all, wholly antagonistic views of women would have been difficult to reconcile with the decision to include women in the order. The view found more commonly in Saidaiji writings is that which constructs women as sinful but helpless lesser beings, as individuals who could, through the compassion of male monastics and through arduous practice, attain the status of "manly persons." In emphasizing images of women as pitiful mothers who must aspire to become "men," Saidaiji priests produced a model that desexualized women as it incorporated them into the order.

Perhaps this move to envision women as men-to-be lessened the perceived danger of women's sexuality, which had long been understood as a threat to the monastic order. For even while Saidaiji priests downplayed images of women as evil temptresses, they did continue to harbor concerns over the possible consequences of welcoming women into the order. The

1273 decision to forbid women from staying at Saidaiji past 10:00 p.m., for example, suggests that Ritsu priests were concerned not only with preventing possible sexual encounters between male and female clerics but also with thwarting the slander of outsiders. Eison's 1249 letter to Jizen, mentioned in chapter 4, expressed this same concern; in fact, he suggested that his reason for refusing to meet with her on a particular occasion stemmed from concern over the possibility that outsiders might misinterpret his visit to the convent.

Saidaiji representations of women as powerless beings who have the potential to become men not only transformed women from dangerous, sexualized enemies to pitiable, desexualized beings, it also imposed a hierarchy in which men—Ritsu priests—were guaranteed a higher stature than women. By teaching women that they must become "men," Ritsu priests projected themselves both as the ultimate model of practice and as the final leaders of the *sangha*. The view that women are helpless beings who must acquire a male state, then, allowed Saidaiji priests to justify the inclusion of women in the Buddhist order while at the same time ensuring that this inclusion was never understood as equality.

The writings of Enkyō and Shinnyo, however, dispel the notion that all Ritsu nuns accepted and thoroughly internalized this rhetoric. Neither Enkyō nor Shinnyo portrayed birth into a female body as a general problem that required a solution. To the contrary, they depicted the founders of their convents, Queen-Consorts Kōmyō and Hashihito, as divine women, women whose bodies were both female *and* perfect. They also reframed Saidaiji discussions of motherhood, shifting attention away from the notion that mothers are passive women in need of salvation and toward an image of mothers as wise leaders, teachers, and saviors. The texts of the convents furthermore accent the agency of women in securing salvation, both for themselves and for others, without the intervention of male priests. Finally, while Ritsu priests' accounts of Hokkeji and Chūgūji tend to portray the priests not only as the initial revivers of the convents but also as the ultimate authority granting legitimacy to these women's institutions, the texts associated with the convents ignore Ritsu priests, focusing instead on their own female leaders: nuns and divine queen-consorts.

As these examples so powerfully indicate, medieval Japanese nuns had the opportunity, through the practices of reading and writing, to construct compelling counterinterpretations of gender, motherhood, and salvation. Against the notion that Ritsu nuns had fully internalized the andocentric rhetoric of the Saidaiji school and practiced Buddhism as supplicants concerned above all else with shedding the female body, the examples above provide evidence that Ritsu nuns, much like the court ladies of the Heian *gosho* discussed in chapter 1, tended to focus on those aspects of Buddhist discourse that did not problematize women or their bodies. By reconfiguring certain motifs, such as that of motherhood, or by drawing attention away from others, such as the notion that women must seek birth into male bodies, Ritsu nuns succeeded in creating images of their convents as communities in which the Buddhist practices of women were affirmed rather than dismissed. By avoiding abstract discussions of gender and instead focusing on mythic figures that even Eison and his disciples respected, nuns like Enkyō and Shinnyo deployed a rhetorical strategy that "talked past" dominant andocentric discourse.

Talking past androcentric discourse is not the same as refuting it; as seen in the example from Jōen's *Chūgūji engi* mentioned above, it is likely that many reformulations of Saidaiji discourse were embedded within certain androcentric assumptions, such as the idea that women faced heavy karmic burdens not encountered by men. What the narratives of Ritsu nuns do so effectively is to exploit powerful images of legendary women of the past—women whom, as shown above, Eison and other priests also venerated—while circumventing abstracted discussions of "women" as sinful and karmically burdened. In this sense, the nuns defined their own interests as remaining largely outside those of Ritsu priests. So while Enkyō and Shinnyo did not necessarily refute certain doctrinal concerns of Ritsu priests, such as the notion that women face heavy karmic burdens, they did, in ignoring these issues, dismiss them as less important than other concerns, such as the merit produced through devotion to Kōmyō and Hashihito, as well as through regular ritual practice, a topic explored in the previous chapter.

Images of autonomous women in positions of authority serve several possible functions in the literature of Hokkeji and Chūgūji. First of all, these images enable Ritsu nuns to assert the right to rule their own institutions, free of supervision from priests. These texts also speak to an audience of court women in transition. Shinnyo and Enkyō offer reminders of a world in which women were at the center of Japan's power structure. Not only were the women of Shinnyo's and Enkyō's day living in a world in which female sovereigns were no longer imaginable, but they were also witnessing the weakening of court women's political influence more broadly: even royal princesses once guaranteed the security of a *nyoin* title were finding that their positions depended upon their biological ability to bear sons (Ōishi 1990; 1997). In romanticizing Hashihito and Kōmyō, Shinnyo and Enkyō make a strong argument for the return to what is understood as the glorious past of Japanese court women, the heyday of which they locate in the Asuka-Nara age. It is easy to see why women of the court—women who envisioned themselves as patrons of Buddhism and as women with some remaining connection to political power—would have been attracted to the legendary queen-consorts venerated by Ritsu nuns.

In short, Ritsu nuns explained the reemergence of female monasticism not in terms of Eison's *vinaya* revival movement but rather in terms of a return to the divine vows of queen-consorts-turned-bodhisattvas. In shifting the focus of these revival narratives, they diverted readers' attention away from the notion that salvation is acquired only through the mediation of male priests and suggested instead that women could rely on the salvific powers of legendary women from Japan's past.

Epilogue

Until recently, studies of Buddhist convents in premodern Japan tended to accept one or both of the following premises: (1) that convents served the social function of housing socially problematic women—illegitimate or unmarriageable daughters, widows, and unwanted wives—and (2) that women who entered convents internalized androcentric doctrines. These assumptions led numerous scholars to the same conclusion: that nuns, forced into convent life, left without better options, and taught to lament the obstacles of their sex, would have found it extremely difficult to create meaningful lives as religious specialists.

Close attention to the discourses and practices taken up by nuns and laywomen at Hokkeji disproves this logic. First, the story of Hokkeji and its restoration sheds light on a group of women not commonly portrayed in earlier studies of convents: women who actively pursued ordination and monastic training. It is not known what exactly brought hundreds of women to Hokkeji and its branch convents in the middle years of the Kamakura period. But as indicated throughout this book, the only explanation offered by the women themselves was that of religious devotion. Other records do suggest, as explained in chapter 2, that at least a few of Hokkeji's first medieval nuns did in fact fall into social categories typically defined as problematic: that is, some were widows, the daughters of illegitimate relationships, or ladies-in-waiting whose mistresses had passed away. It is also possible that some women who became nuns at Hokkeji did so in response to broader historical trends, such as the diminishing of stable court positions for women and losses in women's property rights. But even in those cases in which a functionalist explanation might help describe a woman's initial entry into nunhood, the notion that she would have found it difficult to derive meaning from the religious life is hardly a foregone conclusion. After all, both Jizen and her master Kūnyo, the child of an illegitimate relationship, first took up the nun's life immediately following the deaths of their royal mistresses, yet their monastic lives were not characterized by mourning or hopelessness. These women created their own lineage of nuns and worked to revive Hokkeji both as a center of Kōmyō worship and as a Ritsu convent that carried out official *vinaya* rites. They also fostered a tradition of venerating Buddha relics and restored Hokkeji as a center of cultural production. The story of Hokkeji, then, serves as a powerful reminder of the fact that even women who may have first entered convents for unfortunate reasons or because they were pressured to do so still had the opportunity to create meaningful lives for themselves as nuns. The convent, especially as it was reimagined in the thirteenth and early fourteenth centuries, often operated as a space that allowed women to create significant religious communities and cultural practices.

Also remarkable about narratives describing Hokkeji's medieval revival is the fact that they do not describe the nuns who joined the convent as women who sought nunhood in response to heartbreak, the death of a loved one, or the emergence of an awkward domestic situation. Instead, Hokkeji materials describe the convent as a place for nuns who wanted to pursue religious practice as a vocation. The *Nenjū gyōji,* as well as other records of ritual activity at Hokkeji, confirm that Hokkeji nuns provided professional rituals for the lay community. These rituals, and devotion centered on the legendary figure of Queen-Consort Kōmyō, comprised the core of religious practice at Hokkeji. Heian literary sources may describe nuns as pitiable figures who languished in solitude or sorrow, but Hokkeji materials and related Ritsu materials describe nuns as active participants in a vibrant religious and cultural community.

Studies that approach women's religious lives primarily from the view of doctrine have also missed the mark. In part, this is because few women made the study of doctrinal texts the focal point of their religious lives. As suggested throughout the book, most religious practitioners in premodern Japan, male or female, were driven by a host of other concerns, such as devotional practices, ritual performance, and the pacification of the dead. Doctrine alone cannot explain Kōmyō's symbolic role at Hokkeji; it is only within the context of historical studies of pilgrimage, devotional practice, and religious narrative that her relevance in Hokkeji's long history is made clear. This wider view of religious life at Hokkeji demonstrates that for many of the nuns and pilgrims who practiced at or visited Hokkeji it was Kōmyō's legacy as a divine figure—and not any scriptural teachings on the salvation of women—that shaped their understanding of the relationship between women and Buddhism.

That said, it is not the case that doctrine-oriented studies have been misleading simply because they ignore practices that are difficult to analyze in terms of scriptural and commentarial literature. Doctrinal studies of women in Buddhism have also been problematic insofar as they tend to downplay both diversity and change over time, to present doctrine as singular and static. Another goal of this study has been to reveal the range of doctrinal options open to women at this particular point in Japanese history. As this study indicates, there was never a single Buddhist view of women or women's salvation. Numerous perspectives can be found in doctrinal literature, especially when texts written within China and Japan are taken into consideration. As discussed in chapter 2, for example, Jizen and

Kūnyo, the architects of Hokkeji's Kamakura-period restoration, came of age in court circles in which many women aspired to be reborn, as women, in the Tuṣita Heaven of Maitreya. The view that women must seek rebirth into male bodies in order to gain salvation, then, was only one of many soteriological discourses available to educated women living at this time. Moreover, as late as the thirteenth century, it appears to have remained one of the least popular (and least well-known) discourses on female salvation.

Indeed, Nishiguchi Junko's recent study (2002b) of the *Sutra on Transforming the Female Body (Tennyoshingyō)* has yielded some surprising results, namely, that this text, the one copied and promoted by Eison's disciple Sōji, was extremely rare in premodern Japan. Scholars had long assumed the opposite, primarily because a text with a similar title, *Sutra on Transforming Women into Buddhas (Tennyo jōbutsukyō),* is regularly mentioned in Heian- and Kamakura-period courtier diaries. While the first title appears in the Taishō canon (*Bussetsu tennyoshingyō,* T. no. 564), the second does not. Scholars had long assumed that the second title was in fact a variant of the first and that the *Tennyoshingyō* was both well-known and popular among the elite of the Heian and Kamakura periods.[1] But in a comprehensive comparison of the relevant works, Nishiguchi has proven that these titles refer to two completely different texts. What's more, the first, much lengthier text, which focuses on the notion that women, though bound for buddhahood, must first achieve rebirth into male bodies, gained little popularity in Japan. The text to which courtiers commonly referred in their diaries, the *Tennyo jōbutsukyō,* does not mention transformation into male bodies but instead skips ahead to the notion that women are all destined for the unexcelled enlightenment of the buddhas. Moreover, it teaches that women's salvation is easily achieved. Consider the textual content of this short sutra:

> The Buddha Preaches the Sutra on Transforming Women into Buddhas
> Thus I have heard: Once, when the Buddha was in Śrāvastī together with 1,250 people in the great *bhikṣu* order, Śāriputra spoke to the Buddha, saying, "If we deeply consider women's bodies in the trichiliocosm, not abiding by the precepts, [women] undergo immeasurable eons of suffering. And thus, through what causes and conditions might women speedily transform their female bodies and realize the unsurpassed way [*mujōdō*]?" At that time, the Buddha told Śariputra, "Consider this teaching well: As for the causes and effects associated with women's bodies, because all women's bodies become the mothers of the buddhas of the triple world, they are like the Great Ocean and Great Earth; women's bodies are the storehouses of this Tathāgata, of transformation bodies, and of all myriad things. They are the storehouses of the great bodhisattvas, of all good works, and of all great merit. But the karma of breaking the precepts, lacking faith, acting with indolence, having ill will, being jealous, harboring pride, and holding erroneous views caused them to receive female bodies. When they extinguish the evil karma of previous lives, then they will surely receive the fruit of great bodhisattvahood, and their female bodies will

> achieve the unsurpassed way. If there is a woman who receives and upholds the three refuges, the five precepts, and the ten major bodhisattva precepts and does not break them for seven days or for twenty-one days, or perhaps for one month or two months, or for forty-nine days, or for three months or a half year or three years, if a woman receives and upholds [these precepts] for six calendrical cycles and is not sexually licentious, then when the end of her life draws near, bright light will radiate from her body, she will be born in the Western Pure Land, and she will speedily realize the unsurpassed way. If there is a woman who copies this Mahāyāna sūtra, or reads it aloud, or performs an explanation of it for others, or teaches others to copy and read it aloud, or makes offerings in honor of this sutra and receives and upholds teachers of the Dharma, bestowing them with offerings and paying them respects, then this woman will extinguish all of the grave karma from immeasurable kalpas of past lives and will achieve the Buddha Way." At that time, the Buddha finished preaching this sutra, and the 1,250 members of the great order all rejoiced greatly [in the teaching that had been offered].[2]

It was this sutra, Nishiguchi explains, that had gained wide circulation among Heian- and Kamakura-period elites. Its origin is unknown, but she speculates that it was produced in China or Japan. Its first appearance in Japanese sources dates to the year 884, when the text is mentioned in a *ganmon* attached to the *kanshi* (Sino-Japanese poetry) collection *Kanke bunsō*. From this point through the fourteenth century, both its title and lines from its text are mentioned in numerous courtier diaries and poetry collections. The *Tennyo jōbutsukyō* appears to have been especially popular among aristocratic and royal women, many of whom were buried with copies of the text (2002b, 36–40).

It cannot be denied, of course, that this text contains visibly androcentric rhetoric: it attributes women's birth into female bodies as evidence of evil karma created in past lives and associates women with a number of "feminine vices," including "breaking the precepts, lacking faith, acting with indolence, having ill will, being jealous, harboring pride, and holding erroneous views." One could hardly argue that the text offers a view of women that modern feminists would call empowering. Compared with Buddhist views of women that would become dominant over the course of the late fourteenth and early fifteenth centuries, however, the discourse on women's salvation espoused in the *Tennyo jōbutsukyō* looks rather benign. This is true for two reasons in particular: first, the sutra proclaims that buddhahood is within the reach of all women without emphasizing—or even mentioning—the notion that rebirth into a male body is required before that goal may be reached. Most Mahāyāna texts make assertions of universal buddhahood and include women within those claims, but they typically claim that buddhahood is attained only after one achieves rebirth in a male body.

Secondly, the *Tennyo jōbutsukyō* includes several lines in which the Buddha praises women as the storehouses, or womb-matrixes, of buddhas, bodhisattvas, and merit. The sutra's message about women, then, turns out to be quite mixed. On the one hand, it praises women's bodies as essential to the propagation of the Dharma: they serve as the storehouses of the buddhas and bodhisattvas themselves. But on the other hand, it states that women received these ostensibly praiseworthy bodies due to evil karma from past lives. At this point, the thread in which women's bodies are praised as the storehouses of the buddhas is turned on its head, and the reader is left to conclude that female bodies are the manifestations of past evil. The message is inconsistent, but it gives readers the opportunity to read the text in multiple ways and to emphasize one view of women's bodies over the other. Not surprisingly, Heian- and Kamakura-period elites tended to emphasize the first, more positive reading and to ignore the second. Numerous medieval texts assert, for example, that it is a great sin to slander women, since they are the storehouses of the Buddha-Dharma (Nishiguchi 2002b, 40b; Abe 1998, 118–119). In short, while Heian- and Kamakura-period audiences, male and female, may have accepted the notion, found in Buddhist texts, that male bodies were soteriologically advantageous, they emphasized positive renderings of the female body when possible. Moreover, there is little evidence to suggest that laypeople of the Heian and Kamakura periods viewed women's salvation as a special problem in need of a solution. Indeed, the message of the *Tennyo jōbutsukyō* was that women, though possessing bodies that are simultaneously praiseworthy and reflective of past evil, are certain to achieve buddhahood. All they must do to get there is to receive and uphold basic precepts and to promote the *Tennyo jōbutsukyō*.

In printing and promoting the *Tennyoshingyō*, Sōji and other Saidaiji priests were actively propagating a new and more rigidly androcentric discourse on women's salvation. The *Tennyoshingyō*, which raises questions about women's accessibility to buddhahood, was not well-known during this period, and the views it espouses were not common among Kamakura-period laypeople (Nomura 2004, 112). Against the commonly held assumption that women could easily attain salvation through devotional practices, the sutra suggests that more extreme measures are necessary. Among these more extreme measures, of course, is pursuing rebirth in a male body, a goal the sutra emphasizes.

In many senses, this move toward constructing women's salvation as a problem that requires special handling—and the intervention of male priests—resembles claims made by other popular religious movements that gained ground during this period. Abe Yasurō has observed that the Pure Land priest Hōnen (1133–1212) was the first Japanese priest to actively preach of the need to save women. He suggests that Hōnen presented female salvation as a problem precisely so he could offer its solution, thereby winning himself a larger audience. In other words, Abe argues that Hōnen manufactured a market for himself first by teaching lay audiences that women were extremely difficult to save and then by offering a special means of saving them: *nenbutsu* practice. Educating people about the difficulty of saving women served the necessary function of making the *nenbutsu* teachings relevant (1998, 67–76).

For Saidaiji priests, the *Tennyoshingyō* likely served a similar function. One might view Ritsu efforts to teach laypeople about the great karmic obstacles of women as having helped the group create a niche for itself in the religious landscape of medieval Japan. It is also clear, however, that Ritsu priests, like their Zen colleagues, were attempting to create within Japan a more authentic Buddhist order. Efforts to popularize the *Tennyoshingyō* can likely be understood as part of a broader Ritsu project to spread among Japanese nuns and laypeople certain texts and ideas believed to represent a more authentic version of Buddhism.

Sōji's ambition to spread the *Tennyoshingyō* far and wide does not appear to have met with much success. Although he instructed Hokkeji nuns, in the epigraph he attached to the *Tennyoshingyō,* to "print copies" of the text, to "distribute it into perpetuity," and to "receive and uphold" it with great faith, there is no evidence that Hokkeji nuns followed his directives. As Nishiguchi notes, the only surviving copy of the *Tennyoshingyō* in Japan is a copy from Sōji's woodblock version, and this copy, now held in the Tōshōdaiji archives, bears no signs of usage (2002b, 35a). Moreover, none of the nuns at Hokkeji or its branch convents mentioned the sutra in other documents.

Sōji's attempt to popularize the *Tennyoshingyō* may have failed, but his efforts to introduce new perspectives on women's salvation were part of a larger discourse on Buddhism and women that did eventually take root by the late fourteenth and early fifteenth centuries. As suggested in the last chapter, Ritsu discourses were in a state of flux during the middle years of the thirteenth century. Eison, his disciples, and his colleagues were trying out a number of new teachings and concepts that had been imported from the continent, popularized within Nara circles, or picked up during interactions with Zen groups. Ritsu perspectives on women's salvation were still in their developmental stages during the years of the Hokkeji restoration and had not yet been formulated in a systematic or cohesive way.

But outside sources suggest that by the early decades of the fourteenth century, Ritsu priests had succeeded in articulating and implementing a more rigid view of gender. One indication of this change in Ritsu views of women is found in the diary of Hanazono Tennō. In an entry dated to the nineteenth day of the eleventh month of Genkō 1 (1321), Hanazono describes the tonsure ceremony of a princess *(nyoō)* who had become the adoptive daughter of Fujiwara no Tsuneko (mother of Go-Fushimi Tennō and author of the *Nakatsukasa naishi nikki*). In describing the details of the ceremony, Hanazono notes that the princess's precepts master, Seikan (son of Nijō Noriyoshi, b. 1234), who was the rector of the Taishi Hall at Saidaiji, did not cut the princess's hair himself but instead had one of his novices perform the task. The reason for this, Hanazono explains, is "because those who uphold the *vinaya* do not touch women with their hands" (*Wayaku Hanazono Tennō shinki,* 3:100).[3] This small detail is significant, for it is the first time Saidaiji-related materials mention the notion that precepts-abiding priests should avoid all physical contact with women, even within the context of performing a religious ritual. This remark thus implies that Ritsu priests had begun to adopt increasingly exclusionary views of women. That male members of the clergy were not to touch women is of course a rule that can be found among the two hundred and fifty precepts of the *Four-Part Vinaya,* but it is one that most Japanese priests had ignored for centuries. That Saidaiji priests eventually came to take pride in upholding this precept is illustrative of the degree to which their zeal for the *vinaya* introduced new, and typically more androcentric, views of women into popular discourse.

Another example of the ways in which later Ritsu groups worked to propagate more notably androcentric Buddhist discourse might be found in two large hanging scroll sets that date to the early decades of the fourteenth century. Both works are titled *Hokkekyō mandara* and depict well-known scenes from the *Lotus Sutra.* One dates to the year 1327 and is held in the archives of Honpōji in Toyama; the other belongs to the collection of Hōnkōji in Shizuoka and is dated to the period 1326–1328. Although both of these temples now belong to the Nichiren sect, art historian Haraguchi Shizuko (2009) believes that the paintings were originally associated with, and likely commissioned by, Ritsu priests. What is significant about these paintings is that they both offer a visual interpretation of the Devadatta chapter's dragon girl that diverges from those interpretations that had become standard within Japan. Illustrated versions of the *Lotus* produced in Japan had long followed visual models of the dragon girl's attainment of buddhahood that avoided the question of her sexual transformation. As explained in chapter 2, the *Heike nōkyō* ignores the issue altogether by depicting the dragon girl on the brink of her enlightenment, during the moment in which she is offering a jewel to the Buddha. But the *Hokkekyō mandara* of Honpōji and Hōnkōji introduce a new visual model of the Devadatta chapter. These paintings depict the sexual transformation of the dragon girl, making her rebirth into a male body explicit. A number of visual cues are used to alert the viewer to the dragon girl's sexual transformation: her skin is made darker (a sign of masculinity, since women were typically depicted with milky-white complexions), and her form takes on the shape of a male monk (i.e., she loses her breasts).[4]

These paintings thus serve as another example of how Ritsu priests attempted to introduce more overtly androcentric interpretations of Buddhist doctrine to lay audiences. Much like Sōji's *Tennyoshingyō,* the paintings do not appear to have succeeded in popularizing *henjō nanshi* theory, as the visual model of the dragon girl's rebirth used in these paintings remained extremely rare (Haraguchi 2009, 96). But these small steps toward increasingly more exclusionary views of women and women's salvation are emblematic of broader changes that did begin to crystallize by the late fourteenth and early fifteenth centuries, when practices related to the *Blood Bowl Sutra (Ketsubonkyō)* began to take root in Japan.

As related in the last chapter, the apocryphal *Blood Bowl Sutra,* which appears to have been produced in China during the late twelfth century, introduces yet another obstacle said to hinder women in their pursuit of buddhahood: in retribution for the blood that women spill on the earth during their menses and in the process of giving birth, the text teaches, women are bound for a hell in which they will be submerged in pools of blood (see Soymié 1965). The *Blood Bowl Sutra*'s vision of women's salvation demonizes women's bodies in a manner not visible in earlier discourses. Now, in addition to carrying out practices aimed at gaining transformation into a buddha-body (as the *Tennyo jōbutsukyō* preaches) or a male body (as the *Tennyoshingyō* preaches), women must first carry out practices aimed at saving themselves from the blood bowl hell.

Scholars have struggled in their attempts to date the importation of the *Blood Bowl Sutra* into Japan. Some have suggested that the sutra may have entered Japan as early as the thirteenth century, but most speculate that the text was not known there until at least the middle years of the Muromachi period.[5] Recent archaeological evidence from the Dōnokuchi site in modern-day Sendai has revealed, however, that laywomen in the Tōhoku region were being buried with copies of the text in the early years of the fifteenth century (Tokieda 2007, esp. 36). Current research in this area does not allow scholars to ascertain whether Ritsu priests played any role in the early spread of *Blood Bowl Sutra*–related practices. One of the few surviving copies of the text was discovered among bodily remains at Saidaiji, but that particular text dates to the Edo period (Takemi 1983, 231).[6] What is clear about practices surrounding the *Blood Bowl Sutra,* however, is that their spread in Japan reflects two larger sociopolitical trends of the period: increased interaction with China and the gradual dissemination of patriarchal Confucian values. Late-thirteenth- and early-fourteenth-century Saidaiji discourses on women's salvation foreshadow these later developments. They represent some of the first steps that Japanese priests took toward the development of a cohesive ideology of gender steeped in textual precedents from continental sources.

Ironically, then, the same Ritsu movement that granted women greater levels of institutional inclusion also ushered in discourses on women's salvation that were ultimately more damning of women than Heian- and early-Kamakura-period discourses had been. This outward paradox reflects the degree to which the thirteenth-century restoration of Hokkeji represented the fortuitous convergence of two discrete sets of interests: those of certain female practitioners who sought greater opportunities as members of the clergy and those of Ritsu priests who, like their Zen colleagues, sought to create in Japan a more "authentic" Buddhist order, that is, an order that looked more like Buddhism as it was practiced in China and less like the *kenmitsu* orthodoxy of their contemporaries. As demonstrated in chapter 2, the first group was working from earlier paradigms of female practice and assumptions about women's salvation. Specifically, there is little evidence to suggest that its members viewed women's salvation as something that presented a particular set of difficulties. Most likely, they followed those views of women's salvation that had been popularized in Heian- and Kamakura-period texts like the *Tennyo jōbutsukyō,* which had long been regarded as evidence that women's salvation was easily achieved. But the second group, made up of Ritsu priests committed to the project of implementing Chinese and other continental texts within Japan more fully, would turn against the more benign discourses on women's salvation that had been popularized during the Heian and Kamakura periods and would instead promote the more overtly androcentric texts and discourses they associated with authentic Buddhist practice. The creation of a nuns' order at Hokkeji, then, took place on the cusp of a significant shift in Japanese Buddhist discourse on gender and salvation. Women at Hokkeji and its affiliate convents won greater institutional inclusion in the Buddhist order at the hands of priests who would eventually teach them that the salvation they had viewed as easily accomplished was in fact difficult to attain in female bodies.

These later ideological developments notwithstanding, Hokkeji's mid-thirteenth-century restoration played an important role in granting convents institutional visibility in Japanese society. At the time of Hokkeji's revival, it had been some four centuries since Japanese nuns had had the opportunity to pursue the priesthood as a vocation under the auspices of an official Buddhist institution. Hokkeji was one of the first of many convents to be established during the Kamakura period, and following its revival convents became visible social institutions and remained such throughout the rest of Japanese history. Although convents were always less powerful than male monasteries, and despite the fact that nuns were never allowed to assume the elite posts within sectarian monastic hierarchies, many female members of the clergy did succeed, as was demonstrated in chapter 7, in securing positions that allowed them to serve lay patrons as teachers and ritual specialists.

The story of Hokkeji's medieval restoration offers clear evidence of the ways in which religious women in premodern Japan were able to create meaningful religious lives and rich spiritual communities within a tradition whose canonical texts viewed women in a negative light. Perhaps much of this success is attributable to the fact that Hokkeji nuns did not view doctrine as the centerpiece of their practice; instead, they focused their daily lives on a host of other practices and beliefs, including devotional practices centered on Queen-Consort Kōmyō, the veneration of Buddhist relics, and the performance of pragmatic rituals, such as memorial rites for the dead. In building the reputation of their institution around these practices, Hokkeji nuns succeeded in attracting a large group of lay followers and in promoting themselves as the performers of efficacious priestly rites. Once the broader social and religious functions of the convent were in place, issues of women's salvation were irrelevant. Hokkeji nuns did not doubt their ability to extend salvation to themselves or others. Why, then, would their lay patrons?

In analyzing the restoration of Hokkeji and its place in Japanese religious history, we are also drawn toward a fuller understanding of Buddhism on the ground, Buddhism as it was encountered and reproduced by those not representing the interests of elite scholar-priests. In particular, analysis of nuns' activities at Hokkeji reminds us of the sustained focus within clerical circles, evident throughout the history of monastic Buddhism in Japan, on rites meant to entertain and educate pilgrims; to secure salvation for clergy, patrons, and family members; and to protect the state. That nuns shared in the broader pragmatic goals of Buddhist monasteries helps explain why they were less concerned about the so-called soteriological obstacles of womanhood than scholars have long imagined. Hokkeji nuns went about their business at the convent, offering services to local lay believers and promoting their institution as the center of Kōmyō veneration without even mentioning the notion that women faced difficulties on the Buddhist path. For what the nuns who worked to restore Hokkeji in the thirteenth century hoped to gain from their endeavors was not a special means of saving themselves despite their female state; rather, they were taking advantage of an opportunity to pursue the priesthood as a vocation, to immerse themselves in the religious life. Studies of nuns that infer or deduce women's experience of Buddhism from doctrinal sources alone have failed to recognize the degree to which male and female clerics alike drew upon other forms of religious expression—such as ritual performance, devotional practice, relic veneration, and visions—both to serve their communities and to enrich their daily lives. It is only when discussions of doctrine are tempered with attention to these common, on-the-ground religious practices that we begin to see the depth and complexity of Buddhist monasticism in premodern Japan.

Notes

Introduction

1. Takagi suggests that as many as ten of these provincial nunneries were actually built (1988, 73).

2. The exoteric-esoteric orthodoxy *(kenmitsu)* was represented by the so-called six Nara schools, plus the Tendai and Shingon schools of the Heian period. For an overview of relevant issues, see Abé 1999, esp. 399–428.

3. An ordination platform, or *kaidan,* refers to a physical space sanctioned, usually through purification rites, for ordination ceremonies. Most typically, *kaidan* consisted of large, raised platforms. Sometimes they were made into small halls known as *kaidan-in.*

4. I have adopted Dorothy Ko's (1994) translation of *sanjū* (Chns. *sancong*) as "thrice following."

5. Other convents associated with the movement that were revived or established during this period include Chūgūji, Kōtaiji, Tōrinji, Shōbōji, Dōmyōji, Manishu-in, Sairin-in, Sanka-in, Shana-in, Kaiganji, Mimuradera, Sōji-in, Myōrakuji, and Myōhōji (Ushiyama 1986).

6. Eison's movement stressed strict adherence to the *vinaya* precepts but also embraced the practice of esoteric Buddhism. Its doctrinal position on the precepts is based primarily upon the following texts: the *Four-Part Vinaya* (T. no. 1428), the *Brahma Net Sutra* (Chns. *Fanwang jing,* T. no. 1484), and the *Yuqie shidu lun* (Discourses on the stages of concentration practice, Jpns. *Yugashijiron,* abbr. *Yugaron,* Skt. *Yōgācāra-bhūmi-śāstra,* T. no. 1579).

7. According to Katsuura Noriko (1989, 23), state-authorized ordination platforms for nuns had disappeared by the end of the ninth century. In the eleventh century, an official precepts ordination platform for women was established at Hōjōji, but after the temple burned down in 1058, this platform came to an end.

8. Mount Hiei, a mountain northeast of Heian-kyō (present-day Kyoto), was the center of the Tendai school of Buddhism (Chns. Tian-tai). Mount Hiei's Enryakuji, the main temple of the Tendai school, was founded by the priest Saichō in the year 788. Saichō established a precepts platform at Enryakuji that focused on the ten major and forty-eight minor bodhisattva precepts of the *Brahma Net Sutra.* This ordination platform was distinguished from the Tōdaiji platform in Nara, where the *Four-Part Vinaya* was used. See Groner 1984 and Minowa 1999.

9. See Eison's own remarks about his ordination of women at Hokkeji. *KJGSK* 1999, 350.

10. Here I refer primarily to the *Kongō Busshi Eison kanjin gakushōki (KJGSK),* which is widely recognized as the autobiography of Eison.

11. Gregory Schopen's work, in particular, has revised many long-entrenched scholarly assumptions about monastic life. Drawing on archaeological and epigraphic evidence, he has illustrated the degree to which monastic life as practiced on the ground in ancient India diverged from monastic ideals preserved in classical Buddhist texts. See Schopen 1997, 2004, and 2005. Other recent works that emphasize the need for greater attention to the sociocultural and material realities of monastic life (as opposed to studies that focus only on ideals as presented in doctrinal texts) include Dreyfus 2003 and Hao 1998.

12. Tanaka Takako has lamented the comments of Ishida Mizumaro in particular. Ishida emphasizes the notion that nuns were pitiable figures in the Buddhist world: they occupied the lowest position in the community and were governed by priests. Given such oppression, he surmises, nuns must have lost all will to study Buddhist texts or to train in ritual performance. Women who became nuns, he says, had no choice but to tuck themselves away in some obscure corner of society and to spend their last days lethargically reading through the sutras. Tanaka 2005, 169–171; Ishida Mizumaro 1978.

13. Recent scholarship in this area suggests that *goke-ama,* or "widow nuns," used official document seals that ordinary women may have had a more difficult time using. See Shiga-kenritsu Biwako Bunkakan 2007, 93.

14. Also qtd. in Dobbins 1995. See also Seidensticker's translation: "If only they might share the same lotus in another world.... These are the thoughts, one is told, with which [Genji] tormented himself" (1976, 359).

15. Nomura also counts terms related to *henjō nanshi,* such as *tennyo jōbutsu* (transforming women into buddhas), *tennyo jōnan* (transforming women into men), *nyonin no mi o hanare* (separation from the female body), and *nyonin no mi o itō* (to grow weary of or give up attachment to the female body). These terms and phrases, which had considerable conceptual overlap, were often used interchangeably.

16. As Dobbins suggests, popular literature from the Heian and Kamakura periods indicates that people tended to view birth in paradise as a goal attainable by men and women alike. To give just one example, the authors and compilers of *ōjōden* (accounts of births in paradise) collections—many of whom were male monks—commonly included stories of women who successfully attained birth in Amida's Pure Land.

17. D. Max Moerman (2006) works from the premise that androcentric views of the female body based in Buddhist narratives and doctrines were part of the dominant discourse of medieval Japan. While it is likely the case that images and themes from the *Blood Bowl Sutra* had entered popular discourse by the fifteenth century, we do not know how long exactly it took for knowledge of the *Blood Bowl Sutra* and related practices to gain widespread circulation. This topic will be treated again in chapter 7 and in the epilogue. See also Williams 2004a, 157–158nn56–57.

18. Despite these general tendencies, however, scholars of the Christian West have noted the fluidity of the term "monk." During certain historical periods and in certain regions of the West, monks did perform rites for lay benefactors.

19. Senority was required for the ordination of other priests, however. Only priests who had practiced for ten years as fully ordained *bhikṣu* were to bestow precepts upon others (see Matsuo 2004b, 22). *Kanjō* (Skt. *abhiṣeka*), or Dharma anointment, ordinations constitute another exception to the general rule described above, as these ordinations supplied priests with an additional degree of prestige. See *Bukkyōgo daijiten,* 192d–193a.

20. *Ritsuryō* codes did legislate against monks and nuns stirring up the people, but such laws were rarely enforced, especially after the Nara and early Heian periods. See Abé 1999, 33–34.

21. As in the East Asian case, though, Christian nuns were never the *equal* counterparts of monks. In particular, there is much evidence to suggest that many Christian patrons believed the prayers of monks to be more effective than those of nuns. As Jane Tibbetts Schulenburg has explained, this belief often led those in power to patronize male monasteries over female ones (1989, esp. 285–290). In Buddhist India, too, it is believed that the nuns' order suffered because society held offerings made to monks to be more meritorious than those made to female religious (see Heirman 2001).

It should also be noted here that many scholars of female monasticism in the West have come to view the category "nun" as too narrow. The category "nun," as defined by the male religious order, was limited to women who took solemn vows and accepted the rule of enclosure. But recent research has demonstrated that many women in premodern Europe lived as contemplatives in monastic communities, often without taking solemn vows or enduring claustration. In other words, many women who took up residence in religious communities and dedicated themselves to the devotional life were not viewed as "nuns" in the eyes of Church authorities. To better account for the diversity of religious lifestyles undertaken by women in premodern Europe, scholars have suggested new categories, such as "vowesses," "female monastics," and the even broader "religious women." For a more comprehensive overview of these issues, see Bitel 2008; see also McLaughlin 1989.

22. Although there were some notable exceptions to the general rule of female claustration in Christian monasticism, canon law required that vowed religious women live under enforced rules of enclosure. In 1298, Pope Boniface VIII issued the papal bull *Periculoso,* which declared that all vowed women were to be cloistered. The bull, which remained part of canon law through the early 1970s, led to numerous architectural innovations. As Jessica A. Sheetz puts it, "Claustration included the installation of gates, high walls, shutters, the use of the turntable to receive goods, and the grille separating nuns from their families" (1997, 1378; Hamburger 1992). While Japanese noblewomen, including those who were ordained as nuns, typically sought to conceal themselves behind blinds and in interior rooms far from exterior doorways, they did so primarily as a matter of propriety; laws did not require such practices. Because the concept of claustration was not relevant in the Buddhist case, male monasteries converted into convents did not require architectural refitting.

There were many exceptions in the Christian case, of course. Some European women resisted or disregarded the laws of claustration, creating innovative communities of religious women who, though not recognized as nuns by male authorities, took up religious vocations. One of the more famous cases of such women was that of the Beguines, who emerged around 1200, nearly a century before Boniface VIII's decretal. Although Beguine communities enjoyed local support, church officials viewed them with great suspicion: in fact, the 1311–1312 Council of Vienne denounced the Beguines as heretics who did not live under a sanctified rule (Simons 2001, 133). Another interesting case is that of the women of Corpus Domini, a religious community in Ferrara, Italy. In a study of fifteenth-century documents associated with this community, Mary McLaughlin finds that the women who practiced there "made every effort to avoid" the implementation of strict rules surrounding enclosure, dress, and vows (1989, 298).

Several hundred years later, in the sixteenth and seventeenth centuries, female congregations focused on teaching and nursing, such as the Ursulines and the Sisters of Charity, were founded. Unlike women recognized as nuns, these women were not cloistered and did not take solemn vows (Johnston 2005, 1497).

23. Fróis also claims, just before this comment, that while Western nuns were expected to live in isolation, Japanese convents were more or less prostitution houses. This comment suggests that he was conflating the practices of certain traveling "bikuni" who did offer sexual services with all nuns, a conflation that likely misrepresents the social reality of the time. Still, this contrast between Western nuns as cloistered and Japanese nuns as having relative freedom of movement is worth noting. Okano Akio has published a well-annotated translation of Fróis's treatise (1999, 54). For Portuguese original, see *Kulturgegensätze Europa-Japan,* 128.

24. Samuel Turner, *An Account of an Embassy to the Court of the Teshoo Lama, in Tibet* (1800, II. x. 348; qtd. in the *Oxford English Dictionary*).

Chapter 1—Pilgrimage, Popular Devotion, and the Reemergence of Hokkeji

1. See "Kokushi" and "Kokubunji" in *Nihon kodaishi daijiten,* 251, 253–254.

2. See, for example, *fu* dated to Jōwa 11 (844) 11/15, Kōnin 3 (812) 7/10, and Kōnin 9 (818) 5/29, *Ruijū sandai kyaku,* 3:111–112, 139–140. The Kōnin 9 (818) 5/29 *fu* adds that the mixing of the sexes is permissible in cases when local laypeople are attending lectures or seeking medical treatment. Members of one sex are not to stay overnight in a monastery designated for members of the opposite sex, however.

3. In fact, a *fu* dating to Enryaku 16 (797) 2/2 says that nuns had been vying to enter Hokkeji. This rush for Hokkeji might be understood as a reaction against the trend Ushiyama describes of convents, especially those in Nara, being converted into monasteries. Ushiyama notes that the ecclesiastical policies of Kanmu Tennō appear to have delivered a great blow to women's inclusion in Japan's official monastic community. See Ushiyama 1990, 16–19, and *Ruijū sandai kyaku,* 3:138.

4. According to Nishiguchi, Hokkeji had come under Kōfukuji control by the late medieval period (2004, 137). (Here, she is probably referring to the late fourteenth century or the early fifteenth century.)

5. And in fact it has been shown that these *bettō* were of lower social class than the rector (*chōrō,* literally "elder," a gender-neutral term); it is thought, then, that

the *chōrō* often held superior social and political power in *chōrō-bettō* relations. See Ōishi 1997.

6. Japan's *ritsuryō* state, modeled on the Tang system of governance as expressed in the *lü-ling* codes, was strongest during the early and mid-eighth century. The system established not only legal codes but also a complex set of administrative structures and bureaucratic procedures. It also called for frequent surveys of land and population. A census was to be taken every six years, and rice fields were to be reallocated in reponse to changes in population. This was one of the most cumbersome—and least popular—aspects of the *ritsuryō* system.

7. *Nyoin* (also *nyōin*) was a powerful royal title similar to that of a retired sovereign *(in)*. The title was typically accompanied by a royal *mandokoro,* or household administrative office. The next chapter will discuss *nyoin* in greater depth.

8. Abe 1998 discusses the role of *engi* in women's pilgrimages (8–9).

9. *Shichidaiji junrei shiki,* 47. A version of this same story also appears in the *Three Jewels* (see Kamens 1988, 353).

10. These lines refer to the rhetoric of the neglected or ruined city, as found in Chinese poetic works such as the *Wucheng fu* of Bao Zhao (aka Bao Mingyuan, ca. 414–466) and the *Li gong gao* of Bo Juyi (772–846). These connections are analyzed in greater depth in the notes to chapter 7.

11. *Kenkyū gojunreiki,* 142–143. For more on the role of bathhouses in the institutional history of Japanese Buddhism, see Williams 2004b. Joan Piggott describes the *sangō* as the "three deans" who governed a temple (1997, 217).

12. Although this narrative (*Konjaku monogatarishū,* 11.19) is no longer extant, its title, "Kōmyō kōgō Hokkeji o tatete amadera to nashitamō koto," is included in extant versions of the *Konjaku.* It is likely that the narrative once included here was based on that included in the *Three Jewels.* See *SNKBT* 35, 61.

13. Notable examples include Mount Hiei (Enryakuji), Mount Kōya, Daigoji, and Mount Ōmine.

14. Scholarship on *nyonin kinzei* has demonstrated that the practice did not develop until at least the ninth century. Research in this area has also suggested that the practice was not well-known until after the eleventh century and that it was the thirteenth or fourteenth century before it became truly widespread. Suzuki Masutaka provides a nice overview of this scholarship (2002, 120–130).

15. Abe Yasurō notes that *nenbutsu hijiri,* in particular, played an important role in the spread of the *Taima mandara engi,* as many aspects of this story encouraged women's participation in *nenbutsu* movements (1998, 8–9).

16. This Rinkai appears to have been the Rinkai who had once served as the *bettō* of Hokkeji. This narrative seems to have gained popularity over the course of the medieval period: Mujū Ichien (1226–1312) also mentions it in his 1305 *Zōdanshū* (307–309), and it appears in the 1309 illustrated narrative *Kasuga gongen genki* as well (*Kasuga gongen genki-e,* 48–49).

17. See, for example, the description of Jingoji in *Heike monogatari,* book 5. Very similar diction is employed to relate the decline of Jingoji. Narratives recounting thirteenth-century restorationist efforts at Chūgūji and Kairyūōji also employ nearly identical phrases.

18. The entry goes on to state that the *kesa* worn by these four hundred priests have been preserved in the "northern treasury [*kita no hōzō*]."

19. The date of this text has not been established, but internal evidence demonstrates that it was produced sometime after 1337. (The text contains a reference to a Kenmu 4 [1337] 12/15 inscription.) See *Kōfukuji ranshōki,* 455b.

20. *HMJE* and *Shoji engishū* in *YKT,* 5:43b.

21. Tankū studied together with Shinran as a disciple under Hōnen. He was the grandson of the *sadaijin* (great minister of the left) Fujiwara no Saneyoshi (1096–1157). He studied *mikkyō* on Mount Hiei, later leaving to study with Hōnen. He eventually established the Nison-in in Saga.

22. Jinen is listed as the seventh rector of the revived Hokkeji (*HMJE,* 143a). Since Jizen, who is listed as the first rector of the revived Hokkeji, was regarded as the rector of Hokkeji during the convent's initial interactions with Eison, it is unlikely that Jinen would have been the rector of Hokkeji at this time. By the time Enkyō wrote the *Hokke metsuzaiji engi* in 1304, however, Jinen, who passed away in 1298, had already served as a rector of Hokkeji. Thus, it is likely that she refers to Jinen as "*chōrō*" not to indicate that Jinen was the rector at that time but rather out of a sense of respect. Enkyō was probably a younger member of the order who was not present at Hokkeji during the 1240s, during the early years of the restoration movement. Since this same document indicates that Jinen lived at Hokkeji until the time of her death, at age eighty-six, in 1298, we can surmise that Jinen shared with Enkyō stories of the early years of the Hokkeji revival. Jinen would have been in her early thirties in the 1240s, when the small group of nuns was first interacting with Tankū and Eison.

23. Here, *kebutsu* (transformation buddha, Skt. *nirmāṇa-buddha*) is used to denote a small Buddha image that appears on the head or crown of a larger one. The implication is that although there were eleven small Buddha images atop the Eleven-Faced Kannon's head, there was no Amida in the center. According to the standard iconography of the Jūichimen Kannon, this twelfth miniature Buddha (which is actually larger than the other eleven and placed in the center) is optional and does not occur in all representations of the Eleven-Faced Kannon (see Japanese Architecture and Art Net Users System, s.v. "Juichimen Kannon"). Nishikawa points out that Hokkeji's Eleven-Faced Kannon resembles images held at Dōmyōji (Osaka), Chōenji (Osaka), and Hōshaku-in (Yamagata), insofar as they all include a *kebutsu* that depicts Amida from the waist up (rather than from the neck up) and wearing a priest's robe (1978, 57b).

24. Although there is no need to read too deeply into this particular detail, it is interesting to note that the Eleven-Faced Kannon image is said to have grown an Amida statue just after Master Tankū, a Tendai / Pure Land priest, visited Hokkeji and helped the nuns rebuild the walls and gate. Amida is of course the primary deity associated with Pure Land practice. It is fitting, then, that Amida should appear just after Tankū's visit.

25. The character *miyako* or *kyō* is used, in this instance, to refer to the southern capital of Nara. See Nara Rokudaiji taikan kankō kai 1999, 53–54.

26. Ibid. There has been some uncertainty regarding the character directly following *ama* (Ōta 1978, 40a).

27. See *Nihon kodaishi daijiten* 439d; Tanabe Takao, "Umoreta hotoketachi," no. 291 of Kuroda Kinen Shitsu exhibit, Fukuoka City Museum, http://museum.city.fukuoka.jp/je/html/291-300/291/291_01.htm (accessed Sept. 26, 2007); and Tanaka Minoru 1978a, 84b.

Chapter 2—Envisioning Nuns: Views from the Court

1. This sentiment, which appears throughout Heian and early Kamakura literature, is clearly expressed in the "Writing Practice" (Tenarai) chapter of *Genji.*

2. She took the "ji" character in Jizen from Jiren-bō. See Hosokawa 1999b, 213–215.

3. In a section on miracles associated with the revival of convents, Eison's autobiography mentions a revelatory dream in which Kūnyo appears to Jizen and asks her to perform a Sixteen Arhats *kuyō* on her behalf. This passage explicitly identifies Jizen as the disciple of Kūnyo: "Also, there was a privately professed nun [*zenni*] (a royal daughter of Takamatsu Nyoin. First she was called Takakura-dono; later she was called Daigo-dono. She passed away at Hokkeji). After she closed her eyes for the final time, she informed Jizen Bikuni, the rector of Hokkeji (who had been her disciple), saying: 'There is no one who wishes to pay respects to me. You must perform a Sixteen Arhats *kuyō* [on my behalf]'" (*KJGSK* 1977, 24).

4. This description of Kūnyo as wise, pure, and thoroughly devoted to Buddhism is characteristic of the "eminent priest" genre of Buddhist hagiography. The biographies of many Chinese nuns were modeled on the *Gaoseng zhuan* (Biographies of eminent monks, Jpns. *Kōsō den*) genre employed to describe the lives of famous priests. It seems likely that Eison was modeling his description of Kūnyo on stories of famous Chinese nuns. The *Biqiuni zhuan* (Jpns. *Bikuniden*), compiled in sixth-century China, offers many examples of nuns described in a similar manner. For an English translation of the text, see Tsai 1994. The Shaka *nenbutsu* refers to a practice in which devotees intone the name of Śākyamuni Buddha.

5. A passage from Teika's *Meigetsuki* identifies Shin-Amidabutsu-ni as the daughter of the Chōken's younger sister and states that it was through family connections that Kūnyo was placed at Daigoji. The passage further links both Kūnyo and Jizen (here referred to as Shōe-bō) to Shōkutei-in (*Kundoku Meigetsuki,* Karoku 2/9/11, 4:227b–228a).

6. The more famous child born of this relationship was the priest Kaie of Ninnaji (b. 1172). See Tanaka T. 2006, 162, 186.

7. *The Distribution of the Eight Grains of the Tooth Relic (Gashari bunpu hachiryū)* makes the same claim: "Her [Kūnyo's] mother is the *nyoin* Takamatsu" (qtd. in Tanaka T. 2006, 176). Tanaka Takako (2006) also uncovered a document that explicitly identifies Takakura-dono, or Kūnyo, as the daughter of Chōken Hōin (see "Hokkeji," *Kanazawa bunko komonjo* 3, no. 2285). Translation of "Kongō Busshi Eison kanjin gakushōki" follows Groner 2001, 116.

8. According to Tanaka Takako, careful study of Heian literature reveals the conventions typically followed in response to such embarrassing births. If the product of such a relationship were male, she points out, the child would be sent to train at a temple from a young age; if female, the child would be made a *nyōbō* and would

serve as a lady-in-waiting at a court *gosho* (royal residence). In the case of Takamatsu-in and Chōken, this premise seems to hold: Kaie and other male children did indeed become priests, and Takakura-dono (Kūnyo) did in fact become a *nyōbō*. She served in the *gosho* of *nyoin* Hachijō-in.

9. Shunzei was made the superintendent of the queen-consort's household agency buildings in 1170, meaning that he was, at this time, in the service of Queen-Consort Fujiwara no Yoshiko (d. 1209). See Gomi 1984, 392.

10. Tanaka Takako argues that Takakura-dono (Kūnyo) is the same person as the poet Hachijō-in no Takakura (2005, 162–163). Hosokawa agrees with her argument throughout his work (see, e.g., 1999a, 33). Jizen is known to have maintained close ties with Shunzei's son Teika. See Hosokawa 1987, 132; Ishida Y. 1957.

11. See related documents in *Daigoji shin yōroku,* vol. 3, esp. 747.

12. Studies that focus on the history of nuns' precepts platforms in Japan have tended to dismiss all post-Nara nuns as laywomen who were not recognized by the wider aristocratic and monastic communities as "true" nuns. In his appraisal of ordination platforms in premodern Japan, for example, Matsuo (1995) points to an 1182 Sanron-school document in which monks argue that women in Japan cannot be considered full *bikuni:* since they take only the ten precepts, the monks insist, these women can only be thought of as *shamini* (novice nuns).

13. The actual land transfer document says that Shin-Amidabutsu-ni passed Shōkutei-in down to someone called "Sakato," but several Japanese scholars have compellingly argued that this "Sakato" is indeed Takakura-dono, or Kūnyo. See Tsuchiya 1989, 194–195.

14. The first woman to receive the *nyoin* title was Higashi Sanjō-in, who received it in the year 991. Although early *nyoin* like Jōtōmon-in, the daughter of Fujiwara no Michinaga, were certainly powerful, Nomura's point is that *nyoin* become even more powerful from Bifukumon-in's time, when they, like their male counterparts, the retired sovereigns *(in),* began accumulating massive portfolios of landed estates.

15. Although both of these women had names that read "Fujiwara no Shōshi," the "shō" characters in their names were different.

16. For more on the political and military power of Hachijō-in and other *nyoin,* see Kawai 2007.

17. Gomi Fumihiko argues that the relationship between *nyoin* and their ladies-in-waiting eventually began to mimic the mother-daughter relationship, as *nyoin* came to bequeath land rights upon their ladies-in-waiting with increasing frequency (1984, 385).

18. Among the daughters of clerics, we find the daughter of a Ninnaji priest, a daughter of a priest known as Zenchi Hōin, and a daughter of a *bettō* (chief administrator priest) of a Hachiman complex.

19. For more on *nyoin* participation in relics services, see Ruppert 2000 and Nomura 1989.

20. Nicole Fabricand-Person discusses similar issues as they apply to *Fugen jūrasetsunyo* iconography (2002, 369).

21. Only four of the signatories have been clearly identified, but Komatsu Shigemi's extensive research on the project has allowed him to reconstruct a list of the remaining donors (2005a, 106–107; 2005b; see also Meech-Pekarik 1976, 34–38).

22. *Wuliangyi jing,* an introduction to the *Lotus; Guan puxian jing* (also *Guan puxian pusa xingfa jing*); *Amituo jing* (T no. 366.12.346b–348b); *Bore boluomiduo xinjing* (Skt. *Prajñāpāramitā-hṛdaya sūtra,* T. nos. 253–256).

23. For more on *onna-e,* see Komatsu 1994, 98–118.

24. In her study of the Heian-period songbook *Ryōjin hishō,* Yung-Hee Kim suggests that positive readings of the dragon girl's attainment of buddhahood had spread outside elite circles as well. A number of the *imayō* songs that appear in the collection present plainly positive interpretations of the Devadatta chapter of the *Lotus.* See Kim 1994, 81–82, and *Ryōjin hishō,* nos. 113, 116–117, 208, 292.

25. Fabricand-Person is critical of the view that court ladies enjoyed the "romantic fantasy" of envisioning themselves as "part of Fugen's entourage" (368), but she does offer evidence that court women did in fact commission and create such images. She also offers a thorough synthesis of earlier Japanese scholarship on the issue.

26. The Tuṣita Heaven is the fourth of six heavens that exist within the realm of desire *(kāma-dhātu).* That the Tuṣita Heaven, unlike Amida's Pure Land, is located within the realm of desire helps explain why hair, and female bodies, would be allowed within it.

27. *Akudō* refers to the realms of animals, hungry ghosts, and hell beings.

28. Kimura (2004), too, suggests that in seeking rebirth in the Tuṣita Heaven, court women evaded *henjō nanshi* discourse.

29. There is one known exception: the novice nun Shinmyō does include, in a 1247 *ganmon,* or written prayer request, that all women, beginning with her mother, be separated from their female bodies and made to achieve enlightenment quickly (*Ama Shinmyō Ganmon, SEDS,* 393).

30. Kōfukuji's Jōkei (1155–1213) is famous for his public opposition to the Pure Land movements, especially that of Hōnen, on both political and doctrinal grounds. The degree to which Nara priests identified with forms of non-Amidist forms of *nenbutsu* practice, then, must also be considered in terms of the larger political context. See Ford 2006, 110–113, 159–184.

31. James Ford also mentions the role that belief in *Tosotsuten ōjō* played in the lives and teachings of Nara priests like Jōkei. He offers an insightful discussion of Jōkei's teachings on the merits of Maitreya's Tuṣita Heaven (2006, 110–111).

32. I have relied upon the translations of Sōgō positions created and used by Abé (1999, 30).

33. Ingen was a student of Ryōgen. For more on his life, see McCullough and McCullough 1980, 248, 396.

34. For examples of Ingen's service to elite women, see McCullough and McCullough 1980, 273, 444, 525, 620, 640, 719.

35. Although Ryōnin first trained on Mount Hiei, he eventually started his own movement, which later came to be known as the Yūzū Nenbutsu sect (*Nihon Bukkyō jinmei jiten,* 454–455).

36. It was not always the case that all priests were of lower rank than court aristocrats: by the mid-Heian period, high-ranking priests tended to be of aristocratic stock themselves.

37. Notes and minor changes indicated in brackets.

38. Kubota Jun, the editor of the *SNKBZ* edition of the *Towazugatari,* notes that this particular line conveys Lady Nijō's "*hankan,*" or feelings of antipathy, toward the priest of Kawara-in (47[1999]: 235n14). Misumi Yōichi, editor of the *SNKBT* edition, similarly remarks that this particular line expresses Lady Nijō's critique of this priest's incompetence (50[1994]: 32n5).

39. Although this sentiment can be found throughout Heian literature, one poignant example is that of Ukifune's tonsure in the "Writing Practice" chapter of the *Genji.* See Tyler 2001, esp. 1098–1105.

40. That said, we still find many Kamakura-period examples of the convent as a signifier of destitution, failure, and loneliness. The *Heike monogatari,* for example, portrays Kenreimon-in's life as a nun in a small hermitage in the bleakest of terms.

41. Hosokawa confirms this reading, arguing that medieval nunneries did frequently serve as inns for traveling women (1989a, 182–184). Nishiguchi also demonstrates that nuns' hermitages commonly accepted guests during the Heian period (1987, 158–160).

42. Kamens quotes a passage from the *Murasaki Shikibu nikki* in which Lady Murasaki comments upon the advantages—for an artist—of living in a secluded place. Murasaki makes the job of the great Kamo priestess sound like a stay at an artist's colony and downplays the priestess' feelings of loneliness in having been distanced from court life.

43. Tabuchi has suggested that Abutsu-ni must have herself been considered something of a *Genji* specialist, since Tameie's ladies hired her to copy the text. Abutsu-ni's *Genji* expertise is echoed in her own writing, which contains copious allusions to *Genji* and other *monogatari.* It is also known that her husband Tameie's Mikohidari school of poetry—in which she became quite involved—held the *Genji* in high esteem, producing many poems that refer or respond to *Genji* texts (2000, 118–121).

44. Abutsu-ni wrote *Menoto no fumi* for her daughter, who eventually entered the salon of a *nyoin* (Tabuchi 2000, 232–234; Miner, Odagiri, and Merrell 1985, 141).

45. According to Jien (1155–1225), Tendai abbot and elder brother of Kūjō Kanezane, "These ladies secretly called Anraku and other *nembutsu* priests into their presence to explain the *nembutsu* teaching. Anraku seems to have gone with some colleagues to see these ladies, even staying overnight. Because this was an unspeakable affair, Anraku and Jūren were eventually beheaded. Saint Hōnen was banished [in 1207] and not allowed to reside in the capital" (trans. Brown and Ishida 1979, 172).

46. Abutsu-ni's notes about the roles of nuns as the teachers of wellborn women also suggests, when put in the broader context of her life, that elite pilgrims at institutions like Hokkeji may have been involved in intellectual exchange at several levels. While Abutsu-ni makes it clear that elite women should learn the Dharma from nuns, details from her life have allowed some scholars to suggest that she most likely offered instruction in the writing of *waka* and in the proper reading of the *Genji monogatari* during her time at Hokkeji. Christina Laffin, in particular, has shown that Abutsu-ni managed to attract disciples throughout her travels and posits that she most likely offered instruction to nuns and laywomen alike during her time in residence near Hokkeji (2009). If this were indeed the case, then we can

likely imagine certain convents, and especially those linked to aristocratic women, as intellectual centers where one could pursue not only Buddhist learning but also training in poetry and in the *Genji*.

47. See, for example, *Toganoo Myōe Shōnin denki*, 354–355. Mark Unno discusses Myōe's relationships with female disciples (2004, 129–145). Karen Brock also provides an insightful discussion of Myōe and his female patron-disciples (1990, 205–210).

48. See *Azuma kagami*, Jishō 4 (1180) 8/18, 35. I discuss household-consultant nuns in Meeks 2008. See also Katsuura 2000, 2004.

Chapter 3—Envisioning Nuns: Views from the Male Monastic Order

1. Cook also includes this passage in his translation of sections from the *Shōbōgenzō* (2002, 104). My translation of titles follows the Sōtō Zen Text Project.

2. For a more thorough treatment of tensions between early Buddhist communities in China and the Chinese polity, see Orzech 1998, 107–121. General discussions of these debates can also be found in Zürcher 2007 and Tsukamoto 1985.

3. Certainly this concern is evident in his harsh critique of priests who serve elite female patrons. That Dōgen decided to establish his monastic center, Eiheiji, in the remote province of Echizen has also been understood as indicative of his will to distance himself from worldly power.

4. Here, Eison is referring to the *Da banniepan jing (Mahāparinirvāṇa-sūtra)*.

5. Although the *Brahma Net Sutra*, like the *Lotus*, teaches that bodhisattvas are not to associate closely with those in positions of political or worldly power, it also teaches that bodhisattvas are to bestow the bodhisattva precepts on *all* who request ordination, including kings and rulers (1008b21–22). Earnest requests for ordination were not to be turned down, and thus monks like Eison felt obliged to bestow the bodhisattva precepts on rulers who made sincere, repeated requests. Eison's sermons and autobiography suggest that political pressure was also part of the equation: although Eison did turn down the initial invitations of Go-Saga and of the warrior government regent, he might have faced censure or punishment if he had repeatedly refused to meet with such powerful figures. See *Chōmonshū*, esp. 218, and *KJGSK* 1999, esp. 264–265.

I use the term "warrior government" here to refer to the government initially established in Kamakura by Minamoto no Yoritomo in the 1180s. From this period through the establishment of the Tokugawa government in the early years of the seventeenth century, Japan was ruled by multiple centers of power. The court, based in Kyoto, and the warrior government, based in Kamakura, were the most visible centers of power. But a number of monastic complexes, such as Enryakuji and Kōfukuji, also comprised political power blocs *(kenmon)*, meaning not only that they possessed great administrative and economic power but also that they exercised jurisdiction over their own lands. For more nuanced discussions, see Adolphson 2000, Hurst 1982, and Kuroda T. 1975.

6. In some other versions of this story, Myōe gives the precepts to Kenreimon-in rather than Shikikenmon-in. I relate this same episode in Meeks 2009, 12.

7. Chinkai is known to have studied at both Tōdaiji and Daigoji.

8. From the time Eison began ordaining *bikuni,* he regularly noted how overjoyed he was to have created a genuine *sangha* in Japan (e.g., *Chōmonshū,* 193).

9. See also Reischauer 1955a, 207; 1955b, 171–172. Groner also mentions this passage (2002a, 274). The ten major bodhisattva precepts *(Bonmō no jūjūkai)* require not only that one restrain one's own behavior but also that one help others avert evil actions and commit good ones. Hisao Inagaki summarizes the ten major bodhisattva precepts as follows: "(1) not to kill or induce others to kill, (2) not to steal or make others steal, (3) not to engage in or make others engage in sexual intercourse, (4) not to lie or make others lie, (5) not to sell or make others sell intoxicating liquors, (6) not to talk of or make others talk of a fault in a bodhisattva, monk, or nun, (7) not to praise oneself and abuse others or make others do so, (8) not to be mean or make others be mean, (9) not to give vent to anger and treat others harshly or make others do so, and (10) not to abuse or make others abuse the three treasures [the Buddha, the Dharma, and the Sangha]" (*Dictionary of Japanese Buddhist Terms,* s.v. "*Bonmō no jūjūkai,*" 15–16).

10. Although Adolphson does not treat this particular case, his discussion of the rivalry between the two branches of the Tendai school is helpful for understanding the broader context of the incident. As Mitsuhashi has pointed out, Michinaga patronized both branches of the Tendai school, often pitting them against each other (2000, 468).

11. Eison invited Ryōhen to serve as the *dōshi,* or officiating priest, for the eye-opening ceremony held to commemorate a copy of Seiryōji's statue of Śākyamuni. Eison's group installed the replica, which it had commissioned, at Saidaiji in 1249. Ryōhen's name also appears on the list of the "*biku* order" in the *Saidaiji kyōmyō shingon kechien kakochō.* There, he is listed as Shingan-bō of Chisoku-in (*KJGSK* 1999, 185; Hosokawa 1999b, 196–197).

12. Shunjō is reported to have been a close friend of the great Japanese Zen master Eisai. According to the *Sennyūji Fukaki hōshiden,* a 1244 biography of Shunjō (also known as the master Fukaki), the two met in Hakata. Eisai, hearing that Shunjō was returning to Japan from China, is said to have made the trip down to Hakata to greet Shunjō upon his return. The text says that Eisai entreated Shunjō to join him in an effort to spread the Dharma and benefit sentient beings *(guhō rijō)* (53a).

13. For the relevant sermons, see *Chōmonshū,* 200, 214.

14. It was at Kairyūōji that Eison made his debut as a teacher of the *vinaya* following his ordination as a Ritsu monk. Ultimately, Eison pressed for an interpretation of the precepts that diverged from Shunjō's on several fronts, and these disagreements caused him to face persecution at the hands of Shunjō's disciples. Despite these later differences with Shunjō's disciples, however, it is clear from Eison's writings that he viewed Shunjō with great respect. Eison's early troubles at Kairyūōji are treated at greater length in the next chapter.

15. The excerpt cited is based on a passage in the *Da banniepan jing* (T. no. 374, 422b). Some sentences are cited character-for-character, but the version from Eison's sermon does alter and add to the text in several places. Eison also refers to this same passage in his *Bosatsu kaihon shūyō bugyō monjū,* which was a commentary on the Silla priest Taehyeon's *Fanwang jing* commentary *Beommanggyeong bosalgyebon jongyo.*

16. *Zenni* literally means "meditation nun," but in premodern Japan it was commonly used to refer to privately professed nuns who had taken only novice precepts. Some of these women lived at home and practiced as especially devoted laywomen, while others took up residence in hermitages on the edges of monastic complexes or lived as itinerant pilgrims.

17. The temples were so close, in fact, that Kairyūōji authorities issued a special set of rules in 1232 *(Kairyūōji genseiji)* that specifically forbade Kairyūōji monks from allowing women and nuns to spend the night in the residential quarters of the monastery. That this document was issued at this particular time suggests both that at least a handful of nuns were already in residency at Hokkeji during the 1230s and that Kairyūōji authorities were, like many Nara monks active during this period, actively concerned with reinstating the behavioral norms outlined in the *vinayas.*

18. *Biqiuni chao* is listed as "*Sifenlü biqiuni chao,* in three scrolls," in *Zhiyuan yibian* (X. 59, no. 1104), p. 649a9. It is also listed as a work of six scrolls compiled by Daoxuan in *Sinpyeon jejong gyojang chongrok* (Newly compiled comprehensive record of the scriptures of the various schools), p. 1174a15. (See also DDB, s.v. "*Sinpyeon jejong gyojang chongrok*").

19. Translation of *Shichijūichiban shokunin uta-awase* adapted from Goto's. Scholars have dated the *Shichijūichiban shokunin uta-awase* scroll to the earliest years of the sixteenth century, but the genre of *shokunin uta-awase,* or poetry exchanges exploring the lives of artisans, dates back to the late Kamakura period. It is likely, then, that this particular depiction of nuns as skilled workers was based on social views of nuns established long before the year 1500.

20. The annotator mistakenly identifies Hokkeji as a Nichiren temple here and the Ritsu nun as a Lotus school nun. Wakita and Harada correctly identify the nun as a Ritsu nun (Wakita 2006, 113; Harada 1997, 140).

21. In many Jodō Shin-shū circles, the model that took hold was that of the "half-laywoman, half-nun" who assisted her "half-layman, half-priest" husband in the administration of local *dōjō.* See Endō 2002; Nishiguchi 1999b.

22. Of course, Eison was still in the position of having to make himself mobile, insofar as warrior government officials called him all the way to Kamakura from Nara. But once he arrived at Kamakura, he took up residence within a temple, and those who sought audience with him came to him; he was not expected to spend his days in the personal quarters of elites.

23. She was, in turn, the son of Michikata, meaning that Mino no tsubone was likely the mother of Ichijō no tsubone.

Chapter 4—Hokkeji's Place in Eison's Vinaya Revival Movement

1. For more on Son'en, see Hosokawa 1999b, 60–62.

2. Paul Groner (2005) provides an excellent summary and analysis of the doctrinal issues at play in these self-ordinations.

3. This is Mikael Adolphson's translation of *gōso* (2000, 416).

4. Eison also uses the story of Kakujō crying at Saidaiji's first *fusatsu* as an anecdote in the thirty-ninth of his collected teachings (*Chōmonshū,* 206–207).

5. The Sumiyoshi deity was known as a god who offered protection to those traveling by sea (see Hosokawa 1999b, 174–175). I use the term "shrine" both here and in the case of Hachiman not to suggest a clear division between "Buddhist" and "non-Buddhist" institutions but instead to reflect that these institutions were known as *miya* or *jingū* (shrines or palaces of the deities) rather than *ji* (temples).

6. Tradition regards Cien Ji as the founding patriarch of the Consciousness-Only (Weishi) school, also known as the "Dharma-Character" (Faxiang, Jpns. Hossō) school. Translations follow *DDB,* s.v. "Dharma-character school."

7. The twelve volumes that comprise this work, incidentally, were among those texts retrieved by Eison's disciples who went to Song China.

8. Canonical sources note that this two-year waiting period was meant to confirm that novice nuns were not with child before allowing them to advance to full nunhood. It is for this reason that there are three stages of nunhood but only two stages of monkhood.

9. Hamuro was also the author of the courtier diary *Yōkōki.* For more on his life, see Hosokawa 1999b, 254–255.

10. The Kinai region refers to the capital area of ancient Japan and includes most of those provinces in which royal residences had been established at one time or another: Yamato, Yamashiro, Kawachi, Izumi, and Settsu. According to the tenth-century *Engi-shiki,* the Kingoku region referred to the seventeen provinces that were near the capital area: Iga, Ise, Shima, Owari, Mikawa, Tanba, Inaba, Bizen, Awa, Kii, Sanuki, Ōmi, Mino, Wakasa, Tajima, Harima, and Awaji.

11. For more on the Kōmyō Shingon, see Unno 2004, Abé 2003.

12. As Hosokawa points out, Eison's nephew and close disciple Sōji was in charge of all of the Saidaiji-branch temples in the provinces of Settsu, Kawachi, and Izumi. This means that the convents under his jurisdiction would likely have included Dōmyōji, Keishō-in, Shana-in, and the Izumi temple Maniju-in (see Hosokawa 1989b, 140, 152–153). Little is known about the latter two convents, but the first two are examined in chapter 5. Hosokawa does not explain what he means when he writes that Sōji was in charge of managing these institutions. Clearly, Sōji was responsible for too many temples to have managed the daily affairs of individual convents. He may have instead functioned as a Saidaiji representative in these provinces, relaying information back and forth between Saidaiji and these particular temples. Although he was involved in printing various publications for nuns, there is little evidence to suggest that Sōji treated the convents under his jurisdiction differently than the temples for men.

13. In one of his sermons, Eison tells of how he spent several months on foot, traveling from place to place and offering services during the year 1281. He suggests that this travel was part of his work as a bodhisattva: "I started this practice [of reviving the *vinaya*] from the time I was a little over thirty years old. I have devoted myself entirely to ascetic practice for the benefit of sentient beings. This year, too, from the first month of the year I left this temple [Saidaiji] and walked from place to place, in response to various invitations, until now, the sixteenth day of this [the fourth] month, when I am returning to the temple for the beginning of the summer retreat [*ketsuge*]. Perhaps it is because I have devoted myself to ascetic practice in this way that I have been hearing reports of people seeing dreams in which I force

open the gates of hell [and save sentient beings]" (*Chōmonshū,* 212–213; see also Kōshō Bosatsu Onkyōkai Chōmonshū Kenkyūkai 2003, 135).

14. This argument is somewhat implicit, for example, in Hosokawa 1989b.

15. Sōji's exact birth date is unknown, but Wajima has surmised that since a number of Eison's followers were first ordained as novices at age twelve, Sōji too was likely twelve years old when he took the tonsure in the year 1244. This dating would place Sōji's birth around the year 1225 or 1226. Given that he is known to have died in the year 1312, it seems unlikely that he would have been born much earlier than the mid-1220s; a birth dated to 1225, for example, would mean that Sōji lived for eighty-seven years, which was a remarkably long lifetime for this period. See Hosokawa 1989b, 161n46, and Wajima 1972.

16. For more on Sōji's age, background, and activities, see Hosokawa 1989b, esp. 126–147, and 1987, 85–87.

17. It is not clear when exactly Kairyūōji began to identify itself as a *matsuji,* or branch temple, of Saidaiji. As mentioned earlier in this chapter, Eison was more or less kicked out of this temple in the year 1238, when his critiques of *vinaya* practice there were met with hostility. But Eison appears to have patched things up with Kairyūōji monks by the year 1245, when he began staying there for annual lectures at Hokkeji. He also built a *stupa* at Kairyūōji in the year 1288, enshrining within it relics from Hokkeji's collection. See Ueda 1976, 339.

18. Nishiguchi discusses examples of women and nuns making, washing, and mending the robes of monks (1987, 137–139).

19. That nuns were sometimes asked to wash the robes of monks was likely a carryover from broader social practices. During the Heian period, it was common for men practicing duolocal marriage to entrust sewing and other clothing-related needs to the household(s) of their wives. For more on the construction of washing as a sacred act entrusted to women, see Katsuura 1995, 185–206.

20. Here, I refer to some of the powers ascribed to Buddhist relics as delineated in Ōe no Chikamichi's *Issai sharira shū,* as summarized by Ruppert (2000).

21. As Naitō (2004) points out, Eison's familiarity with Ono-branch doctrines and practices reflects the fact that his early training (during his childhood and teenage years) took place at Daigoji. My translation of "Kinrinbucchō" follows Japanese Architecture and Art Net Users System, s.v. "Ichijikinrin." See *Bukkyōgo daijiten,* 1431a, for the translation of "Nyoihōringe."

22. As its alternative name, the Saidaiji Goshichinichichō Darani-e (Latter Seven-Day-Long Dhāraṇī Ceremony at Saidaiji), suggests, this ritual was seven days in duration and focused largely on the incantation of the Zuishin Nyoihōju Konbon Darani, a Nyoirin Kannon *dhāraṇī.* Like the Latter Seven-Day rite held at Tōji, this rite was held annually during the second week of the New Year. See Ruppert 2000, 102–103.

23. Eison's posthumous name was awarded by royal command.

24. The *Gyōjitsu nenpu* includes the text of this *engi.* An earlier copy of the *engi* also exists as an independent document held in the Hokkeji archives.

25. The notion of using a hammer to determine the authenticity of Buddha relics appears in other narrative collections from China and Japan. The adoption of this motif in the *Hokkeji shari engi* thus reflects knowledge of wider continental

narratives about the nature of Buddha relics, how they can be tested, and what makes them authentic. As Ruppert writes, this same motif was invoked in a narrative about Soga no Umako in the *Nihon shoki.* In this story, Umako tests a relic that appeared spontaneously when three nuns partook of a vegetarian Buddhist meal together with Umako's retainer Shime Dachito. This test, resembling that mentioned in other narratives, involves trying to smash the relic with a hammer. According to the narrative, the indestructibility of the relic deepens Umako's faith and motivates him to erect a temple space within his home (2000, 59; *Nihon shoki,* Bidatsu Tennō [584] 13/9, 68:148–149; *Gangōji garan engi narabi ruki shizaichō,* 11–12). William Deal also includes translations of relevant passages (1998, 220).

26. Members of the *saikai-shū* took the eight pure precepts and lived on the grounds of the temple. These divisions in the Hokkeji community will be discussed in the next chapter.

27. Why did the nuns ask Eison to write out the *engi* for them? Was it because they were unable to write it themselves and needed him to serve as a scribe, or was it because they knew that a document written in the hand of the popular and highly respected Eison would garner more attention than whatever they might have written on their own? Another question, of course, is whether Eison actually composed the narrative or if he merely transcribed an oral version of the narrative (or perhaps a written draft) that the nuns had already fashioned.

28. Eison's record from this visit indicates that a count had been carried out in Bun'ei 7, just several months before this visit. He says that the reason he carried out another count was because there had been something "strange" in the Bun'ei 7 count. Most likely, the concern was that the relics had decreased in number. According to the *Hokkeji shari engi,* a count undertaken earlier, in 1268, had resulted in a calculation of 2,073 relics, 10 more than Eison counted during this visit in 1275. See *Hokkeji shari engi,* 143–144; *Gyōjitsu nenpu,* 167.

29. Ruppert does not divide textual representations of women and relics into three categories; I have categorized the problem this way for heuristic purposes. Bernard Faure has also written extensively on narratives about the "Jewel Woman" or "Jade Maiden" (1998, 2003).

30. According to Ruppert, "By the mid-twelfth century, women, at least in the royal court, were playing a pivotal role in the protection and worship of relics" (2002, 192).

31. Although Abe does not address the relationship between nuns and relics in this article, he does suggest that Hokkeji nuns performed *miko*-like functions within the Nara monastic community.

32. This dream revelation is similar to the dream revelation related by the nun Shinnyo to Eison, a revelation he held to be a divine confirmation of his *vinaya* revival movement. See Meeks 2007, 363–364.

33. "Jimyō *nyoin*" and "Jimyō Dharma prince" are also mentioned. These names likely refer to Kita Shirakawa-in and Go-Takakura-in, respectively.

34. The nun Monshō is listed in the 1280 name register *Jubosatsukai deshi kyōmyō* as the *bikuni* Monshō Hōe-bō.

35. One question worth consideration here is what Hokkeji nuns were using as relics and how they were acquiring relics. Such questions are obviously difficult

to approach, but we do know that many of the objects revered as relics during this period consisted of "small crystalline stones." Certain Shingon lineages, Ruppert explains, compiled texts describing how one could manufacture Buddha relics and wish-fulfilling jewels using "precious stones, medicines, or pebbles" (2000, 5). Given the extremely large number of relics apparently enshrined at Hokkeji, it seems possible to suggest that Hokkeji nuns may have been involved in the process of manufacturing Buddha relics. It is possible to imagine that Kūnyo and Jizen, who had numerous ties in the Shingon community, may have had access to knowledge regarding the production of such objects. Another possibility is that Hokkeji nuns used some of the *chindangu* they discovered on the building site of the Golden Hall at Hokkeji when it was reconstructed in the early 1250s. *Chindangu* were small precious objects buried under building sites during the Nara period in order to appease the gods of the land. Some of the *chindangu* recovered at Hokkeji were used to ornament an image of Rushana reconstructed during this period. But it is possible to imagine that the nuns may have used others as relics, for many *chindangu* consisted of small jewels, stones, and precious objects. For more on *chindangu,* see chapter 1. See also Tanaka Minoru 1978a, 84b.

Chapter 5—Social and Economic Life at Hokkeji and Its Branch Convents

1. The notion that home leavers abandon family names and affiliations to become sons of the Buddha is a common trope in Buddhist literature. See T. no. 125, 658c4–7; T. no. 1425, 456a11–13; T. no. 1719, 177b1–2; T. no. 1805, 408b29–c1; T. no. 1812, 594a23–24, and so forth.

2. In reality, many "widow nuns" retired only in name; they often identified as nuns as a means of publicly claiming that they would not remarry following the death of their husbands. According to the laws of the *Goseibai shikimoku,* women could inherit the property of their husbands only if they did not remarry. In practice, these women often took unofficial lovers, even while maintaining the legal identity of "nun" so as to maintain control of inherited property. See Tonomura 1990; Hosokawa 2006.

3. There is one exception: the fourth of the four *kekkaiki* from Hokkeji does not break the number 119 down into levels of ordinations taken. See Tanaka Minoru 1978c, 89.

4. Eison's reading of Vasubandhu, Daoxuan, and Yuanzhao appear to have inspired his innovative use of these categories. See Minowa 1996a, 78-81; 1999, 321; Meeks 2009.

5. The *hassaikai* include the five lay precepts (which prohibit killing, stealing, inappropriate sexual relations, the misuse of language, and the use of intoxicants) plus precepts forbidding the adornment of the body, listening to music, and dancing; sleeping on a high, wide bed; and eating at forbidden times.

6. The six laws are mentioned in conjunction with *shikishamana* in numerous *vinaya* texts. Especially relevant here are discussions found in the *Four-Part Vinaya (Sifenlü),* in Daoxuan's *Sifenlü shanfanbuque xingshichao,* in Yuanzhao's *Sifenlü xingshichao zichiji,* and in Daoxuan's *Sifenlü shanbu suiji jiemo.* The ten novice precepts

consisted of prohibitions on killing, stealing, engaging in sexual relations, lying, using intoxicants, eating during forbidden times, decorating the body, enjoying song and dance, sleeping on a high, wide bed, and possessing valuables. The six laws include precepts against sexual relations, stealing, killing, lying, using intoxicants, and eating between meals or in the afternoon. See also Minowa 1999, xiv–xv, 316–330.

7. As mentioned in chapter 2, the sobriquet "commander of the gate guards" was likely taken from the title of one of Jizen's male relatives.

8. For more on *ajikan* practice (meditation on the Sanskrit letter "A"), see notes to chapter 6.

9. That so many of the rectors are noted to be *vinaya* masters is worth attention, for it suggests that they were respected for their study and understanding of doctrinal matters.

10. I translate "*nyūmetsu*" as "enter final nirvana" here because Enkyō seems to invoke the term "*shikyo*" in this text when referring to an ordinary death.

11. Although the *YKT* version of the *Hokke metsuzaiji engi* lists the thirteenth nun as Ryōzen, this is a misrendering for Ryōshō.

12. Jakuen-bō's status as a member of the *bikuni* order is confirmed in the *Jubosatsukai deshi kyōmyō,* where she is listed as "Son'e Jakuen-bō" (Matsuo 1996, 96b).

13. The Nikaidō family was a southern Fujiwara branch family founded by Fujiwara no Yukimasa, a cousin of Minamoto no Yoritomo who acted under Yoritomo's direction as one of the architects of the Kamakura shogunate. The family took its name from the Nikaidō district in the city of Kamakura, and Yukimasa's descendants held influential positions within the warrior government through the sixteenth century. Goble refers to members of this family who took administrative positions in the warrior government as "hereditary bureaucrats" (1996, 229, 237).

14. A native of Kyoto, Zonkaku is affiliated with two temples there: Kōshōji (the temple that became Bukkōji), which he helped establish, and Jōrakuji (also known as Jōrakudai), which he founded on his own. The two accounts referred to here are the *Jōrakudaishu rōnō ikkiki* and the *Ōtani Honganji tsūki,* both in *Dai Nihon shiryō,* sect. 6, vol. 37. See 30, 44–45, 176.

15. There may have been one or even several other rectors in between Myōpen and Go-Fukakusa's daughter. Names of several rectors not listed in the *Hokke metsuzaiji engi* appear in the *Hokke metsuzaiji nenjū gyōji.* One of these nuns, the rector Myōi Kōshin-bō (first day, fourth month) also appears in the *Jubosatsukai deshi kyōmyō.* We know, then, that she had already taken *bikuni* precepts by the year 1280. It seems likely that her tenure as rector may have bridged that of Myōpen and Go-Fukakusa's daughter. See *HMJE, Jubosatsukai deshi kyōmyō,* and *Nenjū gyōji.*

16. Goble (1989) offers a comprehensive portrait of Hanazono's pursuit of Buddhist learning.

17. I am grateful to Andrew Goble for having guided me to this passage in Hanazono's diary.

18. This first list of *gyōdō shamini,* which does not indicate affiliation with a particular institution, offers no information as to whether the women were living or deceased in the year 1280. The parallel list on the men's side does indicate at

its end that the men listed in the first set of *gyōdō shami* were deceased, suggesting that perhaps the first list for both the male and female orders did not indicate institutional affiliation because it contained the names of the dead. From this view, we might imagine that the author simply failed to include the phrase "the above are deceased" *(ijō kako)* at the end of this first *gyōdō shamini* list. That said, it is also possible to surmise that this phrase was intentionally left out and that the first list of *gyōdō shamini* might include women who, though still living, were no longer active as *gyōdō shamini.* One such case might have been that of Abutsu-ni, who was active at Hokkeji in the year 1252 but then left the convent to marry Fujiwara no Tameie. There is some speculation that the name "Ji-Amidabutsu," which appears in this first *gyōdō shamini* list, refers to her. But this list was compiled in the year 1280, and Abutsu-ni lived until 1283. If the name does indeed refer to her, then we can assume that this first list of *gyōdō shamini* includes women ordained as *gyōdō shamini* who were either deceased or inactive in the year 1280.

19. Although it would be possible to read these numbers as indicators of "Dharma age," or the number of years that have passed since one's initiation into the order, such a reading seems implausible in this case, as the lowest number in the group is eleven. Since we know that the movement was growing most rapidly during the 1270s and 1280s, it seems impossible that the newest *gyōdō shamini* in 1280 would have been veterans of eleven years. If the numbers indicated Dharma age, lower numbers would surely be present in the list.

20. It is worth noting that from Eison's perspective, the *gyōdō shami* were considered equal to the *daisō* of Mount Hiei, since both groups had taken the ten major bodhisattva precepts (Minowa 1999, 326.) In other words, in Saidaiji's view, even *gyōdō shamini* were considered nuns whose status was roughly equivalent to that of a Tendai monk.

21. Minowa warns that such speculation is difficult but does not address the problem in depth (1999, 338).

22. *Mon* coins were strung in units of 100. Ten of these strings (or 1,000 copper coins) were equivalent to a *kan* or *kanmon.* See Gay 2001, 47.

23. Another question that might emerge here is whether or not ordination as a *gyōdō shamini* became a necessary step in the progression toward full nunhood within the Ritsu group. As mentioned earlier, the first groups to take ordinations at Hokkeji were initially ordained as full novices; Eison did not ordain any women as *gyōdō shamini* until 1249, and on this same occasion he ordained five women as full novices, or *hōdō shamini* (*KJGSK* 1999, 184). This detail suggests that ordination as a *gyōdō shamini* was not required for those who sought ordination as *hōdō shamini,* for the five ordained as full novices in 1249, like the thirteen women ordained as full novices by Eison in 1245, were not ordained as *gyōdō shamini* before receiving ordination as *hōdō shamini.* That said, evidence from the male order indicates that many *gyōdō shami* did go on to seek full ordination as male novices. Since *gyōdō shami* and *shamini* had already shaved their heads and taken the ten major bodhisattva precepts, they needed only to take the ten novice precepts of the *Four-Part Vinaya* to advance to the stage of *hōdō shami* and *shamini.* It is possible that at some later point in the Ritsu movement ordination as a *gyōdō shamini* did become a prerequisite for ordination as a *hōdō shamini,* but such was not the case in 1249.

24. *Dai Nihon shiryō,* sect. 5, vol. 29, 136–137.

25. Ōishi, in particular, feels that it is important to recognize the degree to which women whose status was similar to that of a layperson dominated the Hokkeji population in 1280 (2004, 326–327, 330–334).

26. Eison built new "separate ordination" *(betsuju)* platforms at Saidaiji, Hokkeji, and Ebaraji. ("Comprehensive ordination" and "separate ordination" are Minowa's translations. See 1999, xiv–xv.) The *Saidai chokushi kōshō bosatsu gyōjitsu nenpu,* a diary of Eison's life edited by early modern Jōjūji priests, claims that Eison was also responsible for the establishment of *betsuju* ordination platforms at Jōjūji and Kairyūōji. See Matsuo 1998, 192–196; 2001, 379. Although there is no documentary evidence indicating that the Kairyūōji platform was active during Eison's time, a 1356 diagram of the *betsuju* ordination platform at Kairyūōji suggests that this temple did in fact have an ordination platform of its own operating by the mid-fourteenth century. See *Kairyūōji ama betsuju shito.*

27. Hosokawa's work (1987, 1989a, 1997, 1999a) provides thorough summaries of these branch convents.

28. Eison's *Bonmōkyō koshakki hokō monjū* was a collection of works on the *Beommanggyeong gojeokgi,* one of commentaries on the *Brahma Net Sutra* written by the Silla priest Taehyeon.

29. See *Kanagawa kenshi shiryōhen,* vol. 2., no. 2842.

30. This temple no longer exists. A number of scholars believe that Shōbōji was also known as Sōgōji. In the fifteenth century, it was recognized as a branch temple of Hokkeji. See Tamura 1935 and *Nihon rekishi chimei taikei,* s.v. "Sōgōji ato."

31. The first position is one of the three teachers required, along with seven witnesses, for ordination ceremonies; the second is one of the seven priestly positions *(shichisō)* to be filled in any major Buddhist ceremony. The *dōtatsu* was to transmit to the officiating priest (or nun) liturgical documents to be chanted aloud.

32. Several of the texts featuring variations of the narrative in which Shinnyo discovers the *Tenjukoku mandara* include the *Shōyoshō,* the *Taishi mandara kōshiki* (1275), the *Chūgūji engi* (1274?), and the thirteenth-century *Shōtoku Taishi denki.* Narratives from Shōtoku story collections such as the *Jōgū Shōtoku Sōōtei setsu* explain that the original *Tenjukoku mandara* was produced when the Lady Tachibana, devastated by the prince's passing, ordered her ladies-in-waiting to weave a silk *mandala* that would depict his life in the other world. See "Tenjukoku shūchō" in Nara National Museum 2003, 211; Pradel 1997; Hosokawa 1987, 114–115; and Meeks 2007.

33. "Hōin" (Dharma Seal) is an abbreviation of "Hōin Daioshōi," the highest rank the state bestowed upon Buddhist priests.

34. Some of the material in this paragraph and the three that precede it appears in Meeks 2007, 366–367.

35. For perspective, the Hokkeji group contributed just over 75 *kan,* while the Saidaiji group amassed over 220 *kan.* The total amount raised for the project was just over 715 *kan.* See *Saidaiji nishi sōbō zōei dōshin gōriki hōga chō,* 383–389.

36. The date of the temple's founding is based on Robert Borgen's assessment (2007, 1, 16).

37. The Sixteen-Year-Old Filial Prince Shōtoku was a standard form of Shōtoku iconography popular during this period.

38. Borgen provides a comprehensive treatment of these documents (2007, 39–43).

39. The idea was that the gods directed the *kuji*-drawing process and that those of true faith would draw the lot that they were meant to draw. Eison makes references to *kuji* in several of his sermons, including passages 8, 24, and 35 in the *Chōmonshū* (pp. 192, 199, 205). See also Kōshō Bosatsu Onkyōkai Chōmonshū Kenkyūkai 2003, 100b, 115a, 125a. This particular instance is mentioned in Matsuo 2004b, 24. For more on the use of *kuji* (which later came to be known as *omikuji*), see Oishio 1995.

40. Ninshō's work at *hiden* in Kamakura is mentioned in Eison's *Kantō ōkanki* (78). For more on Daibutsu-dani, see Matsuo 2004a, 129–132. Scholars believe that the Great Buddha of Hase in Kamakura (Hase Daibutsu) was a project spearheaded by a *nenbutsu* priest named Jōkō. The production of the large Amida image, which stands some 11.4 meters in height, was initiated in the year 1252 and appears to have reached completion sometime between 1262 and 1264. Matsuo surmises that Ninshō would have found inspiration in Jōkō's talent for fund-raising and suggests that he may have learned from Jōkō how large-scale fund-raising is done (131).

41. See also Hosokawa 1989a, 143, 158n58. As Hosokawa points out, Hayashi Mikiya dates the letter to the year 1308 (1980, 441).

42. Her name appears toward the end of the list. Since these lists typically place Eison's disciples in the order of their ordinations, Ryōshō's placement suggests that she was likely ordained as a *bikuni* in 1270, not along with the very first generation of nuns at Hokkeji. This would explain why she is not included in the *Hokke metsuzaiji engi*. To view her name on the register, see *Jubosatsukai deshi kyōmyō* in Matsuo 1996, 96a.

43. *HMJE* states that Shin'a died in 1297 at age seventy, which would place her birth in or around the year 1228. (This calculation takes into account the fact that babies were regarded as one-year-olds at the time of birth.)

44. An undated letter written to Junnin and signed by Shin'a can be found in *Kanagawa kenshi shiryōhen*, vol. 2, no. 2559. For one example of an ordination ritual involving monks and nuns from a number of different Ritsu temples in the Kamakura area, see *Kanazawa Bunko komonjo*, no. 5888 ("Shōmyōji juyo kanjō ki").

45. Shinkai was a disciple of Jimyō, who had studied under Kakujō's student Ryōhen. He had been living at Yakushiji in Shimotsuke Province prior to this appointment. See Matsuo 2004a, 180–181.

46. As the charts indicate (Nōdomi 1982, 431–435), Ritsu priests in the Kamakura area bestowed the Dharma transmission initiation on a great number of nuns over the course of the fourteenth century.

47. Here, I refer to the land donation of two *tan* from the *bikuni* Chōzen to Saidaiji for Kōmyō Shingon performances, listed in the *Saidaiji den'en mokuroku*, Kōan 10/9. The attribution of Toyuradera to Suiko is legendary; recent research would not support this attribution. See McCallum 2009, 23–29.

48. Ushiyama has collected information about some fifty-five convents active in the Kamakura and Nanbokuchō periods. He provides a useful summary of this research in his "Chūsei no amadera nōto" (1986).

49. This particular group, "the *gonjūnyo,*" refers to the female *saikai-shū.* Ordinarily it has been assumed that such a group existed only at Hokkeji, but here the section appears directly following a list of donations from male *saikai-shū* members at Saidaiji and several sections before the portion of the document in which Hokkeji's contributions are listed. Does this mean that a female *saikai-shū* group also existed at Saidaiji? It seems unlikely that such was the case, given the degree to which Eison was concerned with separating the sexes so as to avoid the possibility of arousing suspicion among followers. The document is somewhat haphazard in its organization; the Hokkeji section, for example, contains several different subsections that all have the same title of "*hassaikai-shū, saikai-shū, or hassai-shū.*" It is likely the case, then, that donations were recorded as they were received or accounted for and not as part of a single, organized process. This first entry for the *gonjūnyo* likely belongs in the Hokkeji section but was simply recorded before the rest of the Hokkeji contributions.

50. Female *saikai-shū* members number 138 if the early list after Saidaiji is included (see footnote above), 123 if it is not.

51. This passage suggests, of course, that Hokkeji's bathhouse had already been established before the convent's association with Eison's movement. This detail thus lends additional support to the thesis forwarded in chapter 1, namely, that Hokkeji had already begun to flourish as a pilgrimage destination long before its configuration as a Ritsu convent.

52. This title *kōi* refers to the three positions of the Sōgō. It was sometimes used to refer to the second-in-command at monastic institutions, but it could also be used instead of *chōrō,* or rector.

53. Some Ritsu studies were based on texts believed to have been translated by Xuanzang.

54. Fujiwara no Atsuyori (b. 1090) is known to have gone by the name "Novice Dōin," but his dates (he is thought to have died around 1182) seem too late for inclusion in this document. This Dōin appears to have been a different person, and one based in Kamakura.

55. Although the *Nenjū gyōji* identifies Hashimoto as a post-station in Owari Province, it was actually located in Tootōmi Province.

56. Kagami post-station developed in the Kamakura period as a replacement for an earlier station, Shinohara, which had fallen into a state of decline. See "Kagami no shuku," in *Kadokawa Nihon chimei daijiten,* vol. 25: Shigaken, 213. See also "Hashimoto," in *Kadokawa Nihon chimei daijiten,* vol. 22: Shizuoka-ken, 760; "Kagami shuku," in *Nihon rekishi chimei daijiten;* and "Hashimoto shuku," in *Nihon rekishi chimei daijiten.*

57. There is also much evidence to suggest that *asobi* frequently married regional elites. In his description of the post-station at Akasaka, the author of the *Kaidōki,* a 1223 account of a trip taken between Kyoto and Kamakura, recalls the popular story of a beautiful *asobi* who won the heart of Ōe no Sadamoto (d. 1034),

the governor of Mikawa. Ōe is said to have made her his second wife. So in love with her was he that when she passed away, he renounced the world. Taking the Buddhist name Jakushō, he trained under Genshin on Mount Hiei, went to Song China, and died before making it back to Japan (*SNKBZ*, 48:30–31). Versions of this same story also appear in *Konjaku monogatarishū* (19:2) and *Uji shūi monogatari* (4:7).

58. "Bishamonten tainai ganmon," in *Shizuoka-ken shiryō*, 447–450. According to the entry "Ōgaji" in the *Nihon rekishi chimei taikei*, some scholars have raised questions about the authenticity of this *ganmon*.

59. The name "Tortoise Chrysanthemum" (Kamegiku), used by Go-Toba-in's famous *shirabyōshi* lover, is another example of this naming practice. *Shirabyōshi* were dancers who, like *asobi*, provided entertainment and sex for male clients. For more on *shirabyōshi*, see Goodwin 2007.

60. Even while the Hokkeji order may have respected *asobi* as elegant women of financial means, Eison may have viewed them in a different light. His autobiography contains an entry in which he bestows a special form of the *saikai* on "more than seventeen hundred licentious women and the like" in Hyōgo (*KJGSK* 1977, 61). His choice of the word "licentious women" (*injo*, Chns. *yinnü*), a Chinese term used to denote female prostitutes, suggests that he looked down upon women involved in sexual entertainment (see Goodwin 2007, 118). But Eison's use of the term may reflect his immersion in *vinaya* texts as much, if not more than, his everyday attitude toward *asobi*. The term is not commonly found in more general works from Japan's premodern period but is found throughout the Chinese canon, and especially in *vinaya* texts (see T. nos. 1, 26, 125, 1804, and 1813). Moreover, *vinaya* texts sometimes use the derogatory term in ambiguous ways: Ambapālī, who is explicitly identified as a *yinnü* in Chinese *vinaya* texts, is portrayed in a positive light. She shares her extreme wealth with the Buddha by offering him a meal and then bestowing upon him her mango garden. See Shinohara 2009, 19–22.

61. Harada also mentions that many of Zen nuns affiliated with the Gozan (Five Mountain) convents *(amadera gozan)* of the Muromachi period produced accessories for *kesa*, as well as altar cloths, for monks. Some also appear to have washed robes for monks, and others became known for money lending (2004, 157–158). "Monzeki" is used to refer to temples or subtemples headed by members of the royal family. The term may also be used to refer to the member of the royal family holding the chief position at such a temple. The Daijōin was a sub-temple on the grounds of Kōfukuji, and the Daijōin Monzeki, its foremost position, was to be held by a member of the royal family.

62. As mentioned earlier, this same 1280 record does mention that a few Kairyūōji monks also made donations of silk, cotton, and robes to the same campaign, a detail that works against the impression that such donations were particular to the nuns' order at Hokkeji. What should be considered here is the fact that Kairyūōji was physically adjacent to Hokkeji. Given the proximity of the two temples, the fact that Kairyūōji monks were also associated with textile-based contributions actually supports the possibility that a small-scale textile and garment industry existed at medieval Hokkeji: Kairyūōji monks, unlike those at other Saidaiji branch temples, would have had greater access to the materials produced at Hokkeji.

63. Definition of "ordination" from *Encyclopedia of Religion,* ed. Mircea Eliade, 11:97. I would like to thank an extremely helpful anonymous reader of a recent article (Meeks 2009) for drawing my attention both to the need to define ordination more carefully and to this definition in particular.

Chapter 6—Ritual Life at Medieval Hokkeji

Epigraph. Honchō seiki, Tengyō 1 (938) 8/12.

1. *Honchō seiki* is a compilation of earlier sources, mostly private court diaries, but scholars have noted the degree to which Michinori added to and edited these sources as he arranged them in his new history (*Nihonshi bunken kaidai jiten,* 993–994). That he presented the story of this nun in this particular way thus suggests that even in the twelfth century it made sense to explain the nun's punishment in terms of noncompliance rather than heterodoxy.

2. There is some evidence that male spirit mediums were still active during this period (the twelfth-century *Ryōjin hishō* mentions them, for example), but female spirit mediums appear to have been more prevalent. In fact, Yung-Hee Kim writes in her study of the *Ryōjin hishō* that male *miko* were so rare that they would have been considered "aberrant" (1994, 143, 147–148).

3. The major exception is that Ritsu nuns, like all Buddhist nuns, were not allowed to bestow full ordination status on their disciples. Although Ritsu nuns did eventually come to play an active role in the ordination of nuns once the Ritsu group began bestowing *betsuju* ordinations on nuns (as mentioned in the previous chapter's notes), women could not become full-fledged nuns without receiving ordination from priests. Male priests were also regarded as the final teachers of the Dharma: although there are many instances of women teaching other women and perhaps some lay men about the Dharma, nuns are never depicted as the teachers of male monks or priests. Although Saidaiji texts do not address this issue in an explicit or systematic way, their general stance toward female members of the order follows the spirit of the eight special rules *(aṭṭha garu-dhammā)* Śākyamuni is said to have established for nuns when he agreed to admit women into the order. These rules state the following:

> (1) nuns must receive the doctrine from monks, and they should not ridicule it or make fun of it, (2) a nun must always honour and certainly never distract a young monk, (3) nuns and monks should never stay in each other's company, since this will [in]evitably [ignite] the desires, (4) nuns themselves should check the nuns' community for bad habits (without the help, and thus without the presence, of monks), (5) nuns cannot demand justice of a monk; if a monk accuses a nun, the nuns themselves should examine the case without reviling the monk, (6) if there is any doubt among the nuns they can ask the monks for help, but only on *prajñāpāramitā;* they should not consult monks on trivial matters, (7) a nun cannot on her own follow the path; if she offends against a rule, she has to confess it at the fortnightly meeting and reject her arrogant and contemptuous attitude, (8) even when a nun has been ordained for one hundred years, she must rise up from her seat when seeing a newly ordained monk, and she must pay obeisance to him. (Heirman 2001, 286)

Neither Hokkeji nor Saidaiji texts invoke these rules, but documents surrounding the Ritsu movement indicate that the gender hierarchy in place at Ritsu institutions followed the assumption, inherent in these rules, that final authority in the *sangha* always rested with the male members of the order.

4. Hokkeji *bikuni* also had formal roles in the ordination ceremonies of their fellow nuns, part of which they performed alongside Ritsu priests. Such ceremonies are discussed in chapter 5.

5. Examples of Saidaiji manuals that contain the actual textual content of many of the chants that appear in the *Hokke metsuzaiji nenjū gyōji* include *Gongyō hōsoku* (Liturgical procedures, Saidaiji Archives, document no. 62-49, late Muromachi period) and *Sanji hōsoku* (Procedures for the three daily liturgies, Saidaiji Archives, document no. 66-9, late Muromachi period).

6. For an overview of the history of *shōmyō* in Japan, see Iwahara 1986.

7. The Zuigu Dhāraṇī is taught in the *Zuigukyō,* also known by the longer title *Pubian guangming qingjing chicheng ruyi baoyin xinwunengsheng damingwang dasuiqiu tuoluoni jing.*

8. Here, I follow Charles Muller's English translation. See *DDB,* s.v. "Yuigyōkyō."

9. The Sonshō Darani appears in the *Foding zunsheng tuoluoni jing* (Jpns. *Bucchō sonshō daranikyō*). According to this sutra, the Buddha provided this *dhāraṇī* for a prince who sought help after receiving the upsetting prediction that he would die seven days later and be reborn in the animal realm. The Buddha promised that those who heard, held in their mind, and recited this *dhāraṇī* would eradicate all of their karmic obstacles (*Daizōkyō zenkaisetsu daijiten,* 284a–b).

10. The other version is invoked in Shari Kōshiki (Chanted Lecture on the Relics) pieces by both Kakuban (1095–1143) and Gyōnen (*Bukkyō ongaku jiten,* 135b).

11. Here I refer to the *Gongyō hōsoku* and the *Sanji hōsoku* (Saidaiji Archives, document no. 66-9, late Muromachi period).

12. The second and third sets of comments in brackets are Watson's; the others are mine.

13. By the thirteenth century, several priests had postulated that the Kōmyō Shingon could be used to achieve *henjō nanshi,* or transformation into a male body (Taira 1990, 87). Although the Kōmyō Shingon does appear in the Hokkeji liturgy, we cannot assume that the chant was aimed at accomplishing *henjō nanshi* in this case. Eison had popularized the Kōmyō Shingon within his movement and used it frequently in the rituals he performed. Saidaiji monks also performed this *mantra* frequently and included it in their liturgies. The *mantra* was regarded as having many merits, only one of which was *henjō nanshi.* The inclusion of Kōmyō Shingon in the *Hokke metsuzaiji nenjū gyōji* thus reflects Hokkeji's affiliation with Saidaiji but offers no clear evidence that Hokkeji nuns were interested in achieving *henjō nanshi.*

14. The text of the full-length *Jiutiao xizhang* was standardized rather early. It appears in Zhiyi's (538–597) *Fahua chanfa.* The translation above is based on the first few stanzas of Zhiyi's *Jiutiao xizhang* (T. no. 2417, 269a02–a11). There is ample evidence to suggest that medieval Japanese renditions of the *shakujō* chants were based on this same text. We see, for example, in the early-Kamakura-period *Taima mandara kōshiki* an abbreviated *shakujō* that does not include all nine sections. This

text is simply an abridgement of Zhiyi's original (T. no. 2622, 381b13–20). As stated earlier, the textual content of the chant was taken from the *Flower Ornament Sutra in Eighty Fascicles (Dafangguangfo huayan jing).* Zhiyi's contribution was to designate passages from this text as the *Jiutiao xizhang* chant.

15. Here, I follow D. Lusthaus's translation of *sannōhen.*

16. A relevant discussion took place on the PMJS (Premodern Japanese Studies) listserv a number of years ago. See the archives of the PMJS for June 2000 and March 2001 at http://www.meijigakuin.ac.jp/~pmjs/.

17. For more on *ajikan* practice, see Chidō's (fl. late 13th c.) *Dreams of Buddhism (Buppō yume monogatari),* trans. Bodiford 1999, 242–243; Payne 1998; and Stone 2006. As Stone explains, historical examples of *ajikan,* or "A-syllable contemplation," are rare. Although numerous Heian-period ritual manuals and commentaries describe *ajikan* as involving complex breathing and visualization practices, at least several Kamakura-period priests promoted it as a simple practice and claimed that it was even "easier" than chanting the *nenbutsu* (Stone 2006, esp. 168–169, 178).

18. Nijō's phrasing is "*kyō nado yomite*" (*TG,* 104), the "*nado*" likely referring to the other types of chants we see in the Hokkeji liturgies: *dhāraṇī, wasan,* and other incantations, such as the Relics Respects. See *TG,* 40–41, 99, 104; trans. Brazell 1973, 40–41, 103, 108.

19. *TG,* 41; trans. Brazell 1973, 41. (I do not follow Brazell's translation here.)

20. Here, I follow Abé Ryūichi's translation of "Shuni-e." For a thorough discussion of the rite, see Abé 1999, 168–176.

21. At Tōdaiji, the Shuni-e came to be a two-week event, making it much longer than the three-day version listed in Hokkeji's *Nenjū gyōji.* Still, studies of the Shuni-e have indicated that Tōdaiji monks traditionally set aside several weeks to prepare ritual implements used in the ceremony: they made paper flowers by hand, constructed large torches, prepared banners and costumes, practiced chants and choreography, and so on. It is likely that many of Hokkeji's ceremonies, especially those to be performed over a period of several days or a week, also would have required extensive preparation.

22. It should be noted, however, that the oldest surviving ritual calendar of Daianji dates to the year 1448, which is some 144 years later than the *Hokke metsuzaiji nenjū gyōji.* It is possible that this calendar was scaled down as a result of difficult financial times. See Hosokawa 1994, 77–84.

23. For a detailed treatment of ceremonies and their place in the careers of scholar-priests, see Sangō 2007.

24. Kōfukuji hired dancers and musicians from specific *za.* See Nagamura 2001b.

25. The earliest known *kōshiki,* the Nijūgo Zanmai-shiki (Meditation Rite for Twenty-Five), is attributed to Genshin (942–1017). Guelberg has translated the entire text (1999, 101–176). According to many scholars, it was the Sanron-school priest Yōkan who established a standard model for the *kōshiki* genre. His Ōjō Kōshiki (Chanted Lecture on Birth in the Pure Land) set the tone—and established the basic structure—for later *kōshiki* (36). The genre flourished in the Kamakura period, when figures like Jien, Jōkei, and Myōe produced new *kōshiki* texts. Although few new *kōshiki* texts were written after the Kamakura period, clerics and laypeople

alike continued to perform them throughout the Edo period, and they are still performed in some temples today. *Kōshiki* services appear to have been rooted in the regular meetings of lecture confraternities *(kōe)*. The first known confraternity of this sort was formed among twenty-five disciples of Tendai priest Ryōgen (912–985). In 986, they created the Meditation Assembly of Twenty-Five (Nijūgo Zanmai-e). They vowed both to perform monthly chanted lectures in honor of Amida Nyorai (Amitābha Buddha) and to offer each other regular spiritual assistance. During the Heian period, lecture confraternities were often expected to provide deathbed care for their members. Given the gravity of such responsibilities, confraternities governed their membership with great care (Guelberg 2006, esp. 30–31; Ford 2006, 77–78).

26. Laypeople sometimes formed their own lecture confraternities and performed *kōshiki* in their homes as well. One such example is found in the *Heikoki* of Taira no Tsunetaka. Additional examples can be found in courtier diaries (Guelberg 2006, 32–33; *Heikoki*, Ninji 1 [1240] 1/10).

27. Most scholars date the *Genpei jōsuiki* to the late Kamakura or early Nanbokuchō period.

28. Although there is some variation, *kōshiki* are typically divided into five *dan,* or sections. When performed, these *dan* were typically undertaken in order, with a *hyōbyaku* piece (stating the ritual intention) opening the service and with short verses (*kada,* Chns. *qietuo,* Skt. *gāthā*) separating each *dan*. These verses were chanted in *onyomi,* or Chinese pronunciation, but the *dan* were chanted in *kundoku* style. Typically, the fifth *dan* functioned as an *ekō,* but a separate *ekō* was sometimes added to the end of the ceremony as well.

29. Translation taken from Steven G. Nelson, "Buddhist Music in Japan: Music 139A," course reader for the Department of Music, University of California, Berkeley, 2004. Reprinted with Nelson's permission.

30. Eison wrote *kōshiki* for Prince Shōtoku and Mañjuśrī. The Kannon *kōshiki* mentioned here probably refers to the one composed by Jōkei, while the chanted lectures on the arhats and on Ānanda are likely those of Myōe (See the *Kōshiki Dētabēsu*).

31. As Katsuura notes, Faxian specifies that in the case of offerings made to *stupas* of Śāriputra, Maudgalyāyana, and Mahākāśyapa, priests making the offerings hired operatic performers to act out the scenes in which these disciples came to Śākyamuni seeking initiation into the order (2008, 104–106). It seems likely that in the case of nuns making offerings to Ānanda, performers may have acted out the scene in which Ānanda intercedes on behalf of Śākyamuni's foster mother and aunt, Mahāprajāpatī Gautamī, when she seeks entrance into the Buddhist order.

32. The non-Pāli *vinaya* texts containing the story of Ānanda intervening on Mahāprajāpatī's behalf when she seeks entrance into the *sangha* include the *Mahīśāsaka vinaya* (T. no. 1421), the *Mahāsāṃghika vinaya* (T. no. 1425), the *Dharmagipta vinaya* (T. no. 1428), the *Sarvāstivāda vinaya* (T. no. 1435), the *Mūlasarvāstivāda vinaya* (T. no. 1451), and the *Pinimu jing* (T. no. 1463). Heirman has analyzed the narrative as it appears in two other texts as well: the *Vinaya of the Mahāsāṃghika-Lokottaravādins* and the *Sutra on Gautamī* (2001, 278–281). For a discussion of the Pāli sources, see Ohnuma 2006, esp. 863.

33. Ohnuma (2006) argues that this issue of the Buddha's debt to Mahāprajāpātī has been overlooked in past scholarship and deserves greater attention. The four fruits, which describe progress toward arhathood, are stream-enterer, once-returner, non-returner, and arhat (*DDB,* s.v. "Shikō shika").

34. Katsuura suggests that the new dating scheme offered here—and incidentally the same schedule followed by Hokkeji's *Nenjū gyōji*—may have been inspired by the fact that the eighth day of the eighth month was regarded as a day significant in the Buddha's own life. (It was the day he is said to have been born, the day he is said to have turned the Wheel of the Dharma, and the day he is said to have entered nirvana.) As for the eighth day of the second month, Katsuura demonstrates that this day was viewed as a day associated with the eight pure precepts (2008, 109).

35. Katsuura suggests that this misattribution may have been the result of Myōe's having copied the *kōshiki* out as a gift for a patron or patrons. She further speculates that Myōe might have copied the text out for Shumeimon-in (1182–1264), who was one of his most visible patrons (2008, 120).

36. For English scholarship on the Anan Kōshiki, see Arai 2000, 2008.

37. I.e., the six days associated with the *hassaikai:* the eighth, fourteenth, fifteenth, twenty-third, twenty-ninth, and thirtieth.

38. The Buddha's words to Gautamī are rendered a bit differently in the *Dafangbian baoen jing* as it appears in the Taishō canon (T. no. 156, 154b03–154b12).

39. "Raun" is another common transliteration of Rāhula.

40. For more on Yuishin, see Namai 2004, esp. 28.

41. Some scriptures, such as the *Fo benxingji jing* (Skt. *Abhiniṣkramaṇa-sūtra*) give the age of fifteen, but other scriptures, such as the *Weiceng youyinyuan jing,* indicate that Rāhula was nine years old at the time of his entrance into the order. See Sekiguchi 1998, 3.

42. Sekiguchi's study provides the Tōshōdaiji version of the text.

43. Incidentally, the term *gigaku* (Chns. *jile*) is also used in Faxian's description of the rites carried out by priests making offerings to the stupas of Śāriputra, Maudgalyāyana, and Mahākāśyapa. According to Faxian, these monks had *jile ren* (musicians or musical performers) act out the scenes in which these disciples went to the Buddha and asked for initiation into the order. The use of the term *gigaku* here suggests, then, that rites offered in Kōmyō's honor at Hokkeji may have involved some type of dramatic reenactment using music.

44. The *Nenjū gyōji* calls for *gigaku,* but according to scholars of Japanese music, *gigaku* was not performed as late as the fifteenth century. It is likely that *gagaku* was performed instead. See Nelson 2008a, 2008b.

45. For definitions of "priest," see *Encyclopedia of Religion,* 2nd ed., s.v. "Priesthood; An Overview," and *Oxford English Dictionary Online,* 2nd ed., draft revision, March 2008.

46. Borgen provides a more thorough discussion of these documents (2007, 39–42, esp. 34–35).

47. The Nakahara family was known for its special expertise in the "Myōgyōdō," one of the four paths of study under the university program of the *ritsuryō* legal codes.

48. Mantokuji is best known as a "divorce temple" *(enkiridera),* a temple that helped women negotiate legal separation from their husbands in return for service to the convent. As Wright points out, Mantokuji was one of only two officially recognized divorce temples operative in the Edo period. The other was Tōkeiji (2002, 247).

Chapter 7—Representations of Women and Gender in Ritsu Literature

1. Hosokawa (1989b) criticizes Matsuo for describing salvation as something that men performed on behalf of women *(nyonin kyūsai o okonau)* without looking at women's salvation from the other side. While Hosokawa does, in his own work, consider the "women's side," his research still works from the assumption that women were dependent upon priests for salvation. To be fair, though, most of Hosokawa's work on Hokkeji is now twenty years old. Feminist and other scholars of Buddhism within Japan critiqued, in the 1990s, much of his work on the convent, their main contention being that he did not take the agency of women into account. Hosokawa has acknowledged these critiques, and today he admits that the approach he took to Hokkeji in the late 1980s is not the approach he would take today (personal conversation with Hosokawa, June 19, 2007). Unfortunately, however, he has since moved on to other scholarship and has not revised in print his views of Hokkeji. As a result, work on Hokkeji in Japanese still tends to reflect the biases of his older work. See Abe 1991.

2. For a discussion of the important role that female *miko* played in Eison's upbringing and in his religious practice, see Abé 2003.

3. Although the earliest surviving versions of the *Kōshō Bosatsu gyōjitsu nenpu* and the *Kōshō Bosatsu gokyōkai chōmonshū* date from the seventeenth century, Japanese scholars consider them to be generally reliable. For more on the biography edited by Jikō, see Kōbayashi 1977.

4. For the ten vices of women, see the *Jingxin jieguan fa,* 824a. That Daoxuan appears in Hokkeji's calendary ritual guide, the *Hokke metsuzaiji nenjū gyōji,* suggests that Hokkeji nuns may have venerated him. The convent also appears to have sponsored ritual lectures on his *vinaya* commentaries.

Mujū Ichien, the same Buddhist priest who speaks fondly of the nun Shinnyo, provides a summary of Daoxuan's condemnation of women in his own *Tsuma kagami* (Mirror for women). Mujū writes, "Serious instances of the sins of women, among the unregenerate who are all deluded, are cited in the sacred scriptures and commentaries." But because women have such an "abundance" of severe faults, he concludes, "there is no time to discuss these sins in detail." Even after enumerating the many vices of women, however, Mujū retreats with the admission that "there are also among women many instances of deep compassion and religious aspiration." His narrative then recounts stories of virtuous women from the Buddhist sutras: the Lady Vaidehi of the *Sutra of Meditation on the Buddha of Immeasurable Life* (*Guan wuliangshou Fojing,* also *Guan wuliangshou jing*) and the daughter of the *Lotus Sutra*'s dragon king. The secret to gaining redemption as a woman, Mujū explains, is to recognize "the great burden of sin which women bear" and to abandon worldly pursuits in favor of the practice of Buddhism (trans. Morrell 1980, 67–69).

Mujū's treatment of women suggests that Daoxuan's understanding of women both as temptresses and as spiritually and physically impure had gained a certain degree of currency by Eison's time. His attention to figures like Lady Vaidehi and the daughter of the dragon king, as well as instructions explaining how women can overcome their vices, however, suggest that Mujū did understand women as ultimately redeemable through Buddhism, an idea that also runs through the literature of Eison and his disciples.

5. Alan Sponberg notes the "multiplicity" of opinions in early Indian Buddhist literature regarding the relationship between women and Buddhism (1995, 3). He argues that at least four distinct attitudes toward women emerge in such literature: (1) "soteriological inclusiveness," (2) "institutional androcentrism," (3) "ascetic misogyny," and (4) "soteriological androgyny." He suggests that the fourth—soteriological androgyny—represents "in part, a later attempt to resolve the inconsistency and tension among the first three" (8). All four of these voices also appear in the literature of Saidaiji priests. This first voice, that of Eison quoting the *Dazhidu lun,* represents the third category, ascetic misogyny, but as we will see below, Saidaiji priests also put forth views that fit into the other three categories.

6. Although certain contemporary constructivist Buddhist "theological" moves have argued that the teaching of emptiness undercuts social hierarchy, there is very little historical evidence that discourse on nonduality was ever successfully deployed for socially egalitarian ends. As these examples from Jishin and Enkyō suggest, nonduality discourse does not necessarily (and indeed does not usually) translate into the construction of real egalitarian institutions. For examples of contemporary authors who argue for the egalitarianism "inherent" in nonduality discourse, see Schuster 1981, esp. 54–55; Gross 1993, esp. 71; and Paul 1985, esp. 170. Jan Nattier discusses this problem in an insightful article entitled "Gender and Enlightenment: Sexual Transformation in Mahāyāna Sūtras," forthcoming in the *Journal of the International Association of Buddhist Studies.*

7. The excerpt cited is based on a passage in the *Sutra on the Final Nirvana of Śākyamuni* (*Da banniepan jing,* T. no. 374, 422b). Some sentences are cited character-for-character, but the version from Eison's sermon does alter and add to the text in several places. Eison also refers to this same passage in his commentary *Bosatsu kaihon shūyō bugyō monjū* (64a15–b3).

8. The *Tennyoshingyō* refers to the *Foshuo zhuan nushen jing* (T. no. 564; see also T. nos. 562–563 and 565–566). This text teaches that there is "no male or female aspect" and describes the appearance of male and female attributes as mirages created by magicians. It speaks of emptiness at length, focusing especially on the emptiness of maleness and femaleness. If there are women who want to rid themselves of their female bodies and acquire male bodies, the text explains at one point, they need only to give rise to the mind of enlightenment, and then they will realize that there is no such thing as a male body or a female body (920b–c).

9. The ten practices to be carried out in honor of texts include copying the Mahāyāna scriptures, holding offering services *(kuyō)* in their honor, blessing others with them, auditing the sermons of others, reading them fervently on one's own, grasping them, intoning them, teaching them widely for the benefit of others, pondering them carefully on one's own, and cultivating them through repeated

practice (*Bukkyōgo daijiten,* 660d). Sōji's message here is that Hokkeji nuns should engage the *Sutra on Transforming the Female Body* in all ten of these ways.

10. The passage Sōji quotes is from the *Jinguangming zuishengwang jing* (Jpns. *Konkōmyō saishōōkyō,* Skt. *Suvarna-prabhāsa-uttama-sūtra,* Golden light sutra of the most victorious kings), T. no. 665, 413b8–9.

11. Although it cannot be known for certain that Sōji (d. 1312) and Enkyō, the nun who recorded *Hokke metsuzaiji engi* in the year 1304, knew each other personally, they were contemporaries. And given Sōji's involvement in the affairs of Hokkeji and other convents, it is difficult to imagine that the two did not know each other. Moreover, we can safely assume that the Hokkeji nun Enkyō was aware of Sōji's preface to the *Tennyoshingyō,* since he had donated this particular copy of the sutra to Hokkeji. Enkyō's own writing reveals her role as a scholar and archivist. Her 1304 *Hokke metsuzaiji engi* shows that she was reading widely, for she cites and interprets passages from a variety of sources. The *Hokke metsuzaiji engi* not only conveys a high level of erudition, it also confirms that Enkyō had access to an extensive range of literary collections. Given her exposure to the *engi* (karmic origin stories) and *nikki* (diaries) of other temples (monasteries), as well as to state histories like the *Shoku Nihongi,* it is safe to assume that Enkyō would have been aware of—and indeed that she would have had access to—the copy of the *Tennyoshingyō* that Sōji had donated to Hokkeji.

12. Rokkannon, or the Six Manifestations of Avalokiteśvara, include: (1) Shō (Sacred) Kannon; (2) Senju (Thousand-Armed) Kannon; (3) Mezu (Horse-Headed; Skt. Hayagrīva) Kannon; (4) Jūichimen (Eleven-Faced) Kannon; (5) Jundei Kannon (Skt. Cundī or Candī); (6) Nyorin Kannon (Skt. Cintāmaṇi-cakra). Enkyō cites the *Shichidaiji junreiki* here, but this entry does not match any found in surviving copies of the *Shichidaiji junreiki.* As related in chapter 1, the 1191 *Kenkyū gojunreiki* contains a side narrative in which a Gandhāran king, praying that he can worship a living manifestation of Kannon, is told to worship Kōmyō. That story is further linked to the Eleven-Faced Kannon image in an entry from the 1216 *Shoji konryū.* See chapter 1 for more details.

13. For more about *honji/suijaku* and its prevalence in medieval Japan, see Kuroda T. 1999 and Teeuwen and Rambelli 2003. I am grateful to Stephen Bokenkamp for suggesting this alternative translation of *suijaku.*

14. Although I have attributed the *Ama Shinnyo ganmon* to Shinnyo here, Japanese scholars have been unable to determine whether the text is written in Shinnyo's own hand. It is possible, of course, that the *ganmon* itself was composed by a *ganmon* scribe on Shinnyo's behalf. Recent scholarship on *ganmon* indicates that many of these documents were written by specialists trained in Chinese literature. See Yamamoto 2006, esp. 1129–1141. Given the particularities of Shinnyo's case, however (as mentioned in chapter 7, she is known to have added her own *katen* to the difficult *Yogacāra-bhūmi-śāstra*), it hardly seems beyond the realm of possibility that she authored the *ganmon* text herself.

15. There is some evidence that the deification of Queen-Consort Hashihito had occurred within some circles of popular Shōtoku worship in the years preceding Shinnyo's activity at Chūgūji. In particular, a number of prophetic and other apocryphal texts identifying Shōtoku's mother and favored consort, Kashiwade Bunin, as

manifestations of Amida and his attendant bodhisattva Seishi, respectively, may have emerged as early as the mid-eleventh century. But these narratives, which worked to construct a configuration in which Shōtoku (Kannon), his mother (Amida), and his consort (Seishi) were identified with the Amida triad (Amida flanked by attendant bodhisattvas Kannon and Seishi), do not appear in standard literary collections like the ones mentioned above. For more, see Meeks 2007, 369–370.

16. Eison is said to have offered many performances of the Monju Kuyō (Offerings for the Bodhisattva Mañjuśrī)—one of the *kuyō* he is most famous for popularizing—in an effort to provide his mother with a powerful form of posthumous aid. See *KJGSK* 1999, 122. For more on the Mañjuśrī cult within Eison's movement, see Quinter 2006.

17. Reiko Ohnuma's recent study (2006) suggests that this same notion—that children owe a great debt to their mothers—plays a key role in the story of the Buddha's finally agreeing to let Mahāprajāpatī and her disciples enter the order. It is only after Ānanda reminds Śākyamuni of the great debt he owes to the woman who raised him and loved him like a mother that he agrees to the creation of a nuns' order. In this sense, the notion that one can repay debts owed to one's mother by supporting the nuns' order is not an East Asian concept but one that can be traced back to early Indian precedents as well.

18. It is not clear why exactly Japanese priests writing in the premodern period tended to show more concern about saving their mothers than about saving their fathers. The trend is likely rooted in the perception that women face greater obstacles on the Buddhist path (and thus need more help when it comes to salvation), but it is also possible the family structures of this period tended to yield mother-son relations that were emotionally closer than father-son relations. In the early versions of the *Yulanpen jing*, the sin that lands Mulian's mother in hell is her stinginess: she fails to make offerings to the *sangha* when Mulian is away and asks her to do so. Stinginess, of course, was one of the many vices associated with women in Buddhist texts that warned against men's involvement with the members of the female sex. (Some of the others—jealousy, deceit, flattery, and so forth—are listed above in the excerpt from one of Eison's commentaries.) It is likely that these "vices of women" were conflated with the five obstacles and fell under the larger and more general umbrella of the "heavy karmic burdens" associated with women. In the *Tennyoshingyō* preface cited above, for example, Sōji simply invokes the "heavy karmic burdens" of women. These burdens, which are not described in detail, point to a larger set of well-entrenched doctrinal assumptions about the "sinful" *(zaigōteki)* state of women. (See, for example, Taira 1990.) It is likely that priests were more concerned about saving their mothers than their fathers simply because their mothers were understood as facing these extra karmic burdens associated with women. Recent scholarship has suggested that other factors likely complicated the picture as well. Hank Glassman, for example, argues that by the Kamakura period, "the salvation of mothers as represented in popular [Japanese] hagiography was firmly linked to the idea of the fall of the mother due to emotional attachment to her child" (2001, 16). For more on priests and their mothers in other parts of the Buddhist world, see Spiro 1984, Teiser 1988, and Cole 1998.

19. Saichō (767–822) mentions that some monks left their training at Mount Hiei in order to care for their mothers. See "Tendai Hokkeshū nenbun tokudo gakushō myōshō," in *Dengyō daishi zenshū,* 1:250, 252 (qtd. in Groner 2002a, 425n67). For a detailed study of the trope of motherhood in Saidaiji texts, see Nōdomi 1977 and Groner 2002a, 212–213, 385n4. It is worth noting that Groner describes Ryōgen and Genshin as having been concerned primarily with caring for their mothers in their old age, thereby suggesting that the concern over mothers in early Japanese monastic literature may have been based not only in the desire to follow representations of mother-son relations that emerge in Chinese monastic texts but also in the actual social conditions of family life in tenth-century Japan. For more on mothers as sacred figures in Japanese culture, see Nakamura 1997, 68–84.

20. See also *KJGSK* 1999, 103–104. David Quinter offers an insightful treatment of this passage in his PhD dissertation (2006, 56–59).

21. This passage was well-known in East Asian circles and was often cited even in outside discussions of the twentieth minor bodhisattva precept. Daoshi quotes the same passage, for example, in his *Fayuan zhulin* (780b24–27).

22. Eison also refers to this idea in his commentary *Bosatsu kaihon shūyō bugyō monjū* (76a3–9).

23. Matsuo, for example, writes that the priests of Eison's day considered all women to be impure (2001, 372; 1989, 98–99).

24. According to the *Blood Bowl Sutra,* it is the physiological impurity of women that damns them to suffer in a special hell in which women are forced to swim in pools of their own defiling substances.

25. Although some scholars have suggested that the *Ketsubonkyō* may have been imported to Japan as early as the late thirteenth century, the earliest clear reference to the sutra in Japanese literature is from a document dated to the year 1429 (Matsuoka 1998).

26. Mujū lists seven "grave vices of women," while Daoxuan counts ten. See *Jingxin jieguan fa,* 824.

27. English translations from *DDB,* s.v. "Six Perfections."

28. This same narrative is also mentioned in the *Dazhidu lun,* 542c4–13.

29. Chōken's relationship to Kūnyo, the nun who trained Jizen, Hokkeji's first Kamakura-period rector, is discussed in chapter 2.

30. Here, Chōken refers to a well-known phrase from the *Xiaojing* in which it is taught that the hair and skin of one's body is received from one's mother and father. The point here is that in the case of Buddhas manifesting themselves, fathers have no role and thus do not transmit skin or hair to the manifestation bodies of Buddhas.

31. The phrase "All women are [or become] the true mothers of all the Buddhas of the triple world" appears to be a quotation of the following line from the *Tennyo jōbutsukyō:* "All women's bodies are [or become] the mothers of the Buddhas of the triple world." For the *Tennyo jōbutsukyō* text, see Nishiguchi 2002b. The *Tennyo jōbutsukyō* is an apocryphal text likely produced in China or Japan. It was known in Japan by the late ninth century (40b). The *Tennyo jōbutsukyō* is translated and treated in greater depth in the epilogue.

32. The text reads "Jō-Amidabutsu," but I believe the character "Jō" was a mistake for "Shū" and that this line refers to "Shū-Amidabutsu," who is discussed in the Gyōgu narrative. There are no other references to "Jō-Amidabutsu" in the text, so the sudden appearance is likely a mistake.

33. *Kien* can also be translated as "opportunities for encountering the Dharma." I chose this more succinct translation when the same phrase occurred in *Ama Shinnyo ganmon,* 83a.

34. Hashihito is said to have given birth to Prince Umayado, as well as to three other royal princes. Kōmyō was the mother of the female sovereign Kōken-Shōtoku (718–770).

35. The Pure Land of Hashihito is described at great length in the *engi,* and Chūgūji is explained as an earthly manifestation of this Pure Land, as a Pure Land in the samsaric world.

36. Shinnyo was treated more generously by Saidaiji literature once she had receded further into the past and gained mythic stature. The later popularity of the Shinnyo narrative within the Saidaiji tradition is perhaps best illustrated by its inclusion in a handwritten Sengoku-period booklet found in the archives of Saidaiji and included in the Saidaiji monjo collection. The booklet, which is without title, is dated to the Daiei years (1521–1528). Its opening page explains that there are two theories regarding the importation of Buddhism to Japan, a statement that sets the tone for a brief history of Japanese Buddhism. The booklet is over one hundred pages in length and is written almost in the style of *setsuwa,* insofar as it refers to various anecdotes about the history of Buddhism in Japan, various sovereigns, the revival of the temple Hōryūji, the story of the sacred mountain Shigi-san, and the revival of Chūgūji. As Nishiguchi Junko has explained, the writing has a certain rhythm to it, suggesting that it was most likely used for oral storytelling. The language is particularly vernacular, and the author's Chinese character choices reveal not a concern with written presentation but rather a kind of shorthand useful for reading aloud (conversation with Nishiguchi Junko, July 2002; see *Saidaiji monjo,* box 38, no. 6, archives of Saidaiji temple, Nara, Japan).

A full thirty pages is devoted to the story of Chūgūji. The *bikuni* Shinnyo is mentioned in the second line of the narrative, and she remains the focus of the entire story. For the most part, the storyline follows that of the Shinnyo narratives we saw above. This story, however, starts earlier, providing the audience with Shinnyo's complete life story, including the story of her father, the scholar-priest Shōen, who died in a state of poverty, leaving his daughters with a book they were to use for income by charging priests who wanted to copy its contents. It also tells of Shinnyo's interest in Eison's revival movement, of her decision to take the precepts, of her teacher Kakujō's initial refusal to grant her the precepts, of her prayers that he would receive a revelation telling him to allow her to take the precepts, and then of his eventual vision, which led to his decision to give Shinnyo the precepts. The narrative also includes the story of the priest Kyōen's transformation into a woman and his taking of the nuns' precepts. It then proceeds to include many of the episodes we have seen in other narratives of Shinnyo's life: her desire to know the death date of Shōtoku's mother, her continuous prayers leading up to a vision in which she learns of the *Tenjukoku mandara,* the theft at Hōryūji's treasury and her discovery of the mandala, her revival of Chūgūji, and finally, her *kuyō* for Hashihito.

The text also claims that Shinnyo served as rector for three convents: Hokkeji, Shōbōji, and Chūgūji. Shinnyo is clearly the central focus of this narrative: the story begins and ends with her. But the narrative is also a Saidaiji one; as such, it incorporates the story of Eison's precepts revival and suggests that Eison and his movement provided certain stimuli for Shinnyo and her miraculous revival of Chūgūji. What is so remarkable about the narrative included in this Sengoku-period Saidaiji booklet, however, is that Shinnyo's story is never fully subordinated to that of Eison. She is the main character throughout, and the text clearly assumes that its audience is interested in hearing about Shinnyo herself. If this Saidaiji booklet was indeed used for oral storytelling, then Shinnyo's prominent role in the booklet is particularly worth our attention. Many of the Shinnyo episodes that appear in this booklet also appear in the *Shōyoshō*, which had been compiled by the year 1547 (*Bukkyō kaisetsu daijiten*, 5:389d–390a), and in the thirteenth-century *Shōtoku Taishi denki*.

37. For English translations, see Stevenson 1999.

38. "Kōmyō-kō" likely refers to the Chanted Lecture on the Favorable Birth of Our Founder [Queen-Consort Kōmyō] (Hongan Ontsuizen Ōjō-kō), a part of the festivities held for seven days at Hokkeji in honor of Kōmyō's death, from the seventh day of the sixth month. See *Nenjū gyōji*, 87a.

39. It is worth noting here that both Enkyō and Shinnyo seem to embrace the notion that their convents are institutions built exclusively for women. In her *ganmon*, for example, Shinnyo notes that Chūgūji was restored not just as a temple but specifically as a convent for women: "The teachings and actions of the good friends [*zenshiki*] and *bikuni* [fully ordained nuns] of our school will increasingly prosper." She thus constructs Chūgūji as a religious center designated for women in particular, just as Enkyō, in her origin story for Hokkeji, highlights the fact that Hokkeji was built for women and did not allow men to be on its premises (see *HMJE*, 142a). Perhaps this textual construction of the convent as the site of an all-female community where men are not given positions of authority can be read as a partial response to Saidaiji's male-dominated administrative framework.

40. Here, Enkyō is following Jitsuei's 1191 *Kenkyū gojunreiki* (142), where the same argument is made. See chapter 1.

41. Similar passages are found in Jitsuei's 1191 *Kenkyū gojunreiki* (142) and in the *Sanbōe* (3.13, trans. Kamens 1988, 291–294). In this sense, Enkyō is emphasizing earlier narratives, already in circulation, about the autonomy of women at Hokkeji.

42. Portions of this section on Chūgūji literature were previously published as part of a longer study (Meeks 2007).

43. The Kyōen narrative appears in the following sources (in addition to *Shōyoshō*): *Ritsuen sōbōden* (chap. 11, Jichihan's biography), the *Shōdai senzai denki* (365–367), and the 1702 *Honchō kōsōden* (59). See Hosokawa 1987, 107–108.

44. The story may possibly play upon the famous scene in the *Vimalakīrti sūtra* in which Śāriputra rebukes a goddess, asking her, "Why don't you change out of this female body?" She then uses her powers to transform Śāriputra's male body into a female body and asks him the same question. Baffled, Śāriputra admits that the form of his female body both exists and does not exist. Having clarified the fundamental

emptiness of gender distinctions, the goddess reinstates Śāriputra to his masculine form. Trans. Watson 1997, 90–92. But while the "goddess" chapter of the *Vimalakīrti* serves to illustrate the empty and constructed nature of gender distinctions, Kyōen's transformation suggests, in contrast, that gender distinctions are of such vital import that proper ordinations cannot be carried out without them.

45. Yōmei Tennō reigned from 585 through 587.

46. The *kei,* or *uchiishi,* is a traditional Chinese gong used in the performance of liturgy.

47. The rhetoric of decline that emerges in these documents contains references to specific lines from classical Chinese poetry. In particular, the line "the altar is infested by lizards and frogs, and stags and flying squirrels fight in the rock garden" is taken directly, character-for-character, from *Rhapsody on the Ruined City (Wucheng fu),* a rhapsody composed by Bao Zhao (aka Bao Mingyuan, ca. 414–466) during the Six Dynasties period. In these verses, Bao Zhao laments the decline of the ancient Guangling (near modern Yangzhou), a city that had flourished during the Han Dynasty. The rhapsody begins with a description of the city's glorious and lavish past, of the riches and crowds and grand architecture that once filled its streets. It then moves on to describe in painful detail the extreme nature of its currently neglected state. It is from these lines that Shinnyo borrows. (The English translation of this rhapsody's title is David Knechtges's. Knechtges provides lengthy biographical notes on Bao Zhao [1987, 2:354–355].) Shinnyo borrows another line from Bo Juyi's *Li gong gao,* a well-known poem that mourns the decay of the palace that Yang Gui Fei and the Tang emperor Xuan Zong had enjoyed together as lovers. She also uses this line from Bo Juyi: *kaki ni i ari/kawara ni matsu ari.* These phrases, which basically mean that moss has grown on the walls (or fences, depending on how one takes *kaki*) and that overgrowth has sprouted up between the tiles, appear in a number of other Kamakura-period texts, including the *Heike monogatari* and the *Genpei jōsuiki.* Kairyūōji monks also use this imagery in a 1243 petition titled "Nanto Kairyūōji sōtō kinshin" (in *YKT,* 5:123). Although these Kamakura works include only brief references to Chinese verses on the decay and neglect of great cities and palaces, they work to achieve the same emotional effect. At the end of the third section of the *Wucheng fu,* for example, Bao Zhao says that in witnessing the severe neglect of the once glorious city of Guangling, "The heart is pained and broken" (trans. Knechtges 1987). Nara revivalist literature also emphasizes how the sight of a ruined city arouses great sadness; indeed, it is probably fair to say that the purpose of these references is to express this very sentiment. Emotional appeals—inevitably ones using characters for "tears" or "to cry"—are made in each work once the neglect of the temple has been described. Shinnyo tells us in the *Ama Shinnyo ganmon* that when she saw the state of neglect at Chūgūji, she cried as she recalled the temple's former days of glory. The Kairyūōji monks, in their petition, invoke tears, too, suggesting that the dew covering the overgrowth in the temple garden consisted of heaven's tears.

The *Hokke metsuzaiji engi* describes the dilapidated state of Hokkeji at the beginning of its revival is in similar terms. Enkyō writes: "There were only dilapidated remains here and there, and the lecture hall [*kōdō*] alone barely remained. Because the halls had fallen into destruction like this, the spring rain fell upon the Buddhist statues. There was only one person living in the temple, and she turned the door over to the autumn wind. The garden is an exquisite place, [but] that place has become the dwelling place of oxen and horses. Can people who look at this [situation] not be moved to tears?" (142a–b, 143a).

48. Eison identifies the three nuns with the convent Toyuradera.

49. In Hōnen's commentary on the *Guan wuliangshou jing,* for example, he cites the five obstacles and the thrice following as justification for the exclusion of women from certain temples and sacred places. *Hōnen Shōnin zenshū,* 77.

Epilogue

1. Indeed, even the relatively recent reference work for the Taishō canon, *Daizōkyō zenkaisetsu daijiten,* misidentifies *Tennyo jōbutsukyō* as another name for the *Tennyoshingyō.* See *Tennyoshingyō,* 170a.

2. Translated from the *katsuji* provided by Nishiguchi (2002b, 39).

3. The same entry goes on to explain that, as a part of her ordination ceremony, this princess offers two sutras she had copied out in her own hand: the *Amidakyō* and the *Tennyo jōbutsukyō.*

4. Although neither of these paintings explicitly identifies itself as having been commissioned or used by Ritsu priests, Haraguchi makes a compelling argument in favor of their association with the Ritsu group. In the case of the Honpōji scrolls, scenes from other sections depict priests performing charity work, something for which Ritsu priests were well-known. The scrolls also depict scenes in which fully ordained nuns with shaved heads are shown among the members of the order. These scenes, Haraguchi argues, show a fourfold division of the *sangha,* something with which the Ritsu order, more so than any other group, was specifically concerned. The Hōnkōji scrolls, on the other hand, might be identified with the Ritsu group since Hōnkōji was itself a Ritsu temple during the late Kamakura and early Muromachi periods, when the scrolls were produced. See Haraguchi 2009, esp. pp. 94–95. It is likely that the visual interpretation offered here was based on Chinese models, for as Meech-Pekarik has explained, Chinese and very early Japanese depictions of the Devadatta chapter followed a standard iconography in which the dragon girl's rebirth into male form was portrayed in a rather explicit manner (1976, 251–253).

5. Soymié (1965) gives the earliest dates (1250–1350). Takemi (1981) dates the importation of the sutra to the Muromachi period, as does Kōdate Naomi (1988, 1991, 1992–1993). Katsuura also provides a succinct summary of issues relevant to *Ketsubonkyō* studies (2003, 85–89).

6. Katsuura argues that Tendai and Shūgendō priests were among the first to popularize the text (2003, 88). Tokieda (2007) says that there was likely some connection between the Dōnokuchi site in Sendai and a nearby Tendai temple, but he says that no Shūgendō influence is readily visible (2007, 36).

Character Glossary

Aizen-ō Daiju 愛染王大呪
ajari 阿闍梨
ajikan 阿字観
Ashukuji 阿閦寺
ama 尼
amadera gozan 尼寺五山
amashū 尼衆 (Chns. *nizhong*)
Amida Daiju 阿弥陀大呪
Amida-kyō 阿弥陀経 (Chns. *Amituo jing*)
Amituo jing 阿彌陀經 (Jpns. *Amida-kyō*)
Anahobe no Hashihito no Himemiko 穴穂部の間人皇女 (d. 621)
Anan Keka 阿難悔過
Anan-kō 阿難講
Anan Sonja Kōshiki 阿難尊者講式
angobō 安居房
anju 安居
asobi 遊女 (also *yūjo*)
Azuma kagami 吾妻鏡
Bajingjie 八敬戒 (Jpns. Hakkyōkai)
bakufu 幕府
Bao Zhao 鮑照
ba zhaijie 八斎戒 (Jpns. *hassaikai*)
betsuju 別受
bettō 別当
bian-wen 変文 (Jpns. *henbun*)
Biaowubiao zhang 表無表章
biku 比丘 (Chns. *biqiu*)
bikuni 比丘尼 (Chns. *biqiuni*)
bikuni gusokukai 比丘尼具足戒
biqiu 比丘 (Jpns. *biku*)
biqiuni 比丘尼 (Jpns. *bikuni*)
Bishamonten 毗沙門天
bō 坊
bodaiji 菩提寺
Bodaishinron 菩提心論
Bo Juyi 白居易
bonbai 梵唄
Bonmō Fusatsu 梵網布薩
Bonmōkyō 梵網経
Bonmōkyō Kōsan 梵網経講讃
Bonmōkyō koshakki hokō monjū 梵網経古迹記輔行文集
Bonmōkyō koshakki kamon bugyō monjū ehon 梵網経古迹記科文輔行文集会本
Bonmō no jūjūkai 梵網の重十戒
bon'on 梵音
bōzu no amagozen 坊主の尼御前
Bussetsu tennyoshingyō 仏説転女身経 (also *Tennyoshinkyō, Tennyoshingyō*)
busshi 仏師
busshō 仏性
Busshō-e 仏生会
Butsumyō 仏名
Chikurinji 竹林寺
chindangu 鎮壇具
Chinkai 珍海
chishiki 知識
Chisoku-in 知足院
Chisokuji 知足寺
Chōgen 重源
chōja 長者
Chōken 貞顕 (female)
Chōken 澄憲 (male)
chōmonryō 聴聞料
chōrō 長老
Chōzen 澄禅

Chūgūji 中宮寺
chujia 出家 (Jpns. *shukke*)
Chūyūki 中右記
Cien Ji 慈恩基 (Jpns. Jion Ki, 632–682)
Dahui Zonggao 大慧宗杲
Daianji 大安寺
Daibutsu Hiden 大仏悲田
daie 大衣
Daigo-dono 醍醐殿
Daigoji 醍醐寺
Daihannya 大般若
Daiji 大寺
daijōbu 大丈夫 (Chns. *dazhangfu*)
Daijō-in 大乗院
Daijōkan 太政官
daikai 大戒
Dainin'nō-e 大仁王会
daishi 大師
daisō 大僧
Daoxuan 道宣 (Jpns. Dōsen, 596–667)
Dasheng fayuan yilin zhang 大乗法苑義林章
Datang xiyuji 大唐西域記
Dazhidu lun 大智度論
denbō kanjō 伝法灌頂
dengaku 田楽
Dōga 道我
dokushi 読師
Dōmyōji 道明寺
dōshi 導師
dōtatsu 堂達
Eishin 栄真
Eison or Eizon 叡尊
Eizen 永禅
ekō 廻向
enkiridera or *engiridera* 縁切寺
Enkōji 円興寺
Enni Ben'en 圓爾辯圓
Ennin 円仁
Ensen 円晴
Enshō 円性 (daughter)
Enshō 円照 (son)
etoki 絵解き
Ezen 恵善
Fahua chanfa 法華懺法
fu 符
Fudō Jiku 不動慈救
Fugen jūrasetsunyo 普賢十羅刹女
Fujiodera 藤尾寺
Fujiwara no Atsuyori 藤原敦頼
Fujiwara no Yukinari 藤原行成
fusatsu 布薩
fuse 布施
Gakuanji 額安寺
gakunin 楽人
gaku-shū 学衆
ganmon 願文
Ganpōji 岩峰寺
Gaoseng zhuan 高僧傳
Gashari bunpu hachiryū 牙舎利分布八粒
gasshō 合掌
geango 夏安居
Genshin 源信
genze riyaku 現世利益
Gidō Shūshin 義堂周信
gigaku 伎楽
Gion no Nyōgo 祇園女御
Godai Kokūzō hō 五大虚空蔵法
Goji Monju Ju 五字文殊呪
Gokurakuji 極楽寺
gongyang 供養 (Jpns. *kuyō*)
gongyō 勤行
Gongyō hōsoku 勤行法則
gonji 近事
gonjinyo 近事女
gonjū 近住
gonjūnan 近住男
gonjūnyo 近住女
Gonkan 厳寛
Gonki 権記
gonshi 近士
gosho 御所
goshō 五障 (also *itsutsu no sawari*)
Goza-kō 五座講
Guanxin shijie manchaluo 観心十界曼荼羅
Gubodai-in 求菩提院
guhō rijō 弘法利生
gyakushu 逆修
gyōdō shamini 形同沙弥尼
gyōja 行者
gyokujo or *gyokunyo* 玉女

Gyōnen 凝然
Hachijō-in 八条院
Hachijō-in no Takakura 八条院高倉
Hakuun Egyō 白雲慧曉
Hamuro Sadatsugu 葉室定嗣
hassaikai 八斎戒
Heike nōkyō or *nōgyō* 平家納経
henjō nanshi 変成男子
hensan 褊衫
hikimeshi 引飯
himemiya 姫宮
hinin 非人
hōdō shamini 法同沙弥尼
hōe 法会
Hōin Daioshōi 法印大和尚位
Hōjō 放生
Hōjōji 法成寺
Hokke Hakkō 法華八講
Hokkeji 法華寺
Hokke Sen Narabi Ni San 法華懺幷讃
Hōkyō Darani 宝篋陀羅尼
Hōmyō 法妙
Honchō seiki 本朝世紀
hongaku 本覚
Hongan Onkijitsu Bonmō Dai-e 本願御忌日梵網大会
Hongan Ontsuizen Ōjō-kō 本願御追善往生講
Hōon 法音
Hōryūji kyūki ruijū 法隆寺旧記類従
hōshi 法師
Hōtō-in 宝塔院
hyōbyaku 表白
ikoku kitō 異国祈祷
in 院
Ingen 院源
ingō 院号
injo 淫女 or 婬女
Inpumon-in no taifu 殷富門院大輔
ippongyō 一品経
Issaikyō Tendoku 一切経転読
itsutsu no sawari 五障 (also *goshō*)
Jakuen-bō Son'e 寂円房尊恵
Ji-Amidabutsu 慈阿弥陀仏
jibutsudō 持仏堂
Jikyō Kōshiki 持経講式
jingū 神宮
Jinson 尋尊
Jiren-bō 慈蓮房
Jishin 慈眞
jishu 寺主
jisō 寺僧
Jitsudō 実道
Jitsuei 実叡
Jitsuun 実運
Jizen 慈善
Jōadan 成阿旦
Jōen 定円
jojōbu 女丈夫
Jōjūji 浄住寺
Jōkei 貞慶
Jōken 成賢
Jōki-in 常喜院
Jōkō 淨光
Jōnen 定然
jōnin 浄人
Jōrakudaishu rōnō ikkiki 常楽臺主老衲一期記
joryū 女流
jōza 上座
jūhōgyō 十法行
Jūichimen Daiju 十一面大呪
Jukai-e 受戒会
Jukō 壽廣
jūnin 住人
Junna-in 淳和院
Junna Taikō 淳和太后
Junnin 順忍
Jūroku Rakan 十六羅漢
Jūroku Rakan-kō 十六羅漢講
kada 伽陀
kaibyaku 開白
kaichō 開帳
kaidan 戒壇
Kaidan-in 戒壇院
Kaiganji 海岸寺
Kaikōji 戒光寺
Kainyo 戒如
Kairyūōji 海龍王寺
Kairyūōji hassaikai-shū kishiki jōjō 海龍王寺八斎戒衆規式条々
Kaizen-in 戒禅院

Kakuchō 覚澄
Kakuji 角寺
Kakujō 覚盛
Kami no Katsura no shō 上桂庄
kanjin kōgyō 勧進興行
Kanke bunsō 菅家文草
Kankikōji 歓喜光寺
kanni 官尼
kannō 感応
Kannon-kō 観音講
Kannon-kyō 観音経
kanpaku 関白
kansō 官僧
Kantō *kitōji* 関東祈祷寺
kantoku 感得
katen 加点
Kazan-in Morotsugu 花山院諸継
kebutsu 化仏
kechien 結縁
Kegon-e 花厳会
Keiaiji 景愛寺
Keishō-in 敬聖院
kekkaiki 結界記
Ken'a 釼阿
Kengozen 健御前
Kensaku-in 羂索院
Kenshun 賢舜
Ketsubonkyō or *ketsubongyō* 血盆経
kien 機縁
kijitsu kuyō 忌日供養
Kinrinbucchō hō 金輪仏頂法
kishinjō 寄進状
kōbō rijō 興法利生
kobukuro 小袋
kōe 講会
Kōen 皇円
Kōfukuji Daijōin Monzeki 興福寺大乗院門跡
kōgō 皇后
kōi 綱維
koji 小師
kokoro no yami 心の闇
Kokua 国阿
kokubunji 国分寺
kokubunniji 国分尼寺
kokubunniji 国分二寺
koku kōji 国講師
kokushi 国司
Kokūzō 虚空蔵
Kōmyō Shingon 光明真言
konma 羯磨
kōshi 講師
kōshiki 講式
kōsō 籠僧
kōtaigō 皇太后
Kōtaiji 光台寺
kuji 籤
Kujō Shakujō 九条錫杖
kumokudai 供目代
Kūnyo 空如
Kyōbutsu-bō 経仏房
Kyōe 鏡慧
Kyōjin 経尋
kyōju 教授
kyōka 教化
Kyōkōji 教興寺
kyōmyō 交名
kyōshi 經師
Lanxi Daolong 蘭渓道隆 (Jpns. Rankei Dōryū)
Li gong gao 驪宮高
liufashi 六法事 (Jpns. Roppōji)
Manishu-in 摩尼珠院
Mantokuji 万徳寺
Meigetsuki 明月記
Mida Bōgō 弥陀宝号
Mida Jūni Rai 弥陀十二礼
Mieku 御影供
mikkyō 密教
Mimuradera 三村寺
Mimura amadera 三村尼寺
Misai-e 御斎会
Mitsume 光女
mōja kuyō 亡者供養
Monju-kō 文殊講
Monshō 聞勝
montei 門弟
moya 母屋
Mugai Nyodai 無外如大
mujō 無常
mujōdō 無上道
Mulian 目蓮 (Jpns. Mokuren)

Muromachi-in 室町院 (1228–1300)
musō 夢相
Myōgyōdō 明経道
Myōhōji 妙法寺
Myōrakuji 妙楽寺
Myōsō 妙相
nageshi 長押
Nakahara no Moromori 中原師守
Nakatsukasa naishi nikki 中務内侍日記
Nehan-e 涅槃会
Nehan-kō 涅槃講
Nehankyō Kōsan 涅槃経講讃
ni 尼 (also *ama*)
Nii no shō 新井庄
Nijūgo Zanmai-e 二十五三昧会
Nijūgo Zanmai-Shiki 二十五三昧式
Nikaidō Yukifuji 二階堂行藤
nikō 尼公
Ninnō hannyakyō 仁王般若経 (Chns. *Rewang bore jing*)
Ninshō 忍性
niseng 尼僧 (Jpns. *nisō*)
nisō 尼僧 (Chns. *niseng*)
nizhong 尼衆 (Jpns. *ama-shū*)
Nonomiya amadera 野宮尼寺
nyōbō 女房
nyōbō edokoro 女房絵所
Nyoen 如円
nyogō 女業
Nyohō 如法
nyoi hōju 如意宝珠
Nyoihōringe hō 如意宝輪華法
nyoin or *nyōin* 女院
Nyoirin Kannon 如意輪観音
nyonin kekkai 女人結界
nyonin kinsei or *nyonin kinzei* 女人禁制
nyonin no mi o hanare 女人の身を離れ
nyonin no mi o itō 女人の身を厭う
nyoō or *joo* 女王
Nyoshin 如眞
Nyūdō 入道
Ōe no Chikamichi 大江親通
Ōgaji 應賀寺
Ogurusu Jōgyō 小栗栖常暁
ōjōden 往生伝
okashira 御頭
Onsenji 温泉寺
ōoku 大奥
onki 遠忌
Ōtani Honganji tsūki 大谷本願寺通杞
Pinimu jing 毘尼母経
Pini taoyao 毗尼討要
Ragora-kō 羅睺羅講
raiban 礼盤
Raigōkabe Fugen Bosatsu yōgōzu 来迎壁普賢菩薩影向図
Raimon 礼文
Rakan Ku 羅漢供
Raun Kōshiki 羅云講式
Raun Kuyō Gi 羅云供養儀
Raun Sonja Zō 羅雲尊者像
reijōka 霊場化
retsujobu 烈女夫
Rikke 律家
risshi 律師
rippō tōryō 律法棟梁
rokudō 六道
rokumotsu 六物
Ruyin 如因
Ryōgen 良源
Ryōnin 良忍
Ryōshin-bō Shunnin 了信房春忍
Ryōshō 了證
Ryōzenji 霊山寺
Saidaiji 西大寺
Saidaiji *bettō* 西大寺別当
Saidaiji Goshichinichichō Darani-e 西大寺後七日長陀羅尼会
Saifukuji 最福寺
saikai-shū 斎戒衆
Sairin-in 西林院
Saishō-e 最勝会
Sanbōe 三宝絵
Sanbōin teikeizu 三宝院帝系図
Sangaku-in 三学院
sange 散華
sangō 三網
Sanji hōsoku 三時法則
sanjū 三従 (Chns. *sancong*)
sanjujōkai 三聚淨戒
Sanka-in 三箇院
sankei 参詣

sannōhen 三能變
sanrai 三礼
sanzu 三途
sarugaku 猿楽
Seikaku 政覚
Seikan 静観
seng 僧 (Jpns. *sō*)
sengqie 僧伽 (Jpns. *sōka* or *sōgya*)
Senju Darani 千手陀羅尼
Sennyūji 泉涌寺
sesshō kindan 殺生禁断
Shaka Bōgō 釈迦宝号
Shaka Jūni Rai 釈迦十二礼
Shaka *nenbutsu* 釈迦念仏
shakujō 錫杖
shamini 沙彌尼
Shana-in 舎那院
Shanguangsi 善光寺
Shari-kō 舎利講
Shari Rai[mon] 舎利礼[文]
shari shinkō 舎利信仰
Shari Wasan 舎利和讃
Shengjun Budong Mingwang sishibashizhe mimi chengjiu yigui 勝軍不動明王四十八使者秘密成就儀軌
Shibun bikunishō 四分比丘尼鈔 (Chns. *Sifenlü biqiuni chao*)
Shibun Fusatsu 四分布薩
Shibun ritsu 四分律 (Chns. *Sifenlü*)
Shibutsu Shōnin 仕仏上人
Shichijūichiban shokunin uta-awase 七十一番職人歌合
Shiganji 施眼寺
Shijia fangzhi 釈迦方志
shikishamana 式叉摩那 (alt. *shikishamani* 式叉摩尼)
shikken 執権
Shin-Amidabutsu-ni 新阿仏尼
Shin-Amidabutsu-ni 真阿弥陀仏尼
Shinchokusen wakashū 新勅選和歌集
Shingen Ryōshō-bō (真源良性房 or 良照房)
Shinkai 審海 (chap. 5)
Shinkai 真海
shinmon 真文
Shinmyō 真妙
shintaku 神託
Shiōdō 四王堂
Shiō Sōju 四王惣呪
Shishuki 師守記
shōbō 正法
Shōbōji 正法寺
Shō-Kannon 正観音
shokoku dokushi 諸国読師
shokoku kōshi 諸国講師
Shōkutei-in 勝倶胝院
shōmyō 声明
Shōmyōji 称名寺
shōnin 上人 or 聖人
Shōshu 聖守
shōsō 唱相
shōsōzu 少僧都
Shōyūki 小右記
Shuen 修円
shukke 出家 (Chns. *chujia*)
shukkesha 出家者 (Chns. *chujiazhe*)
Shuni-e 修二会
Shunjō 俊仍
Shun'oku Myōha 春屋妙葩
Shushō-e 修正会
Sifenlü 四分律 (Jpns. *Shibun ritsu*)
Sifenlü biqiuni chao 四分律比丘尼鈔 (Jpns. *Shibun bikunishō*)
Sifen shanding biqiuni jieben 四分刪定比丘尼戒本
sō 僧 (Chns. *seng*)
sogan 素願
Sōgō 僧綱
Sōgōji 惣毫寺
Sōji 惣持
Sōji-in 惣持院
sōjō 僧正
Son'en 尊円
Sonnyo 尊如
Sonshō Darani 尊勝陀羅尼
Sonshū Kōei-bō 尊秀光叡房
Sonshun 尊順
sōzu 僧都
Tadano-in 多田院
Taehyeon 太賢 (aka Taehyŏn, Jpns. Taigen)
taie or *daie* 大衣

taikōtaigō 太皇太后
Taira no Tsunetaka 平経高
Taishi-kō 太子講
Takakura-dono 高倉殿
takusen 託宣
Tankū 湛空
tendoku 転読
Tenjin 天神
tennyo jōbutsu 転女成仏
Tennyo jōbutsukyō 転女成仏経
tennyo jōnan 転女成男
Tennyoshingyō 転女身経
tonseisō 遁世僧
Tōrinji 東林寺
Tōshōdaiji 唐招提寺
Tosotsuten ōjō 兜卒天往生
Toyuradera 豊浦寺
Ugon 有厳
uihō 有爲法
Urabon-e 盂蘭盆会
wajō 和上
waniguchi 鰐口
Wucheng fu 蕪城賦
Wuxue Zuyuan 無学祖元 (Jpns. Mugaku Sogen)
Wuzhun Shifan 無準師範
yado 宿
Yakushiji 薬師寺
yashame 夜叉女
Yōkōki 葉黄記
Yōshō 永昭
Yuandun guanxin shifajie 円鈍観心十法界
Yuanzhao 元照 (Jpns. Ganjō)
Yūgan 融観
Yuge Hōō 弓削法皇
Yuigyōkyō 遺教経 (*Yijiao jing*, aka *Fochui boniepan lüeshuo jiaojie jing*)
Yuima-e 維摩会
Yuishaku-kō 遺跡講
[*Yuishiki*] *sanjū*[*ron*]*ju* [唯識]三十[論]頌
Yuishin Shōnin 唯心上人
yūjo 遊女 (also *asobi*)
yūkō 有効
yūkun 遊君
yulu 語録 (Jpns. *goroku*)
za 座
zaichi ryōshu 在地領主
zaike 在家
zaike-shū seshu 在家衆施主
zazen 坐禅
Zekkai Chūshin 絶海中津
zenchishiki 善知識
Zenmyōji 善妙寺
zenni 禅尼
zenshi 禅師
Zenshin 善信
Zenzai Dōji 善財童子
Zenzō 善蔵
Zhiyi 智顗
Zhiyuan yibian 芝園遺編
Zonkaku 存覚
Zuigu Darani 随求陀羅尼
Zuishin Nyoihōju Konbon Darani 随心如意宝珠根本陀羅尼
zushi 厨子

Works Cited and Consulted

Primary Source Collections and Reference Works

Bukkyō daijiten 佛教大辭典. Ed. Oda Tokunō. Tokyo: Ōkura Shoten, 1928.

Bukkyō daijiten 佛教大辞典. Ed. Mochizuki Shinkō. 1909. Expanded and revised by Tsukamoto Zenryū and Sekai Seiten Kankō Kyōkai. 10 vols. Kyoto: Sekai Seiten Kankō Kyōkai, 1954–1971.

Bukkyōgo daijiten 佛教語大辞典. Ed. Nakamura Hajime. 3 vols. Tokyo: Tokyo Shoseki, 1975.

Bukkyō ongaku jiten 仏教音楽辞典. Ed. Amano Denchū et al. Kyoto: Hōzōkan, 1995.

Bussho kaisetsu daijiten 仏書解説大辞典. Ed. Ono Genmyō. 14 vols. Tokyo: Daitō Shuppansha, 1933–1936. Revised, 1964–1967. Supplementary vols. 12 and 13, ed. Maruyama Takao. Reprint, 1974–1978.

The Cambridge History of Japan. Ed. John Whitney Hall, Marius B. Jansen, Madoka Kanai, and Denis Twitchett. 6 vols. Cambridge: Cambridge University Press, 1988–1989.

Dai kanwa jiten 大漢和辞典. Ed. Morohashi Tetsuji. 13 vols. Tokyo: Shōgakukan, 1960. Reedited, 1986.

Dai Nihon Bukkyō zensho (*DNBZ* 1922) 大日本佛教全書. Ed. Bussho Kankōkai. 161 vols. Tokyo: Dai Nihon Bukkyō Zensho Kankōkai, 1912–1922.

Dai Nihon Bukkyō zensho (*DNBZ* 1973) 大日本佛教全書. Ed. Suzuki Gakujutsu Zaidan. 100 vols. Tokyo: Kodansha, 1973.

Dai Nihon komonjo, iewake 大日本古文書・家わけ. Ed. Tokyo Daigaku Shiryō Hensanjo. Tokyo: Tokyo Daigaku Shuppankai, 1968–.

Dai Nihon shiryō 大日本資料. Ed. Tokyo University Shiryō Hensanjo. Tokyo: Tokyo University, 1901–2000.

Daizōkyō zenkaisetsu daijiten 大蔵経全解説大辞典. Ed. Kamata Shigeo et al. Tōkyō: Yūzankaku Shuppan, 1998.

A Dictionary of Japanese Buddhist Terms. By Hisao Inagaki. Rev. U.S. edition with supplement. 5th ed. Berkeley, CA: Stone Bridge Press, 2007.

Digital Dictionary of Buddhism (DDB). Ed. Charles Muller. http://www.buddhism-dict.net/ddb/.

The Encyclopedia of Religion. Ed. Mircea Eliade et al. 16 vols. New York: Macmillan, 1987.

Encyclopedia of Religion. Ed. Lindsay Jones et al. 2nd ed. 15 vols. Detroit: Macmillan Reference USA, 2005.

Hōbō girin: Dictionnaire encyclopédique du bouddhisme d'après les sources chinoises et japonaises. Under the direction of Sylvain Lévi and Takakusu Junjirō. Ed. Paul Demiéville. Tokyo: Maison Franco-Japonaise, 1929–.

Iwanami Bukkyō jiten 岩波仏教辞典. Ed. Nakamura Hajime et al. Tokyo: Iwanami Shoten, 1989.

Japanese Architecture and Art Net Users System. Comp. Mary Neighbour Parent. http://www.aisf.or.jp/~jaanus/.

Jōdoshū zensho. Ed. Jōdoshū Shūten Kankōkai. 23 vols. Kyōto: Jōdoshū Kaishū Happyaku Nen Kinen Kyōsan Junbi Kyoku, 1970–1974.

Kadokawa kogo daijiten 角川古語大辞典. Ed. Nakamura Yukihiko et al. 5 vols. Tokyo: Kadokawa, 1982–1999.

Kadokawa Nihon chimei daijiten 角川日本地名大辞典. Ed. Kadokawa Nihon Chimei Daijiten Hensan Iinkai and Takeuchi Rizō. 47 vols. Tokyo: Kadokawa Shoten, 1978–1991.

Kamakura ibun 鎌倉遺文. Komonjo Hen. Ed. Takeuchi Rizō. 42 vols. Tokyo: Tōkyōdō Shuppan, 1971–1991.

Kamakura kyū Bukkyō 鎌倉舊佛教. Ed. Kamata Shigeo and Tanaka Hisao. Vol. 15 of *Nihon shisō taikei* 日本思想大系. Tokyo: Iwanami Shoten, 1971.

Kanagawa kenshi shiryōhen 神奈川県史資料編. Ed. Kanagawa-ken Kenshi Henshū-shitsu. 21 vols. Yokohama: Kanagawa-ken, 1970–1982.

Kanazawa Bunko komonjo 金澤文庫古文書. By Kanazawa Bunko. Yokohama: Kanazawa Bunko, 1952–1964.

Kanazawa Bunko shiryō zensho 金沢文庫資料全書. By Kanazawa Bunko. Yokohama: Kanagawa Kenritsu Kanazawa Bunko, 1974.

Kodai seiji shakai shisō 古代政治社会思想. Ed. Yamagishi Tokuhei et al. Vol. 8 of *Nihon shisō taikei* 日本思想大系. Tokyo: Iwanami Shoten, 1979.

Kokushi daijiten 國史大辭典. Ed. Kokushi Daijiten Henshū Iinkai. 15 vols. Tokyo: Yoshikawa Kōbunkan, 1979–1997.

Kōshiki Dētabēsu 講式データベース. Ed. Niels Guelberg. Waseda University. http://www.f.waseda.jp/guelberg/koshiki/kdb/main/kousiki.htm. Accessed Feb. 11, 2008.

Nara kankyōshi 寧楽刊経史. Ed. Ōya Tokujō. Tokyo: Kokusho Kankōkai, 1987.

Nihon Bukkyō jinmei jiten 日本仏教人名辞典. By Saitō Akitoshi and Naruse Yoshinori. Tokyo: Shin Jinbutsu Ōraisha, 1986.

Nihon daizōkyō 日本大藏經. Ed. Nihon Daizōkyō Hensankai. 50 vols. Tokyo: Zokyō Shoin, 1914–1922.

Nihon emakimono zenshū 日本繪卷物全集. Ed. Kadokawa Shoten Henshūbu. Tokyo: Kadokawa shoten, 1958–1969.

Nihon kodaishi daijiten 日本古代史大辞典. Ed. Ueda Masaaki. Tokyo: Daiwa Shobo, 2006.

Nihon kokugo daijiten 日本国語大辞典. Ed. Nihon Kokugo Daijiten Dai 2-han Henshū Iinkai. 2nd ed. Tokyo: Shōgakukan, 2000–2002.

Nihon koten bungaku taikei (NKBT) 日本古典文学大系. Ed. Takagi Ichinosuke et al. 102 vols. Tokyo: Iwanami Shoten, 1957–1968.

Nihon koten bungaku zenshū (NKBZ) 日本古典文学全集. 51 vols. Tokyo: Shōgakukan, 1970–1976.

Nihon rekishi chimei taikei 日本歴史地名体系. JK Select Series. Tokyo: Heibonsha. http://rekishi.jkn21.com/.

Nihonshi bunken kaidai jiten 日本史文献解題辞典. Ed. Katō Tomoyasu and Yui Masaomi. Tokyo: Yoshikawa Kōbunkan, 2000.

Nihon shisō taikei 日本思想大系. Ed. Ienaga Saburō et al. 67 vols. Tokyo: Iwanami Shoten, 1970–1982.

Ōbunsha kogojiten 旺文社古語辞典. Ed. Matsumura Akira et al. Tokyo: Ōbunsha, 1981.

Saidaiji Eison denki shūsei (SEDS) 西大寺叡尊傳記集成. Ed. and comp. Kanshū Nara Kokuritsu Bunkazai Kenkyūjo. Kyoto: Hōzōkan, 1977.

Shin Nihon koten bungaku taikei (SNKBT) 新日本古典文学大系. Ed. Satake Akihiro et al. 100 vols. Tokyo: Iwanami Shoten, 1989–.

Shinpen Nihon koten bungaku zenshū (SKNBZ) 新編日本古典文学全集. 88 vols. Tokyo: Shōgakukan, 1994–.

Shizuoka-ken shiryō 静岡県史料. 5 vols. Shizuoka-shi, Japan: Shizukoa-ken, 1932–1941.

Sōgō Bukkyō daijiten 総合仏教大辞典. Ed. Sōgō Bukkyō Daijiten Henshū Iinkai. 3 vols. Kyoto: Hōzōkan, 1987.

Sōtō Zen Text Project. Ed. Carl Bielefeldt and Griffith Foulk. http://hcbss.stanford.edu/research/projects/sztp/index.html. Accessed July 5, 2009.

Taishō shinshū daizōkyō (T.) 大正新修大藏經. Ed. Takakusu Junjirō, Watanabe Kaigyoku, et al. 85 vols. Tokyo: Taishō Issaikyō Kankōkai, 1924–1932.

Xu zangjing (X.) 續蔵経. Taibei: Xinwenfeng, 1968–1970. Reprint of *Dai Nihon zoku zōkyō* 大日本續蔵経, ed. Nakano Tatsue. Kyoto: Zōkyō Shoin, 1905–1912.

Yamato koji taikan (YKT) 大和古寺大觀. 7 vols. Ed. Ōta Hirotarō et al. Tokyo: Iwanami Shoten, 1976–1978.

Zoku gunsho ruijū 續群書類從. Ed. Hanawa Hokiichi. Revised, Ōta Tōshirō. 33 vols. Tokyo: Zoku Gunsho Ruijū Kanseikai, 1923–1928.

Zoku zoku gunsho ruijū 續々群書類従. Ed. Kokusho kankōkai. 16 vols. Tokyo: Kokusho Kankōkai, 1906–1909.

Individual Primary Sources

Ama Shinnyo ganmon 尼信如願文. In *YKT,* 1:82b–83a.

Anan Sonja kōshiki 阿難尊者講式. In the *Kōshiki Dētabēsu,* no. 166.

Azuma kagami 吾妻鏡. 8 vols. In *Nihon koten zenshū.* Tokyo: Nihon Koten Zenshū Kankōkai, 1926.

Baoxing tuoluoni jing 宝星陀羅尼經. T. no. 402.

Beihua jing 悲華經. T. no. 157.

Beommanggyeong gojeokgi 梵網経古跡記. By Taehyeon. T. no. 1815.

Beommanggyeong bosalgyebon jongyo 梵網経菩薩戒本宗要. By Taehyeon. T. no. 2356.

Biqiuni chao 比丘尼鈔. X. no. 724.

Biqiuni zhuan 比丘尼傳. T. no. 2063.

Bodai shinshū 菩提心集. By Chinkai. In *Jōdoshū zensho,* 15:502–532.

Bonmōkyō koshakki kamon bugyō monjū ehon 梵網経古迹記科文輔行文集会本. In *Nihon daizōkyō,* 21:227–536.

Bore boluomiduo xinjing 般若波羅蜜多心經. T. no. 251.

Bosatsu kaihon shūyō bugyō monjū 菩薩戒本宗要輔行文集. By Eison. T. no. 2356.

Bukkō kokushi goroku 仏光国師語録. T. no. 2549.

Chanzha shane yebao jing 占察善惡業報經. T. no. 839.

Cheng weishi lun 成唯識論. T. no. 1585.

Chōshūki 長秋記 (1105–1136). By Minamoto no Morotoki. In *Zōho shiryō taisei,* vols. 16–17, ed. Zōho Shiryō Taisei Kankōkai. Kyoto: Rinsen Shoten, 1965.

Chūgūji engi 中宮寺縁起. In *YKT,* 1:86a–87b.

Chūyūki 中右記. By Fujiwara no Munetada (1062–1131). In *Zōho shiryō taisei,* vols. 9–15, ed. Zōho Shiryō Taisei Kankōkai. Kyoto: Rinsen Shoten, 1965.

Da banniepan jing 大般涅槃經, T. nos. 374–376.

Dabore boluomiduo jing 大般若波羅蜜多經. T. no. 220.

Dafangbian baoen jing 大方便報恩經. T. no. 156.

Dafangguangfo huayan jing 大方広仏華厳経 (also known as the *Bashi huayan* 八十華嚴). T. nos. 278, 279, 293.

Dahui Pujue chanshi yulu 大慧普覺禪師語録. T. no. 1998a.

Daigoji monjo 醍醐寺文書. In *Dainihon komonjo, iewake.*

Daigoji shin yōroku 醍醐寺新要録. Kyoto: Kyoto-fu Kyōiku Iinkai, 1941.

Daijōin jisha zōjiki 大乗院寺社雑事記. In *Zōho shiryō taisei,* vols. 26–37, ed. Zōho Shiryō Taisei Kankōkai. Kyoto: Rinsen Shoten, 1994.

Daitō saiikiki 大唐西域記. T. no. 2057.

Dajijing 大集經 (also *Dafangdeng daijijing* 大方等大集經). T. no. 397.

Dajue chanshi yulu 大覚禅師語録, T. no. 2547.

Dazhidu lun 大智度論. T. no. 1509.

Dengyō daishi zenshū 伝教大師全集. Ed. Hieizan Senshuin Fuzoku Eizan Gakuin. 5 vols. Tokyo: Sekai Seiten Kankō Kyōkai, 1989.

Denryaku 殿暦 (1098–1118). By Fujiwara no Tadazane. In *Dai Nihon Kokiroku,* ed. Tokyo University Shiryō Hensanjo. 5 vols. Tokyo: Iwanami, 1960–1970.

Eiga monogatari 栄華物語 (ca. 1092). In *SNKBZ,* vols. 31–33.

Eison shojō 叡尊書状. In *SEDS,* 331.

Eison shojō santsū 叡尊書状三通. In *SEDS,* 409–411.

Engi-shiki 延喜式. Vol. 26 in *Shintei zōho kokushi taikei.* 66 vols. Tokyo: Yoshikawa Kōbunkan, 1965.

Fanwang jing 梵網經. T. no. 1484.

Fayuan zhulin 法苑珠林. T. no. 2122.

Fo benxingji jing 仏本行集經. T. no. 190.

Fochui boniepan lüeshuo jiaojie jing 佛垂般涅槃略説教誡經. T. no. 389.

Foding zunsheng tuoluoni jing 佛頂尊勝陀羅尼經. T. no. 967.

Foshuo zhuan nushen jing 佛説転女身經. T. no. 564. (See also T. nos. 562–563 and 565–566.)

Fozhi biqiu liuwutu 仏制比丘六物図. By Yuanzhao. T. no. 1900.

Fusō ryakki 扶桑略記. In *Kokushi taikei,* vol. 12. Tokyo: Yoshikawa Kōbunkan, 1999.

Gaoseng Faxian zhuan 高僧法顯傳. T. no. 2085, 859b24–b27.

Gangōji engi 元興寺縁起. In *Shoji engishū,* vol. 1, ed. Tanaka Denzaburō. Kyoto: Benridō, 1930.

Gangōji garan engi narabi ruki shizaichō 元興寺伽藍縁起并流記資財帳. In *Jisha engi,* ed. Sakurai Tokutarō, Hahiwara Tatsuo, and Miyata Noboru, vol. 20 of *Nihon shisō taikei,* ed. Ienaga Saburō et al. Tokyo: Iwanami Shoten, 1971.

Gashō roku 画証録. By Kitamura Nobuyo (1784–1856). In *Shizuka naru amari/Gashō Roku,* vol. 32 of *Nihon zuihitsu taisei.* Tokyo: Yoshikawa Kōbunkan, 1994.

Genji monogatari 源氏物語 (ca. 1008). Ed. Yahai Shigeshi. In *SNKBT,* vols. 19–23.

Genpei seisuiki 源平盛衰記. Ed. Ichiko Teiji et al. 8 vols. Tokyo: Miyai Shoten, 1991–.

Gikeiki 義経記. In *NKBZ,* vol. 31, ed. Kajihara Masaaki. Tokyo: Shōgakukan, 1971.

Gokurakuji garan kozu 極楽寺古図. In *Kanagawa kenshi shiryōhen,* vol. 3.

Gonjū nannyo kyōmyō 近住男女交名. In *SEDS,* 379–383. Also in Matsuo Kenji, "Saidaiji Eisonzō ni nōnyū sareta 'jubosatsukai deshi kyōmyō' to 'gonjū nannyo kyōmyō.'" *Nanto Bukkyō* 73 (Nov. 1996): 87–107.

Gonki 権記 (991–1011). By Fujiwara no Yukinari, ed. Watanabe Naohiko and Atsuya Kazuo. Vols. 57, 82, and 106 of *Shiryō sanshū,* ed. Zoku Gunsho Ruijū Kanseikai. Tokyo: Zoku Gunsho Ruijū Kanseikai, 1978–1996.

Guan Puxian jing 觀普賢經. Also *Guan Puxian Pusa xingfa jing* 觀普賢菩薩行法經. T. no. 2077.

Guan wuliangshou Fojing 觀無量壽佛經. Also *Guan wuliangshou jing.* T. no. 365.

Gukanshō 愚管抄 (1219). By Jien. In *NKBT,* vol. 86, ed. Okami Masao and Akamatsu Toshihide. Tokyo: Iwanami Shoten, 1967.

Gyokuyō 玉葉. By Kujō Kanezane. 3 vols. Tokyo: Kokusho Kankōkai, 1907. See also Takahashi Sadaichi, ed. *Kundoku Gyokuyō.* 8 vols. Tokyo: Takahashi Shoten, 1988.

Hanazono Tennō shinki 花園天皇宸記. In *Zōho shiryō taisei,* vols. 25–26, ed. Zōho Shinryō Taisei Kankōkai. Kyoto: Rinsen Shoten, 1965–1989.

Hasedera Kannon genki 長谷寺観音験記. Annotated by Nagai Yoshinori. Koten Bunko, vol. 72. Tokyo: Koten Bunko, 1953.

Heihanki 兵範記 (1132–1171). By Taira no Nobunori. In *Zōho shiryō taisei,* vols. 18–21, ed. Zōho Shinryō Taisei Kankōkai. Kyoto: Rinsen Shoten, 1965–1989.

Heike monogatari 平家物語 (ca. 1218). Ed. Ichiko Teiji. In *NKBZ,* vol. 29–30. Tokyo: Shōgakukan, 1973–1975.

Heikoki 平戸記. By Taira no Tsunetaka. In *Zōho shiryō taisei,* vols. 32-33, ed. Zōho Shinryō Taisei Kankōkai. Kyoto: Rinsen Shoten, 1965–1989.

Hōbutsushū 宝物集. Attr. to Taira no Yasuyori. In *DNBZ* 1973, vol. 91.

Hokkeji ama betsuju shito 法華寺尼別受指図. In *YTK,* 5:38.

Hokkeji kekkaiki 法華寺結界記. In *Dai Nihon shiryō,* sect. 5, vol. 29, 136–139.

Hokkeji shari engi 法華寺舎利縁起 (1271). By Eison. In *YTK,* 5:143b–144b. Also in *SEDS,* 159–162.

Hokke metsuzaiji engi (HMJE) 法華滅罪寺縁起 (1304). By Enkyō. In *YKT,* 5:140a–143b.

Hokke metsuzaiji nenjū [*or nenchū*] *gyōji* 法華滅罪寺年中行事 (1322). By Yūshi. In *YTK,* 5:86a–87b.

Honchō kōsōden 本朝高僧伝 (1702). By Shiban. In *DNBZ* 1973, vol. 63.

Honchō seiki 本朝世紀. By Fujiwara no Michinori. In *Kokushi taikei,* vol. 9. Tokyo: Yoshikawa Kōbunkan, 1964.

Hōnen Shōnin gyōjō ezu 法然上人行状絵図. By Shunshō (1255–1335). In *Jōdoshū zensho,* vol. 16.

Hōnen Shōnin zenshū 法然上人全集. Kyoto: Heirakuji Shoten, 1955.

Hōryūji bettō shidai 法隆寺別当次第. In *Zoku gunsho ruijū,* vol. 4, ed. Hanawa Hokiichi and rev. Ōta Tōshirō. Tokyo: Zoku Gunsho Ruijū Kanseikai, 1923–1928.

Izayoi nikki 十六夜日記. By Abutsu-ni (d. 1283). In *SNKBZ,* vol. 48.

Izumi Shikibu nikki 和泉式部日記. By Izumi Shikibu (b. 976?). In *SNKBZ,* vol. 26.

Jinguangming zuishengwang jing 金光明最勝王經 (Jpns. *Konkōmyō saishōōkyō*), also known as *Zuishengwang jing* 最勝王經 (Jpns. *Saishōōkyō*). T. no. 665.

Jiaojie xinxue biqiu xinghu lüyi 教誡新学比丘行護律儀. By Daoxuan. T. no. 1897.

Jikaku Daishi den 慈覚大師伝. By Minamoto no Fusaakira. In *Jikaku Daishi den: The Biography of Jikaku Daishi Ennin.* Trans. and annotated by Saito Enshin. Incl. the original text in Japanese. Tokyo: Sankibō Busshorin, 1992.

Jinguangming zuishengwang jing 金光明最勝王経. T. no. 665.

Jingxin jieguan fa 浄心誡観法. T. no. 1893.

Jubosatsukai deshi kyōmyō 授菩薩戒弟子交名. In *SEDS,* 372–379. Also in Matsuo Kenji, "Saidaiji Eisonzō ni nōnyū sareta 'jubosatsukai deshi kyōmyō' to 'gonjū nannyo kyōmyō.'" *Nanto Bukkyō* 73 (Nov. 1996): 87–107.

Kairyūōji ama betsuju shito 海龍王寺尼別受指図. In *YKT,* 5:93.

Kairyūōji genseiji 海龍王寺厳制事. In *YKT,* 5:122–123.

Kanmon gyoki 看聞御記. In *Zoku gonshu ruijū,* supplement vols. 3–4.

Kantō ōkanki 関東往還記. In *SEDS,* 67–91.

Kasuga gongen genki-e 春日権現験記絵. Ed. Noma Seiroku. Vol. 15 of *Nihon emakimono zenshū,* ed. Kadokawa Shoten Henshūbu. Tokyo: Kadokawa Shoten, 1963.

Kenkyū gojunreiki 建久御巡礼記. In *Kōkan bijutsu shiryō,* vol. 1, ed. Fujita Tsuneyo, 125–62. Tokyo: Chuō Kōron Bijutsu Shuppan, 1972.

Kenshunmon-in Chūnagon nikki 建春門院中納言日記 (aka *Tamakiwaru*). By Kenshunmon-in Chūnagon, a daughter of Fujiwara no Shunzei. In *SNKBT,* vol. 50.

Kenyō daikairon 顕揚大戒論. By Ennin. T. no. 2380.

Kōfukuji ranshōki 興福寺濫觴記. In *Zoku zoku gunsho ruijū,* vol. 11, ed. Kokusho Kankōkai.

Kongō Busshi Eison kanjin gakushōki (KJGSK) 金剛仏子叡尊感身学正記. In *Saidaiji Eison denki shūsei,* ed. and comp. Kanshū Nara Kokuritsu Bunkazai Kenkyūjo, 1–76. Kyoto: Hōzōkan, 1977. First two (of three) sections also published as *Kanjin gakushōki: Saidaiji Eison no jiden* 感身学正記：西大寺叡尊の自伝, trans. and annoted by Hosokawa Ryoīchi. Tokyo: Heibonsha, 1999.

Konjaku monogatarishū 今昔物語集 (1110–1125). Attr. to Minamoto no Takakuni (Uji Dainagon, 1004–1077) and disciples. In *NKBT,* vols. 22–26, ed. Yamada Yoshi, Yamada Tadao, Yamada Hideo, and Yamada Toshio. Tokyo: Iwanami Shoten, 1959–1963.

Kōshō Bosatsu gokyōkai chōmonshū (Chōmonshū) 興正菩薩御教誡聴聞集. In *Kamakura kyū Bukkyō,* 199–226.

Kōzanji Myōe Shōnin gyōjō 高山寺明恵上人行状. In *Kōzanji shiryō sōsho* 高山寺資料叢書, vol. 1. Tokyo: Tokyo University Press, 1971.

Kugutsu no ki 傀儡記. By Ōe no Masafusa (1041–1111). In *Kodai shakai shisō,* ed. Yamagishi Tokuhei, Takeuchi Rizō, Ienaga Saburō, and Ōsone Shōsuke. Vol. 8 of *Nihon shisō taikei.* 67 vols. Tokyo: Iwanami Shoten, 1970–1982.

Kujō-ke monjo 九条家文書. Tokyo: Kunaichō Shoryōbu, 1977.

Kulturgegensätze Europa-Japan: Tratado em que se contem muito susinta e abreviadamente algumas contradições e diferenças de custumes antre a gente de Europa e esta provincia de Japão (1585). By Luís Fróis (1532–1597). Trans. Josef Franz Schütte. Monumenta Nipponica no. 15. Tokyo: Sophia Universität, 1955.

Kundoku Meigetsuki 訓読明月記. By Fujiwara no Teika (1162–1241). Trans. Imagawa Fumio. 6 vols. Tokyo: Kawade Shōbo Shinsha.

Makura no sōshi 枕草紙. By Sei Shōnagon (b. ca. 967). In *SNKBT,* vol. 25.

Masukagami 増鏡. Attr. to Nijō Yoshimoto. In *SNKBT.* Tokyo: Iwanami Shoten, 1993. English trans., George Perkins, *The Clear Mirror: A Chronicle of the Japanese Court during the Kamakura Period (1185–1333).* Stanford: Stanford University Press, 1998.

Menoto no fumi 乳母の文. By Abutsu-ni. Published under the title *Niwa no oshie (kōhon)* 庭の訓 (広本), in *Kōchū Abutsu-ni zenshū* 校註阿仏尼全集, enlarged and revised edition, ed. Yanase Kazuo, 107–151. Tokyo: Kazama Shobō, 1984.

Miaofa lianhua jing 妙法蓮華経. T. no. 262.

Midō Kanpakuki 御堂関白記. By Fujiwara no Michinaga. In *Dai Nihon kokiroku,* ed. Tokyo University Shiryō Hensanjo. 3 vols. Tokyo: Iwanami, 1952–1954.

Mumyōzōshi 無名草子. In *SNKBZ,* vol. 40, 173–342.

Murasaki Shikibu nikki 紫式部日記. By Murasaki Shikubu (d. 1014?). In *SNKBZ,* vol. 26.

Muryōju kyōshaku 無量壽経釈. By Hōnen. In *Ōjō yōshū shaku,* ed. Ōhashi Shunnō. Tokyo: Shunjūsha, 2001.

Namu Amidabutsu sazenshū 南無阿弥陀仏作善集. By Chōgen. Reprinted in *Bijutsu kenkyū* 30 (June 1934): 39–51.

Nanto shodaiji engi-shū 南都諸大寺縁起集. In *Zoku zoku gunsho ruijū,* vol. 11, ed. Kokusho Kankōkai.

Niepan jing 涅槃經. T. no. 374. (See *Da banniepan jing.*)

Nihon shoki 日本書紀. In *NKBT,* vols. 67–68. Tokyo: Iwanami Shoten, 1977.

Nittō gubō junrei kōki 入唐求法巡礼行記. By Ennin. In Tōyō Bunko, no. 157. Tokyo: Heibonsha, 1970.

Pubian guangming qingjing chicheng ruyi baoyin xinwunengsheng damingwang dasuiqiu tuoluoni jing 普遍光明清淨熾盛如意寶印心無能勝大明王大隨求陀羅尼經. T. no. 1153.

Ritsuen sōbōden 律苑僧宝伝 (1689). 15 vols. In *DNBZ* 1973, vol. 64; *DNBZ* 1922, vol. 105.

Ruijū kokushi 類聚國史. In *Kokushi taieki,* vols. 5 and 6, ed. Kokushi Taikei Henshūkai. Expanded rev. ed., Tokyo: Yoshikawa Kōbunkan, 1965.

Ruijū sandai kyaku 類従三代格. In *Kokushi taieki,* vol. 25, ed. Kokushi Taikei Henshūkai. Expanded rev. ed., Tokyo: Yoshikawa Kōbunkan, 1965. On-demand ed., 2007.

Ruijū fusenshō 類聚符宣抄. In *Kokushi taieki,* vol. 27, ed. Kokushi Taikei Henshūkai. Tokyo: Yoshikawa Kōbunkan, 1965.

Ryōjin hishō 梁塵秘抄. In *NKBT,* vol. 73.

Ryōjusen-in nenjū gyōji 霊鷲山院年中行事 (1262). By Shinnyo. In *YTK,* 1:81b–82a.

Saidai chokushi Kōshō Bosatsu gyōjitsu nenpu 西大勅謚興正菩薩行實年譜. Ed. 1688–1703 by Jikō. 5 vols. (three main vols., plus two *furoku,* or supplementary vols.). In *SEDS,* 107–206.

Saidaiji den'en mokuroku 西大寺田園目録 (1298). In *SEDS,* 412–444.

Saidaiji kōmyō shingon-e engi 西大寺光明真言会縁起 (1265). In *SEDS,* 148–151.

Saidaiji nishi sōbō zōei dōshin gōriki hōga chō 西大寺西僧房造営同心合力奉加帳. In *SEDS,* 383–389.

Sakeiki 左経記 (1029–1036). By Minamoto no Tsuneyori. In *Zōho shiryō taisei,* vol. 6, ed. Zōho Shiryō Taisei Kankōkai. Kyoto: Rinsen Shoten, 1965.

Sanbōe kotoba 三宝絵詞 (984). By Minamoto no Tamenori (d. 1011). In Yamada Yoshio, *Sanbōe ryakuchū.* Tokyo: Hōbunkan, 1951. English trans., Edward Kamens, *The Three Jewels: A Study and Translation of Minamoto Tamemori's "Sanbōe."* Ann Arbor: Center for Japanese Studies, University of Michigan, 1988.

Sandai jitsuroku 三代実録. By Fujiwara no Tokihira (871–909). In *Kokushi Taikei,* vol. 4. Tokyo: Yoshikawa Kōbunkan, 2000.

Sankaiki 山槐記 (1151–1194). By Fujiwara no Tadachika. In *Zōho shiryō taisei,* vols. 26–28, ed. Zōho Shiryō Taisei Kankōkai. Kyoto: Rinsen Shoten, 1965.

Sarashina nikki 更級日記. By the daughter of Sugawara Takasue (b. 1008). In *NKBZ,* vol. 26.

Sennyūji Fukaki hōshiden 泉涌寺不可棄法師傳. In *Zoku gunsho ruijū,* vol. 9, ed. Hanawa Hokiichi and rev. Ōta Tōshirō, 45–58. Tokyo: Zoku Gunsho Ruijū Kanseikai, 1923–1928.

Shasekishū 沙石集. By Mujū Ichien (1226–1312). 2 vols. Koten Kenkyūkai. Tokyo: Kyūko Shoin, 1973.

Shibun ritsu chū bikuni kaihon 四分律注比丘尼戒本. By Sōji. In *Kanazawa Bunko shiryō zensho,* vol. 5. Yokohama: Kanagawa Kenritsu Kanazawa Bunko, 1974.

Shichidaiji junrei shiki 七大寺巡禮私記. By Ōe no Chikamichi. In vol. 1 of *Kōkan bijutsu shiryō,* ed. Fujita Tsuneyo, 29–63. Tokyo: Chuō Kōron Bijutsu Shuppan, 1972.

Shichidaiji nikki 七大寺日記. In vol. 1 of *Kōkan bijutsu shiryō,* ed. Fujita Tsuneyo, 19–28. Tokyo: Chuō Kōron Bijutsu Shuppan, 1972.

Shien Shōnin donin gyōhō kechigeki 思圓上人度人行法結夏記 (1290). In *SEDS,* 212–215.

Shinjin yōketsu 真心要決. By Ryōhen. T. no. 2313.

Shishuki 師守記. By Nakahara no Moromori. In *Zoku gunsho ruijū* (1968–1982).

Shōbōgenzō 正法眼蔵. By Dōgen. T. no. 2582.

Shōdai senzai denki 招提千歳伝記 (1691–1701). In *Zoku zoku gunsho ruijū,* 11:352–448.

Shoji engishū 諸寺縁起集. In vol. 1 of *Kōkan bijutsu shiryō,* ed. Fujita Tsuneyo, 65–124 (Daigoji-bon), 257–306 (Gokokuji-bon), and 307–384 (Kanke-bon). Tokyo: Chuō Kōron Bijutsu Shuppan, 1972. Also in *DNBZ* 1922, vol. 108.

Shoji konryū shidai 諸寺建立次第 In vol. 1 of *Kōkan bijutsu shiryō,* ed. Fujita Tsuneyo, 163–182. Tokyo: Chuō Kōron Bijutsu Shuppan, 1972.

Shoku Nihongi 続日本紀. In *SNKBT,* vols. 12–16, ed. Aoki Kazuo et al. Tokyo: Iwanami Shoten, 1989–1998. See also Imaizumi Tadayoshi, ed., *Kundoku Shoku Nihongi.* Kyoto: Rinsen Shoten, 1986.

Shōtoku Taishi denki 聖徳太子伝記. In *YKT,* 1:87b–88b.
Shōtoku Taishi mandara kōshiki 聖徳太子曼荼羅講式 (1274–1275?). In *YTK,* 1:88b–89a.
Shōyoshō 聖誉鈔. In *DNBZ* 1973, vol. 72. Also in *DNBZ* 1922, vol. 112.
Shōyūki 小右記 (982–1032). By Fujiwara no Sanesuke. 3 vols. In *Zōho shiryō taisei,* bekkan 1–3, ed. Zōho Shiryō Taisei Kankōkai. Kyoto: Rinsen Shoten, 1965.
Sifenlü 四分律. T. 22, no. 1428.
Sifenlü biqiu hanzhu jieben 四分律比丘含注戒本. By Daoxuan. T. no. 1806.
Sifenlü shanbu suiji jiemo 四分律刪補隨機羯磨. By Daoxuan. T. no. 1808.
Sifenlü shanfanbuque xingshichao 四分律刪繁補闕行事鈔. By Daoxuan. T. no. 1804.
Sifenlü xingshichao zichiji 四分律行事鈔資持記. By Yuanzhao. T. no. 1805.
Sinpyeon jejong gyojang chongrok 新編諸宗教藏總錄. T. no. 2184.
Sōni ganmon rui jūgo shi 僧尼願文類十五紙. In *SEDS,* 393–396.
Taiki 台記. By Fujiwara no Yorinaga (1120–1156). Shiryō-sanshū, Kiroku-hen. Tokyo: Zoku Gunsho Ruijū Kanseikai, 1976.
Taima mandara chū 当麻曼荼羅註. Attr. to Shōku (1177–1247). In *Seizan zensho.* Kyoto: Buneidō Shoten, 1973.
Taishi mandara kōshiki 太子曼荼羅講式. In *YKT,* 1:88b–89a.
Tamakiwaru zenchūshaku たまきはる全注釈. Ed. Kobara Mikio et al. Tokyo: Kasama Shoin, 1983.
Tōdaiji Enshō Shōnin gyōjō 東大寺円照上人行状. Ed. Tōdaiji Kyōgakubu. Nara: Tōdaiji Toshokan, 1977.
Tōdaiji Tōnan-in monjo 東大寺東南院文書. In *Dai Nihon komonjo, iewake,* vol. 18.
Tōdaiji zoku yōroku 東大寺続要録. Annotated by Tsutsui Eishun. Tokyo: Kokusho Kokusho Kankōkai, 1971.
Toganoo Myōe Shōnin denki 栂尾明恵上人伝記. In *Myōe Shōnin shiryō,* ed. Kōzanji Tenseki Monjo Sōgō Chōsadan. Tokyo: Tokyo Daigaku Shuppankai, 1971–1987.
Towazugatari (TG) 問はず語り. By Go-Fukakusa-in Nijō (aka Nakanoin Masatada no Musume, b. 1258). In *SNKBZ,* vol. 47, ed. Kubota Jun. Also in *Towazugatari,* ed. Tomikura Tokujirō. Tokyo: Chikuma Sōsho, 1967.
Tsuma kagami 妻鏡 (1300). By Mujū Ichien (1226–1312). In *Kana hōgo shū,* ed. Miyasaka Yūshō, *NKBT,* vol. 83. Tokyo: Iwanami Shoten, 1964.
Tsunesada Shinnō den 恒貞親王伝. In *Zoku Gunsho ruijū,* vol. 190.
Uji shūi monogatari 宇治拾遺物語. In *SNKBZ,* vol. 50.
Utatane うたたね. By Abutsu-ni (d. 1283). In *Joryū nikki bungaku kōza,* vol. 6, ed. Imai Takuji et al. Tokyo: Benseisha, 1990.
Wayaku Hanazono Tennō shinki 和譯花園天皇宸記. Annotated by Murata Masashi. 3 vols. Tokyo: Zoku Gunsho Ruijū Kanseikai, 1998–2003.
Weiceng youyinyuan jing 未曾有因縁經. T. no. 754.
Wuliangyi jing 無量義經. T. no. 276.
Wuzhun Shifan chanshi yulu 無準師範禪師語錄, X. no. 1382.
Yamato monogatari 大和物語. In *NKBT,* vol. 9.
Yūjoki 遊女記. By Ōe no Masafusa (1041–1111). In *Kodai shakai shisō,* ed. Yamagishi Tokuhei, Takeuchi Rizō, Ienaga Saburō, and Ōsone Shōsuke, *NSTK,* vol. 8. Tokyo: Iwanami Shoten, 1979.
Yulanpen jing shou 盂蘭盆經疏. By Zongmi. T. no. 1792.

Yuqie shidu lun 瑜伽師地論. T. no. 1579.
Zhong ahan jing 中阿含經. T. no. 26.
Zōdanshū 雑談集 (1305). By Mujū Ichien (1226–1312). In Yamada Shōzen and Miki Sumito, eds., *Chūsei no bungaku*. Tokyo: Miyai Shoten, 1973.

Secondary Sources

Abé Ryūichi. 1999. *The Weaving of Mantra: Kūkai and the Construction of Esoteric Buddhist Discourse.* New York: Columbia University Press.

———. 2003. "Mantra, *Hinin,* and the Feminine: On the Salvational Strategies of Myōe and Eizon." *Cahiers d'Extrēme-Asie* 13:101–125.

Abe Yasurō. 1987. "Chūsei Nanto no shūkyō to geinō: Shinnyoni to Wakamiya miko o megurite" 中世南都の宗教と芸能：信如尼と若宮巫女を巡りて. *Kokugo to kokubunngaku* 国語と国文学 64, no. 5 (May): 72–85.

———. 1989. "Nyonin kinsei to suisan" 女人禁制と推参. In *Miko to megami,* vol. 4 of *Shirīzu josei to Bukkyō,* ed. Ōsumi Kazuo and Nishiguchi Junko, 153–240. Tokyo: Heibonsha.

———. 1991. Review of *Onna no chūsei: Ono no komachi, tomoe, sonota0* by Hosokawa Ryōichi. *Nihonshi kenkyū* 343:122–131.

———. 1998. *Yuya no kōgō: Chūsei no sei to seinaru mono* 湯屋の皇后：中世の性と聖なるもの. Nagoya: Nagoya Daigaku Shuppankai.

Abu-Lughod, Lila. 1990. "The Romance of Resistance: Tracing Transformations of Power through Bedouin Women." *American Ethnologist* 17, no. 1 (Feb.): 41–55.

Adolphson, Mikael. 2000. *The Gates of Power: Monks, Courtiers, and Warriors in Premodern Japan.* Honolulu: University of Hawai'i Press.

Adolphson, Mikael, Edward Kamens, and Stacie Matsumoto, eds. 2007. *Heian Japan: Centers and Peripheries.* Honolulu: University of Hawai'i Press.

Akiyama Terukazu. 1990. "Women Painters at the Heian Court." Adapted and trans. by Maribeth Graybill. In *Flowering in the Shadows: Women in the History of Chinese and Japanese Painting,* ed. Marsha Weidner, 159–184. Honolulu: University of Hawai'i Press.

Amino Yoshihiko. 1978. *Muen, kugai, raku: Nihon chūsei no jiyū to heiwa* 無縁・公界・楽：日本中世の自由と平和. Tokyo: Heibonsha.

———. 1989. "Yūjo to hinin, kawaramono" 遊女と非人・河原者. In *Sei to mibun: Jakusha, haisha no seisei to hiun* 性と身分：弱者・敗者の聖性と悲運, ed. Miyata Noboru, 93–128. Tokyo: Shunjūsha.

———. 1991. *Nihon no rekishi o yominaosu* 日本の歴史をよみなおす. Tokyo: Chikuma Shobō.

———. 1994. *Chūsei no hinin to yūjo* 中世の非人と遊女. Tokyo: Akashi Shoten.

Amino Yoshihiko and Gotō Nobuhiko, eds. 2002. *Yūjo, kugutsu, shirabyōshi* 遊女・傀儡・白拍子. Vol. 3 of *Asahi hyakka: Nihon no rekishi.* Tokyo: Asahi Shinbun Shuppan.

Arai, Paula. 1999. *Zen Nuns: Living Treasures of Japanese Buddhism.* New York: Oxford University Press.

———. 2000. "A Case of Ritual Zen: In Gratitude to Ānanda." In *Innovative Buddhist Women: Swimming against the Stream,* ed. Karma Lekshe Tsomo, 123–129. Richmond, Surrey, UK: Curzon.

———. 2008. "Women and Dōgen: Rituals Actualizing Empowerment and Healing." In *Zen Ritual: Studies of Zen Buddhist Theory in Practice,* ed. Steven Heine and Dale S. Wright, 185–204. Oxford: Oxford University Press.

Bernstein, Gail Lee. 1996. Introduction to *Re-imagining Japanese Women,* ed. Anne Imamura, 1–14. Berkeley: University of California Press.

Bielefeldt, Carl. 1988. *Dōgen's Manuals of Zen Meditation.* Berkeley: University of California Press.

Birge, Bettine. 2002. *Women, Property, and Confucian Reaction in Sung and Yüan China.* Cambridge: Cambridge University Press.

Bitel, Lisa. 2008. "Convent Ruins and Christian Profession: Towards a Methodology for the History of Religion and Gender." In *Gender and Christianity in Medieval Europe: New Perspectives,* ed. Lisa Bitel and Felice Lifshitz, 1–15. Philadelphia: University of Pennsylvania Press.

Blacker, Carmen. 1986. *The Catalpa Bow: A Study of Shamanistic Practices in Japan.* London: Harper Collins, Mandala.

Bodiford, William M. 1993. *Sōtō Zen in Medieval Japan.* Honolulu: University of Hawai'i Press.

———. 1994. "The Enlightenment of *Kami* and Ghosts: Spirit Ordinations in Japanese Sōtō Zen." *Cahiers d'Extrême-Asie* 7:267–282.

———. 1999. "Chidō's *Dreams of Buddhism.*" In *Religions of Japan in Practice,* by George Tanabe Jr., 235–245. Princeton: Princeton University Press.

———, ed. 2005. *Going Forth: Visions of Buddhist Vinaya.* Honolulu: University of Hawai'i Press.

Borgen, Robert. 2007. "A History of Dōmyōji to 1572 (or Maybe 1575): An Attempted Reconstruction." *Monumenta Nipponica* 62, no. 1 (Spring): 1–56.

Bourdieu, Pierre. 1977. *Outline of a Theory of Practice.* Trans. Richard Nice. Cambridge: Cambridge University Press.

Bowring, Richard John. 2005. *The Religious Traditions of Japan, 500–1600.* New York: Cambridge University Press.

Brazell, Karen. 1971. "*Towazugatari:* Autobiography of a Kamakura Court Lady." *Harvard Journal of Asiatic Studies* 31:220–233.

———, trans. 1973. *The Confessions of Lady Nijō.* Garden City, NY: Anchor.

Brock, Karen. 1990. "Chinese Maiden, Silla Monk: Zenmyō and Her Thirteenth-Century Japanese Audience." In *Flowering in the Shadows: Women in the History of Chinese and Japanese Painting,* ed. Marsha Weidner, 185–211. Honolulu: University of Hawai'i Press.

Brown, Delmer, and Ichirō Ishida, trans. 1979. *The Future and the Past: A Translation and Study of the "Gukanshō," an Interpretative History of Japan Written in 1219.* Berkeley: University of California Press.

Bynum, Caroline Walker. 1991. *Fragmentation and Redemption: Essays on Gender and the Human Body in Medieval Religion.* New York: Zone.

Chikusa Masaaki. 1989. "Chūgoku ni okeru nisō kyōdan no seiritsu to hatten" 中国における尼僧教団の成立と発展. In *Ama to amadera,* vol. 1 of *Shirīzu josei to Bukkyō,* ed. Ōsumi Kazuo and Nishiguchi Junko, 43–72. Tokyo: Heibonsha.

Childs, Margaret Helen. 1991. *Rethinking Sorrow: Revelatory Tales of Late Medieval Japan.* Ann Arbor: Center for Japanese Studies, University of Michigan.

Coates, Harper H., and Ishizuka Ryugaku. 1925. *Hōnen the Buddhist Saint.* Kyoto: Chionin.

Cole, Alan. 1998. *Mothers and Sons in Chinese Buddhism.* Stanford: Stanford University Press.

———. 2005. *Text as Father: Paternal Seductions in Early Mahāyāna Literature.* Berkeley: University of California Press.

Collcutt, Martin. 2002. "'Nun Shogun': Politics and Religion in the Life of Hōjō Masako (1157–1225)." In *Engendering Faith: Women and Buddhism in the Literary and Visual Arts of Japan,* ed. Barbara Ruch, 165–188. Ann Arbor: Center for Japanese Studies, University of Michigan.

Connelley, Joan Breton. 2007. *Portrait of a Priestess: Women and Ritual in Ancient Greece.* Princeton: Princeton University Press.

Constable, Giles. 1996. *The Reformation of the Twelfth Century.* Cambridge: Cambridge University Press.

Cook, Francis Dojun. 2002. *How to Raise an Ox: Zen Practice as Taught in Master Dogen's "Shobogenzo."* Boston: Wisdom Publications.

Deal, William E. 1998. "Buddhism and the State in Early Japan." In Buddhism in Practice, ed. Donald Lopez, 216–227. Princeton: Princeton University Press.

Dobbins, James C. 1995. "Women's Birth in the Pure Land as Women: Intimations from the Letters of Eshinni." *Eastern Buddhist,* n.s. 28, no. 1 (Spring): 108–122, plus color plate.

———, ed. 1996. The Legacy of Kuroda Toshio. Special issue, *Japanese Journal for Religious Studies* 23, nos. 3–4.

———. 1998. "Envisioning Kamakura Buddhism." In *Re-envisioning "Kamakura" Buddhism,* ed. Richard Payne, 24–42. Honolulu: University of Hawai'i Press.

———. 2002. *Jōdo Shinshū: Shin Buddhism in Medieval Japan.* Honolulu: University of Hawai'i Press.

———. 2004. *Letters of the Nun Eshinni: Images of Pure Land Buddhism in Medieval Japan.* Honolulu: University of Hawai'i Press.

Dreyfus, Georges B.J. 2003. *The Sound of Two Hands Clapping: The Education of a Tibetan Buddhist Monk.* Berkeley: University of California Press.

Dykstra, Yoshiko K. 1976. "Tales of the Compassionate Kannon: The *Hasedera Kannon genki.*" *Monumenta Nipponica* 31 (3): 113–143.

Endō Hajime. 2002. "The Original *Bōmori:* Husband and Wife Congregations in Early Shin Buddhism." In *Engendering Faith: Women and Buddhism in Premodern Japan,* ed. Barbara Ruch, 501–535. Ann Arbor: Center for Japanese Studies, University of Michigan.

Ericson, Joan E. 1996. "The Origin of the Concept of 'Women's Literature.'" In *The Woman's Hand: Gender and Theory in Japanese Women's Writing,* ed. Paul Gordon Schalow and Janet A. Walker, 75–118. Stanford: Stanford University Press.

Evangelisti, Silvia. 2007. *Nuns: A History of Convent Life.* Oxford: Oxford University Press.

Fabricand-Person, Nicole. 2001. "Filling the Void: The *Fugen Jūrasetsunyo* Iconography in Japanese Buddhist Art." PhD diss., Princeton University.

———. 2002. "Demonic Female Guardians of the Faith: The *Fugen Jūrasetsunyo* Iconography in Japanese Buddhist Art." In *Engendering Faith: Women and Buddhism in Premodern Japan,* ed. Barbara Ruch, 343–382. Ann Arbor: Center for Japanese Studies, University of Michigan.

Faure, Bernard. 1998. *The Red Thread: Buddhist Approaches to Sexuality.* Princeton: Princeton University Press.

———. 2003. *The Power of Denial: Buddhism, Purity, and Gender.* Princeton: Princeton University Press.

Foard, James. 1980. "In Search of a Lost Reformation: A Reconsideration of Kamakura Buddhism." *Japanese Journal of Religious Studies* 7, no. 4 (Dec.): 261–291.

Ford, James. 2006. *Jōkei and Buddhist Devotion in Early Medieval Japan.* Oxford: Oxford University Press.

Fowler, Sherry. 2005. *Murōji: Rearranging Art and History at a Japanese Buddhist Temple.* Honolulu: University of Hawai'i Press.

Fujita Tsuneyo. 1972. "Kenkyū gojunreiki" 建久御巡礼記. In vol. 1 of *Kōkan bijutsu shiryō,* ed. Fujita Tsuneyo, 125–130. Tokyo: Chuō Kōron Bijutsu Shuppan.

Fukuhara Toshio. 1987. "Gaisetsu" 概説. In *Shaji sankei mandara* 社寺参詣曼荼羅, ed. Osaka Shiritsu Hakubutsukan, 214–225. Tokyo: Heibonsha.

Fukushima Kaneharu. 1990. "Kanazawa Shōmyōji no nenjū gyōji" 金沢称名寺の年中行事. In *Kodai chūseishi ronshū* 古代中世史論集, ed. Kyūshū Daigaku Kokushigaku Kenkyūshitsu, 353–377. Tokyo: Yoshikawa Kōbunkan.

Fukutō Sanae. 1989. "Bochi saishi to josei: Heian zenki ni okeru kizokusō" 基地祭祀と女性：平安前期における貴族層. In *Shinjin to kuyō,* vol. 3 of *Shirīzu josei to Bukkyō,* ed. Ōsumi Kazuo and Nishiguchi Junko, 81–110. Tokyo: Heibonsha.

———. 1993. "Ie no seiritsu to josei: Konjaku monogatarishū no setsuwa kara" 家の成立と女性：今昔物語集の説話から. In *Chūsei no seikatsu-kūkan* 中世の生活空間, ed. Toda Yoshimi. Tokyo: Yūhikaku.

———. 1997. *Heianchō no ie to josei: Kita no mandokoro no seiritsu* 平安朝の家と女性：北政所の成立. Tokyo: Heibonsha.

Gay, Suzanne. 2001. *The Moneylenders of Late Medieval Kyoto.* Honolulu: University of Hawai'i Press.

Genjō Masayoshi. 1970. "Tōjiryō jōkeishō ni okeru ryōshuken kakuritsu katei ni tsuite" 東寺領上桂庄における領主権確立過程について. In *Chūsei no kenryoku to minshū* 中世の権力と民衆, ed. Nihonshi Kenkyūkai Shiryō Kenkyū, 112–141. Osaka: Sōgensha.

Glassman, Hank. 2001. "The Religious Construction of Motherhood in Medieval Japan." PhD diss., Stanford University.

———. 2002. "The Nude Jizō at Denkōji: Notes on Women's Salvation in Kamakura Buddhism." In *Engendering Faith: Women and Buddhism in Premodern Japan,* ed. Barbara Ruch, 383–416. Ann Arbor: Center for Japanese Studies, University of Michigan.

Goble, Andrew. 1989. "Truth, Contradiction, and Harmony in Medieval Japan: Emperor Hanazono (1297–1348) and Buddhism." *Journal of the International Association of Buddhist Studies* 12 (1): 21–63.

———. 1996. *Kenmu: Go-Daigo's Revolution.* Cambridge, MA: Harvard University Press.

Gómez, Luis O., trans. 1996. *The Longer Sukhāvatīvyūha Sūtra: English Translation of the Chinese Version Attributed to Samghavarman.* Honolulu: University of Hawai'i Press.

Gomi Fumihiko. 1984. *Inseiki shakai no kenkyū* 院政期社会の研究. Tokyo: Yamakawa Shuppansha.

———. 1988. *Kamakura to kyō* 鎌倉と京. Vol. 5 of *Taikei nihon no rekishi,* ed. Nagahara Keiji et al. Tokyo: Shōgakukan.

———. 1992. "Chūsei no ie to kafuchōsei" 中世の家と家父長性. In *Ie to kafuchōsei* 家と家父長性, ed. Nagahara Kenji, Sumitani Kazuhiko, and Kamata Hiroshi, 31–48. Tokyo: Waseda Daigaku Shuppanbu.

Goodwin, Janet R. 1994. *Alms and Vagabonds: Buddhist Temples and Popular Patronage in Medieval Japan.* Honolulu: University of Hawai'i Press.

———. 2007. *Selling Songs and Smiles: The Sex Trade in Heian and Kamakura Japan.* Honolulu: University of Hawai'i Press.

Goto Michiko. 2006. "The Lives and Roles of Women of Various Classes in the *Ie* of Late Medieval Japan." *International Journal of Asian Studies* 3 (2): 183–210.

Gotō Nobuhiko. 2002. "Yūjo to chōtei, kizoku: Chūsei zenki no yūjotachi" 遊女と朝廷・貴族:中世前期の遊女達. In *Yūjo, kugutsu, shirabyōshi* 遊女・傀儡・白拍子. Vol. 3 of *Asahi hyakka: Nihon no rekishi,* ed. Amino Yoshihiko and Gotō Nobuhiko, 70–72. Tokyo: Asahi Shinbun Shuppan.

Grapard, Allan. 1991. "Visions of Excess and Excesses of Vision: Women and Transgression in Japanese Myth." *Japanese Journal of Religious Studies* 18 (1): 3–22.

Grant, Beata. 2003. *Daughters of Emptiness: Poems of Chinese Buddhist Nuns.* Boston: Wisdom Publications.

Graybill, Maribeth, trans. 1990. "Women Painters at the Heian Court," by Akiyama Terukazu. In *Flowering in the Shadows: Women in the History of Chinese and Japanese Painting,* ed. Marsha Weidner, 159–184. Honolulu: University of Hawai'i Press.

Groner, Paul. 1984. *Saichō: The Establishment of the Japanese Tendai School.* Berkeley: Institute of Buddhist Studies, Center for South and Southeast Asian Studies, University of California, Berkeley. Reprint with a new preface, Honolulu: University of Hawai'i Press, 2000.

———. 2001. "Icons and Relics in Eison's Religious Activities." In *Living Images: Japanese Buddhist Icons in Context,* ed. Robert H. Sharf and Elizabeth Horton Sharf, 114–150. Stanford: Stanford University Press.

———. 2002a. *Ryōgen and Mount Hiei: Japanese Tendai in the Tenth Century.* Honolulu: University of Hawai'i Press.

———. 2002b. "Vicissitudes in the Ordination of Japanese 'Nuns' during the Eighth through the Tenth Centuries." In *Engendering Faith: Women and Buddhism in Premodern Japan,* ed. Barbara Ruch, 65–108. Ann Arbor: Center for Japanese Studies, University of Michigan.

———. 2005. "Tradition and Innovation: Eison's Self-Ordinations and the Establishment of New Orders of Buddhist Practitioners." In *Going Forth: Visions of Buddhist Vinaya,* ed. William Bodiford, 210–235. Honolulu: University of Hawai'i Press.

Gross, Rita. 1993. *Buddhism after Patriarchy: A Feminist History, Analysis, and Reconstruction of Buddhism.* Albany: State University of New York Press.

Guelberg, Neils. 1999. *Buddhistische Zeremoniale (Kōshiki) und ihre Bedeutung für die Literatur des Japanischen Mittelalters.* Stuttgart, Ger.: Steiner.

———. 2006. "Kōshiki to wa nanika?" 講式とは何か. In *Shōmyō shiryōshū* 声明資料集, ed. Nishōgakusha Daigaku 21-seiki COE puroguramu [program] chūsei Nihon kanbunhan, 30–40.Tokyo: Nishōgakusha Daigaku 21-seiki COE puroguramu [program].

Gyatso, Janet. 2003. "Two Plus One Makes Three: Buddhist Gender Conception and the Law of the Non-Excluded Middle." *History of Religions* 43, no. 2 (Nov.): 89–115.

———. 2005. "Sex." In *Critical Terms for the Study of Buddhism,* ed. Donald S. Lopez Jr., 271–290. Chicago: University of Chicago Press.

Hagiwara Tatsuo. 1983. *Miko to bukkyōshi* 巫女と仏教史. Tokyo: Yoshikawa Kōbunkan.

Hall, John Whitney. 1966. *Government and Local Power in Japan, 500–1700.* Princeton: Princeton University Press.

Hamburger, John F. 1992. "Art, Enclosure, and the Curia Monialium: Prolegomena in the Guise of a Postscript." *Gesta* 31:108–134.

Handa Satoshi. 1989. "Chūsei ni okeru ie to josei" 中世における家と女性. In *Ie to josei: Yakuwari* 家と女性：役割, ed. Ishikawa Eikichi, Minegishi Sumio, and Miki Taeko, 161–195. Tokyo: Sanseido.

Hao Chunwen. 1998. *Tang houqi Wudai Songchu Dunhuang sengni de shehui shenghuo* 唐後期五代宋初敦煌僧尼的社會生活 [The Social Lives of Monks and Nuns at Dunhuang in the Late Tang, Five Dynasties, and Early Song Periods]. Beijing: Zhongguo Shehui Kexueyuan Chubanshe.

Harada Masatoshi. 1997. "Nyonin to Zenshū" 女人と禅宗. In *Hotoke to onna* 仏と女, ed. Nishiguchi Junko, 140–180. Tokyo: Yoshikawa Kōbunkan.

———. 2004. "Zenshū to josei" 禅宗と女性. *Kokubungaku kaishaku to kanshō* 69, no. 6 (June): 125–132.

Haraguchi Shizuko. 2009. "Hokkekyō mandara to nyonin jōbutsu: Toyama-shi Honpōji shozōhon o chūshin ni" 法華経曼荼羅と女人成仏：富山市本法寺所蔵本を中心に. In *Amadera monjo chōsa no seika o kiban toshita Nihon no josei to Bukkyō no sōgō kenkyū* II, ed. Yoshiko Oka, 91–97. Kyoto: Kyowa Insatsu.

Harrison, Paul. 1998. "Women in the Pure Land: Some Reflections on the Textual Sources." *Journal of Indian Philosophy* 26 (6): 553–572.

Hattori Ryōjun. "Chūsei risshū no rekishiteki igi ni tsuite no ichi kōsatsu" 中世律宗の歴史的意義についての一考察. *Nanto Bukkyō* 70:1–15.

Hayami Tasuku, ed. *Inseiki no Bukkyō* 院政期の仏教. Tokyo: Yoshikawa Kōbunkan, 1998.

Hayashi Michiyoshi. 1990. *Mikoto to miko no shinwagaku: Nihonjin no kokoro no genkei* 尊と巫女の神話学：日本人の心の原型. Tokyo: Meicho Kankōkai.

Hayashi Mikiya. 1980. *Taishi shinkō no kenkyū* 太子信仰の研究. Tokyo: Yoshikawa Kōbunkan.

Heirman, Ann. 2001. "Chinese Nuns and Their Ordination in Fifth-Century China." *Journal of the International Association of Buddhist Studies* 24 (2): 275–304.

———. 2002. *"The Discipline in Four Parts": Rules for Nuns according to the "Dharmaguptakavinaya."* 3 vols. Delhi: Motilal Banarsidass Publishers, 2002.

Hixon, Lex. 1993. *Mother of the Buddhas: Meditation on the Prajnaparamita Sūtra.* Wheaton, IL: Quest.

Hodate Michihisa. 2001. "Josei no shokumin to sen'i seisan" 女性の職民と繊維生産. In *Toshi to shokunōmin* 都市と職能民, ed. Chūsei Toshi Kenkyūkai, 118–137. Tokyo: Shin Jinbutsu Ōraisha.

Hongō Keiko. 2004. *Chūseijin no keizai kankaku: "Okaimono" kara saguru* 中世人の経済感覚:「お買い物」からさぐる. Tokyo: Nihon Hōsō Shuppan Kyōkai.

Hongō Masatsugu. 1989. "'Kokka Bukkyō' to 'kyūtei Bukkyō': Kyūtei josei no yakuwari" 「国家仏教」「と宮廷仏教」:宮廷女性の役割. In *Shinjin to kuyō,* vol. 3 of *Shirīzu josei to Bukkyō,* ed. Ōsumi Kazuo and Nishiguchi Junko, 207–236. Tokyo: Heibonsha.

Hori Yutaka. 2003. "Hōe ni kizamareta kodai no kioku: Daiku to Daisutarasū" 法会に刻まれた古代の記憶:大供と大修多羅衆. *Bukkyō shigaku kenkyū* 46 (1): 47–75.

Horiike Shunpō. 1977. "Enshō Shōnin gyōjō kaisetsu" 円照上人行状解説. In *Tōdaiji Enshō Shōnin gyōjō,* ed. Tōdaiji kyōgakubu. Nara: Tōdaiji Toshokan.

Hosokawa Ryōichi. 1987. *Chūsei no Risshū jiin to minshū* 中世の律宗寺院と民衆. Tokyo: Yoshikawa Kōbunkan.

———. 1989a. *Onna no chūsei: Ono no komachi, tomoe, sono ta* 女の中世:小野小町・巴・その他. Tokyo: Nihon Editasukūru.

———. 1989b. "Sairinji Sōji to ama" 西林寺惣持と尼. In *Sukui to Oshie,* vol. 2 of *Shirīzu josei to Bukkyō,* ed. Ōsumi Kazuo and Nishiguchi Junko, 121–164. Tokyo: Heibonsha.

———. 1993. *Itsudatsu no nihon chūsei: Kyōki, tōsaku, ma no sekai* 逸脱の日本中世:狂気・倒錯・魔の世界. Tokyo: JICC Shuppankyoku.

———. 1994. "Chūsei Daianji no nenjū gyōji" 中世大安寺の年中行事. *Keizaigaku ronsan* 34 (5): 77–84.

———. 1997. *Chūsei no jiin no fūkei: Chūsei minshū no seikatsu to shinsei* 中世の寺院の風景:中世民衆の生活と心性. Tokyo: Shin'yōsha.

———. 1999a. "Kamakura Period Nuns and Convents: Exploring Hokkeji Convent." Trans. Micah Auerback. In *Gender and Japanese History* 1, ed. Wakita Haruko et al., 25–51. Osaka: Osaka University Press.

———, trans. and annotator. 1999b. *Kanjin gakushōki: Saidaiji Eison no jiden* 感身学正記:西大寺叡尊の自伝. Tokyo: Heibonsha, 1999.

———. 1999c. "Medieval Nuns and Nunneries: The Case of Hokkeji." Trans. Paul Groner. In *Women and Class in Japanese History,* ed. Hitomi Tonomura, Anne Walthall, and Wakita Haruko, 67–80. Ann Arbor: Center for Japanese Studies, University of Michigan.

———. 2006. "Nihonshi no josei shin no jitsuryoku: Sōzoku to isan" 日本史の女性真の「実力」:相続と遺産. *Rekishi Tokuhon* 歴史読本 51.11 (August): 54–61.

Hosokawa Ryōichi and Tabata Yasuko. 2002. *Nyonin, rōjin, kodomo* 女人、老人、子ども. Vol. 4 of *Nihon no chūsei,* ed. Amino Yoshihiko and Ishi'i Susumu. Tokyo: Chuō Kōron Shinsha.

Hurst, G. Cameron. 1974. "The Structure of the Heian Court: Some Thoughts on the Nature of 'Familial Authority' in Heian Japan." In *Medieval Japan: Essays in Institutional History,* ed. John W. Hall and Jeffrey P. Mass, 39–59. New Haven: Yale University Press.

———. 1982. "The Kōbu Polity: Court-Bakufu Relations in Kamakura Japan." In *Court and Bakufu in Japan: Essays in Kamakura History,* ed. Jeffrey Mass, 3–28. New Haven: Yale University Press.

Hurvitz, Leon, trans. 1976. *Scripture of the Lotus Blossom of the Fine Dharma.* New York: Columbia University Press.

Igeta Midori. 1983. "The Image of Women in Sermons." *Japanese Journal of Religious Studies* 10 (2–3): 247–272.

Iinuma Kenji. 1992. "Go goke no chikara: Sono seiritsu to yakuwari o megutte" ご後家 の力：その成立と役割を巡って. In *Kazoku to josei: Chūsei o kangaeru* 家族と女性：中世を考える, ed. Minegishi Sumio, 153–78. Tokyo: Yoshikawa Kōbunka.

Imabori Taichi. 1997. "Hōnen no nenbutsu to josei" 法然の念仏と女性. In *Hotoke to onna* 仏と女, ed. Nishiguchi Junko, 67–107. Tokyo: Yoshikawa Kōbunkan.

Imazeki Toshiko. 1987. *Chūsei joryū nikki bungaku ronsō* 中世女流日記文学論争. Osaka: Wasen Shoten.

Inagaki Eizō, ed. 1994. *Daigoji no mikkyō to shakai* 醍醐寺の密教と社会. Tokyo: Sankibō.

Inoue Kiyoshi. 1947. *Nihon joseishi* 日本女性史. Kyoto: San'ichi Shobō.

Inoue Mitsusada. 1985. "Eizon, Ninshō, and the Saidai-ji Order." *Inoue Mitsusada chosakushū* 井上光貞著作集 9:373–344. Tokyo: Iwanami Shoten.

Institute for Medieval Japanese Studies, ed. 2009. *Amamonzeki, a Hidden Heritage: Treasures of the Japanese Imperial Convents.* Tokyo, Sankei Shinbunsha.

Irie Taikichi. 1996. *Matsuri to Saijiki* 祭と歳時記. Vol. 5 of *Irie Taikichi no Yamatoji.* Tokyo: Shogakukan.

Ishida Eiichiro. 1964. "Mother-son Deities." *History of Religions* 4 (1): 30–52.

Ishida Mizumaro. 1978. "Bikuni kaidan: Ama no tokui na seikaku" 比丘尼戒壇：尼の特異な性格. *Musashino Joshi Daigaku Kiyō* 18:1–15.

———. 1995. *Nyobon: Hijiri no sei* 女犯：聖の性. Tokyo: Chikuma Shobō.

Ishida Yoshisada. 1957. *Fujiwara Sadaie (Teika) no Kenkyū* 藤原定家の研究. Tokyo: Bungadō.

Ishi'i Susumu. 1988. *Chūsei no hito to seiji* 中世のひとと政治. Tokyo: Yoshikawa Kōbunkan.

Ishizaki Shōko and Sakurai Yuki, eds. 1998. *Sei to shintai* 性と身体. Vol. 9 of *Nihon joseishi ronshū,* ed. Sōgō Joseishi Kenkyūkai. Tokyo: Yoshikawa Kōbunkan.

Iwahara Taishin. 1986. "Nanzan shinryū shōmyō kyōten" 南山進流声明教典. In vol. 16 (Hōshiki 3) of *Shingonshū sensho* 真言宗選書, ed. Sensho Kankōkai. Kyoto: Shingonshū Sensho Kankōkai.

Iwasa Miyoko. 1991a. "'Menoto no fumi' kō" 乳母のふみ考. *Kokubun Tsurumi* 26:1–10.

———. 1991b. "Chūsei no joryū nikki—Nakatsukasa naishi nikki—yūai no bungaku" 中世の女流日記—中務内侍日記—友愛の文学. *Bungaku* (Iwanami) 2 (3): 80–91.

Johnston, William M. 2005. "Monasticism." In *New Dictionary of the History of Ideas,* by Mary Cline Horowitz, 1497–1501. New York: Charles Scribner's Sons.

Joseishi Sōgō Kenkyūkai, ed. 1982. *Nihon joseishi* 日本女性史. 5 vols. Tokyo: Tokyo Daigaku Shuppankai.

———. 1990. *Nihon josei seikatsushi* 日本女性生活史. 5 vols. Tokyo: Tokyo Daigaku Shuppankai.

Kamens, Edward. 1988. *The Three Jewels: A Study and Translation of Minamoto Tamemori's "Sanbōe."* Ann Arbor: Center for Japanese Studies, University of Michigan.

———. 1990. *The Buddhist Poetry of the Great Kamo Priestess: Daisaiin Senshi and "Hosshin Wakashū."* Ann Arbor: Center for Japanese Studies, University of Michigan.

———. 1993. "Dragon-Girl, Maidenflower, Buddha: The Transformation of a Waka Topos, 'The Five Obstructions.'" *Monumenta Nipponica* 53 (2): 389–442.

Kasahara Kazuo. 1974. *Bukkyō ni miru chūsei to gendai* 仏教にみる中世と現代. Tokyo: Hyōronsha.

———. 1975. *Nyonin ōjōshisō no keifu* 女人往生思想の系譜. Tokyo: Yoshikawa Kōbunkan.

———, ed. 1976. *Higan ni ikiru chūsei no onna* 彼岸に生きる中世の女. In *Nihon joseishi,* vol. 3. Tokyo: Hyōronsha.

Katakura Hisako and Kuroda Kyoko, eds. 1997. *Ie to josei* 家と女性. In *Nihon joseishi ronshū,* by Sōgō Joseishi Kenkyūkai, vol. 3. Tokyo: Yoshikawa Kōbunkan.

Katsuura Noriko. 1986. "Josei to jigoku no nōto" 女性と地獄のノート. In *Nihon no josei to Bukkyō: kaihō* 日本の女性と仏教：会報 3 (August): 3–14.

———. 1989. "Ama sogi kō: Kami gata kara mita ama no sonzai keitai" 尼削ぎ攷：髪型からみた尼の 存在形態. In *Ama to amadera,* vol. 2 of *Shirīzu josei to Bukkyō,* ed. Ōsumi Kazuo and Nishiguchi Junko, 11–42. Tokyo: Heibonsha.

———. 1990. "Josei to kodai shinkō" 女性と古代信仰. In *Genshi, kodai,* vol. 1 of *Nihon josei seikatsushi,* ed. Joseishi Sōgō Kenkyūkai, 69–104. Tokyo: Tokyo Daigaku Shuppankai.

———. 1995. *Onna no shinjin: Tsuma ga shukke shita jidai* 女の信心：妻が出家した時代. Tokyo: Heibonsha, 1995.

———. 1997. "Onna no shigo to sono kyūsai" 女の死後とその救済. In *Hotoke to onna* 仏と女, ed. Nishiguchi Junko, 34–66. Tokyo: Yoshikawa Kōbunkan.

———. 1999. "Kodai no ama to amadera" 古代の尼と尼寺. In *Nihonshi no naka no josei to Bukkyō* 日本史の中の女性と仏教, ed. Yoshida Kazuhiko et al., 86–119. Kyoto: Hōzōkan.

———. 2000. *Nihon kodai no sōni to shakai* 日本古代の僧尼と社会. Tokyo: Yoshikawa Kōbunkan.

———. 2003. *Kodai, chūsei no josei to Bukkyō* 古代・中世の女性と仏教. Tokyo: Yamakawa Shuppan.

———. 2004. "Bukkyō denrai to Higashi Ajia no nisō-tachi" 仏教伝来と東アジアの尼僧たち. *Kaishaku to kanshō* 69 (6): 14–21.

———. 2008. "*Sanbōe* Sai-in Anan keka: Amadera butsuji no keifu" 「三宝絵」西院阿難悔過：尼寺仏事の系譜. In *"Sanbōe" o yomu* 三宝絵を読む, ed. Kojima Takayuki, Kobayashi Mayumi, and Komine Kazuaki, 99–125. Tokyo: Yoshikawa Kōbunkan.

———. 2009. "Josei to kegarekan" 女性と穢れ観. In *Amadera monjo chōsa no seika o kiban toshita Nihon no josei to Bukkyō no sōgō kenkyū* II, ed. Yoshiko Oka, 8–13. Kyoto: Kyowa Insatsu.

Kawai Sachiko. 2007. "The Lady of the Eight Ward: Political, Economic, and Military Power of Nyoin during the Twelfth Century, Japan." M.A. thesis, University of Southern California.

Khandelwal, Meena, Sondra L. Hausner, and Ann Grodzins Gold, eds. 2005. *Women's Renunciation in South Asia: Nuns, Yoginis, Saints, and Singers.* New York: Palgrave Macmillan.

Kiley, Cornelius. 1982. "The Imperial Court as a Legal Authority in the Kamakura Age." In *Court and Bakufu in Japan: Essays in Kamakura History,* ed. Jeffrey Mass, 29–44. New Haven: Yale University Press.

Kim, Yung-Hee. 1994. *Songs to Make the Dust Dance: The Ryōjin Hishō of Twelfth-Century Japan*. Berkeley: University of California Press.

Kimura Saeko. 2004. "Jotei no umareru toki: *Wagami ni tadoru himegimi* ni okeru ōjō o meguru kōsōryoku (imagination)" 女帝の生まれるとき：我身にたどる姫君における往生をめぐる構想力 (imagination). *Gengi jōhō kagaku* 2:67–80.

Knechtges, David, trans. and annotator. 1987. *Wen Xuan, or Selections from Refined Literature,* by Xiao Tong. 2 vols. Princeton: Princeton University Press.

Ko, Dorothy. 1994. *Teachers of the Inner Chambers: Women and Culture in Seventeenth-Century China*. Stanford: Stanford University Press.

———. 2005. *Cinderella's Sisters: A Revisionist History of Footbinding*. Berkeley: University of California Press.

Ko, Dorothy, Jahyun Kim Haboush, and Joan R. Piggott, eds. 2003. *Women and Confucian Cultures in Premodern China, Korea, and Japan*. Berkeley: University of California Press.

Kōbayashi Tsuyoshi. 1977. Notes on primary sources. In *SEDS,* 445–474.

Kobayashi Takeshi and Sugiyama Jirō. 1960. "Dōmyōji Shōtoku Taishi zō: Shōtoku taishizō kenkyū no naka" 道明寺聖徳太子像：聖徳太子像研究の中. In *Bunkashi ronsō* 文化史論争, ed. Nara kokuritsu bunkazai kenkyūjo. Vol. 8 of *Nara kokuritsu bunkazai kenkyūjo gakuhō,* 31–53. Tokyo: Yoshikawa Kōbunkan.

Kōdate Naomi. 1988. "Chi no ike jigoku no esō o meguru oboegaki: Kyūsaisha toshite no Nyoirin Kannon no mondai o chūshin ni" 血の池地獄の絵相をめぐる覚書：救済者としての如意輪観音の問題を中心に. *Etoki kenkyū* 6:667–690.

———. 1991. "*Ketsubongyō* to nyonin kyūsai: 'Chi no ike jigoku no katari' o chūshin ni site" 「血盆経」と女人救済：「血の池地獄の語り」を中心として. *Kokubungaku kaishaku to kanshō* 56 (5): 124–128.

———. 1992. "Ecchū Tateyama ni okeru Ketsubongyō shinkō 1" 越中立山における血盆経信仰 1. In *Toyama-ken Tateyama Hakubutsukan chōsa kenkyū hōkokusho* 富山県博物館調査研究報告書, 1–27. Tateyama: Tateyama Hakubutsukan.

———. 1993. "Ecchū Tateyama ni okeru Ketsubongyō shinkō 2" 越中立山における血盆経信仰 2. In *Toyama-ken Tateyama Hakubutsukan chōsa kenkyū hōkokusho* 富山県博物館調査研究報告書, 1–25. Tateyama: Tateyama Hakubutsukan.

Koida Tomoko. 2004. "Josei no junrei to engi, reigen setsuwa: *Kumano mōde nikki* o megutte" 女性の巡礼と縁起：霊験説話: 熊野詣日記をめぐって. *Junreiki kenkyū* 1:57–71.

Kojima Kyōko and Shiomi Minako, eds. 1998. *Josei to shūkyō* 女性と宗教. Vol. 5 of *Nihon joseishi ronshū,* ed. Sōgō Joseishi Kenkyūkai. Tokyo: Yoshikawa Kōbunkan.

Kojima Shin'ichi. 1989. *Nihon no shāman* 日本のシャーマン. Tokyo: Hachiman Shoten.

Komatsu Shigemi. 1994. "Ōchō no joseitachi to 'onna-e' no sekai" 王朝の女性たちと「女絵」の世界. In vol. 10 of *Nihon no emaki,* ed. Komatsu Shigemi, 98–118. Tokyo: Chuō Kōronsha.

———. 2005a. *Zusetsu heike nōkyō* 図説平家納経. Tokyo: Ebisukōshō Shuppan.

———. 2005b. *Heike nōkyō: Taira no Kiyomori to sono seiritsu* 平家納経:平清盛とその成立. Tokyo: Chūō Kōron Bijutsu Shuppan.

Kōshō Bosatsu Onkyōkai Chōmonshū Kenkyūkai, eds. 2003. "*Kōshō Bosatsu onkyōkai chōmonshū* yakuchū kenkyū" 興正菩薩御教誡聴聞集訳注研究. Matsuo Kenji, supervisor. *Nihon Bukkyō sōgō kenkyū* 2:97–153.

Kubota Jun. 1993. *Chūsei wakashi no kenkyū* 中世和歌史の研究. Tokyo: Meiji Shoin.

Kuroda Hiroko. 1990. "Chūseikōki no mura no onnatachi" 中世後期の村の女達. In *Chūsei,* vol. 2 of *Nihon josei seikatsushi,* ed. Joseishi Sōgō Kenkyūkai, 187–222.

Kuroda Toshio. 1975. "Chūsei ni okeru kenmitsu taisei no tenkai" 中世における顕密体制の展開. In *Nihon chūsei no kokka to shūkyō* 日本中世の国家と宗教, by Kuroda Toshio. Tokyo: Iwanami Shoten.

———. 1980. *Jisha seiryoku: Mō hitotsu no chūsei* 寺社勢力：もう一つの中世社会. Tokyo: Iwanami Shoten.

———. 1996. "The World of Spirit Pacification: Issues of State and Religion." *Japanese Journal of Religious Studies* 23 (3–4): 321–351.

———. 1999. "Shintō in the History of Japanese Religion: An Essay by Kuroda Toshio." Trans. James Dobbins and Suzanne Gay. In *Religions of Japan in Practice,* ed. George J. Tanabe, 451–467. Princeton: Princeton University Press.

Kyōraku Mahoko. 1999. "Taking the Tonsure in Eleventh-Century Heian-kyō: Buddhism, Women, and the City." Trans. Gustav Heldt. In *Women and Class in Japanese History,* ed. Tonomura Hitomi, Anne Walthall, and Wakita Haruko, 3–23. Ann Arbor: University of Michigan Press.

Laffin, Christina Charlotte. 2005. "Women, Travel, and Cultural Production in Kamakura Japan: A Socio-literary Analysis of 'Izayoi nikki' and 'Towazugatari.'" PhD diss., Columbia University.

———. 2009. "What's Nunhood Got to Do with It? Power, Patronage, Poetry, and the Case of Abutsu-ni (1222–1283)." Paper presented at the University of Southern California.

LaFleur, William R. 1983. *The Karma of Words: Buddhism and the Literary Arts in Medieval Japan.* Berkeley: University of California Press.

Lawrence, C. H. 2001. *Medieval Monasticism: Forms of Religious Life in Western Europe in the Middle Ages.* Harlow, UK: Pearson Education.

Li-ying Kuo. 1994. *Confession et contrition dans le bouddhisme chinois du Ve au Xe siècle.* Paris: Ecole française d'Extrēme-Orient.

Lopez, Donald, ed. 1998. *Buddhism in Practice.* Princeton: Princeton University Press.

Macy, Gary. 2008. *The Hidden History of Women's Ordination: Female Clergy in the Medieval West.* Oxford: Oxford University Press.

Mahmood, Saba. 2005. *Politics of Piety: The Islamic Revival and the Feminist Subject.* Princeton: Princeton Univeristy Press.

Marra, Michele. 1984. "*Mumyōzōshi:* Introduction and Translation." *Monumenta Nipponica* 39 (2): 115–145.

———. 1993. "The Buddhist Mythmaking of Defilement: Sacred Courtesans in Medieval Japan." *Journal of Asian Studies* 52, no. 1 (Feb.): 49–65.

Martin, John Hilary. 1986. "The Ordination of Women and the Theologians in the Middle Ages." *Escritos del Vedat* 36:115–177.

Mass, Jeffrey, ed. 1982. *Court and Bakufu in Japan: Essays in Kamakura History.* New Haven: Yale University Press.

———. 1985. "Patterns of Provincial Inheritance in Late Heian Japan." *Journal of Japanese Studies* 9 (1): 67–95.

———. 1988–1989. "The Kamakura Bakufu." In *Medieval Japan,* ed. Kozo Yamamura. Vol. 3 of *The Cambridge History of Japan,* ed. John W. Hall et al., 46–88. New York: Cambridge University Press.

———. 1989. *Lordship and Inheritance in Medieval Japan: A Study of the Kamakura Sōryō System.* Stanford: Stanford University Press.

Matsuhara Junshi. 1998. "Chūsei zenki ni okeru yūjo, kairaishi no 'ie' to chōja" 中世前期における遊女・傀儡子の「家」と長者. In *Sei to shintai* 性と身体, ed. Ishizaki Shōko and Sakurai Yuki, vol. 9 of *Nihon joseishi ronshū,* ed. Sōgō Joseishi Kenkyūkai, 3–26. Tokyo: Yoshikawa Kōbunkan.

Matsumoto Yasushi. 1986. "Abutsu." In *Nihon kotenbungaku daijiten.* Tokyo: Iwanami Shoten.

Matsumura Yūji. 1999. *"Towazugatari" no naka no chūsei* 「とはずがたり」のなかの中世. Kyoto: Nozogawa Shoten.

Matsuo Kenji. 1989. "Tonseisō to josei kyūsai" 遁世僧と女性救済. In *Sukui to Oshie,* vol. 2 of *Shirīzu josei to Bukkyō,* ed. Ōsumi Kazuo and Nishiguchi Junko, 93–120. Tokyo: Heibonsha.

———. 1995. *Kanjin to hakai no chūseishi: Chūsei Bukkyō no jissō* 勧進と破戒の中世史：中世仏教の実相. Tokyo: Yoshikawa Kōbunkan.

———. 1996. "Saidaiji Eisonzō ni nōnyū sareta 'jubosatsukai deshi kōmyō' to 'gonjū nannyo kyōmyō'" 西大寺叡尊像に納入された「授菩薩戒弟子交名」と「近住男女交名」. *Nanto Bukkyō* 73 (Nov.): 87–107.

———. 1998. *Kamakura shin Bukkyō no seiritsu: Nyūmon girei to soshi shinwa* 鎌倉新仏教の成立：入門儀礼と祖師神話. New ed. Tokyo: Yoshikawa Kōbunkan. (Orig. pub. 1988.)

———. 2001. "Official Monks and Reclusive Monks: Focusing on the Salvation of Women." *Bulletin of the School of Oriental and African Studies* 64 (3): 369–80.

———. 2002. *"Obōsan" no Nihonshi* 「お坊さん」の日本史. Tokyo: Nihon Hōsō Shuppan Kyōkai.

———. 2004a. *Ninshō: Jihi ni Sugita* 忍性：慈悲ニ過ギタ. Kyōto: Mineruva Shobō.

———. 2004b. "Eison no shōgai" 叡尊の生涯. In *Eison, Ninshō: Jikai no seija* 叡尊・忍性：持戒の聖者, ed. Matsuo Kenji, 13–44. Tokyo: Yoshikawa Kōbunkan.

Matsuoka Hideaki. 1998. "Wagakuni ni okeru Ketsubonkyō shinkō ni tsuite no ichikōsatsu" 我が国における血梵経信仰についての一考察. In *Josei to shūkyō* 女性と宗教, ed. Kojima Kyōko and Shiomi Minako, vol. 5 of *Nihon joseishi ronshū,* ed. Sōgō Joseishi Kenkyūkai, 257–279. Tokyo: Yoshikawa Kōbunkan.

Matsushita Midori. 2007. "Chūsei kōki ni okeru nyonin jōbutsu shisō" 中世後期における女人成仏思想. *Nihon Bukkyō sōgō kenkyū* 5:33–50.

McCallum, Donald F. 2009. *The Four Great Temples: Buddhist Archaeology, Architecture, and Icons of Seventh-Century Japan.* Honolulu: University of Hawai'i Press.

McCullough, William, and Helen Craig McCullough, trans. 1980. *A Tale of Flowering Fortunes: Annals of Japanese Aristocratic Life in the Heian Period.* Stanford: Stanford University Press.

McLaughlin, Mary Martin. 1989. "Creating and Recreating Communities of Women: The Case of Corpus Domini, Ferrara, 1406–1452." *Signs* 14, no. 2 (Winter): 293–320.

McNamara, Jo Ann Kay. 1996. *Sisters in Arms: Catholic Nuns through Two Millennia.* Cambridge, MA: Harvard University Press.

Meech-Pekarik, Julia. 1976. "Taira Kiyomori and the Heike Nōgyō." PhD diss., Harvard University.

Meeks, Lori. 2006. "Reconfiguring Ritual Authenticity: The Ordination Traditions of Aristocratic Women in Premodern Japan." *Japanese Journal of Religious Studies* 33 (1): 51–74.

———. 2007. "In Her Likeness: Female Divinity and Leadership at Medieval Chūgūji." *Japanese Journal of Religious Studies* 34 (2): 351–392.

———. 2008. "Chūgūji and Female Monasticism in the Age of Shōtoku." In *Hōryūji Reconsidered,* ed. Dorothy Wong, 237–262. Cambridge: Cambridge Scholars Press.

———. 2009. "Vows for the Masses: Eison and the Popular Expansion of Precept-Conferral Ceremonies in Premodern Japan." *Numen* 56, no. 1 (Jan.): 1–43.

Mikoshiba Daisuke. 1989. "Kōmyōshi no Bukkyō shinkō" 光明子の仏教信仰. In *Ama to amadera,* vol. 1 of *Shirīzu josei to Bukkyō,* ed. Ōsumi Kazuo and Nishiguchi Junko, 73–104. Tokyo: Heibonsha.

Milledge Nelson, Sarah, ed. 2007. *Women in Antiquity: Theoretical Approaches to Gender and Archaeology.* New York: Rowman and Littlefield, Alta Mira Press.

Minamoto Junko. 1981. *Kamakura Jōdokyō to josei* 鎌倉浄土教と女性. Kyoto: Nagata Bunshōdō.

———. 1993. "Buddhism and the Historical Construction of Sexuality in Japan." Trans. Hank Glassman. *U.S.-Japan Women's Journal, English Supplement* 5:87–115.

———. 1996. *Bukkyō to sei: Erosu e no ifu to sabetsu* 仏教と性：エロスへの畏怖と差別. Tokyo: San'ichi Shōbō.

Minegishi Sumio, ed. 1992. *Kazoku to josei* 家族と女性. Tokyo: Yoshikawa Kōbunkan.

Miner, Earl, Hiroko Odagiri, and Robert E. Morrell. 1985. *The Princeton Companion to Classical Japanese Literature.* Princeton: Princeton University Press.

Minowa Kenryō. 1996a. "Eison kyōdan ni okeru kōseiin no kaisō: Gonji, gonjū to gyōdō, hōdō shami" 叡尊教団における構成員の階層：近事・近住と形同・法同沙弥. *Shūkyō kenkyū* 309 (Sept.): 75–98.

———. 1996b. "Eison kyōdan ni okeru bosatsukai no juju: Saidaiji zō *Jubosatsukai yōi kikigaki* to *Jubosatsukai sahō* o chūshin ni." 叡尊教団における菩薩戒の授受：西大寺「蔵授菩薩戒用意聞書」と「授菩薩戒作法」を中心に. *Nanto Bukkyō* 73 (Nov.): 60–86.

———. 1999. *Chūsei shoki Nanto kairitsu fukkō no kenkyū* 中世初期南都戒律復興の研究. Kyoto: Hōzōkan.

———. 2005. "Zen and the Precepts in Medieval Nara Buddhism." Paper presented at the annual meeting of the American Academy of Religion, Philadelphia, PA, Nov. 20.

———. 2006. "Chūsei Nanto ni okeru sangaku no fukkō" 中世南都における三学の復興. *Bukkyōgaku* 48 (Dec.): 41–68.

Mitsuhashi Tadashi. 2000. *Heianjidai no shinkō to shūkyō girei* 平安時代の信仰と宗教儀礼. Tokyo: Zoku Gunsho Ruijū Kanseikai.

Miya Tsugio. 1964a. "Megamizō" 女神像. *Nihon bijutsu kōgei* 日本美術工芸 306: 42–50.

———. 1964b. "Kamakura jidai no megami-tachi" 鎌倉時代の女神達. *Nihon bijutsu kōgei* 日本美術工芸 312: 11–19.

Miyake, Lynne K. 1996. "*The Tosa Diary:* In the Interstices of Gender and Criticism." In *The Woman's Hand: Gender and Theory in Japanese Women's Writing,* ed. Paul Gordon Schalow and Janet A. Walker, 41–73. Stanford: Stanford University Press.

Miyamoto Nagajirō and Ariga Yoshitaka. 1978. "Yokobue dō" 横笛堂. In *YKT,* 5:50–51.

Mizuno Keizaburō. 1978. "Yuima koji zazō" 維摩居士坐像. In *YKT,* 5:61–63.

Mizuno Yaoko, annotator. 1990–1993. *Shōbōgenzō* 正法眼蔵. By Dōgen. 4 vols. Tokyo: Iwanami Shoten.

Moerman, D. Max. 2006. *Localizing Paradise: Kumano Pilgrimage and the Religious Landscape of Premodern Japan.* Cambridge, MA: Harvard University Asia Center.

Mori Ikuo. 1976. "Chūgūji no rekishi" 中宮寺の歴史. In *YKT,* 1:55–60.

———. 1978. "Kawara" 瓦. In *YKT,* 5:52–56.

Morrell, Robert. 1980. "Mirror for Women: Mujū Ichien's *Tsuma Kagami.*" *Monumenta Nipponica* 35 (1980): 45–75.

———. 1985. *Sand and Pebbles (Shasekishū): The Tales of Mujū Ichien, a Voice for Pluralism in Kamakura Buddhism.* Albany: State University of New York Press.

Morrell, Sachiko Kaneko, and Robert E. Morrell. 1983. "Sanctuary: Kamakura's Tokeji Convent." *JJRS* 10 (2–3): 195–228.

———. 2006. *Zen Sanctuary of Purple Robes: Japan's Tōkeiji Convent since 1285.* Albany: State University of New York Press.

Morris, Ivan, trans. 1971. *As I Crossed a Bridge of Dreams: Recollections of a Woman in Eleventh-Century Japan (Sarashina nikki).* New York: Dial.

———, trans. 1991. *The Pillow Book of Sei Shōnagon.* New York: Columbia University Press.

Morris, Joan. 1973. *The Lady Was a Bishop: The Hidden History of Women with Clerical Ordination and the Jurisdiction of Bishops.* New York: Macmillan.

Murakami Nobuhiko. 1970. "Joseishi kenkyū no kadai to tenbō" 女性史研究の課題と展望. *Shisō* 549 (Mar.): 83–95.

Nagai Yoshinori. 1967. *Nihon Bukkyō bungaku kenkyū* 日本仏教文学研究. Tokyo: Tōshima Shobō.

Nagamura Makoto. 1976. "Chūsei Tōdaiji shiin no zaisei katsudō: Toku ni Ryōgain o tooshite" 中世東大寺子院の財政活動：特に楞伽院を通して. *Nanto Bukkyō* 7 (36): 54–77.

———. 2001a. "Jiin shakaishi no kanten kara miru chūsei no hōe" 寺院社会史の観点からみる中世の法会. In *Girei ni miru nihon no Bukkyō: Tōdaiji, kōfukuji, yakushiji* 儀礼にみる日本の仏教：東大寺・興福寺・薬師寺, ed. Nara Joshi Daigaku Kodai Gakujutsu Kenkyū Sentā Setsuritsu Junbisitsu, 53–91. Kyōto: Hōzōkan.

———. 2001b. "Chūsei Tōdaiji no gakujin: Maibito" 中世東大寺の学人：舞人. In *Chūsei ongakushi ronsō* 中世音楽史論叢, ed. Fukushima Kazuo, 141–165. Osaka: Izumi Shoin.

Nagata Mizu. 1985. "Butten ni miru boseikan: Bukkyō ha boseiku o dō toita ka" 仏典にみる母性観：仏教は母性苦をどう説いたか. In *Bosei o tō: Rekishiteki henkan* 母性を問う：歴史的変換, ed. Wakita Haruko, 1:259–283. Kyoto: Jinbun Shoin.

———. 1989. "Butten ni okeru joseikan no hensen" 仏典における女性観の変遷. In *Sukui to Oshie,* vol. 2 of *Shirīzu josei to Bukkyō,* ed. Ōsumi Kazuo and Nishiguchi Junko, 11–44. Tokyo: Heibonsha.

Naitō Sakae. 2004. "Eison no shari shinkō to hōjuhō no bijutsu" 叡尊の舎利信仰と宝珠法の美術. In *Eison, Ninshō: Jikai no seija* 叡尊・忍性:持戒の聖者, ed. Matsuo Kenji, 74–110. Tokyo: Yoshikawa Kōbunkan.

Nakamura Kyōko, ed. 1984. Women and Religion in Japan. Special issue, *Japanese Journal of Religious Studies* 10 (1).

Nakamura Kyoko Motomichi. 1997. *Miraculous Stories from the Japanese Buddhist Tradition: The "Nihon ryōiki" of the Monk Kyōkai.* Surrey, UK: Curzon. (Orig. pub. 1973, Harvard University Press.)

Nakao Takashi. 1987. "Eison no kokkakan: Kantō gekō to mōko shūrai o megutte" 叡尊の国家観:関東下向と蒙古襲来を巡って. In *Nihon ni okeru kokka to shūkyo,* ed. Shimode Sekiyo Hakushi Kanreiki Kinenkai, 155–172. Tokyo: Daizōkyō Shuppan.

Namai Mariko. 2004. "Iwashimizu Hachiman no kigi to bungaku" 岩清水八幡の木々と文学. *Doshisha Daigaku bungaku gakkai* 60 (Mar.): 22–34.

Namiki Kazuko. 1998. "Heian josei to jingi shinkō" 平安女性と神祇信仰. In *Josei to shūkyō* 女性と宗教, ed. Kojima Kyōko and Shiomi Minako, vol. 5 of *Nihon joseishi ronshū,* ed. Sōgō Joseishi Kenkyūkai, 229–256. Tokyo: Yoshikawa Kōbunkan.

Naomi Gentetsu. 1989. "Kōgō kara nyotei e: Sokuten bukō to henjō nanshi no ronri" 皇后から女帝へ:則天武后と変成男子の論理. In *Shinjin to kuyō,* vol. 3 of *Shirīzu josei to Bukkyō,* ed. Ōsumi Kazuo and Nishiguchi Junko, 167–206. Tokyo: Heibonsha.

Nara National Museum, ed. 2001a. *Eison: Priest of Saidaiji (1201–90) (Kōshō Bosatsu Eison).* Nara: Nara National Museum. An exhibition catalogue.

———. 2001b. *Treasures of the Omizutori Ritual and Tōdai-ji's Nigatsudo.* Nara: Nara National Museum. An exhibition catalogue.

———. 2003. *Special Exhibition: Women and Buddhism (Josei to Bukkyō: Inori to hohoemi).* Nara: Nara National Museum, 2003. Exhibition held Apr. 15–May 25.

———. 2006. *Omizutori: Treasures of Tōdaiji's Omizutori Ritual.* Nara: Nara National Museum. An exhibition catalogue.

Nara Rokudaiji Taikan Kankō Kai, ed. 1999. *Kōfukuji* 1 興福寺 1. Vol. 7 of *Nara Rokudaiji taikan.* Tokyo: Iwanami Shoten.

———, ed. 2001. *Saidaiji* 西大寺. Vol. 14 of *Nara Rokudaiji taikan.* Tokyo: Iwanami Shoten.

Nasu Kazuo. 1988. "Chinkai no nenbutsu shisō" 珍海の念仏思想. *Journal of Indian and Buddhist Studies* 36:139–144.

Nattier, Jan. 2003. *A Few Good Men: The Bodhisattva Path According to the Inquiry of Ugra (Ugrapariprccha).* Honolulu: University of Hawai'i Press.

Nelson, Steven G. 2008a. "Court and Religious Music (1): History of *gagaku* and *shōmyō.*" In *The Ashgate Research Companion to Japanese Music,* ed. Alison Tokita and David W. Hughes, 35–48. Hampshire, UK: Ashgate.

———. 2008b. "Court and Religious Music (2): Music of *gagaku* and *shōmyō.*" In *The Ashgate Research Companion to Japanese Music,* ed. Alison Tokita and David W. Hughes, 49–76. Hampshire, UK: Ashgate.

Nihon Bukkyō Gakkai, ed. 1991. *Bukkyō to josei* 仏教と女性. Kyoto: Heirakuji Shoten.

Nihon Hōsō Kyōkai (NHK). 1987. *Nara: Omizutori* 奈良：お水取り. Documentary. Tokyo: NHK.

Nishiguchi Junko. 1987. *Onna no chikara: Kodai no josei to Bukkyō* 女の力：古代の女性と仏教. Tokyo: Heibonsha.

———. 1989a. "Sei to chisuji" 性と血筋. In *Miko to megami,* vol. 4 of *Shirīzu josei to Bukkyō,* ed. Ōsumi Kazuo and Nishiguchi Junko, 127–52. Tokyo: Heibonsha.

———. 1989b. "Ōchō Bukkyō ni okeru nyonin kyūsai no ronri" 王朝仏教における女人救済の論理. In *Sei to mibun: Jakusha, haisha no seisei to hiun,* ed. Miyata Noboru, 129–167. Tokyo: Shunjūsha.

———. 1992. "Josei no shukke to jukai" 女性の出家と受戒. *Kenkyū kiyō* (Kyoto Women's University Religion and Culture Research Institute) 5:79–107.

———, ed. 1997. *Hotoke to onna* 仏と女. Tokyo: Yoshikawa Kōbunkan.

———. 1998."Jōbutsusetsu to josei" 成仏説と女性. In *Josei to shūkyō* 女性と宗教, ed. Kojima Kyōko and Shiomi Minako, vol. 5 of *Nihon joseishi ronshū,* ed. Sōgō Joseishi Kenkyūkai, 329–354. Tokyo: Yoshikawa Kōbunkan.

———. 1999a. "Ama to ie" 尼と家. In *Nihonshi no naka no josei to Bukkyō* 日本史の中の女性と仏教, ed. Yoshida Kazuhiko et al., 159–177. Kyoto: Hōzōkan.

———. 1999b. "Shinshūshi no naka no josei" 真宗史のなかの女性. In *Nihonshi no naka no josei to Bukkyō* 日本史の中の女性と仏教, ed. Yoshida Kazuhiko et al., 178–210. Kyoto: Hōzōkan.

———. 2002a. "Where the Bones Go: Death and Burial of Women of the Heian High Aristocracy." Trans. Mimi Yiengpruksawan. In *Engendering Faith: Women and Buddhism in Premodern Japan,* ed. Barbara Ruch, 65–108. Ann Arbor: Center for Japanese Studies, University of Michigan.

———. 2002b. "*Tennyoshingyō* to *Tennyo jōbutsukyō:* Tōkyō Kokuritsu Hakubutsukanzō *Tennyo jōbutsukyō* ni tsuite" 「転女身経」と「転女成仏経」：東京国立博物館蔵「転女成仏経」について. In *Amadera monjo chōsa no seika o kiban toshita Nihon no josei to Bukkyō no sōgō kenkyū* 尼寺文書調査の成果を基盤とした日本の女性と仏教の総合研究, ed. Oka Yoshiko, 33–41. Kyoto: Kyowa Insatsu.

———. 2004. *Heian jidai no jiin to minshū* 平安時代の寺院と民衆. Kyoto: Hōzōkan.

———. 2006. *Chūsei no josei to Bukkyō* 中世の女性と仏教. Kyoto: Hōzōkan.

Nishikawa Kyōtarō. 1978. "Jūichimen Kannon bosatsu ryūzō" 十一面観音菩薩立像. In *YKT,* 5:57–61.

———. 1988. *Chūgūji no bi Yamato Ikaruga* 中宮寺の美：大和いかるが. Kyoto: Nara National Museum.

Nishiyama Atsushi. 2001. *Kōshō Bosatsu Eison* 興正菩薩叡尊. Nara: Nara National Museum.

Nōdomi Jōten. 1977. "Nanto Bukkyō ni okeru nyonin ōjō shisō" 南都仏教における女人往生思想. *Indogaku Bukkyō* 50:32–37.

———. 1982. *Kanazawa Bunko Shiryō no kenkyū,* vol. 1. Kyoto: Hōzōkan.

Nomura Ikuyo. 1989. "Nyoin ron" 女院論. In *Shinjin to kuyō,* vol. 3 of *Shirīzu josei to Bukkyō,* ed. Ōsumi Kazuo and Nishiguchi Junko, 135–166. Tokyo: Heibonsha.

———. 2004. *Bukkyō to onna no seishinshi* 仏教と女の精神史. Tokyo: Yoshikawa Kōbunkan.

Obara Hitoshi. 1989. "Nyonin ōjōsha no tanjō" 女人往生者の誕生. In *Shinjin to kuyō,* vol. 3 of *Shirīzu josei to Bukkyō,* ed. Ōsumi Kazuo and Nishiguchi Junko, 111–134. Tokyo: Heibonsha.

———. 1997. "Kizoku josei no shinkō seikatsu" 貴族女性の信仰生活. In *Hotoke to onna* 仏と女, ed. Nishiguchi Junko, 5–33. Tokyo: Yoshikawa Kōbunkan.

———. 1998. "Tennyo jōbutsu no juyō ni tsuite" 転女成仏の受容について. In *Josei to shūkyō* 女性と宗教, ed. Kojima Kyōko and Shiomi Minako, vol. 5 of *Nihon joseishi ronshū,* ed. Sōgō Joseishi Kenkyūkai, 129–149. Tokyo: Yoshikawa Kōbunkan.

———. 2002. "The Rebirth of Women into Paradise: Women in Fujiwara no Munetada's Diary *Chūyūki* (1087–1138)." Trans. and adapted by Burton Watson. In *Engendering Faith: Women and Buddhism in Premodern Japan,* ed. Barbara Ruch, 441–462. Ann Arbor: Center for Japanese Studies, University of Michigan.

Obeyesekere, Ranjini. 2001. *Portraits of Buddhist Women: Stories from the "Saddharmaratnāvaliya."* Albany: State University of New York Press.

Ōe Atsushi. 1989. "Junna taigō Masako naishinnō to Junna'in." In *Ama to amadera,* vol. 1 of *Shirīzu josei to Bukkyō,* ed. Ōsumi Kazuo and Nishiguchi Junko, 141–174. Tokyo: Heibonsha.

Ogasawara Kyōko. 1987. "'Kanjin' no ba: Kōgyō o chūshin ni" 「勧進」の場：興行を中心に. *Kokubungaku: Kaishaku to kyōzai no kenkyū* 32, no. 7 (June): 127–131.

Ōgoshi Aiko et al. 1990. *Seisabetsu suru Bukkyō* 性差別する仏教. Kyoto: Hōzōkan.

Oguri Junko. 1984. "Views on Women's Salvation in Japanese Buddhism." *Young East* 10 (1): 3–11.

Ohnuma, Reiko. 2001. "Woman, Bodhisattva, and Buddha." *Journal of Feminist Studies in Religion* 17, no. 1 (Spring): 63–83.

———. 2006. "Debt to the Mother: A Neglected Aspect of the Founding of the Buddhist Nuns' Order." *Journal of the American Academy of Religion* 74, no. 4 (Dec.): 861–901.

Ōishi Masaaki. 1990. "Bikuni gosho to Muromachi bakufu: Ama gozan Tsūgenji o chūshin ni shite" 比丘尼御所と室町幕府：尼五山通玄寺を中心にして. *Nihonshi kenkyū* 日本史研究 335 (July): 1–28.

———. 1997. "Ama no Hokkeji to sō no Hokkeji" 尼の法華寺と僧の法華寺. In *Hotoke to onna* 仏と女, ed. Nishiguchi Junko, 181–217. Tokyo: Yoshikawa Kōbunkan.

———. 2001. "Chūsei Risshū kyōdan no tokushitsu to sono katsudō: Saidaijiryū Risshū no katsudō o chūshin ni" 中世律宗教団の特質とその活動：西大寺流律宗の活動を中心に. In *Chūsei setouchi no tera to shakai* 中世瀬戸内の寺と社会, vol. 12 of *Asahi hyakka: Kokuhō to rekishi no tabi,* 42–45. Tokyo: Asahi Shinbun Shuppan.

———. 2004. *Nihon chūsei shakai to jiin: Chūsei o tsūjite shūkyō seiryoku no jittai to sono henyō o kaimei* 日本中世社会と寺院：中世を通じて宗教勢力の実態とその変容を解明. Osaka: Seibundō.

Oishio Chihiro. 1995. *Chūsei no Nanto Bukkyō* 中世の南都仏教. Tokyo: Yoshikawa Kōbunkan.

Okada Hideo. 1978. "Hondō" 本堂. In *YKT,* 5:45–47.

Okada Seishi. 1990. "Kyūtei no miko" 宮廷の巫女. In *Genshi, kodai,* vol. 1 of *Nihon josei seikatsushi,* ed. Joseishi Sōgō Kenkyūkai, 43–74. Tokyo: Tokyo Daigaku Shuppankai.

Okano Akio, trans. 1999. *Yo-roppa bunka to Nihon bunka,* by Luís Fróis. Tokyo: Iwanami Shoten.

Okano Haruko. 1991. "Bukkyō no joseikan (2): Nihonteki tenkai" 仏教の女性観2:日本的展開. *Jissen Joshi Daigaku Bungakubu Kiyō* 33:51–71.

———. 1998. "A Feminist Critique of Japanese Religions." Trans. Alison Watts. In *Women and Religion in Japan,* ed. Akiko Okuda and Haruko Okano, 17–44. Wiesbaden: Harrassowitz Verlag.

Okano Kōji. 1998. "Mudoen senji, isshin ajari, sōzu chokunin" 無度縁宣旨・一身阿闍梨・僧都直任. In *Inseiki no Bukkyō,* ed. Hayami Tasuku, 80–117. Tokyo: Yoshikawa Kōbunkan.

Orzech, Charles D. 1998. *Politics and Transcendent Wisdom: The "Scripture for Humane Kings" in the Creation of Chinese Buddhism.* University Park: Pennsylvania State University.

Osuka, Shigeru. 2005. *The Very Mahāyāna Buddhist Ethics: Introduction and Translation of the "Fan-wang-ching."* Tokyo: Chuo University Press.

Ōsumi Kazuo. 1989. "*Josei to Bukkyō* o meguru oboegaki: *Miko to megami* o megutte" 「女性と仏教」を巡る覚え書き:「巫女と女神」を巡って (afterword). In *Miko to megami,* vol. 4 of *Shirīzu josei to Bukkyō,* ed. Ōsumi Kazuo and Nishiguchi Junko, 300–311. Tokyo: Heibonsha.

Ōsumi Kazuo and Nishiguchi Junko, eds. 1989. *Shirīzu josei to Bukkyō* シリーズ女性と仏教 . 4 vols. (Vol. 1: *Ama to amadera* 尼と尼寺; Vol. 2: *Sukui to Oshie* 救いと教え; Vol. 3: *Shinjin to kuyō* 信心と供養; Vol. 4: *Miko to megami* 巫女と女神). Tokyo: Heibonsha.

Ōta Hirotarō. 1978. "Hokkeji no rekishi" 法華寺の歴史. In *YKT,* 5:35–44.

Ōtsuka Sanetada. 1967a. "Bikuni gosho rekidai 1" 比丘尼御所歴代 1. *Nihon Bukkyō kenkyū* 26:57–59.

———. 1967b. "Bikuni gosho rekidai 2" 比丘尼御所歴代 2. *Nihon Bukkyō kenkyū* 27:61–64.

———. 1968. "Bikuni gosho rekidai 3" 比丘尼御所歴代 3. *Nihon Bukkyō kenkyū,* 28, 41–44.

———. 1970a. "Bikuni gosho rekidai 4" 比丘尼御所歴代 4. *Nihon Bukkyō kenkyū* 31:49–60.

———. 1970b. "Bikuni gosho rekidai 5" 比丘尼御所歴代 5. *Nihon Bukkyō kenkyū* 32:51–55.

Ōya Tokujō. 1987. *Nara kankyōshi* 寧楽刊経史. Vol. 8 of *Ōya Tokujō chosaku shū.* Tokyo: Kokusho Kankōkai.

Paul, Diana. 1985. *Women in Buddhism: Images of the Feminine in the Mahayana Tradition.* 2nd ed. Berkeley: University of California Press.

Payne, Richard. 1998. "*Ajikan:* Ritual and Meditation in the Shingon Tradition." In *Re-envisioning "Kamakura" Buddhism,* ed. Richard Payne, 219–248. Honolulu: University of Hawai'i Press.

Piggott, Joan. 1997. *The Emergence of Japanese Kingship.* Stanford: Stanford University Press.

———. 1999. "Chieftain Pairs and Co-rulers: Female Sovereignty in Early Japan." In *Women and Class in Japanese History,* ed. Tonomura Hitomi, Anne Walthall, and Wakita Haruko, 17–52. Ann Arbor: Center for Japanese Studies, University of Michigan.

Pradel, Maria del Rosario. 1997. "The Fragments of the Tenjukoku Shūchō Mandara: Reconstruction of the Iconography and Historical Contexts." PhD diss., University of California, Los Angeles.

Pruden, Leo M., trans. 1995. *The Essentials of the Vinaya Tradition,* by Gyōnen. In *BDK English Tripiṭaka* 97-I, II. Berkeley: Numata Center for Buddhist Translation and Research.

Quinter, David. 2006. "The Shingon-Ritsu School and the Mañjuśrī Cult in the Kamakura Period: From Eison to Monkan." PhD diss., Stanford University.

Reischauer, Edwin. 1947. "The Izayoi Nikki." *Harvard Jounral of Asiatic Studies* 10 (3–4): 255–387.

———, trans. 1955a. *Ennin's Diary: The Record of a Pilgrimage to China in Search of the Law.* New York: Ronald Press.

———. 1955b. *Ennin's Travels in T'ang China.* New York: Ronald Press.

Rossi, Mary Ann. 1991. "Priesthood, Precedent, and Prejudice: On Recovering the Women Priests of Early Christianity." *Journal of Feminist Studies in Religion* 7, no. 1 (Spring): 73–94.

Ruch, Barbara. 1977. "Medieval Jongleurs and the Making of a National Literature." In *Japan in the Muromachi Age,* ed. John Whitney Hall and Toyoda Takeshi, 279–309. Berkeley: University of California Press. Reprint, Cornell East Asia Series. Ithaca, NY: Cornell East Asia Program, 2001.

———. 1990. "The Other Side of Culture in Medieval Japan." In *Medieval Japan,* ed. Kōzō Yamamura, vol. 3 of *The Cambridge History of Japan,* ed. John Whitney Hall, 500–543. New York: Cambridge University Press.

———. 1991. *Mō hitotsu no chūseizō: Bikuni, otogi zōshi, raise* もう一つの中世像：比丘尼・御伽草子・来世. Kyoto: Shibunkaku Shuppan.

———. 1992. "Coping with Death: Paradigms of Heaven and Hell and the Six Realms in Early Literature and Painting." In *Flowing Traces: Buddhism in the Literary and Visual Arts of Japan,* ed. James Sanford et al., 93–130. Princeton: Princeton University Press.

———, ed. 2002. *Engendering Faith: Women and Buddhism in Premodern Japan.* Ann Arbor: Center for Japanese Studies, University of Michigan.

Ruppert, Brian. 2000. *Jewel in the Ashes: Buddha Relics and Power in Early Medieval Japan.* Cambridge, MA: Harvard University Asia Center, Harvard University Press.

Saeki Junko. 1987. *Yūjo no bunkashi* 遊女の文化史. Tokyo: Chūkōshinsho.

Sakurai Tokutarō. 1974–1977. *Nihon no shāmanizumu* 日本のシャーマニズム. Tokyo: Yoshikawa Kōbunkan.

Saigusa Mitsuyoshi. 2000. *Engi no shisō* 縁起の思想. Kyoto: Hōzōkan.

Sangō Asuka. 2007. "In the Halo of Golden Light: Imperial Authority and Buddhist Ritual in Heian Japan (794–1185)." PhD diss., Princeton University.

Satō Michiko. 2001. "Hōe no katachi: Ima, shūnie o chūshin ni" 法会のかたち：いま、修二会を中心に. In *Girei ni miru Nihon no Bukkyō* 儀礼にみる日本の仏教, ed. Nara Joshi Daigaku, 25–52. Kyoto: Hōzōkan.

Sawa Hirokatsu. 1990. "Saidaiji ni yoru Dōmyōji no 'fukkō' ni tsuite: Dōmyōji Tenmangū shozō no ichi shiryō narabi ni Dōmyōji engi no kentō" 西大寺による道明寺の「復興」について：道明寺天満宮所蔵の1史料並びに道明寺縁起の検討. *Hisutoria* 127:88–105.

Schalow, Paul Gordon, and Janet A. Walker, eds. 1996. *The Woman's Hand: Gender and Theory in Japanese Women's Writing.* Stanford: Stanford University Press.

Schopen, Gregory. 1997. *Bones, Stones, and Buddhist Monks: Collected Papers on the Archaeology, Epigraphy, and Texts of Monastic Buddhism in India.* Honolulu: University of Hawai'i Press.

———. 2004. *Buddhist Monks and Business Matters: Still More Papers on Monastic Buddhism in India.* Honolulu: University of Hawai'i Press.

———. 2005. *Figments and Fragments of Mahāyāna Buddhism in India: More Collected Papers.* Honolulu: University of Hawai'i Press.

Schulenburg, Jane Tibbetts. 1989. "Women's Monastic Communities, 500–1100: Patterns of Expansion and Decline." In Working Together in the Middle Ages: Perspectives on Women's Communities, special issue, *Signs* 14, no. 2 (Winter): 261–292.

Schuster, Nancy. 1981. "Changing the Female Body: Wise Women and the Bodhisattva Career in Some Maharatnakutasutras." *Journal of the International Association of Buddhist Studies* 4 (1): 24–69.

Segal, Ethan. 2003. "Economic Growth Structures and Changes in Elite Power Structures in Medieval Japan, 1150–1500." PhD diss., Stanford University.

Seidensticker, Edward G., trans. 1976. *The Tale of Genji.* New York: Knopf.

Sekiguchi Shizuo. 1998. "Raun kōshiki shōkō" 羅云講式小考. *Ube kokubun kenkyū* 29 (Mar.): 3–20.

Sheetz, Jessica A. 1997. Review of *Catholic Nuns through Two Millennia,* by Jo Ann Kay McNamara. *Sixteenth Century Journal* 28, no. 4 (Winter): 1376–1379.

Shiga-kenritsu Biwako Bunkakan, ed. 2007. *Josei to inori: Shinkō no sugata* 女性と祈り：信仰の姿. Ōtsu, Japan: Shiga-kenritsu Biwako Bunkakan. An exhibition catalogue.

Shimada Tomohiro. 2004. "Chinkai no *Bodai shinshū* ni tsuite" 珍海の「菩提心集」について. *Chizan gakuhō* 53:223–237.

Shinohara, Koichi. 2009. "Taking a Meal at a Lay Supporter's Residence: The Evolution of the Practice in Chinese *Vinaya* Commentaries." In *Buddhist Monasticism in East Asia: Places of Practice,* ed. James Benn, Lori Meeks, and James Robson, 18–42. London: Routledge.

Shirai Yūko. 1989. "Heian jidai shotō no Bukkyō to josei" 平安時代初頭の仏教と女性. In *Ama to amadera,* vol. 1 of *Shirīzu josei to Bukkyō,* ed. Ōsumi Kazuo and Nishiguchi Junko, 105–140. Tokyo: Heibonsha.

Shirato Waka. 1982. "Manshuin-bon *shukke sahō* no mondai: Ryōnin saku to suitei suru koto ni kanshite" 曼殊院本「出家作法」の問題：良忍作と推定することにかんして. *Indogaku Bukkyō kenkyū* 30 (2): 61–66.

Simons, Walter. 2001. *Cities of Ladies: Beguine Communities in the Medieval Low Countries, 1200–1565.* Philadelphia: University of Pennsylvania Press.

Sōgō Joseishi Kenkyūkai, ed. 1993. *Nihon josei no rekishi: Onna no hataraki* 日本女性の歴史：女の働き. Tokyo: Kadokawa Shoten.

Soymié, Michel. 1965. "Ketsubongyō no shiryōteki kenkyū." In *Dōkyō kenkyū,* vol. 1, ed. Michel Soymié and Iraya Yoshitaka, 109–166. Tokyo: Shōshinsha.

Spiro, Melford E. 1984. "Some Reflections on the Family and Religion in East Asia." In *Religion and Family in East Asia,* ed. George DeVos and Takao Sofue, 35–54. Osaka: National Museum of Ethnology.

Sponberg, Alan. 1985. "Attitudes toward Women and the Feminine in Early Buddhism." In *Buddhism, Sexuality, and Gender,* ed. José Ignacio Cabezon, 3–36. Albany: State University of New York Press.

Stanford, James H., William R. LaFleur, and Masatoshi Nagatomi, eds. 1992. *Flowering Traces: Buddhism in the Literary and Visual Arts of Japan.* Princeton: Princeton University Press.

Steenstrup, Carl. 1979. *Hōjō Shigetoki, 1198–1261, and His Role in the History of Political and Ethical Ideas in Japan.* London: Curzon.

Stevenson, Miwa. 1999. "The Founding of the Monastery Gangōji and a List of Its Treasures." In *Religions of Japan in Practice,* ed. George Tanabe Jr., 299–315. Princeton: Princeton University Press.

Stone, Jacqueline I. 1999. *Original Enlightenment Thought and the Transformation of Medieval Japanese Buddhism.* Honolulu: University of Hawai'i Press.

———. 2006. "Just Open Your Mouth and Say 'A': A-Syllable Practice for the Time of Death in Early Medieval Japan." *Pacific World,* 3rd ser., 8:167–189.

Sugimoto Sonoko and Koga Kōshō. 1979. *Hokkeji.* Vol. 3 of *Koji junrei: Nara* 古寺巡礼: 奈良, 3: 法華寺. Kyoto: Tankōsha.

Suzuki Masutaka. 2002. *Nyonin kinsei* 女人禁制. Tokyo: Yoshikawa Kōbunkan.

Tabata Yasuko. 1985. "Kamakuraki ni okeru boshikankei to boseikan" 鎌倉期における母子関係と母性観. In *Bosei o tō: Rekishiteki henkan* 母性を問う：歴史的変換, ed. Wakita Haruko, 1:143–171. Kyoto: Jinbun Shoin.

———. 1987. *Nihon chūsei no josei* 日本中世の女性. Tokyo: Yoshikawa Kōbunkan.

———. 1998. *Nihon chūsei no shakai to josei* 日本中世の社会と女性. Tokyo: Yoshikawa Kōbunkan.

Tabuchi Kumiko. 2000. *Abutsuni to sono jidai: "Utatane" ga kataru chūsei* 阿仏尼とその時代：「うたたね」が語る中世. Kyoto: Nozogawa Shoten.

Taira Masayuki. 1990. "Chūsei Bukkyō to josei" 中世仏教と女性. In *Chūsei,* vol. 2 of *Nihon josei seikatsushi,* ed. Joseishi Sōgō Kenkyūkai, 75–108. Tokyo: Tokyo Daigaku Shuppankai.

———. 1992. *Nihon chūsei shakai to Bukkyō* 日本中世社会と仏教. Tokyo: Hanawa Shobō.

———. 2000–2002. "Nyonin ōjō" 女人往生. In *Nihon kokugo daijiten,* 302–303.

Takagi Yukata. 1988. *Bukkyōshi no naka no nyonin* 仏教史の中の女人. Tokyo: Heibonsha.

Takeda Chōshū. 1979. *Sōsō bosei kenkyū shūsei* 葬送墓制研究集成. Tokyo: Meichō Shuppan.

Takemi Momoko. 1981. "Nihon ni okeru Ketsubongyō shinkō ni tsuite" 日本における血盆経信仰について. *Nihon Bukkyō* 41:37–49.

———. 1983. "Menstruation Sūtra Belief in Japan." *Japanese Journal of Religious Studies* 10 (2–3): 229–245.

Tamura Yoshinaga. 1935. "Chūgūji chūkō Shinnyo kaiki no Shōbōji ni tsuite" 中宮寺中興信如開基の正法寺に就いて. *Yamato kokorozashi* 2, no. 12:270–271.

Tanabe, George, and Willa Tanabe. 1989. *The Lotus Sūtra in Japanese Culture.* Honolulu: University of Hawai'i Press.

Tanabe Takao. "Umoreta hotoketachi" 埋もれた仏たち. Kuroda Kinen Shitsu exhibit, Fukuoka City Museum, item 291. Http://museum.city.fukuoka.jp/je/html/291-300/291/291_01.htm.

Tanabe, Willa Jane. 1984. "The Lotus Lectures: *Hokke Hakkō* in the Heian Period." *Monumenta Nipponica* 39 (4): 393–407.

Tanaka Masako. 1987. "The Myth of Perfect Motherhood: Japanese Women's Dilemma." In *Speaking of Faith,* ed. Diana L. Eck and Devaki Jain, 75–83. Philadelphia: New Society Publishing.

Tanaka Minoru. 1978a. "Hokke metsuzaiji engi" 法華滅罪寺縁起. In *YKT,* 5:84–85.

———. 1978b. "Hokke metsuzaiji nenjū gyōji" 法華滅罪寺年中行事. In *YKT,* 5:85–86.

———. 1978c. "Hokkeji kekkaiki" 法華寺結界記. In *YKT,* 5:89.

Tanaka Takako. 1996. *Sei naru onna: Saigū, megami, Chūjōhime* 聖なる女：斎宮・女神・中将姫. Tokyo: Jinbun Shoin.

———. 1997. *Seiai no nihon chūsei* 性愛の日本中世. Tokyo: Yōsensha.

———. 2005. *Ama ni natta onna-tachi* 尼になった女たち. Tokyo: Daitō Shuppansha.

———. 2006. *Gehō to aihō no chūsei* 外法と愛法の中世. Tokyo: Sunagoya Shobō. (Orig. pub. 1993.)

Teeuwen, Mark, and Fabio Rambelli, eds. 2003. *Buddhas and Kami in Japan: Honji Suijaku as a Combinatory Paradigm.* London: RoutledgeCurzon.

Teiser, Stephen. 1988. *The Ghost Festival in Medieval China.* Princeton: Princeton University Press.

Tokieda Tsutomu. 2007. "Chūsei Tōhoku no Ketsubonkyō shinkō: Sendai-shi Dōnokuchi iseki shutsudo kokera kyō o tegakarini" 中世東北の血盆経信仰：仙台市洞ノ口遺跡出土柿経を手がかりに. *Risshō Daigaku Bungakubu ronsō* 125:17–39.

Tomikura Tokujirō, ed. 1967. *Towazugatari* とはずがたり. By Go-Fukakusa-in Nijō (aka Nakanoin Masatada no Musume, b. 1258). Tokyo: Chikuma Sōsho.

Tonomura Hitomi. 1979. "Women and Property in a Warrior Society: Patterns of Inheritance and Socio-Political Change in Early Medieval Japan." M.A. thesis, University of Oregon.

———. 1990. "Women and Inheritance in Japan's Early Warrior Society." *Comparative Studies in Society and History* 32 (3): 592–623.

———. 1997. "Re-evisioning Women in the Post-Kamakura Age." In *The Origins of Japan's Medieval World: Courtiers, Clerics, and Peasants in the Fourteenth Century,* ed. Jeffrey Mass, 138–169. Stanford: Stanford University Press.

Tonomura Hitomi, Anne Walthall, and Wakita Haruko, eds. 1999. *Women and Class in Japanese History.* Ann Arbor: University of Michigan Press.

Torjesen, Karen Jo. 1995. *When Women Were Priests: Women's Leaderhip in the Early Church and the Scandal of Their Subordination in the Rise of Christianity.* San Francisco: HarperSanFrancisco.

Tsai, Kathryn Ann. 1994. *Lives of the Nuns.* Honolulu: University of Hawai'i Press.

Tsuchiya Megumi. 1989. "Ganshu to ama: Daigoji no josei" 願主と尼：醍醐寺の女性. In *Ama to amadera,* vol. 1 of *Shirīzu josei to Bukkyō,* ed. Ōsumi Kazuo and Nishiguchi Junko, 175–220. Tokyo: Heibonsha.

Tsukamoto Zenryū. 1985. *An Early History of Chinese Buddhism: From Its Introduction to the Death of Hui-yuan.* Tokyo: Kodansha International.

Tyler, Royall. 1990. *The Miracles of the Kasuga Deity.* New York: Columbia University Press.

———, trans. 2001. *The Tale of Genji,* by Murasaki Shikibu. 2 vols. New York: Viking.

Ueda Sachiko. 1976. "Eison to Yamato no Saidaiji matsuji" 叡尊と大和の西大寺末寺. In *Chūsei shakai no seiritsu to tenkai* 中世社会の成立と展開, ed. Osaka Rekishi Gakkai, 333–398. Tokyo: Yoshikawa Kōbunkan.

Uejima Susumu. 2004. "Chūsei kokka to jisha" 中世国家と寺社. In *Chūsei no keisei* 中世の形成, vol. 3 of *Nihonshi kōza,* ed. Rekishigaku Kenkyūkai and Nihonshi Kenkyūkai, 227–261. Tokyo: Tokyo Daigaku Shuppankai.

Umemura Keiko and Owada Michiko, eds. 1998. *Kon'in to josei* 婚姻と女性. Vol. 4 of *Nihon joseishi ronshū,* ed. Sōgō Joseishi Kenkyūkai. Tokyo: Yoshikawa Kōbunkan.

Uno, Kathleen S. 1996. "Women and Changes in the Household Division of Labor." In *Re-imagining Japanese Women,* ed. Anne Imamura, 17–41. Berkeley: University of California Press.

Unno, Mark. 2004. *Shingon Refractions: Myōe and the Mantra of Light.* Somerville, MA: Wisdom Publications.

Ushiyama Yoshiyuki. 1986. "Chūsei no amadera nōto" 中世の尼寺ノート. *Nihon no josei to Bukkyō: Kaihō* 3 (August): 13–31.

———. 1989. "Chūsei no amadera to ama" 中世の尼寺と尼. In *Ama to amadera,* vol. 1 of *Shirīzu josei to Bukkyō,* ed. Ōsumi Kazuo and Nishiguchi Junko, 221–270. Tokyo: Heibonsha. English version available in *Engendering Faith: Women and Buddhism in Premodern Japan,* ed. Barbara Ruch, 131–164. Ann Arbor: Center for Japanese Studies, University of Michigan, 2002.

———. 1990. *Kodai chūsei jiin soshiki no kenkyū* 古代中世寺院組織の研究. Tokyo: Yoshikawa Kōbunkan.

———. 2003. "Chūsei no amadera to sono shūhen" 中世の尼寺とその周辺. *Kokubungaku* 48 (6): 64–69.

Verschuer, Charlotte von. 2006. *Across the Perilous Sea: Japanese Trade with China and Korea from the Seventh to the Sixteenth Centuries.* Trans. Kristen Lee Hunter. Ithaca: East Asia Program, Cornell University.

Wajima Yoshio. 1959. *Jinbutsu sōsho: Eison, Ninshō* 人物叢書:叡尊・忍性. Tokyo: Yoshikawa Kōbunkan.

———. 1972. "Kawachi Sairinji to Ninshō." 河内西琳寺と忍性. *Ōtemae joshi daigaku ronshū* 6:166–177.

Wakita Haruko. 1984. "Marriage and Property in Premodern Japan from the Perspective of Women's History." Trans. Suzanne Gay. *Journal of Japanese Studies* 10 (1): 77–99.

———. 1985. "Bosei sonchō shisō to zaigōkan: Chūsei no bungei o chūshin ni" 母性尊重思想と罪業観:中世の文芸を中心に. In *Bosei o tō: Rekishiteki henkan* 母性を問う:歴史的変換, ed. Wakita Haruko, 1:172–203. Kyoto: Jinbun Shoin.

———. 1992. *Nihon chūsei joseishi no kenkyū: Seibetsu yakuwaribuntan to bosei, kasei, seiai* 日本中世女性史の研究:性別役割分担と母性・家政・性愛. Tokyo: Tokyo Daigaku Shuppankai.

———. 1993. "Women and the Creation of the *Ie* in Japan: An Overview from the Medieval Period to the Present." Trans. David P. Phillips. *U.S.-Japan Women's Journal,* English supplement 4.

———. 1995. *Chūsei ni ikiru onnatachi* 中世に生きる女達. Tokyo: Iwanami Shoten.

———. 2001. *Josei geinō no genryū: Kugutsu, kusemai, shirabyōshi* 女性芸能の源流:傀儡子・曲舞・白拍子. Tokyo: Kakugawa.

———. 2006. *Women in Medieval Japan: Motherhood, Household Management and Sexuality.* Trans. Alison Tokita. Tokyo: University of Tokyo Press.

Wallace, John R. 1988. "Fitful Slumbers: Nun Abutsu's *Utatane*." *Monumenta Nipponica* 43 (4): 391–398.

Walthall, Anne, ed. 2008. *Servants of the Dynasty: Palace Women in World History.* Berkeley: University of California Press.

Warren, Nancy Bradley. 2001. *Spiritual Economies: Female Monasticism in Later Medieval England.* Philadephia: University of Pennsylvania Press.

Watson, Burton, trans. 1997. *The Vimalakīrti Sūtra.* New York: Columbia University Press.

Williams, Duncan Ryūken. 2004a. *The Other Side of Zen: The Social History of Soto Zen in Tokugawa Japan.* Princeton: Princeton University Press.

———. 2004b. "Esoteric Waters: Meritorious Bathing, Kōbō Daishi, and the Legends of Hot Springs Foundings." *Mikkyō bunka kenkyūsho kiyō* 2:195–216.

Wright, Diana. 2002. "Mantokuji: More Than a Divorce Temple." In *Engendering Faith: Women and Buddhism in Premodern Japan,* ed. Barbara Ruch, 247–276. Ann Arbor: Center for Japanese Studies, University of Michigan.

Wu, Pei-jung. 2002. "The Mañjuśrī Statues and Buddhist Practice of Saidaiji: A Study on Iconography, Interior Features of Statues, and Rituals Associated with Buddhist Icons." PhD diss., University of California, Los Angeles.

Yamagishi Tsuneto. 2001. "Kodai jiin no saikō to Risshū" 古代寺院の再興と律宗. In *Chūsei setouchi no tera to shakai* 中世瀬戸内の寺と社会, vol. 12 of *Asahi hyakka: Kokuhō to rekishi no tabi.* Tokyo: Asahi Shinbun shuppan.

———. 2004. *Chūsei jiin no sōdan, hōe, bunsho* 中世寺院の僧団・法会・文書. Tokyo: Tokyo Daigaku Shuppankai.

Yamamoto Hiroko. 1993. *Henjōfu: Chūsei shinbutsu shūgō no sekai* 変成譜・中世神仏習合の世界. Tokyo: Shunjūsha.

Yamamoto Shingo. 2006. *Heian Kamakura jidai ni okeru hyōbyaku, ganmon no buntai no kenkyū* 平安鎌倉時代に於ける表白・願文の文体の研究. Tōkyō: Kyūko Shoin.

Yiengpruksawan, Mimi. 1993. "The House of Gold: Fujiwara Kiyohara's Konjikidō." *Monumenta Nipponica* 48 (1): 33–52.

———. 1994. "What's in a Name? Fujiwara Fixation in Japanese Cultural History." *Monumenta Nipponica* 49 (4): 423–453.

Yokoyama Hiroshi. 1995. *Shinwa no naka no onnatachi* 神話の中の女達. Kyoto: Jinbun Shoin.

Yoshida Kazuhiko. 1989. "Ryūnyo no jōbutsu" 竜女の成仏. In *Sukui to Oshie,* vol. 2 of *Shirīzu josei to Bukkyō,* ed. Ōsumi Kazuo and Nishiguchi Junko, 45–92. Tokyo: Heibonsha.

———. 1999. "Josei to Bukkyō o meguru shomondai" 女性と仏教を巡る諸問題. In *Nihonshi no naka no josei to Bukkyō* 日本史の中の女性と仏教, ed. Yoshida Kazuhiko et al., 4–47. Kyoto: Hōzōkan.

Yoshida Kazuhiko et al., eds. 1999. *Nihonshi no naka no josei to Bukkyō* 日本史の中の女性と仏教. Kyoto: Hōzōkan.

Yoshie Akiko. 1990. "Kodai no mura no seikatsu to josei" 古代の村の生活と女性. In *Genshi, kodai,* vol. 1 of *Nihon josei seikatsushi,* ed. Joseishi Sōgō Kenkyūkai, 143–180. Tokyo: Tokyo Daigaku Shuppankai.

———. 1996. *Nihon kodai no saishi to josei* 日本古代の祭祀と女性. Tokyo: Yoshikawa Kōbunkan.

Yoshimi Kaneko. 1988. *Onna to ie* 女と家. Tokyo: Dōsei.

———. 1994. *Jiritsu suru onnatachi* 自立する女達. Tokyo: Dōsei.

Yü Chün-Fang. 2001. *Kuan-yin: The Chinese Transformation of Avalokiteśvara.* New York: Columbia University Press.

Zürcher, Erik. 2007. *The Buddhist Conquest of China: The Spread and Adaptation of Buddhism in Early Medieval China.* Leiden: Brill.

Index

Fully ordained nuns are identified as *bikuni* unless they are major figures (e.g., Enkyō). The following abbreviations are used: n. = note; nn. = notes; f. = figure; t. = table.

Kuroda Institute
Studies in East Asian Buddhism

Studies in Ch'an and Hua-yen
Robert M. Gimello and Peter N. Gregory, editors

Dōgen Studies
William R. LaFleur, editor

The Northern School and the Formation of Early Ch'an Buddhism
John R. McRae

Traditions of Meditation in Chinese Buddhism
Peter N. Gregory, editor

Sudden and Gradual: Approaches to Enlightenment in Chinese Thought
Peter N. Gregory, editor

Buddhist Hermeneutics
Donald S. Lopez, Jr., editor

Paths to Liberation: The Margā and Its Transformations in Buddhist Thought
Robert E. Buswell, Jr., and Robert M. Gimello, editors

Sōtō Zen in Medieval Japan
William M. Bodiford

The Scripture on the Ten Kings *and the Making of Purgatory in Medieval Chinese Buddhism*
Stephen F. Teiser

The Eminent Monk: Buddhist Ideals in Medieval Chinese Hagiography
John Kieschnick

Re-Visioning "Kamakura" Buddhism
Richard K. Payne, editor

Original Enlightenment and the Transformation of Medieval Japanese Buddhism
Jacqueline I. Stone

Buddhism in the Sung
Peter N. Gregory and Daniel A. Getz, Jr., editors

Coming to Terms with Chinese Buddhism: A Reading of The Treasure Store Treatise
Robert H. Sharf

Ryōgen and Mount Hiei: Japanese Tendai in the Tenth Century
Paul Groner

Tsung-mi and the Sinificataion of Buddhism
Peter N. Gregory

Approaching the Land of Bliss: Religious Praxis in the Cult of Amitābha
Richard K. Payne and Kenneth K. Tanaka, editors

Going Forth: Visions of Buddhist Vinaya
William M. Bodiford, editor

Burning for the Buddha: Self-Immolation in Chinese Buddhism
James A. Benn

The Buddhist Dead: Practices, Discourses, Representations
Bryan J. Cuevas and Jacqueline I. Stone, editors

The Making of a Savior Bodhisattva: Dizang in Medieval China
Zhiru

How Zen Became Zen: The Dispute over Enlightenment and the Formation of Chan Buddhism in Song-Dynasty China
Morten Schlütter

Hokkeji and the Reemergence of Female Monastic Orders in Premodern Japan
Lori Meeks